Edwin Mansfield

University of Pennsylvania

Nariman Behravesh

Wharton Econometric Forecasting Associates, Inc.

W · W · Norton & Company · New York · London

The Annenberg/CPB Project

Copyright © 1986 by Edwin Mansfield, Nariman Behravesh, the Educational Film
Center and the Corporation for Public Broadcasting
All rights reserved.
Printed in the United States of America.

The text of this book is composed in Caledonia & Vega, with display type set in
Caledonia & Vega. Composition by The Haddon Craftsman. Manufacturing by The
Murray Printing Company. Book design by Nancy Dale Muldoon.

First Edition

Library of Congress Cataloging in Publication Data

Mansfield, Edwin.
  Economics U$A.

  1. Economics. 2. United States—Economic
conditions—1945–   I. Behravesh, Nariman.
II. Title.
HB171.M325 1986   330   85-7291

ISBN 0-393-95508-7

W. W. Norton & Company, Inc., 500 Fifth Avenue, New York, N. Y. 10110
W. W. Norton & Company Ltd., 37 Great Russell Street, London WC1B 3NU

1 2 3 4 5 6 7 8 9 0

★ ★ ★ ★ ★ ★

Contents

☆ ☆ ☆ ☆ ☆ ☆ ☆ ☆ ☆ ☆ ☆ ☆ ☆ ☆ ☆ ☆ ☆ ☆ ☆ ☆

PART 1 INTRODUCTION TO ECONOMICS

Prologue Economic Problems: A Sampler **1**

Unemployment and Inflation ★ The Productivity
Slowdown and the Competitiveness of U.S. Goods ★
Government Regulation of Business ★ The
Elimination of Poverty ★ Looking Ahead

Chapter 1 What Is Economics? **9**

What Is Economics? ★ Opportunity Cost: A
Fundamental Concept ★ *Case Study 1.1 Land Use
in Alaska* ★ The Impact of Economics on Society ★
*Case Study 1.2 Adam Smith, Father of Modern
Economics* ★ The Methodology of Economics ★
Graphs and Relationships ★ The Tasks of an
Economic System ★ **Exploring Further: A Simple
Introductory Model of the Economic System** ★ *Case
Study 1.3 Producing Both Guns and Butter in
1939–41* ★ Summary

Chapter 2 Markets and Prices **31**

Consumers and Firms ★ Markets ★ The Demand
Side of a Market ★ The Supply Side of a Market ★

v ★

Equilibrium Price ★ Actual Price ★ The Price System and the Determination of What Is Produced ★ The Price System and the Determination of How Goods Are Produced ★ The Price System and the Determination of Who Gets What ★ *Case Study 2.1 Mini-Mills* ★ The Price System and Economic Growth ★ The Circular Flows of Money and Products ★ Limitations of the Price System ★ *Case Study 2.2 The Food Stamp Program and the Allocation of Resources* ★ **Exploring Further: Effects of Shifts in the Demand and Supply Curves** ★ Summary

☆ ☆

PART 2 NATIONAL INCOME AND OUTPUT

Chapter 3 **National Income and Product** **55**

Gross National Product ★ Adjusting GNP for Price Changes ★ *Case Study 3.1 The First Estimates of GNP in the United States* ★ Using Value-Added to Calculate GNP ★ Net National Product ★ The Limitations of GNP and NNP ★ Two Approaches to GNP ★ The Expenditures Approach to GNP ★ *Case Study 3.2 Using GNP Estimates in World War II* ★ The Income Approach to GNP ★ Summary

Chapter 4 **Business Fluctuations and Unemployment** **74**

Business Fluctuations ★ Aggregate Supply and Demand ★ The Aggregate Demand Curve ★ The Aggregate Supply Curve ★ National Output and the Price Level ★ Unemployment ★ The Costs of Unemployment ★ *Case Study 4.1 Unemployment: The Classical View* ★ *Case Study 4.2 Karl Marx on Unemployment* ★ *Case Study 4.3 John Maynard Keynes and the Great Depression* ★ **Exploring Further: Effects of Shifts in the Aggregate Demand and Supply Curves** ★ Summary

Chapter 5 **The Determination of National Output and the Keynesian Multiplier** **99**

The Consumption Function ★ The Saving Function ★ Determinants of Investment ★ The Investment

Decision ★ The Equilibrium Level of Net National Product ★ Aggregate Flows of Income and Expenditure ★ Reconciling Aggregate Demand and Supply Curves with Income-Expenditure Analysis ★ *Case Study 5.1 Keynes's Criticisms of the Classical View* ★ Changes in Equilibrium Output ★ The Volatility of Investment ★ Effects of Changes in Intended Investment ★ The Multiplier ★ *Case Study 5.2 Investment and a Great Crash* ★ **Exploring Further: Nonincome Determinants of Consumption** ★ Summary

Chapter 6 Fiscal Policy and National Output   **123**

Government Expenditure and Net National Product ★ Taxation and Net National Product ★ The Nature and Objectives of Fiscal Policy ★ *Case Study 6.1 The Employment Act of 1946* ★ Makers of Fiscal Policy ★ Automatic Stabilizers ★ *Case Study 6.2 President Eisenhower and Automatic Stabilizers* ★ The Tools of Discretionary Fiscal Policy ★ *Case Study 6.3 President Kennedy and the Tax Cut of 1964* ★ Size and Nature of Government Activities ★ **Exploring Further: Fiscal Policy and Aggregate Demand** ★ Summary

Chapter 7 Inflation   **144**

Inflation ★ The Measurement of Inflation ★ Impact of Inflation ★ Aggregate Demand and Inflation ★ *Case Study 7.1 Demand-Pull Inflation and the Tax Surcharge of 1968* ★ *Case Study 7.2 Unemployment and Inflation: An International Overview* ★ Summary

☆ ☆

PART 3 MONEY, BANKING, AND STABILIZATION POLICY

Chapter 8 Money and the Banking System   **159**

What Is Money? ★ The Money Supply, Narrowly Defined ★ The Money Supply, Broadly Defined ★ Commercial Banks in the United States ★ How

Banks Operate ★ The Balance Sheet of an
Individual Bank ★ Fractional-Reserve Banking ★
The Safety of the Banks ★ How Banks Can Create
Money ★ *Case Study 8.1 The Failure of the
Knickerbocker Trust in 1907* ★ **Exploring Further:
A General Proposition Concerning the Effect of
Excess Reserves** ★ Summary

Chapter 9   Monetary Policy and the Federal Reserve   179

The Aims of Monetary Policy ★ The Central Role of
Bank Reserves ★ Makers of Monetary Policy ★ The
Federal Reserve System ★ Functions of the Federal
Reserve ★ The Federal Reserve Banks: Their
Consolidated Balance Sheet ★ Open Market
Operations ★ Changes in Legal Reserve
Requirements ★ Changes in the Discount Rate ★
*Case Study 9.1 The Independence of the Federal
Reserve* ★ Other Tools of Monetary Policy ★ *Case
Study 9.2 Monetary Policy in the 1960s* ★
**Exploring Further: More on the Effects of Monetary
Policy** ★ Summary

**Chapter 10   Stabilization Problems and Anti-Inflationary
Measures   197**

Cost-Push Inflation ★ Difficulties in Distinguishing
Cost-Push from Demand-Pull Inflation ★ The
Instability of the Phillips Curve ★ The Long-Run
Phillips Curve ★ *Case Study 10.1 Stagflation* ★
Wage and Price Controls ★ Income Policies ★
Tax-Based Incomes Policies ★ Economic
Stabilization: Where We Stand ★ **Exploring Further:
The Fed and Cost-Push Inflation** ★ Summary

**Chapter 11   Productivity, Growth, and Technology
Policy   214**

Growth of Per Capita Output in the United States
★ The Productivity Slowdown and Its Consequences
★ Causes of the Productivity Slowdown ★ Has
There Been a Decline in the U.S. Innovation Rate?
★ Cutbacks in the Percentage of GNP Devoted to
R and D ★ Various Mechanisms for Additional
Federal Support of Civilian Technology ★ *Case
Study 11.1 Technology Policy in the Carter and*

Reagan Years ★ Importance of Investment in Plant and Equipment ★ Importance of the General Economic Climate ★ *Case Study 11.2 Supply-Side Economics and the Tax Cut of 1981* ★ **Exploring Further: Supply-Side Government Policies and the Aggregate Supply Curve** ★ Summary

Chapter 12 Deficits, Public Debt, and the Federal Budget   **230**

Deficit and Surplus Financing ★ The Full-Employment Budget ★ Effects of How a Deficit Is Financed, or How a Surplus Is Used ★ Government Debt ★ *Case Study 12.1 Should Eisenhower Have Tried to Balance the Budget?* ★ *Case Study 12.2 Martin Feldstein versus Donald Regan* ★ Recent American Experience with Fiscal Policy and Deficits ★ Summary

Chapter 13 Monetary Policy, Interest Rates, and Economic Activity   **247**

The Value of Money ★ Inflation and the Quantity of Money ★ Unemployment and the Quantity of Money ★ Determinants of the Quantity of Money ★ The Demand for Money ★ Changes in the Money Supply and National Output ★ The Monetarists ★ The Velocity of Money ★ The Equation of Exchange ★ The Crude Quantity Theory of Money and Prices ★ *Case Study 13.1 The Velocity of Money and the Fed's 1975 Decision* ★ The Importance of Money ★ When Is Monetary Policy Tight or Easy? ★ Should the Fed Pay More Attention to Interest Rates or the Money Supply? ★ Problems in Formulating Monetary Policy ★ *Case Study 13.2 The Saturday Night Special* ★ How Well Has the Fed Performed? ★ Should the Fed Be Governed by a Rule? ★ **Exploring Further: A More Sophisticated Version of the Quantity Theory** ★ Summary

Chapter 14 Controversies over Stabilization Policy   **276**

Monetarists versus Keynesians: The Historical Background ★ Causes of Business Fluctuations: The Opposing Views ★ Stability of the Economy: The

Opposing Views ★ A Monetary Rule: The Opposing Views ★ The Current State of the Keynesian-Monetarist Debate ★ *Case Study 14.1 The Coordination of Fiscal and Monetary Policy in the Early 1980s* ★ Rational Expectations: Another Element of the Current Debate ★ Supply-Side Economics Enters the Fray ★ *Case Study 14.2 Recession as a Means to Stop Inflation in 1982* ★ *Case Study 14.3 More on the Tax Cut of 1981* ★ Summary

☆ ☆ ☆ ☆ ☆ ☆ ☆ ☆ ☆ ☆ ☆ ☆ ☆ ☆ ☆ ☆ ☆ ☆ ☆

PART 4 ECONOMIC DECISION MAKING: THE FIRM, THE CONSUMER, SOCIETY

Chapter 15 The Business Firm: Organization, Motivation, and Optimal Input Decisions   **291**

General Motors: A Study ★ *Case Study 15.1 Studebaker and the Low-Volume Trap* ★ Characteristics of American Firms: Some Salient Facts ★ Proprietorships ★ Partnerships ★ Corporations ★ Motivation of the Firm ★ Technology, Inputs, and the Production Function ★ Types of Inputs ★ The Short Run and the Long Run ★ Average Product of an Input ★ Marginal Product of an Input ★ *Case Study 15.2 The Coca-Cola Company and Input Costs* ★ The Law of Diminishing Marginal Returns ★ The Optimal Input Decision ★ **Exploring Further: How to Produce Kansas Corn** ★ Summary

Chapter 16 Getting Behind the Demand and Supply Curves   **311**

The Demand Curve ★ Consumer Expenditures ★ A Model of Consumer Behavior ★ The Equilibrium Market Basket ★ *Case Study 16.1 Conserving Water in a California Drought* ★ The Consumer's Demand Curve ★ Deriving the Market Demand Curve ★ The Supply Curve ★ What Are Costs? ★ Short-Run Cost Functions ★ Average Costs in the Short Run ★ Marginal Cost in the Short Run ★ *Case Study 16.2 Oil Price Increases and Drilling*

Chapter 17 Market Demand and Price Elasticity   **336**

Market Demand Curves ★ The Price Elasticity of
Demand ★ Determinants of the Price Elasticity of
Demand ★ *Case Study 17.1 Instability of Farm
Prices and the Price Elasticity of Demand* ★ Price
Elasticity and Total Money Expenditure ★ The
Demand Curve for Automobiles: A Case Study ★
Industry and Firm Demand Curves ★ Income
Elasticity of Demand ★ Cross Elasticity of Demand
★ **Exploring Further: The Farm Problem** ★
Summary

**Chapter 18 Perfect Competition, Market Supply, and
Efficiency**   **359**

Market Structure and Economic Performance ★
Perfect Competition ★ The Output of the Firm ★
Deriving the Market Supply Curve ★ Price and
Output: The Market Period ★ Price and Output:
The Short Run ★ Price and Output: The Long Run
★ The Allocation of Resources under Perfect
Competition: A More Detailed View ★ *Case Study
18.1 Price Ceiling and Price Supports* ★ Summary

Chapter 19 Monopoly and Its Regulation   **379**

Causes of Monopoly ★ Demand Curve and Marginal
Revenue under Monopoly ★ Price and Output: The
Short Run ★ Price and Output: The Long Run ★
Perfect Competition and Monopoly: A Comparison
★ *Case Study 19.1 John D. Rockefeller and
Standard Oil of Ohio* ★ The Case Against
Monopoly ★ Public Regulation of Monopoly ★ *Case
Study 19.2 AT&T and the Kingsbury Agreement* ★
Efficiency Incentives ★ **Exploring Further: The
Defense of Monopoly Power** ★ Summary

**Chapter 20 Monopolistic Competition, Oligopoly, and
Antitrust Policy**   **401**

Monopolistic Competition and Oligopoly: Their
Major Characteristics ★ Monopolistic Competition

★ Price and Output under Monopolistic Competition ★ Oligopoly ★ Oligopoly Behavior and the Stability of Prices ★ Collusion and Cartels ★ Barriers to Collusion ★ *Case Study 20.1 The Electrical Conspiracy* ★ Price Leadership ★ Nonprice Competition ★ *Case Study 20.2 How Ford Became Number Two and General Motors Became Number One* ★ Comparison of Oligopoly with Perfect Competition ★ The Antitrust Laws ★ The Role of the Courts ★ The Role of the Justice Department ★ The Effectiveness of Antitrust Policy ★ Summary

Chapter 21 The Environment   422

Our Environmental Problems ★ The Important Role of External Diseconomies ★ Economic Growth and Environmental Pollution ★ *Case Study 21.1 Reserve Mining: The Price of Cleaner Water* ★ Public Policy toward Pollution ★ Pollution-Control Programs in the United States ★ How Clean Should the Environment Be? ★ *Case Study 21.2 Leaded Gas and Cost-Benefit Analysis* ★ Summary

☆ ☆

PART 5 THE DISTRIBUTION OF INCOME

Chapter 22 The Supply and Demand for Labor   435

The Labor Force and the Price of Labor ★ The Equilibrium Wage and Employment under Perfect Competition ★ The Market Demand Curve for Labor ★ The Market Supply Curve for Labor ★ Equilibrium Price and Quantity of Labor ★ Labor Unions ★ The American Labor Movement ★ How Unions Increase Wages ★ Collective Bargaining ★ *Case Study 22.1 The Closing of the* Herald Tribune ★ Summary

Chapter 23 Interest, Rent, and Profits   452

The Nature of Interest ★ The Determination of the Interest Rate ★ *Case Study 23.1 Anti-Usury Laws*

and Mortgage Activity ★ Functions of the Interest
Rate ★ Capitalization of Assets ★ The Present
Value of Future Income ★ Rent: Nature and
Significance ★ Profits ★ The Functions of Profits ★
The Functional Distribution of Income ★ Summary

Chapter 24 Poverty, Income Inequality, and
Discrimination   **468**

How Much Inequality of Income? ★ Why
Inequality? ★ Effects of the Tax Structure on
Income Inequality ★ Income Inequality: The Pros
and Cons ★ The Tradeoff Between Equality and
Efficiency ★ What Is Poverty? ★ Social Insurance ★
*Case Study 24.1 Job Training Programs and the War
on Poverty* ★ Antipoverty Programs ★ *Case Study
24.2 The Family Assistance Plan* ★ The Problems of
Discrimination ★ Summary

☆ ☆

**PART 6 GROWTH, THE GOVERNMENT, AND
INTERNATIONAL ECONOMICS**

Chapter 25 Economic Growth   **489**

What Is Economic Growth? ★ Economic Growth as
a Policy Objective ★ Thomas Malthus and
Population Growth ★ *Case Study 25.1 The Club of
Rome's "Limits to Growth" Report* ★ David Ricardo
and Capital Formation ★ Capital Formation and
Economic Growth ★ The Role of Human Capital ★
The Role of Technological Change ★ *Case Study
25.2 Computer-Assisted Design and Manufacture at
Boeing Aircraft* ★ Entrepreneurship and the Social
Environment ★ *Case Study 25.3 The Ford Assembly
Line* ★The Gap Between Actual and Potential
Output ★ Summary

Chapter 26 Public Goods and the Role of the
Government   **508**

What Functions Should the Government Perform?
★ Establishing "Rules of the Game" ★

Redistribution of Income ★ Providing Public Goods ★ Externalities ★ *Case Study 26.1 The Tennessee Valley Authority* ★ The Theory of Public Choice ★ Principles of Taxation ★ The Personal Income Tax ★ *Case Study 26.2 Equity and Simplicity in the Income Tax Code* ★ The Property Tax and the Sales Tax ★ *Case Study 26.3 Proposition 13* ★ Tax Incidence ★ Summary

Chapter 27 International Trade   528

America's Foreign Trade ★ Specialization and Trade ★ Absolute Advantage ★ Comparative Advantage ★ The Terms of Trade ★ International Trade and Individual Markets ★ Tariffs and Quotas ★ Arguments for Tariffs and Quotas ★ *Case Study 27.1 Restrictions on U.S. Imports of Japanese Autos* ★ Summary

Chapter 28 Exchange Rates and the Balance of Payments   544

The Effects of Foreign Trade on NNP ★ International Transactions and Exchange Rates ★ Exchange Rates under the Gold Standard ★ The Foreign Exchange Market ★ Fixed Exchange Rates ★ Balance-of-Payments Deficits and Surpluses ★ Exchange Rates: Pre-World War II Experience ★ *Case Study 28.1 The Abandonment of the Gold Standard* ★ The Gold-Exchange Standard ★ U.S. Balance-of-Payments Deficits, 1950–72 ★ Demise of the Bretton Woods System ★ Fixed versus Flexible Exchange Rates ★ How Well Have Floating Exchange Rates Worked? ★ Summary

Glossary of Terms   565

Index   579

Preface

This book has been prepared to accompany the telecourse *Economics U$A*, which was developed under a grant from the Annenberg/CPB Project. The telecourse is designed to use economic events in America, present and past, to help teach the principles of economics. The elements of this telecourse include: a 28-part television series, this textbook, a telecourse study guide, a text review guide, a 28-part audio series, a faculty manual, and a test bank. The aim of this integrated approach to teaching introductory economics is to use actual economic events to motivate study of the principles of economics, and to show how these principles can help us understand the complex and dynamic American economy.

This text is an adaptation of Edwin Mansfield's *Economics: Principles, Problems, Decisions,* 5th edition. The chapters in the text follow the same sequence as the television programs, and there is much overlap in content between text and video. All chapters include case studies that focus on economic events covered in the corresponding television programs. The telecourse also includes a set of audio programs, intended especially for two-semester principles courses, that helps students review major points and explore subjects further through additional interviews. *Economics U$A* integrates text, video, and audio to an unprecedented degree in introductory economics.

As an aid to students enrolled in the telecourse, the Southern California Consortium has prepared a telecourse study guide, which includes learning objectives, key terms, overviews of text and video, questions and problems (with answers), and "Extended Learning" sections for the two-semester course. The telecourse Study Guide will help students bridge the material in the text, the video, and the audio programs.

This book can be used as the text in a telecourse based on the entire *Economics U$A* television series, and can stand on its own as the text in a traditional lecture course. (If they like, teachers of such courses can supplement their lectures with individual television programs from the series.) The text is suitable for the one-semester survey of economics or, with the supplementary "Exploring Further" sections at the ends of chapters, for the two-semester principles course.

In courses where this book is used on its own, many students will want to use the accompanying *Text Review Guide,* prepared by Edwin Mansfield. Each chapter of the *Text Review Guide* contains many completion questions, true-false questions, multiple-choice questions, discussion questions, and problem sets. These batteries of questions can be used by students for review, as well as for classroom discussion. All of these questions have withstood the test of widespread classroom use.

While it is difficult in many jointly authored works to assign responsibility, in this case it is relatively easy. Nariman Behravesh reorganized and edited the material in Mansfield's *Economics* to make it parallel the telecourse; in addition, he was responsible for the case studies that appear over his initials, as well as the glossary of terms. He was assisted in this effort by Mary Yates of Wharton Econometric Forecasting Associates. Edwin Mansfield is responsible for the text itself (other than Behravesh's case studies and glossary); also, he performed a detailed edit of the final version of the manuscript.

We are grateful to the following teachers, who commented in detail on a preliminary version of the manuscript: Robert C. Augur, Pasadena City College; James E. Clark, Wichita State University; Peter Dorman, University of Massachusetts; Ralph F. Lewis, Economics Research, Inc.; James Phillips, Cypress College; and Victor H. Rieck, Miami-Dade Community College. In addition, we would like to thank Steven Forman, Nancy Palmquist, and Amanda Adams for their efficient handling of the publishing end of the work.

Philadelphia, PA

E.M.
N.B.

PART I

☆☆☆☆☆☆☆☆☆☆☆☆☆☆

Introduction to Economics

Economic Problems:
A Sampler

With reference to a famous nineteenth-century German composer, Mark Twain once said that "his music is better than it sounds." Much the same might be said of economics. Although economics sounds like a difficult and dry subject, it is really an interesting field that throws important light on a wide range of issues that are of great interest to consumers, workers, business executives, government officials—essentially everyone.

Perhaps the best way to get an idea of what economics is all about is to look at some of the problems it can help illuminate. In these opening pages you will encounter four fairly typical economic problems. Although this is only a small sample, it is designed to give you a reasonable first impression of how the study of economics bears directly on the real world.

UNEMPLOYMENT AND INFLATION

The history of the American economy is for the most part a story of growth. Our output—the amount of goods and services we produce annually—has grown rapidly over the years, giving us a standard of living that could not have been imagined a century ago. For example, output per person in the United States was about $15,000 in 1984; in 1900, it was about $3,000. Nonetheless, the growth of output has not been steady or uninterrupted; instead, our output has tended to fluctuate—and so has unemployment. In periods when output has fallen, thousands, even millions, of people have been thrown out of work. In the Great Depression of the 1930s, for example, over 20 percent of the labor force was unemployed (see Figure I). Unemployment on this scale results in enormous economic waste and social misery.

Our first example of an economic problem is: *What determines the*

1 ★

**Figure I
Unemployment
Rates, United
States, 1929–84**
The unemployment
rate has varied
substantially from
year to year. In the
Great Depression, it
reached a high of
over 24 percent. In
1984, it exceeded 7
percent.

extent of **unemployment** *in the American economy, and what can be done to reduce it?* This problem is complicated by a related phenomenon: the level of prices may rise when we reduce the level of unemployment. In other words, inflation may occur. Thus the problem is

*Unemployed factory
workers, Indiana*

not only to curb unemployment but to do it without producing an inflation so ruinous to the nation's economic health that the cure proves more dangerous than the ailment. Consequently, another major accompanying question is: *What determines the rate of* **inflation,** *and how can it be reduced?* As Figure II shows, we have experienced considerable inflation since 1929; the dollar has lost over four-fifths of its purchasing power during this period. Moreover, in the 1970s and early 1980s, our economy has been bedeviled by "stagflation": a combination of high unemployment and high inflation.

During the past 50 years, economists have learned a great deal about the factors that determine the extent of unemployment and inflation. Since, contrary to earlier opinion, our economy has no automatic regulator that keeps it moving quickly and dependably toward minimal unemployment with stable prices, the American people, as well as people in other lands, have given their government the responsibility of promoting conditions favoring a high level of employment without serious inflation. Economists have developed techniques to help the government do this job. These techniques are by no means foolproof, as indicated by the relatively high rates of inflation and unemployment in many countries during the 1970s and early 1980s. Everyone agrees that the techniques must be improved. But practically all observers believe that they are useful.

As a responsible citizen, you should understand these techniques. You should understand how the government can use its control over the

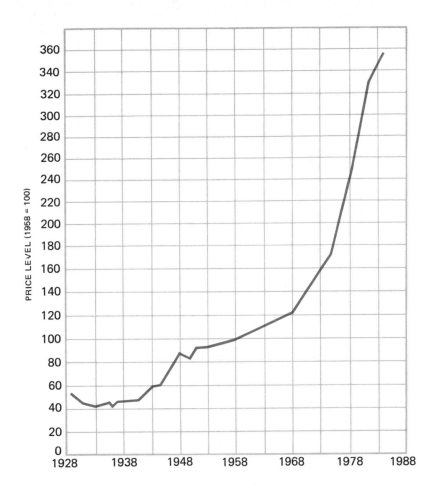

Figure II
Changes in Price Level, United States, 1929–84
The price level has increased steadily since the 1930s, and is now over eight times as high as it was in 1933.

money supply and interest rates, as well as its power to spend and tax, to promote high employment with reasonably stable prices. You should also be aware of the differences of opinion among leading economists on this score. To understand many of the central political issues of the day, and to vote intelligently, this knowledge is essential. Also, to understand the fallacies in many apparently simple remedies for the complex economic problems in this area, you need to know some economics.

THE PRODUCTIVITY SLOWDOWN AND THE COMPETITIVENESS OF U.S. GOODS

Labor productivity is defined as the amount of output that can be obtained per hour of labor. All nations are interested in increasing labor productivity, since it is intimately related to a nation's standard of living. Many factors, including new technologies like microelectronics and biotechnology, influence the rate of increase of labor productivity. Historically, labor productivity has increased relatively rapidly in the United States.

However, beginning in the late 1960s, U.S. labor productivity rose at a slower pace. At first, it was unclear whether this slowdown was only temporary, but experience during the 1970s showed that the situation got worse, not better. Between 1977 and 1980, labor productivity in the United States actually declined. (In other words, less was produced per hour of labor in 1980 than in 1977!) During the early 1980s, productivity growth picked up, but whether it would reach its old level—and stay there —was by no means obvious.

Abandoned steel mill, Pittsburgh, Pennsylvania

FOR LEASE
INDUSTRIAL
PROPERTY
5 ACRES · 20,000 Sq. Ft. Bldg.
681-0754 · Zoned M3 · 521-4257

Many observers regard this productivity slowdown as a very ominous sign for the U.S. economy. Moreover, they worry too about the fact that labor productivity in the United States has been increasing less rapidly than in many other countries like Japan and West Germany. For this and other reasons, there are questions regarding the ability of American firms to compete with their foreign rivals in industries like autos and machine tools.

Our second example of an economic problem is: *What determines the rate of increase of labor productivity? Why has this productivity slowdown occurred in the United States? What measures can and should be adopted to cope with it?* Economics provides a considerable amount of information on this score. Not only does economics tell us a good deal about the broad factors influencing national productivity levels; it also provides rules and principles that are useful in increasing the productivity and efficiency of individual firms (and government agencies).

GOVERNMENT REGULATION OF BUSINESS

The 100 largest manufacturing firms control about half of all manufacturing assets in the United States (and their share of total assets seems to have increased since World War II). In certain industries, like automobiles, the four largest firms have accounted for over 90 percent of the market (see Table I). Nonetheless, although the largest corporations obviously wield considerable power in their markets, the American economic system is built on the idea that firms should compete with one another. In particular, the producers of steel, automobiles, oil, toothpicks, and other goods are expected to set their prices independently and not to collude. Certain acts

Table I
Market Share of
Four Largest Firms,
Selected
Manufacturing
Product Markets,
United States

Industry	Market share of four largest firms (percent)
Automobiles	93
Photographic equipment	72
Soap	59
Tires	70
Aircraft	59
Construction machinery	47
Blast furnaces and steel plants	45

Source: Statistical Abstract of the United States.

of Congress, often referred to as the antitrust laws, make it illegal for firms to get together and set the price of a product.

Our third example of an economic problem is: *Why is competition of this sort socially desirable?* More specifically, why should we be in favor of the antitrust laws? What reasons are there to believe that such laws will result in a more efficient economic system? (And what do we mean by "efficient"?) To a business executive, lawyer, government official, or judge, these questions are very important, since it is likely that at one time or another these people will be concerned with an antitrust case. But these issues also matter to every citizen, because they deal with the basic rules of the game for firms in our economy. Of course, one reason why Americans have traditionally favored competition over collusion, and relatively small firms over giant ones, is that they have mistrusted the concentration of economic power, and obviously this mistrust was based on both political and economic considerations. But beyond this, you should know when competition generally benefits society and when it does not.

One way that society has attempted to control the economic power of corporations that dominate an entire industry is through public regulation. Take the case of radio and TV. The Federal Communications Commission (FCC), a government agency, monitors the activities of broadcasting stations and networks to prevent misuse of the airwaves. Other regulatory commissions have supervised the activities of the power companies, the railroads, and other industries where it has been felt that competition cannot be relied on to produce socially desirable results.

During the late 1970s and early 1980s, there was a notable movement in the United States toward deregulation. At first, the movement was confined largely to the airlines, but then it spread to railroads, trucking, oil, and other industries. In part, this movement reflected a widespread feeling that the regulatory commissions tended to be lax or, worse still, to be more concerned with the industry's interests than with the public good. In addition, it was felt that many aspects of regulation have contributed to inefficiency, both in the regulated industries themselves and in other parts of the economy. Since regulated industries produce about 10 percent of the national output, we all have a big stake in understanding how they operate and whether they should be regulated and, if so, how. This is another aspect of the same general problem of how industries should be organized.

THE ELIMINATION OF POVERTY

As pointed out by Philip Wicksteed, a prominent twentieth-century British economist, "A man can be neither a saint, nor a lover, nor a poet, unless he has comparatively recently had something to eat." Although relatively few people in the United States lack food desperately, about 35 million American people—approximately 15 percent of the population of the United States—live in what is officially designated as *poverty*. These people have frequently been called invisible in a nation where the average yearly income per family is over $25,000; but the poor are invisible only to those who shut their eyes, since they exist in ghettos in the wealthiest American cities like New York, Chicago, and Los Angeles, as well as near Main Street in thousands of small towns. They can also be found in areas where industry has come and gone, as in the former coal-mining towns of Pennsylvania and West Virginia, and in areas where decades of farming have depleted the soil.

Table II shows the distribution of income in the United States in 1983. Clearly, there are very substantial differences among families in income level. Indeed, the cats and dogs of the very rich eat better than some human beings. You as a citizen and a human being need to understand the social mechanisms underlying the distribution of income, both in the United States and in other countries, and how reasonable and just they are.

Table II
Percentage
Distribution of
People, by
Household Monthly
Cash Income,
United States, 1983

Money income (dollars)	Percent of all people
Under 300	4.7
300–599	7.8
600–899	8.0
900–1,199	8.2
1,200–1,599	11.4
1,600–1,999	10.7
2,000–2,999	22.1
3,000–3,999	13.1
4,000 and over	14.1
Total	100[a]

[a]Because of rounding errors, the figures do not sum to total.
Source: U.S. Bureau of the Census. The data pertain to the third quarter of the year.

Our fourth example of an economic problem is: *Why does poverty exist in the world today, and what can be done to abolish it?* To help the poor effectively, we must understand the causes of poverty.

LOOKING AHEAD

Despite the problems described here, the American economy is among the most prosperous in the world. The average American family has plenty of food, clothing, housing, appliances, and luxuries of many kinds, and the average American worker is well educated and well trained. The tremendous strength and vitality of the American economy should be recognized, as well as its shortcomings. Nothing is gained by overlooking either the successes or the faults of our system.

As a first step toward understanding why we are so well off in some respects and so lacking in others, we need to understand how our economy works. Of course, this is a big task. Indeed, you could say that this whole book is devoted to discussing this subject. So we will not try to present a detailed picture of the operation of the American economy at this point. Instead, in the following chapters we will give a basic blueprint of what an economic system must do.

CHAPTER I

★ ★ ★ ★ ★ ★ ★

What Is Economics?

LEARNING OBJECTIVES

In this chapter, you should learn:

★ The definition of economics, including the concepts of resources, scarcity, and choice

★ The four basic tasks that must be accomplished by any economic system

★ The concept of opportunity cost

★ *(Exploring Further)* What a production possibilities curve shows and why the curve is important

In the Prologue we looked at a number of specific economic problems. We must now provide a definition of economics, as well as a description of the basic questions regarding any economic system that are of particular interest to economists. Furthermore, we need to understand the basic methodology of economics.

WHAT IS ECONOMICS?

According to one standard definition, *economics is concerned with the way resources are allocated among alternative uses to satisfy human wants.* This definition is fine, but it does not mean much unless we define what is meant by *human wants* and by *resources.* What do these terms mean?

Human wants are the things, services, goods, and circumstances that people desire. Wants vary greatly among individuals and over time for the same individual. Some people like sports, others like books; some want to travel, others want to putter in the yard. An individual's desire for a particular good during a particular period of time is not infinite, but, in the aggregate, human wants seem to be insatiable. Besides the basic desires for food, shelter, and clothing, which must be fulfilled to some extent if the human organism is to maintain its existence, wants stem from cultural factors. For example, society, often helped along by advertising and other devices to modify tastes, promotes certain images of "the good life," which frequently entails owning an expensive car and living in a $150,000 split-level house in the suburbs.

Resources are the things or services used to produce goods, which then can be used to satisfy wants. *Economic resources* are scarce; *free resources,* such as air, are so abundant that they can be obtained without charge. The test of whether a resource is an economic resource or a free resource is price: economic resources command a nonzero price; free resources do not. The number of free resources is actually quite limited. For instance, although the earth contains a huge amount of water, it is not a free resource to typical urban or suburban home owners, who must pay a local water authority for providing and maintaining their water supply. In a world where all resources were free, there would be no economic problem, since all wants could be satisfied.

Economic resources can be classified into three categories:

1. *Land.* A shorthand expression for natural resources, land includes minerals as well as plots of ground. Clearly, land is an important and valuable resource in both agriculture and industry. Think of the fertile soil of Iowa or Kansas, from which are obtained such abundant crops. Or consider Manhattan island, which supports the skyscrapers, shops, and theaters in the heart of New York. In addition, land is an important part of our environment, and it provides enjoyment above and beyond its contribution to agricultual and industrial output.

2. *Labor.* Human efforts, both physical and mental, are included in the category of labor. Thus, when you study for a final examination or make out an income tax return, this is as much labor as if you were to dig a ditch. In 1986, over 100 million people were employed (or looking for work) in the United States. This vast labor supply is, of course, an extremely important resource, without which our nation could not maintain its current output level.

3. *Capital.* Buildings, equipment, inventories, and other nonhuman producible resources that contribute to the production, marketing, and distribution of goods and services all fall within the economist's definition of capital. Examples are machine tools and warehouses; but not all types of capital are big or bulky: for example, a hand calculator, or a pencil for that matter, is a type of capital. American workers have an enormous amount of capital to work with. Think of the oil refineries in New Jersey and Philadelphia, the blast furnaces and open hearths in Pittsburgh and Cleveland, the aircraft plants in California and Georgia, and the host of

additional types of capital we have and use in this country. Without this capital, the nation's output level would be a great deal less than it is.

Technology and Choice

As pointed out above, economics is concerned with the way resources are allocated among alternative uses to satisfy human wants. An important determinant of the extent to which human wants can be satisfied from the amount of resources at hand is technology. *Technology* is society's pool of knowledge concerning the industrial arts. It includes the knowledge of engineers, scientists, craftsmen, managers, and others concerning how goods and services can be produced. For example, it includes the best existing knowledge regarding the ways in which an automobile plant or a synthetic rubber plant should be designed and operated. The level of technology sets limits on the amount and types of goods and services that can be derived from a given amount of resources.

To see this, suppose that engineers and craftsmen do not know how an automobile can be produced with less than 500 hours of labor being used in its manufacture. Clearly, this sets limits on the number of automobiles that can be produced with the available labor force. Or suppose that scientists and engineers do not know how to produce a ton of synthetic rubber with less than a certain amount of capital being used in its manufacture. This sets limits on the amount of synthetic rubber that can be produced with the available quantity of capital.

Given the existing technology, the fact that resources are scarce means that only a limited amount of goods and services can be produced from them. In other words, the capacity to produce goods and services is limited —*far more limited than human wants.* Thus there arises the necessity for *choice.* Somehow or other, a choice must be made as to how the available resources will be used (or if they will be used at all). And somehow or other a choice must be made as to how the output produced from these resources will be distributed among the population.

Economics is concerned with how such choices are made. Economists have spent a great deal of time, energy, and talent trying to determine how such choices *are* made in various circumstances, and how they *should* be made. Indeed, as we shall see in the next section, the basic questions that economics deals with are problems of choice of this sort. Note that these problems of choice go beyond the problems of particular individuals in choosing how to allocate their resources; they are problems of social choice.

Central Questions in Economics

Economists are particularly concerned with four basic questions regarding the working of any economic system—ours or any other. These questions are: (1) What determines what and how much is produced? (2) What determines how it is produced? (3) What determines how the society's output is distributed among the members? (4) What determines the rate at which the society's per capita income will grow? These questions lie at the core of economics, because they are directed at the most fundamental characteristics of economic systems. And as stressed in the previous section, they are problems of choice.

To illustrate the nature and basic importance of these questions, suppose that because of war or natural catastrophe, your town is isolated from the adjoining territory. No longer is it possible for the town's inhabitants to leave, or for people or goods to enter. (Lest you regard this as fanciful, it is worthwhile to note that Leningrad was under siege in World War II for over two years.) In this situation, you and your fellow townspeople must somehow resolve each of these questions. You must decide what goods and services will be produced, how each will be produced, who will receive what, and how much provision there will be for increased output in the future.

In a situation of this sort, your very survival will depend on how effectively you answer these questions. If a decision is made to produce too much clothing and too little food, some of the townspeople may starve. If a decision is made to allot practically all of the town's output to friends and political cronies of the mayor, those who oppose him may have a very rough time. And if a decision is made to eat, drink, and be merry today, and not to worry about tomorrow, life may be very meager in the days ahead.

Because we are considering a relatively small and isolated population, the importance of these questions may seem more obvious than in a huge country like the United States, which is constantly communicating, trading, and interacting with the rest of the world. But the truth is that these questions are every bit as important to the United States as to the isolated town. And for this reason, it is important that we understand how these decisions are made, and whether they are being made effectively. Just as in the hypothetical case of the isolated town, your survival depends on these decisions—but in the United States the situation isn't hypothetical!

OPPORTUNITY COST: A FUNDAMENTAL CONCEPT

In previous sections, we have emphasized that economics is concerned with the way resources are allocated among alternatives uses to satisfy human wants. To help determine how resources should be allocated, economists often use the concept of *opportunity cost.* We turn now to an introductory discussion of this concept, which should help to acquaint you with how it is used.

Since a specific case is more interesting than abstract discussion, let's return to the case of the town that is isolated from the adjoining territory because of a war or natural catastrophe. Suppose you are a member of the town council that is organized to determine how the town's resources should be utilized. To keep things simple, suppose that only two goods—

food and clothing—can be produced. (This is an innocuous assumption that allows us to strip the problem to its essentials.) You must somehow figure out how much of each good should be produced. How can you go about solving this problem?

Clearly, the first step toward a solution is to list the various resources contained within the town. Using the technology available to the towns-people, each of these resources can be used to produce either food or clothing. Some of these resources are much more effective at producing one good than the other. For example, a tailor probably is better able to produce clothing than to produce food. But nonetheless most resources can be adapted to produce either good. For example, the tailor can be put to work on a farm, even though he may not be very good at farming.

After listing the various available resources and having determined how effective each is at producing food or clothing, the next step is to see how much food the town could produce per year, if it produced nothing but food, and how much clothing it could produce per year, if it produced nothing but clothing. Also, you should determine, if various amounts of food are produced per year, the maximum amount of clothing that the town can produce per year. For example, if the town produces 100 tons of food per year, what is the maximum amount of clothing it can produce per year? If the town produces 200 tons of food per year, what is the maximum amount of clothing it can produce per year? And so on.

Having carried out this step, suppose that the results are as shown in Table 1.1. According to this table, the town can produce (at most) 200 tons of clothing per year if it produces nothing but clothing (possibility A). Or it can produce (at most) 400 tons of food per year if it produces nothing but food (possibility E). Other possible combinations (labeled B, C, and D) of food output and clothing output are specified in Table 1.1.

Possibility	Amount of food produced per year (tons)	Amount of clothing produced per year (tons)
A	0	200
B	100	180
C	200	150
D	300	100
E	400	0

Table 1.1
Combinations of Output of Food and Clothing that the Town Can Produce per Year

Table 1.1 puts in bold relief the basic problem of choice facing you and the other members of the town council. Because the town's resources are limited, the town can only produce limited amounts of each good. There is no way, for example, that the town can produce 200 tons of clothing per year and 200 tons of food per year. This is beyond the capacity of the town's resources. If the town wants to produce 200 tons of clothing, it can produce no food—which is hardly a pleasant prospect. And if the town wants to produce 200 tons of food, it can produce 150 (not 200) tons of clothing per year. Table 1.1 shows what combinations of food and clothing outputs are attainable.

More Food Means Less Clothing

A very important fact illustrated by Table 1.1 is that whenever the town increases its production of one good, it must cut back its production of the other good. For example, if the town increases its production of food from 100 to 200 tons per year, it must cut back its production of clothing from 180 to 150 tons per year. Thus *the cost to the town of increasing its food output from 100 to 200 tons per year is that it must reduce its clothing output from 180 to 150 tons per year.*

Economists refer to this cost as *opportunity cost* (or *alternative cost*); it is one of the most fundamental concepts in economics. *The opportunity cost of using resources in a certain way is the value of what these resources could have produced if they had been used in the best alternative way.* In this case, the opportunity cost of the extra 100 tons of food per year is the 30 tons of clothing per year that must be forgone. This is what the town must give up in order to get the extra 100 tons of food.

Why is opportunity cost so important? Because for you and the other members of the town council to determine which combination of food and clothing is best, you should compare the value of increases in food output with the opportunity costs of such increases. For example, suppose that the town council is considering whether or not to increase food output from 100 to 200 tons per year. To decide this question, the council should compare the value of the extra 100 tons of food with the opportunity cost of the extra food (which is the 30 tons of clothing that must be given up). If the town council feels that the extra 100 tons of food are worth more to the town's welfare than the 30 tons of clothing that are given up, the extra food should be produced. Otherwise it should not be produced.

THE IMPACT OF ECONOMICS ON SOCIETY

In previous sections, we described some of the questions that concern economists. Now we must consider how much influence economics has had. The answer is that economics has influenced generations of states- men, philosophers, and ordinary citizens, and has played a significant role in shaping our society today. Skim through the articles in a daily newspa- per. Chances are that you will find a report of an economist testifying before Congress, perhaps on the costs and benefits of a program to reduce unemployment among black teenagers in the Bedford-Stuyvesant area of New York City, or on the steps to be taken to make American goods more competitive with those of Japan or West Germany. Still another economist may crop up on the editorial page, discussing the pros and cons of various proposed ways to reduce the federal deficit.

Economics and economists play a key role at the highest levels of our government. The president, whether a Democrat or a Republican, relies heavily on his economic advisers in making the decisions that help to shape the future of the country. In Congress, too, economics plays a major role. Economists are frequent witnesses before congressional committees, staff members for the committees, and advisers to individual congressmen and senators. Many congressional committees focus largely on economic matters. For example, in 1985, many congressmen spent large chunks of their time wrestling with budgetary and tax questions.

Positive Economics versus Normative Economics

From the outset, it is essential that we recognize the distinction between positive economics and normative economics. *Positive economics contains descriptive statements, propositions, and predictions about the world.* For instance, an economic theory may predict that the price of copper will increase by $.01 a pound if income per person in the United States rises by 10 percent; this is positive economics. Positive economics tells us only what will happen under certain circumstances. It says nothing about whether the results are good or bad, or about what we should do. *Normative economics, on the other hand, makes statements about what ought to be, or about what a person, organization, or nation ought to do.* For instance, a theory might say that Chile should introduce new technology more quickly in many of its copper mines; this is normative economics.

Clearly, positive economics and normative economics must be treated differently. Positive economics is science in the ordinary sense of the world. Propositions in positive economics can be tested by an appeal to the facts. In a nonexperimental science like economics, it is sometimes difficult to get the facts you need to test particular propositions. For example, if income per person in the United States does not rise by 10 percent, it may be difficult to tell what the effect of such an increase would be on the price of copper. Moreover, even if per capita income does increase by this amount, it may be difficult to separate the effect of the increase in income per person on the price of copper from the effect of other factors. But nonetheless we can, in principle, test propositions in positive economics by an appeal to the facts.

In normative economics, however, this is not the case. *In normative economics, the results you get depend on your values or preferences.* For example, if you believe that reducing unemployment is more important than maintaining the purchasing power of the dollar, you will get one answer to certain questions; if you believe that maintaining the purchasing power of the dollar is more important than reducing unemployment, you are likely to get a different answer to the same questions. This is not at all strange. After all, if people desire different things (which is another way of saying that they have different values), they may well make different decisions and advocate different policies. It would be strange if they did not.

☆ ☆ ☆ ☆ ☆ ☆ ☆ ☆ ☆ ☆ ☆ ☆ ☆

CASE STUDY 1.1 LAND USE IN ALASKA

In November 1980, the Alaska National Interest Lands Conservation Act declared more than 100 million acres of Alaskan wilderness off-limits to extensive mining and resource exploitation. Interior Secretary Cecil Andrus and Arizona Senator Morris Udall supported the bill, but Alaskan representatives such as Senator Mike Gravel sought to have the federally owned lands opened for development.

The bill was the culmination of the environmental battle that started when the conservationists inserted conditions for the preservation of the wilderness in the 1958 Alaska Statehood Act. Environmentalists felt that the value of the land as wilderness—the preservation of the habitat of many plant and animal species, and the use of the land by backpackers—greatly exceeded the potential value of its soil or minerals. Those who sought to postpone the act, including the majority of people in Alaska, argued that the value of the land for mining or logging should be assessed first. They argued in particular that the potential oil reserves should be estimated, in light of the recent doubling in the price of oil caused by the 1979 oil shortage. It would be foolhardy, they said, to reduce artificially the amount of oil available for domestic consumption when the dependence of the United States on foreign oil caused so much harm in terms of inflation and unemployment.

The vote in Congress implicitly maintained that the benefit of keeping the land as wilderness was greater than that of any alternative use. The bill President Carter signed into law sought to "protect the resources of Alaska's crown jewels in perpetuity as national parks, wildlife refuges, forests and wild and scenic rivers." Put in the language of this chapter, the opportunity cost of keeping the land as wilderness was regarded as less than the benefits of doing so.

N.B.

THE METHODOLOGY OF ECONOMICS

Model Building in Economics

Like other types of scientific analysis, economics is based on the formulation of *models. A model is a theory. It is composed of a number of assumptions from which conclusions—or predictions—are deduced.* An astronomer who wants to formulate a model of the solar system might represent each planet by a point in space and assume that each would change position in accord with certain mathematical equations. Based on this model, the astronomer might predict when an eclipse would occur, or estimate the probability of a planetary collision. Economists proceed along similar lines when they set forth a model of economic behavior.

There are several important points to be noted concerning models:

1. *To be useful, a model must simplify the real situation.* The assumptions made by a model need not be exact replicas of reality. If they were, the model would be too complicated to use. The basic reason for using a model is that the real world is so complex that masses of detail often obscure underlying patterns. The economist faces the familiar problem of seeing the forest as distinct from just the trees. Other scientists must do the same; physicists work with simplified models of atoms, just as economists work with simplified models of markets. However, this does not mean that *all* models are good or useful. A model may be so oversimplified and distorted that it is utterly useless. The trick is to construct a model so that irrelevant and unimportant considerations and variables are neglected, but the major factors—those that seriously affect the phenomena the model is designed to predict—are included.

2. *The purpose of a model is to make predictions about the real world; in many respects the most important test of a model is how well it predicts.* In this sense, a model that predicts the price of copper within plus or minus $.01 a pound is better than a model that predicts it within plus or minus $.02 a pound. Of course, this does not mean that a model is useless if it cannot predict very accurately. We do not always need a very accurate prediction. For example, a road map is a model that can be used to make predictions about the route a driver should take to get to a particular destination. Sometimes, a very crude map is good enough to get you where you want to go, but such a map would not, for instance, serve hikers who need to know the characteristics of the terrain through which they plan to walk. How detailed a map you need depends on where you are going and how you want to get there.

3. *A person who wants to predict the outcome of a particular event will be forced to use the model that predicts best, even if this model does not predict very well.* The choice is not between a model and no model; it is between one model and another. After all, a person who must make a forecast will use the most accurate device available—and any such device is a model of some sort. Consequently, when economists make simplifying

assumptions and derive conclusions that are only approximately true, it is somewhat beside the point to complain that the assumptions are simpler than reality or that the predictions are not always accurate. This may be true, but if the predictions based on the economists' model are better than those obtained on the basis of other models, their model must, and will, be used until something better comes along. Thus if a model can predict the price of copper to within plus or minus $.01 per pound, and no other model can do better, this model will be used even if those interested in the predictions bewail the model's limitations and wish it could be improved.

Economic Measurement

To utilize and test their models, economists need facts of many sorts. For example, suppose that an economist constructs a model that predicts that a household's annual clothing expenditure tends to increase by $60 when its income increases by $1,000. To see whether this model is correct, the economist must gather data concerning the incomes and clothing expenditures of a large number of households and study the relationship between them. Suppose that the relationship proves to be as shown in Figure 1.1. The line represents an average relationship between household income and household consumption expenditure. Judging by Figure 1.1, the model is reasonably accurate, at least for households with incomes between $15,000 and $30,000 per year.[1]

**Figure 1.1
Relationship
between Annual
Clothing
Expenditures and
Annual Household
Income**
Each family is represented by a dot. The line shows the average relationship. The line does not fit all families exactly, since all the points do not fall on it. The line does, however, show average clothing expenditure for each income level.

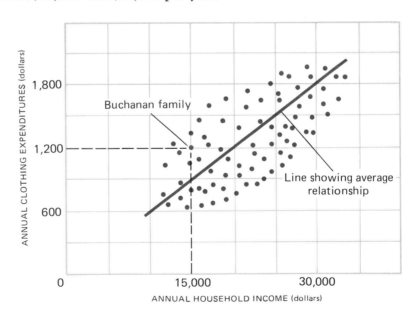

[1]It is worth noting that, although it is useful to see how well a model would have fit the historical facts, this is no substitute for seeing how well it will predict the future. According to one old saying, "It's a darned poor person who can't predict the past."

Measurements like those in Figure 1.1 enable economists to *quantify* their models; in other words, they enable them to construct models that predict *how much* effect one variable has on another. If economists did not quantify their models, they (and their models) would be much less useful. For example, the economist in the previous paragraph might have been content with a model that predicts that higher household income results in higher household clothing expenditures; but this model would not have been interesting or useful, since you do not need an economist to tell you that. A more valuable model is one that is quantitative, that predicts how much clothing expenditure will increase if household income rises by a certain amount. This is the sort of model that economists usually try to construct.

GRAPHS AND RELATIONSHIPS

To conclude our brief discussion of economic methodology, we must describe the construction and interpretation of graphs, such as Figure 1.1, which economists use to present data and relationships.

1. A graph has a horizontal axis and a vertical axis, each of which has a scale of numerical values. For example, in Figure 1.1, the horizontal axis shows a household's annual income, and the vertical axis shows the annual amount spent by the household on clothing. The intersection of the two axes is called the origin and is the point where both the variable measured along the horizontal axis and the variable measured along the vertical axis are zero. In Figure 1.1, the origin is at the lower left-hand corner of the figure, labeled "0."

2. To show the relationship between two variables, one can plot the value of one variable against the value of the other variable. Thus in Figure 1.1 each family is represented by a dot. For example, the dot for the Buchanan family is in the position shown in Figure 1.1 because its income was $15,000 and its clothing expenditure was $1,200. Clearly, the line showing the average relationship does not fit all the families exactly, since all the points do not fall on the line. This line does, however, give the average clothing expenditure for each level of income: it is an average relationship.

3. The relationship between two variables is *direct* if, as in Figure 1.1, the line of average relationship is upward sloping. In other words, if the variable measured along the vertical axis tends to increase (decrease) in response to increases (decreases) in the variable measured along the horizontal axis, the relationship is direct. On the other hand, if the line of average relationship is downward sloping, as in Figure 1.2, the relationship is *inverse.* In other words, if the variable measured along the vertical axis tends to decrease (increase) in response to increases (decreases) in the variable measured along the horizontal axis, the relationship is inverse.

To illustrate how one can graph a relationship between two variables, consider Table 1.2, which shows the quantity of tennis balls demanded in a particular market at various prices. Putting price on the vertical axis and

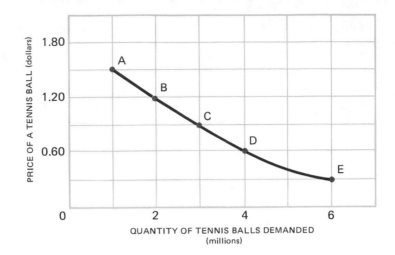

Figure 1.2
Relationship between Quantity Demanded and Price of Tennis Balls (as shown in Table 1.2)

quantity demanded on the horizontal axis, one can plot each combination of price and quantity in this table as a point on a graph; and that is precisely what has been done in Figure 1.2 (points *A* to *E*).

Table 1.2
Quantity of Tennis Balls Demanded in a Particular Market at Various Prices

Price of a tennis ball (dollars)	Quantity of tennis balls demanded (millions)
1.50	1
1.20	2
0.90	3
0.60	4
0.30	6

THE TASKS OF AN ECONOMIC SYSTEM

Having discussed the nature and quantification of economic models, we conclude by describing what an economic system—*ours or any other*—must do. Basically, as we saw earlier in this chapter, there are four tasks that any economic system must perform:

1. *An economic system must determine the level and composition of society's output.* That is, it must answer questions like: To what extent should society's resources be used to produce new aircraft carriers and missiles? To what extent should they be used to produce sewage plants to reduce water pollution? To what extent should they be used to produce swimming pools for the rich? To what extent should they be used to produce low-cost housing for the poor? Pause for a moment to think about how important—and how vast—this function is. Most people simply take for granted that somehow it is decided what we as a society are going to produce, and far too few people really think about the social mechanisms that determine the answers to such questions.

CASE STUDY 1.2 ADAM SMITH, FATHER OF MODERN ECONOMICS

To illustrate the importance of economic ideas, let's consider some of the precepts of Adam Smith (1723–90), the man who is often called the father of modern economics. Much of his masterpiece *The Wealth of Nations** seems trite today because it has been absorbed so thoroughly into modern thought, but it was not trite when it was written. On the contrary, Smith's ideas were revolutionary. *He was among the first to describe how a free, competitive economy can function—without central planning or government interference—to allocate resources efficiently. He recognized the virtues of the "invisible hand" that leads the private interest of firms and individuals toward socially desirable ends, and he was properly suspicious of firms that are sheltered from competition, since he recognized the potentially undesirable effects on resource allocation.*

Adam Smith

In addition, Smith—with the dire poverty of his times staring him in the face—was interested in the forces that determined the evolution of the economy—the forces determining the rate of growth of average income per person. Although Smith did not approve of avarice, he felt that saving was good because it enabled society to invest in machinery and other forms of capital. Accumulating more and more capital would, according to Smith, allow output to grow. In addition, he emphasized the importance of increased specialization and division of labor in producing economic progress. By specializing, people can concentrate on the tasks they do best, with the result that society's total output is raised.

All in all, Smith's views were relatively optimistic. Leave markets alone, said Smith, and beware of firms with too much economic power and government meddling. If this is done, there is no reason why considerable economic progress cannot be achieved. Smith's work has been modified and extended in a variety of ways in the past 200 years. Some of his ideas have been challenged and, in some cases, discarded. But his influence on modern society has been enormous.

*Adam Smith, *The Wealth of Nations.* Originally published in 1776.

☆ ☆ ☆ ☆ ☆ ☆ ☆ ☆ ☆ ☆ ☆ ☆ ☆

2. *An economic system must determine how each good and service is to be produced.* Given existing technology, a society's resources can be used in various ways. Should the skilled labor in Birmingham, Alabama, be used to produce cotton or steel? Should a particular machine tool be used to produce aircraft or automobiles? The way questions of this sort are answered will determine the way each good and service is produced. In other words, it will determine which resources are used to produce which goods and services. If this function is performed badly, society's resources are put to the wrong uses, resulting in less output than if this function is performed well.

3. *An economic system must determine how the goods and services that are produced are to be distributed among the members of society.* In other words, how much of each type of good and service should each person receive? Should there be a considerable amount of income inequality, the rich receiving much more than the poor? Or should income be relatively equal? Take your own case. Somehow or other, the economic system determines how much income you will receive. In our economic system, your income depends on your skills, the property you own, how hard you work, and prevailing prices, as we shall see in succeeding chapters. But in other economic systems, your income might depend on quite different factors. This function of the economic system has generated, and will continue to generate, heated controversy. Some people favor a relatively egalitarian society where the amount received by one family varies little from that received by another family of the same size. Other people favor a society where the amount a family or person receives can vary a great deal. Few people favor a thoroughly egalitarian society, if for no other reason than that some differences in income are required to stimulate workers to do certain types of work.

4. *An economic system must determine the rate of growth of per capita income.* An adequate growth rate has come to be regarded as an important economic goal, particularly in the less developed countries of Africa, Asia, and Latin America. There is very strong pressure in these countries for changes in technology, the adoption of superior techniques, increases in the stock of capital resources, and better and more extensive education and training of the labor force. These are viewed as some of the major ways to promote the growth of per capita income.

☆   ☆   ☆   **EXPLORING FURTHER: A SIMPLE INTRODUCTORY MODEL OF THE ECONOMIC SYSTEM[2]**

The Production Possibilities Curve and the Determination of What Is Produced

In a previous section, we said that economists use models to throw light on economic problems. At this point, let's try our hand at constructing a

[2]Sections titled "Exploring Further" are optional.

simple model to illuminate the basic functions any economic system, ours included, must perform. To keep things simple, suppose that society produces only two goods, food and tractors. This, of course, is unrealistic, but as we stressed in a previous section, a model does not have to be realistic to be useful. Here, by assuming that there are only two goods, we eliminate a lot of unnecessary complexity and lay bare the essentials. In addition, we suppose that society has at its disposal a certain amount of resources, and that this amount is fixed for the duration of the period in question. This assumption is quite realistic. So long as the period is relatively short, the amount of a society's resources is relatively fixed (except, of course, under unusual circumstances, such as if a country annexes additional land). Finally, we suppose as well that society's technology is fixed. So long as the period is relatively short, this assumption too is realistic.

Under these circumstances, it is possible to figure out the various amounts of food and tractors that society can produce. Specifically, we can proceed as we did at the beginning of this chapter to determine the amounts of food and clothing that an isolated town could produce. Let's begin with how many tractors society can produce if all resources are devoted to tractor production. According to Table 1.3, the answer is 15 million tractors. Next, let's consider the opposite extreme, where society devotes all its resources to food production. According to Table 1.3, it can produce 12 million tons of food in this case. Next, let's consider cases where both products are being produced. Such cases are represented by possibilities B to F in the table. As emphasized earlier in this chapter, the more of one good that is produced, the less of the other good that can be produced. Why? Because to produce more of one good, resources must be taken away from the production of the other good, lessening the amount of the other good produced.

Possibility	Food (millions of tons)	Tractors (millions)
A	0	15
B	2	14
C	4	12
D	6	10
E	8	7
F	10	4
G	12	0

Table 1.3
Alternative Combinations of Outputs of Food and Tractors that Can Be Produced

Figure 1.3 shows how we can use a graph to show the various production possibilities society can attain. It is merely a different way of presenting the data in Table 1.3: The output of food is plotted on the horizontal axis and the output of tractors on the vertical axis. The curve in Figure 1.3, which shows the various combinations of output of food and tractors that society can produce, is called a *production possibilities curve.*

The production possibilities curve sheds considerable light on the economic tasks facing any society. It shows the various production possibilities open to society. In Figure 1.3, society can choose to produce 4 million tons

Figure 1.3
**Production
Possibilities Curve**
This curve shows
the various
combinations of
tractors and food
that can be
produced efficiently
with given resources
and technology.
Point *H* is
unattainable.

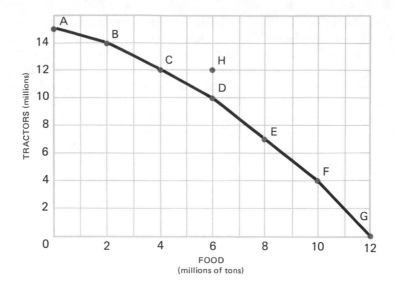

of food and 12 million tractors (point *C*), or 6 million tons of food and 10 million tractors (point *D*), but it cannot choose to produce 6 million tons of food and 12 million tractors (point *H*). Point *H* is inaccessible with this society's resources and technology. Perhaps it will become accessible if the society's resources increase or if its technology improves, but for the present, point *H* is out of reach.

If resources are fully and efficiently utilized, *the first function of any economic system—to determine the level and composition of society's output—is really a problem of determining at what point along the production possibilities curve society should be.* Should society choose point *A, B, C, D, E, F,* or *G?* In making this choice, one thing is obvious from the production possibilities curve: *You cannot get more of one good without giving up some of the other good.* In other words, you cannot escape the problem of choice. So long as resources are limited and technology is less than magic, you must reckon with the fact (emphasized earlier in this chapter) that more of one thing means less of another. The old saw that you don't "get something for nothing" is hackneyed but true, so long as resources are fully and efficiently utilized.

The Production Possibilities Curve and the Determination of How Goods Are Produced

Let's turn now to the second basic function of any economic system: to determine how each good and service should be produced. In Table 1.3 we assumed implicitly that society's resources would be fully utilized and that the available technology would be applied in a way that would get the most out of the available resources. In other words, we assumed that the firms making food and tractors were as efficient as possible and that there was no unemployment of resources. But if there is widespread unemployment of people and machines, will society still be able to choose a point on the production possibilities curve? Clearly, the answer is no. Since society is not using all of its resources, it will not be able to produce as much as if it used them all. Thus *if there is less than full employment of resources, society will have to settle for points inside the production possibilities curve.* For example, the best society may be able to do under these circumstances is to attain point *K* in Figure 1.4. *K* is a less desirable point than *C* or *D*—but that is the price of unemployment.

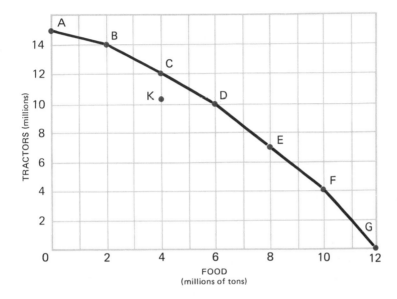

Suppose, on the other hand, that there is full employment of resources but that firms are inefficient. Perhaps they promote relatives of the boss, regardless of their ability; perhaps the managers are lazy or not very interested in efficiency; or perhaps the workers like to take long coffee breaks and are unwilling to work hard. Whatever the reason, will society still be able to choose a point on the production possibilities curve? Again, the answer is no. Since society is not getting as much as it could out of its resources, it will not be able to produce as much as it would if its resources were used efficiently. Thus *if resources are used inefficiently, society will have to settle for points inside the production possibilities curve.* Perhaps in these circumstances too the best society can do may be point *K* in Figure 1.4. This less desirable position is the price of inefficiency.

At this point, it should be obvious that our model at least partially answers the question of how each good and service should be produced. The answer is to *produce each good and service in such a way that you wind up on the production possibilities curve, not on a point inside it.* Of course this is easier said than done, but at least our model indicates a couple of villains to watch out for: unemployment of resources and inefficiency. When these villains are present, we can be sure that society is not on the production possibilities curve. Also, the old saw is wrong, and it *is* possible to "get something for nothing" when society is inside the production possibilities curve. That is, society can increase the output of one good without reducing the output of another good in such a situation. Society need not give up anything—in the way of production of other goods—to increase the production of this good under these circumstances.

The Production Possibilities Curve, Income Distribution, and Growth

The third basic function of any economic system is to distribute the goods and services that are produced among the members of society. Each point on the production possibilities curve in Figure 1.4 represents society's total pie, but to deal with the third function we must know how the pie is divided up among society's members. Since the production possibilities curve does not tell us this, it cannot shed light on this third function.

Fortunately, the production possibilities curve is of more use in analyzing the fourth basic function of any economic system: to determine the society's rate of growth of per capita income. Suppose that the society in Figure 1.4 invests a considerable amount of its resources in developing improved processes and products. It might establish agricultural experiment stations to improve farming techniques and industrial research laboratories to improve tractor designs. As shown in Figure 1.5, the production possibilities curve will be pushed outward. This will be the result of improved technology, enabling more food and/or more tractors to be produced from the same amount of resources. Thus one way for an economy to increase its output—and its per capita income—may be to invest in research and development.

**Figure 1.5
Effect of
Improvement in
Technology on
Production
Possibilities Curve**
An improvement in technology results in an outward shift of the production possibilities curve.

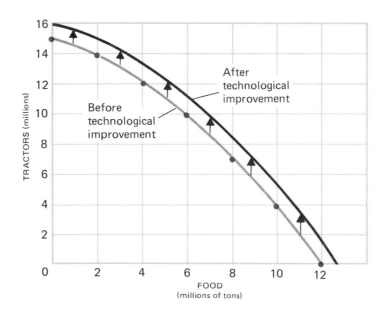

CASE STUDY 1.3 PRODUCING BOTH GUNS AND BUTTER IN 1939–41

Throughout the 1930s, massive amounts of productive resources were wasted. In 1938, even after the economy had recovered from the worst years of the Depression, the unemployment rate was 19 percent; more than 10 million people who were willing and able to work could not find jobs; and the capacity utilization rate for the nation's plant and equipment was very low.

With the outbreak of war in Europe in 1939, the demand for U.S. goods jumped sharply. Orders flowed in, and U.S. firms put their dormant factories to work and increased their hiring. Real national output increased 7.7 percent in 1939, 7.6 percent in 1940, and 16 percent in 1941. Munitions production went from almost zero in 1938 to $3 billion by the end of 1940 and $10 billion by the end of 1941 (all figures are in 1943 dollars).

Because consumers' incomes had increased along with the recovery, the demand for consumer goods also grew. But with the diversion of so much of the labor force and factories into war-related production, what happened to consumer goods production? Consumer expenditures actually increased from $58 billion in 1938 to $70 billion in 1941. By putting existing resources to work, the U.S. economy was able to increase production of *both* guns *and* butter in the early years of the war. Why? Because the United States had been operating at a point inside its production possibilities curve.

By the end of 1941, when the United States officially entered the war, the economy was already producing close to its potential. The unemployment rate had fallen to 4 percent, and capacity utilization had improved dramatically. Only by extending work hours and by upgrading and expanding the nation's capital stock could the economy grow. The United States continued to produce more and more every year of the war, but the gains in both guns and butter were no longer possible. Munitions production increased from $10 billion in 1941 to $64 billion by the end of the war, but there was no further growth in civilian consumption after 1941. In fact, the production of some civilian goods such as autos and appliances was halted completely, and others such as tires, sugar, and coffee were rationed. By 1942, after having taken up the slack of the Depression years, the economy had to face the classic tradeoff between guns and butter.

N.B.

Another way is for the economy to devote more of its resources to the production of capital goods than to consumer goods. *Capital goods* consist of plant and equipment that are used to make other goods; *consumer goods* are items that consumers purchase like clothing, food, and drink. Since capital goods are themselves resources, a society that chooses to produce lots of capital goods and few consumer goods will push out its production possibilities curve much farther than a society that chooses to produce lots of consumer goods and few capital goods.

To illustrate this point, consider our simple society that produces food and tractors. The more tractors (and the less food) this society produces, the more tractors it will have in the next period; and the more tractors it has in the next period, the more of both goods—food and tractors—it will be able to produce. Thus the more tractors (and the less food) this society produces, the farther out it will push its production possibilities curve—and the greater the increase in output (and per capita income) that it will achieve in the next period. If this society chooses point *F* (shown in Figures 1.3 and 1.4), the effect will be entirely different than if it chooses point *C*. If it chooses point *F*, it produces 4 million tractors, which we assume to be the number of tractors worn out each year. Thus if it chooses point *F* it adds nothing to its stock of tractors: it merely replaces those that wear out. Since it has no more tractors in the next period than in the current period, the production possibilities curve does not shift out at all if point *F* is chosen. On the other hand, if point *C* is chosen, the society produces 12 million tractors, which means that it has 8 million additional tractors at the beginning of the next period. Thus, as shown in Figure 1.6, the production possibilities curve is pushed outward. By producing more capital goods (and fewer consumer goods), our society has increased its production possibilities and its per capita income.

**Figure 1.6
Effect of Increase
in Capital Goods
on Production
Possibilities Curve**
An increase in the amount of capital goods results in an outward shift of the production possibilities curve. The choice of point *C* means the production of more capital goods than the choice of point *F*.

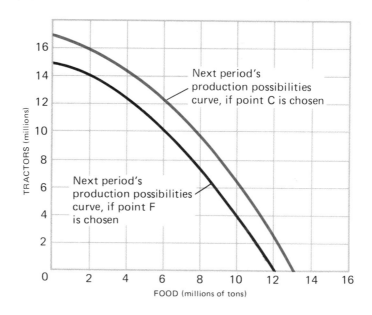

SUMMARY

1. According to one standard definition, economics is concerned with the way resources are allocated among alternative uses to satisfy human wants. A resource is a thing or service used to produce goods (or services) that can satisfy wants. Not all resources are scarce. Free resources, such as air, are so abundant that they can be obtained without charge.

2. Those resources that are scarce are called economic resources. The test of whether a resource is an economic resource or a free resource is price: economic resources command a nonzero price but free resources do not. Economists often classify economic resources into three categories: land, labor, and capital.

3. Since economic resources are scarce, only a limited amount of goods and services can be produced from them, and there arises the necessity for choice. For example, if an isolated town has a certain amount of resources, it must choose how much of each good it will produce from these resources. If it increases the amount produced of one good, it must reduce the amount produced of another good.

4. The opportunity cost (or alternative cost) of using a resource to increase the production of one good is the value of what the resource could have produced had it been used in the best alternative way.

5. Economists are particularly concerned with four basic questions regarding the working of an economic system, ours or any other. These questions are: (1) What determines what (and how much) is produced? (2) What determines how it is produced? (3) What determines how the society's output is distributed among its members? (4) What determines the rate at which the society's per capita income will grow?

6. Economists often distinguish between positive economics and normative economics. Positive economics contains descriptive statements, propositions, and predictions about the world; normative economics contains statements about what ought to be, or about what a person, organization, or nation ought to do.

7. In normative economics, the results you get depend on your basic values and preferences; in positive economics, the results are testable, at least in principle, by an appeal to the facts.

8. The methodology used by economists is much the same as that used in any other kind of scientific analysis. The basic procedure is the formulation and testing of models.

9. A model must in general simplify and abstract from the real world. Its purpose is to make predictions concerning phenomena in the real world, and in many respects the most important test of a model is how well it predicts these phenomena. To test and quantify their models, economists gather data and use various statistical techniques.

*10. The production possibilities curve, which shows the various produc-

*The starred items refer to material covered in the section, "Exploring Further."

tion possibilities a society can attain, is useful in indicating the nature of the economic tasks any society faces. The task of determining the level and composition of society's output is really a problem of determining at what point along the production possibilities curve society should be.

*11. Society has to recognize that it cannot get more of one good without giving up some of another good, if resources are fully and efficiently used. However, if they are not fully and efficiently used, society will have to settle for points inside the production possibilities curve—and it will be possible to obtain more of one good without giving up some of another good.

*12. The task of determining how each good and service should be produced is, to a considerable extent, a problem of keeping society on its production possibilities curve, rather than at points inside the curve. The production possibilities curve does not tell us anything about the distribution of income, but it does indicate various ways that a society can promote growth in per capita income. By doing research and development, or by producing capital goods (rather than consumers' goods), society may push its production possibilities curve outward, thus increasing per capita income.

*The starred items refer to material covered in the section, "Exploring Further."

CHAPTER 2

★ ★ ★ ★ ★ ★ ★ ★ ★

Markets and Prices

LEARNING OBJECTIVES

In this chapter, you should learn:

★ What market demand and market supply curves show

★ The distinction between shifts in a commodity's demand or supply curve and changes in the quantity demanded or supplied of the commodity

★ The significance of equilibrium price

★ How the price system accomplishes the four basic tasks of an economic system, and what general limitations the price system suffers from

★ *(Exploring Further)* The effects of shifts in the demand and supply curves

Capitalist economies use the price system to perform the four basic tasks any economic system must carry out. However, the American economy is a mixed capitalist system, not a pure one. Both government and private decisions are important. This does not mean that the price system is unimportant. On the contrary, the price system plays a vital role in the American economy, and to obtain even a minimal grasp of the workings of our economic system, one must understand how the price system operates. This chapter takes up the nature and functions of the price system, as well as some applications of our theoretical results to real-life problems.

CONSUMERS AND FIRMS

We begin by describing and discussing consumers and firms, the basic building blocks that make up the private, or nongovernmental, sector of **31 ★**

the economy. What is a *consumer*? Sometimes—for example, when a person buys a beer on a warm day—the consumer is an individual. In other cases—for example, when a family buys a new car—the consumer may be an entire household. Consumers purchase the goods and services that are the end products of the economic system. When a man buys tickets to a ball game, he is a consumer; when he buys himself a Coke at the game, he is a consumer; and when he buys his wife a book on baseball for their twentieth wedding anniversary, he is also a consumer.

There are about 16 million *firms* in the United States. About nine-tenths of the goods and services produced in this country are produced by firms. (The rest are provided by government and not-for-profit institutions like universities and hospitals.) A firm is an organization that produces a good or service for sale. In contrast to not-for-profit organizations, firms attempt to make a profit. It is obvious that our economy is centered around the activities of firms.

Like consumers, firms are extremely varied in size, age, power, and purpose. Consider two examples, Peter Amacher's drugstore on Chicago's South Side and the General Motors Corporation. The Amacher drugstore, started in 1922 by Mr. Amacher's father-in-law, is known in the retail drug trade as an independent, because it has no affiliation with a chain-store organization. Mr. Amacher and two other pharmacists keep the store open for business 13 hours a day, except on Sundays. The store sells about $150,000 worth of merchandise per year.

In contrast, General Motors is one of the giants of American industry. It is the largest manufacturer of automobiles in the United States, with sales in 1984 of about $84 billion. Besides cars, it makes trucks, locomotives, aircraft engines, household appliances, and other products. It has long been a leading symbol of American industrial might and success, but recently it has encountered formidable competition from imported Japanese cars.

MARKETS

Consumers and firms come together in a market. The concept of a market is not quite as straightforward as it may seem, since most markets are not well defined geographically or physically. For example, the New York Stock Exchange is an atypical market because it is located principally in a particular building. For present purposes, *a **market** can be defined as a group of firms and individuals that are in touch with each other in order to buy or sell some good.* Of course, not every person in a market has to be in contact with every other person in the market. A person or firm is part of a market even if it is in contact with only a subset of the other persons or firms in the market.

Markets vary enormously in their size and procedures. For some goods like toothpaste, most people who have their own teeth (and are interested in keeping them) are members of the same market; for other goods like Picasso paintings, only a few dealers, collectors, and museums in certain parts of the world may be members of the market. And for still other goods, like lemonade sold by neighborhood children for a nickel a glass at a sidewalk stand, only people who walk by the stand—and are brave enough to drink the stuff—are members of the market. Basically, however, all markets consist primarily of buyers and sellers, although third parties like brokers and agents may be present as well.

Markets also vary in the extent to which they are dominated by a few large buyers or sellers. For example, in the United States, there was for many years only one producer of aluminum. This firm, the Aluminum Company of America, had great power in the market for aluminum. In contrast, the number of buyers and sellers in some other markets is so large that no single buyer or seller has any power over the price of the product. This is true in various agricultural markets, for example. When a market for a product contains so many buyers and sellers that none of them can influence the price, economists call the market *perfectly competitive*. In these introductory chapters, we make the simplifying assumption that markets are perfectly competitive. We will relax that assumption later.

THE DEMAND SIDE OF A MARKET

Every market has a demand side and a supply side. *The* **demand** *side can be represented by a* **market demand curve**, *which shows the amount of the commodity buyers would like to purchase at various prices.* Consider Figure 2.1, which shows the demand curve for wheat in the American market during the mid-1980s.[1] The figure shows that about 2.7 billion bushels of wheat will be demanded annually if the farm price is $3.00 per bushel, about 2.6 billion bushels will be demanded annually if the farm price is $3.30 per bushel, and about 2.5 billion bushels will be demanded annually if the farm price is $3.60 per bushel. The total demand for wheat is of several types: to produce bread and other food products for domestic use, for feed use, for export purposes, and for industrial uses. The demand curve in Figure 2.1 shows the total demand—including all these components—at each price.

Take a good look at the demand curve for wheat in Figure 2.1. This simple, innocent-looking curve influences a great many people's lives. After all, wheat is the principal grain used for direct human consumption in the United States. To states like Kansas, North Dakota, Oklahoma, Montana, Washington, Nebraska, Texas, Illinois, Indiana, and Ohio, wheat is a mighty important cash crop. Note that the demand curve for wheat slopes downward to the right. In other words, the quantity of wheat demanded increases as the price falls. This is true of the demand curve for most commodities: they almost always slope downward to the right. This

---

[1]Officials of the U.S. Department of Agriculture provided this information. Of course, these estimates are only approximations, but they are good enough for present purposes.

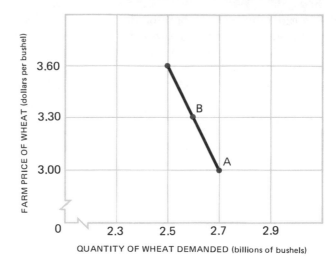

makes sense; one would expect increases in a good's price to result in a smaller quantity demanded.

Any demand curve is based on the assumption that the tastes, incomes, and number of consumers, as well as the prices of other commodities, are held constant. Changes in any of these factors are likely to shift the position of a commodity's demand curve, as indicated below.

CONSUMER TASTES. If consumers show an increasing preference for a product, the demand curve will shift to the right; that is, at each price, consumers will desire to buy more than previously. On the other hand, if consumers show a decreasing preference for a product, the demand curve will shift to the left, since at each price, consumers will desire to buy less than previously. Take wheat: If consumers become convinced that foods containing wheat prolong life and promote happiness, the demand curve may shift, as shown in Figure 2.2; the greater the shift in preferences, the larger the shift in the demand curve.

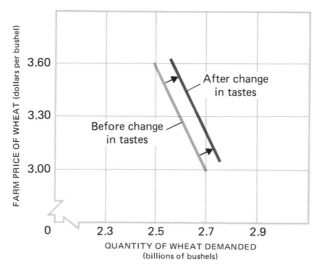

INCOME LEVEL OF CONSUMERS. For some types of products, the demand curve shifts to the right if per capita income increases; for other types of commodities, the demand curve shifts to the left if per capita income rises. Economists can explain why some goods fall into one category and other goods fall into the other, but at present this need not concern us. All that is important here is that changes in per capita income affect the demand curve, the size and direction of this effect varying from product to product. In the case of wheat, a 10 percent increase in per capita income would probably have a relatively small effect on the demand curve, as shown in Figure 2.3.

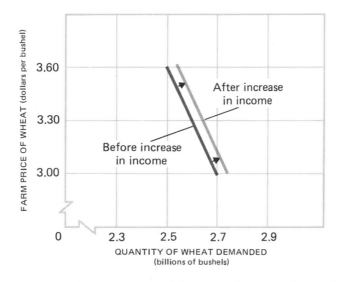

Figure 2.3
Effect of Increase in Income on Market Demand Curve for Wheat
An increase in income would shift the demand curve for wheat to the right, but only slightly.

NUMBER OF CONSUMERS IN THE MARKET. Compare Austria's demand for wheat with the United States'. Austria is a small country with a population of less than 8 million; the United States is a huge country with a population of over 200 million. Clearly, at a given price of wheat, the quantity demanded by American consumers will greatly exceed the quantity demanded by Austrian consumers, as shown in Figure 2.4. Even if consumer tastes, income, and other factors were held constant, this would still be true simply because the United States has so many more consumers in the relevant market.[2]

LEVEL OF OTHER PRICES. A commodity's demand curve can be shifted by a change in the price of other commodities. Whether an increase in the price of good B will shift the demand curve for good A to the right or the left depends on the relationship between the two goods. If they are substitutes, such an increase will shift the demand curve for good A to the right. Consider the case of corn and wheat. If the price of corn goes up, more wheat will be demanded since it will be profitable to substitute wheat for

[2]Note that no figures are given along the horizontal axis in Figure 2.4. This is because we do not have reasonably precise estimates of the demand curve in Austria. Nonetheless, the hypothetical demand curves in Figure 2.4 are close enough to the mark for present purposes.

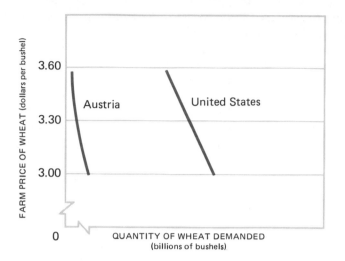
corn. If the price of corn drops, less wheat will be demanded since it will be profitable to substitute corn for wheat. Thus, as shown in Figure 2.5, increases in the price of corn will shift the demand curve for wheat to the right, and decreases in the price of corn will shift it to the left.[3]

**Figure 2.5
Effect of Price of
Corn on Market
Demand Curve for
Wheat**
Price increases for
corn will shift the
demand curve for
wheat to the right.

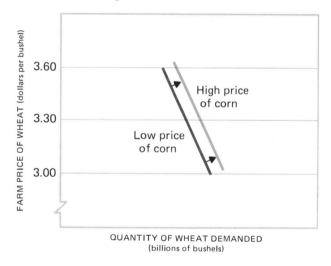

The Distinction between Changes in Demand and Changes in the Quantity Demanded

It is essential to distinguish between a *shift in a commodity's demand curve* and a change in the *quantity demanded of the commodity.* A shift

[3]If goods A and B are complements, an increase in the price of good B will shift the demand curve for good A to the left. Thus an increase in the price of gin is likely to shift the demand curve for tonic to the left. Why? Because gin and tonic tend to be used together. The increase in gin's price will reduce the quantity of gin demanded, which in turn will reduce the amount of tonic that will be demanded at each price of tonic.

in a commodity's demand curve is a change in the *relationship* between price and quantity demanded. Figures 2.2, 2.3, and 2.5 show cases where such a change occurs. A change in the quantity demanded of a commodity may occur even if *no* shift occurs in the commodity's demand curve. For example, in Figure 2.1, if the price of wheat increases from $3.00 to $3.30 per bushel, the quantity demanded falls from 2.7 to 2.6 billion bushels. This change in the quantity demanded is due to a *movement along* the demand curve (from point *A* to point *B* in Figure 2.1), not to a *shift* in the demand curve.

When economists refer to an *increase in demand,* they mean a *rightward shift* in the demand curve. Thus Figures 2.2, 2.3, and 2.5 show increases in demand for wheat. When economists refer to a *decrease in demand,* they mean a *leftward shift* in the demand curve. An increase in demand for a commodity is not the same as an increase in the quantity demanded of the commodity. In Figure 2.1, the quantity demanded of wheat *increases* if the price falls from $3.30 to $3.00 per bushel, but this is not due to an increase in demand, since there is no rightward shift of the demand curve. Similarly, a decrease in demand for a commodity is not the same as a decrease in the quantity demanded of a commodity. In Figure 2.1, the quantity demanded of wheat *decreases* if the price rises from $3.00 to $3.30 per bushel, but this is not due to a decrease in demand, since there is no leftward shift of the demand curve.

THE SUPPLY SIDE OF A MARKET

So much for our first look at demand. What about the other side of the market: supply? *The **supply** side of a market can be represented by a **market supply curve** that shows the amount of the commodity sellers would offer at various prices.* Let's continue with the case of wheat. Figure 2.6 shows the supply curve for wheat in the United States in the mid-1980s, based on estimates made informally by government experts.[4] According to the figure, about 2.4 billion bushels of wheat would be supplied if the farm price were $3.00 per bushel, about 2.6 billion bushels if the farm price were $3.30 per bushel, and about 2.8 billion bushels if the farm price were $3.60 per bushel.

Look carefully at the supply curve shown in Figure 2.6. Although it looks innocuous enough, it summarizes the potential behavior of thousands of American wheat farmers—and their behavior plays an important role in determining the prosperity of many states and communities. Note that the supply curve for wheat slopes upward to the right. In other words, the quantity of wheat supplied increases as the price increases. This seems plausible, since increases in price give a greater incentive for farms to produce wheat and offer it for sale. Empirical studies indicate that the

[4]Officials of the U.S. Department of Agriculture provided these estimates. Although rough approximations, they are good enough for present purposes.

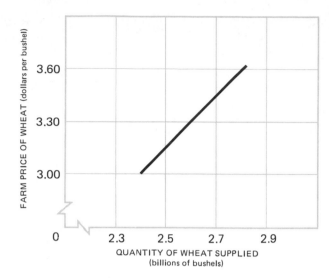

**Figure 2.6
Market Supply
Curve for Wheat,
Mid-1980s**
The curve shows
the amount that
sellers would supply
at various prices. At
$3.60 per bushel,
about 17 percent
more wheat would
be supplied than at
$3.00 per bushel.

supply curves for a great many commodities share this characteristic of sloping upward to the right.

Any supply curve is based on the assumption that technology and input prices are held constant. Changes in these factors are likely to shift the position of a commodity's supply curve.

TECHNOLOGY. Recall that technology was defined in Chapter 1 as society's pool of knowledge concerning the industrial arts. As technology progresses, it becomes possible to produce commodities more cheaply, so firms often are willing to supply a given amount at a lower price than formerly. Thus technological change often causes the supply curve to shift to the right. This certainly has occurred in the case of wheat, as shown in Figure 2.7. There have been many important technological changes in wheat production, ranging from advances in tractors to the development of improved varieties, like semi-dwarf wheats.

**Figure 2.7
Effect of
Technological
Change on Market
Supply Curve for
Wheat**
Improvements in
technology often
shift the supply
curve to the right.

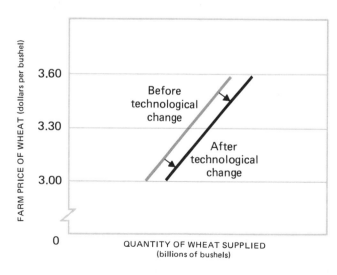

INPUT PRICES. The supply curve for a commodity is affected by the prices of the resources (labor, capital, and land) used to produce it. Decreases in the price of these inputs make it possible to produce commodities more cheaply, so that firms may be willing to supply a given amount at a lower price than they formerly would. Thus decreases in the price of inputs may cause the supply curve to shift to the right. On the other hand, increases in the price of inputs may cause it to shift to the left. For example, if the wage rates of farm labor increase, the supply curve for wheat may shift to the left, as shown in Figure 2.8.

Figure 2.8
Effect of Increase in Farm Wage Rates on Market Supply Curve for Wheat
An increase in the wage rate might shift the supply curve to the left.

An *increase in supply* is defined to be a *rightward shift* in the supply curve; a *decrease in supply* is defined to be a *leftward shift* in the supply curve. A change in supply should be distinguished from a change in the quantity supplied. In Figure 2.6, the quantity supplied of wheat will increase from 2.4 to 2.6 billion bushels if the price increases from $3.00 to $3.30 per bushel, but this is not due to an increase in supply, since there is no rightward shift of the supply curve in Figure 2.6.

EQUILIBRIUM PRICE

The two sides of a market, demand and supply, interact to determine the price of a commodity. Prices in a capitalistic system are important determinants of what is produced, how it is produced, who receives it, and how rapidly per capita income grows. It behooves us, therefore, to look carefully at how prices themselves are determined in a capitalist system. As a first step toward describing this process, we must define the equilibrium price of a product. At various points in this book, you will encounter the concept of an equilibrium, which is very important in economics, as in many other scientific fields.

Put briefly, *an equilibrium is a situation where there is no tendency for change;* in other words, it is a situation that can persist. Thus *an* **equilib-**

rium price *is a price that can be maintained.* Any price that is not an equilibrium price cannot be maintained for long, since there are basic forces at work to stimulate a change in price. The best way to understand what we mean by an equilibrium price is to take a particular case, such as the wheat market. Let's put the demand curve for wheat (in Figure 2.1) and the supply curve for wheat (in Figure 2.6) together in the same diagram. The result, shown in Figure 2.9, will help us determine the equilibrium price of wheat.

Figure 2.9
Determination of the Equilibrium Price of Wheat, Mid-1980s
The equilibrium price is $3.30 per bushel, and the equilibrium quantity is 2.6 billion bushels. At a price of $3.60 per bushel, there would be an excess supply of 300 million bushels. At a price of $3.00 per bushel, there would be an excess demand of 300 million bushels.

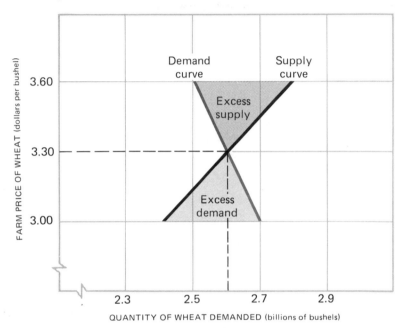

We begin by seeing what would happen if various prices were established in the market. For example, if the price were $3.60 per bushel, the demand curve indicates that 2.5 billion bushels of wheat would be demanded, while the supply curve indicates that 2.8 billion bushels would be supplied. Thus if the price were $3.60 a bushel, there would be a mismatch between the quantity supplied and the quantity demanded per year, since the rate at which wheat is supplied would be greater than the rate at which it is demanded. Specifically, as shown in Figure 2.9, there would be an *excess supply* of 300 million bushels. Under these circumstances, some of the wheat supplied by farmers could not be sold, and as inventories of wheat built up, suppliers would tend to cut their prices in order to get rid of unwanted inventories. Thus a price of $3.60 per bushel would not be maintained for long—and for this reason $3.60 per bushel is not an equilibrium price.

If the price were $3.00 per bushel, on the other hand, the demand curve indicates that 2.7 billion bushels would be demanded, while the supply curve indicates that 2.4 billion bushels would be supplied. Again we find a mismatch between the quantity supplied and the quantity demanded per year, since the rate at which wheat is supplied would be less than the rate at which it is demanded. Specifically, as shown in Figure 2.9, there would be an *excess demand* of 300 million bushels. Under these circumstances, some of the consumers who want wheat at this price would have to be turned away empty-handed. There would be a shortage. And given this shortage, suppliers would find it profitable to increase the price and competition among buyers would bid the price up. Thus a price of $3.00 per bushel could not be maintained for long—so $3.00 per bushel is not an equilibrium price.

Under these circumstances, the equilibrium price must be the price where the quantity demanded equals the quantity supplied. Obviously, this is the only price at which there is no mismatch between the quantity demanded and the quantity supplied; and consequently it is the only price that can be maintained for long. In Figure 2.9, the price at which the quantity supplied equals the quantity demanded is $3.30 per bushel, the price where the demand curve intersects the supply curve. Thus $3.30 per bushel is the equilibrium price of wheat under the circumstances visualized in Figure 2.9, and 2.6 billion bushels is the equilibrium quantity.

ACTUAL PRICE

The price that counts in the real world, however, is the actual price, not the equilibrium price, and it is the actual price that we set out to explain. In general, economists simply assume that the actual price will approximate the equilibrium price, which seems reasonable enough, since the basic forces at work tend to push the actual price toward the equilibrium price. Thus if conditions remain fairly stable for a time, the actual price should move toward the equilibrium price.

So long as the actual price exceeds the equilibrium price, there will be downward pressure on price. Similarly, so long as the actual price is less than the equilibrium price, there will be upward pressure on price. Thus there is always a tendency for the actual price to move toward the equilibrium price. But it should not be assumed that this movement is always rapid. Sometimes it takes a long time for the actual price to get close to the equilibrium price. Sometimes the actual price never gets to the equilibrium price because by the time it gets close, the equilibrium price changes (because of shifts in either the demand curve or the supply curve or both). All that safely can be said is that the actual price will move toward the equilibrium price. But of course this information is of great value, both theoretically and practically. For many purposes, all that is needed is a correct prediction of the direction in which the price will move.

THE PRICE SYSTEM AND THE DETERMINATION OF WHAT IS PRODUCED

Having described how prices are determined in free markets, we can now describe somewhat more fully how the price system goes about performing the four tasks (described in the previous chapter) that face any economic system. Let's begin by considering the determination of what society will produce: How does the price system carry out this task?

A product's demand curve is an important determinant of how much firms will produce of the product, since it indicates the amount of the product that will be demanded at each price. From the point of view of the producers, the demand curve indicates the amount they can sell at each price. In a capitalist economy, firms are in business to make money. Thus the manufacturers of any product will turn it out only if the amount of money they receive from consumers exceeds the cost of putting the product on the market. Acting in accord with the profit motive, firms are led to produce what the consumers desire. We saw in a previous section that if consumers' tastes shift in favor of foods containing wheat, the demand curve for wheat will shift to the right, which will increase the price of wheat. (If this is not obvious, see the section, "Exploring Further," in this chapter.) Given the shift in the demand curve, it is profitable for firms to raise output. Acting in their own self-interest, they are led to make production decisions geared to the wants of the consumers.

Supply and demand in the Eldridge General Store, Fayette County, Illinois

Thus the price system uses the self-interest of the producers to get them to produce what consumers want. Consumers register what they want in the marketplace by their purchasing decisions—which can be represented by their demand curves. Producers can make more money by responding to consumer wants than by ignoring them. Consequently, they are led to produce what consumers want and are willing to pay enough to cover the producers' costs. Note that costs as well as demand determine what will be produced, and that producers are not forced by anyone to do anything. They can produce air conditioners for Eskimos if they like—and if they are prepared to absorb the losses. The price system uses prices to communicate the relevant signals to producers, and metes out the penalties and rewards in the form of losses or profits.

THE PRICE SYSTEM AND THE DETERMINATION OF HOW GOODS ARE PRODUCED

Next, consider how society determines how each good and service is produced. How does the price system carry out this task? The price of each resource gives producers an indication of how scarce this resource is and how valuable it is in other uses. Clearly, firms should produce goods and services at minimum cost. Suppose that there are two ways of producing tables: Technique A and Technique B. Technique A requires four man-hours of labor and $10 worth of wood per table, whereas Technique B requires five man-hours of labor and $8 worth of wood. If the price of a man-hour of labor is $4, Technique A should be used since a table costs $26 with this technique, as opposed to $28 with Technique B.[5] In other words, Technique A uses fewer resources per table.

The price system nudges producers to opt for Technique A rather than Technique B through profits and losses. If each table commands a price of $35, then by using Technique A, producers make a profit of $35 − $26 = $9 per table. If they use Technique B, they make a profit of $35 − $28 = $7 per table. Thus producers, if they maximize profit, will be led to adopt Technique A. Their desire for profit leads them to adopt the techniques that will enable society to get the most out of its resources. No one commands firms to use particular techniques. Washington officials do not order steel plants to substitute the basic oxygen process for open hearths, or petroleum refineries to substitute catalytic cracking for thermal cracking. It is all done through the impersonal marketplace.

You should not, however, get the idea that the price system operates with kid gloves. Suppose all firms producing tables used Technique B until this past year, when Technique A was developed: in other words, Technique A is based on a new technology. Given this technological change, the supply curve for tables will shift to the right, and the price of a table will fall. (If this is not obvious, see the section, "Exploring Further,"in this chapter.) Suppose it drops to $27. If some firm insists on sticking with Technique B, it will lose money at the rate of $1 a table; and as these losses mount, the firm's owners will become increasingly uncomfortable. The firm will either switch to Technique A or go bankrupt. The price system leans awfully hard on producers who try to ignore its signals (as illustrated by Case Study 2.1 on p. 44).

THE PRICE SYSTEM AND THE DETERMINATION OF WHO GETS WHAT

Let's turn now to how society's output will be distributed among the people: How does the price system carry out this task? How much people

---

[5]To obtain these figures, note that the cost with Technique A is four man-hours times $4 plus $10, or $26, while the cost with Technique B is five man-hours times $4 plus $8, or $28.

☆ ☆ ☆ ☆ ☆ ☆ ☆ ☆ ☆ ☆ ☆ ☆ ☆

CASE STUDY 2.1 MINI-MILLS

The 1950s and 1960s were very profitable years for the large steel producers who operated massive integrated facilities; and it appeared that the larger the factory, the more profitable it would be. Steel mills processed the raw materials, produced pig iron in huge blast furnaces, manufactured steel in open hearth, oxygen, or electric furnaces, and then cast and milled the steel into finished shapes and bars. The mill represented a huge investment that was costly to finance and made firms reluctant to develop or utilize new technology.

By the mid-1970s, however, these large mills were no longer the most efficient producers of all types of steel products. It became clear that mini-mills, which had become an important factor in the steel industry in the 1960s, enjoyed a substantial cost advantage over the integrated mills in the production of reinforcing bars, wire rods, and merchant-quality bars and shapes. The mini-mills used electric furnaces and steel scrap rather than huge blast furnaces, iron ore, and coal. The investment was much smaller, since mini-mills did not have to process raw materials or generate their own energy, and the cost of producing a ton of steel was about 75 percent of the cost to the integrated producers.

Mini-mills now dominate the markets for a number of products. U.S. Steel tried to compete with the mini-mills in the production of wire rod by opening a massive plant in its South Chicago works in the 1970s. By 1983, however, the plant was forced to close even though the small mills were operating at capacity. Even the highly efficient Japanese integrated producers could not compete with the mini-mills.

The relative market prices of electric power versus coke, of processing iron ore versus using steel scrap, and so on forced the economy to shift to the more efficient method of production for certain steel products. In this way, the free market pricing mechanism encourages an economy to get the most productivity out of its scarce productive resources.

N.B.

☆ ☆ ☆ ☆ ☆ ☆ ☆ ☆ ☆ ☆ ☆ ☆ ☆

receive in goods and services depends on their money income, which in turn is determined under the price system by the amount of various resources that they own and by the price of each resource. Thus, under the price system, each person's income is determined in the marketplace: people come to the marketplace with certain resources to sell, and their income depends on how much they can get for these resources.

The question of who gets what is solved at two levels by the price system. Consider an individual product: for example, the tables discussed in the previous section. For the individual product, the question of who gets what is solved by the equality of quantity demanded and quantity supplied. If the price of these tables is at its equilibrium level, the quantity demanded will equal the quantity supplied. Consumers who are willing and able to pay the equilibrium price (or more) get the tables, while those who are unwilling or unable to pay it do not get them. It is just as simple —and as impersonal—as that. It doesn't matter whether you are a nice guy or a scoundrel, or whether you are a connoisseur of tables or someone who doesn't know good workmanship from poor; all that matters is whether you are able and willing to pay the equilibrium price.

Next, consider the question of who gets what at a somewhat more fundamental level. After all, whether consumers are able and willing to pay the equilibrium price for a good depends on their money income. As we have already seen, consumers' money income depends on the amount of resources of various kinds that they own and the price that they can get for them. Some people have lots of resources: they are endowed with skill and intelligence and industry, or they have lots of capital or land. Other people have little in the way of resources. Moreover, some people have resources that command a high price, while others have resources that are of little monetary value. The result is that under the price system, some consumers get a lot more of society's output than others.

THE PRICE SYSTEM AND ECONOMIC GROWTH

Let's turn now to the task of determining a society's rate of growth of per capita income. How does the price system do this? A nation's rate of increase of per capita income depends on the rate of growth of its resources and the rate of increase of the efficiency with which they are used. First, consider the rate of growth of society's resources. The price system controls the amount of new capital goods produced much as it controls the amount of consumer goods produced. Similarly, the price system influences the amount society invests in educating, training, and upgrading its labor resources. To a considerable extent, the amount invested in such resource-augmenting activities is determined by the profitability of such investments, which is determined in turn by the pattern of prices.

Next, consider the rate of increase of the efficiency with which a society's resources are used. Clearly, this factor depends heavily on the rate of technological change. If technology is advancing at a rapid rate, it should be possible to get more and more out of a society's resources. But if technology is advancing rather slowly, it is likely to be difficult to get much more out of them. The price system affects the rate of technological change in a variety of ways: it influences the profitability of investing in research and development, the profitability of introducing new processes and products into commercial practice, and the profitability of accepting technological change—as well as the losses involved in spurning it.

The price system establishes strong incentives for firms to introduce new technology. Any firm that can find a cheaper way to produce an existing product, or a way to produce a better product, will have a profitable jump on its competitors. Until its competitors can do the same thing, this firm can reap higher profits than it otherwise could. Of course, these higher profits will eventually be competed away, as other firms begin to imitate this firm's innovation. But lots of money can be made in the period during which this firm has a lead over its competitors. These profits are an important incentive for the introduction of new technology.

THE CIRCULAR FLOWS OF MONEY AND PRODUCTS

So far we have been concerned largely with the workings of a single market. But how do all of the various markets fit together? This is a very important question. Perhaps the best way to begin answering it is to distinguish between product markets and resource markets. As their names indicate, *product markets* are markets where products are bought and sold; and *resource markets* are markets where resources are bought and sold. Let's first consider product markets. As shown in Figure 2.10, firms provide products to consumers in product markets, and receive money in return. The money the firms receive is their receipts; to consumers, on the other hand, it represents their expenditures.

Figure 2.10
The Circular Flows of Money and Products
In product markets, consumers exchange money for products and firms exchange products for money. In resource markets, consumers exchange resources for money and firms exchange money for resources.

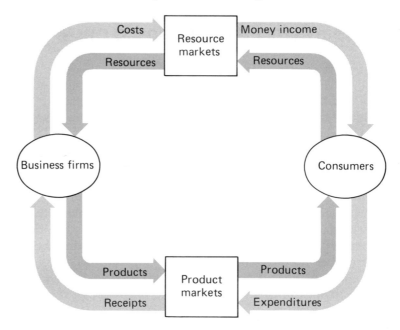

Next, let's consider resource markets. Figure 2.10 shows that consumers provide resources—including labor—to firms in resource markets, and they receive money in return. The money the consumers receive is their income; to firms, on the other hand, it represents their costs. Note that the

resources and products in Figure 2.10 is counterclockwise: *consumers provide resources to firms which in turn provide goods and services to
consumers.* On the other hand, the flow of money in Figure 2.10 is clock-
wise: *firms pay money for resources to consumers who in turn use the
money to buy goods and services from the firms.* Both flows—that of
resources and products and that of money—go on simultaneously and
repeatedly.

So long as consumers spend all their income, the flow of money income
from firms to consumers is exactly equal to the flow of expenditure from
consumers to firms. Thus these circular flows, like Ole' Man River, just
keep rolling along. As a first approximation, this is a perfectly good model.
But capitalist economies have experienced periods of widespread unemployment and severe inflation that this model cannot explain. Also, note
that our simple economy in Figure 2.10 has no government sector. In later
chapters, we will bring the government into the picture. Under pure
capitalism, the government would play a limited role in the economic
system, but in the mixed capitalistic system we have in the United States,
the government plays an important role indeed.

LIMITATIONS OF THE PRICE SYSTEM

Despite its many advantages, the price system suffers from limitations.
Because these limitations are both prominent and well known, no one
believes that the price system, left to its own devices, can be trusted to
solve all society's basic economic problems. To a considerable extent, the
government's role in the economy has developed in response to the limitations of the price system, which are described below.

Distribution of Income

There is no reason to believe that the distribution of income generated
by the price system is *fair* or, in some sense, *best.* Most people feel that
the distribution of income generated by the price system should be altered to suit humanitarian needs—in particular, that help should be
given to the poor. Both liberals and conservatives tend to agree on this
score, although there are arguments over the extent to which the poor
should be helped and the conditions under which they should be eligible
for help. But the general principle that the government should step in to
redistribute income in favor of the poor is generally accepted in the
United States today.[6]

---

[6]Also, because the wealthy have more money to spend than the poor, the sorts of goods and
services that society produces will reflect this fact. Thus luxuries for the rich may be produced in larger amounts and necessities for the poor may be produced in smaller amounts
than some critics regard as sensible and equitable. This is another frequently encountered
criticism of the price system.

CASE STUDY 2.2 THE FOOD STAMP PROGRAM AND THE ALLOCATION OF RESOURCES

Although the free market encourages an efficient allocation of resources, it responds only to those who have money to spend. If people are willing and able to spend money to fulfill a *need* for a good, there is an *effective demand* for that good, and the market will automatically respond to that need. Needs that are not backed up by spending power, however, will not be met by the market.

Clearly, the market system does not ensure that everyone will have money. Income is primarily dependent on one's being able to sell one's services in exchange for a wage. Those who cannot or will not sell their labor services, such as children, the adults who must care for young children, the aged, or the disabled, will have small incomes under the market system. Their needs are not translated into effective demand, so the market will not, by itself, provide for these people.

The government has set up programs that provide varying degrees of assistance to those who have an income below the poverty level. One of the largest, the food stamp program, began as a pilot program in 1961, and was greatly expanded under the Johnson administration in the Food Stamp Act of 1964. Any low-income household meeting the basic eligibility requirements could buy food stamps at a price below their market value. By 1969 there were 3.2 million people using food stamps at a cost to the government of $272 million.

The food stamp program was expanded in 1971 under President Nixon. By the early 1980s, about one out of every eleven Americans was a food stamp recipient, and the program cost $11.3 billion. The rapid growth of the program made it a focus of controversy, and the Reagan administration sought to reduce the growth in outlays. Part of the debate concerned the perennial question of the extent of the federal government's responsibility to help the poor. Should government programs be only a safety net for the truly needy, or should the government create programs of such scope that they would have a major impact on income distribution?

N.B.

Public Goods

Some goods and services *cannot be provided through the price system because there is no way to exclude citizens from consuming the goods whether they pay for them or not.* For example, there is no way to prevent citizens from benefiting from national expenditures on defense, whether they pay money toward defense or not. Consequently, the price system cannot be used to provide such goods; no one will pay for them since they will receive them whether they pay or not. Further, some goods, like the quality of the environment and national defense (and others cited below), *can be enjoyed by one person without depriving others of the same enjoyment.* Such goods are called *public goods*. The government provides many public goods. Such goods are consumed collectively or jointly, and it is inefficient to try to price them in a market. They tend to be indivisible; thus they frequently cannot be split into pieces and be bought and sold in a market.

External Economies and Diseconomies

In cases where *the production or consumption of a good by one firm or consumer has adverse or beneficial uncompensated effects on other firms or consumers, the price system will not operate effectively.* An *external economy* is said to occur when consumption or production by one person or firm results in uncompensated benefits to another person or firm. A good example of an external economy exists where fundamental research carried out by one firm is used by another firm. (To cite one such case, there were external economies from the Bell Telephone Laboratories' invention of the transistor. Many electronics firms, such as Texas Instruments and Fairchild, benefited considerably from Bell's research.) Where external economies exist, it is generally agreed that the price system will produce too little of the good in question and that the government should supplement the amount produced by private enterprise. This is the basic rationale for much of the government's huge investment in basic science. An *external diseconomy* is said to occur when consumption or production by one person or firm results in uncompensated costs to another person or firm. A good example of an external diseconomy occurs when a firm dumps pollutants into a stream and makes the water unfit for use by firms and people downstream. Where activities result in external diseconomies, it is generally agreed that the price system will tolerate too much of the activity and that the government should curb it.

EXPLORING FURTHER: EFFECTS OF SHIFTS IN THE DEMAND AND SUPPLY CURVES

Shifts in the Demand Curve

Heraclitus, the ancient Greek philosopher, said you cannot step in the same stream twice: everything changes, sooner or later. One need not be a disciple of Heraclitus to recognize that demand curves shift. Indeed, we have already seen that demand curves shift in response to changes in tastes, income, population, and prices of other products, and that supply curves shift in response to changes in technology and input prices. Any supply-and-demand diagram like Figure 2.9 is essentially a snapshot of the situation during a particular period of time. The results in Figure 2.9 are limited to a particular period because the demand and supply curves in the figure, like any demand and supply curves, pertain only to a certain period.

What happens to the equilibrium price of a product when its demand curve changes? This is an important question because it sheds a good deal of light on how the price system works. Suppose that consumer tastes shift in favor of foods containing wheat, causing the demand curve for wheat to shift *to the right,* as shown in Figure 2.11. It is not hard to see the effect on the equilibrium price of wheat. Before the shift, the equilibrium price is *OP.* But when the demand curve shifts to the right, a shortage develops at this price: that is, the quantity demanded exceeds the quantity supplied at this price.[7] Consequently, suppliers raise their prices. After some testing of market reactions and trial-and-error adjustments, the price will tend to settle at OP_1, the new equilibrium price, and quantity will tend to settle at OQ_1.

**Figure 2.11
Effect on the
Equilibrium Price
of a Shift to the
Right of the
Market Demand
Curve**
This shift of the demand curve to the right results in an increase in the equilibrium price from *OP* to OP_1 and an increase in the equilibrium quantity from *OQ* to OQ_1.

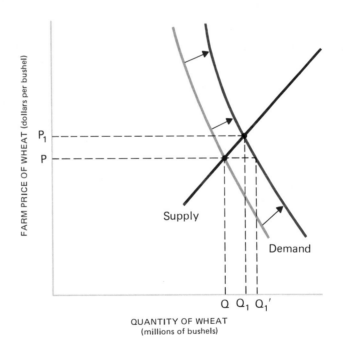

On the other hand, suppose that consumer demand for wheat products falls off, perhaps because of a great drop in the price of corn products. The demand for wheat now shifts *to the left,* as shown in Figure 2.12. What will be the effect on the equilibrium price of wheat? Clearly, the equilibrium price falls to OP_2, where the new demand curve intersects the supply curve.

[7]This shortage is equal to $OQ'_1 - OQ$ in Figure 2.11.

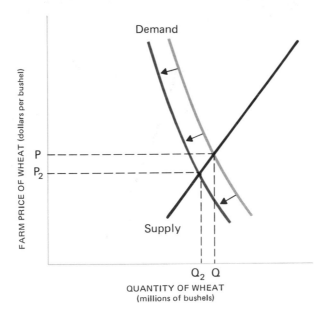

Figure 2.12
Effect on the
Equilibrium Price
of a Shift to the
Left of the Market
Demand Curve
This shift of the
demand curve to
the left results in a
decrease in the
equilibrium price
from *OP* to *OP$_2$* and
a decrease in the
equilibrium quantity
from *OQ* to *OQ$_2$*.

In general, *a shift to the right in the demand curve results in an increase in the equilibrium price, and a shift to the left in the demand curve results in a decrease in the equilibrium price.* This is the lesson of Figures 2.11 and 2.12. Of course, this conclusion depends on the assumption that the supply curve slopes upward to the right, but, as we noted in a previous section, this assumption is generally true.

At this point, since all of this is theory, you may be wondering how well this theory works in practice. In 1972 and 1973, there was a vivid demonstration of the accuracy of this model in various agricultural markets, including wheat. Because of poor harvests abroad and greatly increased foreign demand for American wheat, the demand curve for wheat shifted markedly to the right. What happened to the price of wheat? In accord with our model, the price increased spectacularly, from about $1.35 a bushel in the early summer of 1972 to over $4.00 a year later. Anyone who witnessed this phenomenon could not help but be impressed by the usefulness of this model.

Shifts in the Supply Curve

What happens to the equilibrium price of a product when its supply curve changes? For example, suppose that because of technological advances in wheat production, wheat farmers are willing and able to supply more wheat at a given price than they used to, with the result that the supply curve shifts *to the right,* as shown in Figure 2.13. What will be the effect on the equilibrium price? Clearly, it will fall from *0P* (where the original supply curve intersects the demand curve) to *0P$_3$* (where the new supply curve intersects the demand curve).

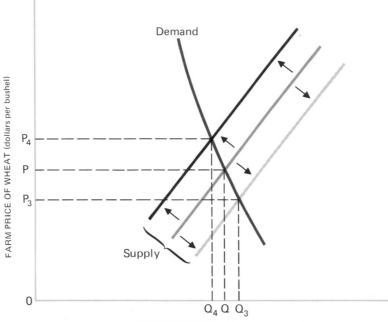

Figure 2.13
Effects on the Equilibrium Price of Shifts in the Market Supply Curve
The shift of the supply curve to the right results in a decrease in the equilibrium price from *OP* to *OP₃*. The shift of the supply curve to the left increases the equilibrium price from *OP* to *OP₄*.

On the other hand, suppose that the weather is poor, with the result that the supply curve shifts *to the left,* as shown in Figure 2.13. What will be the effect? The equilibrium price will increase from *OP* (where the original supply curve intersects the demand curve) to *OP₄* (where the new supply curve intersects the demand curve).

In 1984, law enforcement officers concerned with narcotics consumption in the United States were shown vividly what a shift to the right in the supply curve of a commodity will do. Because of a massive increase in the amount of coca production in South America, the supply curve for cocaine shifted dramatically to the right. The result was just what our theory would predict: a big drop in the price of cocaine. In some parts of the United States, cocaine sold in 1984 for one-half to one-third the price of a year before. According to one federal official, "At no time in the modern history of international drug control has the price of a drug dropped by half so quickly."

In general, *a shift to the right in the supply curve results in a decrease in the equilibrium price, and a shift to the left in the supply curve results in an increase in the equilibrium price.* Of course, this conclusion depends on the assumption that the demand curve slopes downward to the right, but, as we noted in a previous section, this assumption is generally true.

SUMMARY

1. Consumers and firms are the basic units composing the private sector of the economy. A market is a group of firms and individuals that are in touch with each other to buy some commodity or service. When a market for a homogeneous product contains so many buyers and sellers that none of them can influence the price, economists call it a perfectly competitive market.

2. There are two sides to every market: the demand side and the supply side. The demand side can be represented by the market demand curve, which almost always slopes downward to the right and the position of which depends on consumer tastes, the number and income of consumers, and the prices of other commodities.

3. The supply side of the market can be represented by the market supply curve, which generally slopes upward to the right and the position of which depends on technology and resource prices.

4. The equilibrium price and equilibrium quantity of a commodity are given by the intersection of the market demand and market supply curves. If conditions remain reasonably stable for a time, the actual price and quantity should move closer to the equilibrium price and quantity.

5. To determine what goods and services society will produce, the price system sets up incentives for firms to produce what consumers want. To the extent that they produce what consumers want and are willing to pay for, firms reap profits; to the extent that they don't, they experience losses.

6. The price system sets up strong incentives for firms to produce goods at minimum cost. These incentives take the form of profits for firms that minimize costs and losses for firms that operate with relatively high costs.

7. To determine who gets what, the price system results in people's receiving an income that depends on the quantity of resources they own and the prices that these resources command.

8. The price system establishes incentives for activities that result in increases in a society's per capita income. For example, it influences the amount of new capital goods produced, as well as the amount society spends on educating its labor force and improving its technology.

9. There are circular flows of money and products in a capitalist economy. In product markets, firms provide products to consumers and receive money in return. In resource markets, consumers provide resources to firms and receive money in return.

10. The price system, despite its many virtues, suffers from serious limitations. There is no reason to believe that the distribution of income generated by the price system is equitable or optimal. Also, there is no way for the price system to handle public goods properly, and because of external economies or diseconomies, the price system may result in too little or too much of certain goods being produced.

*11. Changes in the position and shape of the demand curve—in response to changes in consumer tastes, income, population, and prices of other commodities—result in changes in the equilibrium price and equilibrium output of a product. Similarly, changes in the position and shape of the supply curve—in response to changes in technology and resource prices, among other things—also result in changes in the equilibrium price and equilibrium output of a product.

*The starred item refers to material covered in the section, "Exploring Further."

PART 2

☆☆☆☆☆☆☆☆☆☆☆☆☆☆☆

National Income
and Output

CHAPTER 3

★ ★ ★ ★ ★ ★ ★ ★ ★

National Income and Product

LEARNING OBJECTIVES

In this chapter, you should learn:

★ What gross national product (GNP) measures and why it is important

★ The nature of a price index and how it can be used

★ Two approaches for measuring GNP

America's *gross national product*—or GNP, as it is often called—was $3,663 billion in 1984, as compared with $3,305 billion in 1983. Put in the simplest terms, the GNP is the value of the total amount of final goods and services produced by our economy during a particular period of time. This measure is important for its own sake and because it helps us to understand both inflation and unemployment. The federal government and the business community watch the GNP figures avidly. Government officials, from the president down, are interested because these figures indicate how prosperous we are, and because they are useful in forecasting the future health of the economy. Business executives are also extremely interested in GNP figures because the sales of their firms are related to the level of the GNP, and so the figures are useful in forecasting the future health of their businesses. All in all, it is no exaggeration to say that the gross national product is one of the most closely watched numbers in existence.

In this chapter, we discuss the measurement, uses, and limitations of the gross national product. At the outset, it is worth noting that measures of national income and national product are of comparatively recent vintage. The Department of Commerce first published such estimates in 1934, after experiments at various universities and at the National Bureau of Economic Research. A leading pioneer in this field was the late Nobel laureate Simon Kuznets, then at the University of Pennsylvania. (See Case Study 3.1.) The concepts that Kuznets and others developed are often called the *national income accounts*, and the Bureau of Economic Analysis of the U.S. Department of Commerce compiles these figures on a continuing basis. Just as the accounts of a firm are used to describe and analyze its financial health, so the national income accounts are used to describe and analyze the economic health of the nation as a whole.

GROSS NATIONAL PRODUCT

As noted above, the gross national product is a measure of how much the economy produces in a particular period of time. But the American economy produces millions of types of goods and services. How can we add together everything from lemon meringue pies to helicopters, from books to houses? The only feasible answer is to use money as a common denominator and to make the price of a good or service—the amount the buyer is willing to pay—the measure of value. In other words, we add up the value in money terms of the total output of goods and services in the economy during a certain period, normally a year, and the result is the gross national product during that period.

Although the measurement of the gross national product may seem straightforward ("just add up the value in money terms of the total output of the economy"), this is by no means the case. Some of the more important pitfalls that must be avoided and problems that must be confronted are the following:

AVOIDANCE OF DOUBLE COUNTING. Gross national product does not include the value of *all* goods and services produced: it includes only the value of *final* goods and services produced. *Final goods and services* are goods and services destined for the ultimate user. For example, flour purchased for family consumption is a final good, but flour to be used in manufacturing bread is an *intermediate good*, not a final good. We would be double counting if we counted both the bread and the flour used to make the bread as output. Thus the output of intermediate goods—goods that are not destined for the ultimate user but are used as inputs in producing final goods and services—must not be included in the gross national product.

VALUATION AT COST. Some final goods and services that must be included in the gross national product are not bought and sold in the marketplace, so they are valued at what they cost. Consider the services performed by government: police protection, fire protection, the use of the courts, defense, and so forth. Such services are not bought and sold in any market (despite the old saw about the New Jersey judge who was "the best that money could buy"). Yet they are an important part of our economy's final output. Economists and statisticians have decided to value them at what they cost the taxpayers. This is by no means ideal, but it is the best practical solution advanced to date.

NONMARKET TRANSACTIONS. It is necessary for practical reasons to omit certain types of final output from the gross national product. In particular, some nonmarketed goods and services, such as the services performed by housewives, are excluded from the gross national product. This is not because economists fail to appreciate these services, but because it would be extremely difficult to get reasonably reliable estimates of the money value of a housewife's services. At first glance, this may seem to be a very important weakness in our measure of total output, but so long as the value of these services does not change much (in relation to total output), the variation in the gross national product will provide a reasonably accurate picture of the variation in total output—and, for our purposes, this is all that is required.

NONPRODUCTIVE TRANSACTIONS. Purely financial transactions are excluded from the gross national product because they do not reflect current production. Such financial transactions include government transfer payments, private transfer payments, and the sale and purchase of securities. *Government transfer payments* are payments made by the government to individuals who do not contribute to production in exchange for them. Payments to welfare recipients are a good example of government transfer payments. Since these payments are not for production, it would be incorrect to include them in the GNP. *Private transfer payments* are gifts or other transfers of wealth from one person or private organization to another. Again these are not payments for production, so there is no reason to include them in the GNP. The sale and purchase of securities are not payments for production, so they too are excluded from the GNP.

SECONDHAND GOODS. Sales of secondhand goods are also excluded from the gross national product. The reason for this is clear. When a good is produced, its value is included in the GNP. If its value is also included when it is sold on the secondhand market, it will be counted twice, thus leading to an overstatement of the true GNP. Suppose that you buy a new bicycle and resell it a year later. The value of the new bicycle is included in the GNP when the bicycle is produced. But the resale value of the bicycle is not included in the GNP; to do so would be double counting.

ADJUSTING GNP FOR PRICE CHANGES

Current Dollars versus Constant Dollars

In the Prologue, we stressed that the general price level has changed over time. (Recall the rapid inflation of the 1970s and early 1980s.) Since the

CASE STUDY 3.1 THE FIRST ESTIMATES OF GNP IN THE UNITED STATES

It is hard to find a copy today of the small report to the United States Senate titled simply "National Income, 1929–32," but when it was first printed in 1934, it was something of a bestseller; 4500 copies sold in eight months—at 20 cents each. It was not yet called the "gross national product"; that title would come later with refinements, but as one expert noted, in terms of looking at the entire American economy, this is when time began.

Senator Robert La Follette of Wisconsin was a key figure in getting the U.S. Department of Commerce to make estimates of GNP for the three previous years, starting with the peak of the nation's growth spurt, 1929. The late Simon Kuznets spearheaded this effort. Born in Russia, Kuznets came to America in 1921, taught himself

Simon Kuznets

English in one summer, and five years later had completed his Ph.D. in economics at Columbia University. He joined the National Bureau of Economic Research where he began looking for ways to refine the statistical measurements of national income and output. Kuznets' work was the foundation of the Commerce Department's estimates.

It took a year to calculate the industry-by-industry income once the definitions had been clarified. On January 4, 1934, the completed report was sent to the Senate and the nation had its first overall measure, one that brought home the bad news. National output had fallen from $89 billion in 1929 to $49 billion at the end of 1931. Simon Kuznets, who was awarded the Nobel Prize in economics in 1971, was the first to warn that GNP did not measure how well off we are as a people. He emphasized that an attempt "to make GNP a gauge of scientifically determined, real welfare of the population involves an unwarranted optimism as to the validity of sciences concerning human nature."

N.B.

gross national product values all goods and services at their current prices, it is bound to be affected by changes in the price level as well as by changes in total output. If all prices doubled tomorrow, this would produce a doubling of the gross national product. Clearly, if the gross national product is to be a reliable measure of changes in total output, we must correct it somehow to eliminate the effects of such changes in the price level.

To make such a correction, economists choose some *base year* and express the value of all goods and services in terms of their prices during the base year. If 1983 is taken as the base year and if the price of beef was $2 per pound in 1983, beef is valued at $2 per pound in all other years. Thus, if 100 million pounds of beef were produced in 1986, this total output is valued at $200 million even though the price of beef in 1986 was actually higher than $2 per pound. In this way, distortions caused by changes in the price level are eliminated.

Gross national product is expressed either in current dollars or in constant dollars. Figures expressed in *current dollars* are actual dollar amounts, whereas those expressed in *constant dollars* are corrected for changes in the price level. Expressed in current dollars, the gross national product is affected by changes in the price level. Expressed in constant dollars, the gross national product is not affected by the price level because the prices of all goods are maintained at their base-year level. The GNP, after being corrected for changes in the price level, is called *real GNP*.

Figure 3.1 shows the behavior of both real GNP and GNP expressed in current dollars. GNP expressed in current dollars has increased more rapidly (due to inflation) than GNP in constant dollars.

Price Indexes

It is often useful to have some measure of how much prices have changed over a certain period of time. One way to obtain such a measure is to divide the value of a set of goods and services expressed in current dollars by the value of the same set of goods and services expressed in constant (or base-year) dollars. Suppose that a set of goods and services costs $100 when valued at 1986 prices, but $70 when valued at 1983 prices. Apparently, prices have risen an average of 43 percent for this set of goods between 1983 and 1986. How do we get 43 percent? The ratio of the cost in 1986 prices to the cost in 1983 prices is $100 \div 70 = 1.43$; thus prices must have risen on the average by 43 percent for this set of goods.

The ratio of the value of a set of goods and services in current dollars to the value of the same set of goods and services in constant (base-year) dollars is a *price index*. Thus 1.43 is a price index in the example above. An important function of a price index is to convert values expressed in current dollars into values expressed in constant dollars. This conversion, known as *deflating*, can be achieved simply by dividing values expressed in current dollars by the price index. In the illustration above, values expressed in 1986 dollars can be converted into constant (i.e., 1983) dollars

**Figure 3.1
Gross National
Product,
Expressed in
Current Dollars
and 1972 Dollars,
United States,
1929–84**
Because of inflation,
GNP expressed in
current dollars has
increased more
rapidly in recent
years than GNP in
constant (1972)
dollars. This was
particularly true in
the 1970s and early
1980s, reflecting the
price surge then.

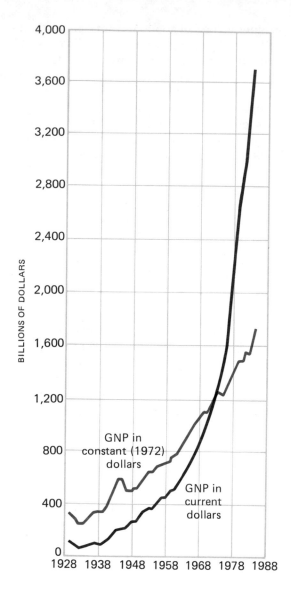

by dividing by 1.43. This procedure is an important one, with applications in many fields other than the measurement of the gross national product. For example, firms use it to compare their output in various years. To correct for price changes, they deflate their sales by a price index for their products.

In many cases, price indexes are multiplied by 100; that is, they are expressed as percentage changes. Thus, in the case described in the previous paragraph, the price index might be expressed as 1.43 × 100, or 143, which would indicate that 1986 prices on the average were 143 percent of their 1983 level. In Chapter 7, we shall say more about price indexes that are expressed in this way. For now, we assume that the price index is not multiplied by 100.

Applications of Price Indexes

To illustrate how a price index can be used to deflate some figures, suppose that we want to measure how much the output of bread rose in *real terms* —that is, in constant dollars—between 1983 and 1987. Let us suppose that the value of output of bread in current dollars during each year was as shown in the first column of Table 3.1, and that the price of bread during each year was as shown in the second column. To determine the value of output of bread in 1983 dollars, we form a price index with 1983 as the base year, as shown in the third column. Then, dividing the figures in the first column by this price index, we get the value of output of bread during each year in 1983 dollars, shown in the fourth column. Thus the fourth column shows how much the output of bread has grown in real terms. The real output of bread has risen by 19 percent—$(1,900 - 1,600) \div 1,600$— between 1983 and 1987.

Year	(1) Output of bread in current dollars	(2) Price of bread (dollars)	(3) Price index (price ÷ 1983 price)	(4) Output of bread in 1983 dollars*
1983	1,600 million	0.50	1.00	1,600 million
1984	1,768 million	0.52	1.04	1,700 million
1985	1,980 million	0.55	1.10	1,800 million
1986	2,090 million	0.55	1.10	1,900 million
1987	2,204 million	0.58	1.16	1,900 million

*This column was derived by dividing column 1 by column 3.

Table 3.1
Use of Price Index to Convert from Current to Constant Dollars

Next, let's take up an actual case. The first column of Table 3.2 shows the gross national product in selected years. The second column shows the relevant price index for the GNP for each of these years. (The base year is 1972.) What was the real GNP in 1981? To answer this question, we must divide the GNP in current dollars in 1981 by the price index for 1981. Thus the answer is $2,938 billion divided by 1.9358, or $1,518 billion. In other words, when expressed in constant 1972 dollars, the GNP in 1981 was $1,518 billion. What was the real GNP in 1978? Applying the

Year	GNP in billions of current dollars	Price index (1972 = 1.0000)	Real GNP (billions of 1972 dollars)
1972	1,171	1.0000	1,171 (= 1,171 ÷ 1.0000)
1975	1,529	1.2718	
1978	2,156	1.5005	1,437 (= 2,156 ÷ 1.5005)
1981	2,938	1.9358	1,518 (= 2,938 ÷ 1.9358)

Table 3.2
Calculation of Real Gross National Product

same principles, the answer is $2,156 billion divided by 1.5005, or $1,437 billion. In other words, when expressed in constant 1972 dollars, the GNP in 1978 was $1,437 billion. To test your understanding, see if you can figure out the value of the real GNP in 1975. (To check your answer, consult footnote 1.)[1]

USING VALUE-ADDED TO CALCULATE GNP

We have pointed out that the gross national product includes the value of only the final goods and services produced. Obviously, however, the output of final goods and services is not due solely to the efforts of the producers of the final goods and services. The total value of an automobile when it leaves the plant, for example, represents the work of many industries besides the automobile manufacturers. The steel, tires, glass, and many other components of the automobile were not produced by the automobile manufacturers. In reality, the automobile manufacturers only added a certain amount of value to the value of the intermediate goods—steel, tires, glass, and so forth—they purchased. This point is basic to an understanding of how the gross national product is calculated.

To measure the contribution of a firm or industry to final output, we use the concept of value-added. *Value-added* means just what it says: *the amount of value added by a firm or industry to the total worth of the product.* It is a measure in money terms of the extent of production taking place in a particular firm or industry. Suppose that $160 million of bread was produced in the United States in 1986. To produce it, farmers harvested $50 million of wheat, which was used as an intermediate product by flour mills, which turned out $80 million of flour. This flour was used as an intermediate product by the bakers who produced the $160 million of bread. What is the value-added at each stage of the process? For simplicity, assume that the farmers did not have to purchase any materials from other firms in order to produce the wheat. Then the value-added by the wheat farmers is $50 million; the value-added by the flour mills is $30 million ($80 million − $50 million); and the value-added by the bakers is $80 million ($160 million − $80 million). The total of the value-added at all stages of the process ($50 million + $30 million + $80 million) must equal the value of the output of final product ($160 million) because each stage's value-added is its contribution to this value.

Table 3.3 shows the value-added by various industrial groups in the United States in 1984. Since the total of the value-added by all industries must equal the value of all final goods and services, which, of course, is the gross national product, it follows that $3,663 billion—the total of the figures in Table 3.3—must have been equal to the gross national product in 1984. It is interesting to note that most of the value-added in the American economy in 1984 was not contributed by manufacturing, min-

---

[1]The real GNP in 1975 equaled $1,529 billion divided by 1.2718, or $1,202 billion in 1972 dollars.

ing, construction, transportation, communication, or electricity or gas. Instead, most of it came from services—wholesale and retail trade, finance, insurance, real estate, government services, and other services. This is a sign of a basic change taking place in the American economy, which is turning more and more toward producing services, rather than goods.

Industry	Value-added (billions of dollars)
Agriculture, forestry and fisheries	91
Mining	118
Construction	148
Manufacturing	776
Transportation	130
Communication	103
Electricity, gas, and sanitation	110
Wholesale and retail trade	602
Finance, insurance, and real estate	598
Other services	529
Government[a]	422
Rest of the world	44
Gross national product	3,663[b]

Table 3.3
Value-Added by Various Industries, United States, 1984

[a]Equals wages and salaries of government workers.
[b]Because of rounding errors and a statistical discrepancy, figures do not sum to total.
Source: U.S. Department of Commerce.

NET NATIONAL PRODUCT

One major drawback of the GNP as a measure of national output must now be faced: it does not take into account the fact that plant and equipment wear out with use, and that a certain amount of each year's national output must be devoted to replacing the capital goods worn out in producing the year's output. Economists have therefore developed another important measure, net national product (NNP), that recognizes what every accountant knows: the relevance of depreciation.

Specifically, the *net national product* equals the gross national product minus depreciation. To obtain the net national product, government statisticians estimate the amount of depreciation—the amount of the nation's plant, equipment, and structures that are worn out during the period—and deduct it from the gross national product. The net national product is a more accurate measure of the economy's output than the gross national product because it takes depreciation into account, but estimates of the net national product contain whatever errors are made in estimating depreciation (which is not easy to measure).

As we shall see in succeeding chapters, data on the gross national product are more often used, even if the net national product may be a somewhat better measure. Actually, since the GNP and the NNP move together quite closely, which one you use doesn't matter much for most practical purposes. (See Figure 3.2.)

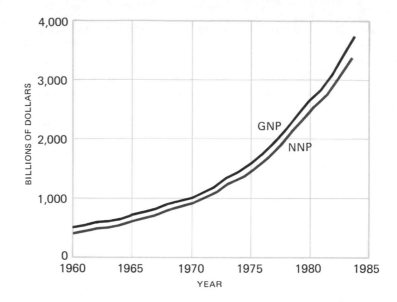

**Figure 3.2
Gross National
Product and Net
National Product,
United States,
1960–84**
It is evident that
GNP and NNP
move together quite
closely. Thus, for
many practical
purposes, which
one you use doesn't
matter much.

THE LIMITATIONS OF GNP AND NNP

It is essential that the limitations of both the gross national product and the net national product be understood. Although they are very useful, these figures are by no means ideal measures of economic well-being. At least five limitations of these measures must always be borne in mind.

POPULATION. GNP and NNP are not very meaningful unless one knows the size of the population of the country in question. For example, the fact that a particular nation's GNP equals $50 billion means one thing if the nation has 10 million inhabitants and quite another thing if it has 500 million inhabitants. To correct for the size of the population, GNP per capita—GNP divided by the population—is often used as a rough measure of output per person in a particular country.

LEISURE. GNP and NNP do not take into account one of mankind's most prized activities; leisure. During the past century, the average work week in the United States has decreased substantially. It has gone from almost 70 hours in 1850 to about 40 hours today. As people have become more affluent, they have chosen to substitute leisure for increased production. Yet this increase in leisure time, which surely contributes to our well-being, does not show up in the GNP or the NNP. Neither does the personal satisfaction (or displeasure and alienation) people get from their jobs.

QUALITY CHANGES. GNP and NNP do not take adequate account of changes in the quality of goods. An improvement in a product is not reflected accurately in the GNP and the NNP unless its price reflects the improvement. For example, if a new type of drug is put on the market at the same price as an old drug, and if the output and cost of the new drug are the same as the old drug, GNP will not increase, even though the new drug is twice as effective as the old one.

VALUE AND DISTRIBUTION. GNP and NNP say nothing about the social desirability of the composition and distribution of the nation's output. Each good and service produced is valued at its price. If the price of a Bible is $10 and the price of a pornographic novel is $10, both are valued at $10, whatever you or I may think about their respective worth. Moreover, GNP and NNP measure only the total quantity of goods and services produced. They tell us nothing about how this output is distributed among the people. If a nation's GNP is $500 billion, this is its GNP whether 90 percent of the output is consumed by a relatively few rich families or whether the output is distributed relatively equally among the citizens.

SOCIAL COSTS. GNP and NNP do not reflect some of the social costs arising from the production of goods and services. In particular, they do not reflect the environmental damage resulting from the operation of our nation's factories, offices, and farms. It is common knowledge that the atmosphere and water supplies are being polluted in various ways by firms, consumers, and governments. Yet these costs are not deducted from GNP or NNP, even though the failure to do so results in an overestimate of our true economic welfare.

Fire on the polluted Cuyahoga River, Cleveland, Ohio

Economists are beginning to correct the GNP figures to eliminate some of these problems. For example, William Nordhaus and James Tobin, both of whom have served on the Council of Economic Advisers, have tried to correct the GNP figures to take proper account of the value of leisure, the value of housewives' services, and the environmental costs of production, among other things.[2]

[2]W. Nordhaus and J. Tobin, "Is Growth Obsolete?" *Fiftieth Anniversary Colloquium,* New York: National Bureau of Economic Research, 1972.

TWO APPROACHES TO GNP

Suppose that we want to measure the market value of an automobile. One way to do this is to look at how much the consumer pays for the automobile. Although this is the most straightforward way to measure the automobile's market value, it is not the only way it can be done. Another, equally valid way is to add up all of the wage, interest, rental, and profit incomes generated in the production of the automobile. As pointed out in the circular flow model in Chapter 2 (Figure 2.10), the amount that the automobile producer receives for this car is equal to its profit (or loss) on the car plus the amount it pays the workers and other resource owners who contributed their resources to its production. Thus, if we add up all of the wage, interest, rental, and profit incomes resulting from the production of the automobile, the result is the same as if we determine how much the consumer pays for the automobile.

By the same token, there are two ways to measure the market value of the output of the economy as a whole. Or, put differently, there are two ways of looking at GNP. One is the *expenditures approach*, which regards GNP as the sum of all the expenditures on the final goods and services produced this year. The other is the *income approach*, which regards GNP as the sum of income derived from the production of this year's total output.

Since both of these approaches are valid, it follows that GNP can be viewed as either the total expenditure on this year's total output or as the total income stemming from the production of this year's total output:

The total expenditure on this year's total output = GNP = The total income stemming from the production of this year's total output

This is an identity; the left-hand side of this equation must equal the right-hand side. (More precisely, the right-hand side should also include depreciation and indirect business taxes, as we will see below. But this refinement can be ignored at this point.)

It is important to understand both the expenditures and the income approaches to GNP. In the following sections we describe both approaches in more detail.

THE EXPENDITURES APPROACH TO GNP

To use the expenditures approach to determine GNP, one must add up all the spending on final goods and services. Economists distinguish among four broad categories of spending, each of which will be taken up.

CASE STUDY 3.2 USING GNP ESTIMATES IN WORLD WAR II

During the Great Depression, policy makers had little idea of what was happening to the economy. In contrast, during World War II economists did have a reasonably accurate picture of the economy's total output thanks to the new estimates of GNP. At the Commerce Department, economists were being pushed by events to come up with predictions on what the American economy could produce. At home, the first mobilization committees were set up under the "Victory" program. And at the Commerce Department, economists went to work to see what kind of arsenal the United States could become and how quickly.

As the war intensified in Europe, the planners went to work. Experts were dispatched to London to find out what the Allies needed to survive. Specifically, the war planners began asking questions like: (1) Could the United States produce enough steel (for ships, guns, and tanks), aluminum (airplanes), and copper (ammunition)? (2) How much of the entire economy could be diverted to the war effort without jeopardizing the basic needs of the American people for food, clothing, housing, and transportation? (3) How much money would the American public be able to pay in taxes to support the war? The effort that went into answering these questions helped to refine the national income and product accounts, and after the end of the war the Commerce Department began to regularly produce estimates of GNP and related measurements.

N.B.

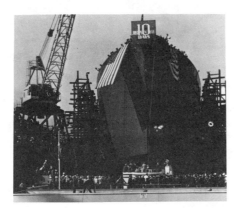

Mobilization during World War II

☆ ☆ ☆ ☆ ☆ ☆ ☆ ☆ ☆ ☆ ☆ ☆ ☆

Personal Consumption Expenditures

Personal consumption expenditures include spending by households on durable goods, nondurable goods, and services. This category of spending includes your expenditures on items like food and drink, which are nondurable goods. It also includes your family's expenditures on a car or on an electric washer or dryer, which are durable goods. Further, it includes your payments to a dentist, who is providing a service (painful though it sometimes may be). Table 3.4 shows that in 1984 personal consumption accounted for about 64 percent of the total amount spent on final goods and services in the United States. Expenditures on consumer durable goods are clearly much less than expenditures on consumer nondurable goods, whereas expenditures on services are now larger than expenditures on either durable or nondurable goods.

Table 3.4
Expenditures on
Final Goods and
Services, United
States, 1984ª

Type of expenditure	Amount (billions of dollars)	
Personal consumption		2,342
Durable goods	319	
Nondurable goods	857	
Services	1,166	
Gross private domestic investment		638
Expenditures on plant and equipment	426	
Residential structures	154	
Increase in inventories	58	
Net exports		−64
Exports	364	
Imports	428	
Government purchases of goods and services		747
Federal	295	
State and local	452	
Gross national product		3,663

ªBecause of rounding error, figures sometimes do not sum to total.
Source: U.S. Department of Commerce.

Gross Private Domestic Investment

Gross private domestic investment consists of all investment spending by U.S. firms. As shown in Table 3.4, three broad types of expenditures are included in this category. First, *all final purchases of tools, equipment, and machinery* are included. Second, *all construction expenditures,* including expenditures on residential housing, are included. (One reason why houses are treated as investment goods is that they can be rented out.) Third, the *change in total inventories* is included. An increase in inventories is a positive investment; a decrease in inventories is a negative investment. The change in inventories must be included, because GNP measures the value of all final goods and services produced, even if they are not sold this year. Thus GNP must include the value of any increases in inventories that occur during the year. On the other hand, if a decrease occurs during the year in the value of inventories, the value of this decrease in inventories must be subtracted in calculating GNP because these goods and services were produced prior to the beginning of this year. In other words, a decline in inventories means that society has purchased more than it has produced during the year.

Gross private domestic investment is "gross" in the sense that it includes all additions to the nation's stock of investment goods, whether or not they are replacements for equipment or plant that are used up in producing the current year's output. Net private domestic investment includes only the addition to the nation's stock of investment goods after allowing for the replacement of used-up plant and equipment. To illustrate the distinction between gross and net private domestic investment, consider the situation in 1984. In that year, the nation produced $638 billion worth of investment goods: thus gross private domestic investment equaled $638 billion. But in producing the 1984 GNP, $403 billion worth of investment goods were used up. Thus net private domestic investment equaled $638 billion minus $403 billion, or $235 billion. This was the net addition to the nation's stock of investment goods.

Net private domestic investment indicates the change in the nation's stock of capital goods. If it is positive, the nation's productive capacity, as gauged by its capital stock, is growing. If it is negative, the nation's productive capacity, as gauged by its capital stock, is declining. As pointed out in Chapter 1, the amount of goods and services that the nation can produce is influenced by the size of its stock of capital goods. (Why? Because these capital goods are one important type of resource.) Thus this year's net private domestic investment is a determinant of how much the nation can produce in the future.

Government Purchases of Goods and Services

This category of spending includes the expenditures of the federal, state, and local governments for the multitude of functions they perform: defense, education, police protection, and so forth. It does not include transfer payments, since they are not payments for current production. Table 3.4 shows that government spending in 1984 accounted for about 20 percent of the total amount spent on final goods and services in the United States. State and local expenditures are bigger than federal expenditures. Many of the expenditures of the federal government are on items like national defense, health, and education, while at the state and local levels the biggest expenditures are for items like education and highways.

Net Exports

Net exports equal the amount spent by other nations on our goods and services less the amount we spent on other nations' goods and services. This factor must be included since some of our national output is destined for foreign markets and since we import some of the goods and services we consume. There is no reason why this component of spending cannot be negative, since imports can exceed exports. The quantity of net exports tends to be quite small. Table 3.4 shows that net exports in 1984 were equal (in absolute terms) to about 2 percent of the total amount spent on final goods and services in the United States. Because net exports are so small, we will generally ignore them until Chapters 27 and 28, where we will focus attention exclusively on international trade and finance.

Putting Together the Spending Components

Finally, because the four categories of expenditures described above include all possible types of spending on final goods and services, their sum equals the gross national product. In other words,

> GNP = personal consumption expenditures +
> gross private domestic investment +
> government purchases of goods and services +
> net exports.

As shown in Table 3.4, the gross national product in 1984 equaled 2,342 + 638 + 747 − 64, or $3,663 billion.

THE INCOME APPROACH TO GNP

To use the income approach to determine GNP, one must add up all the income stemming from the production of this year's output. This income is of various types: compensation of employees, rents, interest, proprietors' income, and corporate profits. In addition, for reasons that need not concern us here,[3] we must also include depreciation and indirect business taxes. Each of these items is defined and discussed below.

Compensation of Employees

This is the largest of the income categories. It includes the wages and salaries paid by firms and government agencies to suppliers of labor. In

---

[3]For a detailed explanation of the reasons why depreciation and indirect business taxes must be included, see E. Mansfield, *Economics: Principles, Problems, Decisions,* 5th ed., New York: Norton, 1986.

addition, it contains a variety of supplementary payments by employers for the benefit of their employees, such as payments into public and private pension and welfare funds. These supplementary payments are part of the employers' costs and are included in the total compensation of employees.

Rents

In the present context, rent is defined as a payment to households for the supply of property resources. For example, it includes house rents received by landlords. Quite different definitions of rent are used by economists in other contexts.

Interest

Interest includes payments of money by private businesses to suppliers of money capital. If you buy a bond issued by General Motors, the interest payments you receive are included. Interest payments made by the government on Treasury bills, savings bonds, and other securities are excluded on the grounds that they are not payments for current goods and services. They are regarded as transfer payments.

Proprietors' Income

What we have referred to as profits are split into two parts in the national income accounts: proprietors' income and corporate profits. Proprietors' income consists of the net income of unincorporated businesses. In other words, it consists of the net income of proprietorships and partnerships (as well as cooperatives).

Corporate Profits

Corporate profits consist of the net income of corporations. This item contains three parts: (1) dividends received by the stockholders, (2) retained earnings, and (3) the amount paid by corporations as income taxes. In other words, this item is equal to corporate profits before the payment of corporate income taxes.

Depreciation

All of the items discussed above—compensation of employees, rents, interest, proprietors' income, and corporate profits—are forms of income. In addition, there are two nonincome items, depreciation and indirect business taxes, that must be added to the sum of the income items to obtain

GNP. As we know from an earlier section, depreciation is the value of the nation's plant, equipment, and structures that are worn out this year. In the national income accounts, depreciation is often called a *capital consumption allowance,* because it measures the value of the capital consumed during the year.

Indirect Business Taxes

The government imposes certain taxes, such as general sales taxes, excise taxes, and customs duties, which firms treat as costs of production. These taxes are called indirect business taxes because they are not imposed directly on the business itself, but on its products or services instead. A good example of an indirect business tax is the tax on cigarettes; another is the general sales tax. Before a firm can pay out income to its workers, suppliers, or stockholders, it must pay these indirect business taxes to the government.

Putting Together the Income Components (Plus Depreciation and Indirect Business Taxes)

As we have stated repeatedly, the sum of the five types of income described above (plus depreciation and indirect business taxes) equals gross national product. In other words,

$$
\begin{aligned}
\text{GNP} = \ &\text{compensation of employees} + \\
&\text{rents} + \\
&\text{interest} + \\
&\text{proprietors' income} + \\
&\text{corporate profits} + \\
&\text{depreciation} + \\
&\text{indirect business taxes.}
\end{aligned}
$$

**Table 3.5
Claims on Output,
United States, 1984**

Type of claim on output	Amount of claim (billions of dollars)
Employee compensation	2,173
Rental income	62
Interest	284
Income of proprietors and professionals	154
Corporate profits	286
Indirect business taxes	304
Depreciation	403
Statistical discrepancy[a]	−3
Gross national product	3,663

[a]This also includes some minor items that need not be of concern here. See the source.
Source: U.S. Department of Commerce.

Table 3.5 shows the total amounts of various types of income paid out
(or owed) during 1984. It also shows depreciation and indirect business taxes. You can see for yourself that the total of these items equals gross national product.

SUMMARY

1. One of the key indicators of the health of any nation's economy is the gross national product, which measures the total value of the final goods and services the nation produces in a particular period. Since gross national product is affected by the price level, it must be deflated by a price index to correct for price-level changes. When deflated in this way, GNP is called real GNP, or GNP in constant dollars.

2. There are many pitfalls in calculating the gross national product. One must avoid counting the same output more than once. Purely financial transactions that do not reflect current production must be excluded. Also, some final goods and services that must be included in GNP are not bought and sold in the marketplace, so they are valued at what they cost.

3. GNP is not an ideal measure of total economic output, let alone a satisfactory measure of economic wellbeing. It takes no account of a nation's population, the amount of leisure time, or the distribution of income. It does not reflect many changes in the quality of goods and many social costs like pollution. Economists are beginning to correct GNP figures to eliminate some of these problems.

4. One approach to GNP is the expenditures approach, which regards GNP as the sum of all the expenditures that are involved in taking the total output of final goods and services off the market. To determine GNP in this way, one must add up all the spending on final goods and services. Economists distinguish among four broad categories of spending; personal consumption expenditures, gross private domestic investment, government purchases, and net exports. GNP equals the sum of these four items.

5. Another approach to GNP is the income approach, which regards GNP as the sum of incomes derived from the production of this year's output (plus depreciation and indirect business taxes). To determine GNP in this way, one must add up all the income stemming from the production of this year's total output (plus depreciation and indirect business taxes). Economists identify five broad categories of income: compensation of employees, rent, interest, proprietors' income, and corporate profits. GNP equals the sum of these five items (plus depreciation and indirect business taxes).

6. Net national product is gross national product minus depreciation. It indicates the value of net output when account is taken of capital used up.

CHAPTER 4

★ ★ ★ ★ ★ ★ ★ ★ ★

Business Fluctuations and Unemployment

LEARNING OBJECTIVES

In this chapter, you should learn:

★ The nature of business fluctuations and their four phases

★ What aggregate demand and aggregate supply curves show

★ The types of unemployment and the costs they impose on society

★ *(Exploring Further)* The effects of shifts in the aggregate demand and aggregate supply curves

While the U.S. economy has grown considerably over the past century, the ascent has not been a smooth one. The path of the American economy can be compared to a roller coaster that keeps moving higher and higher. In subsequent chapters we will discuss, at length, some of the reasons behind economic fluctuations and some of the proposed remedies. But first we need to define what we mean by a business cycle. Given the economic tools that we have developed so far, we can describe in simple terms some of the fundamental forces that bring about business cycles. We also need to consider what the consequences of these fluctuations are for individuals and for the economy as a whole. In particular, we must discuss unemployment.

BUSINESS FLUCTUATIONS

Business executives, government officials, and practically everyone else are interested in business fluctuations because they influence our welfare. Business fluctuations are intimately related to the twin economic evils of unemployment and inflation.

To illustrate what we mean by business fluctuations—or the business cycle—let's look at how national output has grown in the United States since World War I. Figure 4.1 shows the behavior of real GNP (in constant dollars) in the United States since 1919. It is clear that output has grown considerably during this period. Indeed, GNP is more than 5 times what it was 50 years ago. It is also clear that this growth has not been steady. On the contrary, although the long-term trend has been upward, there have been periods—1919–21, 1929–33, 1937–38, 1944–46, 1948–49, 1953–54, 1957–58, 1969–70, 1973–75, January-July 1980, and 1981–82—when national output has declined.

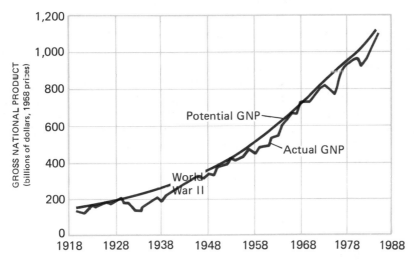

**Figure 4.1
Gross National
Product (in 1958
dollars), United
States, 1919–04,
Excluding World
War II**
Real GNP has not grown steadily. Instead, it has tended to approach its potential level (that is, its full-employment level), then to falter and fall below this level, then to rise once more, and so on. (Note that GNP is expressed in 1958—not 1972—dollars here.)

Potential GNP is the total amount of goods and services that could have been produced if the economy had been operating at full capacity or full employment. Figure 4.1 shows that national output tends to rise and approach its potential level (that is, its full-employment level) for a while, then falter and fall below this level, then rise to approach it once more, then fall below it again, and so on. For example, output remained close to its potential level in the prosperous mid-1920s, fell far below this level in the depressed 1930s, and rose again to this level once we entered World War II. This movement of national output is sometimes called the *business cycle*, but it must be recognized that these cycles are far from regular or consistent. On the contrary, they are very irregular.

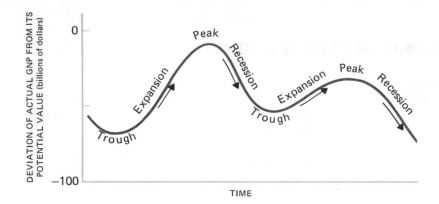

**Figure 4.3
Business
Fluctuations in the
United States,
1860–1980**
To construct this
chart, a single index
of economic activity
was used. After
fitting a trend line to
it, the deviations of
this index from its
trend value were
plotted. The results
show the
fluctuations in
economic activity in
the U.S.

Each cycle can be divided into four phases, as shown in Figure 4.2. The *trough* is the point where national output is lowest relative to its potential level (that is, its full-employment level). *Expansion* is the subsequent phase during which national output rises. The *peak* occurs when national output is highest relative to its potential level. Finally, *recession* is the subsequent phase during which national output falls.[1]

Two other terms are frequently used to describe stages of the business cycle. A *depression* is a period when national output is well below its potential level; it is a severe recession. Depressions are, of course, periods of excessive unemployment. *Prosperity* is a period when national output is close to its potential level. Prosperity, if total spending is too high relative to potential output, can be a time of inflation. (Of course, in some business cycles, the peak may not be a period of prosperity because output may be below its potential level, or the trough may not be a period of depression because output may not be far below its potential level.)

Since World War II, peaks have occurred in 1948, 1953, 1957, 1960, 1969, 1973, 1980 (January), and 1981, while troughs have occurred in

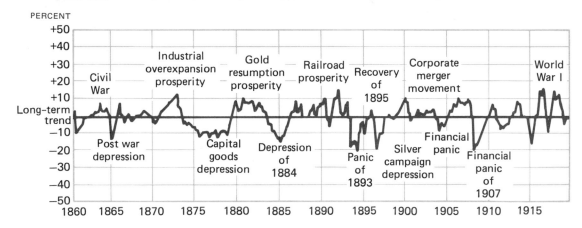

[1]More precisely, the peak and trough are generally defined in terms of deviations from the long-term trend of national output, rather than in terms of deviations from the potential (that is, the full-employment) level of national output.

1949, 1954, 1958, 1961, 1970, 1975, 1980 (July) and 1982 (November). None of these recessions has been very long or very deep (although the 1974–75 and 1981–82 recessions resulted in substantial unemployment). We have done better since the war at avoiding and cushioning recessions, partly because of improvements in economic knowledge of the causes and cures of business cycles.

Although business cycles have certain things in common, they are highly individualistic (see Figure 4.3). For certain classes of phenomena, it may be true that "if you've seen one, you've seen them all," but not for business cycles. They vary too much in length and nature. Moreover, the basic set of factors responsible for the recession and the expansion differs from cycle to cycle. This means that any theory designed to explain them must be broad enough to accommodate their idiosyncracies. In subsequent chapters, much will be said about the causes of business fluctuations; however, using aggregate demand and supply curves we can begin to understand how some of these fluctuations can come about.

AGGREGATE SUPPLY AND DEMAND

In Chapter 2 we described the demand and supply curves for an individual commodity like wheat. Using these demand and supply curves, we analyzed the forces determining the price and output of a commodity in a competitive market. For example, we saw that a shift to the right in the demand curve for wheat tends to increase both the price and output of wheat.

Here, we will analyze the changes in the price level (that is, the average of all prices of goods and services) and output of the entire economy. That is, we are going to determine why the price level increases in some periods but not in others, and why the gross national product soars in some periods

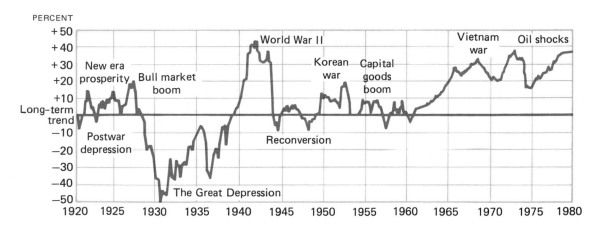

Source: Ameri Trust Company. Adapted with changes.

and plummets in others. To understand the factors underlying inflation and unemployment, we must know why changes occur in the price level and in national output.

Can we use demand and supply curves for the entire economy in much the same way as we did in individual markets? Are there demand and supply curves for the whole economy that are analogous to the demand and supply curves for individual products like wheat? The answer to both questions is yes. And in the next few sections of this chapter, we shall indicate the nature and usefulness of these aggregate demand and supply curves.

THE AGGREGATE DEMAND CURVE

To begin with, consider the *aggregate demand curve.* The aggregate demand curve shows the level of real national output that will be demanded at each price level. (Recall from Chapter 3 that real national output is measured by real gross national product or by real net national product. Thus real national output is composed of the output of food, automobiles, machine tools, ships, and the host of other final goods and services that are produced.) As can be seen in Figure 4.4, the aggregate demand curve slopes downward and to the right. In other words, when other things are held equal, the higher the price level, the smaller the total output demanded will be; and the lower the price level, the higher the total output demanded will be. This might be expected, since the demand curve for an individual product also slopes downward and to the right, as we saw in Chapter 2.

There are two fundamental reasons why the demand curve for an individual commodity like wheat slopes downward and to the right. (1) As the

**Figure 4.4
Aggregate
Demand Curve**
The aggregate demand curve shows the level of total real output that will be demanded at each price level. If the price level is 100, a total real output of $220 billion will be demanded. If the price level is 103, a total real output of $200 billion will be demanded.

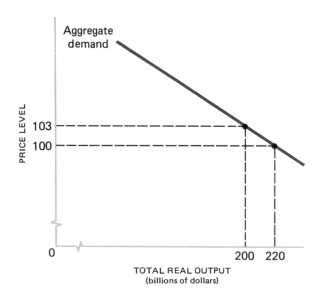

price of the commodity falls, consumers buy more of it because it is less expensive relative to other commodities. (2) As its price falls, each consumer's money income (which is held constant) will buy a larger total amount of goods and services, so it is likely that more will be bought of this commodity.

Neither of these reasons can be used to explain the shape of the aggregate demand curve, which relates the economy's total real output to the price level. When the price level falls, the average price of all goods and services falls.[2] Unlike the demand curve for an individual commodity, there is not just a single price that falls, with the result that consumers find the relevant commodity relatively cheap and buy more of it. Since the aggregate demand curve is concerned with the economy's price level and total real output, not the price and output of a single commodity, the reasons for the downward slope of a demand curve for an individual commodity are not applicable to the aggregate demand curve.

Reasons for the Aggregate Demand Curve's Shape

Why then does the aggregate demand curve slope downward and to the right? The basic reasoning is described in the following two steps. In later chapters, we will fill in many of the details regarding the demand for money and the effects of the supply of money on interest rates and of interest rates on total spending. For present purposes, only a rough sketch is needed.

Step 1: *Increases in the price level will push up interest rates.* In constructing the aggregate demand curve, it is assumed that the quantity of money in the economy is fixed. An increase in the price level increases the average *money* cost of each transaction because the price of each good tends to be higher. Thus, if the price level increases considerably, people will have to hold more money in their wallets and checking accounts to pay for the items they want to buy, since prices will be so much higher. Since the quantity of money is fixed, and the demand for money increases, there will be a shortage of money. In an attempt to increase their money holdings, people will borrow or will sell government securities and other financial assets. As this happens, interest rates—the price paid for borrowing money—will be bid up. (The interest rate is the annual amount that a borrower must pay for the use of a dollar for a year. If the interest rate is 10 percent, a borrower must pay 10 cents per year for the use of a dollar for a year.)

Step 2: *Increases in interest rates will reduce total output.* When the interest rate goes up, firms that borrow money to invest in plant and equipment and consumers that borrow money to buy automobiles or houses tend to cut down on their spending on these items. Due to the higher interest rates, the cost of borrowing money is greater, and hence

[2]Of course, this does not mean that the price of each good and service falls when the price level falls. Only the *average* falls.

some of these investment projects and purchases no longer seem profitable or worthwhile. Because of the reduced spending on these items, the nation's total real output declines.[3]

THE AGGREGATE SUPPLY CURVE

Just as the aggregate demand curve is analogous to the demand curve for an individual product, so the *aggregate supply curve* is analogous to the supply curve for an individual product. *The aggregate supply curve shows the level of real national output that will be supplied at each price level.* As can be seen in Figure 4.5, the aggregate supply curve slopes upward and to the right. In other words, when other things are held equal, the higher the price level, the larger the total output supplied will be; and the lower the price level, the smaller the total output supplied will be. This might be expected since the supply curve for an individual product also slopes upward and to the right, as we saw in Chapter 2.

**Figure 4.5
Aggregate Supply
Curve**
The aggregate supply curve shows the level of total real output that will be supplied at each price level. If the price level is 100, a total real output of $190 billion will be supplied. If the price level is 103, a total real output of $200 billion will be supplied.

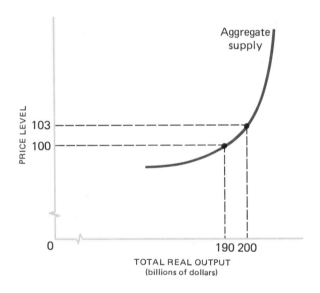

But just as we could not derive the aggregate demand curve simply by adding up the demand curves for all the individual commodities in the economy, so we cannot derive the aggregate supply curve by adding up the supply curves for all the individual commodities. If we did this, we would commit a grave error because the factors held constant in constructing an individual supply curve are not held constant in constructing an aggregate supply curve. In particular, in constructing an individual supply curve, the price of only one commodity is allowed to vary, whereas in constructing an aggregate supply curve, the price level (and thus every price) is allowed to vary.

[3]There are other reasons for the shape of the aggregate demand curve. See E. Mansfield, *Economics: Principles, Problems, Decisions,* 5th ed.

Reasons for the Aggregate Supply Curve's Shape

As indicated in Figure 4.6, the aggregate supply curve can be divided into three ranges: (1) a horizontal range (for output levels up to OQ_0), (2) a vertical range (when output reaches OQ_1), and (3) a positively sloped range (for output levels between OQ_0 and OQ_1). To understand the overall shape of the aggregate supply curve, we must know why each of these ranges exists.

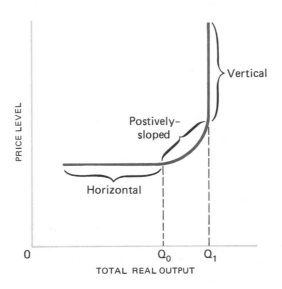

Figure 4.6
Three Ranges of the Aggregate Supply Curve
The aggregate supply curve contains three ranges: (1) a horizontal range, (2) a positively sloped range, and (3) a vertical range.

HORIZONTAL RANGE. In this range, national output can be increased without increasing the price level. This is sometimes called the Keynesian range because it corresponds to a situation of substantial unemployment, which is the situation (during the Great Depression) that concerned John Maynard Keynes, the great British economist. (See Case Study 4.3.) Basically, the horizontal shape of the aggregate supply curve in this range is due to the fact that there is no upward pressure on prices as output increases because there are plenty of unemployed workers, equipment, and other resources. Since these resources can be used to produce additional output at about the same cost per unit of output as the existing volume of output, firms do not have to receive higher prices for their products to be willing to expand production. And since wages and the prices of other resources are relatively fixed, there is little or no downward pressure on prices as output decreases. Of course, the horizontal shape of the curve is a simplification, not an exact description of the behavior of the economy. But it seems to be a useful approximation to reality.

VERTICAL RANGE. In this range, output cannot be expanded, no matter how much the price level increases. Thus, in Figure 4.6, OQ_1 is the maximum amount that the economy can produce. This is sometimes called the classical range because it represents the situation that concerned the classical economists (described in Case Study 4.1 and discussed further in subsequent chapters). It is a situation where the economy's resources are fully employed. In contrast to the Keynesian range, there are no unemployed resources in the classical range.

Of course, this range, like the horizontal range, is a simplification. In fact, it is always possible to get a bit more output from any economic system. People can work longer hours. Equipment can be used around the clock. Children and old people can be brought into the labor force. But under normal conditions there does seem to be a point beyond which further increases in the price level result in little or no increases in output, and this range of the aggregate supply curve approximates this point.

POSITIVELY SLOPED RANGE. In this range, as output increases, shortages of some products begin to develop. Thus the prices of some commodities are pushed up, and the price level—which is the average of all prices of goods and services—rises. For this reason, there is a direct relationship between total real output and the price level.

This is an intermediate range between the horizontal range, where there is considerable unemployment of resources, and the vertical range, where there is full employment. As output rises from the depressed levels in the horizontal range, some sectors of the economy reach relatively full employment before others do. Prices begin to be bid up in some markets, but not in others. As output continues to increase, more and more sectors of the economy reach their capacities, and find it increasingly difficult and costly to increase their output further. Thus the aggregate supply curve becomes steeper as output rises—and eventually it enters the vertical range.

NATIONAL OUTPUT AND THE PRICE LEVEL

The equilibrium level of real national output and the equilibrium price level are given by the intersection of the aggregate demand curve and the aggregate supply curve. In Figure 4.7, the equilibrium level of real national output is $200 billion and the equilibrium price level is 103. The reasoning here is essentially the same as in Chapter 2, where we showed that the equilibrium price and output of a commodity are given by the intersection of the commodity's demand and supply curves. In the present case, an equilibrium can occur only at a price level and level of real national output where aggregate demand equals aggregate supply.

Two Examples

Using aggregate demand and aggregate supply curves, we can begin to understand what has caused some of the swings in the U.S. economy. To

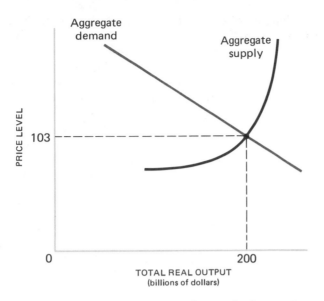

Figure 4.7
Equilibrium Price Level and Total Real Output
The equilibrium level of total real output and the equilibrium price level are given by the intersection of the aggregate demand and supply curves. Here the equilibrium price level is 103 and the equilibrium level of total real output is $200 billion.

illustrate, let's consider how aggregate demand changed in the Great Depression and World War II.

THE GREAT CRASH. Let's begin with the late 1920s. During 1928 and 1929, the American economy was in the midst of prosperity, and the gross national product was approximately equal to its potential value. Unemployment was low. Among the reasons for this prosperity was a relatively strong demand for machinery and equipment to produce new products (like the automobile, radio, telephone, and electric power) and to replace old machinery and equipment that had been worn out or outmoded during World War I and its aftermath.

The New York Stock Exchange, October 1929

The picture changed dramatically in 1929. After the stock market plummeted in October of that year, the economy headed down at a staggering pace. Real GNP fell by almost one-third between 1929 and 1933. Unemployment rose to an enormous 25 percent of the labor force by 1933. One important reason was the severe contraction of gross private domestic investment. (Recall from Chapter 3 that gross private domestic investment is spending on tools, equipment, machinery, construction, and additional inventories.) Whereas gross private domestic investment was about $16 billion in 1929, it fell to about $1 billion in 1933. (The reasons for this decrease will be discussed in later chapters.) Another important factor was the decrease in the supply of money between 1929 and 1933. For reasons discussed in Chapters 9 and 13, this too tended to depress spending and output.

Put in terms of the aggregate demand and supply curves, the situation was as shown in Figure 4.8. For the reasons given in the previous paragraph, the aggregate demand curve shifted markedly to the left; and, as would be expected on the basis of Figure 4.8, total real output and the price level fell between 1929 and 1933.

**Figure 4.8
Shift of the
Aggregate
Demand Curve,
1929–33**
A marked shift to the left in the aggregate demand curve was the principal reason for the onset of the Great Depression. (For simplicity, we assume here that the aggregate supply curve remained fixed.) Output fell drastically (from *OQ₁* to *OQ₂*); the price level fell too (from *OP₂* to *OP₁*).

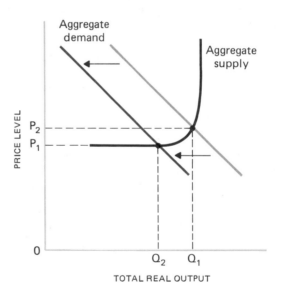

WORLD WAR II. The United States remained mired in the Great Depression until World War II (and the mobilization period that preceded the war). To carry out the war effort, the government spent huge amounts on military personnel and equipment. One result of this increase in spending was a substantial increase in real GNP, which rose by about 75 percent between 1939 and 1945. Another result was a marked reduction in unemployment, as the armed forces expanded and jobs opened up in defense plants and elsewhere. Still another result was the appearance of serious inflationary pressures. As the aggregate demand curve shifted to the right, there was severe upward pressure on the price level as increases in spending pushed national output to its maximum (see Figure 4.9). To counter this pressure, the government instituted price controls (which mandated that firms charge no more than particular amounts) and other measures that kept a temporary lid on prices; but when these controls were lifted after the termination of the war, the price level increased dramatically. Between 1945 and 1948, prices to consumers rose by about 34 percent.

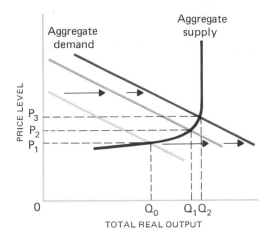

Figure 4.9
Shifts of the Aggregate Demand Curve in World War II
When we entered World War II, the aggregate demand curve shifted to the right as military expenditures mushroomed. Output increased (from OQ_0 to OQ_1 to OQ_2), and inflationary pressures mounted. (For simplicity, we assume that the aggregate supply curve remained fixed.)

UNEMPLOYMENT

In previous sections of this chapter, we have been concerned with business fluctuations. One of the principal reasons why economists and policy makers are so interested in business fluctuations is that the unemployment rate tends to go up during recessions and depressions. As we stressed in the Prologue to this book, unemployment is an economic and social problem that concerns us all. The balance of this chapter is devoted to the definition, measurement, and effects of unemployment.

Almost a century ago, Pope Leo XIII said, "Among the purposes of a society should be to arrange for a continuous supply of work at all times and seasons."[4] The word unemployment is one of the most frightening in the English language —and for good reason. Unemployed people become demoralized, lose prestige and status, and often see their families break apart. Sometimes they are pushed toward crime and drugs; often they feel terrible despair. Their children are innocent

An unemployed Detroit auto worker

[4]Pope Leo XIII, "Encyclical Letter on the Conditions of Labor," May 15, 1891.

victims too. Indeed, perhaps the most devastating effects of unemployment are on children, whose education, health, and security may be ruined. After a few minutes' thought, most people would agree that in this or any other country, every citizen who is able and willing to work should be able to get a job.

We are not saying that all unemployment, whatever its cause or nature, should be eliminated. (For example, some unemployment may be voluntary.) According to the U.S. government, any person 16 years old or older who does not have a job and is actively looking for one is unemployed. Since this definition is necessarily quite broad, it is important that we distinguish among three different kinds of unemployment.

Frictional unemployment occurs because people quit jobs, because ex-students are looking for their first job, or because of seasonal workers. *Structural unemployment* occurs when new goods and new technologies call for different skills than old ones, and workers with older skills cannot find jobs. *Cyclical unemployment* occurs because of business fluctuations of the sort shown in Figure 4.3.

The Unemployment Rate

Each month, the federal government conducts a scientific survey of the American people, asking a carefully selected sample of the population whether they have a job and, if not, whether they are looking for one. According to most experts, the resulting figures are quite reliable but subject to a number of qualifications. One is that the figures do not indicate the extent to which people are underemployed. Some people work only part-time or at jobs well below their level of education or skill, but the government figures count them as fully employed. Also, some people have given up looking for a job and are no longer listed among the unemployed, even though they would be glad to get work if any was offered. To be counted as unemployed in the government figures, one must be actively seeking employment.

To obtain the unemployment rate, the Bureau of Labor Statistics (the government agency responsible for producing the unemployment data) divides the estimated number of people who are unemployed by the estimated number of people in the labor force. To be in the labor force, a person must either be employed or unemployed. Note that the unemployment rate can rise either because people who formerly were employed are thrown out of work or because people who formerly were not in the labor force decide to look for jobs. For example, an increasing number of married women who decide to enter the labor force may tend to raise the unemployment rate.

How Much Unemployment Is There?

To get some idea of the extent of unemployment, we can consult Figure 4.10, which shows the percent of the labor force unemployed during each year from 1929 to 1984. Note the wide fluctuations in the unemployment rate, and the very high unemployment rates during the 1930s. Fortunately, unemployment since World War II has never approached the tragically high levels of the Great Depression of the 1930s. Between 1955 and 1964, it averaged about 6 percent, and then declined steadily until it fell below 4 percent in 1966–69. In 1970–74, it bounced back up to 5 or 6 percent, and then rose to 8½ percent in 1975, after which it receded to 5.8 percent in 1979. In 1981 and 1982 it rose to about 9.5 percent, after which it fell to about 7.4 percent in 1984. Although many of these variations in the unemployment rate may seem small, they are by no means unimportant. With a labor force of over 100 million in the United States, a 1-percentage-point increase in the unemployment rate means that over 1 million more people are unemployed. Any administration, Democratic or Republican, watches these figures closely and tries to avoid significant increases in unemployment.

Figure 4.10
Unemployment Rates, United States, 1929–84
The unemployment rate has varied substantially. Fortunately, since World War II it has not approached the very high levels of the Great Depression of the 1930s. But the recession of 1981 showed that the nation is not immune to severe bouts of unemployment.

THE COSTS OF UNEMPLOYMENT

High levels of unemployment impose great costs on society. In this section, we describe these costs, which are both economic and noneconomic.

Economic Costs

The economic costs of unemployment include the goods and services that could have been produced by the unemployed. Because these people were unemployed, society had to forgo the production of the goods and services they might have produced, with the result that human wants were less effectively fulfilled than would otherwise have been the case. To

CASE STUDY 4.1 UNEMPLOYMENT: THE CLASSICAL VIEW

In early 1914, it was obvious that something was wrong with the U.S. economy. Unemployment was climbing, prices were falling, and factories were closing. While many were quick to blame the Wilson administration for the slump, few thought that the government should intervene to promote higher employment. The prevailing view among classical economists was that, by purchasing more goods and services to take up the slack in business investment, the government might do more harm than good.

Economists of the time saw business cycle fluctuations as temporary aberrations that the price system, left to its own devices, would automatically correct. Classical economic thought held that there could be no such thing as general overproduction. Depressions would cure themselves. If labor was unemployed, workers had only to accept lower wages, whereupon business would gladly rehire them and prosperity would return.

> TRAITÉ
> D'ÉCONOMIE POLITIQUE,
> OU
> SIMPLE EXPOSITION
> DE LA MANIÈRE DONT SE FORMENT, SE DISTRI-
> BUENT, ET SE CONSOMMENT LES RICHESSES.
> Par JEAN-BATISTE SAY, Membre du Tribunat.

Underlying this assumption was a doctrine called Say's Law, after the nineteenth-century French economist J. B. Say. According to this law, the production of a certain amount of goods and services results in the generation of an amount of income which, if spent, is precisely sufficient to buy that output. In other words, *supply creates its own demand. The total amount paid out by the producers of the goods and services to resource owners must equal the value of the goods and services. Thus, if this amount is spent, it must be sufficient to purchase all of the goods and services that are produced.*

But what if resource owners do not spend all of their income, but save some of it instead? How, then, will the necessary spending arise to take all of the output off the market? The answer the classical economists offered is that each dollar saved will be invested. Therefore, investment (expenditures by business firms on plant, equipment, and other productive assets) will restore to the spending stream what resource owners take out through the saving process. The classical economists believed that the amount invested would automatically equal the amount saved because the interest rate—the price paid for borrowing money—would fluctuate in such a way as to maintain equality between them.

Further, the classical economists said that the amount of goods and services firms can sell depends upon the prices they charge, as well as on total spending. For example, $1 million in spending will take 200 cars off the market if the price is $5,000 per car, and 100 cars off the market if the price is $10,000 per car. Recognizing this, the classical economists argued that firms would cut prices to sell their output. Competition among firms would prod them to reduce their prices in this way, with the result that the high-employment level of output would be taken off the market.

The prices of resources must also be reduced under such circumstances. Otherwise firms would incur losses because they would be getting less for their product, but paying no less for resources. The classical economists believed that it was realistic to expect the prices of resources to decline in such a situation. Indeed they were quite willing to assume that the wage rate—the price of labor—would be flexible in this way. Through the processes of competition among laborers, they felt that wage rates would be bid down to the level where everyone who really wanted to work could get a job.

E.M. and N.B.

determine how much society loses in this way by tolerating an unemployment rate above the minimum level resulting from frictional (and some structural) unemployment, economists estimate the *potential GNP*, which is the level of gross national product that can be achieved with full employment. (We first introduced the concept of potential GNP in Figure 4.1). Thus, if *full employment* is defined as a 5 percent unemployment rate, potential GNP can be estimated by multiplying 95 percent of the labor force times the normal hours of work per year times the average output per manhour at the relevant time.

The gap between actual and potential GNP is a measure of what society loses by tolerating less than full employment. Figure 4.11 shows the estimated size of this gap from 1952 to 1984. (Note that both actual and potential GNP are expressed in 1972 prices.) Clearly, the economic costs of unemployment have been very substantial. Consider 1975, a recession year when unemployment was about 8½ percent. As shown in Figure 4.11, society lost about $100 billion in that year alone. Although this estimate is very rough, it is accurate enough to suggest the social waste that accompanies large-scale unemployment.

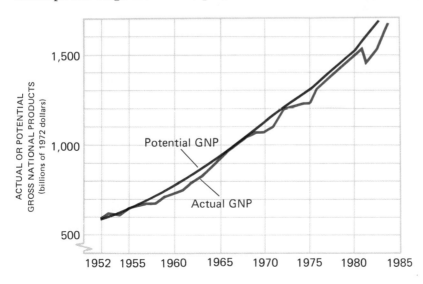

**Figure 4.11
Actual and
Potential GNP,
United States,
1952–84**
The gap between actual and potential GNP is a measure of what society loses because there is less than full employment. In Figure 4.1 we show the size of this gap in earlier years.

☆ ☆ ☆ ☆ ☆ ☆ ☆ ☆ ☆ ☆ ☆ ☆

CASE STUDY 4.2 KARL MARX ON UNEMPLOYMENT

World War I had been good for the American labor movement. But with the armistice, the economy slowed down, the demand for manpower shrank, and support for unions virtually vanished. Unemployment, virtually nonexistent during the war, jumped to 14 percent in 1921. To some workers, angry at unemployment, the views of Karl Marx were appealing. While the classical economists held that depressions were temporary and self-correcting aberrations, Marx argued that economic crises were not accidents but a built-in feature of the capitalist system. A meticulous German scholar who spent much of his life in poverty-ridden circumstances in Britain, Marx (1818–83) wrote a huge, four-volume work on economics, *Das Kapital.* * Eighteen years in the making, it remains one of the most influential books ever written.

Karl Marx

To understand Marx, we need to know something about the times in which he lived. The period was characterized by revolutionary pressures against the ruling classes. In most of the countries of Europe, there was little democracy as we know it. The masses participated little, if at all, in the world of political affairs, and very fully in the world of drudgery. For example, at one factory in Manchester, England, in 1862, people worked an average of about 80 hours per week. For these long hours of toil, the workers generally received small wages. They often could do little more than feed and clothe themselves. Given these circumstances, it is little wonder that revolutionary pressures were manifest.

Marx, viewing the economic system of his day, believed that capitalism was doomed to collapse. He believed that the workers were exploited by the capitalists: the owners of factories, mines, and other types of capital. And he believed that the capitalists, by introducing new labor-saving technology, would throw more and more workers into unemployment. This army of unemployed workers, by competing for jobs, would keep wages at a subsistence level. As machinery was substituted for labor, Marx felt that profits would fall. Unemployment would become more severe. Big firms would absorb small ones. Eventually the capitalistic system was bound to collapse.

According to Marx, the inevitable successor to capitalism would be socialism, an economic system with no private property. Instead, property would be owned by society as a whole. Socialism, constituting a "dictatorship of the proletariat," would be only a transitional step to the promised land of communism. Marx did not spell out the characteristics of communism in detail. He was sure that it would be a classless society where everyone worked and no one owned capital, and he was sure that the state would "wither away," but he did not attempt to go much beyond this in his blueprint for communism. For present purposes, it is not necessary to detail the many places where Marx's theories went astray. The important point here is that although the classical view (discussed in Case Study 4.1) was the dominant one, it did not go unchallenged, even in the nineteenth century.

E.M. and N.B.

*Karl Marx, *Das Kapital,* New York: Modern Library, 1906.

One important problem in estimating this gap stems from the difficulty of defining "full employment." For many years, a common definition of full employment was a 4 percent unemployment rate, since it was felt that frictional and structural unemployment could not be reduced below this level. During the seventies, some argued that an unemployment rate of about 5 percent was a more realistic measure of full employment than 4 percent because there were more young people, women, and minority workers in the labor force. All of these groups find it relatively difficult to secure jobs. In 1979, the Council of Economic Advisers used a figure of 5.1 percent. Since this debate is unresolved, we shall not try to give a precise numerical definition of full employment.[5]

Noneconomic Costs

Unemployment strikes at the social fabric of families and societies; it is not only an economic phenomenon. Since general descriptions of the plight of the unemployed often have relatively little impact, a real-life case study may give you a better feel for what unemployment is like. Consider Joseph Torrio, a New Haven factory worker who was laid off after 18 years on the job. He describes in his own words how he spent several mornings:

> Up at seven, cup of coffee, and off to Sargent's. Like to be there when the gang comes to work, the lucky devils. Employment manager not in. Waited in his outer office. . . . Three others waiting, two reporting for compensation. Other one laid off two weeks ago and said he called at office every day. He inquired what I was doing and when I said "looking for work" he laughed. "You never work here? No? What chance you think you got when 400 like me who belong here out?" Employment manager showed up at 9:30. I had waited two hours.

[5]Note that Figure 4.11 is based on a definition of full employment that sometimes exceeded 4 percent. For example, in 1977, it was 4.8 percent. For the definitions used, see *Economic Report of the President,* 1978, p. 84. Also see *Economic Report of the President,* 1979–85.

☆ ☆ ☆ ☆ ☆ ☆ ☆ ☆ ☆ ☆ ☆ ☆ ☆

CASE STUDY 4.3 JOHN MAYNARD KEYNES AND THE GREAT DEPRESSION

Son of a British economist who was famous in his own right, John Maynard Keynes (1883–1946) was enormously successful in a variety of fields. He published a brilliant book on the theory of probability while still a relatively young man. Working for a half-hour in bed each morning, he made millions of dollars as a stock market specula-tor. He was a distinguished patron of the arts and a member of the Bloomsbury set, a group of London intellectuals who were the intellectual pacesetters for British society. He was a faculty member at Cambridge University and a key figure at the British Treasury.

*John Maynard
Keynes*

Keynes lived and worked almost a century after Marx. His world was quite different from Marx's world; and Keynes himself—polished, successful, a member of the elite—was quite dif-ferent from the poverty-stricken, revolutionary Marx. But the two great economists were linked in at least one important respect. Both were preoccupied with unemployment and the future of the capitalistic system. As we saw in Case Study 4.2, Marx predicted that unemployment would get worse and worse, until at last the capi-talist system would collapse. In the 1930s, when Keynes was at the height of his influence, the Great Depression seemed to many people to be proving Marx right.

In 1936, while the world was still in the throes of this economic disaster, Keynes published his *General Theory of Employment, Interest, and Money.** His purpose in this book was to explain how the capitalist economic system could get stalled in the sort of depressed state of equilibrium that existed in the 1930s. He also tried to indicate how governments might help to solve the problem. Contrary to the classical economists, Keynes concluded that no automatic mechanism in a capitalistic society would generate a high level of employment—or, at least, would generate it quickly enough to be relied on in practice. Instead, the equilibrium level of national output might for a long time be below the level required to achieve high employment. His reasons for believing that this could be the case are discussed in detail in subsequent chapters.

To push the economy toward a higher level of employment, Keynes advocated the conscious, forceful use of the government's power to spend and tax. As we shall see in later chapters, many years passed before these powers became accepted tools of national economic policy, but it was Keynes who provided much of the intellectual stimulus. According to many economists, Keynes made a major contribution to saving the capitalist system.

*John Maynard Keynes, *The General Theory of Employment, Interest, and Money*, New York: Harcourt, Brace, 1936.

My time has no value. A pleasant fellow; told me in a kind but snappy way business was very bad. What about the future, would he take my name? Said he referred only to the present. Nothing more for me to say, so left. Two more had drifted into office. Suppose they got the same story. Must be a lot of men in New Haven that have heard it by now.

On May 21, interview with sales manager of the Real Silk Hosiery Mills. Had seen their ads for salesmen in the paper. Sales manager approached me with his hand sticking out, the first one who had offered to shake hands with me. I told him my name and inquired about the position. He took me into his private office, well furnished, and asked me if I had had any selling experience. I told him that I hadn't any but I thought I could do the work. . . . Asked me to report at 9 A.M. the next morning for further instructions. . . . On May 22, I kept my appointment with the sales manager. Spent the morning learning about different kinds of stockings. Made another appointment for the afternoon which I did not keep because he wanted me to bring along $6 as security on a bag and some stock. I did not have the $6.[6]

No single case study can give you an adequate picture of the impact on people of being without a job. There are a wide variety of responses to unemployment. Some people weather it pretty well, others sink into despair; some people have substantial savings they can draw on, others are hard pressed; some people manage to shield their families from the blow, others allow their misfortunes to spread to the rest of the family. But despite these variations, being without work deals a heavy blow to a person's feeling of worth. It hits hard at a person's self-image, indicating that he or she is not needed, cannot support a family, is not really a full and valuable member of society. The impact of widespread and persistent unemployment is most clearly visible at present among blacks and other racial minorities, where unemployment rates (42.7 percent among non-white teen-agers in 1984) are much higher than among the white population. Unquestionably, the prevalence of unemployment among blacks greatly influences how they view themselves, as well as the way they interact with the rest of the community.

EXPLORING FURTHER: EFFECTS OF SHIFTS IN AGGREGATE DEMAND AND SUPPLY CURVES

Shifts in the Aggregate Demand Curve

In Chapter 2 we saw that shifts in the demand curve for an individual commodity result in changes in the price and output of this commodity. We now see that shifts in the aggregate demand curve result in changes in the price level and total real output.

[6]E. W. Bakke, *The Unemployed Worker,* Hamden, Conn.: Archon, 1969, pp. 168, 169, 174, and 175.

Effect of a Rightward Shift

Suppose that consumers or investors decide to *increase* their spending, perhaps because of a change in their expectations. (They anticipate a marked improvement in economic conditions.) Since the level of total real output demanded at each price level increases, the aggregate demand curve shifts outward and to the right, as shown in Figure 4.12. What is the effect on the price level and on total output? The answer depends on where the aggregate demand curve intersected the aggregate supply curve before the shift in the aggregate demand curve.

HORIZONTAL RANGE OF THE AGGREGATE SUPPLY CURVE. If the intersection occurred in the horizontal range of the aggregate supply curve, the rightward shift of the aggregate demand curve will increase total real output, but have no effect on the price level. (See panel A of Figure 4.12.) As pointed out above, this is because there is considerable unemployment of resources. More output does not entail increased prices.

VERTICAL RANGE OF THE AGGREGATE SUPPLY CURVE. If the intersection occurred in the vertical range of the aggregate supply curve, the rightward shift of the aggregate demand curve will increase the price

**Figure 4.12
Effect of a Shift to
the Right in the
Aggregate
Demand Curve**
Panel A shows that, in the horizontal range of the aggregate supply curve, a rightward shift of the aggregate demand curve increases output, but not the price level. Panel B shows that, in the vertical range of the aggregate supply curve, a rightward shift of the aggregate demand curve increases the price level, but not output. Panel C shows that, in the positively sloped range of the aggregate supply curve, a rightward shift of the aggregate demand curve increases both output and the price level.

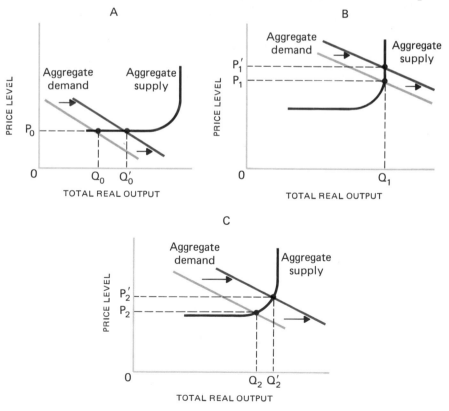

level but have no impact on total real output. (See panel B of Figure 4.12.) As pointed out above, this is because there is full employment of resources. More spending bids up prices, but cannot augment total real output, which is at its maximum level.

POSITIVELY SLOPED RANGE OF THE AGGREGATE SUPPLY CURVE. If the intersection occurred in the positively sloped range of the aggregate supply curve, the rightward shift of the aggregate demand curve will increase both the price level and total real output. (See panel C of Figure 4.12.) This is because increases in output can be attained in this range only if the price level increases, as we saw in a previous section.

Effect of a Leftward Shift

In contrast to the previous situation, suppose that consumers or investors decide to *decrease* their spending. Since the level of total real output demanded at each price level falls, the aggregate demand curve shifts inward and to the left, as shown in Figure 4.13. The effect of this shift depends on where the aggregate demand curve intersected the aggregate supply curve before the shift occurred.

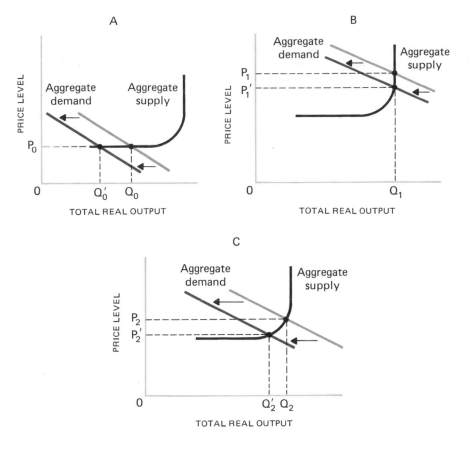

Figure 4.13
Effect of a Shift to the Left in the Aggregate Demand Curve
Panel A shows that, in the horizontal range of the aggregate supply curve, a leftward shift of the aggregate demand curve reduces output, but not the price level. Panel B shows that, in the vertical range of the aggregate supply curve, a leftward shift of the aggregate demand curve reduces the price level, but not output. Panel C shows that, in the positively sloped range of the aggregate supply curve, a leftward shift of the aggregate demand curve reduces both output and the price level.

If the intersection occurred in the horizontal range of the aggregate supply curve, the leftward shift of the aggregate demand curve will reduce total real output, but have no effect on the price level (panel A of Figure 4.13). If the intersection occurred in the vertical range of the aggregate supply curve, this shift will reduce the price level, but have no effect on total real output (panel B of Figure 4.13). If the intersection occurred in the positively sloped range of the aggregate supply curve, this shift will reduce both the price level and total real output.

According to many economists, leftward shifts of the aggregate demand curve generally have much more effect on total real output than on the price level, which (as pointed out below) seldom tends to decline. If this is the case, panel A (or perhaps panel C) in Figure 4.13 is a closer approximation to reality than panel B.

Shifts in the Aggregate Supply Curve

Shifts in the aggregate supply curve, like those in the aggregate demand curve, result in changes in the price level and total real output, as indicated below.

Effect of a Rightward Shift

Suppose that, because of increases in productive capacity or changes in technology, firms are willing and able to supply *more* goods and services (at any given price level) than in the past. Under these circumstances, the aggregate supply curve shifts outward and to the right, as shown in Figure 4.14. What is the effect on the price level and on total output? If prior to this shift the aggregate demand curve intersected the aggregate supply curve at a point where the latter was positively sloped (or vertical), the result will be an increase in total real output and a reduction in the price level, as shown in Figure 4.14.

**Figure 4.14
Effect of a Shift to
the Right in the
Aggregate Supply
Curve**
If the aggregate supply curve shifts to the right, the result will be increased real output (*OQ'* rather than *OQ*) and a lower price level (*OP'* rather than *OP*).

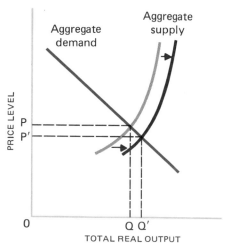

Effect of a Leftward Shift

On the other hand, suppose that firms are willing and able to supply *less* goods and services (at any given price level) than in the past. For example, suppose that there is a worldwide shortage of important raw materials like oil or iron ore that results in increases in their prices. Given that this is the case, a given level of total real output can be produced only at a higher price level than was previously the case. That is, the aggregate supply curve shifts upward and to the left, as shown in Figure 4.15. The effect will be a reduction in total real output and an increase in the price level, as shown in Figure 4.15.

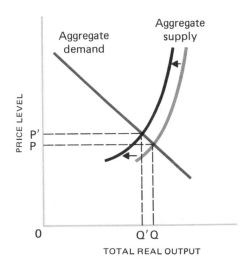

Figure 4.15
Effect of a Shift to the Left in the Aggregate Supply Curve
If the aggregate supply curve shifts to the left, the result will be reduced real output (*OQ'* rather than *OQ*) and a higher price level (*OP'* rather than *OP*).

SUMMARY

1. National output tends to rise and approach its potential (its full-employment) level for a while, then falter and fall below this level, then rise to approach it once more, and so on. These ups and downs are called business fluctuations, or business cycles.

2. Each cycle can be divided into four phases: trough, expansion, peak, recession. These cycles are very irregular and highly variable in length and amplitude. Unemployment tends to be higher at the trough than at the peak; inflation tends to be higher at the peak than at the trough.

3. Until the 1930s, most economists (classical economists) were convinced that the price system, left to its own devices, would ensure the maintenance of full employment. They thought it unlikely that total spending would be too small to purchase the full-employment level of output and argued that prices would be cut if any problem of this sort developed. A notable exception was Karl Marx, who felt that the capitalistic system would suffer from worse and worse unemployment, leading to the system's eventual collapse.

4. John Maynard Keynes, in the 1930s, developed a theory to explain how the capitalist economic system remained mired in the Great Depression, with its tragically high levels of unemployment. Contrary to the classical economists, he concluded that there was no automatic mechanism in a capitalistic system to generate and maintain full employment—or, at least, to generate it quickly enough to be relied on in practice.

5. The aggregate demand curve shows the level of real national output that will be demanded at each price level. It slopes downward and to the right because (1) increases in the price level push up interest rates, and (2) increases in interest rates reduce real national output.

6. The aggregate supply curve shows the level of real national output that will be supplied at each price level. It can be divided into three ranges: (1) the horizontal or Keynesian range where there is considerable unemployment and where output can be increased without increasing the price level, (2) an intermediate range where shortages begin to develop and where increases in output require increases in the price level, and (3) a vertical or classical range where output is at its maximum and where increases in the price level have no effect on output.

7. The equilibrium level of real national output and the equilibrium price level are given by the intersection of the aggregate demand and supply curves.

8. Unemployment is of various types: frictional, structural, and cyclical. The overall unemployment rate conceals considerable differences among types of people. The Bureau of Labor Statistics publishes monthly data concerning the percent of the labor force that is unemployed.

9. High levels of unemployment impose great costs on society. The economic costs of unemployment include the goods and services that could have been produced (but weren't) by the unemployed. Potential GNP is the level of GNP that could have been achieved if full employment had been reached. For many years, a common definition of full employment was a 4 percent unemployment rate, but many economists now believe that a figure of 5 percent or more is more realistic. The gap between actual and potential GNP is a measure of the economic costs of high unemployment.

CHAPTER 5

★ ★ ★ ★ ★ ★ ★ ★ ★

The Determination of National Output and the Keynesian Multiplier

LEARNING OBJECTIVES

In this chapter, you should learn:

★ The nature of the consumption function and the marginal propensity to consume

★ The nature of the saving function and the marginal propensity to save

★ The determinants of the level of net private domestic investment

★ The significance of equilibrium NNP and why it must equal total intended spending

★ How equilibrium NNP can change, and how the multiplier affects these changes

★ *(Exploring Further)* The causes and effects of shifts in the consumption and saving functions

In the previous chapter, we presented an introductory sketch of business fluctuations and indicated how aggregate demand and supply curves can be used to analyze these fluctuations. In this chapter, we go a step further. Rather than simply taking the position of the aggregate demand curve as **99** ★

given, we are concerned with why the equilibrium level of national output is what it is. Why is the aggregate demand curve positioned so as to intersect the aggregate supply curve at this (rather than some other) output? In this chapter we also discuss how the economy can move from one equilibrium to another.

National output is defined in this chapter as net national product, since it is the best measure of how much the economy is producing when depreciation is taken into account. But since net national product and gross national product move up and down together, this theory will also enable us to explain movements in gross national product, and to help forecast them.

Simplifying Assumptions

In this chapter, we shall make three major simplifying assumptions:

1. We assume that there are no government expenditures and that the economy is closed (no exports or imports). Thus *total spending on final output—that is, on net national product—in this simple case equals consumption expenditure plus net investment.* [1] (Why? Because the other two components of total spending—government expenditures and net exports —are zero.)

2. We assume that there are no taxes, no transfer payments, and no undistributed corporate profits. Thus, if we define ***disposable income*** as the total amount of income that people get to keep after paying personal taxes, *NNP equals disposable income in this simple case.* Later chapters relax this and the first assumption.

3. We shall assume that the total amount of intended investment (that is, the total amount that firms and individuals intend to invest) is *independent* of the level of net national product. This, of course, is only a rough simplification, since the amount firms invest will be affected by the level of national output. But this simplification is very convenient, and it is relatively easy to extend the model to eliminate this assumption.

THE CONSUMPTION FUNCTION

An important part of our theory of the determination of national output is the **consumption function,** *which is the relationship between consumption spending and disposable income. It seems clear that consumption expenditures—whether those of a single household or the total consumption expenditures in the entire economy—are influenced heavily by income.* For individual households, Figure 5.1 shows that families with higher incomes spend more on consumption than families with lower incomes. Of course, individual families vary a good deal in their behavior;

[1]Since personal consumption expenditure and net private domestic investment are cumbersome terms, we shall generally use consumption expenditure and net investment instead in this and subsequent chapters.

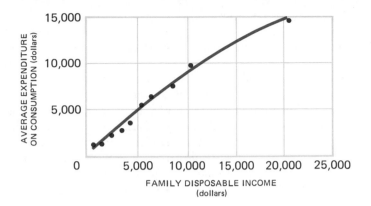

Figure 5.1
Relation between Family Expenditures on Consumption and Family Disposable Income, United States
Families with higher incomes spend more on consumption than families with lower incomes.

some spend more than others even if their incomes are the same. But, on the average, a family's consumption expenditure is tied very closely to its income.

What is true for individual families also holds for the entire economy: total personal consumption expenditures are closely related to disposable income. This fact is shown in Figure 5.2, where personal consumption expenditure in each year (from 1929 to 1984) is plotted against disposable income in the same year (from 1929 to 1984). The points fall very near the straight line drawn in Figure 5.2, but not right on it. For most practical purposes, we can regard the line drawn in Figure 5.2 as representing the relationship between personal consumption expenditure and disposable income. In other words, we can regard this line as the consumption function.

The consumption function is at the heart of the modern theory of the determination of national output. It is a working tool that is used widely and often by economists to analyze and forecast the behavior of the economy.

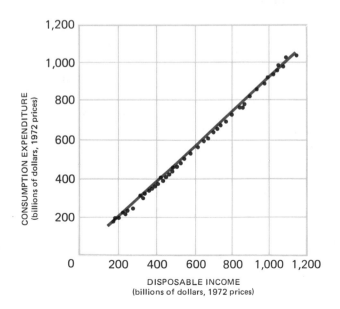

Figure 5.2
Relationship between Personal Consumption Expenditures and Disposable Income, United States, 1929–84 (excluding World War II)
There is a very close relationship between personal consumption expenditure and disposable income in the United States.

The Marginal Propensity to Consume

Suppose that we know what the consumption function for a given society looks like in a particular time period. For example, suppose that it is given by the figures for disposable income and personal consumption expenditure in the first two columns of Table 5.1. Based on our knowledge of the consumption function, we can determine the *extra* amount families will spend on consumption if they receive an *extra* dollar of disposable income. *This amount—the fraction of an extra dollar of income that is spent on consumption—is called the* **marginal propensity to consume.**

**Table 5.1
The Consumption
Function**

Disposable income (billions of dollars)	Personal consumption expenditure (billions of dollars)	Marginal propensity to consume	Average propensity to consume
1,000	950		.95
		$\frac{30}{50} = .60$	
1,050	980		.93
		$\frac{30}{50} = .60$	
1,100	1,010		.92
		$\frac{30}{50} = .60$	
1,150	1,040		.90
		$\frac{30}{50} = .60$	
1,200	1,070		.89
		$\frac{30}{50} = .60$	
1,250	1,100		.88
		$\frac{30}{50} = .60$	
1,300	1,130		.87

To make sure that you understand exactly what the marginal propensity to consume is, consult Table 5.1. What is the marginal propensity to consume when disposable income is between $1,000 billion and $1,050 billion? The second column shows that when income rises from $1,000 billion to $1,050 billion, consumption expenditure rises from $950 billion to $980 billion. Consequently, the fraction of the extra $50 billion of income that is consumed is $30 billion ÷ $50 billion, or 0.60. Thus the marginal propensity to consume is 0.60. Based on similar calculations, the marginal propensity to consume when disposable income is between $1,050 billion and $1,100 billion is 0.60; the marginal propensity to consume when disposable income is between $1,100 billion and $1,150 billion is 0.60; and so forth.

The marginal propensity to consume can be interpreted geometrically as the slope of the consumption function. The slope of any line is the ratio of the vertical change to the horizontal change when a small movement occurs along the line. As shown in Figure 5.3, the vertical change is the change in personal consumption expenditure, and the horizontal change is the change in disposable income. Thus the ratio of the vertical change to the horizontal change must equal the marginal propensity to consume.

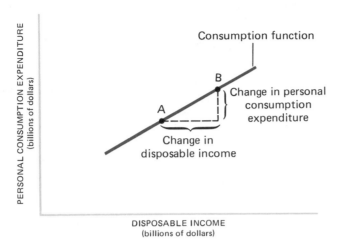

In the figure:
- PERSONAL CONSUMPTION EXPENDITURE (billions of dollars) — vertical axis
- Consumption function
- B
- Change in personal consumption expenditure
- A
- Change in disposable income
- DISPOSABLE INCOME (billions of dollars) — horizontal axis

Figure 5.3
The Marginal Propensity to Consume Equals the Slope of the Consumption Function
The slope of the consumption function between points *A* and *B* equals the vertical change (which is the change in personal consumption expenditure) divided by the horizontal change (which is the change in disposable income).

In general, the marginal propensity to consume can differ, depending on the level of disposable income. For example, the marginal propensity to consume may be higher at lower levels than at higher levels of disposable income. Only if the consumption function is a straight line, as in Figure 5.2 and Table 5.1, will the marginal propensity to consume be the same at all levels of income. For simplicity, we assume in much of the subsequent analysis that the consumption function is a straight line, but this assumption can easily be relaxed without affecting the essential aspects of our conclusions.

The Average Propensity to Consume

It is important to distinguish between the marginal propensity to consume and the *average propensity to consume*. The average propensity to consume equals the proportion of disposable income that is consumed. In other words, it equals

$$\frac{\text{personal consumption expenditure}}{\text{disposable income}}$$

Clearly, this will not in general equal the marginal propensity to consume, which is

$$\frac{\text{change in personal consumption expenditure}}{\text{change in disposable income}}$$

The point is that the marginal propensity to consume is the proportion of *extra* income consumed; this proportion is generally quite different from the proportion of *total* income consumed. For example, in Table 5.1, the average propensity to consume when disposable income is $1,100 billion is 0.92; but the marginal propensity to consume when disposable income is between $1,050 billion and $1,100 billion is 0.60.

THE SAVING FUNCTION

If people don't devote their disposable income to personal consumption expenditure, what else can they do with it? They can save it. When families refrain from spending their income on consumption goods and services—that is, when they forgo present consumption to provide for larger consumption in the future—they save. Thus we can derive from the consumption function the total amount people will save at each level of disposable income. All we have to do is subtract the total personal consumption expenditure from disposable income at each level of disposable income. The difference is the total amount of saving at each level of disposable income. This difference is shown in the third column of Table 5.2. We can plot the total amount of saving against disposable income, as in Figure 5.4. The resulting relationship between total saving and disposable income is the *saving function.* Like the consumption function, it plays a major role in the theory of national output determination.

**Table 5.2
The Saving
Function**

Disposable income (billions of dollars)	Personal consumption expenditure (billions of dollars)	Saving (billions of dollars)	Marginal propensity to save
1,000	950	50	
			$\frac{20}{50} = .40$
1,050	980	70	
			$\frac{20}{50} = .40$
1,100	1,010	90	
			$\frac{20}{50} = .40$
1,150	1,040	110	
			$\frac{20}{50} = .40$
1,200	1,070	130	
			$\frac{20}{50} = .40$
1,250	1,100	150	
			$\frac{20}{50} = .40$
1,300	1,130	170	

**Figure 5.4
The Saving
Function**
The saving function describes the total amount of saving at each level of disposable income. The slope of the saving function equals the change in saving divided by the change in disposable income. Thus the slope of the saving function equals the marginal propensity to save.

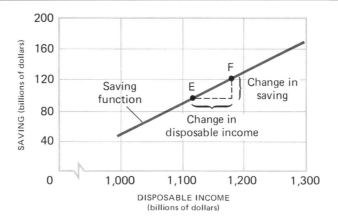

The Marginal Propensity to Save

If we know the saving function, we can calculate the marginal propensity to save at any level of disposable income. *The* **marginal propensity to save** *is the proportion of an extra dollar of disposable income that is saved.* To see how to calculate it, consult Table 5.2. The third column shows that when income rises from $1,000 billion to $1,050 billion, saving rises from $50 billion to $70 billion. Consequently, the fraction of the extra $50 billion of income that is saved is $20 billion ÷ $50 billion, or 0.40. Thus the marginal propensity to save is 0.40. Similar calculations show that the marginal propensity to save when disposable income is between $1,050 billion and $1,100 billion is 0.40; the marginal propensity to save when disposable income is between $1,100 billion and $1,150 billion is 0.40; and so forth.

Note that *at any particular level of disposable income, the marginal propensity to save plus the marginal propensity to consume must equal one.* By definition, the marginal propensity to save equals the proportion of an extra dollar of disposable income that is saved, and the marginal propensity to consume equals the proportion of an extra dollar of income that is consumed. The sum of these two proportions must equal one, for, as stated above, the only things that people can do with an extra dollar of disposable income are consume it or save it. Table 5.2 shows this fact clearly.

Finally, it is worth noting that the marginal propensity to save equals the slope of the saving function—just as the marginal propensity to consume equals the slope of the consumption function. As pointed out above, the slope of a line equals the vertical distance between any two points on the line divided by the horizontal distance between them. Since (as shown in Figure 5.4) the vertical distance is the change in saving and the horizontal distance is the change in disposable income, the slope of the saving function must equal the marginal propensity to save.

DETERMINANTS OF INVESTMENT

In Chapter 3, we stressed that investment consists largely of the amount firms spend on new buildings and factories, new equipment, and increases in inventory. Investment plays a central role in the modern theory of output and employment. To understand this theory, it is essential that you understand the factors determining the level of net private domestic investment (which is gross

*New office
buildings in
Alexandria, Virginia*

private domestic investment less depreciation). Basically, there are two broad determinants of the level of net private domestic investment: the expected rate of return from capital and the interest rate.

Rate of Return

The *expected rate of return* from capital is the perceived rate of return that businesses believe they can obtain if they put up new buildings or factories, add new equipment, or increase their inventories. Each of these forms of investment requires the expenditure of money. The rate of return measures the profitability of such an expenditure; it shows the annual profits to be obtained per dollar invested. Thus a rate of return of 10 percent means that, for every dollar invested, an annual profit of 10 cents is obtained. Clearly, the higher the expected rate of return from a particular investment, the more profitable the investment is expected to be.

Interest Rate

The *interest rate* is the cost of borrowing money. As pointed out in Chapter 4, it is the annual amount that a borrower must pay for the use of a dollar for a year. Thus, if the interest rate is 8 percent, a borrower must pay 8 cents per year for the use of a dollar. And if the interest rate is 12 percent, a borrower must pay 12 cents per year for the use of a dollar. Anyone with a savings account knows what it is to earn interest; anyone who has borrowed money from a bank knows what it is to pay interest.

THE INVESTMENT DECISION

To determine whether to invest in a particular project (a new building, piece of equipment, or other form of investment), a firm must compare the expected rate of return from the project with the interest rate. If the expected rate of return is less than the interest rate, the firm will lose money if it borrows money to carry out the project. For example, if the firm invests in a project with a 10 percent rate of return and borrows the money to finance the project at 12 percent interest, it will receive profits of 10 cents per dollar invested and pay out interest of 12 cents per dollar invested. So it will lose 2 cents (12 cents minus 10 cents) per dollar invested.

Even if the firm does not borrow money to finance the project, it will be unlikely to invest in a project where the expected rate of return is less than the interest rate. Why? Because, if the firm can lend money to others at the prevailing interest rate, it can obtain a greater return from its money by doing this than by investing in the project. Thus if the interest rate is 12 percent and an investment project has an expected rate of return of 10 percent, a firm will do better, if it has a certain amount of money, to lend it out at 12 percent than to earn 10 percent from the investment project.

Since firms are likely to invest only in projects where the expected rate of return exceeds the interest rate, it is obvious that the *level of both gross and net private domestic investment depends on the total volume of investment projects where the expected rate of return exceeds the interest rate.* For example, if the interest rate is 10 percent, the level of (gross and net) investment depends on the total volume of investment projects where the expected rate of return exceeds 10 percent. The more such projects there are, the higher will be the level of (gross and net) investment. Also, the higher the interest rate, the lower will be the level of (gross and net) investment.

THE EQUILIBRIUM LEVEL OF NET NATIONAL PRODUCT

As stressed in Chapter 2, an equilibrium is a situation where there is no tendency for change; it is a situation that can persist. In Chapter 2, we studied the equilibrium value of a product's price. Here we are interested in the equilibrium value of net national product. In Chapter 2, we saw that price is at its equilibrium value when the quantity demanded equals the quantity supplied. Here we shall see that NNP is at its equilibrium value when the flow of income (generated by this value of NNP) results in a level of spending that is just sufficient (not too high, not too low) to take this level of output off the market. To understand this equilibrium condition, it is essential to keep three points in mind:

1. *The production of goods and services results in a flow of income to the workers, resource owners, and managers that help to produce them.* Each level of NNP results in a certain flow of income. More specifically, under the assumptions made here, NNP equals disposable income. Thus whatever the level of NNP may be, we can be sure that the level of disposable income will be equivalent to it.

2. *The level of spending on final goods and services is dependent on the level of disposable income.* As we saw earlier in this chapter, consumption expenditure depends on the level of disposable income. (For the moment, we assume that investment is independent of the level of output in the economy.) Thus if we know the level of disposable income, we can predict what level of spending will be forthcoming.

3. *The level of production is dependent mainly on the level of spending.* If producers find that they are selling goods faster than they are producing them, their inventories will decline. If they find that they are selling goods slower than they are producing them, their inventories will rise. *If NNP is at its equilibrium value, the intended level of spending must be just equal to NNP.* Why? Because otherwise there will be an unintended increase or decrease in producers' inventories—a situation that cannot persist. Much more will be said on this score in the sections that follow.

AGGREGATE FLOWS OF INCOME AND EXPENDITURE

Output Determines Income

Let's look in more detail at the process whereby national output (that is, NNP) determines the level of income, which in turn determines the level of spending. Suppose that the first column of Table 5.3 shows the various possible output levels—that is, the various possible values of NNP—that the economy might produce this year. This column shows the various output levels that might be produced, *if producers expect that there will be enough spending to take this much output off the market at the existing price level.* And, as stressed above, disposable income equals NNP.

Table 5.3
Determination of
Equilibrium Level of
Net National
Product (Billions of
Dollars)

(1) Net national product (= disposable income)	(2) Intended consumption expenditure	(3) Intended saving	(4) Intended investment	(5) Total intended spending (2) + (4)	(6) Tendency of national output
1,000	950	50	90	1,040	Upward
1,050	980	70	90	1,070	Upward
1,100	1,010	90	90	1,100	No change
1,150	1,040	110	90	1,130	Downward
1,200	1,070	130	90	1,160	Downward
1,250	1,100	150	90	1,190	Downward

Income Determines Spending

Since disposable income equals NNP (under our current assumptions), the first column of Table 5.3 also shows the level of disposable income corresponding to each possible level of NNP. From this it should be possible to determine the level of spending corresponding to each level of NNP. Specifically, suppose that the consumption function is as shown in Table 5.1. In this case, intended consumption expenditure at each level of NNP will be shown in column 2 of Table 5.3. For example, if NNP equals $1,000 billion, intended consumption expenditure equals $950 billion.

But consumption expenditure is not the only type of spending. What about investment? Suppose that firms want to invest $90 billion (net of depreciation) regardless of the level of NNP. Under these circumstances, total spending at each level of NNP will be as shown in column 5 of Table 5.3. (Since total intended spending equals intended consumption expenditure plus intended investment, column 5 equals column 2 plus column 4.)

Output Must Equal Spending

Column 5 of Table 5.3 shows the level of total intended spending at each level of national output (and income). *If NNP is at its equilibrium value, total intended spending must equal total output.* In other words, *if NNP is at its equilibrium value, total intended spending must equal NNP.* The easiest way to show this is to show that if intended spending is not equal to NNP, NNP is not at its equilibrium value. The following discussion provides such a proof. First we show that if intended spending is greater than NNP, NNP is not at its equilibrium level. Then we show that if intended spending is less than NNP, NNP is not at its equilibrium level.

If intended spending is greater than NNP, what will happen? Since the total amount that will be spent on final goods and services exceeds the total amount of final goods and services produced (the latter being, by definition, NNP), firms' inventories will be reduced. Consequently, firms will increase their output rate to avoid continued depletion of their inventories and to bring their output into balance with the rate of aggregate demand. Since an increase in the output rate means an increase in NNP, it follows that NNP will tend to increase if intended spending is greater than NNP. NNP therefore is not at its equilibrium level.

On the other hand, what will happen if intended spending is less than NNP? Since the total amount that will be spent on final goods and services falls short of the total amount of final goods and services produced (the latter being, by definition, NNP), firms' inventories will increase. As inventories pile up unexpectedly, firms will cut back their output to bring it into better balance with aggregate demand. Since a reduction in output means a reduction in NNP, it follows that NNP will tend to fall if intended spending is less than NNP. Once again, NNP is not at its equilibrium level.

Since NNP is not at its equilibrium value when it exceeds or falls short of intended spending, it must be at its equilibrium value only when it equals intended spending.

Why NNP Must Equal Intended Spending: Three Cases

To get a better idea of why NNP will be at its equilibrium value only if it equals intended spending, consider three possible values of NNP—$1,050 billion, $1,100 billion, and $1,150 billion—and see what would happen in our simple economy (in Table 5.3) if these values of NNP prevailed.

CASE 1: NNP = $1,050 BILLION. What would happen if firms produced $1,050 billion of final goods and services? Given our assumptions, disposable income would also equal $1,050 billion (since disposable income equals NNP), so consumers would spend $980 billion on consumption goods and services. (This follows from the nature of the consumption function: see column 2 of Table 5.3.) Since firms want to invest $90 billion, total intended spending would be $1,070 billion ($980 billion + $90 billion, as shown in column 5). But the total amount spent on final goods and services under these circumstances would exceed the total value of final goods and services produced by $20 billion ($1,070 billion − $1,050 billion), so firms' inventories would be drawn down by $20 billion. Clearly, this situation could not persist for long. As firms saw their inventories becoming depleted, they would step up their production rates, so that the value of output of final goods and services—NNP—would increase.

CASE 2: NNP = $1,150 BILLION. What would happen if firms produced $1,150 billion of final goods and services? Given our assumptions, disposable income would also equal $1,150 billion (since disposable income equals NNP), with the result that consumers would spend $1,040 billion on consumption goods and services. (Again, this follows from the consumption function: see column 2 of Table 5.3.) Since firms want to invest $90 billion, total spending would be $1,130 billion ($1,040 billion + $90 billion, as shown in column 5). But the total amount spent on final goods and services under these circumstances would fall short of the total value of final goods and services produced by $20 billion ($1,150 billion − $1,130 billion), so that firms' inventories would increase by $20 billion. Clearly, this situation, like the previous one, could not continue for long. When firms saw their inventories increasing, they would reduce their production rates, causing the value of output of final goods and services—NNP—to decrease.

CASE 3: NNP = $1,100 BILLION. What would happen if firms produced $1,100 billion of final goods and services? Disposable income would also equal $1,100 billion (since disposable income equals NNP), so consumers would spend $1,010 billion on consumption goods and services. (Once again, this follows from the consumption function: see column 2 of Table 5.3.) Since firms want to invest $90 billion, total spending would be $1,100 billion ($1,010 billion + $90 billion, as shown in column 5). Thus the total amount spent on final goods and services under these circumstances would exactly equal the total value of final goods and services produced. Consequently, there would be no reason for firms to alter their production rates. This would be an equilibrium situation—a set of circumstances where there is no tendency for NNP to change—and the equilibrium level of NNP in this situation would be $1,100 billion.

These three cases illustrate the process that pushes NNP toward its equilibrium value (and maintains it there). So long as NNP is below its equilibrium value, the situation is like that described in our first case. So long as NNP is above its equilibrium value, the situation is like that described in our second case. Whether NNP is below or above its equilibrium value, there is a tendency for production rates to be altered so that NNP moves toward its equilibrium value. Eventually, NNP will reach its equilibrium value, and the situation will be like that described in our third case. The important aspect of the third case—the equilibrium situation—is that for it to occur, intended spending must equal NNP.

Using a Graph to Determine Equilibrium NNP

We can represent the same argument in a diagrammatic, rather than tabular, analysis. Let's show again that the equilibrium level of NNP is at the point where intended spending equals NNP, but now using a graph. Since disposable income equals net national product in this simple case, we can plot consumption expenditure (on the vertical axis) versus net national product (on the horizontal axis), as shown in Figure 5.5. This is the consumption function. Also, we can plot the sum of consumption expenditure and investment expenditure against NNP, as shown in Figure 5.5. This relationship, shown by the $C + I$ line, indicates the level of total intended spending on final goods and services for various amounts of NNP. Finally, we can plot a 45-degree line, as shown in Figure 5.5. This line contains all points where the amount on the horizontal axis equals the amount on the vertical axis. Thus since NNP is on the horizontal axis and intended spending is on the vertical axis, it contains all points where total intended spending equals net national product.

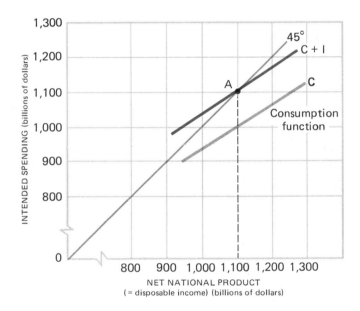

Figure 5.5
Determination of Equilibrium Value of Net National Product
The consumption function is C, and the sum of consumption and investment expenditure is $C + I$. The equilibrium value of NNP is at the point where the $C + I$ line intersects the 45-degree line, here $1,100 billion.

The equilibrium level of net national product will be at the point where total intended spending equals NNP. Consequently, the equilibrium level of NNP will be at the point on the horizontal axis where the $C + I$ line intersects the 45-degree line. In Figure 5.5, this occurs at $1,100 billion. Under the conditions assumed here, no other level of NNP can be maintained for any considerable period of time.

Why can we be sure that the point where the $C + I$ line intersects the 45-degree line is the point where intended spending equals NNP? Because a **45-degree line** is, by construction, a line that includes all points where the amount on the horizontal axis equals the amount on the vertical axis. In this case, as noted above, intended spending is on the vertical axis and NNP is on the horizontal axis. Thus at point A, the point where the $C + I$ line intersects the 45-degree line, intended spending must equal NNP, because point A is on the 45-degree line.

RECONCILING AGGREGATE DEMAND AND SUPPLY CURVES WITH INCOME-EXPENDITURE ANALYSIS

At this point, we must reconcile and integrate the income-expenditure analysis presented here with the aggregate demand-aggregate supply analysis presented in Chapter 4. According to the *income-expenditure analysis*, the equilibrium level of NNP occurs at the point where the $C + I$ line intersects the 45-degree line, as shown in panel A of Figure 5.6. This analysis assumes that firms set their output levels in accord with the level of demand at current prices. If intended spending increases, firms increase their output levels; if intended spending falls, firms cut their output levels.

**Figure 5.6
Relationship
between Income-
Expenditure
Analysis and
Aggregate
Demand-
Aggregate Supply
Analysis**
Income-
expenditure analysis
uses the
intersection of the *C*
+ *I* line and the
45-degree line to
find the equilibrium
level of NNP.
Aggregate
demand-aggregate
supply analysis uses
the intersection of
the aggregate
demand and supply
curves to find the
equilibrium level of
NNP. Both types of
analysis yield the
same result—
namely, that the
equilibrium value of
NNP is *OY*.

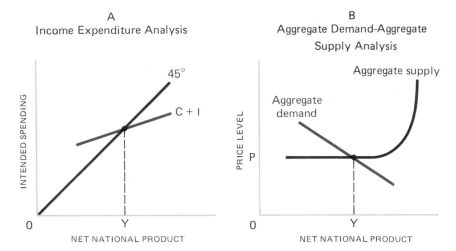

The income-expenditure analysis assumes that firms will produce whatever is demanded at the going price level. In other words, it assumes that the economy is situated on the horizontal range of its aggregate supply curve. As shown in panel B of Figure 5.6, the aggregate demand curve intersects the aggregate supply curve in this range. Put differently, the income-expenditure analysis assumes that the equilibrium level of output is demand-determined and that supply adjusts passively to demand.

If the economy is experiencing considerable unemployment, and the horizontal range of the aggregate supply curve is the relevant one, the income-expenditure analysis tends to be a more revealing way of looking at the determinants of national output than the aggregate demand-aggregate supply analysis. It shows the nature of the changes in spending, which are the prime movers in the model.

But if the economy is operating at a point where the aggregate supply curve is vertical (or close to it), the aggregate demand-aggregate supply analysis is more relevant than the income-expenditure analysis because it

CASE STUDY 5.1 KEYNES'S CRITICISMS OF THE CLASSICAL VIEW

There were at least two basic flaws in the classical model, as Keynes and his followers saw it. First, in their view, *there is no assurance that total intended spending will equal NNP at a level ensuring high employment.* The people and firms who save are often not the same people and firms who invest, and they often have quite different motivations. In particular, a considerable amount of saving is done by families who want to put something aside for a rainy day or for a car or appliance. On the other hand, a considerable amount of investment is done by firms interested in increasing their profits by expanding their plants or by installing new equipment. According to Keynes, one cannot be sure that changes in the interest rate will bring about the equality of saving and investment visualized by the classical economists. Total intended spending may equal NNP at a level corresponding to considerable unemployment (or to considerable inflation). Thus a purely capitalist economic system, in the absence of appropriate government policies, has no dependable rudder to keep it clear of the shoals of serious unemployment or of serious inflation.

Second, *Keynes and his followers pointed out the unreality of the classical economists' assumption that prices and wages are flexible.* Contrary to the classical economists' argument, the modern economy contains many departures from perfect competition that are barriers to downward flexibility of prices and wages. In particular, many important industries are dominated by a few producers who try hard to avoid cutting prices. Even in the face of a considerable drop in demand, such industries have sometimes maintained extraordinarily stable prices. Moreover, the labor unions fight tooth and nail to avoid wage cuts. In view of these facts, the classical assumption of wage and price flexibility seems unrealistic. According to Keynes, it is unlikely that price and wage reductions can be depended on to maintain full employment.

focuses on changes in the price level, which are not included or shown in the income-expenditure analysis.

In subsequent chapters, both of these types of analysis will be used. They both are important parts of the economist's tool kit.

CHANGES IN EQUILIBRIUM OUTPUT

Based on the simple model we have constructed in the previous sections, we can see that equilibrium output can be altered by changes in investment or by changes in consumption that are not due to changes in income.

We conclude this chapter by discussing the volatility of investment spending and how changes in such spending have an amplified—multiplier—effect on output. In the section, "Exploring Further," we show that shifts in the consumption function have similar effects on national output.

THE VOLATILITY OF INVESTMENT

As shown in Figure 5.7, investment expenditure tends to be relatively unstable. That is, it varies from year to year by greater percentages than does consumption expenditure. There are many reasons for this.

**Figure 5.7
Gross Private Domestic Investment, United States, 1940–84**
Gross investment varies considerably from year to year. So does net investment.

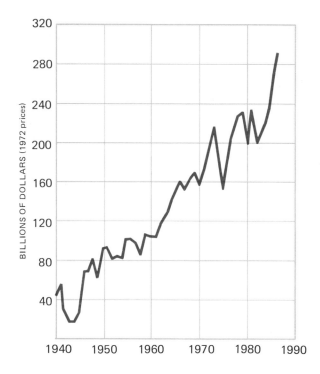

IRREGULARITY OF INNOVATION RATE. Technological innovation occurs irregularly—in fits and starts—not at a constant rate. Thus investment, which is dependent on the rate of technological change, also tends to occur irregularly. Investment booms seem to have occurred in response to major innovations like the railroad and the automobile. According to some forecasts, important innovations are likely to occur during the 1980s and 1990s in robotics and biotechnology. If so, they may also be major stimuli to investment.

DURABILITY OF CAPITAL GOODS. Because capital goods tend to be quite durable, firms frequently can postpone investment decisions. For example, they can postpone the replacement of a piece of equipment by using it even though it is not as reliable as it once was. Or they can postpone the construction of a new building by tolerating crowded conditions in their existing buildings. Since many investment decisions are postponable, the exact time when projects are accepted may depend on the state of business expectations and the level of firms' profits, both of which are highly variable. Also, since the optimism or pessimism of business expectations tends to be contagious, firms often tend to invest at the same time.

CAPACITY UTILIZATION. There are great differences from one year to the next in the extent to which existing productive capacity is being utilized. In some years, sales are so great that firms are working their plants at full capacity. In other years, sales are so slack that firms have plenty of excess capacity. In periods when the existing stock of capital goods is more than sufficient to meet current sales, the level of investment will tend to be lower than in periods when the existing stock of capital goods is only barely sufficient to meet current sales. Because of the year-to-year variation in the extent to which sales levels press against productive capacity, there is considerable variation in the level of investment.

EFFECTS OF CHANGES IN INTENDED INVESTMENT

Looking at the highly simplified model we constructed in previous sections to explain the level of national output, what is the effect of a change in the amount of intended investment? Specifically, if the firms increase their intended investment by $1 billion, what effect will this increase have on the equilibrium value of net national product?

This is a very important question, the answer to which sheds considerable light on the reasons for changes in national output. In the following sections devoted to answering this question, we assume that the change in investment is autonomous, not induced. An *autonomous* change in spending is one that *is not* due to a change in income or NNP. An *induced* change in spending is one that *is* due to a change in income or NNP.

The Spending Chain: One Stage After Another

If there is a $1 billion increase in intended investment, the effects can be divided into a number of stages. In the first stage, firms spend an additional $1 billion on plant, equipment, or inventories. This extra $1 billion is received by workers and suppliers as extra income, which results in a second stage of extra spending on final goods and services. How much of their extra $1 billion in income will the workers and suppliers spend? If the marginal propensity to consume is 0.6, they will spend 0.6 times $1 billion, or $.6 billion. This extra expenditure of $.6 billion is received by firms and disbursed to workers, suppliers, and owners as extra income, bringing about a third stage of extra spending on final goods and services. How much of this extra income of $.6 billion will be spent? Since the marginal propensity to consume is 0.6, they will spend 60 percent of this $.6 billion, or $.36 billion. This extra expenditure of $.36 billion is received by firms and disbursed to workers, suppliers, and owners as extra income, which results in a fourth state of spending, then a fifth stage, a sixth stage, and so on.

TOTALING UP THE STAGES Table 5.4 shows the total increase in expenditure on final goods and services arising from the original $1 billion increase in intended investment. The total increase in expenditures is the increase in the first stage, plus the increase in the second stage, plus the increase in the third stage, and so on. Since there is an endless chain of stages, we cannot list all the increases. But because the successive increases in spending get smaller and smaller, we can determine their sum, which in this case is $2.5 billion. Thus the $1 billion increase in intended investment results—after all stages of the spending and responding process have worked themselves out—in a $2.5 billion increase in total expenditures on final goods and services. In other words, it results in a $2.5 billion increase in NNP.

Table 5.4
The Multiplier
Process

Stage	Amount of extra spending (billions of dollars)
1	1.00
2	.60
3	.36
4	.22
5	.13
6	.08
7	.05
8	.03
9 and beyond	.03
Total	2.50

THE MULTIPLIER

In general, *a $1 billion increase in intended investment results in an increase in equilibrium NNP of (1/MPS) billions of dollars, where MPS is the marginal propensity to save.* This is a very important conclusion. To understand more clearly what it means, let's consider a couple of numerical examples involving values of the marginal propensity to save other than 0.4. For instance, if the marginal propensity to save is $\frac{1}{3}$, a $1 billion increase in intended investment will increase equilibrium NNP by $1 \div \frac{1}{3}$ billion dollars; that is, by $3 billion. Or take a case where the marginal propensity to consume equals $\frac{3}{4}$. What is the effect of a $1 billion increase in intended investment? Since the marginal propensity to save must equal $1 - \frac{3}{4}$, or $\frac{1}{4}$, the answer must be $1 \div \frac{1}{4}$ billion dollars. That is, equilibrium NNP will increase by $4 billion.

Since a dollar of extra intended investment results in (1/MPS) dollars of extra NNP, (1/MPS) is called the **multiplier**. If you want to estimate the effect of a given increase in intended investment on NNP, multiply the increase in intended investment by (1/MPS). The result will be the in-

CASE STUDY 5.2 INVESTMENT AND A GREAT CRASH

Between 1929 and 1933, annual investment spending in the United States fell by about $50 billion (1972 dollars). To get some idea of how a Great Crash, such as occurred then, can take place, let's consider a simple economy with no government or foreign trade. Suppose that intended investment in this economy falls from $52 billion to $2 billion. Assume that the saving function is as shown below:

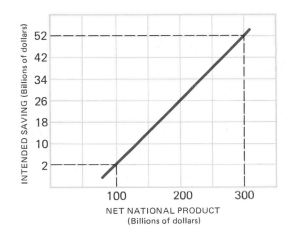

According to the graph, intended saving equals $2 billion when NNP is $100 billion, and it equals $52 billion when NNP is $300 billion. Thus since NNP equals disposable income under the assumed (highly simplified) conditions, the marginal propensity to save equals (52 − 2) ÷ (300 − 100) = 0.25. The multiplier equals the reciprocal of the marginal propensity to save, or 1/0.25 = 4 in this highly simplified case. The drop in investment ($50 billion) times the multiplier (4) is equal to the drop in NNP ($200 billion). So, in this example NNP must have dropped by $200 billion.

This is an illustration of how the multiplier can be used. Knowing the marginal propensity to save (0.25), we can calculate the multiplier (4), which enables us to determine the change in NNP ($200 billion).

crease in NNP. Moreover, it is easy to show that the same multiplier holds for decreases in intended investment as well as for increases. That is, a dollar less of intended investment results in (1/MPS) dollars less of NNP. Consequently, if you want to estimate the effect of a given change in intended investment (positive or negative) on NNP, multiply the change in intended investment by (1/MPS).

It is important to note that since MPS is less than one, *the multiplier must be greater than one.* In other words, an increase in intended investment of $1 will result in an increase in NNP of more than $1. This means that NNP is relatively sensitive to changes in intended investment. Moreover, since the multiplier is the reciprocal of the marginal propensity to save, the smaller the marginal propensity to save, the higher the multiplier—and the more sensitive is NNP to changes in intended investment. As we shall see, this result has important implications for public policy. For example, because our system of taxes and transfer payments tends to increase the marginal propensity to save out of NNP, the destabilizing effect of a sharp change in investment expenditures frequently is reduced.

☆   ☆   ☆   **EXPLORING FURTHER: NONINCOME DETERMINANTS OF CONSUMPTION**

In previous sections of this chapter, we were concerned with the effects on NNP of changes in investment spending. Now we must consider the effects of changes in consumption expenditure. It is important to recognize that many other factors besides disposable income have an effect on personal consumption expenditure. Holding disposable income constant, personal consumption expenditure is likely to vary with the amount of wealth in the hands of the public, the ease and cheapness with which consumers can borrow money, the expectations of the public, the amount of durable goods on hand, the income distribution, and the size of the population. In this section, we discuss the effects of these nonincome factors on consumption expenditure.

Shifts in the Consumption and Saving Functions

Suppose that a change occurs in one of these nonincome factors. For example, suppose that there is a marked increase in the amount of wealth in the hands of the public. What effect will this have on the consumption function? Obviously, it will shift the consumption function upward, as from position 1 to position 2 in Figure 5.8A. Or suppose that it becomes more difficult and expensive for consumers to borrow money. What effect will this have on the consumption function? Obviously, it will shift the consumption function downward, as from position 1 to position 3 in Figure 5.8A.

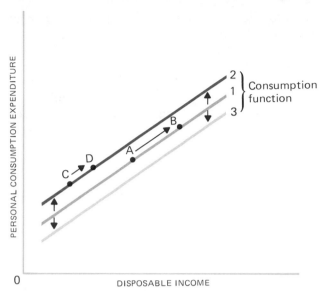

Figure 5.8A
A Shift versus a Movement in the Consumption Function
If the consumption function moves from position 1 to position 2 (or position 3), this is a shift in the consumption function. A movement from *A* to *B* (or from *C* to *D*) is a movement along a given consumption function.

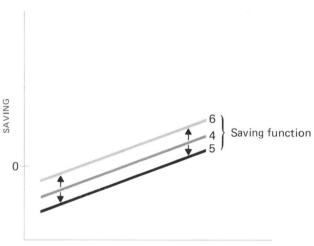

Figure 5.8B
Effects of Shifts in Consumption Function on Saving Function
An upward shift in the consumption function (as from position 1 to position 2 in panel A) is accompanied by a downward shift in the saving function (from position 4 to position 5 in panel B). A downward shift in the consumption function (as from position 1 to position 3 in panel A) is accompanied by an upward shift in the saving function (from position 4 to position 6 in panel B).

Shifts in Functions versus Movements Along Them

It is important to distinguish between a *shift* in the consumption function and a *movement along* a given consumption function. A shift in the consumption function means that the public wants to spend a different amount on consumption goods out of a given amount of disposable income than in the past. Thus if the consumption function shifts to position 2 in Figure 5.8A, this means that the public wants to spend more on consumption goods out of a given amount of disposable income than when the consumption function was at position 1. And if the consumption function shifts to position 3 in Figure 5.8A, this means that the public wants to spend less on consumption goods out of a given amount of disposable income than when the consumption function was at position 1.

In contrast, a movement along a given consumption function is a change in personal consumption expenditure induced by a change in disposable income, with no change in the relationship between personal consumption expenditure and disposable income. For example, the movement from point A to point B is a movement along a consumption function (in position 1). Similarly, the movement from point C to point D is a movement along a consumption function (in position 2).

How Shifts in the Consumption Function Are Related to Shifts in the Saving Function

Note that an *upward* shift in the consumption function must be accompanied by a *downward* shift in the saving function. If the public wants to spend *more* on consumption goods out of a given amount of disposable income, it must want to save *less* out of that amount of disposable income. (Why? Because personal consumption expenditure plus saving equals disposable income.) Thus if the consumption function shifts upward from position 1 to position 2 in Figure 5.8A, the saving function must shift downward from position 4 to position 5 in Figure 5.8B.

Also, a *downward* shift in the consumption function must be accompanied by an *upward* shift in the saving function. If the public wants to spend *less* on consumption goods out of a given amount of disposable income, it must want to save *more* out of that amount of disposable income. (Why? Because personal consumption expenditure plus saving equals disposable income.) Thus if the consumption function shifts downward from position 1 to position 3 in Figure 5.8A, the saving function must shift upward from position 4 to position 6 in Figure 5.8B.

Effects of Shifts in the Consumption Function

Earlier in this chapter, we showed that changes in intended investment have an amplified effect on NNP, with the extent of the amplification measured by the multiplier. But it is important to note at this point that a shift in the consumption function will also have such an amplified effect on NNP. For example, in Figure 5.9, if the consumption function shifts from C_1 to C_2, this means that at each level of disposable income, consumers intend to spend $1 billion more on consumption goods and services than they did before. *This $1 billion upward shift in the consumption function will have precisely the same effect on equilibrium NNP as a $1 billion increase in intended investment.*

Moreover, a *$1 billion downward shift in the consumption function will have precisely the same effect on equilibrium NNP as a $1 billion decrease in intended investment.* Thus both upward and downward shifts in the consumption function—due to changes in tastes, assets, price, popu-

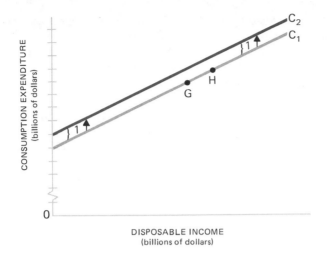

Figure 5.9
Shift in the Consumption Function
If the consumption function shifts from C_1 to C_2, this means that, at each level of disposable income, consumers intend to spend $1 billion more on consumption goods and services. Such a shift results in an increase of $\frac{1}{MPS}$ billions of dollars in equilibrium NNP.

lation, and other things—will have a magnified effect on NNP. NNP is sensitive to shifts in the consumption function in the same way that it is sensitive to changes in intended investment. This is an important point. Finally, to prevent misunderstanding, recall from the previous sections that a *shift* in the consumption function is quite different from a *movement along* a given consumption function. (An example of the latter would be the movement from point G to point H in Figure 5.9.) We are concerned here with shifts in the consumption function, not movements along a given consumption function.

SUMMARY

1. The consumption function—the relation between personal consumption expenditure and disposable income—is at the heart of the modern theory of the determination of national output. From the consumption function, one can determine the marginal propensity to consume, which is the proportion of an extra dollar of income that is spent on consumption, as well as the saving function (the relationship between total saving and disposable income) and the marginal propensity to save (the proportion of an extra dollar of income that is saved).

2. The level of both gross and net private domestic investment is determined by the expected rate of return from capital and the interest rate. The expected rate of return from capital is the perceived rate of return that businesses expect to obtain if new buildings are put up, new equipment is added, or inventories are increased. The interest rate is the cost of borrowing money. The level of investment is directly related to the expected rate of return from capital, and inversely related to the interest rate.

3. The equilibrium level of net national product will be at the point where intended spending on final goods and services equals NNP. If in-

tended spending exceeds NNP, NNP will tend to increase. If intended spending falls short of NNP, NNP will tend to fall.

4. If NNP is below its equilibrium level, the total amount spent on goods and services will exceed the total amount produced, so firms' inventories will be reduced. Firms will step up their output rates, thus increasing NNP.

5. If NNP is above its equilibrium value, the total amount spent on goods and services will fall short of the total amount produced, so firms' inventories will increase. Firms will cut their output rates, thus reducing NNP.

6. Investment expenditure tends to vary from year to year by greater percentages than does consumption expenditure. This is due in part to the irregularity of innovation, the durability of capital goods, and the differences from year to year in the extent to which existing productive capacity is utilized.

7. A $1 billion change in intended investment will result in a change in equilibrium NNP of (1/MPS) billions of dollars, where MPS is the marginal propensity to save. In other words, the multiplier is (1/MPS). The multiplier can be interpreted in terms of—and derived from—the successive stages of the spending process.

*8. Holding disposable income constant, personal consumption expenditure is likely to depend on the amount of wealth in the hands of the public, the ease and cheapness with which consumers can borrow money, the expectations of the public, the amount of durable goods on hand, the income distribution, and the size of the population. Changes in these factors are likely to cause shifts in the consumption function.

*9. A shift in the consumption function will also have an amplified effect on NNP, a $1 billion shift in the consumption function resulting in a change of (1/MPS) billions of dollars in NNP.

*The starred items relate to material covered in the section, "Exploring Further."

CHAPTER 6

★ ★ ★ ★ ★ ★ ★ ★

Fiscal Policy and National Output

LEARNING OBJECTIVES

In this chapter, you should learn:

★ How government spending and taxation affect the level of NNP

★ The objectives and methods of fiscal policy

★ The pros and cons of fiscal policy

★ The types of expenditures made and taxes collected by the federal, state, and local levels of government

★ *(Exploring Further)* How fiscal policy affects the aggregate demand curve

In the period since World War II, the idea that the government's power to spend and tax should be used to stabilize the economy—that is, to reduce unemployment and fight inflation—has gained acceptance throughout the world. Most economists believe that this idea is essentially correct. However, time has also revealed that fiscal policy (the use of government spending and taxation for stabilization purposes) is far from a panacea. Witness the severe inflationary pressures and the high unemployment rates that plagued the American economy in the late 1970s and early 1980s. Both the power and the limitations of fiscal policy must be recognized. This chapter presents a first look at fiscal policy, in the context of the simplest Keynesian model. In Chapters 12 and 14, a more sophisticated analysis of fiscal policy is presented.

GOVERNMENT EXPENDITURE AND NET NATIONAL PRODUCT

In the previous chapters, we showed how the equilibrium level of net national product was determined in a simplified economy without government spending or taxation. We must now extend this theory to include both government spending and taxation. As we shall see, the results form the basis for some of our nation's past and present economic policy. In this section, we incorporate government spending into the theory of the determination of net national product. In so doing, we assume that government spending will not affect the consumption function or the level of intended investment. In other words, we assume that government spending does not reduce or increase private desires to spend out of each level of income. (Government here includes federal, state, and local.)

Suppose that the government purchases $50 billion worth of goods and services and that it will purchase this amount whatever the level of NNP. (As pointed out in Chapter 3, only government purchases, not transfer payments, are included here.) Clearly, adding this public expenditure to the private expenditures on consumption and investment results in a higher total level of intended spending. In an economy with government spending (but no net exports) total intended spending on output equals consumption expenditure plus intended investment expenditure plus intended government expenditure. Since an increase in government expenditure (like increases in consumption or investment expenditure) results in an increase in total intended spending, and since the equilibrium value of net national product is at the point where total intended spending equals NNP, it follows that an increase in government expenditure, as well as the induced increase in private spending, brings about an increase in the equilibrium value of NNP.

To see the effects of government expenditure on the equilibrium value of NNP, we can use a graph similar to those in Chapter 5. We begin by plotting the consumption function, which shows intended consumption expenditure at each level of NNP (since NNP equals disposable income under our assumptions): the result is line C in Figure 6.1. Then we can plot the sum of intended consumption expenditure and investment expenditure at each level of NNP. The result is line $C + I$. Next, we plot the sum of intended consumption expenditure, investment expenditure, and government expenditure at each level of NNP, to get line $C + I + G$. Since the **C + I + G** *line* shows total intended spending, and since, as we stressed in Chapter 5, the equilibrium value of NNP is at the point where total intended spending equals NNP, it follows that the equilibrium value of NNP is at the point where the $C + I + G$ line intersects the 45-degree line. This is at an output of $1,225 billion.

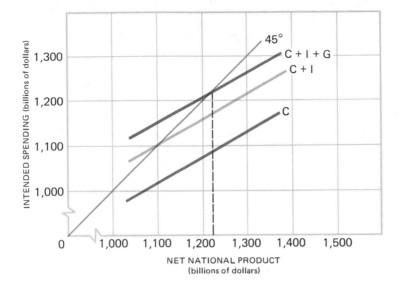

Figure 6.1
Determination of Net National Product, Including Government Expenditure
The consumption function is C, the sum of consumption and investment expenditures is $C + I$, and the sum of consumption, investment, and government expenditures is $C + I + G$. The equilibrium value of NNP is at the point where the $C + I + G$ line intersects the 45-degree line, which here is $1,225 billion.

Effect of Increased Government Expenditure

What happens to the equilibrium level of NNP if government expenditure increases? Figure 6.2 shows the results of a $5 billion increase in government spending. The increased government expenditure (G_1) will raise the $C + I + G$ line by $5 billion, as the figure shows. Since the $C + I + G_1$ line must intersect the 45-degree line at a higher level of NNP, increases in government expenditure result in increases in the equilibrium level of NNP. In Figure 6.2, the $5 billion increase in government expenditure raises the equilibrium value of NNP from $1,225 billion to $1,237.5 billion.

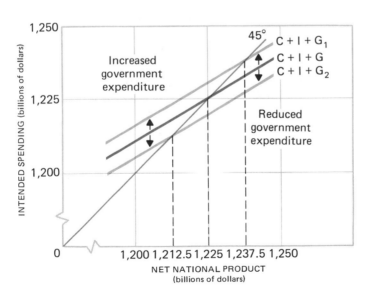

Figure 6.2
Effects on Equilibrium Net National Product of a $5 Billion Increase and Decrease in Government Expenditure
A $5 billion increase raises the equilibrium value of NNP from $1,225 billion to $1,237.5 billion. A $5 billion decrease reduces the equilibrium value of NNP from $1,225 billion to $1,212.5 billion.

Effect of Decreased Government Expenditure

Figure 6.2 also shows what happens when government spending goes down by $5 billion (to G_2). The new $C + I + G_2$ line is $5 billion lower than the old $C + I + G$ line. Since the new $C + I + G_2$ line intersects the 45-degree line at a lower level of NNP, decreases in government expenditure result in decreases in the equilibrium level of NNP. In Figure 6.2 the $5 billion decrease in government expenditure reduces the equilibrium value of NNP from $1,225 billion to $1,212.5 billion.

What Is the Multiplier Effect for Government Expenditure?

How sensitive is the equilibrium level of NNP to changes in government spending? In the previous chapter, we found that a $1 billion change in intended investment—or a $1 billion shift in the consumption function—results in a change in equilibrium NNP of (1/MPS) billions of dollars, where MPS is the marginal propensity to save. The effect of a $1 billion change in government expenditure is exactly the same. It will result in a change in equilibrium NNP of (1/MPS) billion dollars. Thus a change in government expenditure has the same multiplier effect on NNP as a change in investment or a shift in the consumption function. For example, if the marginal propensity to consume is 0.6, an extra $1 billion in government expenditure will increase equilibrium NNP by $2.5 billion.

TAXATION AND NET NATIONAL PRODUCT

The previous section added government expenditures to our theory, but it did not include taxes. (Here we assume taxes to be net of transfer payments.) For simplicity, assume that all tax revenues stem from personal taxes. How do tax collections influence the equilibrium value of net national product? For example, if consumers pay 16 ⅔ percent of their income to the government in taxes, what effect does this have on NNP? Clearly, the imposition of this tax means that for each level of NNP, people have less disposable income than they would with no taxes. In particular, disposable income now equals 83 ⅓ percent of NNP, whereas without taxes it equaled NNP. Thus *the relationship between consumption expenditure and NNP is altered by the imposition of the tax.* Before the tax was levied, the relationship was given by line C_0 in Figure 6.3; after the imposition of the tax, it is given by line C_1.

The relationship between consumption expenditure and national output changes in this way because consumption expenditure is determined by the level of disposable income. For instance, in the case in Figure 6.3, consumption expenditure equals $350 billion plus 60 percent of disposable

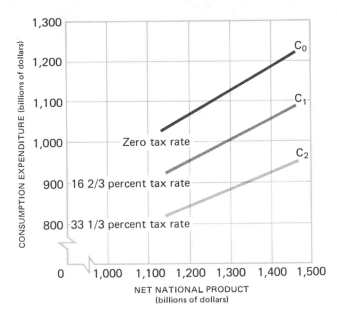

**Figure 6.3
Relationship
between
Consumption
Expenditure and
Net National
Product, Given
Three Tax Rates**
If taxes are zero, C_0
is the relationship
between
consumption
expenditure and
NNP. If consumers
pay 16⅔ percent of
their income in
taxes, C_1 is the
relationship; and if
consumers pay
33⅓ percent of
their income in
taxes, C_2 is the
relationship. Clearly,
the higher the tax
rate, the less
consumers spend
on consumption
from a given NNP.

income. Thus since the tax reduces the amount of disposable income at each level of NNP, it also reduces the amount of consumption expenditure at each level of NNP. In other words, since people have less after-tax income to spend at each level of NNP, they spend less on consumption goods and services at each level of NNP. This seems reasonable. It is illustrated in Figure 6.3, where at each level of NNP, consumption expenditure after tax (given by line C_1) is less than before the tax (given by line C_0).

Because the imposition of the tax influences the relationship between consumption expenditure and NNP, it also influences the equilibrium value of NNP. As we have stressed, the equilibrium value of NNP is at the point where intended spending on output equals NNP. Lines C_0 and C_1 in Figure 6.3 show intended consumption expenditure at each level of NNP, before and after the tax. Adding intended investment and government expenditure to each of these lines, we get the total intended spending before and after the tax. The results are shown in Figure 6.4, under the assumption that the sum of intended investment and government spending equals $140 billion. The $C_0 + I + G$ line shows intended spending before the tax, while the $C_1 + I + G$ line shows intended spending after the tax.

Effect of the Tax

The equilibrium level of NNP is appreciably lower after the imposition of the tax than before. Specifically, as shown in Figure 6.4, it is $980 billion after the imposition of the tax and $1,225 billion before. The tax reduced the equilibrium level of NNP because it lowered the $C + I + G$ line from

Figure 6.4
Determination of
Equilibrium Value
of Net National
Product, with Zero
and 16⅔ Percent
Tax Rates
The tax rate
influences the
relationship between
consumption
expenditure and
NNP. (C_0 is this
relationship with a
zero tax rate, while
C_1 is the
relationship with a
16⅔ percent tax
rate. See Figure
6.3.) Consequently,
the equilibrium value
of NNP is $1,225
billion if the tax rate
is zero, and $980
billion if it is 16⅔
percent.

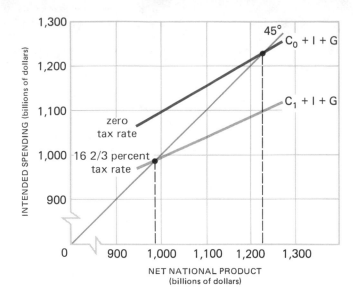

$C_0 + I + G$ to $C_1 + I + G$. It did this because it reduced the amount people wanted to spend on consumption goods at each level of NNP. People still wanted to spend the same amount *from each (after-tax) income level* but, because of the tax, their spending decisions had to be based on a *reduced (after-tax) income,* so that they spent less on consumption goods and services at each level of NNP.

Effect of a Tax Increase

Going a step further, *the higher the tax rate, the lower the equilibrium value of NNP; and the lower the tax rate, the higher the equilibrium value of NNP.* This is a very important proposition, as we shall see in subsequent sections. To demonstrate it, let's see what will happen to the equilibrium value of NNP when the tax rate is increased from 16 ⅔ percent of NNP to 33 ⅓ percent of NNP. If the tax rate is 33 ⅓ percent, total intended spending at each level of NNP will be given by line $C_2 + I + G$ in Figure 6.5.

Since the equilibrium value of NNP will be at the point where the $C_2 + I + G$ line intersects the 45-degree line, the equilibrium value of NNP will be $816 ⅔ billion, rather than $980 billion (which was the equilibrium value when the tax rate was 16 ⅔ percent). Thus the increase in the tax rate will reduce the equilibrium value of NNP. By reducing the amount people want to spend on consumption at each level of NNP, the increase in the tax rate will lower the $C + I + G$ line from $C_1 + I + G$ to $C_2 + I + G$.

Effect of a Tax Cut

On the other hand, suppose that the tax rate is made lower than 16 ⅔ percent of NNP. What will happen to the equilibrium value of NNP? If the

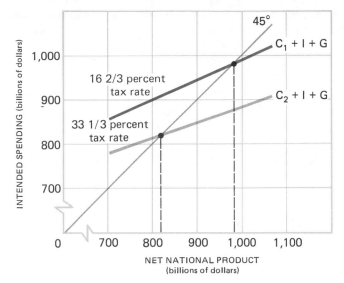

Figure 6.5
Determination of Equilibrium Value of Net National Product, with 16⅔ Percent and 33⅓ Percent Tax Rates
The $C_1 + I + G$ line shows total intended spending at each level of NNP if the tax rate is 16⅔ percent, and the $C_2 + I + G$ line shows total intended spending at each level of NNP if the tax rate is 33⅓ percent. Consequently, the equilibrium value of NNP is $980 billion if the tax rate is 16⅔ percent and $816⅔ billion if it is 33⅓ percent.

tax rate is lower than 16 ⅔ percent, the intended spending on output at each level of NNP will be given by a $C + I + G$ line that lies between $C_0 + I + G$ and $C_1 + I + G$ in Figure 6.4. Since the equilibrium value of NNP will be at the point where this line intersects the 45-degree line, the equilibrium value of NNP will be greater than $980 billion. Thus the decrease in the tax rate will increase the equilibrium value of NNP. By increasing the amount people want to spend on consumption at each level of NNP, it will raise the $C + I + G$ line from $C_1 + I + G$ to a higher level.

THE NATURE AND OBJECTIVES OF FISCAL POLICY

Our discussions in previous sections make it easy to understand the basic ideas underlying modern fiscal policy. For example, suppose that the economy is suffering from an undesirably high unemployment rate. What should the government do? The economy needs increased spending. In other words, the economy needs an upward lift of the $C + I + G$ line, which by increasing NNP will increase employment as well. There are three ways that the government can try to bring this about. First, *it can reduce taxes,* which, as shown in a previous section, will shift the relation between consumption expenditure and NNP—and consequently the $C + I + G$ line—upward. Second, *it can increase government expenditures,* which will also shift the $C + I + G$ line upward. Third, *the government can encourage firms to invest more,* perhaps by enacting tax credits to make investment more profitable for them. The resulting increase in intended investment will shift the $C + I + G$ line upward too.

On the other hand, perhaps we are suffering from a high rate of inflation. What should the government do? The economy needs reduced spending. In other words, what is required is a downward shift of the $C + I + G$ line. The government has three ways to try to bring this about.

First, *it can increase taxes.* This, as shown in a previous section, will shift the relation between consumption expenditure and NNP—and consequently the $C + I + G$ line—downward. Second, *it can cut government expenditures,* which will also shift the $C + I + G$ curve downward. Third, *it can change the tax laws and do other things to discourage firms from investing in plant and equipment or inventories.* The resulting decrease in intended investment will shift the $C + I + G$ line downward too.

CASE STUDY 6.1 THE EMPLOYMENT ACT OF 1946

As previous chapters have indicated, the experiences of the Depression and the war convinced many Americans that the government had both the duty and the power to guarantee jobs for all its citizens. And the theoretical basis for this belief came from John Maynard Keynes. (See Case Study 4.3.) Keynes argued that an industrial economy could stabilize at high levels of unemployment, and the length and depth of the Great Depression bore him out. He argued that massive government intervention could restore prosperity to a stalled economy, and the wartime experience seemed to prove him right. When prosperity was threatened at the end of the war, a Full Employment Bill was introduced in the U.S. Senate in January 1945.

The first shot had been fired in a year-long legislative battle. While everyone had been anxious to talk about full employment during the political campaigns of 1944, there was still plenty of resistance to the idea of this much government intervention in the economy. A year of compromises saw many changes in the language of the bill. The words "full employment" were replaced by the phrase "maximum employment, production and purchasing power." Gone were the original instructions to the president to initiate spending programs to guarantee employment. Conservatives rejoiced in a watered-down bill. Liberals denied that there was any retreat involved.

The bill that President Truman signed into law on February 20, 1946, was called The Employment Act of 1946. It instructed the federal government "to promote maximum employment, production and purchasing power." The president was instructed to form a Council of Economic Advisers to assist him in preparing economic forecasts. The idea of a right to a job, and a spending program to guarantee that right, disappeared from the final bill. By the time the Employment Act became law, the war was over, but the prosperity continued. Dire predictions of hard times and high unemployment vanished in the explosion of pent-up consumer demand. The end of the war marked the beginning of a long period of prosperity. And the Employment Act of 1946 marked the commitment of the government to use its considerable power to ensure a continuation of this prosperity.

N.B.

Certainly, these ideas do not seem very hard to understand. Advocates of fiscal policy maintain that *if there is too much unemployment, the government should promote, directly or indirectly, additional public and /or private spending, which will result in additional output and jobs.* On the other hand, *if there is too much inflation, the government should reduce, directly or indirectly, spending (public and/or private), which will curb the inflationary pressure on prices.* Most economists believe that these propositions are useful—although by themselves they cannot deal as effectively as one would like with times like the 1970s and early 1980s, when excessive unemployment and inflation have occurred together. (We shall discuss such situations in detail in Chapter 10.)

MAKERS OF FISCAL POLICY

When you go to a ball game, you generally get a program telling you who on each team is playing each position. To understand the formulation and implementation of fiscal policy in the United States, we need the same kind of information. Who are the people who establish our fiscal policy? Who decides that in view of the current and prospective economic situation, tax rates or government expenditures should be changed? This is not a simple question because many individuals and groups play important roles. In the Congress, the House and Senate Budget Committees—as well as the Congressional Budget Office—have been charged with important responsibilities in this area. The Appropriations Committees, the House Ways and Means Committee, and the Senate Finance Committee also have considerable influence. In addition, another congressional committee is of importance: the Joint Economic Committee of Congress. Established by the Employment Act of 1946, this committee goes over the annual Economic Report of the President on the state of the economy and, through its hearings, provides a major forum for review of economic issues.

In the executive branch of government, the most important person in the establishment of fiscal policy is, of course, the president. Although he must operate in the context of the tax and expenditure laws passed by Congress, he and his advisers are the country's principal analysts of the need for fiscal expansion or restraint and its leading spokesmen for legislative changes to meet these needs. Needless to say, he doesn't pore over the latest economic data and make the decisions all by himself. The Office of Management and Budget, which is part of the Executive Office of the President, is a very powerful adviser to the president on expenditure policy, as is the Treasury Department on tax policy.

In addition, there is the *Council of Economic Advisers,* which is part of the Executive Office of the President. Established by the Employment Act of 1946, its job is to help the president carry out the objectives of that act. During the past 30 years, the Council of Economic Advisers (CEA), headed by a series of distinguished economists who left academic and other posts to contribute to public policy, has become a very important actor on the national economic policy stage.

AUTOMATIC STABILIZERS

Now that we have met some of the major players, we must point out that, in their efforts to fight serious unemployment or inflation, they get help from some *automatic stabilizers:* structural features of our economy that tend to stabilize national output. Although these economic stabilizers cannot do all that is required to keep the economy on an even keel, they help a lot. As soon as the economy turns down and unemployment mounts, they give the economy a helpful shot in the arm. As soon as the economy gets overheated and inflation breaks out, they tend to restrain it. These stabilizers are automatic because they come into play without the need for new legislation or administrative decisions.

Tax Revenues

Changes in income tax revenues are an important automatic stabilizer. Our federal system relies heavily on the income tax. The amount of income tax collected by the federal government goes up with increases in NNP and goes down with decreases in NNP. Moreover, the average tax rate goes up with increases in NNP, and goes down with decreases in NNP. This, of course, is just what we want to occur. When output falls off and unemployment mounts, tax collections fall off too, so disposable income falls less than NNP. This means less of a fall in consumption expenditure, which tends to break the fall in NNP. When output rises too fast and the economy begins to suffer from serious inflation, tax collections rise too—which tends to restrain the increase in NNP. Of course, corporate income taxes, as well as personal income taxes, play a significant role here.

Unemployment Compensation and Welfare Payments

Unemployment compensation is paid to workers who are laid off, according to a system that has evolved over the past 50 years. When unemployed workers go back to work, they stop receiving unemployment compensation. Thus when NNP falls off and unemployment mounts, the tax collections to finance unemployment compensation go down (because of lower employment), while the amount paid out to unemployed workers goes up. On the other hand, when NNP rises too fast and the economy begins to suffer from serious inflation, the tax collections to finance unemployment compensation go up, while the amount paid out goes down because there is less unemployment. Again, this is just what we want to see happen. The fall in spending is moderated when unemployment is high, and the in-

CASE STUDY 6.2 PRESIDENT EISENHOWER AND AUTOMATIC STABILIZERS

When Dwight Eisenhower took office in 1953, he inherited a prosperity that had been bubbling along since the postwar boom. But by August 1953, there were signs that the economy was headed for a recession. By 1954 the unemployment rate was 6 percent, the highest since the Great Depression. Although Eisenhower remained outwardly confident, there was concern behind the scenes about the deepening recession and a debate about what the government should do. Because the recession reduced tax revenues, the government was running a deficit, and some people felt that taxes should be raised.

But President Eisenhower was getting other advice. In 1954 the Committee for Economic Development (composed largely of top business executives) urged the president to forget about balancing the budget and to leave the economy alone. As 1954 wore on and the Democrats and the labor unions demanded action, the economy stumbled, sputtered, then took off in an upward direction. The first Republican recession since 1929 had come and gone, and even dedicated Democrats had to admit that the nation had survived. But we survived by doing nothing. And in hindsight, nothing turns out to have been just the thing to do.

An important factor in promoting recovery was the existence of our economy's automatic stabilizers. The concept of automatic stabilizers had been brought to the Eisenhower administration by Arthur F. Burns, who chaired the Council of Economic Advisers. Ironically, in 1952 Congress had tried to kill the Council by cutting off its funding. By the end of 1954 it was clear that the Council, its chairman, and its stabilizing budget policy had passed a major test with honors.

President Dwight Eisenhower

N.B.

crease in spending is curbed when there are serious inflationary pressures. Various welfare programs have the same kind of automatic stabilizing effect on the economy.

Corporate Dividends, Family Saving, and Farm Programs

Since corporations tend to maintain their dividends when their sales fall off, and moderate the increase in their dividends when their sales soar, their dividend policy tends to stabilize the economy. This is very important. Also, to the extent that consumers tend to be slow to raise or lower their spending in response to increases or decreases in their income, this too tends to stabilize the economy. Finally, there are agricultural support programs. The government has buttressed farm prices and income when business was bad and unemployment was high. When output was high and inflation occurred, the government distributed the commodities in its warehouses and received dollars. In both cases, these programs acted as stabilizers.

Having painted such a glowing picture of the economy's automatic stabilizers, we are in danger of suggesting that they can stabilize the economy all by themselves. It would be nice if this were true, but it isn't. All the automatic stabilizers do is *cut down* on variations in unemployment and inflation, not *eliminate* them. Discretionary tax and spending programs are needed to supplement the effects of these automatic stabilizers. Some economists wish strongly that it were possible to set well-defined rules for government action, rather than leave things to the discretion of policy makers. Indeed, the economist Milton Friedman, Stanford's Nobel laureate, forcefully argues for greater reliance on such rules, but most economists feel that it is impossible to formulate a set of rules flexible and comprehensive enough to let us do away with the discretionary powers of policy makers. Instead their concern is with sharpening the tools available to government economic decision makers.

THE TOOLS OF DISCRETIONARY FISCAL POLICY

Suppose that the Council of Economic Advisers, on the basis of information concerning recent economic developments, believes that national output may decline soon, causing serious unemployment, and that other agencies, like the Treasury and the Federal Reserve System, agree. What specific measures can the council recommend the government take under such circumstances?

1. *The government can vary its expenditure for public works and other programs.* If increased unemployment seems to be in the wind, it can step up outlays on roads, urban reconstruction, and other public programs. Of course, these programs must be well thought out and socially productive. There is no sense in pushing through wasteful and foolish public works programs merely to make jobs. Or if, as in 1969, the economy is plagued

by inflation, it can (as President Nixon ordered) stop new federal construction programs temporarily.

2. *The government can vary welfare payments and other types of transfer payments.* For example, a hike in Social Security benefits may provide a very healthy shot in the arm for an economy with too much unemployment. An increase in veterans' benefits or in aid to dependent children may do the same thing. The federal government has sometimes helped the states to extend the length of time that the unemployed can receive unemployment compensation; this too will have the desired effect. On the other hand, if there is full employment and inflation is a dangerous problem, it may be worthwhile to cut back on certain kinds of transfer payments. For example, if it is agreed that some veterans' benefits should be reduced, this reduction might be timed to occur during a period when inflationary pressures are evident.

3. *The government can vary tax rates.* For example, if there is considerable unemployment, the government may cut tax rates, as it did in 1975. Or if inflation is the problem, the government may increase taxes, as it did in 1968 when, after considerable political maneuvering and buck-passing, Congress was finally persuaded to put through a 10 percent tax surcharge to try to moderate the inflation caused by the Vietnam War. However, temporary tax changes may have less effect than permanent ones, since consumption expenditure may be influenced less by transitory changes in income than by permanent changes.

Pros and Cons of Various Fiscal Policy Tools

Of course there are advantages and disadvantages in each of these tools of fiscal policy. *One of the big disadvantages of public works and similar spending programs is that they take so long to get started.* Plans must be made, land must be acquired, and preliminary construction studies must be carried out. By the time the expenditures are finally made and have the desired effect, the dangers of excessive unemployment may have given way to dangers of inflation, so that the spending, coming too late, does more harm than good. To some extent, this problem may be ameliorated by having a backlog of productive projects ready to go at all times. In this way, at least a portion of the lag can be eliminated.

In recent years, there has been a widespread feeling that government expenditures should be set on the basis of their long-run desirability and productivity and not on the basis of short-term stabilization considerations. The optimal level of government expenditure is at the point where the value of the extra benefits to be derived from an extra dollar of government expenditure is at least equal to the dollar of cost. This optimal level is unlikely to change much in the short run, and it would be wasteful to spend more—or less—than this amount for stabilization purposes when tax changes could be used instead. Thus many economists believe that tax cuts or tax increases should be the primary fiscal weapons to fight unemployment or inflation.

☆ ☆ ☆ ☆ ☆ ☆ ☆ ☆ ☆ ☆ ☆ ☆ ☆

CASE STUDY 6.3 PRESIDENT KENNEDY AND THE TAX CUT OF 1964

When the Kennedy administration took office in 1961, it was confronted with a relatively high unemployment rate—about 7 percent in mid-1961. By 1962, although unemployment was somewhat lower (about 6 percent), the president's advisers, led by Walter W. Heller, chairman of the Council of Economic Advisers, pushed for a tax cut to reduce unemployment further. The president, after considerable discussion of the effects of such a tax cut, announced in June 1962 that he would propose such a measure to the Congress; and in January 1963, the bill was finally sent to Congress.

The proposed tax bill was a victory for Heller and the CEA. Even though it would mean a deliberately large deficit, the president had been persuaded to cut taxes to push the economy closer to full employment. But the Congress was not so easily

President John F. Kennedy and Walter Heller

convinced. Many congressmen labeled the proposal irresponsible and reckless. Others wanted to couple tax reform with tax reduction. It was not until 1964, after President Kennedy's death, that the tax bill was enacted. It took a year from the time the bill was sent to Congress for it to be passed, and during this interval, there was a continuous debate in the executive branch and the Congress. The secretary of the Treasury, Douglas Dillon, the chairman of the Federal Reserve Board, William M. Martin, and numerous congressmen—all powerful and all initially cool to the proposal—were eventually won over. The result was a tax reduction of about $10 billion per year.

The effects of the tax cut are by no means easy to measure, in part because the rate of growth of the money supply increased at the same time, which should also affect GNP. But in line with the theory presented in earlier sections, consumption expenditure did increase sharply during 1964. Moreover, the additional consumption expenditure undoubtedly induced additional investment. According to some estimates, the tax cut resulted in an increase in GNP of about $24 billion in 1965 and more in subsequent years.* The unemployment rate, which had been about 5 ½ to 6 percent during 1962 and 1963, fell to 5 percent during 1964 and to 4.7 percent in the spring of 1965. It is fair to say that most economists were extremely pleased with themselves in 1965. Fiscal policy based on their theories seemed to work very well indeed!

*Arthur Okun, "Measuring the Impact of the 1964 Tax Reduction," in Walter W. Heller, *Perspectives on Economic Growth,* New York: Random House, 1968, p. 33.

☆ ☆ ☆ ☆ ☆ ☆ ☆ ☆ ☆ ☆ ☆ ☆ ☆

However, *one of the big problems with tax changes is that it sometimes is difficult to get Congress to take speedy action.* There is often considerable debate over a tax bill, and sometimes it becomes a political football. Another difficulty with tax changes is that it generally is much easier to reduce taxes than it is to get them back up again. To politicians, lower taxes are attractive because they are popular, and higher taxes are dangerous because they may hurt a politician's chances of re-election. In discussing fiscal policy (or most other aspects of government operations, for that matter), to ignore politics is to risk losing touch with reality.

SIZE AND NATURE OF GOVERNMENT ACTIVITIES

How Big Is the Government?

Up to this point, we have been concerned primarily with fiscal policy and the role of the government in stabilizing economic fluctuations. We have made no attempt to describe the size and nature of the functions of the U.S. government in quantitative terms. It is time now to turn to some of the relevant facts. One useful measure of the extent of the government's role in the American economy is the size of government expenditures, both in absolute terms and as a percentage of our nation's total output.

The sum total of government expenditures—federal, state, and local—was about $1.2 trillion in 1983. Since the nation's total output was about $3.3 trillion, this means that government expenditures were about one-third of our total output. The ratio of government expenditures to total output in the United States has not always been this large, as Figure 6.6 shows. In 1929, the ratio was about 10 percent, as contrasted with over 30 percent in 1983. (Of course, the ratio of government spending to total output is smaller now than during World War II, but in a wartime economy, one would expect this ratio to be abnormally high.)

There are many reasons why government expenditures have grown so much faster than total output. Three of these are particularly important. First, *the United States did not maintain anything like the kind of military force in pre-World War II days that it does now.* In earlier days, when weapons were relatively simple and cheap, and when we viewed our military and political responsibilities much more narrowly than we do now, our military budget was relatively small. The cost of being a superpower in the days of nuclear weaponry is high by any standards. Second, *there has been a long-term increase in the demand for the services provided by government,* like more and better schooling, more extensive highways, more complete police and fire protection, and so forth. As incomes rise, people want more of these services. Third, **government transfer payments**—*payments in return for no products or services—have grown substantially.* For example, various types of welfare payments have increased markedly. (Another transfer payment, Social Security, increased from about $20 billion in 1965 to about $180 billion in 1984.) Since

**Figure 6.6
Government
Spending as a
Percent of Total
Output, United
States**
Government
expenditures—
federal, state, and
local—totaled about
$1.2 trillion in 1983.
These expenditures,
which include
transfer payments,
have grown more
rapidly than total
output in this period.

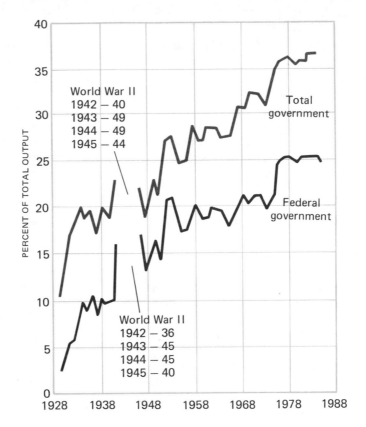

transfer payments do not entail any reallocation of resources from private to public goods, but a transfer of income from one private citizen or group to another, Figure 6.6 is, in some respects, an overstatement of the role of the public sector.

How the Federal, State, and Local Governments Spend Money

There are three levels of government in the United States: federal, state, and local. The state governments spend the least, while the federal government spends the most. This was not always the case. Before World War I, local governments spent more than the federal government. In those days, the federal government did not maintain the large military establishment it does now, nor did it engage in the many programs in health, education, welfare, and other areas that it currently does. Figure 6.6 shows that federal spending is now a much larger percentage of the total than it was 40 years ago. Table 6.1 shows how the federal government spends its money. *About one-third of the federal expenditures goes for defense and other items connected with international relations and national security. About one-half goes for social security, welfare (and other income security) programs, health, and education. The rest goes to support farm,*

Purpose	Amount (billions of dollars)	Percent of total
National defense	286	29
International affairs	18	2
Energy	5	1
Veterans' benefits	27	3
General science, space, and technology	9	1
Agriculture	13	1
Education, training, employment, and social services	29	3
Health	35	4
Natural resources and environment	12	1
Commerce and housing credit	2	b
Transportation	26	3
Community and regional development	7	1
Interest	143	15
General government	5	1
Income security	116	12
Administration of justice	5	1
General purpose fiscal assistance	3	b
Social security and medicare	269	28
Offsetting receipts	−37	−4
Total[a]	974	100

Table 6.1
Federal Expenditures, Fiscal 1986

[a]Because of rounding errors, the figures may not sum to totals.
[b]Less than ½ of 1 percent.
Source: Economic Report of the President, 1985. These are estimates made in 1985.

transportation, housing, and other such programs, as well as to run Congress, the courts, and the executive branch of the federal government.

What about local and state governments? On what do they spend their money? Table 6.2 shows that *the biggest expenditure of state and local governments is on schooling.* After the end of World War II, these expenditures increased greatly because of the baby boom—the explosion in the number of school-age children. Traditionally, schools in the United States have been a responsibility of local governments: cities and towns. *State governments spend most of their money on education; welfare, old age, and unemployment benefits; and highways.* (Besides supporting education directly, they help localities to cover the costs of schooling.) In addition local and state governments support hospitals, redevelopment programs, courts, and police and fire departments.

Type of expenditure	Amount (billions of dollars)	Percent of total
Education	164	35
Highways	37	8
Public welfare	60	13
Other	205	44
Total	466	100

Table 6.2
Expenditures of State and Local Governments, United States, 1983

Source: Economic Report of the President, 1985.

What the Federal, State, and Local Governments Receive in Taxes

To get the money to cover most of the expenditures discussed in previous sections, governments collect taxes from individuals and firms. As Table 6.3 shows, *at the federal level the personal income tax is the biggest single money raiser.* It brings in almost one-half of the tax revenue collected by the federal government. The next most important taxes at the federal level are the Social Security, payroll, and employment taxes. Other important taxes are the corporation income taxes, excise taxes—levied on the sale of tobacco, liquor, imports, and certain other items—and death and gift taxes. (Even when the Grim Reaper shows up, the Tax Man is not far behind.)

**Table 6.3
Federal Receipts by
Tax, Fiscal 1986**

Type of tax	Amount (billions of dollars)	Percent of total
Personal income tax	359	45
Corporation income tax	74	9
Employment taxes	289	36
Excise taxes	35	4
Estate and gift taxes	5	1
Other revenues	31	4
Total·	794	100

·Because of rounding errors, figures may not sum to totals.
Source: Economic Report of the President, 1985. These are estimates made in 1985.

At the local level, on the other hand, the most important form of taxation and source of revenue is the property tax. This is a tax levied primarily on real estate. Other important local taxes—although dwarfed in importance by the property tax—are local sales taxes and local income taxes. Many cities—for example, New York City—levy a sales tax, equal to a certain percent—4 percent in New York City—of the value of each retail sale. The tax is simply added on to the amount charged the customer. Also, many cities—for example, Philadelphia and Pittsburgh—levy an income (or wage) tax on their residents and even on people who work in the city but live outside it. *At the state level, sales (and excise) taxes are the biggest money raiser,* followed by income taxes and highway-user taxes. The latter include taxes on gasoline and license fees for vehicles and drivers. Often they exceed the amount spent on roads, and the balance is used for a variety of nonhighway uses. (See Table 6.4.)

Source	Revenues (billions of dollars)	Percent of total
General sales tax	100	25
Property tax	89	22
Personal income tax	55	14
Corporate income tax	14	4
Other taxes	138	35
Total	396	100

Table 6.4
State and Local Tax
Revenues, by
Source, 1983

ªBecause of rounding errors, the figures may not sum to the totals.
Source: Economic Report of the President, 1985.

EXPLORING FURTHER: FISCAL POLICY AND AGGREGATE DEMAND

Fiscal Policy and Aggregate Demand

How can fiscal policy be included in the aggregate demand-aggregate supply analysis presented in Chapter 4? Clearly, *an anti-unemployment fiscal policy* (where government spending is increased and/or taxes are reduced) *tends to push the aggregate demand curve to the right. An anti-inflationary fiscal policy* (where government spending is reduced and/or taxes are increased) *tends to push the aggregate demand curve to the left.*

ANTI-UNEMPLOYMENT POLICY. Suppose that the unemployment rate is very high, and that the nation's most important economic problem is to get its citizens back to work. This was the case in the Great Depression of the thirties, as well as in subsequent serious recessions. Clearly, under these circumstances, the sensible strategy is for the government to shift the aggregate demand curve to the right. This situation is shown in Figure 6.7. A rightward shift of the aggregate demand curve will increase total real output and have little or no effect on the price level, since the economy is in the horizontal range of the aggregate supply curve (because there is substantial unemployment). The increase in total real output will reduce unemployment because more workers and other resources will have to be employed to produce the extra output.

In fact, this is the sort of strategy that both Democratic and Republican administrations have adopted on many occasions to try to reduce unemployment. For example, in the early 1960s, President John Kennedy's (and President Lyndon Johnson's) tax policies resulted in a rightward shift in the aggregate demand curve, thus helping to reduce unemployment from about 5.7 percent in 1963 to 4.5 percent in 1965. (Recall Case Study 6.3.) And in the mid-1970s, President Gerald Ford's economic policies pushed the aggregate demand curve to the right, with the result that unemployment fell from 8.7 percent in March 1975 to 7.5 percent in March 1976.

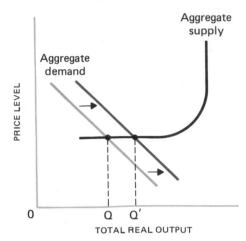

ANTI-INFLATIONARY POLICY. In the late 1970s and early 1980s, many American people felt that inflation, not unemployment, was the number one problem. Since the price level was increasing at over 10 percent per year during 1979–81, this concern over inflation was not hard to understand. If the government anticipates that the price level is going to rise because of a rightward shift of the aggregate demand curve, it can reduce the prospective increase in the price level by using fiscal policy to shift the aggregate demand curve to the left. This situation is shown in Figure 6.8. If the government does not intervene, the equilibrium will be at point A, and the price level will be OP, which presumably is much higher than it is at present. To avoid reaching point A, the government shifts the aggregate demand curve to the left, with the result that the equilibrium will be at point B, and the price level will be OP', which is considerably lower than OP. Although this results in less real output (OQ' versus OQ), less inflation occurs than would otherwise be the case.

Both Democratic and Republican administrations have used this sort of anti-inflationary strategy. For example, in the early 1980s, the Reagan administration adopted policies resulting in a leftward shift in the aggre-

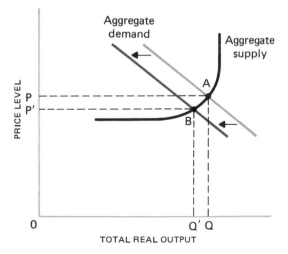

gate demand curve. By discouraging and cutting back spending, inflation was reduced in the 1980s.

SUMMARY

1. The equilibrium level of net national product is the level where intended consumption plus intended investment plus intended government spending equal net national product. A $1 billion change in government purchases will result in a change in equilibrium NNP of the same amount as a $1 billion change in intended investment or a $1 billion shift in the relation between consumption expenditures and NNP. In any of these cases, there is a multiplier effect.

2. An increase in the tax rate shifts the relationship between consumption expenditure and NNP downward, thus reducing the equilibrium value of NNP. A decrease in the tax rate shifts the relationship upward, thus increasing the equilibrium value of NNP.

3. Policy makers receive a lot of help in stabilizing the economy from our automatic stabilizers—automatic changes in tax revenues, unemployment compensation and welfare payments, corporate dividends, family saving, and farm aid. However, the automatic stabilizers can only cut down on variations in unemployment and inflation, not eliminate them.

4. Discretionary programs are needed to supplement the effects of these automatic stabilizers. Such discretionary actions include changing government expenditure on public works and other programs, changing welfare payments and other such transfers, and changing tax rates. An important problem with some of these tools of fiscal policy is the lag in time before they can be brought into play.

5. In the past 50 years, government spending has increased considerably both in absolute terms and as a percentage of total output. (It is now about one-third of our total output.) To a large extent, this increase has been due to our greater military responsibilities as well as to the fact that, as their incomes have risen, our citizens have demanded more schools, highways, and other goods and services provided by government. Also, government transfer payments have grown substantially.

6. To get the money to cover most of these expenditures, governments collect taxes from individuals and firms. At the federal level, the most important form of taxation is the personal income tax; at the local level, the property tax is very important; and at the state level, sales (and excise) taxes are the biggest money raisers.

*7. If a depression is imminent, or if a considerable amount of resources is unemployed, governments frequently try to push the aggregate demand curve to the right. Fiscal policy is often used for this purpose.

*8. If it appears likely that there will be a substantial increase in the price level, the government is likely to try to use fiscal policy to induce a leftward shift of the aggregate demand curve, thus causing the price level to be lower than it otherwise would be.

*The starred items refer to material covered in the section, "Exploring Further."

CHAPTER 7

★ ★ ★ ★ ★ ★ ★ ★ ★

Inflation

LEARNING OBJECTIVES

In this chapter, you should learn:

★ The nature and effects of inflation

★ How inflation is measured

★ The relationship between aggregate demand and inflation

★ The nature and significance of the Phillips curve

At the very beginning of this book, we stressed that unemployment and inflation are two major economic evils. Up to this point, we have devoted much more attention to unemployment than to inflation. As we also pointed out, inflation and unemployment are inextricably linked. Unfortunately, this linkage is a complex one and has consequently been the subject of much debate among economists. Inflation, its costs, and its causes cannot be covered in one chapter alone. This chapter contains part of the relevant discussion; the rest is in Chapter 10.

INFLATION

It is hard to find anyone these days who does not know the meaning of inflation firsthand. Try to think of goods you regularly purchase that cost less now than they did several years ago. Chances are that you can come up with precious few. *Inflation* is a general upward movement of prices. In other words, inflation means that goods and services that currently cost

$10 may soon be priced at $11 or even $12, and that wages and other input prices will increase as well. It is essential to distinguish between the movements of individual prices and the movement of the entire price level. As we saw in Chapter 2, the price of an individual commodity can move up or down with the shifts in the commodity's demand or supply curve. If the price of a particular good—corn, say—goes up, this need not be a sign of inflation: if the prices of other goods are going down at the same time, the overall price level—the general average level of prices—remains much the same. Inflation occurs only if the prices for most goods and services in a society move upward—that is, if the average level of prices increases.

In periods of inflation, the value of money is reduced. A dollar is worth what it will buy, and what it will buy is determined by the price level. Thus a dollar was more valuable in 1940, when the price of a Hershey chocolate bar was 5 cents, than in 1986, when it was about 40 cents. But it is important to recognize that inflations may vary in severity. **Runaway inflation** wipes out the value of money quickly and thoroughly, while **creeping inflation** erodes its value gradually and slowly. The following examples indicate the important differences between runaway inflation and creeping inflation.

Runaway Inflation

The case of Germany after World War I is a good example of runaway inflation. Germany was required to pay large reparations to the victorious Allies after the war. Rather than attempting to tax its people to pay these amounts, the German government merely printed additional quantities of paper money. This new money increased total spending in Germany, and this in turn, resulted in higher prices because the war-devastated economy could not increase output substantially. As more and more money was printed, prices rose higher and higher, reaching utterly fantastic levels. By 1923, it took a *trillion* marks (the unit of German currency) to buy what one mark would buy before the war began in 1914.

The effect of this runaway inflation was to disrupt the economy. Prices had to be adjusted from day to day. People rushed to the stores to spend the money they received as soon as possible, since very soon it would buy much less. Speculation was rampant. This inflation was a terrible blow to Germany. The middle class was wiped out; its savings became completely worthless. It is no wonder that Germany has in recent years been more sensitive than many other countries to the evils of inflation.

Creeping Inflation

For the past 40 years, the price level in the United States has tended to go one way only—up. In practically all years during this period, prices have risen. Since 1955, there hasn't been a single year when the price level has fallen. Certainly, this has not been a runaway inflation, but it has resulted in a very substantial erosion in the value of the dollar. Like a beach slowly worn away by ocean waves, the dollar has gradually lost a considerable portion of its value. Specifically, prices now tend to be about 6 times what they were 40 years ago. Thus the dollar now is worth about a sixth of what it was worth then. Although a creeping inflation of this sort is much less harmful than a runaway inflation, it has a number of unfortunate social consequences, which are described in detail in subsequent sections of this chapter.

THE MEASUREMENT OF INFLATION

The most widely quoted measure of inflation in the United States is the *Consumer Price Index,* published monthly by the Bureau of Labor Statistics. Until 1978, the purpose of this index was to measure changes in the prices of goods and services purchased by urban wage earners and clerical workers and their families. In 1978, the index was expanded to include all urban consumers (although the narrower index was not discontinued). The first step in calculating the index is to find out how much it costs in a particular month to buy a market basket of goods and services that is representative of the buying patterns of these consumers. This amount is then expressed as a ratio of what it would have cost to buy the same market basket of goods and services in the base period (1967 at present), and this ratio is multiplied by 100. This (like most commonly used indexes) shows the *percentage,* not the proportional, change in the price level. For example, the Consumer Price Index equaled 315.5 in December 1984, which meant that it cost 215.5 percent more to buy this market basket in December 1984 than in 1967. To obtain results based on Chapter 3's definition of a price index, all we have to do is divide this index by 100.

The market basket of goods and services that is included in the Consumer Price Index is chosen with great care and is the result of an extensive survey of people's buying patterns. Among the items that are included are food, automobiles, clothing, homes, furniture, home supplies, drugs, fuel, doctors' fees, legal fees, rent, repairs, transportation fares, recreational goods, and so forth. Prices, as defined in the index, include sales and excise taxes. Also, real estate taxes, but not income or personal property taxes, are included in the index. Besides the overall index, a separate price index is computed for various types of goods or services, such as food, rent, new cars, medical services, and a variety of other items. Also, a separate index is computed for each of 28 metropolitan areas, as well as for the entire urban population.

The Consumer Price Index is widely used by industry and government. Labor agreements often stipulate that, to offset inflation, wages must increase in accord with changes in the index. Similarly, pensions, welfare payments, royalties, and even alimony payments are sometimes related to the index. However, this does not mean that it is an ideal, all-purpose measure of inflation. For one thing, it does not include the prices of industrial machinery or raw materials. For another thing, it is not confined to currently produced goods and services.

Figure 7.1 shows the behavior of the Consumer Price Index since 1929. As pointed out in the previous section, the price level has increased considerably in the United States in the past 40 years. Substantial inflation followed World War II: the price level increased by about 34 percent between 1945 and 1948. Bursts of inflation recurred during the Korean War and then during the Vietnam War. The 1970s were a period of particularly high inflation; between 1969 and 1979 the price level doubled. The 1980s began with double-digit inflation, but there was a reduction in the inflation rate in 1982–1985. How long this respite will continue is not clear.

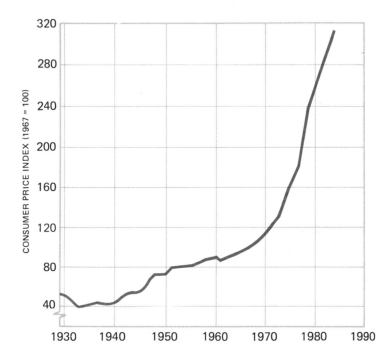

IMPACT OF INFLATION

Citizens and policy makers generally agree that inflation, like unemployment, should be minimized. For example, in 1981, the Council of Economic Advisers identified inflation as the chief economic problem confronting the United States. Why is inflation so widely feared? What are its effects? Inflation affects the distribution of income and wealth, as well as the level of output, as we will see below.

Redistributive Effects

Perhaps the most important impact of inflation is on the distribution of income and wealth. To understand the redistributive effects of inflation, it is necessary to distinguish between *money income* and *real income*. A family's money income is its income measured in current dollars, whereas its real income is adjusted for changes in the price level. Suppose that the Murphy family earned $22,000 this year and $20,000 last year, and that the price level is 10 percent higher this year than last year. Under these circumstances, the Murphy family's money income has increased by $2,000 (or 10 percent of last year's income), but its real income has not increased at all (because its money income has risen by the same percentage as the price level). The distinction between money income and real income plays an important role in understanding the effects of inflation on people with relatively fixed incomes, lenders, and savers—three groups that tend to be hit hard by inflation.

FIXED MONEY INCOMES. Inflation may seem no more than a petty annoyance; after all, most people care about relative, not absolute, prices. For example, if the Murphy family's money income increases at the same rate as the price level, the Murphy family may be no better or worse off under inflation than if its money income remained constant and no inflation occurred. But not all people are as fortunate as the Murphys. Some people cannot increase their wages to compensate for price increases because, for instance, they work under long-term contracts. These people take a considerable beating from inflation.

Elderly citizen hurt by inflation

The elderly tend to be particularly hard-hit by inflation. Older people often must live on pensions and other relatively fixed forms of income. According to a study carried out by Joseph Minarik of the Urban Institute, the effect of a 2 percent increase in the rate of inflation is to reduce the real income of elderly households (with incomes over $10,000) by about 10 percent.[1] This is a substantial, inequitable, and unwelcome impact of inflation on our older citizens.

LENDERS. Inflation hurts lenders and benefits borrowers, since its results in the depreciation of money. A dollar is worth what it will buy, and what it will buy is determined by the price level. If the price level in-

---

[1] J. Minarik, "Who Wins, Who Loses from Inflation," *The Brookings Bulletin*, Summer 1978.

creases, a dollar is worth less than it was before. Consequently, if you lend Bill Dvorak $100 in 1985 and he pays you $100 in 1995—when a dollar will buy much less than it did in 1985—you are losing on the deal. In terms of what the money will buy, he is paying you less than what he borrowed. Of course, if you anticipate considerable inflation, you may be able to recoup by charging him a high enough interest rate to offset the depreciation of the dollar, but it is not so easy to forecast the rate of inflation and protect yourself.

SAVERS. Inflation can have a devastating and inequitable effect on savers. The family that works hard and saves for retirement (and a rainy day) finds that its savings are worth far less, when it finally spends them, than the amount it saved. Consider the well-meaning souls who invested $1,000 of their savings in United States savings bonds in 1939. By 1949, these bonds were worth only about 800 1939 dollars, including the interest received in that 10-year period. Thus these people had $200 taken away from them, in just as real a sense as if someone had picked their pockets.[2]

An Arbitrary "Tax"

While inflation hurts some people, it benefits others. Those who are lucky enough to invest in goods, land, equipment, and other items that experience particularly rapid increases in price may make a killing. For this reason, speculation tends to be rampant during severe inflations. However, it is important to recognize that the rewards and penalties resulting from inflation are meted out with little or no regard for society's values or goals. As the late Arthur Okun, a former chairman of the Council of Economic Advisers, put it, " 'sharpies' . . . make sophisticated choices and often reap gains on inflation which do not seem to reflect any real contribution to economic growth. On the other hand, the unsophisticated saver who is merely preparing for the proverbial rainy day becomes a sucker."[3] This is one of the most undesirable features of inflation, and it helps to account for inflation's sometimes being called an arbitrary "tax."

Effects on Output

Creeping inflation, unlike unemployment, does not seem to reduce national output; in the short run, output may increase, for reasons taken up in a later section. But although a mild upward creep of prices at the rate of a few percent per year is not likely to reduce output, a major inflation can have adverse effects on production. For one thing, it encourages

---

[2]However, it is important to recognize that the form of the savings matters. If people can put their savings in a form where its monetary value increases as rapidly as the price level, savers are not harmed by inflation. But this isn't always easy to do.

[3]Arthur Okun, "The Costs of Inflation," in *The Battle Against Unemployment and Inflation,* 3rd ed., New York: Norton, 1982.

speculation rather than productive uses of savings. People find it more profitable to invest in gold, diamonds, real estate, and art (all of which tend to rise in monetary value during inflations) than in many kinds of productive activity. Also, businesses tend to be discouraged from carrying out long-range projects because of the difficulty of forecasting what future prices will be. If the rate of inflation reaches the catastrophic heights that prevailed in Germany after World War I, the monetary system may break down. People may be unwilling to accept money. They may insist on trading goods or services directly for other goods and services. The result is likely to be considerable inefficiency and substantially reduced output.

AGGREGATE DEMAND AND INFLATION

One way in which inflation can get started is via demand pressures. If aggregate demand is growing more rapidly than potential GNP, then sooner or later the economy is going to run into bottlenecks and shortages. This inevitably leads to wage and price increases. If these demand pressures are maintained, wages and prices will continue to increase, and we have inflation. During the postwar period, the times in which the gap between actual GNP and potential GNP has been small (see Figure 4.1) have also been the times during which inflation has accelerated.

This relationship is illustrated in Figure 7.2. Both the unemployment rate and the inflation rate are determined by the total level of spending on the goods and services produced by the economy. Consumers, firms, and governments all spend money on the goods and services the nation produces. The level of output in our economy depends on how much money they spend. If their expenditures are very low, this means that the economy will operate in Range A in Figure 7.2, where national output is far below its maximum. Because the low level of expenditure means a low level of demand for the nation's goods and services, firms cannot sell enough goods and services to make it profitable to hire many of the workers who want to work. Thus the unemployment rate is high. The inflation rate is low, since there are plenty of excess capacity and unemployed resources. It is no time to raise prices.

**Figure 7.2
Output,
Employment, and
the Rate of
Inflation**
In Range *A*, the rate of inflation is very low but the unemployment rate is very high. In Range *B*, the unemployment rate is substantially less than in Range *A*, but the price level begins to rise. In Range *C*, national output is at its maximum, and increases in total spending result only in inflation.

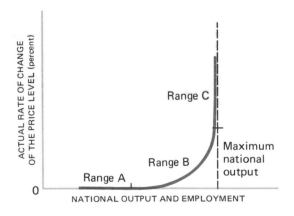

Under these circumstances, suppose that an increase occurs in the total level of spending. National output and employment will rise, and the unemployment rate will fall, but there will be little or no increase in the price level since output can be increased without bidding up the prices of labor and other inputs. When the level of expenditure increases to the point where output and employment are in Range B, the unemployment rate will be substantially lower than in Range A, but the price level will begin to rise. Why? Because bottlenecks occur in some parts of the economy, and labor pushes harder for wage increases (and firms are more willing to agree to such increases).

Finally, if the level of spending increases to the point where output and employment are in Range C, there will be no further decreases in the unemployment rate, since national output, which has reached its maximum, can grow no more. In this range, the rate of inflation is very high, since total spending far exceeds the value of national output at initial prices. There are "too many dollars chasing too few goods."

In order to better understand demand-induced inflation, let's use the analytical tools we have developed in Chapters 4 to 6.

Inflationary Gap

Using the analysis developed in Chapter 5 we see from Figure 7.3 that the inflationary gap is the reduction in intended spending required to *push the equilibrium NNP down to the full-employment level.* For example, if the full-employment level of NNP is $1,400 billion in Figure 7.3, the inflationary gap is $40 billion. Why? Because this is the amount by which intended spending must be reduced if NNP is to fall from its current equilibrium level, $1,500 billion, to its full-employment level of $1,400 billion. In other words, as shown in Figure 7.3, this is the amount by which the $C + I + G$ line must fall in order to reduce the equilibrium level of NNP from $1,500 billion to $1,400 billion. Assuming that $1,400 billion is the maximum value of real NNP (in initial prices) that can be achieved,

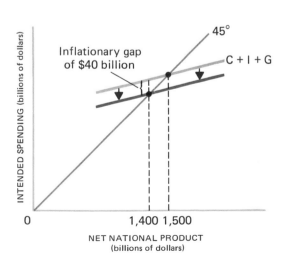

Figure 7.3
Inflationary Gap
To reduce the equilibrium NNP from $1,500 billion (its current level) to $1,400 billion, intended spending must be reduced by $40 billion. In other words, the $C + I + G$ line must be lowered by $40 billion. This amount —the vertical distance between the 45-degree line and the $C + I + G$ line at the full employment level of NNP—is called the inflationary gap.

any increase of the money value of NNP above $1,400 billion is due entirely to inflation. Thus, *to curb inflationary pressures, such an inflationary gap should be eliminated.*

Demand-Pull Inflation

Demand-induced inflation has also been called **demand-pull inflation.** Using the aggregate demand and supply curves introduced in Chapter 4, demand-pull inflation can be viewed, in the extreme, as the case when the aggregate demand curve is shifting up along the vertical portion of the aggregate supply curve. We have had many inflations of this kind. The major inflations during the Revolutionary War and the Civil War were basically caused by demand-pull factors; and so, much more recently, was the inflation arising from the Vietnam War.

In those extreme cases in which all resources are utilized, the rise in the price level that occurs in demand-pull inflation can be viewed as a matter of arithmetic: since national output is fixed, the rise in the price level must be proportional to the increase in total spending. This is the situation shown in Figure 7.4, in which the economy is assumed to be on the vertical segment of its aggregate supply curve before the increase in aggregate demand.

Figure 7.4
Increase in the Price Level Due to a Shift in the Aggregate Demand Curve
Major inflations during the Revolutionary and Civil Wars were due in considerable part to shifts upward and to the right in the aggregate demand curve. Such a shift results in an increase in the price level from OP_0 to OP_1.

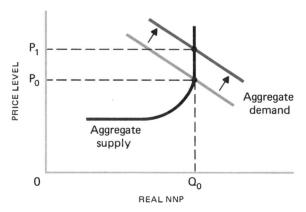

The Phillips Curve

Some economists also believe that inflation can result from the power of labor to push up wages and the power of companies to pass on higher wage costs to consumers in the form of higher prices. What determines the rate at which labor can push up wages? If you think about it for a while, you will probably agree that *labor's ability to increase wages depends on the level of unemployment. The more unemployment, the more difficult it is for labor to increase wages.* Although perfect competition by no means prevails in the labor market, there is enough competition so that the presence of a pool of unemployed workers puts some damper on wage

CASE STUDY 7.1 DEMAND-PULL INFLATION AND THE TAX SURCHARGE OF 1968

The economic policies carried out under Presidents Kennedy and Johnson did succeed in stimulating growth in demand; business was thriving, plants were operating close to capacity, and there were plenty of jobs. But many felt that by mid-1965, the economy showed signs of overheating.

Besides the boost to private demand, government spending was beginning to grow rapidly. President Johnson had succeeded in getting many of his programs to reduce domestic poverty passed. In addition, military spending rose as dark war clouds began to gather in Southeast Asia. In late July 1965, President Johnson announced that the United States would send 50,000 more men to Vietnam. From fiscal 1965 to fiscal 1966, defense expenditures rose from $50 billion to $60 billion—a large increase in government expenditure, and one that took place at a time of relatively full employment. Such an increase in government expenditure could be expected to cause inflationary pressures. The Council of Economic Advisers recognized this danger and recommended in late 1965 that the president urge Congress to increase taxes. Johnson was reluctant. Inflationary pressures mounted during 1966, and little was done by fiscal policy makers to quell them.

President Lyndon Johnson with economic adviser Walter Heller

Even in 1967, the Congress was unwilling to raise taxes. The case for fiscal restraint was, it felt, not clear enough. As for the president, he said, "It is not a popular thing for a president to do . . . to ask for a penny out of a dollar to pay for a war that is not popular either." Finally, in mid-1968, a 10 percent surcharge on income taxes, together with some restraint in government spending, was enacted. This increase in taxes was obviously the right medicine, but it was at least two years too late, and its effects were delayed and insufficient. In the meantime, the rate of inflation had risen from 2 percent in 1965 to 6 percent in 1969.

E.M. and N.B.

increases. In nonunion industries and occupations, workers are much less inclined to push for wage increases—and employers are much less inclined to accept them—when lots of people are looking for work. In unionized industries and occupations, unions are less likely to put their members through the hardship of a strike—and firms have less to lose from a strike—when business is bad and unemployment is high.

Because wages tend to increase more rapidly when unemployment is low, one would expect the rate of increase of wages in any year to be inversely related to the level of unemployment. Suppose that the rate of increase in wages in a particular period is related to the level of unemployment in the way shown in Figure 7.5. According to this figure, which is based on hypothetical but reasonable numbers, wages tend to rise by about 6 percent per year when 9 percent of the labor force is unemployed, by about 7 ½ percent per year when 7 percent of the labor force is unemployed, and by about 9 percent per year when 6 percent of the labor force is unemployed. *The relationship between the rate of increase of wages and the level of unemployment is known as the* **Phillips curve.** It was named after A. W. Phillips, the British economist who first called attention to it.

Figure 7.5
The Phillips Curve
The Phillips curve shows the relationship between the rate of increase of wages and the level of unemployment. This curve is drawn on the assumption that moderate inflation is expected.

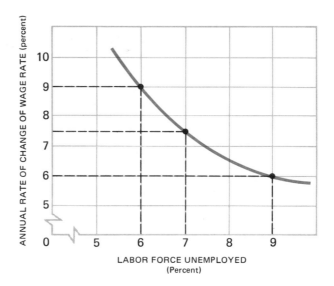

The Relationship between Inflation and Unemployment

Given the Phillips curve in Figure 7.5, one can determine the relationship between the rate of inflation and the level of unemployment. Under reasonable assumptions, *the rate of increase of prices equals the rate of increase of wages minus the rate of increase of output per hour of labor.*[4] Suppose, for example, that the rate of increase of output per hour of labor (that is, *labor productivity*) is 2 percent per year. Then the rate

---

[4]For these assumptions, see E. Mansfield, *Economics: Principles, Problems, Decisions,* 5th ed. For present purposes, it is sufficient to note that total cost per unit of output equals total cost per hour of labor divided by output per hour of labor. Thus the rate of increase of total cost per unit of output equals the rate of increase of total cost per hour of labor minus the rate of increase of output per hour of labor.

of increase of prices equals the rate of increase of wages minus 2 percent. Consequently, the relationship between the rate of increase in prices and the level of unemployment is as shown in Figure 7.6.

There is, of course, a simple relationship between the curve in Figure 7.5 and the curve in Figure 7.6. The curve in Figure 7.6 (which shows the relationship between price increases and unemployment) is always 2 percentage points below the curve in Figure 7.5 (which shows the relationship between wage increases and unemployment). Why? Because the rate of increase of prices—under the assumptions set forth above—always equals the rate of increase of wages minus 2 percent.

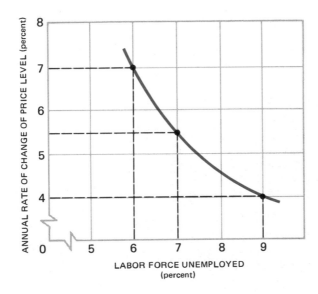

Figure 7.6
Relationship between Unemployment Rate and Rate of Inflation
This relationship can, under the conditions assumed in the text, be deduced from the Phillips curve.

The Policy Menu

If the curve in Figure 7.6 remains fixed, the government is faced with a fundamental choice. It can reduce unemployment only if it is willing to accept a higher rate of inflation, and it can reduce the rate of inflation only if it is willing to accept a higher rate of unemployment. For example, in Figure 7.6, if the unemployment rate is 7 percent and the inflation rate is 5 ½ percent, the government will be anxious to reduce unemployment, but if it reduces it to 6 percent, the inflation rate will jump to 7 percent. The government will also want to reduce inflation, but if it cuts inflation to 4 percent, the unemployment rate will jump to 9 percent. This poses a difficult problem for the government (and for society as a whole), since it would be desirable to reduce both inflation and unemployment.

But contrary to the assumption underlying the previous paragraph, the curve in Figure 7.6 has not remained fixed. Instead, during the 1970s and early 1980s, the curve in Figure 7.6 shifted upward and to the right. High unemployment co-existed with high inflation. In recent years, more and more economists seem to have become persuaded that the reductions in

☆ ☆ ☆ ☆ ☆ ☆ ☆ ☆ ☆ ☆ ☆ ☆ ☆

CASE STUDY 7.2 UNEMPLOYMENT AND INFLATION: AN INTERNATIONAL OVERVIEW

Economic problems, like smugglers, have no respect for international boundaries. In the 1980s, unemployment and inflation afflicted most of the industrialized world.

Relative to previous experience since World War II, unemployment rates in 1984 were high in all major industrialized countries in Europe and Asia. For example, in 1969, West Germany's unemployment rate was only 0.9 percent, but in 1984 it was 7.4 percent. Comparing the U.S. unemployment rate with that in other countries, our 1984 unemployment rate was lower than that in Canada, France, and Great Britain, and higher than that in Germany, Italy, and Japan. To some extent, these international differences in unemployment rates are because unemployment is defined differently in one country than in another. In some countries, to be counted as unemployed, you must register with government unemployment exchanges. Another reason for the international differences in unemployment rates is that institutional and cultural arrangements differ from country to country. In Japan, many large firms commit themselves to a policy of lifetime employment for workers. This is one reason for Japan's relatively low unemployment rates. Still another reason is differences among countries in their fiscal and monetary policies (discussed in Chapters 9, 12, and 13).

As for the rate of inflation, the U.S. performance in 1984 seemed better than in a number of the other countries. While France and Italy experienced increases in consumer prices of over 7 percent per year during 1984, we managed to keep the rate of inflation down to about 4 percent per year during that period. But a 4 percent annual rate of inflation is high, relative to 25 years ago. Many economists, and citizens as well, would be glad to return to the days when the price level seldom rose at more than a couple of percentage points per year, and unemployment rarely exceeded 4 or 5 percent.

unemployment due to increased inflation are only transitory, and that increases in inflation bring little in the way of reduced unemployment in the long run. Much more will be said on this score in Chapter 10.

SUMMARY

1. Inflation is a general upward movement of prices. Runaway inflation occurs when the price level increases very rapidly, as in Germany after World War I. Creeping inflation occurs when the price level rises a few percent per year, as in the United States during the 1950s and 1960s. The

Consumer Price Index, published monthly by the Bureau of Labor Statistics, is a key measure of the rate of inflation.

2. High rates of inflation produce considerable redistribution of income and wealth. People with relatively fixed incomes, such as the elderly, tend to take a beating from inflation. Inflation hurts lenders and benefits borrowers, since it results in the depreciation of money. Inflation can also have a devastating effect on savers. The penalties (and rewards) resulting from inflation are meted out arbitrarily, with no regard for society's values or goals. Substantial rates of inflation may also reduce efficiency and total output.

3. Demand-induced or demand-pull inflation can be viewed, in the extreme, as a case where the aggregate demand curve is shifting up along the vertical portion of the aggregate supply curve.

4. The Phillips curve shows the relationship between the rate of increase of wages and the level of unemployment. If the Phillips curve remains fixed, it poses an awkward dilemma for policy makers. If they reduce unemployment, inflation increases; if they reduce inflation, unemployment increases. During 1955–69, there was a fairly close relationship between the inflation rate and the unemployment rate.

5. During the 1970s and early 1980s, the Phillips curve shifted upward and to the right. High unemployment and high inflation occurred simultaneously.

PART 3

☆☆☆☆☆☆☆☆☆☆☆☆☆☆☆☆☆

Money, Banking, and Stabilization Policy

CHAPTER 8

Money and the Banking System

LEARNING OBJECTIVES

In this chapter, you should learn:

★ The nature and functions of money

★ What the money supply is and how it is measured

★ How commercial banks operate, including the concept of fractional reserve banking

★ How banks can increase or decrease the money supply

In this chapter, we are concerned with the nature of money and the key economic role played by banks and the banking system. Banking is often viewed as a colorless, dull profession whose practitioners are knee-deep in deposit slips and canceled checks. Bankers are also often viewed as heartless skinflints when the time comes to reject a loan application. Yet despite these notions, most people recognize the importance of the banks in our economy, perhaps because banks deal in such an important and fascinating commodity: money. One purpose of this chapter is to introduce you to the operations of the banking system, which is neither as colorless nor as mysterious as is sometimes assumed.

WHAT IS MONEY?

We begin by defining money. At first, it may seem natural to define it by its physical characteristics, and to say that money consists of bills of a certain size and color with certain words and symbols printed on them, as well as coins of a certain type. But this definition would be too restrictive, since money in other societies has consisted of whale teeth, wampum, and a variety of other things. Thus it seems better to define money by its functions than by its physical characteristics. Like beauty, money is as money does.

Medium of Exchange

Money acts as a medium of exchange. People exchange their goods and services for something called money, and then use this money to buy the goods and services they want. To see how important money is as a medium of exchange, let's suppose that it did not exist. To exchange the goods and services they produce for the goods and services they want to consume, people would resort to *barter,* or direct exchange. If you were a wheat farmer, you would have to contact the people who produce the meat, clothes, and other goods and services you want, and swap some of your wheat for each of these goods and services. Of course this would be a very cumbersome procedure, since it would take lots of time and effort to locate and make individual bargains with each of these people. To get some idea of the extent to which money greases the process of exchange in any highly developed economy, consider all the purchases your family made last year: cheese from Wisconsin and France, automobiles from Detroit or Japan, oil from Texas and the Middle East, books from New York, and thousands of other items from all over the world. Imagine how few of these exchanges would have been feasible without money.

Standard of Value, Store of Value

Money acts as a standard of value. It is the unit in which the prices of goods and services are measured. How do we express the price of coffee or tea or shirts or suits? In dollars and cents. Thus money prices tell us the rates at which goods and services can be exchanged. If the money price of a shirt is $30 and the money price of a tie is $10, a shirt will exchange for three ties. Put differently, a shirt will be "worth" three times as much as a tie.

Money acts as a store of value. A person can hold on to money and use it to buy things later. You often hear stories about people who hoard a lot of money under their mattresses or bury it in their backyards. These people have an overdeveloped appreciation of the role of money as a store of value. But even those of us who are less miserly use this function of money when we carry some money with us or keep some in the bank to make future purchases.

Finally, it should be recognized that money is a social invention. It is easy to assume that money has always existed, but this is not the case. Someone had to get the idea, and people had to come to accept it. Nor has money always had the characteristics it has today. In ancient Greece and Rome, money consisted of gold and silver coins. By the end of the seventeenth century, paper money was established in England; but this paper currency, unlike today's currency, could be exchanged for a stipulated amount of gold. Only recently has the transition been made to money that is not convertible into a fixed amount of gold or silver. But regardless of its form or characteristics, anything that is a medium of exchange, a standard of value, and a store of value, is money.

THE MONEY SUPPLY, NARROWLY DEFINED

In practice, it is not easy to draw a hard-and-fast line between what is money and what is not money, for reasons discussed below. But everyone agrees that coins, currency, demand deposits (that is, checking accounts), and other checkable deposits are money. And the sum total of coins, currency, demand deposits, and other checkable deposits is called the money supply, narrowly defined.[1]

Coins and Currency

Coins are a small proportion of the total quantity of money in the United States. This is mainly because coins come in such small denominations. It takes a small mountain of pennies, nickels, dimes, quarters, and half-dollars to make a billion dollars. Of course, the metal in each of these coins is worth less than the face value of the coin; otherwise people would melt them down and make money by selling the metal. In the 1960s, when silver prices rose, the government stopped using silver in dimes and quarters to prevent coins from meeting this fate.

Currency—paper money like the $5 and $10 bills everyone likes to have on hand—constitutes a second and far larger share of the total money supply. Together, currency and coins outstanding totaled about $159 billion in 1984, as shown in Table 8.1. The Federal Reserve System, described in detail in the next chapter, issues practically all of our currency in the form of Federal Reserve notes. Before 1933, it was possible to exchange currency for a stipulated amount of gold, but this is no longer the case. (The price of gold on the free market varies; thus the amount of gold one can buy for a dollar varies too.) All American currency (and coin) is presently "fiat" money. It is money because the government says so, and because the people accept it. There is no metallic backing of the currency any more. But this does not mean that we should be suspicious of the soundness of our currency, since gold backing is not what gives money its

[1]In addition, travelers checks are included in the money supply, narrowly defined, since one can pay for goods and services about as easily with travelers checks as with cash. As indicated in Table 8.1, travelers checks are only about 1 percent of the money supply, narrowly defined. Since they are so small a percentage of the money supply, we ignore them in the following discussion.

value. (In fact, to some extent, cause and effect work the other way. The use of gold to back currencies has in the past increased the value of gold.) Basically, the value of currency depends on its acceptability by people. And the government, to ensure its acceptability, must limit its quantity.

Table 8.1
Money Supply,
November 1984

	Amount (billions of dollars)
Demand deposits	248
Currency and coins[a]	159
Other checkable deposits[b]	142
Travelers checks[c]	5
Total	553

[a]Only currency and coins outside bank vaults (and the Treasury and Federal Reserve) are included.
[b]Includes ATS and NOW balances at all institutions, credit union, share draft, and other minor items.
[c]See footnote 1.

Demand Deposits and Other Checkable Deposits

Demand deposits—bank deposits subject to payment on demand—are the third part of the narrowly defined money supply. They are much larger than the other two parts, as shown in Table 8.1. At first you may question whether these demand deposits—or checking accounts, as they are commonly called—are money at all. In everyday speech, they often are not considered money. But economists include demand deposits as part of the money supply, and for good reason. After all, you can pay for goods and services just as easily by check as with cash. Indeed, the public pays for more things by check than with cash. This means that checking accounts are just as much a medium of exchange—and just as much a standard of value and a store of value—as cash. Thus, since they perform all of the functions of money, they should be included as money.

Other checkable deposits include negotiable order of withdrawal (NOW) accounts and other accounts that are very close to being demand deposits. A *NOW account* is essentially an interest-bearing checking account available at banks, savings banks and other thrift institutions. First created in 1972 by a Massachusetts savings bank, such accounts became available in more and more states, particularly in the Northeast. In 1980, Congress passed a financial reform act that permitted federally chartered thrift institutions to have NOW accounts. Banking innovations like NOW accounts have blurred the distinction between checking and savings accounts. Since many savings and loan associations, mutual savings banks, and credit unions are now providing accounts against which checks can be drawn, it would make no sense to include as money only demand deposits in commercial banks. Instead, all such checkable deposits are included.

Figure 8.1 shows how the narrowly defined money supply—the sum total of coins, paper currency, demand deposits, and other checkable deposits—has behaved since World War II. You can see that the quantity of money has generally increased from one year to the next, and that the increase has been at an average rate of about 4 or 5 percent per year. However, the rate of increase of the quantity of money has not been constant. In some years, like 1972, the quantity of money increased by about 9 percent; in others, like 1984, it increased by about 5 percent. A great deal will be said later about the importance and determinants of changes in the quantity of money.

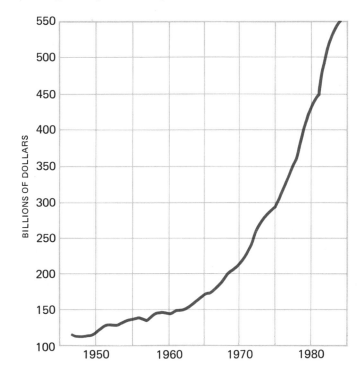

Figure 8.1
Behavior of Money Supply (Narrowly Defined), United States, 1947–84
The money supply, about $550 billion in 1984, has generally increased from year to year, but the rate of increase has by no means been constant.

THE MONEY SUPPLY, BROADLY DEFINED

The narrowly defined money supply (which includes coins, currency, demand deposits, and other checkable deposits) is not the only definition of the money supply that is used by economists. There is also the money supply, broadly defined, which includes savings and small time deposits (under $100,000) and money market mutual fund balances and money market deposit accounts, as well as coins, currency, demand deposits, and other checkable deposits. The money supply, narrowly defined, is often called *M-1*, while the money supply, broadly defined, is often called *M-2*.

The traditional reason for excluding time and savings deposits from the narrow definition of money has been that, in most instances, you could not pay for anything with them. For example, suppose that you had a savings account at a commercial bank. You could not draw a check against it, as you could with a demand deposit. And to withdraw your money from the account, you might have to give the bank a certain amount of notice (although in practice this right might be waived and the bank would ordinarily let you withdraw your money when you desired). Nonetheless, since this savings account could so readily be transformed into cash, it was almost like a checking account. Not quite, but almost.

Besides time and savings accounts, many other assets can also be transformed into cash without much difficulty—though not quite as easily as time and savings deposits. There is no way to draw a hard-and-fast dividing line between money and nonmoney, since many assets have some of the characteristics of money. Consequently, there are still other definitions of the money supply that are more inclusive than *M*-2. Any dividing line between money and nonmoney must be arbitrary. In this book, we shall use the narrow definition, *M*-1, when we refer to the money supply.

COMMERCIAL BANKS IN THE UNITED STATES

There are thousands of commercial banks in the United States. This testifies to the fact that in contrast to countries like England, where a few banks with many branches dominate the banking scene, the United States has promoted the growth of a great many local banks. In part, this has stemmed from a traditional suspicion in this country of "big bankers."

Commercial banks have two primary functions. First, *banks hold demand deposits and permit checks to be drawn on these deposits.* This function is familiar to practically everyone. Most people have a checking account in some commercial bank, and draw checks on this account. Second, *banks lend money to industrialists, merchants, homeowners, and other individuals and firms.* At one time or another, you will probably apply for a loan to finance some project for business, home, or education.

Commercial banks are not the only kind of financial institution. Mutual savings banks and savings and loan associations hold savings and time deposits and various forms of checkable deposits; "consumer finance" companies lend money to individuals; insurance companies lend money to firms and governments; "factors" provide firms with working capital; and investment bankers help firms sell their securities to the public. All these types of financial institutions play an important role in the American economy. In general, they all act as intermediaries between savers and investors; that is, they all turn over to investors money that they receive from savers. This process of converting savings into investment is very important in determining net national product.

HOW BANKS OPERATE

Although it is difficult to generalize about the operation of commercial banks because they vary so much, certain principles and propositions generally hold.

1. *Banks generally make loans to both firms and individuals, and invest in securities, particularly the bonds (which are essentially IOUs) of state and local governments, as well as federal government bonds.* The relationship between a business firm and its bank is often a close and continuing one. The firm keeps a reasonably large deposit with the bank for long periods of time, while the bank provides the firm with needed and prudent loans. The relationship between individuals and their banks is much more casual, but banks like consumer loans because they tend to be relatively profitable. Besides lending to firms and individuals, banks buy large quantities of government bonds. For example, in the early 1970s, commercial banks held about $60 billion in state and local government bonds.

2. *Banks, like other firms, operate to make a profit.* They don't do it by producing and selling a good, like automobiles or steel. Instead, they perform various services, including lending money, making investments, clearing checks, keeping records, and so on. They manage to make a profit from these activities by lending money and making investments that yield a higher rate of interest than they must pay their depositors. For example, the Bank of America, the nation's largest bank, may be able to get 15 percent interest on the loans it makes, while it must pay only 9 percent interest to its depositors. (Commercial banks pay interest on some, but not all, deposits.) If so, it receives the difference of 6 percent, which goes to meet its expenses—and to provide it with some profits.

3. *Banks must constantly balance their desire for high returns from their loans and investments against the requirement that these loans and investments be safe and easily turned into cash.* Since a bank's profits increase if it makes loans or investments that yield a high interest rate, it is clear why a bank favors high returns from its loans and investments. But those that yield a high interest rate often are relatively risky, which means that they may not be repaid in full. Because a bank lends out its depositor's money, it must be careful to limit the riskiness of the loans and investments it makes. Otherwise it may fail. (As we shall see below, the Penn Square Bank of Oklahoma City failed in the early 1980s.)

Until about 50 years ago, banks

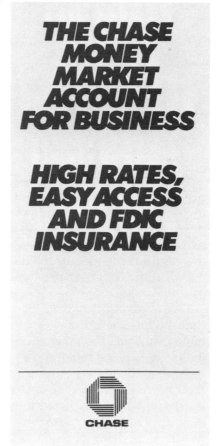

*The Chase
Manhattan Bank
advertises its
services*

used to fail in large numbers during recessions, causing depositors to lose their money. Even during the prosperous 1920s, over 500 banks failed per year. It is no wonder that the public viewed the banks with less than complete confidence. Since the mid-1930s, bank failures have been far fewer, in part because of tighter standards of regulation by federal and state authorities. For example, bank examiners audit the books and practices of the banks. In addition, confidence in the banks was strengthened by the creation in 1934 of the Federal Deposit Insurance Corporation, which insures over 99 percent of all commercial bank depositors. At present, each deposit is insured up to $100,000.

THE BALANCE SHEET OF AN INDIVIDUAL BANK

A good way to understand how a bank operates is to look at its balance sheet. A firm's balance sheet shows the nature of its assets, tangible and intangible, at a certain point in time. Table 8.2 shows the balance sheet of the nation's largest commercial bank, the Bank of America, as of the end of 1983.

Table 8.2
**Balance Sheet,
Bank of America,
December 31, 1983
(Billions of Dollars)**

Assets		Liabilities and net worth	
Cash	15.6	Deposits	89.9
Securities	8.4	Other liabilities	15.1
Loans	73.0	Net worth	4.5
Other assets	12.5		
Total	109.5	Total	109.5

Source: Annual Report, Bank of America.

THE LEFT-HAND SIDE. The left-hand side shows that the total assets of the Bank of America were $109.5 billion, and that these assets were made up as follows: $15.6 billion in cash, $8.4 billion in bonds and other securities, $73.0 billion in loans, and $12.5 billion in other assets. In particular, note that the loans included among the assets of the Bank of America are the loans it made to firms and individuals. As we have emphasized, lending money is one of the major functions of a commercial bank.

THE RIGHT-HAND SIDE. The right-hand side of the balance sheet says that the total *liabilities*—or debts—of the Bank of America were $105.0 billion, and that these liabilites were made up of $89.9 billion in deposits (both demand and time), and $15.1 billion in other liabilities. Note that the deposits at the Bank of America are included among its liabilities, since the Bank of America owes the depositors the amount of money in their deposits. It will be recalled from the previous sections that maintaining these deposits is one of the major functions of a commercial bank. The difference between the Bank of America's total assets and its total liabilities—$4.5 billion—is its net worth. (A firm's *net worth* is the value of the firm's owners' claims against the firm's assets.)

Cash Less than Deposits

One noteworthy characteristic of any bank's balance sheet is the fact that *a very large percentage of its liabilities must be paid on demand.* For example, if all the depositors of the Bank of America tried to withdraw their demand deposits, a substantial proportion of its liabilities would be due on demand. Of course, the chance of all depositors wanting to draw out their money at once is infinitesimally small. Instead, on a given day some depositors withdraw some money, while others make deposits, and most neither withdraw nor deposit money. Consequently, any bank can get along with an amount of cash to cover withdrawals that is much smaller than the total amount of its deposits. For example, the Bank of America's cash equaled about one-sixth of its total deposits.[2]

The Bank of America's practice of holding an amount of cash much less than the amount it owes its depositors may strike you as dangerous. Indeed, if you have a deposit at the Bank of America, you may be tempted to go over and withdraw the money in your account and deposit it in some bank that does have cash equal to the amount it owes its depositors. But you won't be able to do this because *all banks hold much less cash than the amount they owe their depositors.* This is a perfectly sound banking practice, as we shall see.

FRACTIONAL-RESERVE BANKING

To understand the crucial significance of ***fractional-reserve banking***, as this practice is called, let's compare two situations: one where a bank must hold as reserves an amount equal to the amount it owes its depositors, another where its reserves do not have to match the amount it owes its depositors. In the first case, the bank's balance sheet might be as shown in Table 8.3, if demand deposits equal $2 million and net worth equals $500,000. The bank's loans and investments in this case are made entirely with funds put up by the owners of the bank. To see this, note that loans and investments equal $500,000, and that the bank's net worth also equals $500,000. Thus, if some of these loans are not repaid or if some of these investments lose money, the losses are borne entirely by the bank's stock-

Assets		Liabilities and net worth	
Reserves	2.0	Demand deposits	2.0
Loans and investments	0.5	Net worth	0.5
Total	2.5	Total	2.5

Table 8.3
Bank Balance
Sheet: Case Where
Reserves Equal
Demand Deposits
(Millions of Dollars)

[2]Note that "cash" here includes the bank's deposit with the Federal Reserve and its deposits with other banks, as well as cash in its vault. The Federal Reserve is our nation's central bank, and will be described below and in subsequent chapters.

holders. The depositors are protected completely because every cent of their deposits is covered by the bank's reserves.

Now let's turn to the case of fractional-reserve banking. In this case, the bank's balance sheet might be as shown in Table 8.4, if deposits equal $2 million and net worth equals $500,000. Some of the loans and investments made by the bank are not made with funds put up by the owners of the bank, but with funds deposited in the bank by depositors. Thus though depositors deposited $2 million in the bank, the reserves are only $400,000. What happened to the remaining $1.6 million? Since the bank (in this simple case) has only two kinds of assets, loans (and investments) and reserves, the bank must have lent out (or invested) the remaining $1.6 million.

**Table 8.4
Bank Balance
Sheet: Fractional
Reserves (Millions
of Dollars)**

Assets		Liabilities and net worth	
Reserves	0.4	Demand Deposits	2.0
Loans and		Net worth	0.5
investments	2.1		
Total	2.5	Total	2.5

Origins of Fractional-Reserve Banking

The early history of banking is the story of an evolution from the first to the second situation. The earliest banks held reserves equal to the amounts they owed depositors, and were simply places where people stored their gold. But as time went on, banks began to practice fractional-reserve banking. It is easy to see how this evolution could take place. Suppose that you owned a bank of the first type. You would almost certainly be struck by the fact that most of the gold entrusted to you was not demanded on any given day. Sooner or later, you might be tempted to lend out some of the gold and obtain some interest. Eventually, as experience indicated that this procedure did not inconvenience your depositors, you and other bankers might make this practice common knowledge.

You might use several arguments to defend this practice. First, you would probably point out that none of the depositors had lost any money. (To the depositors, this would be a rather important argument.) Second, you could show that the interest you earned on the loans made it possible for you to charge depositors less for storing their gold. Consequently, you would argue that it was to the depositors' advantage (because of the savings that accrued to them) for you to lend out some of the gold. Third, you would probably argue that putting the money to work benefited the community and the economy. After all, in many cases, firms can make highly productive investments only if they can borrow the money, and by lending out your depositors' gold, you would enable such investments to be made.

Legal Reserve Requirements

Arguments of this sort have led society to permit fractional-reserve banking. In other words, banks are allowed to hold less in reserves than the amount they owe their depositors. But what determines how much banks hold in reserves? For example, the Bank of America, according to Table 8.2, held cash equal to about 17 percent of its total deposits. It probably could have gotten away with holding much less in reserves, so long as there was no panic among depositors and it made sound loans and investments. The Bank of America held this much cash for a very simple reason: *The Federal Reserve System requires every commercial bank (whether or not it is a member of the system) to hold a certain percentage of its deposits as reserves.*

What is the Federal Reserve System (commonly called the Fed)? It is our nation's central bank, and its most important functions are to help control the quantity of money, provide facilities for the collection of checks, supply the public with currency, and supervise the operation of commercial banks. Much more will be said about the Fed below and in subsequent chapters.

According to the 1980 financial reform act, the Fed can set the percentage of deposits that a bank must hold as reserves between the limits of 8 and 14 percent for checkable deposits (that is, deposits subject to direct or indirect transfer by check).[3] Also, on the affirmative action of five of the seven members of the Fed's board of governors, it can impose an additional reserve requirement of up to 4 percent. And in extraordinary circumstances the Fed can for 180 days set the percentage at any level it deems necessary. These are *legal reserve requirements*; they also exist for time deposits (of businesses and nonprofit institutions), but are lower than for checkable deposits.

The Federal Reserve System in recent years has dictated that the average bank should hold about $1 in reserves for every $6 of demand deposits. Most of these reserves are held in the form of deposits by banks at the Federal Reserve. Thus, for example, a great deal of the Bank of America's reserves are held in its deposit with the Federal Reserve. In addition, some of any bank's reserves are held in cash on the bank's premises. However, its legal reserves are less than the "cash" entry on its balance sheet since its deposits with other banks do not count as legal reserves.

The most obvious reason why the Fed imposes these legal reserve requirements would seem to be to keep the banks safe, but in this case the obvious answer isn't the right one. Instead, *the most important reason for legal reserve requirements is to control the money supply.* It will take some more discussion before this becomes clear.

[3]For up to $25 million in checkable deposits, this percentage is 3 percent. Note too that the 1980 law also applies these reserve requirements to deposits in other thrift institutions (savings and loan associations, mutual savings banks, and credit unions), not just banks.

THE SAFETY OF THE BANKS

We have just argued that the reserve requirements imposed by the Federal Reserve System exceed what would be required under normal circumstances to ensure the safety of the banks. To support our argument, we might cite some authorities who claim that a bank would be quite safe if it had reserves equal only to about 2 percent of its deposits. Under these circumstances it still would be able to meet its depositors' everyday demands for cash. Obviously this level of reserves is much lower than the legally required level.

The Role of Bank Management

But high reserve requirements will not by themselves ensure bank safety. For example, suppose that a bank lends money to every budding inventor with a scheme for producing perpetual-motion machines, and that it grants particularly large loans to those who propose to market these machines in the suburbs of Missoula, Montana. This bank is going to fail eventually, even if it holds reserves equal to 20 percent—or 50 percent, for that matter—of its demand deposits. It will fail simply because the loans it makes will not be repaid, and eventually these losses will accumulate to more than the bank's net worth. In other words, if the bank is sufficiently inept in making loans and investments, it will lose all the owners' money and some of the depositors' money besides.

The well-managed bank must make sensible loans and investments. In addition, it must protect itself against short-term withdrawals of large amounts of money. Although much-larger-than-usual withdrawals are not very likely to occur, the bank must be prepared to meet a temporary upswing in withdrawals. One way is to invest in securities that can readily be turned into cash. For example, the bank may invest in short-term government securities that can readily be sold at a price that varies only moderately from day to day. Such securities are often referred to as *secondary reserves.*

The Role of Government

There can be no doubt that banks are much safer today than they were 50 or 100 years ago. The reason is that the government has put its power squarely behind the banking system. It used to be that "runs" occurred on the banks; depositors, frightened that their banks would fail and that they would lose some of their money, would line up at the teller's windows and withdraw as much money as they could. Faced with runs of this sort, banks were sometimes forced to close because they could not satisfy all demands for withdrawals. Needless to say, no fractional-reserve banking system can satisfy demands for total withdrawal of funds.

Runs on banks are rare now, for several reasons. One is that the government—including the Federal Deposit Insurance Corporation (FDIC), the Federal Reserve, and other public agencies—has made it clear that it will not stand by and tolerate the panics that used to occur periodically in this country. The FDIC insures the accounts of depositors in practically all banks so that even if a bank fails, depositors will get their money back—up to $100,000. Another reason is that the banks themselves are better managed and regulated. For example, bank examiners are sent out to look over the bankers' shoulders and determine whether they are solvent.

Nonetheless, this does not mean that bank regulation is all that it might be. In 1984, the Continental Illinois Bank, the eighth largest in the United States, required a multi-billion-dollar rescue operation by federal agencies to keep it in operation. Continental Illinois bought up more than $1 billion in loans made by Penn Square Bank of Oklahoma City. When these loans went sour (and Penn Square Bank failed), Continental's depositors became worried and began to withdraw their funds. Federal agencies tried to arrange a merger between Continental and some other bank, but no partner could be found. To keep Continental going, the FDIC put up billions of dollars and established what is essentially a new bank.

Depositors worried about the safety of their deposits at a savings and loan association in Baltimore, Maryland

HOW BANKS CAN CREATE MONEY

Genesis tells us that God created heaven and earth. Economists tell us that banks create money. To many people, the latter process is as mysterious as the former.

To see how banks can create money, imagine the following scenario. First, suppose that someone deposits $10,000 of newly printed money in a particular bank, which we'll call Bank A. Second, suppose that Bank A lends Ms. Smith $8,333, and that Ms. Smith uses this money to purchase some equipment from Mr. Jones, who deposits Ms. Smith's check in his account at Bank B. Third, Bank B buys a bond for $6,944 from Ms. Stone, who uses the money to pay Mr. Green for some furniture. Mr. Green deposits the check to his account at Bank C. We assume that the legal reserve requirements are that $1 in reserves must be held for every $6 in demand deposits.

CASE STUDY 8.1 THE FAILURE OF THE KNICKERBOCKER TRUST IN 1907

The Knickerbocker Trust in New York City was a successful bank at the turn of the century. The Knickerbocker Trust's main branch was at a fashionable Fifth Avenue address, where many well-to-do people (including the writer Mark Twain) kept their accounts. At its downtown office near Wall Street, the Knickerbocker Trust held some of the deposits of large corporations like General Electric and the Pennsylvania Railroad. In turn, the bank made loans to numerous growing businesses. Under its dynamic president, Charles T. Barney, the Knickerbocker held city bonds and invested in the development of the transit system, in new hotels along Fifth Avenue, and in elegant apartment buildings on the Upper West Side. Not all of the bank's loans paid off. But most did, and the bank prospered.

KNICKERBOCKER WILL NOT OPEN

Conference of Bankers Deems It Unwise to Aid the Trust Company Further To-day.

EIGHT MILLIONS WITHDRAWN

An opportunity then came along for Charles Barney to make a lot of money, if he was willing to take some major risks. Barney had connections with a speculator named Charles Morse. Morse and his partner, Frederick Heinze, formulated a scheme to manipulate the price of copper stock on Wall Street in 1907. The extent of Barney's involvement is debatable, but many believed he made behind-the-scenes arrangements for the Morse-Heinze combine, which, on October 15, 1907, tried and failed to squeeze the copper market, and the syndicate went under. There was no evidence that Barney had overcommitted loans to Morse, but there were rumors to this effect, and Barney, like any banker of the day, realized that gossip could lead to the death of his bank before any facts were proven. He knew that as the word spread that the Knickerbocker was in trouble, the depositors would start a run of withdrawals. Like any banker caught in that situation, Barney also knew that, if he could temporarily pull enough cash together, he might be able to calm his customers. If they were made to believe that the bank could make its payouts, his bank might be saved.

On Sunday, October 20, Charles Barney left his home on Park Avenue to try to borrow the cash he needed. He went to appeal to the only person who could save him: J. P. Morgan. Morgan had helped tide over banks in trouble before, and he was one of the few men who had the reputation and resources to do it. Morgan had been friendly with Barney, and owned some Knickerbocker stock. But Morgan refused even to see him. For Barney, disaster was inescapable. Trying to forestall the rumors, the bank's board of directors on Monday forced Barney's resignation. It didn't help. The run on the Knickerbocker began. On Tuesday morning, bank officials announced they had $8 million cash in their vaults, but most of it was gone before the end of the day. The Knickerbocker closed its doors. Those customers who hadn't withdrawn their money were out of luck for an unforeseeable future. The failure of the Knickerbocker Trust led to doubts about other banks, and snowballed into the Panic of 1907.

Realizing that the ensuing bank failures could endanger the entire system—including his own holdings—J. P. Morgan subsequently stepped in, and under his leadership, a large reserve fund was pooled together. But by the time the panic was over, 246 banks had closed, and a disgraced, distraught Charles Barney had killed himself. Ironically, the Knickerbocker Trust was not all that bad a bank—it was to reopen five months later, and depositors got most of their money back.

N.B.

Money Creation at Bank A

The first step in our drama occurs when someone deposits $10,000 in newly printed money in Bank A. The effect of this deposit is shown in the first panel of Table 8.5: Bank A's demand deposits and its reserves both go up by $10,000. Now, Bank A can make a loan of $8,333, since this is the amount of its *excess reserves* (those in excess of legal requirements). Because of the $10,000 increase in its deposits, its legally required reserves increase by ($10,000/6) or $1,667. (Recall that $1 in reserves must be held for every $6 in deposits.) Thus, if it had no excess reserves before, *it now has excess reserves of $10,000 − $1,667, or $8,333.* When Ms. Smith asks one of the loan officers of the bank for a loan to purchase equipment, the loan officer approves a loan of $8,333. Ms. Smith is given a checking account of $8,333 at Bank A.

How can Bank A get away with this loan of $8,333 without winding up with less than the legally required reserves? The answer is given in the rest

	Assets		Liabilities and net worth	
Bank receives deposit	Reserves	+10,000	Demand deposits	+10,000
	Loans & investments	No change	Net worth	No change
	Total	+10,000	Total	+10,000
Bank makes loan	Reserves	No change	Demand deposits	+ 8,333
	Loans & investments	+ 8,333	Net worth	No change
	Total	+ 8,333	Total	+ 8,333
Ms. Smith spends $8,333	Reserves	− 8,333	Demand deposits	− 8,333
	Loans & investments	No change	Net worth	No change
	Total	− 8,333	Total	− 8,333
Total effect	Reserves	+ 1,667	Demand deposits	+10,000
	Loans & investments	+ 8,333	Net worth	No change
	Total	+10,000	Total	+10,000

Table 8.5
Changes in Bank A's Balance Sheet (Dollars)

of Table 8.5. The second panel of this table shows what happens to Bank A's balance sheet when Bank A makes the $8,333 loan and creates a new demand deposit of $8,333. Obviously, both demand deposits and loans go up by $8,333. Next, look at the third panel of Table 8.5, which shows what happens when Ms. Smith spends the $8,333 on equipment. As pointed out above, she purchases this equipment from Mr. Jones. Mr. Jones deposits Ms. Smith's check in his account in Bank B, which presents the check to Bank A for payment. After Bank A pays Bank B (through the Federal Reserve System), the result—as shown in the third panel—is that Bank A's deposits go down by $8,333, since Ms. Smith no longer has the deposit. Bank A's reserves also go down by $8,333, since Bank A has to transfer these reserves to Bank B to pay the amount of the check.

As shown in the bottom panel of Table 8.5, the total effect on Bank A is to increase its deposits by the $10,000 that was deposited originally and to increase its reserves by $10,000 minus $8,333, or $1,667. In other words, reserves have increased by one-sixth as much as demand deposits. This means that Bank A will meet its legal reserve requirements.

It is important to recognize that Bank A *has now created $8,333 in new money.* To see this, note that Mr. Jones winds up with a demand deposit of this amount that he didn't have before; this is a net addition to the money supply, since the person who originally deposited the $10,000 in currency still has his $10,000, although it is in the form of a demand deposit rather than currency.

Money Creation at Bank B

The effects of the $10,000 deposit at Bank A are not limited to Bank A. Instead, as we shall see, other banks can also create new money as a consequence of the original $10,000 deposit at Bank A. Let's begin with Bank B. Recall from the previous section that the $8,333 check made out by Ms. Smith to Mr. Jones is deposited by the latter in his account at Bank B. This is a new deposit of funds at Bank B. As pointed out in the previous section, Bank B gets $8,333 in reserves from Bank A when Bank A pays Bank B to get back the check. Thus the effect on Bank B's balance sheet, as shown in the first panel of Table 8.6, is to increase both demand deposits and reserves by $8,333.

Bank B is in much the same position as was Bank A when the latter received the original deposit of $10,000. Bank B can make loans or investments equal to its excess reserves, which are $6,944. (The way we derive $6,944 is explained in the footnote below.)[4] Specifically, it decides to buy a bond for $6,944 from Ms. Stone and credits her checking account at Bank B for this amount. Thus, as shown in the second panel of Table 8.6,

---

[4]Since Bank B's deposits increase by $8,333, its legally required reserves increase by ($8,333/6), or $1,389. Thus $1,389 of its increase in reserves is legally required, and the rest ($8,333 − $1,389 = $6,944) is excess reserves.

	Assets		Liabilities and net worth	
Bank receives deposit	Reserves	+8,333	Demand deposits	+8,333
	Loans & investments	No change	Net worth	No change
	Total	+8,333	Total	+8,333
Bank buys bond	Reserves	No change	Demand deposits	+6,944
	Loans & investments	+6,944	Net worth	No change
	Total	+6,944	Total	+6,944
Mr. Green deposits money in Bank C	Reserves	−6,944	Demand deposits	−6,944
	Loans & investments	No change	Net worth	No change
	Total	−6,944	Total	−6,944
Total effect	Reserves	+1,389	Demand deposits	+8,333
	Loans & investments	+6,944	Net worth	No change
	Total	+8,333	Total	+8,333

Table 8.6
Changes in Bank B's Balance Sheet (Dollars)

the effect of this transaction is to increase Bank B's investments by $6,944 and to increase its demand deposits by $6,944. Ms. Stone writes a check for $6,944 to Mr. Green to pay for some furniture. Mr. Green deposits the check in Bank C. Bank B's demand deposits and its reserves are decreased by $6,944 when it transfers this amount of reserves to Bank C to pay for the check. When the total effects of the transaction are summed up, Bank B, like Bank A, continues to meet its legal reserve requirements, since, as shown in the bottom panel of Table 8.6, the increase in reserves ($1,389) equals one-sixth of its increase in demand deposits ($8,333).

Bank B has also created some money—$6,944, to be exact. Mr. Green has $6,944 in demand deposits that he didn't have before; this is a net addition to the money supply, since the person who originally deposited the currency in Bank A still has his $10,000, and Mr. Jones still has the $8,333 he deposited in Bank B.

The Total Effect of the Original $8,333 in Excess Reserves

How big an increase in the money supply can the entire banking system support as a consequence of the original $8,333 of excess reserves arising from the $10,000 deposit in Bank A? Clearly, the effects of the original injection of excess reserves into the banking system spread from one bank to another, since each bank hands new reserves (and deposits) to another bank, which in turn hands them to another bank. For example, Bank C now has $6,944 more in deposits and reserves and so can create $5,787 in new money[5] by making a loan or investment of this amount. This process

[5]Why $5,787? Because it must hold ($6,944/6) = $1,157 as reserves to support the new demand deposit of $6,944. Thus it has excess reserves of $5,787, and it can create another new demand deposit of this amount.

goes on indefinitely, and it would be impossible to describe each of the multitude of steps involved. Fortunately, it isn't necessary to do so. We can figure out the total amount of new money the entire banking system can support as a consequence of the original excess reserves at Bank A without going through all these steps. *When the process works itself out, the entire banking system can support $50,000 in new money as a consequence of the original injection of $8,333 of excess reserves.*[6]

☆　　☆　　☆　　## EXPLORING FURTHER: A GENERAL PROPOSITION CONCERNING THE EFFECT OF EXCESS RESERVES

In general, *if a certain amount of excess reserves is made available to the banking system, the banking system as a whole can increase the money supply by an amount equal to the amount of excess reserves multiplied by the reciprocal of the required ratio of reserves to deposits.* In other words, to obtain the total increase in the money supply that can be achieved from a certain amount of excess reserves, multiply the amount of excess reserves by the reciprocal of the required ratio of reserves to deposits—or, what amounts to the same thing, *divide the amount of excess reserves by the legally required ratio of reserves to deposits.*

Let's apply this proposition to a couple of specific cases. Suppose that the banking system gains excess reserves of $10,000 and that the required ratio of reserves to deposits is $\frac{1}{6}$. To determine how much the banking system can increase the money supply, we must divide the amount of the excess reserves, $10,000, by the required ratio of reserves to deposits, $\frac{1}{6}$, to get the answer: $60,000. Now suppose that the required ratio of reserves to deposits is $\frac{1}{5}$. By how much can the banking system increase the money supply? Dividing $10,000 by $\frac{1}{5}$, we get the answer: $50,000. Note that the higher the required ratio of reserves to deposits, the smaller the amount by which the banking system can increase the money supply on the basis of a given amount of excess reserves. More will be said about this in the next chapter.

In reality, an increase in reserves generally affects a great many banks at about the same time. For expository purposes, it is useful to trace through the effect of an increase in the reserves of a single bank—Bank A in our previous case. But usually this is not what happens. Instead, lots of banks experience an increase in reserves at about the same time. Thus they all have excess reserves at about the same time, and they all make loans or investments at about the same time. The result is that when the people who borrow money spend it, each bank tends both to gain and to

[6]The proof of this is as follows. The total amount of new money supported by the $8,333 in excess reserves is $8,333 + $6,944 + $5,787 + . . . , which equals $8,333 + $\frac{5}{6}$ × $8,333 + ($\frac{5}{6}$)^2 × $8,333 + ($\frac{5}{6}$)^3 × $8,333 + . . . , which equals $8,333 × (1 + $\frac{5}{6}$ + ($\frac{5}{6}$)^2 + ($\frac{5}{6}$)^3 + . . .) = $8,333 × $\left(\dfrac{1}{1-\frac{5}{6}} \right)$ = $50,000, since $1 + \frac{5}{6} + (\frac{5}{6})^2 + (\frac{5}{6})^3 + . . . = \left(\dfrac{1}{1-\frac{5}{6}} \right)$.

lose reserves. On balance, each bank need not lose reserves. In real life the amount of bank money often *expands simultaneously* throughout the banking system until the legally required ratio of deposits to reserves is approached.

The Effect of a Decrease in Reserves

Up to this point, we have been talking only about the effect of an increase in reserves. What happens to the quantity of money if reserves decrease? *In general, if the banking system has a deficiency of reserves of a certain amount, the banking system as a whole will reduce demand deposits by an amount equal to the deficiency in reserves multiplied by the reciprocal of the required ratio of reserves to deposits.*

In other words, to obtain the total decrease in demand deposits resulting from a deficiency in reserves, *divide the deficiency by the legally required ratio of reserves to deposits.* Although there is often a simultaneous contraction of money on the part of many banks (just as there is often a simultaneous expansion) this doesn't affect the result.

Let's apply this proposition to a particular case. Suppose that the banking system experiences a deficiency in reserves of $8,333 and that the required ratio of reserves to deposits is ⅙. Applying this rule, we must divide the deficiency in reserves, $8,333, by the required ratio of reserves to deposits, ⅙, to get the answer, which is a $50,000 reduction in demand deposits. Note that the effect of a $1 deficiency in reserves is equal in absolute terms to the effect of $1 in excess reserves.[7]

SUMMARY

1. Money performs several basic functions. It serves as a medium of exchange, a standard of value, and a store of value. The money supply, narrowly defined, is composed of coins, currency, demand deposits, and other checkable deposits. Economists include demand (and other checkable) deposits as part of the money supply because you can pay for goods and services about as easily by check as with cash.

2. Besides this narrow definition of money, broader definitions include savings and time deposits (and money market mutual fund shares). It is not easy to draw a line between money and nonmoney, since many assets have some of the characteristics of money.

3. Commercial banks have two primary functions. First, they hold demand (and other checkable) deposits and permit checks to be drawn on them. Second, they lend money to firms and individuals. Most of our

[7]The results set forth in this chapter are based on a number of simplifying assumptions. For a discussion of these assumptions, see E. Mansfield, *Economics: Principles, Problems, Decisions,* 5th ed.

money supply is not coin and paper currency, but bank money—demand (and other checkable) deposits. This money can be created by banks.

4. Whereas the earliest banks held reserves equal to deposits, modern banks practice fractional-reserve banking. That is, their reserves equal only a fraction of their deposits. The Federal Reserve System requires every commercial bank (and other thrift institutions with checkable deposits) to hold a certain percentage of its deposits as reserves. The major purpose of these legal reserve requirements is to control the money supply.

5. Banks have become much safer in recent years, in part because of better management and regulation as well as the government's stated willingness to insure and stand behind their deposits. However, bank failures still occur, and bank regulation is not as stringent as it might be.

*6. The banking system as a whole can increase its demand deposits by an amount equal to its excess reserves divided by the legally required ratio of reserves to deposits. Thus, if excess reserves in the banking system equal a certain amount, the banking system as a whole can increase demand deposits by the amount of the excess reserves divided by the legally required ratio of reserves to deposits.

*7. If there is a deficiency in reserves in the banking system, the system as a whole must decrease demand deposits by the amount of this deficiency divided by the legally required ratio of reserves to deposits.

*The starred items refer to material in the section, "Exploring Further."

CHAPTER 9

★ ★ ★ ★ ★ ★ ★ ★ ★

The Federal Reserve and Monetary Policy

LEARNING OBJECTIVES

In this chapter, you should learn:

★ The aims and nature of monetary policy

★ The groups empowered to make monetary policy

★ The workings and importance of the Federal Reserve System

★ The pros and cons of monetary policy

★ *(Exploring Further)* The effects of monetary policy on the aggregate demand curve

Like fiscal policy, monetary policy is no panacea, but it is a very important tool for stabilizing the economy. In recent years, monetary policy has been the subject of considerable controversy. For example, in early 1984, when the Federal Reserve loosened up on the money supply, some economists felt that improper monetary policy would rekindle very serious inflation in the United States, while others argued that a less restrictive monetary policy of this sort was needed to reduce unemployment. Such controversies will continue in the future, since one thing is certain: Economists of all persuasions agree that monetary policy has a major impact on the economy.

179 ★

THE AIMS OF MONETARY POLICY

Monetary policy is the exercise of the central bank's control over the quantity of money and interest rates to promote the objectives of national economic policy. (In the United States, the central bank is the Federal Reserve, as we saw in the previous chapter.) If the economy is at considerably less than full employment, increases in the money supply tend to increase real NNP, and decreases in the money supply tend to decrease real NNP, with relatively little effect on the price level. As full employment is approached, increases in the money supply tend to affect the price level as well as real output. Once full employment is reached, increases in the money supply result primarily in increases in the price level, since real output cannot increase appreciably.

In formulating monetary policy, the government's objectives are to attain and maintain reasonably full employment without excessive inflation. In other words, when a recession seems imminent and unemployment begins to rise, the monetary authorities are likely to increase the money supply and push down interest rates. That is, they will "ease credit" or "ease money," as the newspapers put it. This tends to push the aggregate demand curve to the right, thus increasing net national product. On the other hand, when the economy is in danger of overheating and serious inflation threatens, the monetary authorities will probably rein in the money supply and push up interest rates. In newspaper terms, they will "tighten credit" or "tighten money." This tends to push the aggregate demand curve to the left, thus curbing the upward pressure on the price level.

At this point, you may be muttering to yourself, "But the aims of monetary policy are essentially the same as those of fiscal policy!" You are right. Monetary policy and fiscal policy are both aimed at promoting full employment without inflation. But they use different methods to attain this goal. Fiscal policy uses the spending and taxing powers of the government, whereas monetary policy uses the government's power over the money supply.

THE CENTRAL ROLE OF BANK RESERVES

In view of the importance of monetary policy, it is essential that we understand how the Federal Reserve can promote its aims. Although there are differences of views concerning the processes by which changes in the money supply affect NNP and the price level, economists of all persuasions would agree that a fundamental question is: How can the Federal Reserve influence the money supply? And they would agree that the answer is: *by managing the reserves of the banking system.*

To see what this means in practice, suppose that the Federal Reserve thinks that a recession is about to develop and that, to prevent it, it wants to increase the money supply more rapidly than it would otherwise. How can it accomplish this objective? By providing the banks with plenty of excess reserves. As we saw in the previous chapter, excess reserves enable the banks to increase the money supply. Indeed, we learned that the banks could increase the money supply by $6 for every $1 of excess reserves.[1] Thus, the $8,333 of excess reserves at Bank A enabled the banking system as a whole to increase the money supply by $50,000. (The ways in which the monetary authorities can increase the reserves of the banking system —and thus provide excess reserves—are discussed at length in subsequent sections.)

On the other hand, suppose that the Federal Reserve smells a strong whiff of unacceptable inflation in the economic wind, and so decides to cut back on the rate of increase of the money supply. To do so, it can slow down the rate of increase of bank reserves. As we saw in the section, "Exploring Further," in the previous chapter, this will force the banks to curtail the rate of growth of their demand deposits by easing off on the rate of growth of their loans and investments. Indeed, if the Federal Reserve goes so far as to reduce the reserves of the banking system, this will tend to reduce the money supply. Under the assumptions made in the previous chapter, the banks must cut back the money supply by $6 for every $1 deficiency in reserves.

MAKERS OF MONETARY POLICY

Who establishes our monetary policy? Who decides that, in view of the current and prospective economic situations, the money supply should be increased (or decreased) at a certain rate? As in the case of fiscal policy, this is not a simple question to answer; many individuals and groups play an important role. Certainly, however, *the leading role is played by the Federal Reserve Board and the Federal Open Market Committee,* both of which are described in detail in subsequent sections. The chairman of the Federal Reserve Board is the chief spokesman for the Federal Reserve System. The recent chairmen—Paul A. Volcker, G. William Miller, Arthur F. Burns, and William McChesney Martin—undoubtedly have had considerable influence over monetary policy.

Although the Federal Reserve (the "Fed") is responsible to Congress, Congress has established no clear guidelines for its behavior. Thus the Federal Reserve has wide discretionary powers over monetary policy. But the Federal Reserve System is a huge organization, and it is not easy to figure out exactly who influences whom and who decides what. Formal actions can be taken by a majority of the board and of the Federal Open Market Committee. However, this tells only part of the story.

[1]This assumes that the legal reserve requirement is 16⅔ percent. If the legal reserve requirement were 20 percent, a $5 increase in the money supply could be supported by $1 of excess reserves. As pointed out in more advanced texts, a much smaller increase in the money supply may result from a dollar of reserves if banks want to hold excess reserves and if currency is withdrawn.

To get a more complete picture, it is essential to note too that many agencies and groups other than the Fed have an effect on monetary policy, although it is difficult to measure their respective influences. The Treasury Department frequently has an important voice in the formulation of monetary policy. The Fed must take into account the problems of the Treasury, which is faced with the task of selling huge amounts of government securities (that is, government IOUs) each year. Also, congressional committees hold hearings and issue reports on monetary policy and the operations of the Federal Reserve. These hearings and reports cannot fail to have some effect on Fed policy. In addition, since 1975 Congress has stipulated that the Fed must publish its long-term targets for growth in the money supply, the purpose being to establish somewhat more control over monetary policy. Finally, the president may attempt to influence the Federal Reserve Board. To keep the board as free as possible from political pressure, members are appointed for long terms—14 years—and a term expires every two years. But since members frequently do not serve out their full terms, a president may be able to name more than two members during each of his terms in office.

THE FEDERAL RESERVE SYSTEM

In this and the previous chapter, we have referred repeatedly to the Federal Reserve, and stressed its importance. Now we must look in some detail at its organization and functions. After a severe financial panic in 1907, when many banks failed (recall Case Study 8.1), there was strong public pressure to do something to strengthen our banking system. At the same time, many people feared the centralized domination of the nation's banks. The result—after six years of negotiation and discussion—was the establishment by Congress of the ***Federal Reserve System*** in 1913.

**Figure 9.1
Organization of
the Federal
Reserve System**
The Federal
Reserve System
contains over
5,000 commercial
banks, the 12
regional Federal
Reserve Banks, and
the Board of
Governors, as well
as the Federal
Open Market
Committee and
various advisory
councils and
committees.

Member Banks

As shown in Figure 9.1, the organization of the Federal Reserve System can be viewed as a triangle. At the base are the commercial banks that belong to the system: the ***member banks.*** All ***national banks*** (so called because they receive their charters from the federal government) have to be members, and many of the larger ***state banks*** (chartered by the states) are members too.

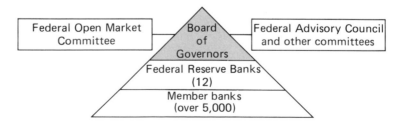

Federal Reserve Banks

In the middle of the triangle in Figure 9.1 are the 12 Federal Reserve Banks, each located in its own Federal Reserve district. The entire nation is divided into 12 Federal Reserve districts, with Federal Reserve Banks in New York, Chicago, Philadelphia, San Francisco, Boston, Cleveland, St. Louis, Kansas City, Atlanta, Richmond, Minneapolis, and Dallas. Though each of these banks is a corporation owned by the member banks, the member banks do not in any sense act as owners of the Federal Reserve Bank in their district. Instead, each Federal Reserve Bank is a public agency. These Federal Reserve Banks act as "bankers' banks," performing much the same sorts of functions for commercial banks that commercial banks perform for the public. That is, they hold the deposits of member banks and make loans to them. In addition, the Federal Reserve Banks perform a function no commercial bank can perform: They issue Federal Reserve notes, which are the nation's currency.

The Board of Governors

At the top of the triangle in Figure 9.1 is the Board of Governors of the Federal Reserve System. Located in Washington, this board—generally called the *Federal Reserve Board*—has seven members appointed by the president for 14-year terms. The board, which coordinates the activities of the Federal Reserve System, is supposed to be independent of partisan politics and to act to promote the nation's general economic welfare. It is responsible for supervising the operation of the money and banking system of the United States. The board is assisted by the *Federal Open Market Committee*, which establishes policy concerning the purchase and sale of government securities. The Federal Open Market Committee is composed of the board plus the presidents of five Federal Reserve Banks. The board is also assisted by the Federal Advisory Council, a group of 12 commercial bankers that advises the board on banking policy.

FUNCTIONS OF THE FEDERAL RESERVE

As pointed out in the previous chapter, the Federal Reserve Board, with the 12 Federal Reserve Banks, constitutes the central bank of the United States. Every major country has a central bank. England has the Bank of England, and France has the Bank of France. *Central banks* are very important organizations, and their most important function is to help control the quantity of money. But this is not their only function. A central bank also handles the government's financial transactions, and coordinates and controls the country's commercial banks. Specifically, the Federal Reserve System is charged with the following responsibilities.

MEMBER BANK RESERVES. The Federal Reserve Banks hold deposits, or reserves, of the member banks. As we have seen, these reserves play an important role in the process whereby the Fed controls the quantity of money.

CHECK COLLECTION. The Federal Reserve System provides facilities for check collection. In other words, it enables a bank to collect funds for checks drawn on other banks.

CURRENCY. The Federal Reserve Banks supply the public with currency by issuing Federal Reserve notes.

GOVERNMENT FISCAL AGENT. The Federal Reserve Banks act as fiscal agents for the federal government. They hold some of the checking accounts of the U.S. Treasury, and aid in the purchase and sale of government securities.

BANK SUPERVISION. Federal Reserve Banks supervise the operation of the member commercial banks. Recall our discussion of the nature of bank supervision and regulation in the previous chapter.

THE FEDERAL RESERVE BANKS: THEIR CONSOLIDATED BALANCE SHEET

We know that the Federal Reserve controls the money supply largely by controlling the quantity of member bank reserves. To understand how the Federal Reserve can control the quantity of member bank reserves, we must begin by examining the consolidated balance sheet of the 12 regional Federal Reserve Banks. Such a consolidated balance sheet is shown in Table 9.1. It pertains to November 30, 1984.

As shown in Table 9.1, the assets of the Federal Reserve Banks are largely of three kinds: gold certificates, securities, and loans to commercial banks.

1. *Gold certificates* are warehouse receipts issued by the Treasury for gold bullion. For present purposes, this item is less important than securities or loans to commercial banks.

Table 9.1
Consolidated
Balance Sheet of
the 12 Federal
Reserve Banks,
November 30, 1984
(Billions of Dollars)

Assets		Liabilities and net worth	
Gold certificates·	11	Reserves of member banks	25
Securities	158	Treasury deposits	2
Loans to commercial banks	5	Outstanding Federal Reserve notes	164
Other assets	31	Other liabilities and net worth	14
Total	205	Total	205

ªCash is included here too.
Source: Federal Reserve Bulletin.

2. The *securities* listed on the Federal Reserve Banks' balance sheet are U.S. government bonds, notes, and bills. (Bonds are long-term IOUs, notes are medium-term IOUs, and bills are short-term IOUs.) By buying and selling these securities, the Federal Reserve exercises considerable leverage on the quantity of member bank reserves, as we will see below.

3. The *loans to commercial banks* listed on the Federal Reserve Banks' balance sheet are loans of reserves that the Fed has made to commercial banks that are members of the Federal Reserve System. The Fed can make such loans if it wants to. The interest rate charged for such loans— the discount rate—is discussed below.

According to the right-hand side of the balance sheet in Table 9.1, the liabilities of the Federal Reserve Banks are largely of three kinds: outstanding Federal Reserve notes, Treasury deposits, and reserves of member banks.

1. The *outstanding Federal Reserve notes* are the paper currency that we use. Since these notes are debts of the Federal Reserve Banks, they are included among the banks' liabilities.

2. *Treasury deposits* are the deposits that the U.S. Treasury maintains at the Federal Reserve Banks. The Treasury draws checks on these deposits to pay its bills.

3. The *reserves of member banks* were discussed in some detail in the previous chapter. Although these reserves are assets from the point of view of the commercial banks, they are liabilities from the point of view of the Federal Reserve Banks.

OPEN MARKET OPERATIONS

Table 9.1 shows that government securities constitute about 75 percent of the assets held by the Federal Reserve Banks. The market for government securities is huge and well developed. The Federal Reserve is part of this market. Sometimes it buys government securities, sometimes it sells them. Whether it is buying or selling—and how much—can have a heavy impact on the quantity of bank reserves. Indeed, the most important means the Federal Reserve has to control the quantity of bank reserves (and thus the quantity of excess reserves) are *open market operations*, which is the name given to the purchase and sale by the Federal Reserve of U.S. government securities in the open market.

Buying Securities

Suppose that the Federal Reserve buys $1 million worth of government securities in the open market, and that the seller of these securities is General Motors.[2] To determine the effect of this transaction on the quantity of bank reserves, let's look at the effect on the balance sheet of the Fed

[2] Large corporations often hold quantities of government securities.

and on the balance sheet of the Chase Manhattan Bank, General Motors' bank.[3] In this transaction, the Fed receives $1 million in government securities and gives General Motors a check for $1 million. When General Motors deposits this check to its account at the Chase Manhattan Bank, the bank's demand deposits and reserves increase by $1 million.

Thus, as shown in Table 9.2, the left-hand side of the Fed's balance sheet shows a $1 million increase in government securities, and the right-hand side shows a $1 million increase in bank reserves. The left-hand side of the Chase Manhattan Bank's balance sheet shows a $1 million increase in reserves, and the right-hand side shows a $1 million increase in demand deposits. Clearly, *the Fed has added $1 million to the banks' reserves.* The situation is somewhat analogous to the $10,000 deposit at Bank A in the previous chapter.

Table 9.2
Effect of Fed's Purchasing $1 Million of Government Securities (Millions of Dollars)

A. Effect on Fed's balance sheet:

Assets		Liabilities and net worth	
Government securities	+1	Member bank reserves	+1

B. Effect on balance sheet of the Chase Manhattan Bank:

Assets		Liabilities and net worth	
Reserves	+1	Demand deposits	+1

Selling Securities

Suppose that the Federal Reserve sells $1 million worth of government securities in the open market. They are bought by Merrill Lynch, Pierce, Fenner, and Smith, a huge brokerage firm. What effect does this transaction have on the quantity of bank reserves? To find out, let's look at the balance sheet of the Fed and the balance sheet of Merrill Lynch's bank, which we again assume to be Chase Manhattan. When Merrill Lynch buys the government securities from the Fed, the Fed gives Merrill Lynch the securities in exchange for Merrill Lynch's check for $1 million. When the Fed presents this check to the Chase Manhattan Bank for payment, Chase Manhattan's demand deposits and reserves decrease by $1 million.

Thus, as shown in Table 9.3, the left-hand side of the Fed's balance sheet shows a $1 million decrease in government securities, and the right-hand side shows a $1 million decrease in reserves. The left-hand side of the Chase Manhattan Bank's balance sheet shows a $1 million decrease in reserves, and the right-hand side shows a $1 million decrease in demand deposits. Clearly, *the Fed has reduced the reserves of the banks by $1 million.*

[3]For simplicity, we assume that General Motors has only one bank, the Chase Manhattan Bank. Needless to say, this may not be the case, but it makes no difference to the point we are making here. We make a similar assumption regarding the investment firm of Merrill Lynch in the next section.

Table 9.3
Effect of Fed's
Selling $1 Million of
Government
Securities (Millions
of Dollars)

A. Effect on Fed's balance sheet:			
Assets		Liabilities and net worth	
Government securities	−1	Member bank reserves	−1

B. Effect on balance sheet of the Chase Manhattan Bank:			
Assets		Liabilities and net worth	
Reserves	−1	Demand deposits	−1

The Federal Open Market Committee

As indicated above, open market operations are the Fed's most important method for controlling the money supply. The Federal Reserve adds to bank reserves when it buys government securities and reduces bank reserves when it sells them. Obviously, the extent to which the Federal Reserve increases or reduces bank reserves depends in an important way on the amount of government securities it buys or sells. The greater the amount, the greater the increase or decrease in bank reserves.

The power to decide on the amount of government securities the Fed should buy or sell at any given moment rests with the *Federal Open Market Committee.* This group wields an extremely powerful influence over bank reserves and the nation's money supply. Every three or four weeks, the Federal Open Market Committee meets to discuss the current situation and trends, and gives instructions to the manager of the Open Market Account at the Federal Reserve Bank of New York, who actually buys and sells the government securities.

CHANGES IN LEGAL RESERVE REQUIREMENTS

Open market operations are not the only means the Federal Reserve has to influence the money supply. Another way is *to change the legal reserve requirements.* In other words, *the Federal Reserve Board can change the amount of reserves banks must hold for every dollar of demand deposits.* In 1934, Congress gave the Federal Reserve Board the power to set —within certain broad limits—the legally required ratio of reserves to deposits for both demand and time deposits. From time to time, the Fed uses this power to change legal reserve requirements. For example, in 1958 it cut the legally required ratio of reserves to deposits in big city banks from 17½ percent to 16½ percent; the ratio remained at 16½ percent until 1968, when it was raised to 17 percent. Table 9.4 shows the legal reserve requirements in 1985. According to the 1980 financial reform act, the Fed can set the legally required ratio of reserves to deposits between the limits of 8 and 14 percent for checkable deposits. Also, on the affirmative action of five of the seven members of the Fed's board of governors, it can impose an additional reserve requirement of up to 4 percent. And in extraordinary conditions it can set the percentage at any level it deems necessary.

Table 9.4
Legal Reserve
Requirements of
Depository
Institutions, 1985

Type and size of deposits	Reserve requirements (percent of deposits)
Net transaction accounts	
Up to $28.9 million	3
Over $28.9 million	12
Nonpersonal time deposits, by original maturity	
Less than 1½ years	3
1½ years or more	0

Source: *Federal Reserve Bulletin.*

Effect of an Increase in Reserve Requirements

The effect of an increase in the legally required ratio of reserves to deposits is that banks must hold larger reserves to support the existing amount of demand deposits. This in turn means that banks with little or no excess reserves will have to sell securities, refuse to renew loans, and reduce their demand deposits to meet the new reserve requirements. For example, suppose that a member bank has $1 million in reserves and $6 million in demand deposits. If the legal reserve requirement is 16 percent, it has excess reserves of $1 million minus $960,000 (.16 × $6 million), or $40,000. It is in good shape. If the legal reserve requirement is increased to 20 percent, this bank now needs $1.2 million (.20 × $6 million) in reserves. Since it only has $1 million in reserves, it must sell securities or refuse to renew loans.

Consider now what happens to the banking system as a whole. Clearly, an increase in the legally required ratio of reserves to deposits means that with a given amount of reserves, the banking system can maintain less demand deposits than before. For example, if the banking system has $1 billion in total reserves, it can support $1 billion/.16, or $6.25 billion in demand deposits when the legal reserve requirement is 16 percent. But it can support only $1 billion/.20, or $5 billion in demand deposits when the legal reserve requirement is 20 percent (see Table 9.5).[4] Thus *in-*

Table 9.5
Consolidated
Balance Sheet of
All Member Banks,
Before and After an
Increase (from 16
to 20 Percent) in
the Legal Reserve
Requirement
(Billions of Dollars)

A. Before the increase in the legal reserve requirement:

Assets		Liabilities	
Reserves	1.00	Demand deposits	6.25
Loans and investments	7.25	Net worth	2.00
Total	8.25		8.25

B. After the increase in the legal reserve requirement:

Assets		Liabilities	
Reserves	1.00	Demand deposits	5.00
Loans and investments	6.00	Net worth	2.00
Total	7.00		7.00

[4]We assume arbitrarily in Table 9.5 that the total net worth of the banks is $2 billion. Obviously, this assumption concerning the amount of total net worth makes no difference

creases in the legal reserve requirement tend to reduce the amount of
demand deposits—bank money—the banking system can support.

189 ★
Changes in the
Discount Rate

Effect of a Decrease in Reserve Requirements

What is the effect of a decrease in the legally required ratio of reserves to deposits? It means that banks must hold less reserves to support the existing amount of demand deposits, which in turn means that banks will suddenly find themselves with excess reserves. If the banking system has $1 billion in reserves and $5 billion in demand deposits, there are no excess reserves when the legal reserve requirement is 20 percent. But suppose the Federal Reserve lowers the legal reserve requirement to 16 percent. Now the amount of legally required reserves is $800 million ($5 billion × .16), so the banks have $200 million in excess reserves—which means that they can increase the amount of their demand deposits. Thus *decreases in the legal reserve requirements tend to increase the amount of demand deposits—bank money—the banking system can support.*

Changes in legal reserve requirements are a rather drastic way to influence the money supply; they are to open market operations as a cleaver is to a scalpel, and so are made infrequently. For example, for about ten years—from April 1958 to January 1968—no change at all was made in legal reserve requirements for demand deposits in city banks. Nonetheless, the Fed can change legal reserve requirements if it wants to. And there can be no doubt about the potential impact of such changes. Large changes in reserve requirements can rapidly alter bank reserves and the money supply.

CHANGES IN THE DISCOUNT RATE

Still another way that the Federal Reserve can influence the money supply is through changes in the discount rate. As shown by the balance sheet of the Federal Reserve Banks (in Table 9.1), commercial banks that are members of the Federal Reserve System can borrow from the Federal Reserve when their reserves are low (if the Fed is willing). This is one of the functions of the Federal Reserve. The interest rate the Fed charges the banks for loans is called the *discount rate*, and the Fed can increase or decrease the discount rate whenever it chooses. Increases in the discount rate discourage borrowing from the Fed, while decreases in the discount rate encourage it.

The discount rate can change substantially and fairly often (Table 9.6). For instance, the discount rate was increased from 12 to 13 percent in early 1980, then reduced to 12 percent in May, 11 percent in June, and 10 percent in July, after which it was raised back to 13 percent by Decem-

---

to the point we are making here. Also, for simplicity, here and below we ignore checkable deposits other than demand deposits.

☆ ☆ ☆ ☆ ☆ ☆ ☆ ☆ ☆ ☆ ☆ ☆ ☆

CASE STUDY 9.1 THE INDEPENDENCE OF THE FEDERAL RESERVE

During World War II, the Federal Reserve was called upon to buy up Treasury securities to aid the Treasury in financing the war. Buying bonds pumped lots of money into circulation—which could have caused inflation, had not the high employment of the war effort, combined with wage and price controls, offset the inflationary pressure. When the war ended, the Treasury insisted on continuing this arrangement with the Fed. In effect, the Fed lost control of the money supply, and Marriner Eccles, Fed chairman in the late 1940s, called the agreement an "Engine of Inflation."

In 1951, the Fed and the Treasury worked out an accord that gave the Fed a freer hand in conducting monetary policy: The Fed would temporarily support long-term government securities, but would thereafter be free to follow a more flexible policy consistent with noninflationary growth. Nevertheless, the independence of the Fed has been and will continue to be the subject of much debate.

Paul Volcker

Some say the Fed is responsible to Congress. Its enabling legislation was passed by Congress in 1913, and it could presumably be reorganized should it sufficiently rouse Congress's wrath. But Congress moves with nothing if not deliberate speed, and it seldom has sought to influence the Federal Reserve through major new legislation. The president fills vacancies on the Board of Governors, but since terms on the board run for 14 years, presidents may have to wait until their second term to appoint a majority of the board.

In fact, as knowledgeable observers often agree, there are two groups that, without appearing prominently on the organization chart, exercise considerable influence over the policies of the Fed. One is the business community—a group with a definite interest in preserving the value of a dollar. The second is the board's professional staff of senior economists. Administrations come and go, but staff economists remain, and their uniquely detailed knowledge of the workings of the Fed assure them a hearing at 20th and Constitution.

All chairmen of the Fed—such as Paul Volcker, G. William Miller, and Arthur Burns in recent years—have been sensitive to the ultimate vulnerability of the Fed's independence, and so have been reluctant to buck administration policy too dramatically. Whether the Federal Reserve's current procedures can survive a general call for more accountability is an open question. In early 1975, Congress passed a resolution that the Federal Reserve must publish its targets for growth in the money supply. But the extent to which this really has tied the Fed's hands is by no means clear.

E.M. and N.B.

Table 9.6
Average Discount
Rate, 1960–84

Year	Discount rate (percent)	Year	Discount rate (percent)
1960	3.53	1973	6.45
1961	3.00	1974	7.83
1962	3.00	1975	6.25
1963	3.23	1976	5.50
1964	3.55	1977	5.46
1965	4.04	1978	7.46
1966	4.50	1979	10.28
1967	4.19	1980	11.77
1968	5.17	1981	13.41
1969	5.87	1982	11.02
1970	5.95	1983	8.50
1971	4.88	1984	8.80
1972	4.50		

Source: Economic Report of the President.

ber 1980. When the Fed increases the discount rate (relative to other interest rates), it makes it more expensive for banks to augment their reserves by borrowing from the Fed; hence it tightens up a bit on the money supply. On the other hand, when the Fed decreases the discount rate, it is cheaper for banks to augment their reserves in this way; hence the money supply eases up a bit.

The Fed is largely passive in these relations with the banks. It cannot make the banks borrow. It can only set the discount rate and see how many banks show up at the "discount window" to borrow. Also, the Fed will not allow banks to borrow on a permanent or long-term basis. They are expected to use this privilege only to tide themselves over for short periods, not to borrow in order to relend at a profit. To discourage banks from excessive use of the borrowing privilege, the discount rate is kept relatively close to short-term market interest rates.

Most economists agree that changes in the discount rate have relatively little direct impact, and that the Fed's open market operations can and do offset easily the amount the banks borrow. Certainly changes in the discount rate cannot have anything like the direct effect on bank reserves of open market operations or changes in legal reserve requirements. *The principal importance of changes in the discount rate lies in their effects on people's expectations.* When the Fed increases the discount rate, this is generally interpreted as a sign that the Fed will tighten credit and the money supply. A cut in the discount rate is generally interpreted as a sign of easier money and lower interest rates.

OTHER TOOLS OF MONETARY POLICY

In addition, the Federal Reserve has several other tools it can use, each of which is discussed below. These tools are generally less important than open market operations, changes in legal reserve requirements, and changes in the discount rate.

CASE STUDY 9.2 MONETARY POLICY IN THE 1960s

To illustrate how monetary policy has been conducted, consider the decade of the 1960s. When the Kennedy administration took office in 1961, it inherited a weak economy. To stimulate it, the Federal Reserve added generously to bank reserves, thus permitting rapid growth in the money supply. However, monetary policy did not play a leading role in economic policy in the Kennedy years. Instead, the Kennedy administration pushed hard for a large tax cut, which was the cornerstone of its economic policy. Monetary policy played a supporting role. Leading administration economists felt that the money supply should grow in such a way as to accommodate the desired growth in national product, but that the growth in national product was to be brought about largely by the tax cut.*

In fact, the Federal Reserve expanded the money supply during the early 1960s at a substantially higher average annual rate than during the late 1950s. In later years, some monetarists—including Milton Friedman—were to argue that this increase in the money supply, and not the tax cut, was responsible for the growth of national product in the mid-1960s.

When government spending in Vietnam began to skyrocket in 1965, monetary policy began to push itself to the fore. The Federal Reserve Board, faced with strong inflationary pressures stemming from a highly destabilizing fiscal policy, committed itself to a strong deflationary stance, after which it eased credit considerably. Indeed, in a rapid about-face, the Fed began to expand credit very rapidly in 1967 and 1968. In the latter part of 1967, the money supply was increasing at 10 percent per year. The tax surcharge of 1968 was expected (incorrectly) to reduce spending so much that the Fed was encouraged to increase the money supply to offset it partially. Alarmed by this apparent shift to an inflationary posture, critics in Congress and elsewhere belabored the Fed for its "stop–go" policies.

When the Nixon administration came into office in 1969, inflation was unquestionably the nation's principal economic problem. Thus practically everyone, both Republicans and Democrats, agreed that monetary policy should be tight. In accord with this view, the Federal Reserve kept a close rein on the money supply during 1969. The result, however, was to slow the growth of national output and to increase unemployment.

*During much of the 1960s, monetary policy was formulated with one eye on the balance of payments, discussed in Chapter 28. If the Fed had attempted to stimulate the economy, interest rates would have fallen, and capital would have gone abroad in response to higher yields there. The result would have been a worsening of our balance-of-payments problems.

Moral Suasion

Moral suasion is a fancy term to describe various expressions of pleasure or displeasure by the Fed. In other words, the Fed tells the banks what it would like them to do or not do, and exhorts them to go along with its wishes. Banks may be asked not to "overexpand" credit. The Fed may appeal to the patriotism of the bankers, or it may make some statements that could be regarded as threats. Although the Fed does not have the power to force banks to comply with its wishes, the banks don't want to get into difficulties with the Fed. Thus moral suasion can have a definite impact, particularly for short periods. But banks are profit-oriented enterprises, and when the Fed's wishes conflict strongly with the profit motive, moral suasion may not work very well for very long.

Interest-Rate Ceilings

The Fed has been able to vary the maximum interest rate commercial banks can pay on time deposits. Since the 1930s, the Fed has had the power, under *Regulation Q*, to establish a ceiling on the interest rates commercial banks can pay. And the level at which this ceiling is set can have an important influence on the flow of funds into time deposits, savings and loan associations, and other financial institutions. In particular, by preventing commercial banks from paying more than a certain rate of interest on time deposits, the Fed can protect the savings and loan associations, which are important sources of funds for the construction industry. In other words, the Fed can prevent the commercial banks from drawing too many deposits away from the savings and loan associations.

Because it has been so closely keyed to the needs of the construction industry, Regulation Q is often regarded as a selective credit control, not as a general tool of monetary policy. A *selective credit control* is a control aimed at the use of credit for specific purposes. Most economists favor the elimination of such interest ceilings on the grounds that they interfere with the functioning of free markets for funds. In 1980, Congress passed a financial reform act to phase out Regulation Q over a six-year period.

EXPLORING FURTHER: MORE ON THE EFFECTS OF MONETARY POLICY

In this section we describe how monetary policy influences the aggregate demand curve. We discuss the view that changes in the money supply were an important cause of the Great Depression, and we present some evidence concerning the lags in the effects of monetary policy.

Monetary Policy and the Aggregate Demand Curve

Monetary policy has an important effect on the aggregate demand curve. As you will recall from Chapter 4, the aggregate demand curve is drawn on the assumption that the money supply is fixed. An increase in the money supply shifts the aggregate demand curve to the right. A decrease in the money supply shifts the aggregate demand curve to the left. Because an increase in the money supply lowers interest rates and increases investment, it raises aggregate demand (when the price level is held constant).

Suppose that the economy is experiencing inflationary pressures. Specifically, assume that the price level is OP and the aggregate demand curve is AD_1, as shown in Figure 9.2.

Figure 9.2
Effect of Increase in the Money Supply
If the Fed increases the money supply so that the aggregate demand curve shifts from AD_1 to AD_2, the price level will increase from OP_1 to OP_2.

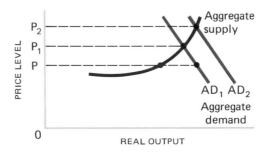

If the money supply remains fixed, the price level will increase to OP_1, at which point aggregate demand and aggregate supply will be equal.

Suppose that the Fed increases the money supply to such an extent that the aggregate demand curve shifts from AD_1 to AD_2.

When the price level increases from OP to OP_1, there still are inflationary pressures. The price level must increase from OP_1 to OP_2, at which point aggregate demand and supply will be equal. Thus inflation does not abate after the increase in the price level to OP_1. (And so long as the Fed continues to increase the money supply at a relatively rapid rate, it will not abate.)

What Caused the Great Depression?

There has been much disagreement over the causes of the Great Depression of the 1930s. According to Milton Friedman and Anna Schwartz, the Great Depression was due in large measure to changes in the money supply, indicated below:

Year	Money supply (billions of dollars)	
	M-1	M-2
1929	26.6	46.6
1930	25.8	45.7
1931	24.1	42.7
1932	21.1	36.0
1933	19.9	32.2
1934	21.9	34.4

In response to the substantial drop in NNP after 1929, the Fed, according to Friedman and Schwartz, did not undertake large-scale open market purchases until 1932. Friedman and Schwartz, among others, argue that it was an incorrect policy and that the Fed should have adopted a more expansionary policy in the early 1930s. The Friedman-Schwartz interpretation of the Great Depression has been challenged by MIT's Peter Temin, who argues that the decline in the money supply in 1929–33 was due to a reduction in the demand for money. A drop in investment or a downward shift in the consumption function might have reduced NNP. The reduction in NNP would have reduced the demand for money. The result: a decrease in interest rates, which could reduce the money supply. For example, banks might be induced to hold more excess reserves.

How Quickly Does Monetary Policy Work?

An enormous amount of statistical and econometric research has been carried out to determine how quickly an unanticipated recession can be combated by monetary policy. According to Robert Gordon of Northwestern University, the total lag between the occurrence of such an unanticipated slowdown in economic activity and the impact of monetary policy is about 14 months. In other words, it takes about 14 months for the Federal Reserve to become aware of the slowdown, to take the appropriate actions, and to have these actions affect real GNP. According to Gordon, the lags are approximately as follows:

Lag	Months
From slowdown to reflection in economic data	2
From reflection in economic data to change in money supply	3
From change in money supply to effect on real GNP	9
Total	14

By the time the effects of the expansionary monetary policy are felt, the economy may not need additional stimulus. Suppose you were driving a car in which the wheels responded to steering wheel turns with a substantial lag. The problems would be analogous to those confronting the Fed.

SUMMARY

1. The Federal Reserve System is responsible for regulating and controlling the money supply. Established in 1913, the Federal Reserve System is composed of the member banks, 12 regional Federal Reserve Banks, and the Federal Reserve Board, which coordinates the activities of the system. The Federal Reserve is the central bank of the United States.

2. Monetary policy is concerned with the money supply and interest rates. Its purpose is to attain and maintain full employment without inflation. When a recession seems imminent, the monetary authorities are likely to increase the money supply and reduce interest rates. On the other hand, when the economy is in danger of overheating and inflation threatens, the monetary authorities are likely to rein in the money supply and push up interest rates.

3. Monetary policy and fiscal policy are aimed at much the same goals, but they use different methods to promote them. One advantage of monetary policy over fiscal policy is that the lag between decision and action is relatively short. In view of the time involved in getting tax (and spending) changes enacted, this is an important point.

4. Although monetary policy is influenced by Congress, the Treasury, and other segments of the government and the public at large, the chief responsibility for the formulation of monetary policy lies with the Federal Reserve Board and the Federal Open Market Committee. To a very large extent, monetary policy operates by changing the quantity of bank reserves.

5. The most important tool of monetary policy is open market operations, which involve the buying and selling of government securities in the open market by the Federal Reserve. When the Fed buys government securities, this increases bank reserves. When the Fed sells government securities, this reduces bank reserves.

6. The Fed can also tighten or ease money by increasing or decreasing the discount rate or by increasing or decreasing legal reserve requirements. In addition, the Fed can use moral suasion, and it has had power over maximum interest rates on time deposits.

CHAPTER 10

★ ★ ★ ★ ★ ★ ★ ★

Stagflation and Anti-Inflationary Measures

LEARNING OBJECTIVES

In this chapter, you should learn:

★ What cost-push inflation is and its relation to demand-pull inflation

★ The nature of stagflation

★ The kinds of incomes policies that have been proposed

★ The disadvantages of wage and price controls

★ *(Exploring Further)* How the Fed may accommodate cost-push inflation

Policy makers in the 1970s and early 1980s found it very difficult to maintain reasonably full employment with reasonably stable prices. Inflation galloped along at close to double-digit rates even when the unemployment rate was relatively high. It was a period of considerable economic discomfort for the nation—as well as a period of discomfort for economists, since they had difficulty in coming up with any solutions that were acceptable to policy makers. Between 1962 and 1981, when the problem of inflation was at its worst, the Consumer Price Index tripled!

COST-PUSH INFLATION

In the view of many economists, demand-pull inflation is not the only kind of inflation. There is another kind: *cost-push inflation*. The process underlying cost-push inflation is not as well understood as it should be, but, according to many economists, it works something like this. While GNP is below its potential level, costs increase, perhaps because unions push up wages; and, in an attempt to protect their profit margins, firms push up the prices of their goods and services. These price increases affect the costs of other firms and the consumer's cost of living. As the cost of living goes up, labor feels entitled to, and obtains, higher wages to offset the higher living costs. Firms again pass on the cost increase to the consumer in the form of a price increase. This so-called *wage-price spiral* is at the heart of cost-push inflation.

One case of fairly pure cost-push inflation occurred in the late 1950s. This was a period of considerable slack in the economy. You will recall from Chapter 4 that a recession occurred in 1957–58. By 1958 6.8 percent of the labor force was unemployed. Nonetheless, wage increases took place during the late 1950s, and at a rate in excess of the rate of increase of labor productivity (output per hour of labor).[1] For example, average earnings (outside agriculture) went up by 4 percent between 1957 and 1961, while labor productivity went up by 2½ percent. Moreover, prices increased each year: by 3 percent from 1956 to 1957, and by 2 percent from 1957 to 1958.

Certainly this seemed to be a different phenomenon than the demand-pull inflation described in Chapter 7. There was no evidence that too much money was chasing too few goods. Instead, this was apparently a case of cost-push inflation. Commenting on the situation in the middle and late 1950s, the Council of Economic Advisers concluded: "The movement of wages during this period reflected in part the power exercised in labor markets by strong unions and the power possessed by large companies to pass on higher wage costs in higher prices."[2]

In some cases, increases in the prices of materials may play a major role in cost-push inflation. When the oil-producing countries increased the price of crude oil in 1974 and 1979, this resulted in price increases in a wide variety of products made directly or indirectly from petroleum. Because these price increases were not offset by price reductions elsewhere in the economy, the overall price level increased (and at a very rapid rate) in 1974 and 1979. Of course, the price hike for crude oil (and other materials) was by no means the sole reason for this inflation. But

[1]In Chapter 7, we discussed the importance of the rate of increase of output per hour of labor. For present purposes, it is sufficient to note that the greater the rate of increase of output per hour of labor, the larger the rate of increase of cost per hour of labor that can be absorbed without an increase in cost per unit of output. See footnote 4, Chapter 7.

[2]*1962 Annual Report of the Council of Economic Advisers,* Washington, D.C.: Government Printing Office, p. 175.

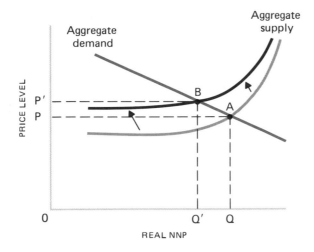

Figure 10.1
Increase in the Price Level Due to a Shift in the Aggregate Supply Curve
According to many economists, the inflation of the middle and late 1970s was due in considerable part to shifts upward and to the left in the aggregate supply curve because of shortages and price increases in oil and other materials. Such a shift results in an increase in the price level from *OP* to *OP'*.

unquestionably it did play a noteworthy role in shifting the aggregate supply curve upward and to the left, as shown in Figure 10.1.

DIFFICULTIES IN DISTINGUISHING COST-PUSH FROM DEMAND-PULL INFLATION

Generally, it is difficult, if not impossible, to sort out cost-push inflation from demand-pull inflation. For example, an increase in aggregate demand may raise firms' demand for labor, causing workers to demand higher wages, which in turn leads firms to raise their prices. In such a case, the inflation may be demand-pull in the sense that the ultimate cause was an increase in aggregate demand, but it is cost-push in the sense that the proximate cause of the increase in the price level was an increase in wages.

Also, it is important to note that a cost-push inflation of the sort shown in Figure 10.1 is unlikely to continue for a long period of time unless the Fed "accommodates" or "validates" it by following policies that shift the aggregate demand curve to the right. If the aggregate demand curve does not shift, the inflation will die out. (In Figure 10.1, once the economy moves from point *A* to point *B*, the inflation will be over. There will be no further increases in the price level.) For further discussion, see p. 212.

THE INSTABILITY OF THE PHILLIPS CURVE

In Chapter 7 we introduced the Phillips curve and discussed the tradeoff between inflation and unemployment that it implied. During the 1960s economists came to believe that the Phillips curve was a stable, predictable relationship. Panel A of Figure 10.2 shows the relationship between the inflation rate and the unemployment rate in the United States during 1955 to 1969. As you can see, there was a fairly close relationship between them in this period. Economists relied heavily on these data to buttress their belief that the Phillips curve really existed and that it had the hypothesized shape. It is no exaggeration to say that the Phillips curve in Figure 10.2 (the heavy line) had a major influence on both economic analysis and economic policy in the sixties.

But then something unforeseen (by most economists) occurred. *The inflation and unemployment rates in the seventies and early eighties did not conform at all closely to the relationship that prevailed in the sixties.* As shown in panel B of Figure 10.2, the points for 1970 to 1984 lie

**Figure 10.2
Relationship
between Inflation
Rate and
Unemployment
Rate**
*Source: Economic
Report of the
President,*
Washington, D.C.:
Government Printing
Office, 1979 and
1985.

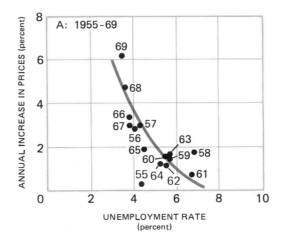

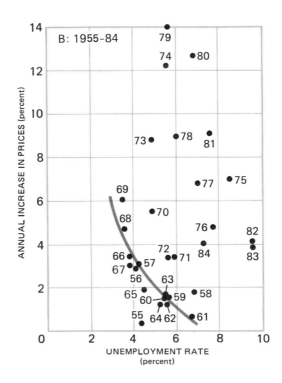

far above and to the right of the relationship that prevailed earlier. In other words, holding constant the unemployment rate, the inflation rate tended to be much higher in the seventies than in the sixties. Or, holding the inflation rate constant, the unemployment rate tended to be much higher in the seventies than in the sixties. Whichever way you look at it, this departure from the earlier relationship between inflation and unemployment was bad news.

A Reason for Instability

Why did this departure from the earlier relationship occur? As stressed in a previous section, one reason was the shift to the left in the aggregate supply curve due to price hikes in oil, food, and raw materials. Because of this shift, both the inflation rate and the unemployment rate increased. And the rapid inflation of the seventies helped to bring on higher levels of unemployment. The oil price hikes acted like an excise tax levied on the consumer: they reduced the amount that consumers could spend on other things. The general inflation raised people's money incomes, thus pushing them into higher income tax brackets and increasing the amount they had to pay in taxes. (Similarly, the inflation swelled the paper profits of many firms, and increased their tax bills.) Because of the oil price increases and the effective increase in taxes, as well as other factors such as the decline in the stock market, consumers cut back on their spending. Thus the $C + I + G$ line was pushed downward, and the equilibrium value of NNP fell.

THE LONG-RUN PHILLIPS CURVE

Many leading economists, like Milton Friedman and Edmund Phelps, deny that the Phillips curve exists as a stable "long-run" phenomenon. To them, the Phillips curve in Figure 7.5 is only a short-run relationship; in the long run, they believe that the Phillips curve is vertical. Thus they are not surprised that, holding constant the unemployment rate, the rate of inflation was higher in the seventies than in the sixties. In their view, expansionary monetary and fiscal policies that result in inflation will only reduce unemployment temporarily, with the result that the rate of inflation will tend to accelerate, for reasons given below. Thus these economists are often called *accelerationists*.

"Natural" Rate of Unemployment

According to the accelerationists, there is a certain "natural" (or full-employment) rate of unemployment, which is determined by how long workers search before taking a new job. The more reluctant they are to take unattractive or low-paying jobs, the higher the "natural" rate of

☆ ☆ ☆ ☆ ☆ ☆ ☆ ☆ ☆ ☆ ☆ ☆ ☆

CASE STUDY 10.1 STAGFLATION

The 1970s and early 1980s were characterized by a combination of high unemployment and high inflation: stagflation. (The term "stagflation" was coined by combining stagnation and inflation.) What caused this turn of events? According to many economists, it was because the aggregate supply curve shifted upward and to the left, as shown in Figure 10.1. Since a reduction in national output means high unemployment, and an increase in the price level means inflation, it is easy to see that such a shift in the aggregate supply curve might result in stagflation.

But why did the aggregate supply curve shift upward and to the left during the seventies? The following reasons are among those frequently cited. (1) Food prices

A meeting of the OPEC oil ministers

shot up, beginning in late 1972, because of bad crops around the world (and the disappearance of Peruvian anchovies, which caused a drop in the fish catch off the South American coast). (2) Many other raw material prices increased rapidly because of worldwide shortages. (3) As pointed out in a previous section, the price of crude oil increased greatly in 1974, 1979, and other years, because of the actions of Arab and other oil-producing countries. Because of these factors, a given level of NNP could be produced only at a higher price level than was previously the case. That is, the aggregate supply curve shifted upward and to the left.

☆ ☆ ☆ ☆ ☆ ☆ ☆ ☆ ☆ ☆ ☆ ☆ ☆

unemployment. Economists who stress the importance of structural unemployment argue that the "natural" rate of unemployment depends too on the rate at which changes in technology and tastes occur and the speed with which workers in declining industries can be retrained for jobs in expanding industries.

Suppose that this "natural" rate is 5½ percent, and that the government, not realizing that it is this high, uses expansionary monetary and fiscal policies to reduce unemployment to 4 percent. Because of the resulting increase in aggregate demand, the price level rises; and *if the level of money wages remains relatively constant,* firms' profits

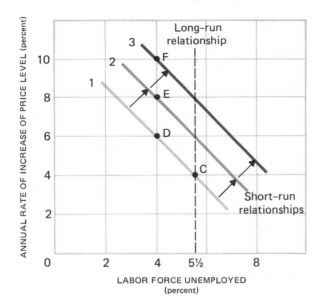

Figure 10.3
A Simplified
Accelerationist
Model
According to the accelerationists, if the government persists in trying to reduce the unemployment rate below the natural rate of 5½ percent, all that it will achieve is a higher and higher rate of inflation. In the long run, the unemployment rate returns to the natural rate (5½ percent in this case). Thus the long-run relationship between the unemployment rate and inflation rate is vertical.

go up. Higher profits lead to expanded output and more employment. Thus the economy moves from point *C* (where it was before the government's expansionary policies) to point *D* in Figure 10.3. This movement is entirely in accord with the concept of the Phillips curve; a reduction in unemployment is gained at the expense of more inflation (6 percent rather than 4 percent).[3]

However, the accelerationists go on to argue that this movement is only temporary. To see why, it is essential to recognize that the short-run Phillips curve reflects people's expectations concerning the future rate of inflation. If people have come to expect a higher rate of inflation than in the past, this will shift the Phillips curve upward and to the right. To illustrate, let's compare two situations, one where workers and firms expect that prices will increase by 10 percent per year in the immediate future, the other where they expect no inflation at all. In the former case, unions will not be content to obtain less than a 10 percent increase in money wages, since a smaller increase would mean a cut in real wages. In the latter case, unions can afford to settle for a much more moderate increase in money wages, since none of the money wage increase is expected to be offset by inflation. Thus the rate of increase of wages is likely to be greater in the former than the latter case, if the unemployment rate is the same.

In summary, *the more inflation people expect, the further upward and*

[3]To prevent confusion, note that we are not assuming that the short-run relationship between the inflation rate and the unemployment rate (curve 1 in Figure 10.3) is the same as the curve in Figure 7.6. Instead, we assume that it is below and to the left of the curve in Figure 7.6. In succeeding paragraphs, we will show how it moves toward the position shown in Figure 7.6.

out from the origin the short-run Phillips curve is likely to be. And the less inflation people expect, the further downward and close to the origin the short-run Phillips curve will be.

According to the accelerationists, the movement from point C to point D in Figure 10.3 is only temporary because workers adjust their expectations concerning inflation. Before the government's expansionary monetary and fiscal policies were adopted, the inflation rate was 4 percent, and this was (more or less) what workers expected. The movement from point C to point D means an increase in the inflation rate to 6 percent, which the workers do not expect. Although they are fooled at first, people *adapt* their expectations; that is, the rate of inflation they expect is adjusted upward toward the new 6 percent rate. As pointed out in the previous paragraph, this increase in the expected amount of inflation will shift the short-run Phillips curve upward and out from the origin. The short-run relationship between the unemployment rate and the inflation rate will shift from curve 1 to curve 2 in Figure 10.3. Faced with this new short-run curve, the government will raise the inflation rate to 8 percent if it persists in trying to maintain the unemployment rate at 4 percent. That is, it will have to move to point E in Figure 10.3.

A Second Try

Suppose that the government continues to try to maintain a 4 percent unemployment rate. Since the inflation rate increases to 8 percent as a consequence, people once more begin to adapt their expectations to the new inflation rate. Workers, trying to compensate for the higher inflation rate, ask for bigger wage increases, and firms are more willing to grant such increases because they recognize that the inflation rate has risen. Once again, the short-run Phillips curve shifts upward and outward from the origin. The short-run relationship between the unemployment rate and the inflation rate will shift from curve 2 to curve 3 in Figure 10.3. Thus the government will have increased the inflation rate to 10 percent if it persists in trying to keep the unemployment rate at 4 percent. That is, it will have to move to point F in Figure 10.3.

The Long-Run Relationship

If the government persists in trying to reduce the unemployment rate below the natural rate of $5\frac{1}{2}$ percent, it will continually fail to do so. All that it will achieve is a higher and higher rate of inflation. Thus, according to the accelerationists, the Phillips curve really does not exist, except in the short run, and governments that believe in its existence can cause considerable mischief. It is not possible for the economy to remain permanently at any point on the short-run curves in Figure 10.3 other than at the natural rate of unemployment ($5\frac{1}{2}$ percent in this case). Thus the long-run relationship between the unemployment rate and the inflation rate is a vertical line, as shown in Figure 10.3.[4]

Not all economists agree with the accelerationists' view that the long-run relationship between the unemployment rate and the inflation rate is a vertical line. Some believe that even in the long run, this relationship is inverse. However, there seems to be little doubt that the long-run relationship is a lot steeper than the short-run relationship. Thus much, though perhaps not all, of the reduction in unemployment due to increases in inflation is likely to be illusory.

WAGE AND PRICE CONTROLS

One aim of government policy is to lower the inflation rate corresponding to a given unemployment rate—or to lower the unemployment rate corresponding to a given inflation rate. One way that the government can try to do this is by adopting *wage and price controls*. During 1971–74 (as well as various wartime emergencies), the government imposed controls of this sort. The government intervened directly in the marketplace to make sure that wages and prices did not increase by more than a certain amount. The economics profession has little enthusiasm for direct controls of wages and prices, for several reasons.

1. *Such controls are likely to result in a distorted allocation of resources.* Wage and price controls do not permit prices to perform their functions in allocating resources, and the result is inefficiency and waste.

2. *Such controls are likely to be expensive to administer.* For example, during the Korean War, the Economic Stabilization Agency had 16,000 employees; even so, it was difficult to prevent violation or evasion of the controls.

3. *There is widespread opposition to detailed government regulation and control of this sort, on the grounds that it impairs our economic freedom.* The Council of Economic Advisers undoubtedly spoke for most of the economics profession when it said in 1968:

> The most obvious—and least desirable—way of attempting to stabilize prices is to impose mandatory controls on prices and wages. While such controls may be necessary under conditions of an all-out war, it would be folly to consider them as a solution to the inflationary pressures that accompany high employment under any other circumstance. . . . Although such controls may be unfortunately popular when they are not in effect, the appeal quickly disappears once people live under them.[5]

---

[4]The available evidence seems to indicate that the natural rate of unemployment has been higher in more recent years than in the 1960s, in considerable part because women and teenagers have been a larger percentage of the labor force than in the 1960s. This increase in the natural rate of unemployment is another factor that is partly responsible for the recent stagflation, but it is by no means the whole story.

[5]*1968 Annual Report of the Council of Economic Advisers,* Washington, D.C.: Government Printing Office, p. 119.

INCOMES POLICIES

As we have stressed, the 1970s and early 1980s were a period of uncomfortably high inflation. For example, in 1980, the price level in the United States was increasing by more than 10 percent per year. Such high rates of inflation spurred considerable interest, both here and abroad, in using incomes policies to help curb inflation without cutting back on aggregate demand. According to one common definition, an *incomes policy* contains three elements:

1. *An incomes policy includes targets for wages (and other forms of income) and prices for the economy as a whole.* For example, the target may be to stabilize the price level, or to permit the Consumer Price Index to increase by less than 2 percent per year, or to allow wage increases not exceeding a certain percentage.

2. *An incomes policy gives particular firms and industries more detailed guides for decision making on wages (and other forms of income and prices).* These guides are set in such a way that the overall targets for the entire economy will be fulfilled. For example, if the aim is price stability, these guides tell firms and unions what kinds of decisions are compatible with this target. To be useful, the guides must be specific and understandable enough to be applied in particular cases. There obviously is little point in telling firms and unions to avoid "inflationary" wage and price decisions if they don't know whether a particular decision is "inflationary" or not.

3. *An incomes policy contains mechanisms to get firms and unions to follow its guidelines.* An incomes policy differs from wage and price controls in that it seeks to induce firms and unions to follow these guides voluntarily. But if it is to have any effect, clearly the government must be prepared to use certain forms of persuasion beyond moral suasion. In fact, governments sometimes have publicly condemned decisions by firms and unions that were regarded as violating the guides. Government stockpiles of materials and government purchasing policies have also been used to penalize or reward particular firms and industries. Other pressures too have been brought to bear in an attempt to induce firms to follow the established guides. Thus the difference between an incomes policy and wage and price controls is one of degree and emphasis, not a clear-cut difference in kind.

An example of an incomes policy in the United States was the so-called Kennedy-Johnson guidelines. Although earlier administrations (for example, the Eisenhower and Truman administrations) had often appealed to business and labor to limit wage and price increases, the first systematic attempt at a fairly specific incomes policy in the United States occurred during the Kennedy administration. In 1961, President Kennedy's Council of Economic Advisers issued the following wage-price guidelines:

The general guide for noninflationary wage behavior is that the rate of increase in wage rates (including fringe benefits) in each industry be equal to the trend rate of *over-all productivity advance*. General acceptance of this guide would maintain stability of labor cost per unit of output for the economy as a whole—though not of course for individual industries. The general guide for noninflationary price behavior calls for price reduction if the industry's rate of productivity increase exceeds the over-all rate—for this would mean declining unit labor costs; it calls for an appropriate increase in price if the opposite relationship prevails; and it calls for stable prices if the two rates of productivity increase are equal. [Note once again that productivity equals output per hour of labor.][6]

To see just what this means, let's consider prices and wages in the auto industry. Suppose that labor productivity in the economy as a whole was increasing at 3.2 percent per year. Then according to the guidelines, *wages in the automobile industry should increase by 3.2 percent per year.* If labor productivity in the auto industry increased by 4.2 percent per year, then, if the auto makers applied this guideline, the labor cost of producing a unit of output would decrease by 1 percent per year in the auto industry (since the 3.2 percent rate of increase of wages minus the 4.2 percent rate of increase of labor productivity equals −1 percent). Thus the guidelines specified that *prices in the auto industry should decrease,* perhaps by about 1 percent per year.

The Steel Price Increase: Incomes Policy in Action

To conform to our definition of an incomes policy, the Kennedy-Johnson wage-price policy had to have an overall target, more detailed guides for wage and price decisions, and a mechanism to get firms and unions to observe these guides. The overall target was the stabilization of prices, and the more detailed guides for wage and price decisions were described in the previous section. But what about the mechanisms to induce acceptance of these guides? How did the government get industry and labor to go along?

The famous confrontation in 1962 between President Kennedy and the steel industry is an interesting case study of how pressure was brought to bear. Before the wage-price guidelines were issued, President Kennedy asked the major steel companies to avoid raising prices, and no price increases occurred. Then, after the issuance of the guidelines, he asked the steel union for restraint in the wage negotiations coming up in March 1962. Arthur Goldberg, Kennedy's secretary of labor, played an important role in persuading the union to accept a 2.5 percent increase in compensation, which was clearly noninflationary. At this point, government and the press felt quite optimistic about the apparent success of the president's program.

In the week following the wage agreement, however, the United States Steel Corporation increased all its prices by 3½ percent, and most of the

[6]*1962 Annual Report of the Council of Economic Advisers,* Washington, D.C.: Government Printing Office, p. 189.

major steel companies followed suit. The price increase was clearly a violation of the president's guidelines. It almost seemed as if the steel companies were trying to demonstrate once and for all that pricing was up to them, and them alone. Their action elicited a wrathful speech by the president publicly denouncing them. Roger M. Blough, chairman of U.S. Steel, tried to rebut the president's arguments by claiming that U.S. Steel's profits were too low to attract new capital.

Three of the major steel producers—Armco, Inland, and Kaiser—did not follow U.S. Steel's lead in the day or so after its price increase. Government officials, noting this fact as well as prior public arguments against price increases by Inland officials, quickly began to apply pressure on these three producers to hold their prices constant. Government officials who knew executives of these firms called them and tried to persuade them to do so. The firms were also informed that government contracts would be directed to firms that held their prices constant. Apparently, the government's campaign succeeded. Inland and Kaiser made public statements that they would not raise prices. Faced with this fact, the other steel companies had no choice but to rescind the price increase.

This is an example of how presidential pressure can induce firms to go along with wage and price guidelines. Often Kennedy's Council of Economic Advisers tried to head off price increases before they were announced. The council would learn of an impending price increase, sometimes from the companies themselves, and then ask the firms to meet to discuss the situation. In these meetings, the council would explain the importance of price stability and both parties would discuss the proposed increase. It is difficult, of course, to measure the impact of such discussions, but according to the council, they sometimes resulted in the postponement or reduction of planned price increases.

The Kennedy-Johnson Guidelines: Criticism and Experience

Soon after the announcement of the guidelines, critics began to point out the following problems in them.

INEFFICIENCY. Some observers feared that the guidelines would result in inefficiency and waste. In a free-enterprise economy, we rely on price changes to direct resources into the most productive uses and to signal shortages or surpluses in various markets. If the guidelines were accepted by industry and labor, prices would not be free to perform this function. Of course, the guidelines specified that modifications of the general rules could be made in case of shortages, but critics of the guidelines felt that this escape hatch was too vague to be very useful.

FREEDOM. Many observers were concerned about the reduction in economic freedom. Of course, the guidelines were presented in the hope that they would be observed voluntarily. But a time was sure to come when they would be in serious contradiction with the interests of firms and unions. In such a situation, what would happen if the firms or unions decided not to follow them? To the extent that the government applied pressure on the firms or unions, there would certainly be a reduction in economic freedom; and to some observers, it seemed likely that the next step might well be direct government controls. Moreover, the nonlegislated character of the guidelines and the arbitrary choice of whom to pursue by the government raised important political questions.

FEASIBILITY. Many people felt that the guidelines really were not workable. In other words, even if the public went along with them, in many cases they would be impossible to apply, because accurate and relevant data on changes in labor productivity in particular industries were often unobtainable, and the situations where exceptions were allowed were so vaguely specified.

SYMPTOMS. Some economists felt that reliance on the guidelines was dangerous because it focused attention on the symptoms rather than the causes of inflation. In their view, inflation was largely the result of improper monetary and fiscal policies. In other words, the basic causes had to be laid at the government's door. But by setting up guidelines, the government seemed to be saying that the fault lay with industry and labor. Thus some critics felt that the guidelines tended to cloud the real issues and so let the government escape responsibility for its actions.

From 1962 to 1964 the government claimed that the guidelines were working well. Their success during this period may have been because the economy still had considerable slack, and because of the noninflationary expectations of firms and individuals engendered by several years of relative price stability. By 1965, as labor markets tightened and prices rose in response to the Vietnam buildup, it became much more difficult to use the guidelines. Union leaders fought the guidelines tooth and nail, mainly because consumer prices were rising. In various important labor negotiations, unions demanded and got higher wage increases than the guidelines called for. The airline machinists, for example, got a 4.9 percent increase in 1966. By 1968, the guidelines were dead. No one was paying any attention to them.

What effect did the guidelines have? Some people claim that they had no real effect at all, while others claim that they reduced cost-push inflation in the early 1960s by a considerable amount. Since it is difficult to separate the effects of the guidelines from the effects of other factors, there is considerable dispute over the question. Considering the level of unemployment in the early 1960s, wages increased less rapidly then than in earlier or later periods. Prices too increased less rapidly during that period—holding unemployment constant—than earlier or later. But whether these developments were due to the guidelines, or to noninflationary expectations, or to some other factors, is hard to say.

The guidelines broke down largely because they could not deal with the strong demand-pull inflation of the late 1960s. Even the strongest defenders of the guidelines are quick to point out that they are no substitute for proper monetary and fiscal policy. *If fiscal or monetary policy is generating strong inflationary pressures, such as existed in the late 1960s, it is foolish to think that guidelines can save the situation.* Perhaps they can cut down on the rate of inflation for a while; but in the long run, the dike is sure to burst. If the guidelines are voluntary, firms and unions will ignore them, and the government will find it difficult, if not impossible, to do anything. *Even wage and price controls won't contain the strong inflationary pressures generated by an overly expansive fiscal or monetary policy. Such controls may temporarily suppress the symptoms of inflation, but over the long haul these inflationary pressures will have their effect.*

TAX-BASED INCOMES POLICIES

In the past ten years, a number of influential economists have recommended tax-based incomes policies to slow the rate of inflation. Such incomes policies use the tax system or subsidies to induce firms to hold down prices and workers to hold down wages. Some tax-based incomes policies use a "carrot" while others use a "stick." To illustrate the nature of those that use a "stick," suppose that a target of 6 percent were established for overall pay increases. If a firm's average pay increase was less than or equal to the 6 percent target, it would pay the basic corporate income tax rate (about 46 percent). But if its average pay increase exceeded the 6 percent target, it would be subject to a higher tax rate. For example, its income tax might be 51 percent of its profits if its pay increase was 7 percent, 56 percent of its profits if its pay increase was 8 percent, and so on. Clearly, the firm would be penalized for granting large pay increases. If it allowed pay increases far in excess of the target, its after-tax profits would be cut severely.

Although tax-based incomes policies have attracted considerable interest and attention in the late 1970s and early 1980s, they are not free of problems. For one thing, the administrative difficulties in implementing these policies are significant. The job of the Internal Revenue Service would be complicated considerably if such policies were adopted, and firms might have difficulties in complying with them. Neither business nor labor has expressed enthusiasm for tax-based incomes policies. Labor leaders have been cool to them, because they feel that such policies imply (unfairly, in their view) that inflation is due primarily to wage increases. They feel that these policies are an unwelcome interference with collective bargaining. Business leaders have been wary of them, because they fear that these policies would complicate wage negotiations and personnel management. They also fear that some firms (small or unincorporated businesses, in particular) may be exempt from the program and that these firms may thereby gain a competitive edge.

Despite these problems, some form of tax-based incomes policy may eventually be tried, if for no other reason that it may seem preferable to other policies. As Henry Wallich has put it, "Of course, nobody likes tax-based incomes policies *per se*. It is really a question of the alternatives."

ECONOMIC STABILIZATION: WHERE WE STAND

Where do we stand in the struggle to achieve full employment without inflation? Clearly, we know much more than we did 40 years ago about how to use monetary and fiscal policies to attain this objective. Given the more advanced state of economics, it is very unlikely that a catastrophe like the Great Depression of the 1930s will occur again. But on the other hand, economists were overly optimistic in the mid-1960s when they talked about "fine-tuning" the economy. Our experience since then makes it clear that we have a long way to go before we understand the workings of the economy well enough to achieve continuous full employment without considerable inflation. Equally important, we have seen that even if the advice of its economists were always correct, the government might still pursue destabilizing policies, as it did in the late 1960s.

The 1970s and early 1980s were characterized by both excessive inflation and excessive unemployment. Throughout the Western industrialized world, governments were perplexed by this phenomenon of "stagflation." The standard economic remedies—monetary and fiscal policy—are not very effective in treating this combination of ailments. Although they can deal with either excessive unemployment or excessive inflation, they are not well designed to remedy both of them simultaneously.

To some economists, the answer (or at least a partial answer) is to rely more heavily on some form of incomes policy to fight inflation. But the evidence, here and abroad, seems to highlight the problems in formulating an effective incomes policy. The unfortunate truth is that although our understanding of the factors causing stagflation is more complete than the newspapers frequently imply, it is not complete enough to provide a workable cure that most economists can agree on. Until we obtain a better basic understanding of this phenomenon, the chances are that policy makers, both here and abroad, will continue to find economic stabilization difficult—and that there will be a good deal of floundering. If the rate of inflation takes an alarming upturn, it is likely that some form of wage and price controls will once again be applied in the United States. But it must be recognized that such controls have had limited success in restraining inflation more than temporarily in the United States as well as in other countries.[7]

Finally, there has been a shift in emphasis in many public policy discussions by economists and others. During recent decades, these discussions focused almost exclusively on the government's management of aggregate demand in its effort to maintain full employment. Now more attention is being given to the supply side of the economy. This is due in part to the commodity shortages, sluggish productivity growth, and relatively low

[7]The Reagan administration has put less emphasis on incomes policies than did the Carter administration. As for wage and price controls, President Reagan is on record as believing that they don't work. But this does not mean that such measures will not be adopted sometime in the future.

rates of capital investment that troubled the United States during the 1970s. We will say much more about these developments in the next chapter.

EXPLORING FURTHER: THE FED AND COST-PUSH INFLATION

Suppose that labor unions suddenly demand that their wage rate (in money, not real terms) be doubled. Since firms must increase prices if they are to be willing to produce the same output as before, the aggregate supply curve will shift upward and to the left, as shown in Figure 10.4.

If the Federal Reserve holds the money supply at its initial level, as shown in Figure 10.4, the economy will move from point A to point B. Thus real output will fall from OQ_0 to OQ_1 and the decrease in real output will increase unemployment. Because the price level at point B is higher than at point A, although the money wage has doubled, the real wage has less than doubled.

Figure 10.4
Accommodation of
Cost-Push Inflation
by the Fed
By increasing the money supply, the Fed can maintain real output at OQ_0, but the price level will increase greatly.

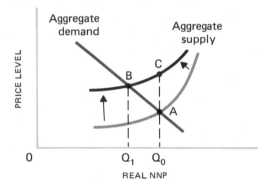

By increasing the money supply, the Fed can push the aggregate demand curve to the right. If it pushes it far enough to the right, it can make it intersect the new aggregate supply curve at point C, where real NNP is at its original level, OQ_0. The price level will rise considerably. As shown in the diagram, the price level at point C is much higher than at point A. The Fed, by enabling the cost-push action of the unions to increase the price level without resulting in additional unemployment, is said to have *accommodated* the cost-push.

SUMMARY

1. The Phillips curve shows the relationship between the rate of increase of wages and the level of unemployment. If the Phillips curve remains

fixed, it poses an awkward dilemma for policy makers. If they reduce unemployment, inflation increases; if they reduce inflation, unemployment increases. During 1955–69, there was a fairly close relationship between the inflation rate and the unemployment rate. But then something unforeseen by most economists occurred. The inflation and unemployment rates in the 1970s did not conform at all closely to the relationship that prevailed in the 1960s. Both the unemployment rate and the inflation rate tended to be much higher in the seventies than in the sixties.

2. The accelerationists, led by Milton Friedman, believe that the downward-sloping Phillips curve is only a short-run relationship. In the long run, they believe that it is vertical. In their view, expansionary policies that result in inflation will reduce unemployment only temporarily, with the result that the government, if it sets out to reduce unemployment to below its natural level, will have to permit higher and higher rates of inflation.

3. To reduce the inflation rate (at a given unemployment rate), governments have tried wage and price controls. Although a few economists favor such controls during peacetime, most do not. Such controls are likely to distort the allocation of resources, to be difficult to administer, and to run counter to our desire for economic freedom.

4. Many countries have experimented with various kinds of incomes policies. An incomes policy contains targets for wages and prices for the economy as a whole, more detailed guides for wage and price decisions in particular industries, and some mechanisms to get firms and unions to follow these guides. The Kennedy-Johnson guidelines were one form of incomes policy. Although guidelines of this sort have a short-term effect on the price level, how much effect they have in the long run is hard to say.

5. A variety of types of tax-based incomes policies has been proposed in recent years. Such policies use the tax system or subsidies to induce firms to hold down prices and workers to hold down wages.

6. Although it is unlikely that a catastrophe like the Great Depression will recur, our recent experience indicates that we have a long way to go before we understand the workings of the economy well enough to achieve continuous full employment without inflation. Also, even with consistently correct advice from its economists, there is no assurance that the government would always pursue policies that lead toward economic stabilization.

CHAPTER 11

★ ★ ★ ★ ★ ★ ★ ★ ★

Productivity, Growth, and Technology Policy

LEARNING OBJECTIVES

In this chapter, you should learn:

★ The importance of productivity and what causes it to increase or decrease

★ The nature of the productivity slowdown in the United States and its effects on the economy

★ The sorts of public policies that can be used to stimulate productivity

★ *(Exploring Further)* The effects of supply-side government policies

Productivity in the United States has not increased at a constant rate. The rate of growth of output per man-hour was significantly higher after World War I than before, and significantly higher after World War II than before. Such changes in the rate of growth of labor productivity are due in part to changes in the rate of technological change and changes in the amount of capital per worker.

During the late 1960s and the 1970s, the United States experienced a notable slowdown in its rate of increase of output per man-hour. As this slowdown continued for almost two decades, economists viewed it with increasing concern and considered it one of the factors behind the stagflation of the 1970s.

GROWTH OF PER CAPITA OUTPUT IN THE UNITED STATES

Let's begin by looking at the salient facts about the rate at which per capita output in the American economy has grown in the past. Soon after its emergence as an independent nation, the United States achieved a relatively high level of economic development. By 1840, it ranked fourth in per capita output, behind England, France, and Germany. During the next 30 years, the United States experienced relatively rapid economic growth. By 1870, it ranked second only to England in per capita output. Over the next 40 years, the American economy continued to grow rapidly. National product per person employed grew by about 2.2 percent per year between 1871 and 1913. This growth rate was higher than for practically any other major industrialized nation; and well before the turn of the century, output per capita was greater in the United States than in any other nation in the world.

Between 1913 and 1959, the American growth rate was somewhat lower than in previous years. National product per person employed grew by about 1.8 percent per year. Nonetheless, although we grew less rapidly than in earlier years, we pulled further ahead of most other industrialized countries, because we continued to grow faster than they did. Of course, our rate of economic growth varied from decade to decade. (By the rate of economic growth we mean the rate of growth of real GNP per capita.) Economic growth does not proceed at a steady rate. In some decades (like the 1920s), our economy grew rapidly, while in others (like the 1930s), it grew little, if at all. During periods of recovery and prosperity, the growth rate was high; during depressions, it was low. In the 1950s, the growth rate in the United States was lower than in many other countries, and this caused considerable controversy and some alarm.

During the 1960s our growth rate increased perceptibly. But our present growth rate is by no means the highest among the major industrialized nations. That honor belongs to Japan, which has long experienced rapid economic growth. Table 11.1 shows the annual rates of growth of per capita real GNP in the United States and other major Western industrialized countries during the last century. You can see that, for the period as

Country	1870–1964	1929–70
United States	1.9	1.9
Canada	1.7	2.1
France	1.5	2.0
Germany	1.7	3.0
Italy	1.4	2.5
United Kingdom	1.3	1.7

Source: U.S. Department of Commerce. *Long-Term Economic Growth*, 1966, and *Statistical Abstract of the United States.*

Table 11.1
Average Annual
Growth Rates of
Per Capita Real
GNP, Selected
Western
Industrialized
Countries (Percent)

a whole, per capita real GNP in the United States grew at an average rate of about 2 percent per year. Compared with Germany, France, Italy, Canada, and the United Kingdom, our growth rate was impressive. In recent years, however, many industrialized countries have shown growth rates larger than or equal to ours. And many observers have been concerned about the slowdown of our rate of productivity increase. Much more will be said below about our recent performance.

Technological Change

Technological change takes the form of new methods of producing existing products; new designs that make it possible to create new products; and new techniques for organization, marketing, and management. America's economic growth has been due in very considerable part to technological change. Table 11.2 shows that according to Denison, the advance of knowledge contributed about one-eighth of the growth in real output during 1909–29, about one-fifth of this growth during 1929–57, and even a larger share of this growth in 1969–73. (However, in 1973–76, this factor seemed to contribute little or nothing to economic growth.) Such estimates are rough but useful. It is very difficult to separate the effects of technological change on economic growth from those of investment in physical capital, since in order to be used, new technology must be embodied in physical capital, such as new machines and equipment. For example, a nuclear power plant must obviously be built to take advantage of nuclear power plant technology. Nor can the effects of technological change easily be separated from those of education. After all, the returns from increased education are enhanced by technological change, and the rate of technological change is influenced by the extent and nature of a society's investment in education. Nonetheless, the estimates in Table 11.2 are useful.

In interpreting America's economic growth, we must recognize that the United States has long been a technological leader. Even before 1850, scattered evidence gives the impression that the United States was ahead

Table 11.2
Estimated Sources
of Growth in Real
National Income in
the United States,
1909–73

Source	1909–29	Period 1929–57 (percent of total growth)	1969–73
Increase in quantity of labor	39	27	33
Increase in quantity of capital	26	15	16
Improved education and training	13	27	20
Advance of knowledge	12	20	48
Other factors	10	11	−17
Total	100	100	100

Source: E. Denison, *The Sources of Economic Growth in the United States,* New York: Committee for Economic Development, 1962; and his *Accounting for Slower Economic Growth,* Washington, D.C.: Brookings 1979. The 1969–73 figures pertain to nonresidential business output.

of other countries in many technological areas. And after 1850, the available evidence indicates that productivity was higher in the United States than in Europe, that the United States had a strong position in technically progressive industries, and that Europeans tended to imitate American techniques. Needless to say, the United States did not lead in all fields, but it appears to have held a technological lead in many important aspects of manufacturing. This was in contrast to pure science where, until World War II, the United States was not a leader.

Recent decades have witnessed tremendous growth in the amount spent on *research and development*. R and D expenditures in the United States in 1985 were over 20 times what they were in 1945. Although the bulk of these expenditures go for rather minor improvements rather than major advances, this vast increase in research and development has generated much economic growth. As shown in Table 11.3, the federal government is the source of about half of all R and D funds, which are heavily concentrated on defense and space technology. In the eyes of many economists, this vast investment in R and D would probably have had a bigger impact on the rate of economic growth if more of it had been directed at civilian rather than military and political objectives.

A National Aeronautics and Space Administration (NASA) satellite

Table 11.3
Transfers of Funds for Research and Development, United States, 1980 (Billions of Dollars)

| | Performers | | | | | |
Sources of funds	Federal government	Industry	Universities and colleges	FFRDC's[a]	Other nonprofit institutions	Total[b]
Federal government	7.8	14.0	4.1	2.0	1.5	29.4
Industry	—	28.3	0.2	—	0.2	28.7
Universities and colleges	—	—	1.3	—	—	1.3
Other nonprofit institutions	—	—	0.4	—	0.5	1.0
Total[b]	7.8	42.3	6.0	2.0	2.2	60.4

[a]Federally funded research and development centers. These are organizations exclusively or substantially financed by the federal government to meet a particular requirement or to provide major facilities for research and training purposes. Those that are administered by industry (such as Oak Ridge National Laboratory or Sandia Laboratory) or nonprofit institutions (such as the RAND Corporation) are included in the respective totals for industry or nonprofit institutions.
[b]Because of rounding errors, items do not always sum to total.
Source: National Science Foundation, *National Patterns of Science and Technology Resources,* 1980, Washington, D.C.: Government Printing Office, 1980.

THE PRODUCTIVITY SLOWDOWN AND ITS CONSEQUENCES

During the 1970s, U.S. policy makers became increasingly concerned about the decreasing rate of growth of output per hour of labor. According

Table 11.4
Output Per Hour of
Labor, United
States, Percent
Change from
Previous Year,
1948–84

Year	Percent change	Year	Percent change	Year	Percent change	Year	Percent change
1948	5.3	1957	2.5	1966	3.1	1975	2.2
1949	1.5	1958	3.1	1967	2.3	1976	3.3
1950	7.9	1959	3.2	1968	3.3	1977	2.4
1951	2.8	1960	1.5	1969	0.2	1978	0.5
1952	3.2	1961	3.3	1970	0.8	1979	−1.2
1953	3.2	1962	3.8	1971	3.6	1980	−0.5
1954	1.6	1963	3.7	1972	3.5	1981	1.9
1955	4.0	1964	4.3	1973	2.6	1982	0.2
1956	1.0	1965	3.5	1974	−2.4	1983	2.7
						1984	3.6

Source: Economic Report of the President, 1985.

to the Bureau of Labor Statistics, output per hour of labor (in the business sector) grew at an average annual rate of about 3.3 percent from 1947 to 1966, but at an average annual rate of about 1.9 percent from 1967 to 1976. In 1979–80, the annual growth rate of productivity fell further, as productivity actually declined (see Table 11.4).

This slowdown in the rate of productivity increase worried policy makers for at least two reasons. First, *to the extent that it reflected a decrease in the rate of technological change, it spelled trouble for our rate of economic growth, since the latter is dependent on our rate of technological change.* Second, *since higher productivity can offset the effect of higher wages on average cost (recall Chapter 10), the slowdown in productivity increase was likely to contribute to a higher rate of inflation.*

Besides being concerned about the slowdown in our rate of increase of productivity, many observers are concerned about the apparent reduction of America's technological lead over other nations, and about the slow rate of productivity growth in the United States relative to other major countries. During 1960–82, the percentage gain in output per hour of labor was smaller in the United States than in France, West Germany, Japan, or the United Kingdom (see Table 11.5). *In some industries, like autos, there are worries over the ability of American firms to compete with foreign rivals.*

Table 11.5
Output Per
Man-Hour in
Manufacturing,
Selected Countries,
1960–82 (1977 =
100)

Country	1960	1965	1970	1975	1982
United States	60.1	74.6	79.2	93.5	103.6
France	40.0	51.5	70.6	88.4	122.3
Germany	40.0	53.5	68.5	89.3	114.7
Japan	21.7	32.8	60.7	84.0	127.6
United Kingdom	58.3	69.9	83.2	95.0	118.2

CAUSES OF THE PRODUCTIVITY SLOWDOWN

What factors have been responsible for this significant slackening of U.S. productivity growth? According to various studies, the following factors should be noted.

INCREASE IN THE PROPORTION OF YOUTHS AND WOMEN IN THE LABOR FORCE. Output per hour of labor tends to be relatively low among women and among new entrants into the labor force, in part because of their limited experience and training and the sort of work they get. During the late 1960s, women and new entrants increased as a proportion of the labor force. Based on calculations by the Bureau of Labor Statistics, this change in labor force composition may have been responsible for 0.2 to 0.3 percentage point of the difference between the average rate of productivity increase in 1947–66 and that in 1966–73.

REDUCTION IN THE RATE OF GROWTH OF THE CAPITAL-LABOR RATIO. During 1948–73, relatively high rates of private investment resulted in a growth of the capital-labor ratio of almost 3 percent per year. After 1973, relatively low rates of investment resulted in the growth of the capital-labor ratio by only about 1 ¾ percent per year. According to the Council of Economic Advisers, this reduction in the rate of growth of the capital-labor ratio may have reduced the rate of productivity increase by up to 0.5 percentage point per year.

INCREASED GOVERNMENT REGULATION. A variety of new environmental, health, and safety regulations have been adopted in recent years. Because reduced pollution, enhanced safety, and better health are generally not included in measured output, the use of more of society's resources to meet these regulations is likely to result in a reduction in measured productivity growth. Also, the litigation and uncertainty associated with new regulations may discourage investment and efficiency, and the form of the regulations sometimes may inhibit socially desirable adaptations by firms. According to the Council of Economic Advisers, the direct costs of compliance with environmental health and safety regulations may have reduced the growth of productivity by about 0.4 percentage point per year since 1973.

REDUCTION IN THE PROPORTION OF GROSS NATIONAL PRODUCT DEVOTED TO RESEARCH AND DEVELOPMENT. In a later section, we will look closely at the changes over time in the level of R and D expenditures in the United States. For now, it is enough to say that R and D expenditures in America decreased, as a percentage of gross national product, from 3.0 percent in 1964 to 2.2 percent in 1978.

SHIFT OF NATIONAL OUTPUT TOWARD SERVICES AND AWAY FROM GOODS. There is considerable disagreement over whether the shift in the composition of national output toward services and away from goods is responsible for much of the productivity slowdown. For example, some economists argue that it is more difficult to increase productivity in service industries than in manufacturing industries. Others feel that this factor is of relatively little importance.

HAS THERE BEEN A DECLINE IN THE U.S. INNOVATION RATE?

According to many observers, the productivity slowdown has been due in part to a decline in the rate of *innovation* in the United States. In their opinion, the rate of introduction of new products and processes has fallen. There is evidence supporting this view, but it should be viewed with caution.

The Available Evidence

Some studies use the patent rate to shed light on the rate of innovation. (A patent is a document issued by the government granting exclusive use of an invention—if the invention meets certain conditions.) The patent rate in the United States has been falling since about 1969. In practically all of the 52 product fields for which data are available, the number of patents granted annually (by year of application) to U.S. inventors declined during the 1970s. But patent statistics are a crude measure of the rate of innovation. The average importance of the patents granted at one time and place may differ widely from the importance of those granted at another time and place. The proportion of total inventions that are patented may also vary significantly.

Direct evidence of a fall in the rate of innovation exists in some industries where one can measure the number of major innovations that are carried out per unit of time. In the pharmaceutical industry, for example, the number of new chemical entities introduced per year in the United States declined relative to the 1950s and early 1960s. The significance of this measure is limited by difficulties in assessing the relative importance of different innovations, and by the related problem of the small innovations that have a bigger cumulative effect than some of the more spectacular discoveries. Still, many of the available bits and scraps of data suggest a slackening in the pace of innovation in the United States.

Differences Among Sectors of the Economy

Without denying that a slackening of the rate of innovation may have occurred in some industries, there is little evidence of such a slackening in other important sectors of the economy. For example, in pharmaceuticals and agricultural chemicals, there may very well have been a decrease in the rate of innovation, in large part because of increases in regulatory requirements. But in other parts of the economy, such as microelectronics, the rate of innovation seems to be hale and hearty. Recent advances in microprocessors and microcomputers are regarded by experts as extremely important, and should have widespread effects on many areas of the economy. Computers should become cheaper, smaller, and smarter. Another potentially important area is biotechnology, where many major advances are expected. For instance, new biological techniques may allow the development of new plants.

A microchip manufactured by IBM

The Diminishing U.S. Technological Lead

It is also important to distinguish between a reduction in the rate of technological change in the United States and a reduction in the *U.S. technological lead* over other countries. According to expert opinion, the United States no longer has the commanding technological lead it enjoyed during the 1950s and 1960s. As countries like Japan and West Germany completed their recoveries from World War II and devoted more attention to transferring, adapting, and extending technology, they narrowed the technological gap considerably, and in some areas surpassed the United States. But this does not mean that the U.S. rate of innovation necessarily declined. Even in microelectronics, where there is little or no evidence of a decline in the U.S. rate of innovation, the gap between the United States and Japan has been reduced considerably, because, according to many experts, the Japanese rate of advance (from a lower level) has exceeded our own.

CUTBACKS IN THE PERCENTAGE OF GNP DEVOTED TO R AND D

Some economists believe that the productivity slowdown in the United States has been due in part to the fact that R and D expenditures, as a percentage of gross national product, fell from 1964 onward. In their view, more R and D would have produced more technological innovations, which in turn would have promoted higher productivity. The nation's total R and D expenditures (including government, industry, and others), when inflation is taken into account, remained essentially constant from 1966 to 1977. As a percentage of gross national product, R and D expenditures fell from about 3.0 percent in 1964 to about 2.2 percent in 1978. This decline occurred almost continually from 1964 to 1978, each year's percentage generally being lower than the previous year's percentage. (This decline is in contrast to the increase in other major countries like Germany and Japan, shown in Table 11.6.)

Table 11.6
Expenditures on
R and D as a
Percentage of
Gross National
Product, Selected
Countries, 1963 and
1980

Country	1963	1980
United States	2.87	2.33
France	1.53	1.76ᵇ
Germany	1.40	2.36ᶜ
Japan	1.44	1.93ᵇ
United Kingdomᵃ	2.29	2.11
Soviet Union	2.40	3.47

ᵃFigures pertain to 1964 and 1978.
ᵇFigures pertain to 1978.
ᶜFigure pertains to 1979.
Source: National Science Foundation.

In large part, this decline was due to cutbacks in government R and D expenditures. In the late 1960s, in part because of the tightening of federal fiscal constraints caused by the Vietnam War, federal expenditures on R and D (in 1972 dollars) decreased. From $18.2 billion in 1967, they fell to $14.5 billion in 1974. Accounting for much of this reduction was the winding down of the space program and the reduction (in constant dollars) of defense R and D expenditures. During the late 1970s, there once again were increases in federal R and D expenditures, but in constant dollars they remained below their 1969 level.

Industry's expenditures on R and D (in 1972 dollars) increased from 1967 to 1978, but at a much slower rate than in 1960–67. In 1960, industry's R and D expenditures (in 1972 dollars) were $6.6 billion; in 1967, they were $10.3 billion; in 1978, they were $14.9 billion. The slower rate of increase may have reflected a stabilization or decline of the profitability of R and D. By 1983, industry's R and D expenditures were about $20 billion.

VARIOUS MECHANISMS FOR ADDITIONAL FEDERAL SUPPORT OF CIVILIAN TECHNOLOGY

There are various means by which the federal government can encourage investment in civilian technology.

R and D Tax Credits

In 1981 Congress passed a 25 percent incremental tax credit to encourage industrial R and D. (See Case Study 11.1.) Such an R and D tax credit reduces the after-tax cost of R and D, and thus encourages R and D. Perhaps the most important advantages of this mechanism are that it requires less direct government control than some of the other mechanisms, and in some respects it is relatively easy to administer. Its most important disadvantages are that it rewards firms for doing R and D that they would have done anyhow, and that it does not help firms that have no profits. Moreover, any program of this sort may run into difficulties in

CASE STUDY 11.1 TECHNOLOGY POLICY IN THE CARTER AND REAGAN YEARS

In 1978 and 1979, the federal government carried out a Domestic Policy Review on Industrial Innovation. Draft reports were prepared on (1) federal procurement, (2) direct support of R and D, (3) environmental, health, and safety regulations, (4) industry structure, (5) economic and trade policy, (6) patents, and (7) information policy. These drafts were discussed and criticized by many academic, business, and labor experts involved in the review, as well as by a large number of government agencies. The overall result was a large and far-flung effort to come up with policy recommendations to stimulate the rate of innovation in the United States.

One theme that ran through many of the drafts by industry experts was that many aspects of environmental, health, and safety regulations deterred innovation. As pointed out in previous sections, there was a strong feeling that this was the case in a number of industries, although it was recognized that we lack very dependable or precise estimates of the effects of particular regulatory rules on the rate of innovation. Another theme found in some of the drafts by industry experts was that tax credits for R and D expenditures should be considered seriously. Other groups, including the U.S. Treasury Department, did not warm to this proposal.

On October 31, 1979, President Carter put forth a number of proposals, based on the Domestic Policy Review. He asked Congress to establish a consistent policy with respect to patents arising from government R and D, and advocated exclusive licenses for firms that would commercialize inventions of this sort. Also, he asked the Justice Department to write guidelines indicating the conditions under which firms in the same industry can carry out joint research projects without running afoul of the antitrust laws. Further, to reduce regulatory uncertainties, he asked environmental, health, and safety agencies to formulate a five-year forecast of what rules would be adopted. In addition, he proposed the creation of four "generic technology centers" at universities or other sites in the private sector to develop and transfer technologies where the social returns far exceed the private returns. Each center would be jointly financed by industry and government. Also, he proposed that government procurement policies put more stress on performance standards rather than on specific design specifications.

When President Reagan's administration entered Washington in early 1981, more reliance was placed on market mechanisms than on government intervention to achieve desired goals. In August 1981, Congress passed a major tax bill, which, among other things, provided for a 25 percent incremental tax credit for R and D. That is, a firm could reduce its income tax liability by an amount equal to 25 percent of the difference between its R and D expenditure and the average amount of its R and D expenditure in the previous three years. Expenditures qualifying for this new incremental R and D tax credit are "in-house" expenditures for R and D wages, supplies, and the use of equipment, 65 percent of the amount paid for contract research, and 65 percent of corporate grants to universities and certain scientific research organizations for basic research.

defining R and D, since firms have an incentive to use as wide a definition as possible. Studies of such tax credits, both in the United States and in other countries (like Canada and Sweden) seem to indicate that they have only a modest effect on industrial R and D expenditures.

Federal Grants and Contracts

It has also been proposed that the federal government make grants and contracts in support of civilian technology. This, of course, is the route taken by the Department of Defense and the National Aeronautics and Space Administration in much of their work. It has the advantage of being direct and selective, but it can involve political problems in the choice of contractors, as well as problems relative to the disposition of patents resulting from such contracts and grants. Still another, more fundamental difficulty with this mechanism for supporting private sector R and D is that it is so difficult to predict the social costs and benefits of a proposed R and D project, and that government agencies may not be very adept at making what are essentially commercial development decisions.

Expanded Responsibility of Federal Laboratories

The federal government could support additional civilian R and D by initiating and expanding work of the relevant sorts in its own government laboratories. While this approach has the advantage of being direct and selective, there are great problems when R and D is conducted by organizations that are not in close touch with the production and marketing of the product. It is very important that there be unimpeded flows of information and good coordination of R and D on the one hand, and production and marketing on the other.

IMPORTANCE OF INVESTMENT IN PLANT AND EQUIPMENT

Since investment in plant and equipment accounts for a relatively large proportion of the cost of many innovations, measures which encourage investment are likely to encourage innovation. And since the profitability of R and D is dependent upon the profitability of the entire business venture of which the R and D is a part, measures that reduce the after-tax costs to the firm of plant and equipment are likely to increase the profitability of R and D.

Encouragement of investment in plant and equipment also is likely to increase the rate of diffusion of new techniques, thus increasing the rate of growth of productivity. Many new techniques cannot be employed unless new plant or equipment is constructed and utilized. Thus public policies that encourage investment are likely to encourage both innovation and the diffusion of new technology.

During the late 1970s, many suggested that investment be encouraged with a policy of accelerated depreciation. (The cost of a firm's plant and equipment is not charged entirely against a firm's earnings in the year they are bought. Instead, this cost is spread gradually over their life. The amount that is charged each year is called *depreciation.*) According to its proponents, accelerated depreciation would increase the profitability of investment in plant and equipment and increase the cash flow that firms could use for these purposes. In August 1981, the Congress passed a tax bill that allows firms to depreciate assets much more quickly than in the past. Although relatively little is known about the quantitative impact of such tax changes on the rate of innovation, it seems likely that they would have some positive effect on it. As indicated in Table 11.7, America's investment rate has tended to be considerably lower than some of its major international competitors, such as Germany and Japan.

Country	Total Economy		Manufacturing	
	1960–69	1970–77	1960–69	1970–77
		(percentages)		
United States	14.9	14.5	8.8	9.6
Canada	20.0	19.3	14.4	15.1
Japan	28.8	26.7	29.9	26.5[b]
France	19.5	18.8	N.A.	N.A.
Germany	20.1	18.7	16.3	15.2[c]
United Kingdom	16.5	17.6	13.4	13.6

[a]Capital investment excludes residential construction in these figures.
[b]1970–74 figure.
[c]1970–76 figure.
Source: Committee for Economic Development.

Table 11.7
Capital Investment as Percentage of Output,[a] Total Economy and Manufacturing, Selected Countries, 1960–69 and 1970–77

IMPORTANCE OF THE GENERAL ECONOMIC CLIMATE

Even broader measures can have a major impact on innovation. One of the strongest influences on technological innovation is the general economic climate; measures that encourage economic growth, saving and investment, and price stability are quite likely to enhance our technological position. Indeed, improvements in our general economic climate may have more impact on the state of U.S. technology than many of the specific measures that have been proposed to stimulate technological change.

As an illustration, consider the effects of the high rate of inflation in the United States during the late 1970s and early 1980s. Inflation that is high on the average tends to be very variable in its rate; as Milton Friedman pointed out in his Nobel lecture, this reduces the efficiency of the price system as a mechanism for coordinating economic activity. In particular,

☆ ☆ ☆ ☆ ☆ ☆ ☆ ☆ ☆ ☆ ☆ ☆ ☆

CASE STUDY 11.2 SUPPLY-SIDE ECONOMICS AND THE TAX CUT OF 1981

In the late 1970s and early 1980s, some economists advocated tax reductions in order to stimulate national output. Their views came to be known as "supply-side economics," and received considerable attention when some of them received high-level posts in the Reagan administration. They played an important role in formulating and helping to push through the very large tax cut passed in August 1981. The "supply-siders" advocated cuts in taxes on labor income on the grounds that people would then work longer and harder. Many economists are skeptical of this proposition. The available evidence seems to indicate that the hours worked by prime-age males would not be affected much by tax changes. But the amount of work done by married women seems more responsive to changes in tax rates. (If the marginal tax rate—the proportion of an extra dollar of income paid in taxes—is high, some women feel it is not worthwhile to work outside their home.)

"Supply-siders" also advocated reductions in taxes on capital income. For example, they called for cuts in taxes on dividends, interest income, and capital gains. (Capital gains are increases in the value of assets.) In their view, such cuts would encourage additional saving. Although economists agree that saving and investment tend to promote the growth of an economy, there is considerable controversy over the extent to which saving is influenced by tax cuts. Early studies of consumption and saving found saving behavior to be relatively insensitive to changes in the rate of return that savers receive. (That is, if people can obtain a 15 percent annual return from their savings in banks and elsewhere, they may not save much more than if they can obtain only 10 percent.) Recent studies, particularly by Stanford's Michael Boskin, challenge this conclusion, but critics respond that the 1981 tax cut has not increased the percent of total income devoted to saving.

Some "supply-siders" argue that the tax burden is currently so high that further increases in the marginal tax rate would result in lower, not higher, total tax revenue. To explain why they believe this to be true, they use the *Laffer curve,* which relates the amount of income tax revenue collected by the government to the marginal tax rate. According to USC's Arthur Laffer (after whom the curve was named), tax revenues will be zero if the tax rate is zero. This is indisputable. Also, he points out that tax revenues will be zero if the marginal tax rate is 100 percent. Why? Because if the government takes all the income in taxes, an individual has no incentive to earn taxable income.

According to the Laffer curve (shown on the next page), the maximum tax revenue is reached when the tax rate is at some intermediate level between zero and 100 percent. This level is *Oa.* According to Laffer, U.S. tax rates already have reached or exceeded this level. Many other economists deny this. Although they admit that a reduction in tax rates could reduce the incentive to cheat on taxes and to find tax loopholes (as well as encourage people to work harder and save more), they feel that Laffer's evidence is too weak to support his conclusions. It seems fair to say that there is considerable uncertainty about the shape of the Laffer curve and where the United States is located on it. Even the existence and usefulness of such a curve is a matter of dispute. (More will be said on this score in Chapter 14.)

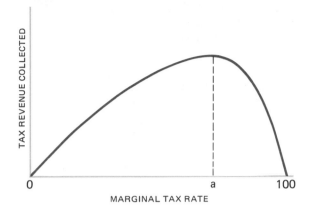

economists, both liberals and conservatives, worry about the effect of high rates of inflation on investment. Thus Washington consultant Robert Nathan has stated: "There are many serious consequences of an economic, social, and political nature flowing from high rates of inflation. Perhaps its most clearly identifiable negative impact has to do with investment. High interest rates, . . . the tendency of government policies to fight inflation with recessions, the drop in the value of the dollar, all relate to inflation and all serve to discourage new investment."

Of course, very high unemployment rates, as well as very high inflation rates, will tend to discourage innovation. When sales are depressed and the future looks grim, the climate for innovation is not bright. Neither severe and prolonged recession nor double-digit inflation constitutes a benign climate for industrial innovation.

EXPLORING FURTHER: SUPPLY-SIDE GOVERNMENT POLICIES AND THE AGGREGATE SUPPLY CURVE

It is clear that rightward shifts of the aggregate supply curve are likely to result in more output and a quelling of inflationary pressures. (See Figure 11.1.) Since these are desirable goals, it is not surprising that government policies have begun to emphasize measures designed to push the aggregate supply curve outward and to the right. This emphasis on the aggregate supply curve is not new; in fact, in 1776 Adam Smith recognized the importance of such shifts in the aggregate supply curve, although he did

Figure 11.1
**Effect of a Shift to
the Right in the
Aggregate Supply
Curve**
If the aggregate
supply curve shifts
to the right, the
result will be
increased real
output (*OQ'* rather
than *OQ*) and a
lower price level
(*OP'* rather than
OP). In the early
1980s, there was
much discussion of
supply-side policies
to achieve such a
shift in the
aggregate supply
curve.

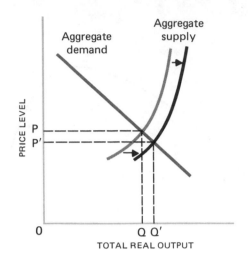

not couch his discussion in precisely these terms. But in the late 1970s and early 1980s, much more talk was heard about the supply side—that is, shifts in the aggregate supply curve—than in previous decades. (See Case Study 11.2.)

When the Reagan administration took office, it pushed through Congress a number of measures that it felt would help to shift the aggregate supply curve to the right. In particular, the 25 percent cut in the personal income tax and the accelerated depreciation of plant and equipment (both included in the 1981 tax bill) were supposed to further this aim. According to the administration, the important thing was to encourage people and firms to work, invest, and take prudent risks. There has been considerable controversy inside and outside the economic profession as to the effectiveness and side-effects of some of these proposals. All that we want to emphasize here is that the Reagan administration promoted measures to shift the aggregate supply curve. (Much more will be said about supply-side economics in Chapter 14.)

SUMMARY

1. Compared with other major industrial countries, America's rate of growth of per capita output has been impressive over the past century, because of rapid technological change, increases in education and training, investment in plant and equipment, plentiful natural resources, and our social and entrepreneurial climate.

2. During the late 1960s and the 1970s, the United States experienced a notable slowdown in its rate of increase of output per man-hour. Among the factors that are often cited as being responsible for the slowdown are: (1) the increase in the proportion of youths and women in the labor force,

(2) the reduction in the rate of growth of the capital-labor ratio, (3) increased government regulation, and (4) the reduction in the proportion of GNP devoted to research and development.

3. According to many observers, the productivity slowdown is due in part to a decline in the rate of innovation in the United States. R and D tax credits, federal R and D grants and contracts, and expanded work by federal laboratories are among the measures that have been proposed to help deal with whatever underinvestment in R and D exists. In 1981, a 25 percent incremental R and D tax credit was enacted.

4. America's investment in plant and equipment (as a percentage of output) is considerably lower than that of some of its major international competitors, such as Germany and Japan. In 1981, Congress passed a tax bill that permitted accelerated depreciation of assets. This bill was intended to encourage such investment.

5. One of the strongest influences on the rate of innovation is the general economic climate. Measures that encourage economic growth, saving and investment, and price stability are likely to enhance our technological position. Indeed, improvements in our general economic climate may have more impact on the state of U.S. technology than many of the specific measures that have been proposed to stimulate technological change.

*6. The Reagan administration pushed through Congress some very large tax cuts in 1981, the idea being to shift the aggregate supply curve to the right.

---

*The starred item refers to material covered in the section, "Exploring Further."

CHAPTER 12

★ ★ ★ ★ ★ ★ ★ ★ ★

Deficits, Public Debt, and the Federal Budget

LEARNING OBJECTIVES

In this chapter, you should learn:

★ The issues concerning a balanced federal budget

★ The significance of the full employment budget

★ The nature of the federal budgetary process

★ The fiscal policies employed by recent American presidents

In the early 1980s the federal deficit—that is, the difference between federal expenditures and federal revenue—exploded. By 1985, it was about $200 billion. This sharp increase in the deficit was financed through government borrowing, which added to the national debt (the amount owed by the federal government). The rise in both the deficit and the debt rekindled the controversy about how government spending should be financed and whether the federal budget should be in balance at all times.

In this chapter we consider under what circumstances the government's budget should or should not be balanced and how the deficit or surplus should be measured. We also discuss how deficits can be financed

and the impact of the national debt.

DEFICIT AND SURPLUS FINANCING

In Chapter 6 we studied the basic elements of fiscal policy. Now let's see how well we would fare with some of the problems that confront our nation's top policy makers.

Case 1: An Imminent Recession

Suppose that, through some inexplicable malfunctioning of the democratic process, you are elected president of the United States. Your Council of Economic Advisers reports to you that, on the basis of various forecasts, national output is likely to drop next year and unemployment is likely to be much higher. Naturally you are concerned; and having absorbed the ideas presented in Chapter 6, you ask your advisers—the Council of Economic Advisers, the Treasury, and the Office of Management and Budget—what sort of fiscal policy should be adopted to head off this undesirable turn of events. On the basis of their advice, you suggest to Congress that taxes should be cut and government expenditures should be increased.

When they receive your message, a number of key congressmen point out that if the government cuts taxes and raises expenditures it will operate in the red. In other words, government revenue will fall short of government spending—there will be a *deficit*. They warn that such fiscal behavior is irresponsible, since it violates the fundamental tenet of public finance that the budget should be balanced. Income should cover outgo. For further clarification on this point, you call in your advisers, who deny that the budget should be balanced each year. They point out that, if a deficit is run in a particular year, the government can borrow the difference; and they claim that the national debt is in no sense dangerously large in the United States at present. Whose advice would you follow: that of your economic advisers or that of the congressmen?

Case 2: Inflationary Signals

Suppose your advisers tell you that inflation is a growing problem and that you should cut back government spending and raise taxes. Since this advice seems sensible, based on the principles set forth in Chapter 6, you propose this course of action to Congress. Some prominent newspapers point out that by raising taxes and cutting expenditures, the government will take in more than it spends. In other words, there will be a *surplus.* They say that there is no reason for the government to take more money from the people than it needs to pay for the services it performs, and they argue that taxes should not be increased because the government can cover its expenditures without such an increase. Whose advice would you follow: that of your economic advisers or that of the newspapers?

What Should You Do?

You would be wise to go along with your economic advisers in both cases. Why? Because for reasons discussed in more detail in the next section, it is not essential or necessarily desirable for the budget to be balanced each year. Although it may well be prudent for individuals and families not to spend more than they earn, this does not carry over to the federal government. When we need to stimulate the economy and raise national output, it is perfectly legitimate and desirable for the federal government to run a deficit, provided it gets its full money's worth for what it spends. Thus in the first case, you should not have been worried by the fact that a deficit would result. And in the second case, while it is true that the government could support its expenditures with lower taxes, this would defeat your purpose. What you want to do is cut total spending, public and private; and raising taxes will cut private spending.

Should the Budget Be Balanced Annually?

At least three policies concerning the government budget are worthy of detailed examination. The first policy says that *the government's budget should be* **balanced** *(that is, revenues should equal expenditures) each and every year.* This is the philosophy that generally prevailed, here and abroad, until a few decades ago. Superficially, it seems reasonable. After all, won't a family or firm go bankrupt if it continues to spend more than it takes in? Why should the government be any different? However, the truth is that the government has economic capabilities, powers, and responsibilities that are entirely different from those of any family or firm, and it is misleading—sometimes even dangerous—to assume that what is sensible for a family or firm is also sensible for the government.

If this policy of balancing the budget is accepted, the government cannot use fiscal policy as a tool to stabilize the economy. Indeed, if the government attempts to balance its budget each year, it is likely to make unemployment or inflation worse rather than better. For example, suppose that severe unemployment occurs because of a drop in national output. Since incomes drop, tax receipts drop as well. Thus if the government attempts to balance its budget, it must cut its spending and/or increase tax rates, both of which will tend to lower, not raise, national output. On the other hand, suppose that inflation occurs because spending increases too rapidly. Since incomes increase, tax receipts increase too. Thus for the government to balance its budget, it must increase its spending and/or decrease tax rates, both of which will tend to raise, not lower, spending.

Despite these considerations, there has been a considerable amount of political support for a constitutional amendment to mandate a balanced federal budget. In large part, this seems to be a reaction to persistent, large deficits which are widely regarded as being inflationary. No doubt the federal government, through inappropriate fiscal or monetary policies, has frequently been responsible for excessive inflation. Some economists go so far as to say that the real problem is how to prevent the government from creating disturbances, rather than how to use the government budget (and monetary policy) to offset disturbances arising from the private sector. But for the reasons discussed above, most economists would not conclude that the government should balance its budget each year.

Should the Budget Be Balanced over the Business Cycle?

A second budgetary philosophy holds that *the government's budget should be balanced over the course of each business cycle.* As we have seen in previous chapters, the rate of growth of national output tends to behave cyclically. It tends to increase for a while, then drop, then increase, then drop. Unemployment also tends to ebb and flow in a similar cyclical fashion. According to this second budgetary policy, the government is not expected to balance its budget each year, but is expected to run a big enough surplus during periods of high employment to offset the deficit it runs during the ensuing period of excessive unemployment. This policy seems to give the government enough flexibility to run the deficits or surpluses needed to stabilize the economy, while at the same time allaying any public fear of a chronically unbalanced budget. It certainly seems to be a neat way to reconcile the government's use of fiscal policy to promote noninflationary full employment with the public's uneasiness over chronically unbalanced budgets.

Unfortunately, however, it does contain one fundamental flaw. There is no reason to believe that the size of the deficits required to eliminate excessive unemployment will equal the size of the surpluses required to moderate the subsequent inflation. Suppose that national output falls sharply, causing severe and prolonged unemployment, then regains its full-employment level only briefly, then falls again. In such a case, the deficits incurred to get the economy back to full employment are likely to far exceed the surpluses run during the brief period of full employment. Thus there would be no way to stabilize the economy without running an unbalanced budget over the course of this business cycle. If this policy were adopted, and if the government attempted to balance the budget over the course of each business cycle, this would interfere with an effective fiscal policy designed to promote full employment with stable prices.

Should We Worry about Balancing the Budget?

Finally, a third budgetary policy says that *the government's budget should be set so as to promote whatever attainable combination of unemployment and inflation seems socially optimal,* even if this means that the budget is unbalanced over considerable periods of time. This policy is sometimes called *functional finance*.[1] Proponents of functional finance point out that, although this policy may mean a continual growth in the public debt, the problems caused by a moderate growth in the public debt are small when compared with the social costs of unemployment and inflation.

Changes in Public Attitudes

Certainly, the history of the past 40 years has been characterized by enormous changes in the nation's attitude toward the government budget. Forty years ago, the prevailing attitude was that the government's budget should be balanced. The emergence of the Keynesian theory of the determination of national output and employment shook this attitude, at least to the point where it became respectable to advocate a balanced budget over the business cycle, rather than in each year. In many circles, functional finance was advocated.

In the late 1970s and early 1980s, there was some movement back toward earlier views favoring balanced budgets. Conservatives emphasized the usefulness of the balanced budget as a device to limit government spending, which they regarded as excessive. The public tended to blame very high rates of inflation on large deficits. Although neither political party was prepared (even remotely) to renounce deficits, considerable lip service was paid to the desirability of a balanced budget.

THE FULL-EMPLOYMENT BUDGET

Some of the misconceptions about budget deficits and surpluses can be avoided by the use of the *full-employment budget*, which shows the difference between tax revenues and government expenditures that would result if we had full employment. For example, in 1958, the Eisenhower administration ran a deficit of about $10 billion—a reasonably large deficit by historical standards. Basically, the reason for this deficit was that with the unemployment rate at about 7 percent, there was a substantial gap between actual and potential output. Net national product fell from 1957 to 1958, and, as a result, incomes and federal tax collections fell, and the government ran a deficit. But this $10 billion deficit was entirely due to the high level of unemployment the country was experiencing.

Had we been at full employment, there would have been a surplus of about $5 billion in 1958. NNP, incomes, and federal tax receipts would all have been higher. Government spending and the tax rates in 1958 were

[1]See Abba Lerner, *Economics of Control,* New York: Macmillan, 1944.

not such as to produce a deficit if full employment had been attained. On the contrary, the full-employment budget shows that, if full employment had prevailed, tax receipts would have increased so that federal revenues would have exceeded expenditures by about $5 billion. It is important to distinguish between the full-employment budget and the actual budget. When, as in 1958, the actual budget shows a deficit but the full-employment budget does not, most economists feel that fiscal policy is not too expansionary, since at full employment the federal government would be running a surplus.

Recognizing these considerations, recent administrations have officially adopted the full-employment budget as their measure of the stabilization impact of the actual budget. As you can see in Figure 12.1, President Nixon ran a full-employment surplus during his first term in office to combat inflation. In 1972, there was a full-employment deficit, but in 1973, and to a greater extent in 1974, there were full-employment surpluses. This is in contrast to the actual budget, which was in deficit in 1975 to

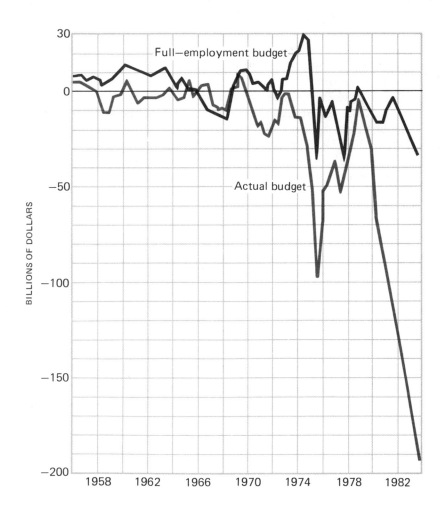

**Figure 12.1
Full-Employment
and Actual Budget
Deficits and
Surpluses, 1956–83**
The full-employment budget shows the difference between tax revenues and government expenditures that would result if there was full employment.

promote recovery from the recession. In subsequent years, President Carter incurred full-employment deficits too (for example, in the recession of 1980).

As you can see in Figure 12.1, the full-employment budget can differ substantially from the actual budget. To understand whether fiscal policy is restrictive or stimulative, you must understand the difference.

EFFECTS OF HOW A DEFICIT IS FINANCED, OR HOW A SURPLUS IS USED

Before leaving the topic of budget deficits and surpluses, it is important to note that the effect of a deficit may depend on how it is financed, as well as on its size. One way for the government to finance a deficit is *to borrow from consumers and business firms.* (Such borrowing results in increases in the national debt.) When the government borrows from consumers and business firms, it takes funds from them that might otherwise be spent on consumption or investment goods. Thus some of the expansionary effect of a budget deficit may be offset by reduced private spending, if a deficit is financed by borrowing from the public.[2]

A second way for the government to finance a budget deficit is *to create new money.* For example, the government can simply print additional money to meet the deficit. (A similar result may be obtained if the government borrows from the central bank, the Federal Reserve in the United States.) When the government spends newly created money, it does not use funds that might otherwise be spent by the private sector. Consequently, *the expansionary effects of a deficit may be greater if it is financed by the creation of new money than if it is financed by borrowing from the public.*

Similarly, the effect of a surplus may depend on how it is used, as well as on its size. One way that the government can use a surplus is *to buy back some of its bonds from the public.* (Such purchases reduce the national debt.) When the government buys back some of its bonds, it provides the sellers of the bonds (consumers and firms) with additional spendable funds. Thus some of the anti-inflationary effects of a surplus may be offset by additional private spending.

Another way that the government can use a surplus is to *impound the funds,* that is, keep the funds idle. Since this latter use of the surplus does not provide the private sector with additional spendable funds, there is no such offset to the surplus's anti-inflationary effect. Consequently, *the anti-inflationary effects of a surplus may be greater if the surplus is impounded than if it is used to reduce the national debt.*

---

[2]A deficit financed by borrowing from the public tends to increase interest rates, which is likely to reduce investment and possibly shift the consumption function downward. This will reduce the net increase in spending due to the increase in government expenditures. In other words, the increase in interest rates will reduce private spending.

GOVERNMENT DEBT

The National Debt: Size and Growth

No subject in economics has more confused the public than the national debt. When the federal government spends more than it receives in taxes, it borrows money to cover the difference. The *national debt*—composed of bonds, notes, and other government IOUs of various kinds—is the result of such borrowing. These IOUs are held by individuals, firms, banks, and public agencies both domestic and foreign. There is a large and very

CASE STUDY 12.1 SHOULD EISENHOWER HAVE TRIED TO BALANCE THE BUDGET?

1958 was a recession year in the United States. Tax revenues declined. Unemployment compensation payments rose. The budget deficit for the year approached $10 billion. The large deficit helped to get the recovery going, but when the recession was over President Eisenhower set out to recoup his losses by balancing the budget. As the president forged ahead with his plan for a budget surplus, voices were raised in warning. Some of these warnings came from a group of top business executives, the Committee for Economic Development.

Another person urging caution in the drive for a big surplus was Vice President Richard Nixon. During the recession of 1958, Nixon had urged a tax cut to stimulate the economy. His advice was not heeded. Now, as he prepared to run for president in 1960, he urged a more expansionary budget policy. Again his advice was rejected because the administration was more concerned about fighting inflation. Eisenhower in his last year in office was willing to take the political risk of pinching off growth. He assumed that the next administration would be able to carry on with the expansionary policy—a next administration that was expected to be Republican.

By the summer of 1960, the recovery had ground to a halt, stopping well short of the goal of full employment. As the ranks of the jobless increased, Democratic presidential candidate John Kennedy was helped politically, while Richard Nixon watched the economy slide back into recession and victory slip through his fingers. Historians still argue whether it was the budget surplus and the unexpected recession that cost him the victory; but most economists agree that a budget deficit in 1960 would have generated more jobs and more growth in the economy.

N. B.

important market for government securities, which are relatively riskless and highly liquid. If you look at the *New York Times* or *Wall Street Journal*, for example, you can find each day the prices at which each of a large number of issues of these bonds, notes, and bills are quoted.

How large is the national debt? In 1984, as shown in Figure 12.2, it was about $1.6 trillion. This certainly seems to be a large amount, but it is important to relate the size of the national debt to the size of our national output. After all, a $1.6-trillion debt means one thing if our annual output is $2 trillion, and another thing if our annual output is $200 billion. As a percentage of output, the national debt is smaller now than in 1939, and no larger now than shortly after the Civil War. In 1984, the debt was about 40 percent of output; in 1939, it was about 50 percent of output; and in 1868, it was about 40 percent of output. The debt—expressed as a percent-

**Figure 12.2
Size of the
National Debt,
United States,
1929–84**
The national debt is
currently over
$1 trillion.

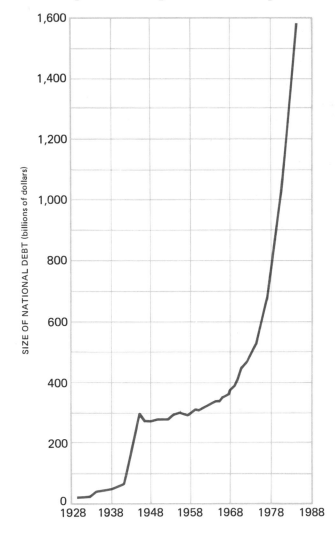

Figure 12.3
National Debt as a
Percent of
National Output,
United States,
1929–84
As a percent of
national output, the
national debt was
smaller in 1984 than
in 1939.

age of output—is shown in Figure 12.3. Surely the figures do not seem to provide any cause for immediate alarm.[3] (However, many economists have warned that there are problems in incurring the large deficits that were responsible for the rapid rate of increase in the national debt during the 1980s. For example, see Case Study 12.2.)

A Burden on Future Generations?

Why has the public has been so agitated about the debt's size? One important reason has been that they have felt that the debt was a burden that was being thrust on future generations. To evaluate this idea it is important to recognize that a public debt is not like your debt or mine, which must be paid off at a certain time in the future. In practice, new government debt is issued by the government to pay off maturing public debt. There never comes a time when we must collectively reach into our pockets to pay off the debt. And even if we did pay it off, the same generation would collect as the one that paid.

Effects of Externally Held Debt

Of course, this does not mean that the debt is of no economic consequence. On the contrary, to the extent that the debt is held by foreigners, we must send goods and services overseas to pay the interest on it. This means that fewer goods and services are available for our citizens. Thus if we finance a particular government activity by borrowing from foreigners, the costs may be transferred to future generations, since they must pay the interest. But from the point of view of the world as a whole, the

---

[3]Note too that much of the public debt is in the hands of government agencies, not held by the public. For example, in 1984, only about $1 trillion was held by private investors.

current generation sacrifices goods and services, since the lending country forgoes current goods and services. Also, it must be recognized that if the debt is incurred to purchase capital goods, they may produce enough extra output to cover the interest payments.

Effects of Internally Held Debt

Even if the debt is internally held, it may have some undesirable effects. Taxes must be collected from the public to pay interest to the holders of the government bonds, notes, and other obligations. To the extent that the bondholders receiving the interest are wealthier than the public as a whole, there is some redistribution of income from the poor to the rich. To the extent that the taxes needed to obtain the money to pay interest on the debt reduce incentives, the result also may be a smaller national output.

A final word should be added about the idea that the national debt imposes a burden on future generations. *The principal way in which one generation can impose such a burden on another is by using up some of the country's productive capacity or by failing to add a normal increment to this capacity.* This, of course, is quite different from incurring debt. For example, World War II would have imposed a burden on subsequent generations whether or not the national debt was increased. However it was financed, the war would have meant that our resources had to be used for tanks and war planes rather than for keeping up and expanding our productive capacity during 1941–45. And this imposed a burden, a real burden, on Americans living after 1945—as well, of course, as on those living during the war.

The Federal Budgetary Process

Determining how much the federal government should spend is a mammoth undertaking, involving literally thousands of people and hundreds of thousands of man-hours. Decisions on expenditures are part of the budgetary process. The *federal budget* is a statement of the government's anticipated expenditures and revenues. The federal budget is for a fiscal year, from October 1 to September 30.

About 15 months before the beginning of a particular fiscal year, the various agencies of the federal government begin to prepare their program proposals for that year. Then they make detailed budget requests which the president, with his Office of Management and Budget, goes over. Since the agencies generally want more than the president wants to spend, he usually cuts down their requests.

In January (preceding the beginning of the fiscal year), the president submits his budget to Congress. Congress then spends several months in intensive deliberation and negotiation. Congressional committees con-

CASE STUDY 12.2 MARTIN FELDSTEIN VERSUS DONALD REGAN

In early 1984, unemployment was receding, sales and profits were rising substantially, and inflation remained at moderate levels. Yet President Reagan's economic advisers were engaged in a public debate that reached the front pages of the nation's newspapers and magazines. What was the fracas about? The huge and growing federal deficit.

The projected 1984 deficit was estimated to be about $200 billion; and by the Reagan administration's own projections, the cumulative deficits from 1984 through 1989 were expected to total a whopping $1 trillion. According to Martin Feldstein, chairman of President Reagan's Council of Economic Advisers, these deficits were very dangerous to the long-term health of the American economy. If they were allowed to occur, they would push up interest rates and result in a crowding out of private investment on plant and equipment. Also, U.S. exports would be hurt, because high U.S. interest rates would push up the value of the dollar relative to other currencies, thus making our exports more expensive to foreign purchasers.

Martin
Feldstein

Donald
Regan

In contrast, Donald Regan, who in 1984 was Secretary of the Treasury, played down the importance of the deficit. In his view, deficits do not push up interest rates and they did not result in an overvaluation of the dollar relative to other currencies. In part, his arguments seemed to be based on studies carried out by some supply-side economists, including members of the Treasury staff. But most economists did not buy these arguments. If the government increases its demands for credit because of very large deficits, the interest rate (the price of borrowing money) will rise.

The contrast between the two combatants, as well as the acidity of the squabble, fascinated news commentators as well as the general public. Feldstein, the whistle blower, was a highly respected economics professor on leave from Harvard University, and a former president of the National Bureau of Economic Research. Regan, the defender of the president's program, was the former head of Merrill Lynch, the huge brokerage firm, and one of the leading lights on Wall Street. Many observers were surprised that the president allowed it to continue so openly for so long. Finally, in the summer of 1984, Feldstein resigned his post and returned to Harvard. Regan remained in the second Reagan administration and in 1985 was given the key job as White House Chief of Staff.

cerned with particular areas like defense or education recommend changes in the president's budget. The Congressional Budget Office, headed in 1985 by Rudolph Penner, makes various economic analyses to help senators and representatives evaluate alternative programs. By mid-May, Congress is supposed to pass a resolution setting tentative targets for overall spending and revenues; this resolution is based on the joint recommendations by the House and Senate Budget Committees. The targets in the resolution are to be kept in mind by the various congressional committees dealing with specific spending or tax actions. If these actions add up to bigger totals than the resolution called for, the budget committees and Congress are supposed to decide how the discrepancies are to be reconciled: by changes in expenditures, taxes, or initial targets. Before late September, Congress is supposed to adopt a second resolution, setting final ceilings for overall expenditure and a floor on revenues.[5]

The Federal Tax Legislative Process

It is one thing for the federal government to decide how much to spend and on what; it is another to raise the money to underwrite these programs. This section describes how the federal government decides how much to tax. Of course, this problem is not solved from scratch every year. Instead, the government takes the existing tax structure and changes it from time to time as desirable. Frequently the major initiative leading to a change in the tax laws comes from the president, who requests tax changes in his State of the Union message, his budget message, or a special tax message. (For example, in January 1985 President Reagan announced a proposal for tax simplification.) Much of the spadework underlying his proposals will have been carried out by the Treasury Department, particularly the Treasury's Office of Tax Analysis, Office of the Tax Legislative Counsel, and Internal Revenue Service.

The proposal of a major tax change generally brings about considerable public debate. Representatives of labor, industry, agriculture, and other economic and social groups present their opinions. Newspaper articles, radio shows, and television commentators analyze the issues. By the time Congress begins to look seriously at the proposal, the battle lines between those who favor the change and those who oppose it are generally clearly drawn. The tax bill incorporating the change is first considered by the Ways and Means Committee of the House of Representatives, a very powerful committee composed of members drawn from both political parties. After public hearings, the committee goes into executive session and reviews each proposed change with its staff and with the Treasury staff. After careful study, the committee arrives at a bill it recommends— though this bill may or may not conform to what the president asked for. Then the bill is referred to the entire House of Representatives for ap-

[5]However, it should not be assumed that this process necessarily works according to schedule. For example, in 1981, the second budget resolution was not passed until December by Congress.

proval. Only rarely is a major tax bill recommended by the committee turned down by the House.

Next, the bill is sent to the Senate. There it is referred to the Finance Committee, which is organized like the House Ways and Means Committee. The Finance Committee also holds hearings, discusses the bill at length, makes changes in it, and sends its version of the bill to the entire Senate, where there frequently is considerable debate. Ultimately, it is brought to a vote. If it does not pass, that ends the process. If it does pass (and if it differs from the House version of the bill, which is generally the case), then a conference committee must be formed to iron out the differences between the House and Senate versions. Finally, when this compromise is worked out, the result must be passed by both houses and sent to the president. The president rarely vetoes a tax bill, although it has occasionally been done.

RECENT AMERICAN EXPERIENCE WITH FISCAL POLICY AND DEFICITS

It should be evident by now that much more is known today about the impact of deficits—and of fiscal policy generally—than at the time when the economy was staggered by the Great Depression. But this does not mean that economists have all (or nearly all) the answers. Enough is known to keep the economy from careening off a bumpy road; avoiding the potholes (some of which are very large) is another matter.

The Nixon Years

The hard choices faced by economists in the top councils of government can be demonstrated by a close inspection of recent attempts to give the economy a smoother ride. Let's begin with the situation in the late 1960s, when there was mounting inflation due partly to government spending on the Vietnam War. During 1969 and 1970, the Nixon administration restricted government expenditures and tried to run a surplus. Yet despite the administration's efforts, the rate of inflation was not decreasing as fast as desired. Between 1969 and 1970, the index of consumer prices rose by about 6 percent. During the first half of 1971, it rose at an annual rate of about 4½ percent. Although this was an improvement, the inflationary process was proving difficult to quell.

In August 1971, the Nixon administration, reversing its previous attitudes, established controls on wages, prices, and rents. This was the first time that such controls had been adopted by an American government in peacetime. At the same time, the administration switched to a more expansionary fiscal policy in order to reduce the relatively high level of unemployment. Specifically, the president called for a tax reduction of about $7 or $8 billion. Included in his tax package was an investment tax credit, which encouraged investment by business firms, as well as a reduction in personal income taxes. By late 1972, the unemployment rate was down to 5½ percent, and the rate of inflation declined to about 3 percent during the year.

After his re-election in November 1972, President Nixon phased out the wage and price controls he had imposed in 1971. Inflation, which never had been quelled, increased after the phaseout of the controls, and during early 1973 the economy was in the midst of a boom. In June 1973, the president imposed another price freeze, this time for 60 days. Then he instituted a program that attempted to limit price increases to an amount equal to cost increases. This program was largely ineffectual, and was phased out in 1974.

The Ford Years

In early 1974, the price of foreign oil was increased very substantially by the OPEC countries. This price increase, as well as considerable increases in farm prices, spearheaded a bewildering inflationary spurt. During 1974, consumer prices rose by about 12 percent! From the point of view of inflation, this was the worst year in decades. At the same time, the nation's real output fell as the economy dropped into the most serious recession since World War II. The result was a marked increase in unemployment. By March 1975, the unemployment rate was 8.7 percent, as compared with 4.9 percent in December 1973.

Faced with a combination of excessive unemployment and excessive inflation, President Ford proposed a $16 billion tax cut, and Congress passed a $23 billion tax cut in March 1975. The economy began to revive in mid-1975, and unemployment fell from 8.7 percent in March 1975 to 7.5 percent in March 1976. However, stagflation was by no means vanquished. On the contrary, both unemployment and inflation continued to be excessive.

The Carter Years

In 1977, the federal government ran a deficit of about $50 billion; the full-employment deficit was about $20 billion. And in January 1978, President Carter proposed personal tax reductions of $24 billion. But during 1978, the rate of inflation increased sharply, and approached double-digit levels. Since the inflation rate was higher than expected, the Carter administration scaled back its proposed tax cut to $20 billion, and the Congress actually passed a $19 billion tax cut. (About $14 billion of this tax cut went to individuals, the rest to corporations.)

In the face of heightened inflation, fiscal policy did not attempt to rein in the economy very much. The deficit in 1978 was about $30 billion; the full-employment deficit was over $10 billion. Some observers were not sure that the inflation rate could be reduced substantially without a recession. In 1979, there was a continuing debate within the administration and in public over this question. In 1980, there was a very brief recession, but it did little to cool off inflation. As in previous years, the federal government ran a full-employment deficit.

The Reagan Years

When the Reagan administration took office in 1981, it was committed to cut both government expenditures and taxes. In August 1981, the administration pushed through Congress a huge tax cut for both individuals and businesses. At the same time, it reduced federal expenditures (relative to the level that former president Carter had proposed). However, the tax cuts were far in excess of the spending cuts, particularly since reductions in GNP in late 1981 also tended to reduce tax receipts. Thus the administration was faced with record deficits of over $100 billion in fiscal 1982 and $150 billion in fiscal 1983. In early 1982, President Reagan said he would try to cut spending further in an attempt to soak up some of the red ink. But the economy was in a recession (with an unemployment rate of 9 percent) and there was little sympathy on Capitol Hill for further spending cuts. Since inflation had fallen to well under double digits, unemployment once again seemed to be Public Enemy Number One.

In November 1982, the economy pulled out of the recession, and the expansion began. Economists of all schools, but particularly supply-side economists (recall Chapter 11), gave the 1981 tax cut considerable credit for increasing real NNP and reducing unemployment. During 1983 and 1984, both years of healthy expansion, the federal government ran huge deficits of about $200 billion. President Reagan vowed that he would not raise taxes, and proposed cuts in nonmilitary government expenditures. In December 1985, a bill mandating that the budget be balanced in annual steps over the next five years was passed, but there were doubts about its effectiveness and constitutionality.

Clearly, judging from our recent history, fiscal policy is no panacea. Policy makers are continually confronted with difficult choices, and the tools of fiscal policy, at least as they are currently understood and used, are not sufficient to solve or dispel many of the problems at hand. However, it is important to recognize that fiscal policy is not the only available means by which policy makers attempt to stabilize the economy. There is also monetary policy, which we discussed in detail in Chapter 9. A sensible fiscal policy can be formulated only in conjunction with monetary policy, and although it is convenient to discuss them separately, in real life they must be coordinated. Also, lest you become overly pessimistic, you should note that despite the problems that remain unsolved, our improved understanding of fiscal and monetary policy has enabled us to steer a better and more stable course than in the days before World War II. So far at least, bouts of severe unemployment and double-digit inflation seem to have been moderated by government action, imperfect though such action may have been.

SUMMARY

1. At least three policies concerning the government budget have had serious proponents. First, the budget should be balanced each and every year. Second, the budget should be balanced over the course of the business cycle. Third, the budget should be set in a way that will promote full employment with stable prices whether or not this means that the budget is unbalanced over considerable periods of time.

2. The history of the past 40 years has seen enormous changes in the public's attitude toward the federal budget. Forty years ago, the prevailing doctrine was that the budget should be balanced each year. Now (although a balanced budget has more support than a few years ago) the attitude seems to be that the budget should be used as a tool to reduce unemployment and inflation.

3. Some of the popular misconceptions concerning budget deficits and budget surpluses can be avoided by the use of the full-employment budget, which shows the difference between tax revenue and government expenditure that would result if we had full employment. When the actual budget shows a deficit but the full-employment budget does not, most economists feel that fiscal policy is not too expansionary.

4. When the government spends more than it receives in revenues, the government borrows money to cover the difference. It could simply print money for this purpose, but it has chosen to borrow a considerable proportion of what has been needed. The resulting debt is often called the national debt.

5. Despite public worry over the size of the national debt, as a percentage of national output it is lower now than in 1939. There are important differences between government debt and private debt. Although the size of the debt is certainly of consequence, it is not true that it somehow leads to bankruptcy.

6. The spending decisions of the federal government take place in the context of the budgetary process. The president submits his budget, which is a statement of anticipated expenditures and revenues, to Congress, which votes appropriations. The Ways and Means Committee of the House of Representatives and the Senate Finance Committee play important roles in the federal tax legislative process.

CHAPTER 13

★ ★ ★ ★ ★ ★ ★ ★ ★

Monetary Policy, Interest Rates, and Economic Activity

LEARNING OBJECTIVES

In this chapter, you should learn:

★ How the quantity of money affects national output

★ The relation between the interest rate and the quantity of money

★ The importance and the limitations of the crude quantity theory

★ The Fed's performance in managing the money supply

In previous chapters we discussed in general terms the impact of money on the economy. In this chapter we give a more detailed picture of how changes in the quantity of money affect interest rates and economic activity. We also consider how effective monetary policy has been in recent years. In particular, we consider questions like: What determines the value of money? What factors influence the demand for money, and what factors influence its quantity? What is the relationship between the quantity of money and the price level? What is the relationship between the quantity of money and the level of net national product? To more fully understand the workings of our economy and the nature of our government's economic policies, you must be able to answer these questions.

THE VALUE OF MONEY

Let's go back to one very important point that was mentioned briefly in Chapter 8. There is no gold backing for our money. In other words, there is no way that you can exchange a $10 bill for so many ounces of gold. (If you look at a $10 bill, you will see that it says nothing about what the government will give you in exchange for it.) Currency and demand (and other checkable) deposits are really just debts or IOUs. Currency is the debt of the government, while demand deposits are the debts of the banks. Intrinsically, neither currency nor deposits has any real value. A $10 bill is merely a small piece of paper, and a deposit is merely an entry in a bank's accounts. And, as we have seen, even coins are worth far less as metal than their monetary value.

All this may make you feel a bit uncomfortable. After all, if our coins, currency, demand deposits, and other checkable deposits have little or no intrinsic value, doesn't this mean that they can easily become worthless? To answer this question, we must realize that basically, *money has value because people will accept it in payment for goods and services.* If your college will accept your check in payment for your tuition, and your grocer will accept a $20 bill in payment for your groceries, your demand deposit and your currency have value. You can exchange them for goods and services you want. And your university or your grocer accepts this money only because they have confidence that they can spend it for goods and services they want.

Money's Value Depends on the Price Level

Thus money is valuable because it will buy things. But how valuable is it? For example, how valuable is $1? Clearly, *the value of a dollar is equivalent to what a dollar will buy. And what a dollar will buy depends on the price level.* If all prices doubled, the value of a dollar would be cut in half, because a dollar would be able to buy only half as many goods and services as it formerly could. On the other hand, if all prices were reduced by 50 percent, the value of a dollar would double, because a dollar would be able to buy twice as many goods and services as it formerly could. You often hear people say that today's dollar is worth only $.50. What they mean is that it will buy only half of what a dollar could buy at some specified date in the past.

It is interesting and important to see how the value of the dollar, as measured by its purchasing power, has varied over time. Figure 13.1 shows how an index of the price level in the United States has changed since 1779. Over time, prices have fluctuated sharply, and the greatest fluctuations have resulted from wars. For example, the price level fell sharply after the Revolutionary War, and our next war—the War of 1812 —sent prices skyrocketing, after which there was another postwar drop in

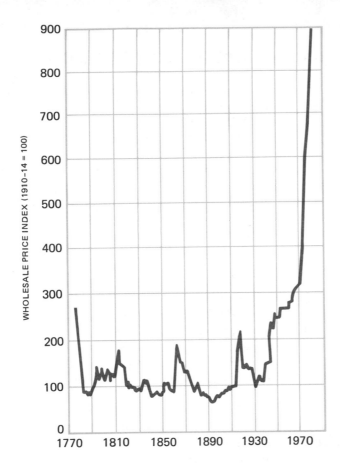

Figure 13.1
**Index of
Wholesale Prices,
United States,
1779–1984
(1910–14 = 100)**
The price level has
fluctuated
considerably, sharp
increases generally
occurring during
wars. Since World
War II, the price
level has tended to
go only one way—
up. In the past 20
years, the price
level has more than
tripled.

prices. The period from about 1820 to about 1860 was marked by relative
price stability, but the Civil War resulted in an upward burst followed by
a postwar drop in prices. After a period of relative price stability from
1875 to 1915, there was a doubling of prices during World War I and the
usual postwar drop. World War II saw a price increase of about 40 percent,
but there was no postwar drop in prices. Instead there has been a very
sharp inflation; during the past 20 years, the price level has more than
tripled.

The value of money is inversely related to the price level. In inflationary
times, the value of money decreases; the opposite is true when the price
level falls (an infrequent phenomenon in the past three decades). Thus the
wartime periods when the price level rose greatly were periods when the
value of the dollar decreased greatly. The doubling of prices during World
War I meant that the value of the dollar was chopped in half. Similarly,
the postwar periods when the price level fell greatly were periods when
the value of the dollar increased. The 50 percent decline in prices after
the Civil War meant a doubling in the value of the dollar. Given the extent
of the variation of the price level shown in Figure 13.1, it is clear that the
value of the dollar has varied enormously during our history.

INFLATION AND THE QUANTITY OF MONEY

If the value of money is reduced in periods of inflation, its value can be largely wiped out in periods of runaway inflation, as in Germany after World War I. (Recall Chapter 7.) Our own country suffered from runaway inflations during the Revolutionary War and the Civil War. You may have heard the expression that something is "not worth a continental." It comes from the fact that the inflated dollars in use during the Revolutionary War were called continentals.

Generally, such severe inflations have occurred because the government increased the money supply at an enormously rapid rate. It is not hard to see why a tremendous increase in the quantity of money will result in a runaway inflation. Other things held constant, increases in the quantity of money will result in increases in total intended spending, and once full employment is achieved, such increases in intended spending will cause more and more inflation.

Eventually, when the inflation is severe enough, households and businesses may refuse to accept money for goods and services because they fear that it will depreciate significantly before they have a chance to spend it. Instead, they may insist on being paid in merchandise or services. Thus the economy will turn to barter, with the accompanying inconveniences and inefficiency.

To prevent such an economic catastrophe, the government must manage the money supply responsibly. If the value of money depends basically on the public's willingness to accept it, then the public's willingness to accept it depends on money's being reasonably stable in value. If the government increases the quantity of money at a rapid rate, thus causing a severe inflation and an accompanying precipitous fall in the value of money, public confidence in money will be shaken, and the value of money will be destroyed. The moral is clear: *the government must restrict the quantity of money and conduct its economic policies so as to maintain a reasonably stable value of money.*

UNEMPLOYMENT AND THE QUANTITY OF MONEY

In the previous section, we were concerned primarily with what happens when the quantity of money grows too rapidly. The result is inflation. But this is only part of the story. The quantity of money can grow too slowly as well as too rapidly. When this happens the result is increased unemployment. If the money supply grows very slowly, or decreases, there will be a tendency for total intended spending to grow very slowly or decrease. This in turn will cause national output to grow very slowly or decrease, thus causing unemployment to increase. The result will be the social waste and human misery associated with excessive unemployment.

According to many economists, the recession of 1974–75 was due partly to an inadequate growth of the money supply. The Federal Reserve, trying to stem the inflationary tide in 1974, cut back on the rate of increase of the money supply. Looking back over past business fluctuations, it appears that an inadequate rate of increase in the quantity of money was responsible, at least in part, for many recessions. According to Harvard economist James Duesenberry: "Every major depression has been accompanied by a substantial decline in the money supply, and often by a complete collapse of the banking system. Among the many causes responsible for our major depressions, money and banking difficulties have always been prominent."[1]

DETERMINANTS OF THE QUANTITY OF MONEY

Judging from our discussion thus far, it is clear that, to avoid excessive unemployment or excessive inflation, the quantity of money must not grow too slowly or too fast. But what determines the quantity of money? To a considerable extent, it is determined by the Federal Reserve, which, as we have noted before, is our nation's central bank. Within limits, the Federal Reserve can and does control the quantity of money. But to some extent the private sector of the economy also determines the quantity of money. For example, the nation's commercial banks, through their lending (and other) decisions, can influence the money supply.[2] In the remainder of this chapter, we shall make the simplifying assumption that the money supply is governed solely by the Federal Reserve.

THE DEMAND FOR MONEY

We have discussed in general terms how changes in the quantity of money affect the tempo of economic activity. Now let's look in detail at how changes in the quantity of money affect net national product. The first step in doing this is to discuss the demand for money. Why does a family or firm want to hold money? Certainly, a family can be wealthy without holding much money. We all know stories about very rich people who hold very little money, since virtually all of their wealth is tied up in factories, farms, and other nonmonetary assets. Unlike assets that yield profits or interest, money produces no direct return; so why do people and firms want to hold money rather than other kinds of assets? Two of the most important reasons are the following.

[1] J. Duesenberry, *Money and Credit: Impact and Control,* Englewood Cliffs, N.J.: Prentice-Hall, 1972, p 3.
[2] Of course, banks do not create money all by themselves. The public's preferences and actions, as well as bank behavior, influence the amount of demand deposits. Also, commercial banks may not be as unique in this respect as it appears at first sight. See James Tobin, "Commercial Banks as Creators of Money," in R. Teigen, ed., *Readings in Money, National Income, and Stabilization Policy,* 4th ed., Homewood, Ill.: Irwin, 1978.

TRANSACTIONS DEMAND FOR MONEY. To carry out most transactions, money is required. People and firms like to keep some money on their person and in their checking accounts to buy things. The higher a person's income—in dollars, not real terms—the more money he or she will want to hold for transactions purposes. For example, in 1985, when a doctor made perhaps $90,000 a year, the average physician would want to keep more money on hand for transactions purposes than in the days, many years before, when a doctor made perhaps $10,000 a year. Because the quantity of money demanded by a household or firm increases with its income, it follows that the total quantity of money demanded for transactions purposes in the economy as a whole is directly related to net national product. That is, the higher (lower) the level of NNP, the greater (less) the quantity of money demanded for transactions purposes.

PRECAUTIONARY DEMAND FOR MONEY. Besides the transactions motive, households and firms like to hold money because they are uncertain concerning the timing and size of future disbursements and receipts. Unpredictable events often require money. People get sick, and houses need repairs. Also, receipts frequently do not come in exactly when expected. To meet such contingencies, people and firms like to put a certain amount of their wealth into money and near-money. In the economy as a whole, the total quantity of money demanded for precautionary purposes (like the quantity demanded for transactions purposes) is likely to vary directly with NNP. If NNP goes up, households and firms will want to hold more money for precautionary purposes, because their incomes and sales will be higher than before the increase in NNP.[3]

The Interest Rate and the Demand Curve for Money

Up to this point, we have discussed why individuals and firms want to hold money. But we must recognize that there are disadvantages, as well as advantages, in holding money. One disadvantage is that the real value of money will fall if inflation occurs. Another is that an important cost of holding money is the interest or profit one loses, since instead of holding money one might have invested it in assets that would have yielded interest or profit. For example, the annual cost of holding $5,000 in money if one can obtain 6 percent on existing investments, is $300, the amount of interest or profit forgone.

With NNP constant, the amount of money demanded by individuals and

---

[3]Still another motive for holding money is the speculative motive. People like to hold some of their assets in a form in which they can be sure of its monetary value and can take advantage of future price reductions. The amount of money individuals and firms will keep on hand for speculative reasons will vary with their expectations concerning future price movements. In particular, if people feel that the prices of bonds and stocks are about to drop soon, they are likely to demand a great deal of money for speculative reasons. By holding money, they can obtain such securities at lower prices than at present.

firms is *inversely* related to the interest rate. *The higher the interest rate, the smaller the amount of money demanded. The lower the interest rate, the greater the amount of money demanded.* This is because the cost of holding money increases as the interest rate or yield on existing investments increases. For example, if the interest rate were 7 percent rather than 6 percent, the cost of holding $5,000 in money for one year would be $350 rather than $300. Thus as the interest rate or profit rate increases, people try harder to minimize the amount of money they hold. So do firms. Big corporations like General Motors or U.S. Steel are very conscious of the cost of holding cash balances.

Figure 13.2 summarizes two important conclusions of our discussion in this and the previous section. Panel A of Figure 13.2 shows that, *holding the interest rate constant, the quantity of money demanded is directly related to NNP.* The higher (lower) the level of NNP, the greater (less) the quantity of money demanded. Panel B of Figure 13.2 shows that, *with NNP constant, the quantity of money demanded is inversely related to the interest rate.*[4] This latter relationship, described in this section, is called the *demand curve for money*.

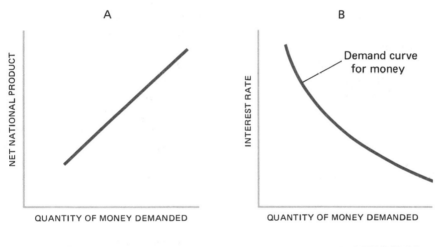

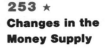

Figure 13.2
The Demand for Money
Holding the interest rate constant, the quantity of money demanded is directly related to NNP, as shown in panel A. Holding NNP constant, the quantity of money demanded is inversely related to the interest rate, as shown in panel B. The latter relationship is known as the demand curve for money.

CHANGES IN THE MONEY SUPPLY AND NATIONAL OUTPUT

Effects of an Increase in the Money Supply: The Keynesian Model

Now that we have investigated the demand for money, we are ready to show how changes in the quantity of money influence the value of NNP.

[4]However, this relationship between the quantity of money and the interest rate is only in the short run. In the long run, increases in the money supply, if they result in increased inflation, may *raise* interest rates, because lenders will require a greater return to offset the greater rate of depreciation of the real value of the dollar. Still, however, the real rate of interest—the rate of interest adjusted for inflation—may decline.

Given the demand curve for money, it is a simple matter to show how the money supply can be inserted into the Keynesian model (in Chapters 5 and 6) aimed at explaining the level of NNP. The results of our analysis will provide an important underpinning for, and link to, our earlier discussions of monetary policy.

To begin with, let's trace the effects of an increase in the money supply from $200 billion to $250 billion. If the demand curve for money is as shown in panel A of Figure 13.3, the result will be a *decrease in the interest rate* from 8 percent to 6 percent. Why? Because if the interest rate is 8 percent, people will demand only $200 billion of money, not the $250 billion that is supplied. Having more money on hand than they want, they will invest the excess in bonds, stocks, and other financial assets, with the result that the price of bonds, stocks, and other financial assets will rise.[5] *Such a rise in the price of bonds is equivalent to a fall in the rate of interest.* (To see why, suppose that a very long-term bond pays interest of $300 per year. If the price of the bond is $3,000, the interest rate on the bond is 10 percent. If the price of the bond rises to $4,000, the interest rate on the bond falls to 7½ percent. The increase in price amounts to a reduction in the interest rate.) When the interest rate has fallen to 6 percent, people will be willing to hold the $250 billion in money. At this interest rate, the quantity of money demanded will equal the quantity of money supplied.

The decrease in the interest rate from 8 percent to 6 percent affects the investment function (which is the relationship between investment and NNP).[6] Recall from Chapter 5 that the level of investment is inversely related to the interest rate. Because it is less costly to invest—and because credit is more readily available[7]—*the investment function will shift upward,* as shown in panel B of Figure 13.3. This occurs because, at each level of net national product, firms will want to invest more, since investment is more profitable (because of the cuts in the interest rate) and funds are more readily available.[8]

---

[5]For simplicity, we assume that when people have excess money balances they use the money to buy financial assets. (In the next section, we assume that when people have smaller money balances than they want, they sell financial assets to get more money.) A more complete analysis is provided in E. Mansfield, *Economics: Principles, Problems, Decisions,* 5th ed., Chap. 15.

[6]Changes in the money supply, interest rates, and credit availability affect the consumption function and government spending, as well as the investment function. For example, *increases (decreases) in interest rates shift the consumption function and the level of government spending downward (upward).* These factors augment the effect of monetary policy described in the text. We focus attention on the investment function in Figures 13.3 and 13.4 merely because this simplifies the exposition.

[7]Note that it is not just a matter of interest rates. Availability of credit is also important. In times when money is tight, some potential borrowers may find that they cannot get a loan, regardless of what interest rate they are prepared to pay. In times when money is easy, people who otherwise might find it difficult to get a loan may be granted one by the banks. Both availability and interest rates are important.

[8]Many firms depend to a considerable extent on retained earnings to finance their investment projects. Thus since they do not borrow externally, the effect of changes in interest rates and credit availability on their investment plans may be reduced. However, since

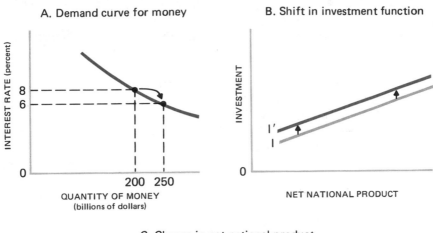

A. Demand curve for money

B. Shift in investment function

Figure 13.3
Effect of an Increase in the Money Supply
If the money supply increases from $200 billion to $250 billion, the interest rate drops from 8 percent to 6 percent (panel A). Because of the decrease in the interest rate, the investment function shifts upward (panel B) and the equilibrium level of NNP increases from D to E (panel C).

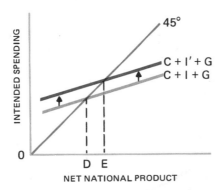

C. Change in net national product

This shift in the investment function then affects the equilibrium level of net national product. As shown in panel C of Figure 13.3, *the equilibrium level of net national product will increase* from *D* to *E*, in accord with the principles discussed in Chapter 6. (Recall that the equilibrium value of NNP is at the point where the *C + I + G* line intersects the 45-degree line.) Thus *the effect of the increase in the money supply is to increase net national product.*

This, in simplified fashion, is how an increase in the money supply affects NNP, according to the Keynesian model.[9] To summarize, *the increase in the money supply results in a reduction in the interest rate, which results in an increase in investment, which results in an increase in NNP.* Obviously, this theory is of great importance in helping us to understand more completely why our economy behaves the way it does. For example, we can now understand better why vast increases in the quantity of money will result in runaway inflation. NNP (in money terms) will be pushed upward at a very rapid rate, driving the price level out of sight.

---

changes in the interest rate reflect changes in the opportunity cost of using funds to finance investment projects, they still may have an appreciable effect on the investment function.
[9]The alert reader will recognize that the increase in NNP in panel C will shift the demand curve for money in panel A of Figure 13.3. For simplicity, we ignore this feedback.

Effects of a Decrease in the Money Supply: The Keynesian Model

Next, let's trace the effects of a decrease in the money supply from $200 billion to $160 billion. If the demand curve for money is as shown in panel A of Figure 13.4, the result will be an *increase in the interest rate* from 8 percent to 10 percent. Why? Because if the interest rate is 8 percent, people will demand $200 billion in money, not the $160 billion that is supplied. Having less money on hand than they want, they will sell some of their bonds, stocks, and other financial assets to build up their money balances, with the result that the prices of bonds, stocks, and other financial assets will fall. *Such a fall in the price of bonds is equivalent to a rise in the rate of interest.* (To see why, suppose that a very long-term bond pays interest of $300 per year. If the price of the bond is $3,000, the interest rate on the bond is 10 percent. If the price of the bond falls to $2,400, the interest rate on the bond is 12½ percent. Thus the fall in price amounts to an increase in the interest rate.) When the interest rate has

**Figure 13.4
Effect of a
Decrease in the
Money Supply**
If the money supply
decreases from
$200 billion to $160
billion, the interest
rate increases from
8 percent to 10
percent (panel A).
Because of the
increase in the
interest rate, the
investment function
shifts downward
(panel B) and the
equilibrium level of
NNP decreases
from *D* to *F*
(panel C).

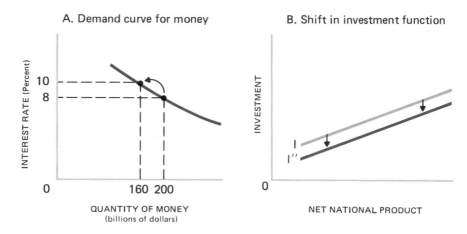

A. Demand curve for money

B. Shift in investment function

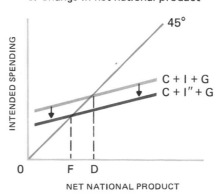

C. Change in net national product

increased to 10 percent, people will be willing to hold only the $160 billion in money. At this interest rate, the quantity of money demanded will equal the quantity of money supplied.

The increase in the interest rate from 8 percent to 10 percent affects the investment function. Because it is more costly for firms to invest—and more difficult to obtain credit—*the investment function will shift downward,* as shown in panel B of Figure 13.4. This shift occurs because, at every level of net national product, firms want to invest less. The reasons why an increase in the interest rate reduces investment were given in Chapter 5.

This downward shift in the investment function has an effect in turn on the equilibrium level of net national product. As shown in panel C of Figure 13.4, *the equilibrium level of net national product will decrease from* D *to* F (since the equilibrium level of NNP is at the point where the $C + I + G$ line intersects the 45-degree line). Thus *the effect of the decrease in the money supply is to decrease net national product.*

This, in simplified fashion, is how a decrease in the money supply affects NNP, according to the Keynesian model.[10] To summarize, *the decrease in the money supply results in an increase in the interest rate, which results in a decrease in investment, which results in a decrease in NNP.* This theory helps to explain, among other things, why an inadequate rate of growth of the money supply can lead to excessive unemployment. If the money supply is too small, NNP will not reach its potential level (that is, its full-employment level).[11]

THE MONETARISTS

Some prominent economists, led by Milton Friedman of Stanford University's Hoover Institution, have expressed disagreement with the models in the previous section. They have formulated a different view of the way in which the quantity of money affects NNP. Since their criticisms of Keynesian economics have extended to many topics besides the way in which the quantity of money affects NNP, we must postpone a complete discussion of their controversies with the Keynesians to Chapter 14. Here we take up their view concerning the effects of the quantity of money on NNP.

These economists share a point of view called monetarism; hence they are called monetarists. It is not easy to summarize the differences between the monetarists and the Keynesians because all monetarists do not agree

[10]For simplicity, we ignore the fact that the decrease in NNP in panel C will shift the demand curve for money in panel A of Figure 13.4.
[11]Harking back to Chapter 4, we are in a better position to understand now why the aggregate demand curve slopes downward and to the right. An increase in the price level increases the transactions demand for money because the average money cost of each transaction tends to go up. Thus the demand curve for money shifts to the right, with the result that the interest rate increases. As indicated in this section, the higher interest rate results in reduced spending on output. Thus there is an inverse relationship between the price level and aggregate demand.

on all aspects of their theory; neither do all Keynesians agree on all aspects of theirs. Consequently, not all monetarists disagree in the same way with all Keynesians. Equally important, the differences between the monetarists and Keynesians have tended to change over time. As we will see in Chapter 14, many of the points of disagreement during the 1950s and 1960s have become less important in the 1970s and 1980s, as one side or the other has changed its position or as economic conditions have changed. (Because of revisions in the Keynesian view, Keynesians are often called neo-Keynesians.)

Milton Friedman

The differences between the monetarists and Keynesians lie in at least two areas. First, the monetarists couch their theory in a different set of concepts than the Keynesians. Rather than use the theory set forth in Chapters 5 and 6, they use the so-called quantity theory of money, which is described below. Second, the monetarists have hypothesized that certain central relationships, such as the demand curve for money, have a somewhat different shape than posited by the Keynesians.

Monetarists regard the rate of growth of the money supply as the principal determinant of nominal NNP. (*Nominal NNP* means NNP in money, not real terms. In other words, nominal NNP is NNP measured in current, not constant, dollars.) Some monetarists have gone so far as to say that fiscal policy, although it will alter the composition of net national product, may have little or no long-run effect on the size of nominal NNP unless it influences the money supply. This latter view, explained in more detail in Chapter 14, is not now accepted by most economists.

The monetarists have had a great impact on economic thought in the postwar period, even though theirs remains a minority view. Milton Friedman's most severe critics admit that his research in this area (which helped win him a Nobel prize) has been pathbreaking and extremely important. According to his findings,

> the rate of change of the money supply shows well-marked cycles that match closely those in economic activity in general and precede the latter by a long interval. On the average, the rate of change of the money supply has reached its peak nearly 16 months before the peak in general business and has reached its trough over 12 months before the trough in general business.[12]

---

[12]Milton Friedman, testimony before the Joint Economic Committee, "The Relationship of Prices to Economic Stability and Growth," 85th Congress, 2d Session, 1958.

THE VELOCITY OF MONEY

As noted above, the monetarists have revived interest in the so-called quantity theory of money, which was developed many years ago by such titans of economics as Alfred Marshall of Cambridge and Irving Fisher at Yale. To understand this theory, it is useful to begin by defining a new term: the velocity of circulation of money. The **velocity of circulation of money** is the rate at which the money supply is used to make transactions for final goods and services. It equals the average number of times per year that a dollar is used to buy the final goods and services produced by the economy. In other words,

$$V = NNP/M \qquad [13.1]$$

where V is velocity, NNP is the nominal net national product, and M is the money supply. For example, if our nominal net national product is $1 trillion and our money supply is $200 billion, the velocity of circulation of money is 5, which means that, on the average, each dollar of our money consummates $5 worth of purchases of net national product.

Nominal net national product can be expressed as the product of real net national product and the price level. In other words,

$$NNP = P \times Q \qquad [13.2]$$

where P is the price level—the average price at which final goods and services are sold—and Q is net national product in real terms. For example, suppose that national output in real terms consists of 200 tons of steel. If the price of a ton of steel is $100, then nominal NNP equals $P \times Q$, or 100×200, or $20,000.[13]

If we substitute $P \times Q$ for NNP in Equation (13.1), we have

$$V = P \times Q/M. \qquad [13.3]$$

That is, velocity equals the price level *(P)* times the real NNP *(Q)* divided by the money supply *(M)*. This is another way to define the velocity of circulation of money—a way that will prove very useful.

THE EQUATION OF EXCHANGE

Now that we have a definition of the velocity of circulation of money, our next step is to present the so-called equation of exchange. The *equation*

[13]Since real NNP is measured here in physical units (tons), P is the price level. If real NNP had been measured in constant dollars, P would have been a price index. In either event, our conclusions would be basically the same.

of exchange is nothing more than a restatement, in somewhat different form, of our definition of the velocity of circulation of money. To obtain the equation of exchange, all we have to do is multiply both sides of Equation (13.3) by M. The result is

$$MV = PQ. \qquad [13.4]$$

To understand exactly what this equation means, let's look more closely at each side. *The right-hand side equals the amount received for final goods and services during the period,* because Q is the output of final goods and services during the period and P is their average price. Thus the product of P and Q must equal the total amount received for final goods and services during the period: nominal NNP. For example, if national output in real terms equals 200 tons of steel, and if the price of a ton of steel is \$100, then \$100 × 200—that is, $P \times Q$— must equal the total amount received for final goods and services during the period.

The left-hand side of Equation (13.4) equals the total amount spent on final goods and services during the period. Why? Because the left-hand side equals the money supply—M—times the average number of times during the period that a dollar was spent on final goods and services: V. Consequently, $M \times V$ must equal the amount spent on final goods and services during the period. For example, if the money supply equals \$10,000 and velocity equals 2, the total amount spent on final goods and services during the period must equal \$10,000 × 2, or \$20,000.

Thus, since the *amount received for* final goods and services during the period must equal the *amount spent on* final goods and services during the period, the left-hand side must equal the right-hand side.

The equation of exchange—Equation (13.4)—holds by definition. Yet it is not useless. On the contrary, economists regard the equation of exchange as very valuable, because it sets forth some of the fundamental factors that influence NNP and the price level. This equation has been used by economists for many years. It is the basis for the crude quantity theory of money used by the classical economists, as well as the recent theories put forth by the monetarists.

THE CRUDE QUANTITY THEORY OF MONEY AND PRICES

The classical economists discussed in Chapter 4 assumed that both V and Q were constant. They believed that V was constant because it was determined by the population's stable habits of holding money, and they believed that Q would remain constant at its full-employment value.[14] On the basis of these assumptions, they propounded the *crude quantity*

[14]In some cases, they did not really assume continual full employment. Instead, they were concerned with the long-run changes in the economy and compared the peaks of the business cycle, where full employment frequently occurs.

CASE STUDY 13.1 THE VELOCITY OF MONEY AND THE FED'S 1975 DECISION

In view of the weakness of the economy at the end of 1974, the Federal Reserve and the Ford administration decided that stimulative measures were necessary. The administration asked for, and quickly got, a large retroactive tax cut in March 1975, and the Fed set a goal for a higher money growth rate. The inflation rate had been in the double digits in 1974 and was expected to be about 7 to 8 percent in 1975, but the Fed was targeting money supply growth at only 5 to 7 percent. Why did the Fed set such a low target? How could a 5 to 7 percent growth in the money supply finance an expansion of 3 to 4 percent real growth with 7 to 8 percent inflation? Many economists agreed that the Fed was embarking on a very restrictive policy and that the expansion would be choked off.

Arthur Burns

Federal Reserve Chairman Arthur Burns argued that a dollar typically finances more transactions (and therefore supports a higher nominal income) during a business recovery than during a recession. "We knew from a careful reading of history," he said, "that the turnover of money balances tends to rise rapidly in the early stages of economic upswing. Consequently, we resisted the advice of those who wanted to open the tap and let money flow out in greater abundance." It turned out that Burns was correct. From the second quarter of 1975 to the first quarter of 1976, the velocity of money increased even more rapidly than the Fed had predicted, and the relatively low rate of monetary growth was sufficient to accommodate a growth rate of more than 14 percent for nominal GNP—6 percent in real terms.

N.B.

theory of money and prices, a theory that received a great deal of attention and exerted considerable influence in its day.

If these assumptions hold, it follows from the equation of exchange—$MV = PQ$—that the price level (P) must be proportional to the money supply (M), because V and Q have been assumed to be constant. (In the short run, the full-employment level of real net national product (Q) will not change much.) Thus we can rewrite Equation (13.4) as

$$P = (V/Q) M \qquad [13.5]$$

where *(V/Q)* is a constant. So *P* must be proportional to *M* if these assumptions hold.

The conclusion reached by the crude quantity theorists—*that the price level will be proportional to the money supply*—is very important if true. To see how they came to this conclusion, one must recognize that they stressed the transactions motive for holding money. Recall that, based on this motive, one would expect the quantity of money demanded to be directly related to the level of nominal NNP. Further, the demand for money was assumed to be stable, and little or no attention was paid to the effect of the interest rate on the demand for money. Indeed, the crude quantity theorists went so far as to assume that the quantity of money demanded was *proportional* to the level of nominal NNP. This amounted to assuming that velocity was constant.

Suppose there is a 10 percent increase in the quantity of money. Why would the crude quantity theorists predict a 10 percent increase in the price level? To begin with, they would assert that, since the quantity of money has increased relative to the value of nominal NNP, households and firms now hold more money than they want to hold. Further, they would argue that households and firms will spend their excess money balances on commodities and services, and that the resulting increase in total intended spending will increase the nominal value, but not the real value, of NNP (since full employment is assumed). In other words, the increase in aggregate demand will bid up prices. More specifically, they would argue that prices will continue to be bid up until they have increased by 10 percent, since only then will the nominal value of NNP be big enough so that households and firms will be content to hold the new quantity of money.

Evaluation of the Crude Quantity Theory

The crude quantity theory is true to its name: it is only a crude approximation to reality. One important weakness is its assumption that velocity is constant. Another is its assumption that the economy is always at full employment, which we know from previous chapters to be far from true. (For a more sophisticated version of the quantity theory, see "Exploring Further" in this chapter.) But despite its limitations the crude quantity theory points to a very important truth. If the government finances its expenditures by an enormous increase in the money supply, the result will be drastic inflation. For example, if the money supply is increased tenfold, there will be a marked increase in the price level. If we take the crude quantity theory at face value, we would expect a tenfold increase in the price level; but that is a case of spurious accuracy. Perhaps the price level will go up only eightfold. Perhaps it will go up twelvefold. The important thing is that it will go up a lot.

There is a great deal of evidence to show that the crude quantity theory is a useful predictor during periods of runaway inflation, such as in Germany after World War I. The German inflation occurred because the

German government printed and spent large bundles of additional money. You often hear people warn of the dangers in this country of the government's "resorting to the printing presses" and flooding the country with a vast increase in the money supply. It is a danger in any country. And one great value of the crude quantity theory is that it predicts correctly what will occur as a consequence: rapid inflation.

There is also considerable evidence that the crude quantity theory works reasonably well in predicting long-term trends in the price level. For example, during the sixteenth and seventeenth centuries, gold and silver were imported by the Spanish from the New World, resulting in a great increase in Europe's money supply. The crude quantity theory would predict a great increase in the price level, and this is what occurred. Or consider the period during the nineteenth century, when the discovery of gold in the United States, South Africa, and Canada brought about a large increase in the money supply. As the crude quantity theory would lead us to expect, the price level rose considerably as a consequence.

THE IMPORTANCE OF MONEY

Whether one is a Keynesian using the model presented in Figures 13.3 and 13.4 or a monetarist using a sophisticated form of quantity theory can make a considerable difference, as we shall see in Chapter 14. But it is important to underscore the fact that *the effect of the money supply on nominal NNP is qualitatively the same in both the Keynesian and monetarist models.* Whatever theory you look at, you get the same qualitative result.

Increases in the money supply would be expected to increase nominal NNP, and decreases in the money supply would be expected to decrease nominal NNP.

Furthermore, no matter which view is accepted, it would be expected that, as the economy approaches full employment, a bigger and bigger share of the increase in nominal NNP due to increases in the money supply will reflect price increases, not increases in real output. *If the economy is at considerably less than full employment, increases in the money supply would be expected to increase real NNP, while decreases in the money supply would be expected to reduce real NNP. However, once full employment is approached, increases in the money supply result more and more in increases in the price level, as distinct from increases in real NNP.*

These expectations are shared by economists of many types, which is fortunate since, as we have seen, they are important guides to the formulation of monetary policy, both here and abroad.

WHEN IS MONETARY POLICY TIGHT OR EASY?

In previous sections of this chapter, we have focused attention on the ways in which the money supply affects economic activity. Now we must look in more detail at the difficulties faced by the Federal Reserve in conducting monetary policy in the United States. Given what we have learned in previous sections of this chapter, we can understand these difficulties more clearly.

Everyone daydreams about being powerful and important. It is a safe bet, however, that few people daydream about being members of the Federal Reserve Board or the Federal Open Market Committee. Yet the truth is that the members of the board and the committee are among the most powerful people in the nation. Suppose you were appointed to the Federal Reserve Board. As a member, you would have to decide—month by month, year by year—exactly how many government securities the Fed should buy or sell, as well as whether and when changes should be made in the discount rate, legal reserve requirements, and the other instruments of Federal Reserve policy. How would you go about making your choices?

Obviously you would need lots of data. Fortunately, the Fed has a very large and able research staff to provide you with plenty of the latest information about what is going on in the economy. But what sorts of data should you look at? One thing you would want is some information on the extent to which monetary policy is inflationary or deflationary—that is, the extent to which it is *easy* or *tight*. This is not simple to measure, but there is general agreement that the members of the Federal Reserve Board—and other members of the financial and academic communities—look closely at short-term interest rates and the rate of increase of the money supply.

The Level of Short-Term Interest Rates

As indicated earlier, Keynesians have tended to believe that changes in the quantity of money affect aggregate demand via their effects on the interest rate. High interest rates tend to reduce investment, which in turn reduces NNP. Low interest rates tend to increase investment, which in turn increases NNP. Because of their emphasis on these relationships, Keynesians tend to view monetary tightness or ease in terms of the behavior of interest rates. High interest rates are interpreted as meaning that monetary policy is tight. Low interest rates are interpreted as meaning that monetary policy is easy.

According to many economists, the *real interest rate,* not the *nominal interest rate,* is what counts in this context. The *real* interest rate is the percentage increase in *real* purchasing power that the lender receives from the borrower in return for making the loan. The *nominal* interest rate is the percentage increase in *money* that the lender receives from the borrower in return for making the loan. The crucial difference between the real rate of interest and the nominal rate of interest is that the former is *adjusted for inflation* whereas the latter is not.

Suppose that a firm borrows $1,000 for a year at 12 percent interest, and that the rate of inflation is 9 percent. When the firm repays the lender

$1,120 at the end of the year, this amount of money is worth only $1,120 ÷ 1.09, or about $1,030 when corrected for inflation. Thus the real rate of interest on this loan is 3 percent, not 12 percent (the nominal rate). Why? Because the lender receives $30 in constant dollars (which is 3 percent of the amount lent) in return for making the loan. The real rate of interest is of importance in investment decisions because it measures the real cost of borrowing money.[15]

The Rate of Increase of the Money Supply

As indicated earlier, monetarists have tended to link changes in the quantity of money directly to changes in NNP. Consequently, they have tended to view monetary tightness or ease in terms of the behavior of the money supply. When the money supply is growing at a relatively slow rate (much less than 4 or 5 percent per year), this is interpreted as meaning that monetary policy is tight. A relatively rapid rate of growth in the money supply (much more than 4 or 5 percent per year) is taken to mean that monetary policy is easy.

Another measure stressed by the monetarists is the *monetary base*, which by definition equals member bank reserves plus currency outside member banks. The monetary base is important because the total money supply is dependent upon, and made from, it. A relatively slow rate of growth in the monetary base (much less than 4 or 5 percent per year) is interpreted as a sign of tight money. A relatively rapid rate of growth (much more than 4 or 5 percent per year) is taken to mean that monetary policy is easy.

SHOULD THE FED PAY MORE ATTENTION TO INTEREST RATES OR THE MONEY SUPPLY?

We have just seen that the level of interest rates and the rate of growth of the money supply are the two principal indicators of monetary tightness or ease. Unfortunately, the Fed may not be able to control them both. To see this, suppose that the existing money supply equals $300 billion, and that the public's demand curve for money shifts upward and to the right, as shown in Figure 13.5. At each level of the rate of interest, the public demands a greater amount of money than before. If the interest rate remains at 12 percent, the quantity of money demanded by the public will exceed $300 billion, the existing quantity supplied. Thus the level of interest rates will rise from 12 to 14 percent, as shown in Figure 13.5. Economists who favor the use of interest rates as an indicator are likely to warn that unless interest rates are reduced, a recession will ensue.

[15]Expressed as an equation, $i_r = i_n - p$, where i_r is the real rate of interest, i_n is the nominal rate of interest, and p is the rate of inflation. In the example in the text, $i_n = 12$ percent and $p = 9$ percent; thus $i_r = 3$ percent.

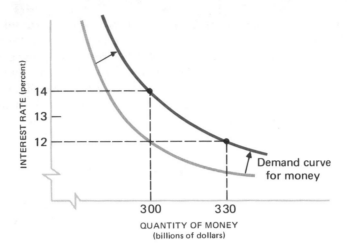

Figure 13.5
Effect of a Shift in the Demand Curve for Money
If the demand curve for money shifts upward and to the right, as shown here, the equilibrium value of the interest rate will increase from 12 to 14 percent, if the quantity of money supplied remains $300 billion. If the Fed wants to push the equilibrium level of the interest rate back to 12 percent, it must increase the quantity of money supplied to $330 billion.

The Fed can push the level of interest rates back down by increasing the quantity of money. The equilibrium value of the interest rate is the one where the quantity of money demanded equals the quantity of money supplied. If the demand curve for money remains fixed at its new higher level, the Fed can push the interest rate back down to 12 percent by increasing the quantity of money to $330 billion. With this quantity of money, the equilibrium interest rate is 12 percent, as shown in Figure 13.5. However, by doing so, the Fed no longer is increasing the money supply in accord with its previous objectives. Economists who favor the use of the rate of growth of the money supply as an indicator are likely to warn that the Fed is increasing the money supply at too rapid a rate.

Thus the Fed is faced with a dilemma. If it does not push interest rates back down to their former level, some economists will claim it is promoting recession. If it does do so, other economists will claim it is promoting inflation. Unfortunately, it is very difficult for the Fed (or anyone else) to tell exactly how much weight should be attached to each of these indicators. In the 1950s and 1960s, the Fed paid much more attention to interest rates than to the rate of increase of the money supply. In the 1970s and early 1980s, because of the growing influence of the monetarists, the Fed has put more emphasis on the rate of growth of the money supply, although it continues to pay close attention to interest rates.

PROBLEMS IN FORMULATING MONETARY POLICY

Before attempting to evaluate the Fed's record, we must recognize the three major kinds of decisions it must continually make. First, the Fed must maintain a constant watch on the economy, checking for signs that the economy is sliding into a recession, being propelled into an inflationary boom, or growing satisfactorily. There is no foolproof way to forecast the economy's short-term movements. Recognizing the fallibility of existing

VIEWS
OF
ECONOMICS
U$A

Superstar Reggie Jackson electrifies the fans in Yankee Stadium with his third home run during the final game of the 1977 World Series against the Los Angeles Dodgers.

The salaries of their favorite players are as familiar to most fans today as their batting averages or ERAs. Why do grown men playing a boy's game earn millions of dollars per year? The answer has to do with the way markets determine prices. See "Markets and Prices: Do They Meet Our Needs?" Program #2 of ECONOMICS U$A.

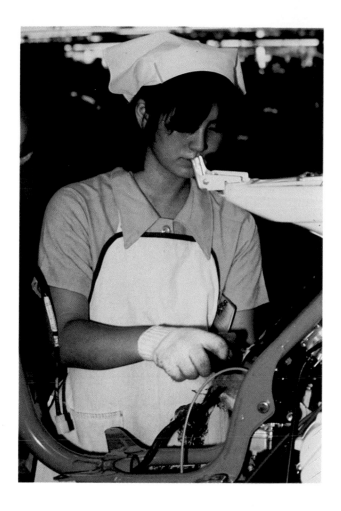

A worker assembling motorbikes at Japan's Yamaha Motor Company plant.

In recent years the productivity of American industry has lagged, falling behind Japan, Germany, and France in the rate of productivity growth. What are the effects of America's productivity slowdown and what policies can address the problem? For answers, see "Productivity: Can We Get More for Less?" Program #11 of ECONOMICS U$A.

☆ ☆ ☆ ☆ ☆ ☆ ☆ ☆ ☆ ☆ ☆ ☆ ☆ ☆ ☆ ☆ ☆

President Ronald Reagan signs H.R. 4170, the Deficit Reduction Act of 1984.

During the Reagan administration the federal deficit reached the unprecedented level of $200 billion. Why has the deficit exploded in recent years, and what dangers does it pose for the American economy? See "Federal Deficits: Can We Live with Them?" Program #12 of ECONOMICS U$A.

☆ ☆ ☆ ☆ ☆ ☆ ☆ ☆ ☆ ☆ ☆ ☆ ☆ ☆ ☆ ☆ ☆

Angry farmers halt the foreclosure sale of a farm in Glenwood, Minnesota.

Caught between high interest costs and fluctuating crop prices, many of America's farmers face bankruptcy and foreclosure. What causes the perennial crises that beset the American farm, and what can be done about them? See "Perfect Competition and Inelastic Demand: Can the Farmer Make a Profit?" Program #17 of ECONOMICS U$A.

☆ ☆ ☆ ☆ ☆ ☆ ☆ ☆ ☆ ☆ ☆ ☆ ☆ ☆ ☆ ☆

A choking layer of pollution clouds the sky over New York City.

In the past twenty years Americans have become painfully aware of the health hazards posed by environmental pollution. Yet the fight against pollution can be costly. How much is a clean environment worth to us? How should the private and public sectors share these costs? See "Pollution: How Much Is a Clean Environment Worth?" Program #21 of ECONOMICS U$A.

☆ ☆ ☆ ☆ ☆ ☆ ☆ ☆ ☆ ☆ ☆ ☆ ☆ ☆ ☆ ☆ ☆

On a pier in Port Elizabeth, New Jersey, brand new Hondas from Japan await delivery to anxious dealers and consumers.

Over the past fifteen years the American automobile industry has been fighting a grim battle with its Japanese competition. Are restrictions on the import of Japanese cars beneficial to the American economy? See "International Trade: For Whose Benefit?" Program #27 of ECONOMICS U$A.

In May 1986 heads of state from around the world convened at Tokyo's Akasaka Palace for the annual economic summit. Pictured, from left, are: Jacques Delors (European Economic Community), Bettino Craxi (Italy), Ruud Lubbers (Netherlands), Helmut Kohl (West Germany), Ronald Reagan (United States), Yasuhiro Nakasone (Japan), François Mitterrand (France), Margaret Thatcher (England), and Brian Mulroney (Canada).

Heading the agenda at the Tokyo economic summit were questions of trade, the balance of payments, and currency exchange rates. For explanations of these basic elements of the international economy, see "International Trade" and "Exchange Rates: What in the World Is a Dollar Worth?" Programs #27 and #28 of ECONOMICS U$A.

forecasting techniques all too well, the Fed must nonetheless use these techniques as best it can to guide its actions.

Second, having come to some tentative conclusion about the direction in which the economy is heading, the Fed must decide to what extent it should tighten or ease money. The answer depends on the Fed's estimates of when monetary changes will take effect and the magnitude of their impact, as well as on its forecasts of the economy's future direction. Also, the answer depends on the Fed's evaluation of the relative importance of full employment and price stability as national goals. If it regards full employment as much more important than price stability, it will probably want to err in the direction of easy money. On the other hand, if it thinks price stability is at least as important as full employment, it may want to err in the direction of tight money.

Third, once the Fed has decided what it wants to do, it must figure out how to do it. Should open market operations do the whole job? If so, how big must be the purchase or sale of government securities? Should a change be made in the discount rate, or in legal reserve requirements? How big a change? Should moral suasion be resorted to? These are the operational questions the Fed continually must answer.

In answering these questions, the Fed must reckon with two very inconvenient facts, both of which make life difficult.

1. *There is often a long lag between an action by the Fed and its effect on the economy.* Although the available evidence indicates that monetary policy affects some types of expenditures more rapidly than others, it is not uncommon for the bulk of the total effects to occur a year or more after the change in monetary policy.[16] Thus the Fed may act to head off an imminent recession, but find that some of the consequences of its action are not felt until later, when inflation, not recession, is the problem. Conversely, the Fed may act to curb an imminent inflation, but find that the consequences of its action are not felt until some time later, when recession, not inflation, has become the problem. In either case, the Fed can wind up doing more harm than good. (Recall our discussion in the section, "Exploring Further," in Chapter 9.)

2. *Experts disagree about which of the available measures—such as interest rates, the rate of increase of the money supply, or the rate of increase of the monetary base—is the best measure of how tight or easy monetary policy is.* Fortunately, these measures often point in the same direction; but when they point in different directions, the Fed can be misled. During 1967–68, the Fed wanted to tighten money. Using interest rates as the primary measure of the tightness of monetary policy, it increased interest rates. However, at the same time, it permitted a substantial rate of increase in the money supply and the monetary base. By doing so, the Fed, in the eyes of many experts, really eased, not tightened money.

---

[16]Robert Gordon has estimated that it takes about 9 months for a change in the money supply to affect real GNP. (See the section, "Exploring Further," in Chapter 9.)

☆ ☆ ☆ ☆ ☆ ☆ ☆ ☆ ☆ ☆ ☆ ☆ ☆

CASE STUDY 13.2 THE SATURDAY NIGHT SPECIAL

In 1979 the inflation rate began to hit double digits. In the second quarter of 1979, the money supply began to rise sharply. Financial managers here and abroad issued statements that inflation was reaching dangerous levels. Fiscal policy was not used to curb this inflation. Consequently, much of the responsibility for fighting inflation fell to the Federal Reserve. What actions did it take?

On Saturday, October 6, 1979, the Federal Open Market Committee held a special meeting where the members were quartered in different hotels to avoid attracting public attention. Feeling that extraordinary measures were required, the committee raised reserve requirements and increased the discount rate from 11 to 12 percent, even though it was widely believed that the economy had entered a recession. At the same time, the committee indicated that it would try to reduce the rate of growth of the money supply. Some people on Wall Street called the announcement the Saturday Night Special, since it hit the financial community hard.

In the last quarter of 1979, the rate of growth of the money supply fell to about 5 percent. Interest rates rose sharply. The prime rate, which had been about 13 percent in September 1979, hit 20 percent in April 1980. However, inflationary pressures were still great. Between December 1979 and February 1980, the Consumer Price Index rose at an annual rate of 17 percent. Financial markets were demoralized. Since there was the risk of inflation getting even worse, and of interest rates therefore going through the roof, it was difficult, if not impossible, for market participants to determine what interest rate to set on new bonds. Consequently, the long-term bond market in large part suspended operations for a while.

Uphill Racer. *A 1980 cartoon shows the peril of soaring prices*

UPHILL RACER

DOUBLE-DIGIT INFLATION

©1980 HERBLOCK

It was hoped that the widely anticipated recession, which finally began in January 1980, would bring down the inflation rate, as well as interest rates. When asked whether monetary tightening would result in a recession, Federal Reserve Chairman Volcker is reported to have said, "yes, and the sooner the better." Apparently, policy makers felt that the most important thing was to reduce inflation, even if a slight or moderate recession ensued. In March 1980, President Carter announced a new anti-inflation plan. The Fed's role in the new program was to tighten monetary policy further.

Clearly, the Fed did pretty much what one would have expected. It cut down on the rate of increase of the money supply, and pushed up interest rates. Unfortunately, such actions may reduce real output (and increase unemployment), as well as cut the inflation rate. Some liberals criticized the Fed's actions on these grounds. Others, particularly conservatives, said that the Fed moved too slowly and not vigorously enough to quell inflation. In fact, inflation, while subsiding significantly, remained at historically high levels during the early 1980s. But in early 1982, it declined substantially.

HOW WELL HAS THE FED PERFORMED?

Given the difficult problems the Federal Reserve faces and the fact that its performance cannot be measured by any simple standard, it would be naive to expect that its achievement could be graded like an arithmetic quiz. Nonetheless, just as war is too important to be left to the generals, so monetary policy is too important to be left solely to the monetary authorities. According to recent studies of Federal Reserve policy making, what have been the strengths and weaknesses of the Fed's decisions?

FORECASTING. If one takes into account the limitations in existing forecasting techniques, the Fed seems to have done a reasonably good job in recent years of recognizing changes in economic conditions. Of course, it sometimes was a bit slow to see that the economy was sinking into a recession, or that inflationary pressures were dominant. But hindsight is always much clearer than foresight (which is why Monday-morning quarterbacks make so few mistakes—and get paid so little). Because the Fed has done a creditable job of recognizing changes in economic conditions, the time interval between changes in economic conditions and changes in policy has been rather short, particularly when compared with the corresponding time interval for fiscal policy.

RECOGNITION OF LAGS. The Fed does not seem to have taken much account of the long—and seemingly quite variable—lags between changes in monetary policy and their effects on the economy. Instead, it has simply reacted quickly to changes in business conditions. As pointed out in a previous section, such a policy can in reality be quite destabilizing. For example, the Fed may act to suppress inflationary pressures, but find that the consequences of its action are not felt until some time later when recession, not inflation, is the problem. Unfortunately, the truth is that, despite advances in knowledge in the past decade, economists do not have a firm understanding of these lags. Thus the Fed is only partly to blame.

COORDINATION. With a few notable exceptions, there generally seems to have been reasonably good coordination between the Federal Reserve and the executive branch (the Treasury and the Council of Economic

Advisers, in particular). This is important because monetary policy and fiscal policy should work together, not march off in separate directions. The fact that the Fed and the executive branch have generally been aware of one another's views and probable actions does not mean that there has always been agreement between them. Nor does it mean that even when they've agreed, they've always been able to point monetary and fiscal policy in the same direction. But at least the left hand has had a pretty good idea of what the right hand was doing.

EMPHASIS. The Fed is often criticized for putting too much emphasis on preventing inflation and too little on preventing unemployment. According to various studies, it probably is true that the Fed has been more sensitive to the dangers of inflation than has Congress or the administration. Liberals, emphasizing the great social costs of excessive unemployment, tend to denounce the Fed for such behavior. Without question, the costs of unemployment are high, as stressed in Chapter 4. Conservatives, on the other hand, argue that governments are tempted to resort to inflation in order to produce the short-term appearance of prosperity, even though the long-term effects may be undesirable. They say that in the short run (when the next election is decided), unemployment is more likely than inflation to result in defeat at the polls. Whether you think that the Fed has put too much emphasis on restraining inflation will depend on the relative importance that you attach to reducing unemployment, on the one hand, and reducing inflation, on the other.[17]

SHOULD THE FED BE GOVERNED BY A RULE?

Many monetarists, led by Milton Friedman, go so far as to say that the Fed's attempts to "lean against the wind"—by easing money when the economy begins to dip and tightening money when the economy begins to overheat—really do more harm than good. In their view, the Fed actually intensifies business fluctuations by changing the rate of growth of the money supply. Why? Partly because the Fed sometimes pays too much attention to measures other than the money supply. But more fundamentally, because the Fed tends to overreact to ephemeral changes and because the effects of changes in the money supply on the economy occur with a long and highly variable lag. In the view of these monetarists, this lag is so unpredictable that the Fed—no matter how laudatory its intent —tends to intensify business fluctuations.

According to Professor Friedman and his followers, the Fed should abandon its attempts to lean against the wind. *The Fed should conform to a rule that the money supply should increase at some fixed, agreed-upon rate, such as 4 or 5 percent per year. The Fed's job would be simply to see that the money supply grows at approximately this rate.* The monetarists

---

[17]For a good discussion of monetary policy, see T. Mayer, J. Duesenberry, and R. Aliber, *Money, Banking, and the Economy,* 2d ed. New York: Norton, 1984.

do not claim that a rule of this sort would prevent all business fluctuations, but they do claim that it would work better than the existing system. In particular, they feel that it would prevent the sorts of major depressions and inflations we have experienced in the past. Without major decreases in the money supply (such as occurred during the crash of 1929–33), major depressions could not occur. Without major increases in the money supply (such as occurred during World War II), major inflations could not occur. Of course, it would be nice if monetary policy could iron out minor business fluctuations as well, but in their view this simply cannot be done at present.

This proposal has received considerable attention from both economists and politicians. A number of studies have been carried out to try to estimate what would have happened if Friedman's rule had been used in the past. The results, although by no means free of criticism, seem to indicate that such a rule might have done better than discretionary action did in preventing the Great Depression of the 1930s and the inflation during World War II. But in the period since World War II, the evidence in favor of such a rule is less persuasive. Most economists believe that it would be a mistake to handcuff the Fed to a simple rule of this sort. They think that a discretionary monetary policy can outperform Friedman's rule.

Nonetheless, the debate over rules versus discretionary action goes on, and the issues are still very much alive. Professor Friedman has been able to gain important converts, including the Federal Reserve Bank of St. Louis and members of the Joint Economic Committee of Congress. Indeed, after the Fed's "stop-go" policies of 1966–68 (when the Fed tightened money sharply in 1966 and eased it rapidly in 1967–68), the Joint Economic Committee urged the Fed to adopt a rule of the sort advocated by Friedman. In 1968, the committee complained that its advice was not being followed, and special hearings were held. The Council of Economic Advisers and the secretary of the Treasury sided with the Fed against adopting such a rule. Some academic economists favor such a rule, others oppose it, and considerable economic research is being carried out to try to clarify and resolve the questions involved.

EXPLORING FURTHER: A MORE SOPHISTICATED VERSION OF THE QUANTITY THEORY   ☆ ☆ ☆

The crude quantity theory was based on two simplifying assumptions, both of which are questionable. One assumption was that real net national product (Q) remains fixed at its full-employment level. The other was that the velocity of circulation of money (V) remains constant. A more sophisticated version of the quantity theory can be derived by relaxing the first assumption. This version of the quantity theory recognizes that the economy is often at less than full employment and consequently that real net national product (Q) may vary a good deal.

So long as velocity remains constant, the equation of exchange—$MV =$

PQ—can be used to determine the relationship between net national product in current dollars and *M,* even if *Q* is allowed to vary. On the basis of the equation of exchange, it is obvious that $P \times Q$ should be proportional to *M,* if the velocity of circulation of money *(V)* remains constant. Since $P \times Q$ is nominal net national product, it follows that, if this assumption holds, *nominal net national product should be proportional to the money supply.* In other words,

$$NNP = aM \qquad [13.6]$$

where NNP is nominal net national product and *V* is assumed to equal a constant: *a.* Thus, if the money supply increases by 10 percent, the nominal value of NNP should increase by 10 percent. If the money supply increases by 20 percent, the nominal value of NNP should increase by 20 percent. And so forth.

If velocity is constant, this version of the quantity theory should enable us to predict nominal net national product if we know the money supply. Also, if velocity is constant, this version of the quantity theory should enable us to control nominal net national product by controlling the money supply. Clearly, if velocity is constant, Equation (13.6) is an extremely important economic relationship, one that will go a long way toward helping to forecast and control NNP. But is velocity constant? Since Equation (13.6) is based on this assumption, we must find out.

Figure 13.6 shows how the velocity of circulation of money has behaved since 1920.[18] Obviously, velocity has not been constant. But on the other hand, it has not varied enormously. Excluding the war years, it has generally been between 2.5 and 6.5 in the United States. It has changed rather slowly, although it has varied a good deal over the business cycle. Velocity tends to decrease during depressions and increase during booms. *One must conclude from Figure 13.6 that although velocity has not varied enormously, it is not so stable that Equation (13.6) alone can be used in any precise way to forecast or control net national product.*[19]

However, this does not mean that Equation (13.6) is useless, or that the more sophisticated quantity theory is without value. On the contrary, this version of the quantity theory points out a very important truth, which is that *the money supply has an important effect on net national product (in money terms). Increases in the quantity of money are likely to increase nominal NNP, while decreases in the quantity of money are likely to decrease nominal NNP.* Because velocity is not constant, the relationship between the money supply and net national product is not as neat and

[18]The velocity figures in Figure 13.6 are based on gross national product, not net national product. But for present purposes this makes little real difference.

[19]It is important to note that the velocity figures in Figure 13.6 are based on the narrow definition of the money supply, *M*-1. If *M*-2 is used instead, velocity is more nearly constant. For example, between 1960 and 1976, velocity based on *M*-2 varied within a very narrow range.

Figure 13.6
Velocity of Circulation of Money, United States, 1920–84
The velocity of circulation of money has generally been between 2.5 and 6.5, except during World War II.

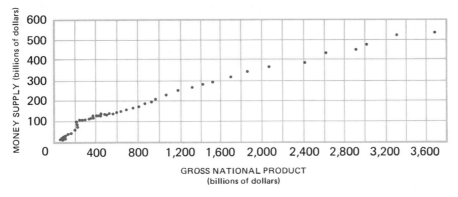

Figure 13.7
Relationship between Money Supply and National Product, United States, 1929–84
There is a reasonably close relationship between the money supply and the money value of national product. As one goes up, the other tends to go up too.

simple as that predicted by Equation (13.6), but there is a relationship—as shown in Figure 13.7.

Going a step further, sophisticated monetarists often relax the assumption that V is constant, and assert that it is possible to predict V as a function of other variables, like the frequency with which people are paid, the level of business confidence, and the cost of holding money (the interest rate). According to some economists, one of Friedman's major contributions was to replace the constancy of V with its predictability. Other economists feel that changes in V reflect, rather than cause, changes in NNP.

SUMMARY

1. America's history has seen many sharp fluctuations in the price level. Generally, severe inflations have occurred because the government expanded the money supply far too rapidly. However, too small a rate of growth of the money supply can also be a mistake, resulting in excessive unemployment.

2. Most economists believe that the lower the interest rate, the greater the amount of money demanded. Thus increases in the quantity of money result in lower interest rates, which result in increased investment (and other types of spending), which results in a higher NNP. Conversely, decreases in the quantity of money result in higher interest rates, which result in decreased investment (and other types of spending), which result in a lower NNP. This is the Keynesian approach.

3. The equation of exchange is $MV = PQ$, where M is the money supply, V is velocity, P is the price level, and Q is net national product in real terms. The velocity of circulation of money is the rate at which the money supply is used to make transactions for final goods and services. Specifically, it equals NNP in money terms divided by the money supply.

4. If the velocity of circulation of money remains constant and if real net national product is fixed at its full-employment level, it follows from the equation of exchange that the price level will be proportional to the money supply. This is the crude quantity theory, which is a reasonably good approximation during periods of runaway inflation, and works reasonably well in predicting long-term trends in the price level.

5. The monetarists, led by Milton Friedman, prefer the quantity theory to the Keynesian model. There have been many disagreements between the monetarists and the Keynesians, but both approaches agree that increases in the money supply will tend to increase nominal NNP while decreases in the money supply will tend to decrease nominal NNP.

6. As indicators of how tight or easy monetary policy is, the Fed has looked at the level of short-term interest rates, the rate of growth of the money supply, and the rate of growth of the monetary base. During the 1950s and 1960s, the Fed paid most attention to the first indicator; in the 1970s and early 1980s, the Fed increased the amount of attention paid to the last two.

7. The Federal Reserve is faced with many difficult problems in formulating and carrying out monetary policy. It must try to see where the economy is heading and whether—and to what extent—it should tighten or ease money to stabilize the economy. This task is made very difficult by the fact that there is often a long—and highly variable—lag between an action by the Fed and its effect on the economy. There is also considerable

disagreement over the best way to measure how tight or easy monetary policy is.

8. There has been criticism of various kinds regarding the performance of the Federal Reserve. Often, the Fed is criticized for paying too little attention to the long lags between its actions and their effects on the economy. Some monetarists, led by Milton Friedman, believe that monetary policy would be improved if discretionary policy were replaced by a rule that the Fed should increase the money supply at some fixed, agreed-on rate, such as 4 or 5 percent per year.

* 9. A more sophisticated version of the quantity theory recognizes that real net national product is often less than its full-employment value; consequently, Q is not fixed. Thus, if velocity remains constant, net national product in money terms should be proportional to the money supply. In fact, velocity has by no means remained constant over time. However, nominal NNP has been fairly closely related to the money supply, and the monetarists assert that velocity is predictable.

*The starred item refers to material covered in the section, "Exploring Further."

CHAPTER 14

★ ★ ★ ★ ★ ★ ★ ★

Controversies over Stabilization Policy

LEARNING OBJECTIVES

In this chapter, you should learn:

★ The disagreements between monetarists and Keynesians over business fluctuations, the stability of the economy, and the use of a monetary rule

★ The nature of rational expectations theory and its effects on economic policy

★ The nature and effects of supply-side economic policies

During the past several decades, there has been a continuing controversy among economists over the effects of monetary and fiscal policy on output and employment, as well as over the kinds of public policies that the government should adopt. This controversy has engaged the attention of many leading economists and has had a strong influence on the thinking of policy makers in both the public and private sectors of the economy. In previous chapters, we have discussed particular aspects of this controversy. Now we can look at it in more detail.

This chapter compares the views of various groups of economists: Keynesians, monetarists, rational expectations theorists, and "supply-side" economists. At the outset, it is important to recognize that within each of these groups there is a great deal of disagreement. For example, Keynesians differ considerably among themselves, and so do monetarists. More-over, as times have changed and evidence has accumulated, each group has changed its position. Thus the Keynesian views of the 1980s are not the same as those of the 1950s, and labels like neo-Keynesian or non-monetarist are often used to represent the recent views of the Keynesians.

In the first part of this chapter, we describe the traditional differences between the Keynesians and monetarists. In particular, we discuss their disagreements over the causes of business fluctuations, the stability of the economy, and the effects of monetary and fiscal policy. Then, in the second half of this chapter, we describe the current state of the Keynesian-monetarist debate, as well as the views of the rational expectations and "supply-side" economists. The latter groups have been influential in the late 1970s and early 1980s.

MONETARISTS VERSUS KEYNESIANS: THE HISTORICAL BACKGROUND

The debate between the monetarists and the Keynesians has not been limited to the classroom and scholarly gatherings. It has spilled over onto the pages of daily newspapers and aroused considerable interest in Congress and other parts of the government. At heart, the argument has been over what determines the level of output, employment, and prices. The *Keynesians* have put more emphasis on the federal budget than have the monetarists; the *monetarists* have put more emphasis on the money supply than have the Keynesians. To understand this debate, we need to know something about the recent development of economic thought. Until the Great Depression of the 1930s, the prevailing theory was that NNP, expressed in real terms, would tend automatically to its full-employment level. (Recall from Chapter 4 the classical economists' reasons for clinging to this belief.) Moreover, the prevailing theory was that the price level could be explained by the crude quantity theory of money. In other words, the price level (P) was assumed to be proportional to the quantity of money (M) because $MV = PQ$, and both Q (real NNP) and V (the velocity of money) were thought to be essentially constant.

During the Great Depression of the 1930s, this body of theory seemed inadequate to many economists. NNP was not tending automatically toward its full-employment level. And the crude quantity theory seemed to have little value. In contrast, Keynes's ideas seemed to offer the theoretical guidance and policy prescriptions that were needed. Keynesians did not neglect the use of monetary policy entirely, but they felt that it should play a subsidiary role. Particularly in depressions, monetary policy seemed to be of relatively little value, since you can't push on a string. In other words, monetary policy can make money available, but it cannot ensure that it will be spent. To Keynesians, fiscal policy was of central importance.

During the 1940s, 1950s, and early 1960s, the Keynesian view was definitely predominant, here and abroad. But by the mid-1960s, it was being challenged seriously by the monetarists, led by Milton Friedman and his supporters. The monetarist view harked back to the pre-Keynesian doctrine in many respects. In particular, it emphasized the importance of the equation of exchange as an analytical device and the importance of the quantity of money as a tool of economic policy. The monetarist view gained adherents in the late 1960s, partly because of the long delay in passing the federal tax increase of 1968. The reluctance of the administration to propose and the reluctance of Congress to enact this tax increase vividly illustrated some of the difficulties in using fiscal policy for stabilization. Even more important was the fact that the tax increase, when finally enacted, failed to have the restrictive effect on NNP (in the face of expansionary monetary policy) that some Keynesians had predicted.

CAUSES OF BUSINESS FLUCTUATIONS: THE OPPOSING VIEWS

Monetarists and Keynesians have tended to disagree over the basic causes of business fluctuations.

The Monetarist View

As seen by monetarists, major depressions, such as that which occurred during 1929–33, are due to decreases in the money supply. Between 1929 and 1933, the money supply contracted by over one-quarter. Similarly, major inflations, in their view, are due to increases in the money supply. Looking at recent developments, they assert that the inflation of the late 1960s and the middle and late 1970s and early 1980s was due to increases in the money supply.

The Keynesian View

Keynesians, on the other hand, have tended to reject the monetarist view that money is the predominant factor accounting for business fluctuations. To Keynesians, both monetary and nonmonetary factors cause business fluctuations. Among the important nonmonetary factors are changes (other than those predicted by changes in the money supply) in investment or shifts in the consumption function. Thus, in explaining the severe depression of 1929–33, Keynesians emphasize the fact that investment declined by about 90 percent during this period.

The Keynesians have not denied that there is a correlation between changes in the money supply and changes in NNP, but they have argued that the monetarists tend to mix up cause and effect. The Keynesians have suggested that increases in intended spending may bring about a greater demand for money, which in turn causes the money supply to increase. Under these circumstances, the line of causation may be the opposite of that posited by the monetarists.

STABILITY OF THE ECONOMY: THE OPPOSING VIEWS

Monetarists and Keynesians also tend to differ over the extent to which our economy is stable.

The Monetarist View

The monetarists are generally more inclined to believe that, if the money supply is managed properly by the government, the free-market economy will tend automatically toward full employment with reasonably stable prices. Although the monetarists are by no means unanimous in this respect, they tend to emphasize the self-regulating characteristics of a free-enterprise economy. In their view, business fluctuations must often be laid at the door of the monetary authorities, whose well-meaning attempts to stabilize the economy frequently do more harm than good.

The Keynesian View

In contrast, the Keynesians are convinced that a free-enterprise economy has relatively weak self-regulating mechanisms. Like Keynes himself, they argue that the equilibrium level of national output may remain for a long time below the level required for full employment. (See Chapter 4 for Keynes's views.) Also, they have argued that there is nothing in the modern economy to prevent considerable inflation, even if the money supply does not increase greatly. Thus, in their view, the government has a much more positive discretionary role to play in stabilizing the economy than that visualized by the monetarists.

A MONETARY RULE: THE OPPOSING VIEWS

The Monetarist View

Many but not all leading monetarists advocate the establishment of a rule to govern monetary policy. In the previous chapter, we discussed the arguments of Milton Friedman and his supporters for such a rule. You will recall their charge that the Federal Reserve's monetary policies have often caused economic instability. Because of the difficulties in forecasting the future state of the economy, and the fairly long and variable time lag in the effect of changes in the money supply, the Fed, in the eyes of many leading monetarists, frequently has caused excessive inflation or unemployment with its discretionary policies. According to the monetarists, we would be better off with a rule stipulating that the money supply should grow steadily at a constant rate, say 4 or 5 percent per year.[1]

The Keynesian View

The Keynesians retort that such a rule would handcuff the monetary authorities and contribute to economic instability, since discretionary monetary policies are required to keep the economy on a reasonably even keel. The Keynesians grant that the Fed sometimes makes mistakes, but they assert that things would be worse if the Fed could not pursue the policies that a given set of circumstances seems to call for.

THE CURRENT STATE OF THE KEYNESIAN-MONETARIST DEBATE

The controversy between the Keynesians and monetarists has been going on for decades. At this point, the debate no longer focuses on some of the issues that were paramount 20 years ago. At that time, the controversy centered on the choice between monetary and fiscal policy. The more partisan monetarists claimed that fiscal policy was relatively impotent; the more partisan Keynesians claimed the same regarding monetary policy.

During the 1970s, as more and more evidence accumulated, this issue seemed to wane in importance. At present, most monetarists concede that fiscal policy can affect output and the price level; most Keynesians concede the same regarding monetary policy. Although it would be incorrect to say that no differences remain on this score, there seems to be a growing recognition that the differences have narrowed considerably. Thus Milton Friedman, the leading monetarist, has been quoted as saying, "We are all Keynesians now." And 1985 Nobel laureate Franco Modigliani, a leading Keynesian, responded in his 1976 presidential address to the American Economic Association by saying, "We are all monetarists now."

During the late 1970s and 1980s, the focus of the debate has tended to shift. Now the clash between the monetarists and the Keynesians (who in more recent years have tended to prefer such labels as neo-Keynesian, post-Keynesian, or nonmonetarist) seems to be traceable largely to the following basic disagreements.

STABILITY OF PRIVATE SPENDING. The monetarists believe that, if the government's economic policies did not destabilize the economy, private spending would be quite stable. Keynesians, on the other hand, believe

---

[1]When he accepted the Nobel prize in 1976, Milton Friedman jokingly said: "My monetary studies have led me to the conclusion that central banks could profitably be replaced by computers geared to provide a steady rate of growth in the quantity of money. Fortunately for me personally, and for a select group of fellow economists, the conclusion has had no practical impact . . . else there would have been no Central Bank of Sweden to have established the award I am honored to receive." (The Central Bank of Sweden donated the money for the Nobel prize in economics.)

☆ ☆ ☆ ☆ ☆ ☆ ☆ ☆ ☆ ☆ ☆ ☆ ☆ ☆

281 ★
**The Current State
of the Keynesian-
Monetarist
Debate**

CASE STUDY 14.1 THE COORDINATION OF FISCAL AND MONETARY POLICY IN THE EARLY 1980s

Traditionally, Keynesians have emphasized fiscal policy, while monetarists have emphasized monetary policy. In recent years economists have been concerned about the coordination of fiscal and monetary policy.

In 1981, President Reagan's program to reduce inflation and promote growth called for a steady reduction in the rate of growth of the money supply, a reduction in federal taxation, and a reduction in federal spending. The spending reduction was not achieved, since the president's request for additional defense spending passed but his planned cutbacks in other sectors of government were only partially approved by Congress. And a massive tax cut did go through, resulting in a deficit that could only have been eliminated if the U.S. economy grew faster than ever before. Meanwhile, the slowing of money growth that Reagan advocated was instituted by the Fed, so by late 1981 fiscal and monetary policies were pushing in opposite directions: the deficit was highly stimulative, but monetary policy was extremely restrictive.

The amount of savings in the economy is roughly a constant proportion of income. If the federal government, in borrowing to finance the deficit, demands a large percentage of the pool of savings available, there is less available for other purposes such as business investment on plant and equipment, housing finance, and so on. Real interest rates (the nominal interest rate minus the expected inflation rate) tend to be pushed up if private sector demands are competing with government demand for funds. The higher interest rates mean that some private sector uses will be crowded out.

Real interest rates will jump especially high if a large deficit is accompanied by a tight monetary policy. This in fact is what occurred. In 1979, the real short-term interest rate was about 2 percent. In 1982, after the bulk of Reagan's policies were in place, the real short-term rate jumped to 7 percent. Even after the Fed loosened up somewhat on monetary policy, real rates remained high, apparently because of the massive federal deficit. Such persistently high real interest rates inhibit the long-term growth of the economy by discouraging investment spending. As Yale's Nobel laureate James Tobin noted in February 1982, "To achieve a solid recovery . . . and to achieve it without astronomical interest rates and serious crowding out, we need an easier monetary policy combined with a tighter fiscal policy."

However, the political difficulties of achieving such a policy mix were enormous. Even in an atmosphere of fiscal stringency, Congress and the Reagan administration were unable to agree to budget cuts that would come close to reducing significantly the projected deficits over the next few years. Tax increases were also difficult to agree upon. With politics apparently having blocked the efficacy of discretionary fiscal policy, the burden of controlling inflation fell to the Federal Reserve by default.

N.B.

that business and consumer spending represents a substantial source of economic instability that should be offset by monetary and fiscal policy.

FLEXIBILITY OF PRICES. Even if intended private spending is not entirely stable, flexible prices tend to stabilize it, according to the monetarists. The Keynesians reply that prices are relatively inflexible downward, as shown by the fact that despite widespread unemployment, prices did not decline during the late 1930s. In their view, the length of time that would be required for the economy to get itself out of a severe recession would be intolerably long. Monetarists seem more inclined than Keynesians to believe that high unemployment will cause wages and input prices to fall, shifting the aggregate supply curve downward and increasing output in a reasonable period of time.

RULES VERSUS ACTIVISM. Monetarists believe that, even if intended private spending is not entirely stable and if prices are not entirely flexible, an activist monetary and fiscal policy to stabilize the economy is likely to do more harm than good. As pointed out above, they favor a rule stipulating that the money supply should grow steadily at a constant rate, because of the difficulties in forecasting the future state of the economy and because of the long and variable time lag in the effect of changes in the quantity of money on output and prices. The Keynesians, while admitting that monetary and fiscal policy have sometimes been destabilizing, are much more optimistic about the efficacy of such policies in the future.

To a considerable extent, the differences between the Keynesians and the monetarists stem from divergent political beliefs. The Keynesians tend to be optimistic concerning the extent to which the government can be trusted to formulate and carry out a responsible set of monetary and fiscal policies. They recognize that some politicians are willing to win votes in the next election by destabilizing the economy, but they nonetheless believe that discretionary action by elected officials will generally be more effective than automatic rules. The monetarists, on the other hand, are skeptical of the willingness of politicians to do what is required to stabilize the economy, rather than what is politically expedient. Since this aspect of the debate is difficult to resolve (in any scientific way), a complete resolution of the Keynesian-monetarist controversy is not likely any time soon. However, many other aspects of the controversy are more amenable to scientific analysis, and these aspects almost surely will be clarified substantially in the years to come.[2]

RATIONAL EXPECTATIONS: ANOTHER ELEMENT OF THE CURRENT DEBATE

It should not be assumed that the debate between monetarists and Keynesians is the only controversy regarding stabilization policy. In recent years,

[2]This section has benefited from the discussion in Robert J. Gordon, *Macroeconomics.*

there has been considerable argument over the theory of rational expectations as well.

Can Stabilization Policies Work?

During the 1970s, a small band of young economists, led by Robert Lucas of the University of Chicago and Thomas Sargent and Neil Wallace of the University of Minnesota, formulated a theory of *rational expectations* that already has had a substantial impact on economic analysis and policy. This theory suggests that *the government cannot use monetary and fiscal policies in the way described in previous chapters, because the models presented in those chapters do not recognize that the expectations of firms and individuals concerning their incomes, job prospects, sales, and other relevant variables are influenced by government policies.* If firms and individuals formulate their expectations rationally (that is, if they make the most efficient use of all information provided by history), they will tend to frustrate the government's attempts to use activist stabilization policies.

To illustrate what these economists are saying, suppose that the economy is in a recession and that the government, in accord with the models in Chapters 6 and 9, increases the amount that it spends on goods and services and increases the money supply. Because prices tend to move up while wages do not, profits tend to rise and firms find it profitable to expand. But this model is based on the supposition that labor is not smart enough to foresee that prices are going to go up and that labor's real wage is going to diminish. If labor does foresee this (that is, if its expectations are rational), it will insist on an increase in its money wage, which will mean that firms will not find it profitable to expand, and that the government's antirecession policy will not work as expected.

Unemployment and Business Fluctuations

According to the rational expectations theorists, high rates of unemployment are not evidence of a gap between actual and potential output that can be reduced; instead, output fluctuations result from random and irreducible errors. Markets are assumed to work efficiently; and firms, acting to maximize their profits, are assumed to make the best possible decisions. According to Lucas, since unemployed workers have the option of accepting pay cuts to get jobs, excess unemployment is essentially voluntary.

Fluctuations in aggregate demand are due principally to erratic and unpredictable government policy, in Lucas's view. Changes in the quantity of money induce cyclical fluctuations in the economy. But the power of policy changes to affect real NNP is limited. People come to learn the way in which policy is made, and only unanticipated government policy changes can have a substantial impact on output or employment. Once firms and individuals learn of any systematic rule for adjusting government policy to events, the rule will have no effect.

Reactions Pro and Con

These views have received considerable attention, and in the late 1970s the Federal Reserve Bank of Minneapolis stated its acceptance of them. In its annual report, the bank stated,

> The rational expectations view conjectures that some amount of cyclical swing in production and employment is inherent in the micro-level processes of the economy that no government macro policies can, or should attempt to, smooth out. Expected additions to money growth certainly won't smooth out cycles, if the arguments in this paper are correct. Surprise additions to money growth have the potential to make matters worse. . . . One strategy that seems consistent with the significant, though largely negative, findings of rational expectations would have monetary policy focus its attention on inflation and announce, and stick to, a policy that would bring the rate of increase in the general price level to some specified low figure.[3]

Given the fact that the rational expectations theorists have challenged the core of the theory underlying current stabilization policies, it is not surprising that many economists, particularly liberals, have challenged their conclusions. Franco Modigliani, for instance, has claimed that the rational expectations model is inconsistent "with the evidence: if it were valid, deviations of unemployment from the natural rate would be small and transitory—in which case Keynes's *General Theory* would not have been written."[4] Since the rational expectations theory makes excess unemployment the result of purely unexpected events, one would think that unemployment would fluctuate randomly around its equilibrium level, if this theory is true. However, as we have seen, recessions often last quite a long time.

Critics also claim that the rational expectations theory neglects the inertia in wages and prices. Contracts are written for long periods of time. Workers stick with firms for considerable periods. Consequently, wages and prices do not adjust as rapidly as is assumed by the rational expectations theorists. According to the critics, most empirical analysis does not support the rational expectations model. Contrary to the theory, price movements show only slow and adaptive changes.

Only the future will tell how successful the rational expectations theorists will be in their attack on conventional doctrines, but there can be no doubt that they have caused a remarkable stir in the economics profession.

[3]The Federal Reserve Bank of Minneapolis, *Rational Expectations—Fresh Ideas That Challenge Some Established Views of Policy Making,* Minneapolis, 1977, pp. 12–13.
[4]F. Modligliani, "The Monetarist Controversy, or, Should We Forsake Stabilization Policies," *American Economic Review,* March 1977, p. 6.

SUPPLY-SIDE ECONOMICS ENTERS THE FRAY

The theory of rational expectations is not the only newcomer to the scene. In the late 1970s and 1980s, *supply-side economics* also entered the fray. To a considerable extent, as we have seen, economic policy since World War II has been dominated by measures aimed at managing aggregate demand, the two traditional tools of demand management being monetary and fiscal policy. In contrast, *supply-side economics is concerned primarily with influencing aggregate supply.*

Supply-side economics really is not new. Major economists of the eighteenth and nineteenth (as well as twentieth) centuries were concerned with the stimulation of aggregate supply. But one new twist is that some people seem to believe that the emphasis in combatting inflation should be on pushing the aggregate supply curve to the right rather than on curbing the rightward movement of the aggregate demand curve. (Recall our discussions of aggregate demand and supply curves, beginning in Chapter 4.)

Supply-Side Prescriptions

To stimulate such a rightward shift in the aggregate supply curve, *supply-siders favor the use of various financial incentives, particularly tax cuts.* In their view, the reduction of tax rates will encourage people to work longer and harder, thus increasing the level of full-employment output. Also, reduced tax rates and regulations are likely to entice firms to make risky investments in research and new plant and equipment. Further, tax reductions are likely to cut the amount of time and resources invested in finding and exploiting tax loopholes; more would be invested in productive activities.

Supply-siders argue too that tax reductions will increase saving. By cutting taxes on income from capital, the government can increase the after-tax return to capital, and encourage saving. Supply-siders emphasize that saving is a very important activity that permits and encourages investment, which in turn increases the nation's productive capacity. Keynes took a somewhat different view of saving, emphasizing its negative effects on aggregate demand.

There is considerable uncertainty regarding the extent to which more work, risk-taking, and saving will result from tax reductions. For example, take the case of saving. In a well-known study, Stanford's Michael Boskin found that a 10-percent increase in the real after-tax rate of return will result in an increase of 2 to 4 percent in saving per year. On the other hand, other economists, such as Phillip Howrey and Saul Hymans of the University of Michigan, have criticized Boskin's findings, and have themselves come to quite different conclusions. Although the jury is still out

☆ ☆ ☆ ☆ ☆ ☆ ☆ ☆ ☆ ☆ ☆ ☆ ☆

CASE STUDY 14.2 RECESSION AS A MEANS TO STOP INFLATION IN 1982

When President Reagan came into office in 1981, the inflation rate was 11 percent. The combination of President Carter's efforts to stimulate the economy in 1977–78 and the oil price shock of 1979 had apparently created an underlying inflation rate of about 8 percent. In his campaign, Reagan had promised to reduce inflation by encouraging the Federal Reserve to reduce the rate of growth of the money supply and by creating greater incentives for the economy to produce more goods. He would therefore attack the traditional causes of inflation, "too much money chasing too few goods," from both sides.

*President Ronald
Reagan presenting
his tax package*

By the 1980s, most economists believed that people's expectations about the possible effects of future government policies could affect how well the policies worked. For example, if the government tried to stimulate the economy by increasing the rate of growth of the money supply, its policy would fail if firms and labor unions simply raised prices and wages in expectation of higher inflation. The additional money supplied to the economy would go into higher prices rather than toward stimulating more production.

One group of economists felt that it would take a long time to get business and labor to reduce their expectations of future inflation. In addition, wage increases tended to be set in advance, by multi-year contracts, so wage gains could not be easily reduced even if expectations of future inflation fell. Because of this, the only way to reduce price increases and wage demands quickly, this group argued, would be to create a large increase in unemployment.

In contrast, another group of economists felt that inflation could be reduced without a large increase in unemployment if the government's resolve to stick to inflation-fighting policies was credible. These economists argued that the problem with the government's anti-inflation efforts in the past was that they were not steady enough. At the first sign of a recession, the Fed would back off and rekindle inflation with an easy money policy.

In fact the Fed did adhere to a tight money policy long after the recession of 1982 became quite severe. Fed Chairman Paul Volcker had tightened up on the money supply in the summer of 1981. Interest rates rose, and the economy slid into recession. In early 1982, the unemployment rate was over 9 percent, but Volcker still maintained a tight policy. It was not until October 1982 that the Fed eased up.

By that time, the rate of inflation had fallen from the 11 percent level of early 1981 to 3.5 percent. But the cost of reducing inflation had been a severe downturn in business activity. According to many observers, the Fed had no choice but to take a strong stand against inflation. Nonetheless, the results suggested that, once inflation becomes embedded, it is difficult to reduce it because expectations of continued inflation can be halted only by deep recession.

N.B.

regarding many of the relevant points, it seems fair to say that many economists are skeptical of the claims made by the more extreme supply-siders.

The Need for Demand Management

In particular, many economists seem to question the idea that supply-side policies alone can make much of a dent in our inflation problems in any reasonable time frame. For example, suppose that we accept the supply-siders' contention that their policies would increase full-employment output substantially. In a period of two or three years, it seems doubtful that these policies could increase full-employment output enough to offset the sorts of inflationary pressures experienced in the late 1970s. Even if supply-side policies could increase the annual rate of growth of full-employment output by one-half of a percentage point (a stellar performance indeed), this would be too little to make much headway against such inflationary pressures.

Supply-side policies should not be viewed as a replacement for demand management. This does not mean that such policies cannot be worthwhile or important. On the contrary, it is of the utmost importance that our

CASE STUDY 14.3 MORE ON THE TAX CUT OF 1981

As indicated in previous chapters, supply-side economists played an important role in formulating and arguing for the huge tax cut in 1981. Individual income taxes were cut 25 percent across the board over three years. Corporate taxes were reduced as a consequence of an increase in the pace at which depreciation can be charged against current income. Other tax reductions were enacted as well.

The first phase of the tax cut occurred in 1981 and was discounted by the administration, because it was only 5 percent and did not prevent the recession of 1981–82. Economic policy makers in the Reagan administration, therefore, counted on the large tax cut of 10 percent in 1982 to stimulate the economy. They argued that the Reagan Economic Recovery Program could only be judged after the successive 10 percent tax cuts in 1982 and 1983 had occurred. They were banking on the success of the successive 10 percent tax cuts to show up in a strong recovery.

In fact, there was a strong recovery in 1983 and 1984; particularly at the beginning of 1984, the supply-siders were often more accurate than other economists in forecasting how strong it would be. However, according to critics of supply-side economics, this substantial increase in real NNP should have been expected on the basis of the Keynesian model described in Chapter 6. To them, the strong recovery of 1983 and 1984 was testimony to the continued usefulness of the Keynesian model, highly simplified though it is.

Also, critics of supply-side economics point out that some supply-siders claimed that the 1981 tax cut would increase output so dramatically that there would be no substantial increase in the federal deficit because output would rise sufficiently to offset the cut in tax rates. Instead, the deficit for fiscal 1985 was about $200 billion. In response to such criticisms, the supply-siders blame the Fed's tight-money policies for the fact that output did not grow as much as they expected.

nation devote attention to pushing its aggregate supply curve to the right. But it is incorrect to view such policies as adequate counter-cyclical measures. The need to influence the aggregate demand curve remains.

SUMMARY

1. Keynesians have tended to view the private sector of the economy as inherently unstable, and they have favored the use of fiscal policy to offset this instability. They have tended to feel that fiscal policy was more important, relative to monetary policy, than have monetarists. Keynesians

have based their analysis of business fluctuations on the sorts of concepts taken up in Chapters 5 and 6.

2. Monetarists have tended to view the private sector of the economy as inherently quite stable, and they have blamed much of the economy's instability on clumsy or ill-conceived policies of the government. They have emphasized the importance of monetary policy. Monetarists have based their analysis of business fluctuations on the equation of exchange, discussed in Chapter 13.

3. Many leading monetarists feel that the Federal Reserve, in its attempts to stabilize the economy, does more harm than good. They favor the establishment of a rule to govern monetary policy, an idea most Keynesians oppose.

4. During the 1970s, as more evidence accumulated, the choice between monetary and fiscal policy, which had been at the center of the debate for so long, seemed to wane in importance. At present, most monetarists concede that fiscal policy can affect output and the price level, and most Keynesians concede the same regarding monetary policy.

5. At present, the debate seems to focus on the stability of private spending, the flexibility of prices, and the desirability of rules rather than discretionary government action. Monetarists tend to feel that: if the government's economic policies did not destabilize the economy, private spending would be quite stable; even if intended private spending is not entirely stable, flexible prices tend to stabilize it; and an activist monetary and fiscal policy is likely to do more harm than good.

6. Keynesians tend to feel that: business and consumer spending represents a substantial source of economic instability that should be offset by monetary and fiscal policy; price flexibility cannot be depended on to promote economic stability in a reasonable length of time; and an activist monetary and fiscal policy is likely to do more good than harm.

7. According to rational expectations theorists, the government cannot use monetary and fiscal policies in the way described in previous chapters because the models presented in these chapters do not recognize that the expectations of firms and individuals concerning their incomes, job prospects, sales, and other relevant variables are influenced by government policies.

8. Supply-side economics is concerned primarily with influencing aggregate supply. To stimulate rightward shifts in the aggregate supply curve, supply-siders favor the use of various financial incentives, particularly tax cuts. Supply-side policies cannot be viewed as a replacement for demand management.

PART 4

☆☆☆☆☆☆☆☆☆☆☆☆☆☆☆☆☆

Economic Decision Making: The Firm, the Consumer, Society

CHAPTER 15

★ ★ ★ ★ ★ ★ ★ ★

The Business Firm: Organization, Motivation, and Optimal Input Decisions

LEARNING OBJECTIVES

In this chapter, you should learn:

★ The pros and cons of various types of business organizations (proprietorships, partnerships, corporations)

★ The concept of the production function

★ The law of diminishing marginal returns

★ How firms should make input decisions, if they want to maximize profit

It is hard to overstate the importance of business firms in the American economy. They produce the bulk of our goods and services, hire most of the nation's workers, and issue stocks and bonds that represent a large percentage of the nation's wealth. Judged by any yardstick—even less complimentary ones like the responsibility for environmental pollution—business firms are an extremely important part of the American economy.

In economies based largely on free enterprise, like our own, the managers of business firms have considerable responsibility for deciding where, when, and how various resources are used. Thus the manager's job is a central one, from both a social and private point of view. Fortunately, the United States has been able to develop large cadres of effective managerial talent, in large part because management and business have been highly esteemed professions in the United States. As President Calvin Coolidge put it, with characteristic brevity and uncharacteristic overstatement, "The business of America is business."

Firms compete in an annual race sponsored by a New York bank

In this chapter, we will take a close look at the decision-making process within the firm. We begin by discussing the organization, motivation, and technology of the firm, and then focus particular attention on the following central question: If a firm attempts to maximize profits, what production technique—that is, what combination of inputs—should it choose to produce a particular quantity of output? Two points should be noted at the outset. First, when finding the optimal input combination, we take as given the quantity of output that the firm will produce. In subsequent chapters, we shall discuss how the firm should choose this output quantity. Second, an important purpose of this chapter and Chapters 16 and 18 is to show how a product's supply curve can be derived. In this chapter, we present some of the concepts and findings required for this purpose.

GENERAL MOTORS: A STUDY

In Chapter 2, when we first discussed the role of the business firm in the American economy, we cited two examples of American business firms: Peter Amacher's drugstore and the General Motors Corporation. Now that we are considering the operations of the business firm in more detail, let's look more closely at the General Motors Corporation.

The Early Years

General Motors was formed in 1908 by William C. Durant, an energetic and imaginative businessman who made over a million dollars in the carriage business before he was 40. After taking over the bankrupt Buick Motor Company in 1904, Durant built it into a very successful operation. Then, in 1908, he gained control of a number of small automobile companies (including Cadillac and Olds), several truck firms, and 10 parts and accessory firms. The resulting amalgamation was General Motors.

In 1910, General Motors's sales fell and Durant lacked the funds to pay his work force and suppliers. To get the money he needed, he went to a banking syndicate, which lent him $15 million but required him to turn over the management of the company to them. By 1915, Durant had acquired another auto producer, Chevrolet, and had picked up formidable financial allies in the Du Ponts, the owners of the famous chemical firm. Using both these levers, Durant regained full control of General Motors in 1916; and between 1916 and 1920, he concentrated on expanding the productive capacity of the General Motors Corporation. A man of extraordinary vision, he recognized, as did few of his contemporaries, a great potential demand for moderately priced cars, and he devoted his energy to putting General Motors in a position to satisfy this demand.

Reorganization of the Firm

Although Durant was a man of great vision, he was not the sort of administrator who created a tidy organizational structure. The General Motors Corporation under Durant was a large agglomeration of companies in a variety of product lines, with somewhat tangled lines of communication and diffuse control. When automobile sales did not come up to expectations in 1920, the firm suffered a reduction in profits. The resulting crisis led to Durant's retirement as president of General Motors, and the adoption by the firm of a new organizational plan created by Alfred Sloan, a young M.I.T.-trained engineer, who soon became president.

Alfred Sloan

This plan divided General Motors into a number of divisions: the Buick division, the Chevrolet division, the accessory division, and so forth. Each division was given considerable freedom, but greater attention was devoted to central control and coordination than under Durant's more anarchic organization. Sloan's organizational plan, an important innovation in its day, remained in effect with little change for many years. (Figure 15.1 shows how General Motors has been organized.)

Figure 15.1
Organization Chart for General Motors Corporation
General Motors has been divided into a number of divisions —Buick, Chevrolet, GMC Truck, Allison, and so on. Although the bulk of GM's sales comes from automobiles, it also manufactures refrigerators and a variety of other types of equipment. In the 1980s, the organization has changed, with the acquisition of Electronic Data Systems and the evolution of the firm's Saturn project.

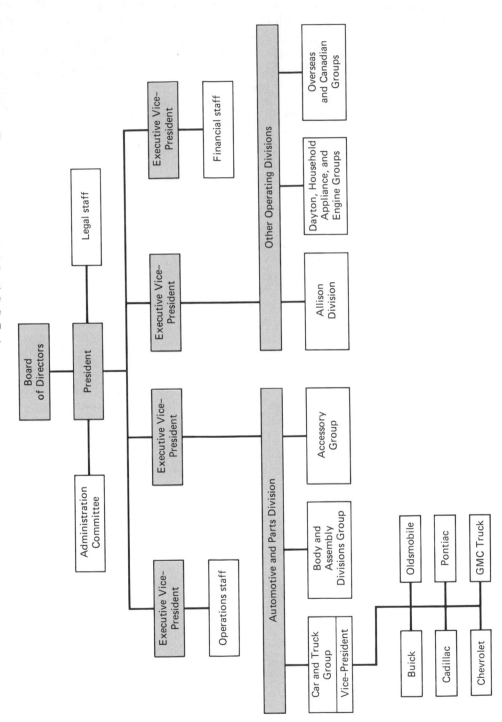

Prosperity and New Challenges

During the 1920s General Motors prospered. Its sales rose from $600 million in 1920 to $1,500 million in 1929, and its profits rose from about $38 million in 1920 to about $248 million in 1929. The next decade was different. The 1930s were the years of the Great Depression, when sales

CASE STUDY 15.1 STUDEBAKER AND THE LOW-VOLUME TRAP

In this case study, we turn from General Motors to another major auto producer, Studebaker, which, after having had its ups and downs before World War II, started off the postwar period in good shape. Flush with cash, Studebaker capitalized on the pent-up demand of the war years by being the first to come out with a new model— a streamlined car of the future. The firm prospered in the late 1940s and early 1950s, and in 1952 it had its best year ever.

As the seller's market of the early postwar years disappeared, however, serious weaknesses in Studebaker's position became obvious. The auto industry was very competitive in the mid-1950s. There were eight major manufacturers (today's Big Three and Studebaker, plus Nash, Hudson, Packard, and Willys). Studebaker suffered from bad management and high-cost labor, but one of its major problems could not have been easily solved by either management or labor—its inability to capture the cost savings that result from a large scale of production.

General Motors and the other large manufacturers had begun to introduce new models every year. While these firms could spread the costs of new model development (about $30 million) over the 1–2 million units they produced each year, Studebaker was selling fewer than 300,000 cars a year. The company could not reach the minimum cost per car that was possible through large volume. In 1953, it scheduled production of 350,000 cars but built only 186,000. By 1954, Studebaker had set its break-even point at 108,000 per year and was trying to reduce the figure still further.

In 1963, Studebaker's sales dipped to 66,000 as the temporary success of the Lark slowed when the Big Three brought out compacts of their own. If the company had plowed its profits back into expansion in the late 1940s, it might have been able to reach a scale of production that would have enabled it to compete with the larger manufacturers. But its small size made it impossible for Studebaker to weather its other problems, and the company was forced to close in 1964.

N.B.

and profits of most firms, including General Motors, were hard hit. But during the 1940s General Motors entered another period of prosperity and growth. Its sales rose from about $1.8 billion in 1940 to about $5.7 billion in 1949, and its profits rose from about $196 million in 1940 to about $656 million in 1949. The 1950s and 1960s saw the prosperity of General Motors continue. Of course there were short intervals when sales and profits fell, but the trend was upward—in part because of population growth and in part because higher incomes meant bigger sales of automobiles. The firm experienced no prolonged period of low profits or considerable excess capacity, as was the case in the 1930s.

However, in the 1970s trouble began to appear in the form of imported Japanese cars. By 1981, the trouble was serious, as evidenced by General Motors' third-quarter loss of about $500 million. Quotas on Japanese imported cars helped the firm to get back into the black, and in 1984 the firm seemed healthier than it had been. But for the foreseeable future, General Motors will have to work hard to compete successfully against the Japanese imports. The stakes are large, since the somewhat jumbled organization William Durant assembled in 1908 is now one of the biggest industrial companies in the United States.

CHARACTERISTICS OF AMERICAN FIRMS: SOME SALIENT FACTS

General Motors is an economic colossus, a huge organization with over 700,000 employees. Of course it is not typical of American business firms. If we broaden our focus to take in the entire population of business firms in the United States, the first thing we note is their tremendous number; according to government statistics, there are about 16 million. The vast majority of these firms, as one would expect, are very small. There are lots of grocery stores, gas stations, auto dealers, drugstores (like Mr. Amacher's), clothing shops, restaurants, and so on. You see hundreds of them as you walk along practically any downtown city street. But these small firms, although numerous, do not control the bulk of the nation's productive capacity. The several hundred largest firms have great economic power, measured by their sales, assets, employment, or other such indexes. The small firms tend to be weak and short-lived. Although some prosper, many small firms go out of business after only a few years of existence.

The next thing to note is that *most of the nation's business firms are engaged in agriculture, services, and retail trade.* Table 15.1 shows that about three-quarters of the firms in the United States are in these industries, an understandable figure since these industries tend to be composed of small businesses. *Although manufacturing firms constitute only about 3 percent of all American firms, they account for more than one-third of all business receipts.* On the other hand, agriculture (including forestry and fisheries) includes about 25 percent of the nation's business firms, but accounts for only 3 percent of the total receipts. Clearly, this is because manufacturing firms tend to be much bigger in terms of receipts, employment, and assets, than agricultural firms. Think, for example, of the steel plants in Pittsburgh or Cleveland, or of the aircraft plants in California or Georgia. They dwarf the typical farm—and they are only part of a larger manufacturing firm.

Industry	Number of firms (millions)	Receipts of firms (billions of dollars)
Agriculture, forestry, and fisheries	4.0	170
Mining	0.1	143
Construction	1.4	318
Manufacturing	0.5	2,099
Transportation, communication[b]	0.5	456
Wholesale and retail trade	3.4	1,968
Financial	2.1	353
Services	4.5	368
Total	16.2	5,877

[a]Figures may not sum to total due to rounding.
[b]Includes electric and gas.
Source: Statistical Abstract of the United States.

Table 15.1
Number and Receipts of Business Firms, by Industry, United States[a]

Finally, note that *most of the nation's business firms are proprietorships;* indeed, almost four-fifths fall into this category, while about 14 percent are corporations, and about 8 percent are partnerships. You often hear the terms *proprietorship, partnership, and corporation.* What do these terms mean?

PROPRIETORSHIPS

A proprietorship is a legal form of business organization—the most common form and also the simplest. Specifically, a ***proprietorship*** is a firm owned by a single individual. A great many of the nation's small businesses are proprietorships. For example, the corner drugstore may well be one. If so, it has a single owner. He hires the people he needs to wait on customers, deliver orders, do the bookkeeping, and so forth. He borrows, if he can, whatever money he feels he needs. He reaps the profits, or incurs the losses. All his personal assets—his house, his furniture, his car—can be taken by creditors to meet the drugstore's bills; he has unlimited liability for the debts of the business.

PROS. What President Lincoln said about the common man applies as well to proprietorships: God must love them, or He wouldn't have created so many of them. If proprietorships didn't have advantages over other legal forms of business organization under many sorts of circumstances, there wouldn't be so many of them. What are these advantages? First, *owners of proprietorships have complete control over their businesses.* They don't have to negotiate with partners or other co-owners. They are the boss—and the only boss. Anyone who has been in a position of complete authority knows the joy it can bring. Many proprietors treasure this feeling of independence. Second, *a proprietorship is easy and inexpensive to establish:* all you have to do is hang out your shingle and announce you are in business. This too is a great advantage.

CONS. But proprietorships have important disadvantages as well, and for this reason they are seldom found in many important industries. One disadvantage is that *it is difficult for a proprietor to put together enough financial resources to enter industries like automobiles or steel.* No one in the world has enough money to establish, by himself or herself, a firm of General Motors' present size. Another disadvantage is that *proprietors are liable for all of the debts of the firm.* If their business fails, their personal assets can be taken by their creditors, and they can be completely wiped out.

PARTNERSHIPS

A *partnership* is more complicated than a proprietorship. As its name implies, it is a form of business organization where two or more people agree to own and conduct a business. Each partner agrees to contribute some proportion of the capital and labor used by the business, and to receive some proportion of the profits or losses. There are many types of partnerships. In some cases, one or more of the partners may be "silent partners" who put up some of the money but have little or nothing to do with the operations of the firm. The partnership is a common form of business organization in some industries and professions, such as the law. But as we saw in a previous section, partnerships are found less frequently than proprietorships or corporations in the United States.

PROS. A partnership has certain advantages. Like a proprietorship, *it can be established without great expense or legal red tape.* (However, if you ever go into a partnership with someone, you would be well advised to have a good lawyer draw up a written agreement establishing such things as the salaries of each partner and how profits are to be shared.) In addition, a partnership can avoid some of the problems involved in a proprietorship. *It can usually put together more financial resources and specialized knowhow than a proprietorship,* and this can be an important advantage.

CONS. But the partnership also has certain drawbacks. First, *each partner is liable without limit for the bills of the firm.* For example, even if one partner of a law firm has only a 30 percent share of the firm, he or she may be called upon to pay all the firm's debts if the other partners cannot do so. Second, *there is some red tape in keeping a partnership in existence.* Whenever a partner dies or withdraws, or whenever a new partner is admitted, a new partnership must be established. Third, though preferable to a proprietorship, *the partnership is still not a very effective way to obtain the large amounts of capital required for some modern industries.*

299 ★
Corporations

A modern automobile plant may cost $500 million, and not many partnerships could assemble that much capital. For these reasons, as well as for others discussed in the next section, the corporation has become the dominant form of business organization in America.

CORPORATIONS

A far more complicated form of business organization than either the proprietorship or partnership, the *corporation* is a fictitious legal person, separate and distinct from its owners. A corporation is formed by having lawyers draw up the necessary papers stating (in general terms) what sorts of activities the owners of the corporation intend to engage in. The owners of the corporation are the stockholders. Stock, pieces of paper signifying ownership of the corporation, is issued to the owners, generally in exchange for their cash. The corporation's board of directors, which is responsible for setting overall policy for the firm, is elected by the stockholders. Ordinarily, each share of stock gives its owner one vote. The firm's owners can, if they are dissatisfied with the company's policies or think they have better opportunities elsewhere, sell their stock to someone else, assuming, of course, that they can find a buyer.

PROS. The corporation has many advantages over the partnership or proprietorship. In particular, *each of the corporation's owners has limited, not unlimited, liability.* If I decide to become one of the owners of General Motors and if a share of General Motors stock sells for $70, I can buy ten shares of General Motors stock for $700. And I can be sure that if General Motors falls on hard times, I cannot lose more than the $700 I paid for the stock. There is no way that I can be assessed beyond this. Moreover, *the corporation, unlike the partnership or proprietorship, has unlimited life.* If several stockholders want to withdraw from the firm, they simply sell their stock. The corporation goes on, although the identity of the owners changes. For these reasons, *the corporation is clearly a better device for raising large sums of money than the partnership or proprietorship.* This is an enormous advantage of the corporation, particularly in such industries as automobiles and steel, which could not otherwise finance their operations.

CONS. Without question, the corporation is a very important social invention. It permits people to assemble the large quantities of capital required for efficient production in many industries. Without limited liability and the other advantages of the corporation, it is doubtful that the opportunities and benefits of large-scale production could have been reaped. This does not mean that the corporate form will work for all firms. If a firm requires only a modest amount of capital, there is no reason to go to the extra trouble and expense of establishing a corporation. Moreover, one disadvantage of the corporation is double taxation of income, since corporations themselves pay income taxes—and the tax rate is often almost one-half of every extra dollar earned. Thus every dollar earned by a corporation and distributed to stockholders is taxed twice by the federal government—once when it is counted as income by the corporation, and once when the remainder is counted as income by the stockholders.

MOTIVATION OF THE FIRM

What determines the behavior of the business firm? As a first approximation, *economists generally assume that firms attempt to maximize* **profits,** which are defined as the difference between the firm's revenue and its costs. In other words, economists generally assume that firms try to make as much money as possible. This assumption does not seem unreasonable; most businesses appear to be interested in making money. Nonetheless, the assumption of profit maximization oversimplifies the situation. Although businesses certainly want profits, they are interested in other things as well. Some firms claim that they want to promote better cultural activities or better racial relations in their community. At a less lofty level, other firms say that their aim is to increase their share of the market. Whether or not one takes these self-proclaimed goals very seriously, it is clear that firms are not interested *only* in making money.

TECHNOLOGY, INPUTS, AND THE PRODUCTION FUNCTION

The decisions a firm should make in order to maximize its profits are determined by the current state of technology.

Technology

Technology is the sum total of society's knowledge concerning the industrial arts. Just as consumers are limited by their income, firms are limited by the current state of technology. If the current state of technology is such that we do not know how to produce more than 40 bushels of corn per year from an acre of land and 2 man-years of labor, then this is as much as the firm can produce from this combination of land and labor. In making its decisions, the firm must take this into account.

Inputs

In constructing a model of the profit-maximizing firm, economists must somehow represent the state of technology and include it in their model. As a first step toward this end, we must define an **input.** Perhaps the simplest definition of an input is that it is anything the firm uses in its production process. Some of the inputs of a farm producing corn might be seed, land, labor, water, fertilizer, and various types of machinery, as well as the time of the people managing the farm.

Production Function

Having defined an input, we can now describe how economists represent the state of technology. The basic concept economists use for this purpose is the production function.

For any commodity, *the* **production function** *is the relationship between the quantities of various inputs used per period of time and the maximum quantity of the commodity that can be produced per period of time.* More specifically, the production function is a table, a graph, or an equation showing the maximum output rate that can be achieved from any specified set of usage rates of inputs. The production function summarizes the characteristics of existing technology at a given point in time. It reflects the technological constraints the firm must reckon with.

To see more clearly what we mean by a production function, consider the Milwaukee Machine Company, a hypothetical machine shop that produces a simple metal part. Suppose that we are considering a period of time that is so short that the firm's basic plant and equipment cannot be altered. For simplicity, suppose that the only input whose quantity can be altered in this period is the amount of labor used by the machine shop. Suppose that the firm collects data showing the relationship between the quantity of its output and the quantity of labor it uses. This relationship, given in Table 15.2, is the firm's production function. It shows that when 1 worker is employed, 100 parts are produced per month; when 2 workers are employed, 210 parts are produced per month; and so on. Information concerning a firm's production function is often obtained from the firm's engineers, as well as its craftsmen and technicians.

Table 15.2
Production Function, Milwaukee Machine Company

Quantity of labor used per month (number of men employed)	Output per month (number of parts)
0	0
1	100
2	210
3	315
4	415
5	500

TYPES OF INPUTS

In analyzing production processes, we suppose that all inputs can be classified into two categories: fixed and variable inputs.

A fixed input *is one whose quantity cannot change during the period of time under consideration.* This period will vary. It may be six months in one case, six years in another case. Among the most important inputs often included as fixed are the firm's plant and equipment—its factory and office buildings, its machinery, its tooling, and its transportation facilities. In the simple example of the wheat farm in Table 15.3, land is a fixed input since its quantity is assumed to be fixed at 1 acre.

Table 15.3
Relationship
between Labor
Input and Output on
1-Acre Wheat Farm

Number of man-years of labor	Bushels of wheat produced per year
0	0
1	30
2	70
3	100
4	125
5	145

A **variable input** *is one whose quantity can be changed during the relevant period.* It is generally possible to increase or decrease the number of workers engaged in a particular activity (although this is not always the case, since they may have long-term contracts). Similarly, it frequently is possible to alter the amount of raw material that is used. In the case of the wheat farm in Table 15.3, labor clearly is a variable input since its quantity can be varied from 0 to 5 man-years.

THE SHORT RUN AND THE LONG RUN

Whether an input is considered variable or fixed depends on the length of the period under consideration. The longer the period, the more inputs are variable, not fixed. Although the length of the period varies from case to case, economists have found it very useful to focus special attention on two time periods: the short run and the long run. *The* **short run** *is defined as the period of time in which at least one of the firm's inputs is fixed.* More specifically, since the firm's plant and equipment are among the most difficult inputs to change quickly, *the short run is generally understood to mean the length of time during which the firm's plant and equipment are fixed.* On the other hand, *the* **long run** *is that period of time in which all inputs are variable.* In the long run, the firm can make a complete adjustment to any change in its environment.

To illustrate the distinction between the short run and the long run, let's consider General Motors. Any period of time during which GM's plant and equipment cannot be altered freely is the short run. A period of one year is certainly a case of the short run, because in a year GM could not vary the quantity of its plant and equipment. It takes longer than a year to construct an automotive plant, or to alter an existing plant to produce a new kind of automobile. For example, the tooling phase of the model changeover cycle currently takes about 2 years. Also, because some of its existing contracts with suppliers and workers extend for more than a year, GM cannot vary all its inputs in a year without violating these contracts. On the other hand, any period of time during which GM can vary the quantity of all inputs is the long run. A period of 50 years is certainly a case of the long run. Whether a shorter period of time—10 years, say—is a long-run situation depends on the problem at hand. If all the relevant inputs can be varied, it is a long-run situation; if not, it is a short-run situation.

A useful way to look at the long run is to consider it a *planning horizon*. While operating in the short run, the firm must continually be planning ahead and deciding its strategy for the long run. Its decisions concerning the long run determine the sort of short-run position the firm will occupy in the future. Before a firm makes the decision to add a new type of product to its line, the firm is in a long-run situation (with regard to the new product), since it can choose among a wide variety of types and sizes of equipment to produce the new product. But once the investment is made, the firm is confronted with a short-run situation, since the type and size of equipment is, to a considerable extent, frozen.

AVERAGE PRODUCT OF AN INPUT

In order to determine which production technique—that is, which combination of inputs—a firm should use, it is necessary to define the average product and marginal product of an input. *The average product of an input is the firm's total output divided by the amount of input used to produce this amount of output.* The average product of an input can be calculated from the production function. Consider the wheat farm in Table 15.3. The average product of labor is 30 bushels per man-year of labor when 1 man-year of labor is used, 35 bushels per man-year of labor when 2 man-years are used, 33⅓ bushels per man-year of labor when 3 man-years are used, and so forth.

MARGINAL PRODUCT OF AN INPUT

As the amount of labor used on the farm increases, so does the farm's output; but the amount of extra output from the addition of an extra man-year of labor varies depending on how much labor is already being used. The extra output from the addition of the first man-year of labor is $30 - 0 = 30$ bushels per man-year of labor. The extra output due to the addition of the second man-year of labor is $70 - 30 = 40$ bushels per man-year of labor. And the extra output from the addition of the fifth man-year of labor is $145 - 125 = 20$ bushels per man-year of labor. *The* **marginal product** *of an input is the addition to total output due to the addition of the last unit of input, the quantity of other inputs used being* *held constant.* Thus the marginal product of labor is 30 bushels when between 0 and 1 man-years of labor are used, 40 bushels when between 1 and 2 man-years of labor are used, and so on.

Table 15.4 shows the average and marginal products of labor at various levels of utilization of labor; Figure 15.2 shows the same thing graphically. The data in both Table 15.4 and Figure 15.2 concerning the average and marginal products of labor are derived from the production function. Given the production function, shown in Table 15.3 and reproduced in Table 15.4, the average and marginal products at each level of utilization of labor can be determined in the way we have indicated.

In Figure 15.2, as in the case of most production processes, the average product of the variable input (labor in this case) rises, reaches a maximum, and then falls. The marginal product of labor also rises, reaches a maxi-

Table 15.4
Average and Marginal Products of Labor, 1-Acre Wheat Farm

Number of man-years of labor	Total output (bushels per year)	Marginal product (bushels per man-year)	Average product (bushels per man-year)
0	0		—
		30	
1	30		30
		40	
2	70		35
		30	
3	100		$33\frac{1}{3}$
		25	
4	125		31¼
		20	
5	145		29

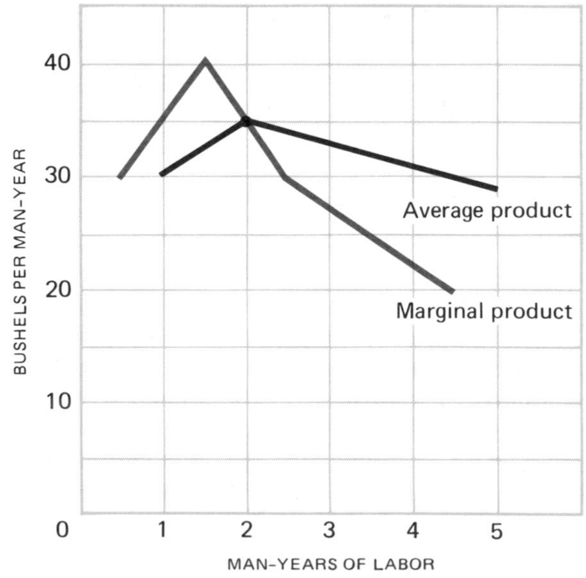

Figure 15.2
Average and Marginal Products of Labor, 1-Acre Wheat Farm
The marginal product of the first man-year of labor (which, according to Table 15.4, equals 30 bushels per man-year) is plotted at the midpoint between 0 and 1 man-year of labor. The marginal product of the second man-year of labor is plotted at the midpoint between 1 and 2 man-years of labor. The marginal product curve connects these and other points showing the marginal product of various amounts of labor.

mum, and falls. This too is typical of many production processes. Why do average and marginal product behave in this way? Because of the law of diminishing marginal returns, to which we now turn.

305 ★
Law of
Diminishing
Marginal Returns

THE LAW OF DIMINISHING MARGINAL RETURNS

Perhaps the best-known, and certainly one of the least understood, laws of economics is the so-called *law of diminishing marginal returns*. Put in a single sentence, this law states that *if equal increments of an input are added, the quantities of other inputs being held constant, the resulting increments of product will decrease beyond some point;* that is, the marginal product of the input will diminish.

Suppose that a small factory that manufactures a metal automobile component has eight machine tools. If this firm hires only one or two workers, total output and output per worker will be quite low. These workers will have a number of quite different tasks to perform, and the advantages of specialization will be sacrificed. Workers will spend considerable time switching from one machine to another, and many of the eight machine tools will be idle much of the time. What happens as the firm increases its work force? As more and more workers are added, the marginal product (that is, the extra product) of each will tend to rise, as the work force grows to the point where it can operate the fixed amount of equipment effectively. However, if the firm continues to increase the number of workers, the marginal product of a worker will eventually begin to decrease. Why? Because workers will have to wait in line to use the fixed number of machine tools, and because the extra workers will have to be assigned to less and less important tasks. Eventually, if enough workers are hired (and utilized within the plant), they may get in each other's way to such an extent that production may grind to a halt.

Returning to the wheat farm discussed in the previous section, Table 15.4 shows that the law of diminishing marginal returns applies in this case too. The third column of this table indicates that beyond 2 man-years of labor, the marginal product of labor falls. Certainly, it seems entirely reasonable that as more and more of a variable input (in this case, labor) is combined with a fixed amount of another input (in this case, land), the additional output to be derived from an additional unit of the variable input will eventually decrease. In the case of a 1 acre wheat farm, one would expect that as more and more labor is added, the extra workers' functions eventually would become less and less important and productive.

The law of diminishing marginal returns plays a major part in determining the firm's optimal input combination and the shape of the firm's cost functions, as we shall see in this and the next chapter. To prevent misunderstanding and confusion, several points about this law should be stressed. First, *it is assumed that technology remains fixed.* If technology changes, the law of diminishing marginal returns cannot predict the effect of an additional unit of input. Second, *at least one input must be fixed in quantity,* since the law of diminishing marginal returns is not applicable to cases where there is a proportional increase in all inputs. Third, *it must be possible to vary the proportions in which the various inputs are utilized.* This is generally possible in industry and agriculture.

THE OPTIMAL INPUT DECISION

Now we are in a position to answer the question posed at the beginning of this chapter: Given that a firm is going to produce a particular quantity of output, what production technique—that is, what combination of inputs —should it choose to maximize profits? Note first that if the firm maximizes its profits it must minimize the cost of producing this quantity of output. This seems obvious enough. But what combination of inputs (that will produce the required quantity of output) will minimize the firm's costs? The answer can be stated like this: *The firm will minimize cost by combining inputs in such a way that the marginal product of a dollar's worth of any one input equals the marginal product of a dollar's worth of any other input used.*

Another way to say the same thing is: *The firm will minimize cost by combining inputs in such a way that, for every input used, the marginal product of the input is proportional to its price.* Why does this say the same thing? Because the marginal product of a dollar's worth of an input equals the marginal product of the input divided by its price. If the marginal product of a man-year of labor is 40 units of output, and if the price of labor is $4,000 per man-year, the marginal product of a dollar's worth of labor is 40 ÷ $4,000 = .01 units of output. Thus, if the firm is satisfying the rule for cost minimization in the previous paragraph—if it is combining inputs so that the marginal product of a dollar's worth of any one input equals the marginal product of a dollar's worth of any other input used— it must at the same time be combining inputs so that for every input used, the marginal product of the input is proportional to its price.

The Wheat Farm: A Numerical Example

To illustrate the application of this rule, let's take a numerical example from the wheat farm cited above. Suppose that the farm can vary the amount of labor and land it uses. Table 15.5 shows the marginal product of each input when various combinations of inputs (all combinations being able to produce the specified quantity of output) are used. Suppose that the price of labor is $4,000 per man-year and that the annual price of using land is $1,000 per acre. (We assume that the firm takes the prices of inputs as given and that it can buy all it wants of the inputs at these prices.) For each combination of inputs, Table 15.5 shows the marginal product of each input divided by its price. Based on our rule, the optimal input combination is 4.1 acres of land and 1 man-year of labor, since this is the

CASE STUDY 15.2 THE COCA-COLA COMPANY AND INPUT COSTS

In 1985 the Coca-Cola company made a well-publicized change in its formula for Coke. The company touted the change with a huge marketing campaign. In fact, the formula for Coke had been quietly changed six years earlier.

Because of worldwide shortages, the price of beet and cane sugar jumped from 19 cents per pound in September 1978 to 26 cents per pound in January 1979. While such a price hike does not dramatically affect most sugar buyers, for Coke it was catastrophic. A change of 1 cent per pound in sugar prices can cause a $20 million swing in Coke's operating profits. The bottling empire is America's largest sugar buyer, taking a million tons per year or about 10 percent of all the sugar sold in the United States.

Because of the efficiencies of corn production in this country, a sweetener made by refining corn into sugar makes high-fructose corn sweeteners about 10 percent cheaper than beet and cane sugar when prices are normal. By using a 55 percent fructose sweetener, Coca-Cola can realize substantial cost savings, particularly when sugar prices are abnormally high. Coke publicly announced the switch to corn sweeteners in January 1979, but other than sugar producers and traders, no one seemed to notice. Eight months later, 7-Up followed suit and decided to increase its use of corn sweeteners, and Pepsi also considered such a move.

The response of the soft drink companies to the high price of sugar is typical of any firm faced with a high-priced input. Firms try to reduce the use of expensive inputs in order to maintain profits or to avoid having to raise the price of their products (and risk losing sales to competitors). The higher the price of an input, the more incentive there is for a profit-maximizing firm to conserve on its use of that input.

N.B.

| Amount of input used | | Marginal product | | Marginal product ÷ price of input | | Total cost |
Labor (man-years)	Land (acres)	Labor	Land	Labor	Land	(dollars)
0.5	7.0	50	5	50 ÷ 4,000	5 ÷ 1,000	9,000
1.0	4.1	40	10	40 ÷ 4,000	10 ÷ 1,000	8,100
1.5	3.0	30	30	30 ÷ 4,000	30 ÷ 1,000	9,000
2.5	2.0	20	50	20 ÷ 4,000	50 ÷ 1,000	12,000

Table 15.5
Determination of Optimal Input Combination

only combination (capable of producing the required output) where the marginal product of labor divided by the price of labor equals the marginal product of land divided by the price of land.

Is this rule correct? Does it really result in a least-cost combination of inputs? Let's look at the cost of the various input combinations in Table 15.5. The first combination (0.5 man-years of labor and 7 acres of land) costs $9,000; the second combination (1.0 man-years of labor and 4.1 acres of land) costs $8,100; and so on. An examination of the total cost of each input combination shows that the input combination chosen by our rule (1.0 man-years of labor and 4.1 acres of land) is indeed the least-cost input combination, the one for the profit-maximizing firm to use.

 **EXPLORING FURTHER: HOW TO PRODUCE KANSAS CORN**

To illustrate the practical payoff from the sort of analysis discussed in this chapter, let's consider how a distinguished agricultural economist, Earl Heady of Iowa State University, has used these methods to help farmers make better production decisions. Table 15.6 shows the various amounts of land and fertilizer that will produce 82.6 bushels of corn on Kansas Verdigras soil. As you can see, this amount of corn can be produced if 1.19 acres of land and no fertilizer are used, or if 1.11 acres of land and 20 pounds of fertilizer are used, or if .99 acres of land and 60 pounds of fertilizer are used, and so forth.

Table 15.6
Combinations of Fertilizer and Land Required to Produce 82.6 Bushels of Corn, and Ratio of Marginal Products at Each Such Combination

| Amount of input used | | Marginal product of fertilizer ÷ Marginal product of land |
Fertilizer (pounds)	Land (acres)	
0	1.19	.0045
20	1.11	.0038
40	1.04	.0030
60	0.99	.0019
80	0.96	.0010
100	0.95	.0003

Source: E. Heady and L. Tweeten, *Resource Demand and Structure of the Agricultural Industry,* Ames: Iowa State University Press, 1963, p. 111.

The third column of Table 15.6 shows the ratio of the marginal product of a pound of fertilizer to the marginal product of an acre of land, when each of these input combinations is used. For example, when 1.19 acres of land and no fertilizer are used, this ratio equals .0045. Based on the rule discussed in previous sections, a firm, if it minimizes costs, must set this ratio equal to the ratio of the price of a pound of fertilizer to the price of an acre of land. Why? Because the rule discussed above stipulates that the firm should choose an input combination so that

$$\frac{\text{marginal product of fertilizer}}{\text{price of fertilizer}} = \frac{\text{marginal product of land}}{\text{price of land}}$$

So, if we multiply both sides of this equation by the price of fertilizer, and divide both sides by the marginal product of land, we get

$$\frac{\text{marginal product of fertilizer}}{\text{marginal product of land}} = \frac{\text{price of fertilizer}}{\text{price of land}}$$

Thus to minimize costs a firm should set the ratio in the third column of this table equal to the ratio of the price of fertilizer to the price of land.

Heady and his coworkers, having obtained the results in the above table, used this technique to determine the optimal input combination farmers should use to minimize their costs.[1] The optimal input combination depends on the price of land and the price of fertilizer. Suppose that a pound of fertilizer costs .003 times as much as an acre of land. Under these circumstances, the minimum-cost input combination would be 40 pounds of fertilizer and 1.04 acres of land—since, as shown in the table, this is the input combination where the ratio of the marginal product of fertilizer to the marginal product of land is .003. No matter what the ratio of the price of fertilizer to the price of land may be, the least-cost input combination can be derived this way.

Such results are of considerable practical value to farmers. Moreover, the same kind of analysis can be used by organizations in other sectors of the economy, not just agriculture. Studies of how the Defense Department can reduce its costs have utilized concepts and techniques of essentially this sort. In a more peaceful vein, this same kind of analysis has been used by various manufacturing firms. For example, steel firms have made many such studies to determine least-cost ways to produce steel, and auto firms have made similar studies to reduce their own costs.

SUMMARY

1. There are three principal types of business firms: proprietorships, partnerships, and corporations. The corporation has many advantages

---

[1]E. Heady and L. Tweeten, *Resource Demand and Structure of the Agricultural Industry,* Ames: Iowa State University Press, 1963. It is assumed that a certain amount of labor is used, this amount being proportional to the number of acres of land.

over the other two: limited liability, unlimited life, and greater ability to raise large sums of money. Nonetheless, because the corporation also has disadvantages, many firms are not corporations.

2. As a first approximation, economists generally assume that firms attempt to maximize profits. In large part, this is because it is a close enough approximation to reality for many of the most important purposes of economics. Also, economists are interested in the theory of the profit-maximizing firm because it provides rules of behavior for firms that do want to maximize profits.

3. To summarize the characteristics of existing technology at a given point in time, economists use the concept of the production function, which shows the maximum output rate of a given commodity that can be achieved from any specified set of usage rates of inputs.

4. Inputs can be classified into two categories: fixed and variable. A fixed input is one whose quantity cannot be changed during the period of time under consideration. A variable input is one whose quantity can be changed during the relevant period.

5. Whether an input is considered variable or fixed depends on the length of the period under consideration. The longer the period, the more inputs are variable, not fixed. The short run is defined as the period of time in which some of the firm's inputs (generally its plant and equipment) are fixed. The long run is the period of time in which all inputs are variable.

6. The average product of an input is the firm's total output divided by the amount of input used to produce this amount of output. The marginal product of an input is the addition to total output due to the addition of the last unit of input, the quantity of other inputs used being held constant.

7. The law of diminishing marginal returns states that if equal increments of an input are added (and the quantities of other inputs are held constant) the resulting increments of product will decrease beyond some point; the marginal product of the input will diminish.

8. To minimize its costs, a firm must choose its input combination so that the marginal product of a dollar's worth of any one input equals the marginal product of a dollar's worth of any other input used. Put differently, the firm should combine inputs so that for every input used, the marginal product of the input is proportional to its price. As an illustration, we showed in the section, "Exploring Further," how this sort of model can be used to determine the optimal combination of fertilizer and land in the production of Kansas corn.

CHAPTER 16

★ ★ ★ ★ ★ ★ ★ ★ ★

Getting behind the Demand and Supply Curves

LEARNING OBJECTIVES

In this chapter, you should learn:

★ How economists explain consumer behavior

★ The concept of marginal utility

★ The relation between an individual's demand curve and the market demand curve

★ The nature of the cost curves that underlie firms' decisions on supply

In a market economy, consumers decide how much to buy based on their income, their tastes, and market prices; firms decide how much to produce based on their costs and what they can charge for their products. In this chapter we look behind the individual's demand and the firm's supply curves by outlining, first, the basic model of consumer demand and, second, the role that costs play in firms' decisions of how much to produce and, therefore, supply. In Chapters 17 and 18 we will expand our discussions of supply and demand and consider what determines the characteristics of market demand and supply.

THE DEMAND CURVE

To a considerable extent, consumers, voting with their pocketbooks, are the masters of our economic system. No wonder, then, that economists spend much of their time describing and analyzing how consumers act. In addition, economists are interested in determining how consumers, as well as other decision-making units, should go about making rational choices. In this chapter, we present the basic model economists use to analyze consumer behavior.

CONSUMER EXPENDITURES

The Walters of San Diego

Since we are concerned here with consumer behavior, let's begin by looking at the behavior of a particular consumer. It is hard to find any consumer who is "typical." There are hundreds of millions of consumers in the United States, and their behavior varies enormously. But how does one particular American family—the Walters of San Diego[1]—spend its money? The Walters are in their mid-thirties, have two children (ages 8 and 6), and have Mrs. Walter's younger brother living with them. They own their own home, and both work. Mr. Walter manages a small clothing firm in San Diego, and Mrs. Walter is a designer at the same firm. Together, the Walters make about $43,000 a year.

How do the Walters spend their money? For most consumers, we cannot answer this question with any accuracy, because the people in question simply do not tell anyone what they do with their money. But because the Walters and their buying habits were scrutinized in a series of articles in a national magazine, it is possible to describe quite accurately where their money goes. As shown in Table 16.1, the Walters spend about $1,250 a month—about 35 percent of their income—on housing. They spend about $500 a month—about 14 percent of their income—on food and drink. About $250 a month—about 7 percent of their income—goes to domestic help, which is needed since both parents work.

In addition, the Walters spend about $260 a month—about 7 percent of their income—on private schools and other lessons for their children. Another $260 a month goes for entertainment and clothing. Because of the mild weather in San Diego (and perhaps because they can get clothing at a discount since they are in the clothing business), their expenditures

---

[1]For obvious reasons, we have changed the name and residence of the family in question. Otherwise, however, the facts given in the following paragraphs are as they were stated in a series of articles in a national magazine. To correct for inflation, we have increased the figures in the articles by the (approximate) percentage by which the price level has risen since the article appeared.

Table 16.1
Monthly Spending
Pattern of Mr. and
Mrs. Walter of San
Diego, California

Item	Amount (dollars)	Percent of income
Housing	1,250	35
Food and drink	500	14
Domestic help	250	7
Private school and education	260	7
Entertainment and clothing	260	7
Medical, dental, and insurance expenses	250	7
Transportation	85	2
Taxes and savings·	745	21
Monthly income	3,600	100

ᵃEstimated by deducting other items from monthly income.

on clothing are not very large. Medical, dental, and insurance expenses consume about $250 a month—again, about 7 percent of income—and $85 a month—or about 2 percent of their income—is spent on transportation. Finally, the Walters allocate about $745 a month—about 21 percent of their income—for taxes and savings.

This, in a nutshell, is how the Walters spend their money. The Walters exchange their resources (mostly labor) in the resource markets for $43,000 a year. They take this money into the product markets and spend about four-fifths of it for the goods and services described above. The remaining one-fifth of their income goes for taxes and saving. The Walters, like practically every family, keep a watchful eye on where their money goes and what they are getting in exchange for their labor and other resources.

Aggregate Data for the United States

How does the way that the Walters spend their money compare with consumer behavior in general? In Table 16.2, we provide data on how all consumers allocated their aggregate income in 1983. These data tell us much more about the typical behavior of American consumers than our case study of the Walters. Note first of all that American households paid about 15 percent of their income in taxes. This, of course, is the price of government services. In addition, American households saved about 4 percent of their income. In other words, they refrained from spending 4 percent of their income on goods and services; instead, they put this amount into stocks, bonds, bank accounts, or other such channels for saving. Also, about 2 percent of their income went for interest payments to banks and other institutions from which they had borrowed money.

American consumers spent the remaining 79 percent of their income on goods and services. Table 16.2 makes it clear that they allocated much of their expenditures to housing, food and drink, and transportation. Spending on housing, household operations, and furniture and other dura-

Table 16.2
Allocation of Income
by U.S. Households,
1983

	Percent of total[a]
Personal taxes	15
Personal saving	4
Interest payments	2
Consumption expenditures	
Autos and parts	5
Furniture and household equipment	4
Other durable goods	2
Food and drink	15
Clothing and shoes	5
Gasoline and oil	3
Other nondurable goods	6
Housing	13
Household operations	6
Transportation	3
Other services	18
Total income	100

[a]Because of rounding errors, figures do not sum to total.
Source: Survey of Current Business, July 1984.

ble household equipment accounted for about 23 percent of American consumers' total income. Spending on food and beverages accounted for about 15 percent of total income. Spending on automobiles and parts, gasoline and oil, and other transportation accounted for about 11 percent of total income. Thus taxes, savings, housing, food and drink, and transportation accounted for about 70 percent of the total income of all households in the United States.

The data in Table 16.2 make it obvious that the Walter family is not very typical of American consumers. For example, it spends a much larger percentage of its income on housing, domestic help, and education than do consumers as a whole. To some degree, this is because the Walters are more affluent than most American families, but this is only part of the reason. To a large extent, it simply reflects the fact that people want different things. Looking around you, you see considerable diversity in the way consumers spend their money. Take your own family as an example. It is a good bet that your family spends its money quite differently from the nation as a whole. If you like to live in a big house, your family may spend much more than the average on housing. Or if you like to go to sports events, your expenditures on such entertainment may be much higher than average.

A MODEL OF CONSUMER BEHAVIOR

Why do consumers spend their money the way they do? The economist answers this question with the aid of a *model of consumer behavior*, which is useful both for analysis and for decision making. To construct this model, the economist obviously must consider the tastes of the consumer which clearly influence the amount a consumer purchases of a particular commodity. Some people like beef, others like pork. Some people like the opera, others would trade a ticket to hear Luciano Pavarotti for a ticket to the Dallas Cowboys game any day of the week.

In Chapter 1, we pointed out that a model, to be useful, must omit many unimportant factors, concentrate on the basic factors at work, and simplify in order to illuminate. To focus on the important factors at work here, let's assume that there are only two goods, food and clothing. This is an innocuous assumption, since the results we shall obtain can be generalized to include cases where any number of goods exist. For simplicity, food is measured in pounds, and clothing is measured in number of pieces of clothing.

Consider Mrs. Walter, making choices for her family. Undoubtedly, she regards certain market baskets—that is, certain combinations of food and clothing (the only commodities)—to be more desirable than others. She certainly regards 2 pounds of food and 1 piece of clothing to be more desirable than 1 pound of food and 1 piece of clothing. For simplicity, suppose that it is possible to measure the amount of satisfaction that she gets from each market basket by its utility. *A utility is a number that represents the level of satisfaction that the consumer derives from a particular market basket.* For example, the utility attached to the market basket containing 2 pounds of food and 1 piece of clothing may be 10 utils, and the utility attached to the market basket containing 1 pound of food and 1 piece of clothing may be 6 utils. (A util is the traditional unit in which utility is expressed.)

Marginal Utility

It is important to distinguish between total utility and marginal utility. The total utility of a market basket is the number described in the previous paragraph; *the **marginal utility** measures the additional satisfaction derived from an additional unit of a commodity.* To see how marginal utility is obtained, let's take a close look at Table 16.3. The total utility the Walter family derives from the consumption of various amounts of food is given in the middle column of this table. (For simplicity, we assume for the moment that the Walters consume only food.) The marginal utility,

Pounds of food	Total utility	Marginal utility
0	0	
		3 (=3−0)
1	3	
		4 (=7−3)
2	7	
		2 (=9−7)
3	9	
		1 (=10−9)
4	10	

Table 16.3
Total Utility and Marginal Utility Derived by the Walters from Consuming Various Amounts of Food Per Day.ª

ªThis table assumes that no clothing is consumed. If a nonzero amount of clothing is consumed, the figures in this table will probably be altered since the marginal utility of a certain amount of food is likely to depend on the amount of clothing consumed.

shown in the right-hand column, is the extra utility derived from each amount of food over and above the utility derived from 1 less pound of food. Thus it equals the difference between the total utility of a certain amount of food and the total utility of 1 less pound of food.

For example, as shown in Table 16.3, the *total* utility of 3 pounds of food is 9 utils, which is a measure of the total amount of satisfaction that the Walters get from this much food. In contrast, the *marginal* utility of 3 pounds of food is the extra utility obtained from the third pound of food —that is, the total utility of 3 pounds of food less the total utility of 2 pounds of food. Specifically, as shown in Table 16.3, it is 2 utils. Similarly, the *total* utility of 2 pounds of food is 7 utils, which is a measure of the total amount of satisfaction that the Walters get from this much food. In contrast, the *marginal* utility of 2 pounds of food is the extra utility obtained from the second pound of food—that is, the total utility of 2 pounds of food less the total utility of 1 pound of food. Specifically, as shown in Table 16.3, it is 4 utils.

The Law of Diminishing Marginal Utility

Economists generally assume that, as a person consumes more and more of a particular commodity, there is, beyond some point, a decline in the extra satisfaction derived from the last unit of the commodity consumed. For example, if the Walters consume 2 pounds of food in a particular period of time, it may be just enough to meet their basic physical needs. If they consume 3 pounds of food in the same period of time, the third pound of food is likely to yield less satisfaction than the second. If they consume 4 pounds of food in the same period of time, the fourth pound of food is likely to yield less satisfaction than the third. And so on.

**Figure 16.1
Total and Marginal
Utility from Food
Consumption,
Walter Family**
The marginal utility of the first pound of food (which, according to Table 16.3, equals 3 utils) is plotted at the midpoint between 0 and 1 pounds of food. The marginal utility of the second pound of food (which, according to Table 16.3, equals 4 utils) is plotted at the midpoint between 1 and 2 pounds of food. The marginal-utility curve connects these and other points showing the marginal utility of various amounts of food consumed.

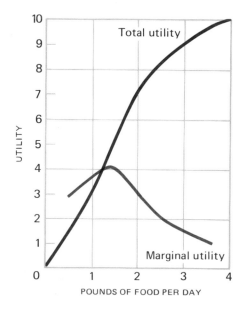

This assumption or hypothesis is often called the *law of diminishing marginal utility*. This law states that, *as a person consumes more and more of a given commodity (the consumption of other commodities being held constant), the marginal utility of the commodity eventually will tend to decline.* The figures concerning the Walter family in Table 16.3 are in accord with this law, as shown in Figure 16.1, which plots the marginal utility of food against the amount consumed. Once the daily consumption of food exceeds about 1½ pounds, the marginal utility of food declines.

THE EQUILIBRIUM MARKET BASKET

Preferences alone do not determine consumers' actions. *Besides knowing consumers' preferences, we must also know their income and the prices of commodities to predict which market basket they will buy.* Consumers' money income is the amount of money they can spend per unit of time, and this amount constrains consumers' choice of a market basket. For example, although Mr. Walter may regard a Hickey Freeman as his favorite suit, he may not buy it because he may not have sufficient funds. The prices of commodities also influence the consumer's choice of a market basket. If the Hickey Freeman suit were offered by a discount store at $100, rather than at its list price of $400, Mr. Walter might purchase it after all.

Given consumers' tastes, economists assume that they attempt to maximize utility. In other words, *consumers are assumed to be rational in the sense that they choose the market basket—or more generally, the course of action—that is most to their liking.* As previously noted, consumers cannot choose whatever market basket they please. Instead, they must maximize their utility subject to the constraints imposed by the size of their money income and the nature of commodity prices.

What is the optimal market basket, the one that maximizes utility subject to these constraints? It is the one where *the consumer's income is allocated among commodities so that, for every commodity purchased, the marginal utility of the commodity is proportional to its price.* Thus, in the case of the Walter family, the optimal market basket is the one where

$$MU_F/P_F = MU_C/P_C \qquad [16.1]$$

where MU_F is the marginal utility of food, MU_C is the marginal utility of clothing, P_F is the price of a pound of food, and P_C is the price of a piece of clothing.

Why Is this Rule Correct?

To understand why the rule in Equation (16.1) is correct, it is convenient to begin by pointing out that $MU_F \div P_F$ is the marginal utility of the *last dollar's worth* of food, and that $MU_C \div P_C$ is the marginal utility of the *last dollar's worth* of clothing. To see why this is so, take the case of food. Since MU_F is the extra utility of the *last pound* of food bought, and since P_F is the price of this *last pound,* the extra utility of the *last dollar's worth* of food must be $MU_F \div P_F$. For example, if the last pound of food results in an extra utility of 4 utils and this pound costs $2, then the extra utility from the last dollar's worth of food must be $4 \div 2$, or 2 utils. In other words, the marginal utility of the last dollar's worth of food is 2 utils.

Since $MU_F \div P_F$ is the marginal utility of the last dollar's worth of food, and $MU_C \div P_C$ is the marginal utility of the last dollar's worth of clothing, what Equation (16.1) really says is that *the rational consumer will choose a market basket where the marginal utility of the last dollar spent on all commodities purchased is the same.* To see why this must be so, consider the numerical example in Table 16.4, which shows the marginal utility the Walters derive from various amounts of food and clothing. Rather than measuring food and clothing in physical units, we measure them in Table 16.4 in terms of the amount of money spent on them.

**Table 16.4
Marginal Utility
Derived by the
Walters from
Various Quantities
of Food and
Clothing**

Commodity	1	2	Dollars worth 3	4	5
			Marginal utility (utils)		
Food	20	16	12	10	7
Clothing	12	10	7	5	3

Given the information in Table 16.4, how much of each commodity should Mrs. Walter buy if her money income is only $4 (a ridiculous assumption but one that will help to make our point)? Clearly, the first dollar she spends should be on food since it will yield her a marginal utility of 20. The second dollar she spends should also be on food since a second dollar's worth of food has a marginal utility of 16. (Thus the total utility derived from the $2 of expenditure is $20 + 16 = 36$.)[2] The marginal utility of the third dollar is 12 if it is spent on more food, and 12 too if it is spent on clothing (since it would be the first dollar spent on clothing). Suppose that she chooses more food. (The total utility derived from the $3 of expenditure is $20 + 16 + 12 = 48$.) What about the final dollar? Its marginal utility is 10 if it is spent on more food and 12 if it is spent on clothing; thus she will spend it on clothing. (The total utility derived from all $4 of expenditure is then $20 + 16 + 12 + 12 = 60$.)

Thus Mrs. Walter, if she is rational, will allocate $3 of her income to food and $1 to clothing. This is the **equilibrium market basket**, the market basket that maximizes consumer satisfaction. The important thing to note is that this market basket demonstrates the principle set forth earlier in Equation (16.1.) As shown in Table 16.4, the marginal utility derived from

[2]Since the marginal utility is the extra utility obtained from each dollar spent, the total utility from the total expenditure must be the sum of the marginal utilities of the individual dollars of expenditure.

the last dollar spent on food is equal to the marginal utility derived from the last dollar spent on clothing. (Both are 12.) Thus this market basket has the characteristics described above: the marginal utility of the last dollar spent on all commodities purchased is the same.

CASE STUDY 16.1 CONSERVING WATER IN A CALIFORNIA DROUGHT

From 1975 to 1977, California suffered a series of droughts. Many communities embarked on water conservation programs. Washing cars and watering lawns were forbidden. Farmers were notified that there might be a cutback of 25 percent in water allotment for the spring, and that they should reduce planting. Marin County, a wealthy community just north of San Francisco, was one of the hardest-hit California communities. By the second year of the drought, residents were rationed to 46 gallons per day, one-third of their normal usage.

To maintain rationing quotas, stiff new water rates were imposed. The basic rate was doubled; anyone who used up twice the quota paid more than eight times the old rate, and usage beyond that amount cost forty times the predrought rate. People reduced their water consumption by 25 percent in the first year and by 65 percent in the second. Water was saved for its most valued uses. Low-volume shower heads and other apparatus were installed to reduce water usage in toilets and sinks.

Torrential rains in the final days of 1977 marked the end of this drought, but its legacy lingered on. Several conservation measures were written into law, and the people of Marin County continued to pay—and willingly pay—more for water than they had before the drought. Total water usage stayed well below the predrought levels for years, both because the higher price of water reduced the quantity demanded and because the demand curve for water had shifted to the left.

The California drought is a good illustration of marginal utility. As water became scarce, its marginal utility to the average consumer rose. People cut back on uses of water that added little to their satisfaction, such as washing cars and watering lawns, and the available water was used in ways that had a high marginal utility: drinking, cooking, and bathing.

N.B.

THE CONSUMER'S DEMAND CURVE

In analyzing consumer behavior, economists often use the concept of an *individual demand curve*. Like the market demand curve, the individual demand curve is the relationship between the quantity demanded of a good and the good's price. But whereas the market demand curve shows the quantity demanded in the *entire market* at various prices, the individual demand curve shows the quantity demanded by a *particular consumer* at various prices. Applying the theory of consumer behavior presented earlier in this chapter, we can derive a particular consumer's demand curve for a particular good. To see this, let's turn to Mrs. Walter and show how we can derive the relationship between the price of food and the amount of food she will buy per month.

Assuming that food and clothing are the only goods, that Mrs. Walter's monthly income is $400, and that the price of clothing is $40 per piece of clothing, we confront Mrs. Walter with a variety of prices of food. First, we confront her with a price of $1 per pound of food. How much food will she buy? Next, we confront her with a price of $2 per pound of food. How much food will she buy? The theory of consumer behavior shows how, under each of these sets of circumstances, she will allocate her income between food and clothing. From Equation 16.1, we know that she will choose an allocation where the marginal utility of the last dollar spent on food will equal the marginal utility of the last dollar spent on clothing. Suppose that she will buy 200 pounds of food when the price is $1 per pound, and 100 pounds of food when the price is $2 per pound. These are two points on Mrs. Walter's individual demand curve for food—those corresponding to prices of $1 and $2 per pound. Figure 16.2 shows these two points, X and Y.

It is no trick to obtain more points on her individual demand curve for food. All we have to do is confront her with other prices of food, and see how much food she buys at each price. Plotting the amount of food she buys against the price, we obtain new points on her individual demand curve for food. Connecting up all these points, we get her complete individual demand curve for food, shown in Figure 16.2.

Figure 16.2
Mrs. Walter's
Individual Demand
Curve for Food
The consumer's individual demand curve for a commodity shows the amount of the commodity the consumer will buy at various prices.

PRICE OF FOOD (dollars per pound)

POUNDS OF FOOD CONSUMED PER MONTH

DERIVING THE MARKET DEMAND CURVE

In the previous section we described how a consumer's individual demand curve for a commodity can be derived, given the consumer's tastes and income, as well as the prices of other commodities. Suppose that we have obtained the individual demand curve for each of the consumers in the market. How can these individual demand curves be used to derive the market demand curve? The answer is simple. *To derive the market demand curve, we obtain the horizontal sum of all the individual demand curves.* In other words, to find the total quantity demanded in the market at a certain price, we add up the quantities demanded by the individual consumers at that price.

Table 16.5 shows the individual demand curves for food of four families: the Walters, Joneses, Smiths, and Kleins. For simplicity, suppose that these four families constitute the entire market for food. (This assumption can easily be relaxed; it just makes things simple.) Then the market demand curve for food is shown in the last column of Table 16.5. Figure 16.3 shows the families' individual demand curves for food, as well as the resulting market demand curve. To illustrate how the market demand curve is derived from the individual demand curves, suppose that the price of food is $1 per pound. The total quantity demanded in the market is 102 hun-

| Price of food (dollars per pound) | | Individual demand | | | Market demand |
| | Jones | Klein | Smith | Walter | |
		(hundreds of pounds per month)			
1.00	50.0	45.0	5.0	2.0	102
1.20	43.0	44.0	4.2	1.8	93
1.40	36.0	43.0	3.4	1.6	84
1.60	30.0	42.0	2.6	1.4	76
1.80	25.0	41.4	2.4	1.2	70
2.00	20.0	41.0	2.0	1.0	64

Table 16.5
Individual Demand Curves and Market Demand Curve for Food

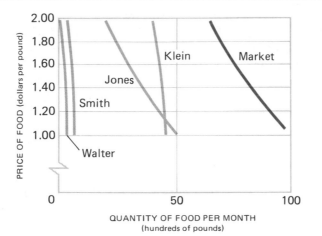

Figure 16.3
Individual Demand Curves and Market Demand Curve for Food
The market demand curve is the horizontal sum of all the individual demand curves.

dreds of pounds per month, since this is the sum of the quantities demanded at this price by the four families. (As shown in Table 16.5, this sum equals 50.0 + 45.0 + 5.0 + 2.0, or 102.)

Since individual demand curves for a commodity almost always slope downward to the right, it follows that *market demand curves too almost always slope downward to the right.* (Why? Because, as stressed above, the market demand curve is the horizontal sum of all of the individual demand curves.) However, the shape and location of the market demand curve vary greatly from commodity to commodity and from market to market. Market demand curves, like people, do not look alike.

THE SUPPLY CURVE

We turn now from the demand to the supply curve. When we look behind the supply curve, it is obvious that a firm's decision about how much to produce is dependent on its costs. In the rest of this chapter, we shall analyze a firm's costs in some detail. Then in Chapter 18 we will show how the results enable us to derive the market supply curve.

WHAT ARE COSTS?

What do we mean by cost? Although this question may seem foolishly simple, it is in fact tricky. *Fundamentally, the cost of a certain course of action is the value of the best alternative course of action that could have been adopted instead.* The cost of producing automobiles is the value of the goods and services that could be obtained from the resources used currently in automobile production if these resources were no longer used to produce automobiles. In general, the costs of a firm's inputs—that is, anything the firm uses in its production process—are their values in their most valuable alternative uses. This is the *opportunity cost,* or *alternative cost,* doctrine. (Recall our discussion of opportunity cost in Chapter 1.)

Suppose that a firm's owner devotes 50 hours a week to the firm's business, and that, because he is the owner, he pays himself no salary. According to the usual rules of accounting, the costs of his labor are not included in the firm's income statement. But according to the economist's opportunity cost doctrine, the cost of his labor is by no means zero. Instead, this cost equals whatever amount he could obtain if he worked 50 hours a week for someone else. Both economists and sophisticated accountants agree that opportunity costs are the relevant costs for many types of problems, and that failure to use the proper concept of cost can result in serious mistakes.

Costs for the individual firm are the necessary payments to the owners of resources to get them to provide these resources to the firm. To obtain these resources as inputs, the firm must bid them away from alternative uses. The payments made to the owners of these resources may be either explicit or implicit costs. If a payment is made to a supplier, laborer, or some other resource owner besides the firm's owner, this is an explicit cost, which is paid for in an explicit way. But if a resource is owned by the firm's owner, there may be no explicit payment for it, as in the case of the labor of the owner who paid himself no salary. The *costs of such owner-supplied resources are called* **implicit costs**. As we stressed above, such implicit costs equal what these resources could bring if they were used in their most valuable alternative employments. And the firm's profits (or losses), as defined by economists, are the difference between the firm's revenues and its total costs, both explicit and implicit.

SHORT-RUN COST FUNCTIONS

In order to maximize its profits, a firm must determine the least-cost combination of inputs to produce any quantity of output. The previous chapter showed how this least-cost input combination can be found; with this information, it is easy to determine the minimum cost of producing each quantity of output. *Knowing the (minimum) cost of producing each quantity of output, we can define and measure the firm's* **cost func-tions**, *which show how various types of costs are related to the firm's output.*

A firm's cost functions will vary, depending on whether they are based on the short or long run. As we saw from the previous chapter, *the* **short run** *is defined as the period of time in which at least one of the firm's inputs is fixed.* On the other hand, *the* **long run** *is that period of time in which all inputs are variable.* In the long run, the firm can make a complete adjustment to any change in its environment.

In the following sections, we will concentrate on the short run, where the firm cannot vary the quantities of plant and equipment it uses. These are the firm's fixed inputs, and they determine the scale of its operations.

Total Fixed Cost

Three kinds of costs are important in the short run: total fixed cost, total variable cost, and total cost. **Total fixed cost** *is the total expenditure per period of time by the firm for fixed inputs.* Since the quantity of the fixed inputs is unvarying (by definition), the total fixed cost will be the same whatever the firm's level of output. Among the firm's fixed costs in the short run are property taxes and interest on bonds issued in the past. If the firm has contracts with suppliers and workers that cannot be renegotiated (without dire consequences) in the short run, the expenses involved in meeting these contracts are also fixed costs.

Consider a hypothetical firm: the Bugsbane Music Box Company. This firm produces a high-priced line of music boxes that, when opened, play your favorite rock song, show tune, or hymn, and emit a deadly gas that

Table 16.6
Fixed, Variable, and
Total Costs,
Bugsbane Music
Box Company

Number of music boxes produced per day	Total fixed cost	Total variable cost (dollars)	Total cost
0	300	0	300
1	300	60	360
2	300	110	410
3	300	160	460
4	300	200	500
5	300	260	560
6	300	360	660
7	300	510	810
8	300	710	1,010
9	300	1,060	1,360

Figure 16.4
Total Fixed Cost,
Bugsbane Music
Box Company
The total fixed cost function is always a horizontal line, since fixed costs do not vary with output.

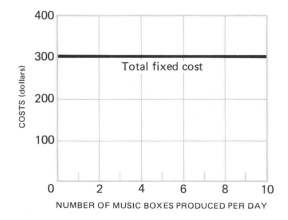

kills all insects, rodents, or pests within a 50-foot radius. Table 16.6 shows that Bugsbane's fixed costs are $300 per day; the firm's total fixed cost function is shown in Figure 16.4.

Total Variable Cost

Total variable cost is the firm's total expenditure on variable inputs per period of time. Since by definition a firm cannot vary its fixed inputs in the short run, it will have to increase its variable inputs if it wants to increase its output. And since higher output rates require greater utilization of variable inputs, they mean a higher total variable cost. Thus if Bugsbane increases its daily production of music boxes, it must increase the amount it spends per day on metal (for the components), wood (for the outside of the boxes), labor (for the assembly of the boxes), and other variable inputs. Table 16.6 shows Bugsbane's total variable costs at various output rates; Figure 16.5 shows the firm's total variable cost function.

Beyond an output rate of 4 music boxes per day, total variable cost increases at an increasing rate. It is important to understand that this characteristic of the total variable cost function results from the operation of the **law of diminishing marginal returns**. This law states that, *if equal*

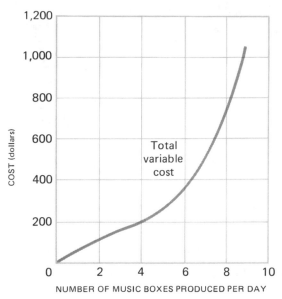

Figure 16.5
Total Variable
Cost, Bugsbane
Music Box
Company
Total variable cost
is the total
expenditure per
period of time on
variable inputs. Due
to the law of
diminishing marginal
returns, total
variable cost
increases first at a
decreasing rate,
then at an
increasing rate.

increments of an input are added, the quantities of other inputs being held constant, the resulting increments of product will decrease beyond some point; that is, the marginal product of the input will diminish. At small output rates, increases in the utilization of variable inputs may bring about increases in their productivity, causing total variable cost to increase with output, but at a decreasing rate. Beyond a point, however, there are diminishing marginal returns from the variable input, with the result that total variable costs increase at an increasing rate.

Total Cost

Total cost *is the sum of total fixed cost and total variable cost.* Thus to obtain the Bugsbane company's total cost at a given output, we need only add its total fixed cost and its total variable cost at that output. The result is shown in Table 16.6, and the corresponding total cost function is shown in Figure 16.6. Since the total cost function and the total variable cost

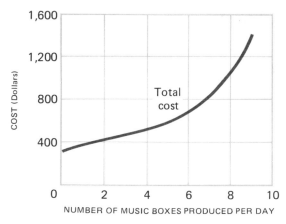

Figure 16.6
Total Cost,
Bugsbane Music
Box Company
Total cost is the
sum of total fixed
cost and total
variable cost. It has
the same shape as
the total variable
cost curve, since
they differ by only a
constant amount
(equal to total fixed
cost).

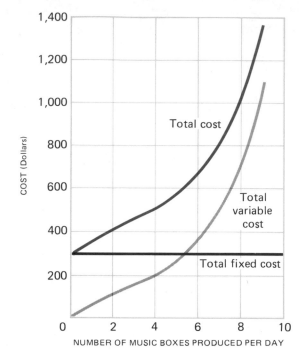

**Figure 16.7
Fixed, Variable, and Total Costs, Bugsbane Music Box Company**
All three cost functions, presented in Figures 16.4–16.6, are brought back for a curtain call.

function differ by only a constant amount (equal to total fixed cost), they have the same shape, as shown in Figure 16.7, which brings together all three of the total cost functions (or cost curves, as they are often called).

AVERAGE COSTS IN THE SHORT RUN

The president of Bugsbane unquestionably cares about the average cost of a music box as well as the total cost incurred; so do economists. *Average cost tells you how much a product costs per unit of output.* There are three average cost functions, one corresponding to each of the three total cost functions.

Average Fixed Cost

Let's begin with **average fixed cost,** *which is simply the total fixed cost divided by the firm's output.* Table 16.7 and Figure 16.8 show the average fixed cost function for the Bugsbane Music Box company. Average fixed cost must decline with increases in output, since it equals a constant—total fixed cost—divided by the output rate.

Average Variable Cost

The next type of average cost is **average variable cost,** *which is total variable cost divided by output.* For Bugsbane, the average variable cost function is shown in Table 16.7 and Figure 16.9. At first, increases in the

Number of music boxes produced per day	Average fixed cost	Average variable cost (dollars)	Average total cost	
1	300(=300 ÷ 1)	60(=60 ÷ 1)	360(=360 ÷ 1)	
2	150(=300 ÷ 2)	55(=110 ÷ 2)	205(=410 ÷ 2)	
3	100(=300 ÷ 3)	53(=160 ÷ 3)	153(=460 ÷ 3)	
4	75(=300 ÷ 4)	50(=200 ÷ 4)	125(=500 ÷ 4)	
5	60(=300 ÷ 5)	52(=260 ÷ 5)	112(=560 ÷ 5)	
6	50(=300 ÷ 6)	60(=360 ÷ 6)	110(=660 ÷ 6)	
7	43(=300 ÷ 7)	73(=510 ÷ 7)	116(=810 ÷ 7)	
8	38(=300 ÷ 8)	89(=710 ÷ 8)	126(=1010 ÷ 8)	
9	33(=300 ÷ 9)	118(=1060 ÷ 9)	151(=1360 ÷ 9)	

Table 16.7
Average Fixed Cost, Average Variable Cost, and Average Total Cost, Bugsbane Music Box Company

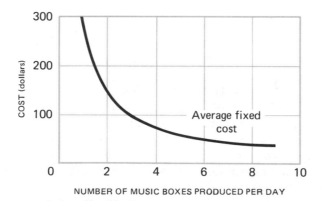

Figure 16.8
Average Fixed Cost, Bugsbane Music Box Company
Average fixed cost is total fixed cost divided by the firm's output. Since it equals a constant (total fixed cost) divided by the output rate, it must decline with increases in output.

output rate result in decreases in average variable cost, but beyond a point they result in higher average variable cost. This is because the law of diminishing marginal returns is in operation. As more and more of the variable inputs are utilized, the extra output they produce declines beyond some point, so that the amount spent on variable inputs per unit of output tends to increase.

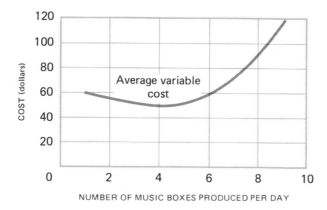

Figure 16.9
Average Variable Cost, Bugsbane Music Box Company
Average variable cost is total variable cost divided by the firm's output. Beyond a point (in this case, about 4 music boxes per day), average variable cost rises with increases in output because of the law of diminishing marginal returns.

Average Total Cost

The third type of average cost is **average total cost,** *which is total cost divided by output.* For Bugsbane, the average total cost function is shown

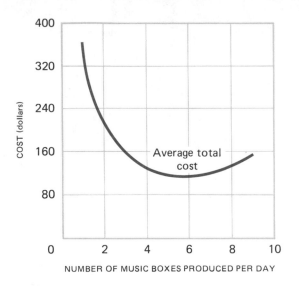

Figure 16.10
**Average Total
Cost, Bugsbane
Music Box
Company**
Average total cost
is total cost divided
by output. It equals
average fixed cost
plus average
variable cost.

COST (dollars)

400

320

240

160

80

Average total
cost

0   2   4   6   8   10

NUMBER OF MUSIC BOXES PRODUCED PER DAY

in Table 16.7 and Figure 16.10. At any level of output, *average total cost equals average fixed cost plus average variable cost.*

The fact that average total cost is the sum of average fixed cost and average variable cost helps explain the shape of the average cost function. If, as the output rate goes up, both average fixed cost and average variable cost decrease, average total cost must decrease too. But beyond some point average total cost must increase, because increases in average variable cost eventually more than offset decreases in average fixed cost. However, average total cost achieves its minimum after average variable cost, because the increases in average variable cost are for a time more than offset by decreases in average fixed cost. (All the average cost functions are shown in Figure 16.12.)

MARGINAL COST IN THE SHORT RUN

No one can really understand the operations of a business firm without understanding the concept of **marginal cost,** *the addition to total cost resulting from the addition of the last unit of output.* To see how marginal cost is calculated, look at Table 16.8, which shows the total cost function of the Bugsbane Music Box Company. When output is between 0 and 1 music box per day, the firm's marginal cost is $60, since this is the *extra cost* of producing the first music box per day. In other words, $60 equals marginal cost in this situation, because it is the difference between the total cost of producing 1 music box per day ($360) and the total cost of producing 0 music boxes per day ($300, which is the firm's total fixed cost).

In general, marginal cost will vary depending on the firm's output level. Thus Table 16.8 shows that at Bugsbane marginal cost is $50 when the firm produces between 1 and 2 music boxes per day, $100 when the firm produces between 5 and 6 music boxes per day, and $350 when the firm produces between 8 and 9 music boxes per day. Table 16.8, and Figure

Number of music boxes produced per day	Total cost	Marginal cost (dollars)
0	300	
		60 (= 360 − 300)
1	360	
		50 (= 410 − 360)
2	410	
		50 (= 460 − 410)
3	460	
		40 (= 500 − 460)
4	500	
		60 (= 560 − 500)
5	560	
		100 (= 660 − 560)
6	660	
		150 (= 810 − 660)
7	810	
		200 (= 1,010 − 810)
8	1,010	
		350 (= 1,360 − 1,010)
9	1,360	

Table 16.8
Calculation of Marginal Cost, Bugsbane Music Box Company

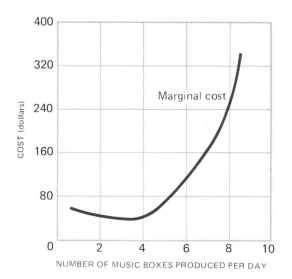

Figure 16.11
Marginal Cost, Bugsbane Music Box Company
The marginal cost of the first unit of output (which according to Table 16.8, is $60) is plotted at the midpoint between 0 and 1 units of output. The marginal cost of the second unit of output is plotted at the midpoint between 1 and 2 units of output. The marginal cost function connects these and other points showing the marginal cost of various amounts of output.

16.11, which shows the marginal cost function graphically, indicates that marginal cost, after decreasing with increases in output at low output levels, increases with further increases in output. In other words, *beyond some point it becomes more and more costly for the firm to produce yet another unit of output.*

Increasing Marginal Cost and Diminishing Returns

The reason why marginal cost increases beyond some output level is to be found in the law of *diminishing marginal returns. If (beyond some point) increases in variable inputs result in less and less extra output, it follows that a larger and larger quantity of variable inputs must be added to produce an extra unit of output. Thus the cost of producing an extra unit of output must increase.*

Relationship between Marginal Cost and Average Cost Functions

The relationship between the marginal cost function and the average cost functions must be noted. Figure 16.12 shows the marginal cost curve together with the three average cost curves. *The marginal cost curve intersects both the average variable cost curve and the average total cost curve at their minimum points.* The reason for this is simple. If the extra cost of a unit of output is greater (less) than the average cost of the units of output already produced, the addition of the extra unit of output clearly must raise (lower) the average cost of production. Thus if marginal cost is greater (less) than average cost, average cost must be rising (falling). And if this is so, average cost can be a minimum only when it equals marginal cost. (The same reasoning holds for both average total cost and average variable cost, and for the short and long runs.)

To make sure that you understand this point, consider the following numerical example. Suppose that the average total cost of producing 4

Figure 16.12 Average Fixed Cost, Average Variable Cost, Average Total Cost, and Marginal Cost, Bugsbane Music Box Company
All of the curves presented in Figures 16.8–16.11 are brought together for review. Note that the marginal cost curve intersects both the average variable cost curve and the average total cost curve at their minimum points.

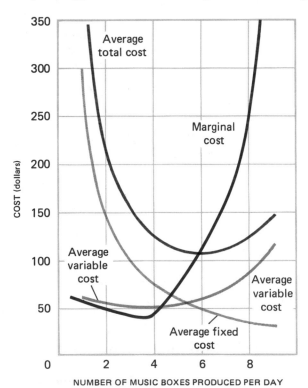

CASE STUDY 16.2 OIL PRICE INCREASES AND DRILLING ACTIVITY

In the decade prior to 1973, independent domestic oil producers were finding it increasingly difficult to compete with OPEC's low world oil prices. Domestic oil production had leveled off, and many suppliers had left the industry. In the wake of the 1973–74 oil embargo and the quadrupling of oil prices, many producers were spurred to jump into the oil patch; new companies, speculative investors, and existing companies expanded their drilling. The new price and profit potential were the main motivating factors for this expansion. The lust for undiscovered "new" oil was greater than ever.

In 1979 the Carter administration announced the gradual phase-out of control on domestic oil prices. The new high price for oil and government decontrol were the financial carrots needed to lure new suppliers back into domestic oil production. The number of active rigs had gone from under 1,000 in 1971 to over 4,000 in 1981. Over 16,500 wildcat wells were drilled in 1982, as opposed to 7,000 in 1971. As one producer put it, "Just about anywhere you went in that period, you stumbled over

A new oil-recovery unit in Long Beach, California

someone behind a bush, drilling." In the decade following the first oil crisis in 1973, oil exploration almost doubled. Independent companies, wildcatters, accounted for roughly 90 percent of the drillings. In accord with the basic economic models presented in this text, the amount of drilling activity increased in response to higher oil prices, which acted both as signals and as incentives for such resource re-allocation.

The marginal cost of extracting additional barrels of oil rises steeply after a point. Drillers have to resort to more expensive techniques for secondary and tertiary recovery—that is, recovering the oil from a given well that is hard to reach. As the price of oil rose, these more expensive techniques became more affordable. Similarly, the drilling of new, deeper, and more expensive wells could be justified because the higher costs could be covered by the higher price of oil.

N.B.

☆ ☆ ☆ ☆ ☆ ☆ ☆ ☆ ☆ ☆ ☆ ☆ ☆

units of output is $10, and that the marginal cost of the fifth unit of output is less than $10. Will the average total cost be less for 5 units of output than for 4 units? It will be less, because the fifth unit's cost will pull down the average. On the other hand, if the marginal cost of the fifth unit of output had been greater than $10, the average total cost for 5 units of output would have been greater than for 4 units of output, because the fifth unit's cost would pull up the average. Thus *average total cost will fall when it is above marginal cost, and it will rise when it is below marginal cost.* Consequently, *when it is a minimum, average total cost must equal marginal cost,* as shown in Figure 16.12.

THE LONG-RUN AVERAGE COST FUNCTION

We have held to the last one additional kind of cost function that plays a very important role in economic analysis. This is the firm's **long-run average cost function,** *which shows the minimum average cost of producing each output level when any desired type or scale of plant can be built.* Unlike the cost functions discussed in the previous sections, this cost function pertains to the long run—*to a period long enough so that all inputs are variable and none is fixed.* In the long run, a firm can make any adjustments in its production techniques, to suit changes in its environment.

Suppose a firm can build plants of three sizes: small, medium, and large. The short-run average total cost functions corresponding to these plants are *AA', BB',* and *DD'* in Figure 16.13. If the firm is still in the planning stage of plant construction, it can choose whichever plant has the lowest costs. Consequently, the firm will choose the small plant if it believes that its output rate will be smaller than $0Q_1$, the medium plant if it believes that its output rate will be above $0Q_1$ but below $0Q_2$, and the large plant if it believes that its output rate will be above $0Q_2$. Thus the long-run average cost curve is *AUVD'.* And if, as is generally the case, there are many possible types of plants, the long-run average cost curve looks like

Figure 16.13
Short-Run Average Cost Curves and Long-Run Average Cost Curve
The short-run average total cost functions for three plants—small, medium, and large —are *AA', BB',* and *DD'.* The long-run average cost function is *AUVD',* if these are the only three types of plant that can be built.

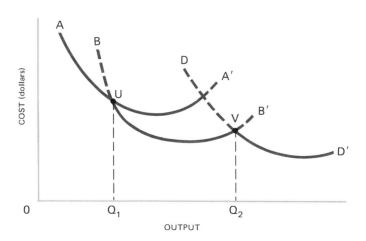

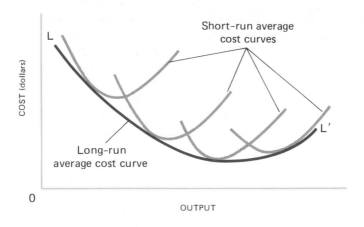

Figure 16.14
Long-Run Average Cost Curve
If many possible types of plants can be built, the long-run average cost function is *LL'*.

LL' in Figure 16.14. (Only a few of the short-run average cost curves are shown in Figure 16.14.)

RETURNS TO SCALE

What determines the shape of the long-run average cost function in a particular industry? Its shape must depend upon the characteristics of the *production function,* which shows the most output that existing technology permits the firm to extract from each quantity of inputs. Specifically, the shape of the long-run average cost function depends upon whether there are increasing, decreasing, or constant returns to scale. To understand what these terms mean, consider a long-run situation and suppose that the firm increases the amount of all inputs by the same proportion. What will happen to output? *If output increases by a larger proportion than each of the inputs, this is a case of* **increasing returns to scale.** *If output increases by a smaller proportion than each of the inputs, this is a case of* **decreasing returns to scale.** *If output increases by the same proportion as each of the inputs, this is a case of* **constant returns to scale.**

At first glance it may seem that constant returns to scale must always prevail. After all, if two factories are built with the same equipment and use the same type and number of workers, it would seem obvious that they can produce twice as much output as one such factory. But things are not that simple. If a firm doubles its scale, it may be able to use techniques that could not be used at the smaller scale. Some inputs are not available in small units; for example, we cannot install half a robot. Because of indivisibilities of this sort, increasing returns to scale may occur. Thus, although one could double a firm's size by simply building two small factories, this may be inefficient. One large factory may be more efficient than two smaller factories of the same total capacity because it is large enough to use certain techniques and inputs that the smaller factories cannot use.

Another reason for increasing returns to scale stems from certain *geo-*

metrical relations. For example, since the volume of a box that is $3 \times 3 \times 3$ feet is 27 times as great as the volume of a box that is $1 \times 1 \times 1$ foot, the former box can carry 27 times as much as the latter box. But since the area of the six sides of the $3 \times 3 \times 3$-foot box is 54 square feet and the area of the six sides of the $1 \times 1 \times 1$-foot box is 6 square feet, the former box only requires 9 times as much wood as the latter. Greater *specialization* also can result in increasing returns to scale. As more men and machines are used, it is possible to subdivide tasks and allow various inputs to specialize.

Decreasing returns to scale can also occur; the most frequently cited reason is *the difficulty of coordinating a large enterprise.* It can be difficult even in a small firm to obtain the information required to make important decisions; in a large firm, the difficulties tend to be greater. It can be difficult even in a small firm to be certain that management's wishes are being carried out; in a larger firm these difficulties too tend to be greater. Although the advantages of a large organization seem to have captured the public fancy, there are often very great disadvantages as well.

Whether there are increasing, decreasing, or constant returns to scale in a particular situation must be settled case by case. Moreover, the answer is likely to depend on the particular range of output considered. There frequently are increasing returns to scale up to some level of output, then perhaps constant returns to scale up to a higher level of output, beyond which there may be decreasing returns to scale. This pattern is responsible in part for the U-shaped long-run average cost functions in Figure 16.14. At relatively small output levels, there are increasing returns to scale, and long-run average cost decreases as output rises. At relatively high output levels, there are decreasing returns to scale, and long-run average cost increases as output rises.

The U-shaped pattern is not found in all industries. Within the range covered by the available data, there is little or no evidence in many industries that long-run average cost increases as output rises. But this may be because the data do not cover a wide enough range. Eventually, one would expect long-run average cost to rise because of problems of coordination, increased red tape, and reduced flexibility. Firms as large as General Motors or U.S. Steel are continually bedeviled by the very real difficulties of enormous size.

SUMMARY

1. Utility is a number that represents the level of satisfaction derived by the consumer from a particular market basket. Market baskets with higher utilities are preferred over market baskets with lower utilities.

2. The model of consumer behavior recognizes that preferences alone do not determine the consumer's actions. Choices are dictated by the size of the consumer's money income and the nature of commodity prices. These factors, as well as the consumer's preferences, determine choice.

3. If consumers maximize utility, their income is allocated among commodities so that, for every commodity purchased, the marginal utility of the commodity is proportional to its price. In other words, the marginal utility of the last dollar spent on each commodity is made equal for all commodities purchased.

4. The individual demand curve shows the quantity of a good demanded by a particular consumer at various prices of the good. The individual demand curve for practically all goods slopes downward and to the right. Its location depends on the consumer's income and tastes and the prices of other goods.

5. To derive the market demand curve, we obtain the horizontal sum of all the individual demand curves of the people in the market. Since individual demand curves for a commodity almost always slope downward to the right, it follows that market demand curves too almost always slope downward to the right.

6. The cost of a certain course of action is the value of the best alternative course of action that could have been pursued instead. This is the doctrine of opportunity cost or alternative cost.

7. Three kinds of total cost functions are important in the short run: total fixed cost, total variable cost, and total cost. In addition, there are three kinds of average cost functions (corresponding to each of the total cost functions): average fixed cost, average variable cost, and average total cost.

8. Marginal cost—the addition to total cost due to the addition of the last unit of output—is of enormous significance in the firm's decison-making process. Because of the law of diminishing marginal returns, marginal cost tends to increase beyond some output level.

9. The firm's long-run average cost curve shows the minimum average cost of producing each output level when any desired type or scale of plant can be built. The shape of the long-run average cost curve is determined in part by whether there are increasing, decreasing, or constant returns to scale.

10. Suppose that a firm increases the amount of all inputs by the same percentage. If output increases by more than this percentage, this is a case of increasing returns to scale. If output increases by less than this percentage, this is a case of decreasing returns to scale. If output increases by this same percentage, this is a case of constant returns to scale.

CHAPTER 17

Market Demand and Price Elasticity

LEARNING OBJECTIVES

In this chapter, you should learn:

★ What the price elasticity of demand is, and what it means for a good to be price elastic or price inelastic

★ The nature of the income elasticity of demand

★ What product substitutes and complements are

★ *(Exploring Further)* The market conditions that present perennial problems for farmers

What do Corfam (Du Pont's synthetic leather) and the Edsel (the make of automobile Ford introduced in the 1950s) have in common? Both were new products that were unsuccessful because the market demand for them was too small. In a capitalist economy, market demand is a fundamental determinant of what is produced and how. The market demand curve for a commodity plays an important role in the decision-making process within each firm that produces the commodity, as well as in the economy as a whole. It is no exaggeration to say that firms spend enormous time and effort trying to cater to, estimate, and influence market demand.

MARKET DEMAND CURVES

Let's review what a *market demand curve* is. You will recall from Chapters 2 and 16 that a commodity's market demand curve shows how much of the commodity will be purchased during a particular period of time at various prices. Figure 17.1 ought to be familiar; it is the market demand curve for wheat in the mid-1980s, which figured prominently in our discussion of the price system in Chapter 2. Among other things, it shows that during the mid-1980s about 2.7 billion bushels of American wheat would have been purchased per year if the price was $3.00 per bushel, that about 2.6 billion bushels would have been purchased per year if the price was $3.30 per bushel, and that about 2.5 billion bushels would have been purchased if the price was $3.60 per bushel.

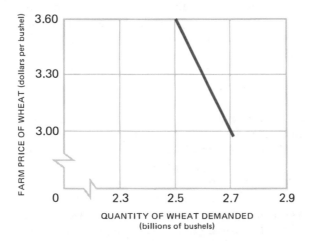

Since the market demand curve reflects what consumers want and are willing to pay for, when the market demand curve for wheat shifts upward to the right, this indicates that consumers want more wheat at the existing price. On the other hand, when the curve shifts downward to the left, this indicates that consumers want less wheat at the existing price. Such shifts in the market demand curve for a commodity trigger changes in the behavior of the commodity's producers. When the market demand curve shifts upward to the right, the price of wheat will tend to rise, thus inducing farmers to produce more wheat, because they will find that, given the price increase, their profits will increase if they raise their output levels. The same process occurs in other parts of the economy. Shifts in the demand curve reflecting the fact that consumers want more (less) of a commodity set in motion a sequence of events leading to more (less) production of the commodity.

Measuring Market Demand Curves

To be of practical use, market demand curves must be based on careful measurements. Let's look briefly at some of the techniques used to estimate the market demand curve for particular commodities. At first glance, a quick and easy way to estimate the demand curve might seem to be interviewing consumers about their buying habits and intentions. However, although more subtle variants of this approach sometimes may pay off, simply asking people how much they would buy of a certain commodity at particular prices does not usually seem very useful, since off-the-cuff answers to such questions are rarely very accurate. Thus marketing researchers and econometricians interested in measuring market demand curves have been forced to use more complex procedures.

One such procedure is the direct market experiment. Although the designs of such experiments vary greatly and are often quite complicated, the basic idea is simple: see the effects on the quantity demanded of actual variations in the price of the product. (Researchers attempt to hold other market factors constant or to take into account whatever changes may occur.) The Parker Pen company conducted an experiment a number of years ago to estimate the demand curve for their ink, Quink. They increased the price from $.15 to $.25 in four cities, and found that the quantity demanded was quite insensitive to the price. Experiments like this are frequently made to try to estimate a product's market demand curve.

Still another technique is to use statistical methods to estimate demand curves from historical data on price and quantity purchased of the commodity. For example, one might plot the price of slingshots in various periods in the past against the quantity sold, as shown in Figure 17.2. Judging from the results, curve *D* in Figure 17.2 seems a reasonable approximation to the demand curve. Although this simple analysis provides some insight into how statistical methods are used to estimate demand curves from historical data, it is a vast oversimplification. For one thing, the market demand curve may have shifted over time, so that curve *D* is not a proper estimate. Fortunately, modern statistical techniques recognize this possibility and allow us to estimate the position and shape of this curve (at each point in time) in spite of it.

**Figure 17.2
Estimated Demand
Curve for
Slingshots**
One very crude way to estimate the market demand curve is to plot the amount sold of a commodity in each year against its price in that year, and draw a curve, like *D*, that seems to fit the points reasonably well. However, this technique is generally too crude to be reliable.

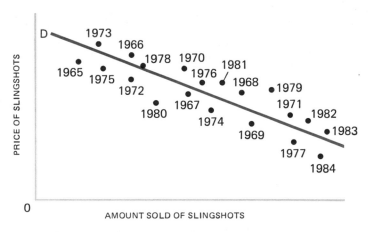

THE PRICE ELASTICITY OF DEMAND

The quantity demanded of some commodities, like beef in Figure 17.3, is fairly sensitive to changes in the commodity's price. That is, changes in

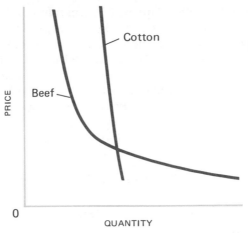

Figure 17.3
**Market Demand
Curves, Beef and
Cotton**
The quantity
demanded of beef
is much more
sensitive to price
than is the quantity
demanded of
cotton.

price result in significant changes in quantity demanded. On the other hand, the quantity demanded of other commodities, like cotton in Figure 17.3, is very insensitive to changes in the price. Large changes in price result in small changes in the quantity demanded.

To discuss this subject more rigorously, we must have some measure of the sensitivity of quantity demanded to changes in price. The measure customarily used for this purpose is the **price elasticity of demand**, *defined as the percentage change in quantity demanded resulting from a 1 percent change in price.*[1] For example, suppose that a 1 percent reduction in the price of slingshots results in a 2 percent increase in quantity demanded. Then, using this definition, the price elasticity of demand for slingshots is 2. (Convention dictates that we give the elasticity a positive sign even though the change in price is negative and the change in quantity demanded is positive.) The price elasticity of demand is likely to vary from one point to another on the market demand curve. For example, the price elasticity of demand for slingshots may be higher when a slingshot costs $1.00 than when it costs $0.25.

Note that the price elasticity of demand is expressed in terms of *relative* —that is, proportional or percentage—changes in price and quantity demanded, not *absolute* changes in price and quantity demanded. Thus, in studying the slingshot market, we look at the *percentage* change in quantity demanded resulting from a 1 *percent* change in price. This is because absolute changes depend on the units in which price and quantity are measured. Suppose that a reduction in the price of good Y from $100 to $99 results in an increase in the quantity demanded from 200 to 210 pounds per month. If price is measured in dollars, the quantity demanded of good Y seems quite sensitive to price changes, since a decrease in price

[1]What if price does not change by 1 percent? Then the price elasticity of demand is defined as the *percentage change in quantity demanded divided by the percentage change in price.* This definition will be used in the next section. Put in terms of symbols, the price elasticity of demand equals $(\frac{-\Delta Q}{\Delta P}) \times (P/Q)$, where P is price, ΔP is the change in price, Q is quantity demanded, and ΔQ is the change in the quantity demanded.

of "1" results in an increase in quantity demanded of "10". On the other hand, if price is measured in cents, the quantity demanded of good Y seems quite insensitive to price changes, since a decrease in price of "100" results in an increase in quantity demanded of "10." By using relative changes, we avoid this problem. Relative changes do not depend on the units of measurement. Thus the percentage reduction in the price of good Y is 1 percent, regardless of whether price is measured in dollars or cents. And the percentage increase in the quantity demanded of good Y is 5 percent, regardless of whether it is measured in pounds or tons.

Calculating the Price Elasticity of Demand

The price elasticity of demand is a very important concept and one that economists use often, so it is worthwhile to spend some time explaining exactly how it is computed. Suppose that you have a table showing various points on a market demand curve. For example, Table 17.1 shows the quantity of wheat demanded at various prices, as estimated by Professor Karl Fox of Iowa State University during the early 1960s.[2] Given these data, how do you go about computing the price elasticity of demand for wheat? Since the price elasticity of demand for any product generally varies from point to point on its market demand curve, you must first determine at what point on the demand curve you want to measure the price elasticity of demand.

**Table 17.1
Market Demand for
Wheat, Early 1960s**

Farm price of wheat (dollars per bushel)	Quantity of wheat demanded (millions of bushels)
1.00	1,500
1.20	1,300
1.40	1,100
1.60	900
1.80	800
2.00	700
2.20	675

Source: K. Fox, V. Ruttan, and L. Witt, *Farming, Farmers, and Markets for Farm Goods.* New York: Committee for Economic Development, 1962.

Let us assume that you want to estimate the price elasticity of demand for wheat when the price of wheat is between $2.00 and $2.20 per bushel. To do this, you can use the following formula:

$$\text{price elasticity} = \text{percentage change in quantity demanded} \div \text{percentage change in price}$$

$$= \frac{\text{change in quantity demanded}}{\text{original quantity demanded}} \div \frac{\text{change in price}}{\text{original price}}.$$

[2]Note that Table 17.1 pertains to the early 1960s whereas Figure 17.1 pertains to the mid-1980s. Consequently, the demand curves are quite different, as you can see.

Table 17.1 shows that the quantity demanded equals 700 million bushels when the price is $2.00, and that it equals 675 million bushels when the price is $2.20. But should we use $2.00 and 700 million bushels as the original price and quantity? Or should we use $2.20 and 675 million bushels as the original price and quantity? If we choose the former,

$$\text{price elasticity} = \frac{-(675 - 700)}{700} \div \frac{(2.20 - 2.00)}{2.00} = .36.$$

The price elasticity of demand is estimated to be .36. (The minus sign at the beginning of this equation is due to the fact, noted above, that convention dictates that the elasticity be given a positive sign.)

But we could just as well have used $2.20 and 675 million bushels as the original price and quantity. If this had been our choice, the answer would be

$$\text{price elasticity} = \frac{-(700 - 675)}{675} \div \frac{(2.00 - 2.20)}{2.20} = .41$$

which is somewhat different from the answer we got in the previous paragraph.

To get around this difficulty, the generally accepted procedure is to use the average values of price and quantity as the original price and quantity. In other words, we use the following:

$$\text{price elasticity} = \frac{\text{change in quantity demanded}}{\text{sum of quantities}/2} \div \frac{\text{change in price}}{\text{sum of prices}/2}$$

This is the *arc elasticity of demand*. In the specific case we are considering, the arc elasticity is

$$\text{price elasticity} = -\frac{(675 - 700)}{\frac{(675 + 700)}{2}} \div \frac{(2.20 - 2.00)}{\frac{(2.20 + 2.00)}{2}} = .38.$$

This is the answer to our problem.

DETERMINANTS OF THE PRICE ELASTICITY OF DEMAND

Many studies have been made of the price elasticity of demand for particular commodities. Table 17.2 reproduces the results of some of them. Note the substantial differences among products. For example, the estimated price elasticity of demand for women's hats is about 3.00, while for cotton it is only about 0.12. Think for a few minutes about these results, and try to figure out why these differences exist. If you rack your brains for a while, chances are that you will agree that the following factors are important

Table 17.2
Estimated Price
Elasticities of
Demand for
Selected
Commodities,
United States

Commodity	Price elasticity
Women's hats	3.00
Gasoline	0.30
Sugar	0.31
Corn	0.49
Cotton	0.12
Hay	0.43
Potatoes	0.31
Oats	0.56
Barley	0.39
Buckwheat	0.99
Refrigerators	1.40
Airline travel	2.40
Radio and TV sets	1.20
Legal services	0.50
Pleasure boats	1.30
Canned tomatoes	2.50
Newspapers	0.10
Tires	0.60
Beef	0.92
Shoes	0.40

Source: H. Schultz, *Theory and Measurement of Demand.* Chicago: University of Chicago Press. 1938; M. Spencer and L. Siegelman, *Managerial Economics,* Homewood, Ill.: Irwin, 1959; H. Houthakker and L. Taylor, *Consumer Demand in the United States, 1929–1970.* Cambridge, Mass.: Harvard, 1966; and U.S. Department of Agriculture.

determinants of whether a commodity's price elasticity of demand is high or low.

NUMBER AND CLOSENESS OF AVAILABLE SUBSTITUTES. *If a commodity has many close substitutes, its demand is likely to be highly elastic—* that is, the price elasticity is likely to be high. If the price of the product increases, a large proportion of its buyers will turn to the close substitutes that are available. If its price decreases, a great many buyers of substitutes will switch to this product. Naturally, the closeness of the substitutes depends on how narrowly the commodity is defined. In general, one would expect that, as the definition of the product becomes narrower and more specific, the product has more close substitutes and its price elasticity of demand is higher. Thus the demand for a particular brand of motor oil is more price elastic than the overall demand for oil, and the demand for oil is more price elastic than the demand for fuel as a whole. If a commodity is defined so that it has perfect substitutes, its price elasticity of demand approaches infinity. Thus if one farmer's wheat is exactly like that grown by other farmers and if the farmer raises the price slightly (to a point above the market level), the farmer's sales will be reduced to nothing.

IMPORTANCE IN CONSUMERS' BUDGETS. It is often asserted that the price elasticity of demand for a commodity is likely to depend on the

CASE STUDY 17.1 INSTABILITY OF FARM PRICES AND THE PRICE ELASTICITY OF DEMAND

To illustrate the importance of the price elasticity of demand, let's consider the nation's farms. One of the most difficult problems for farmers is that, under a free market, farm incomes vary enormously between good times and bad, the variation being much greater than for nonfarm incomes. This is so because while farm prices vary a great deal between good times and bad, farm output is much more stable than industrial output. Why is agriculture like this?

The answer lies in considerable part with the price elasticity of demand for farm products. Food is a necessity with few good substitutes. Thus we would expect the demand for farm products to be price inelastic. And as Table 17.2 suggests, this expectation is borne out by the facts. Given that the demand curve for farm products is price inelastic—and that the quantity supplied of farm products is also relatively insensitive to price—it follows that relatively small shifts in either the supply curve or the demand curve result in big changes in price. This is why farm prices are so unstable. Panel A of the figure below shows a market where the demand curve is much more inelastic than in panel B. As you can see, a small shift to the left in the demand curve results in a much larger drop in price in panel A than in panel B.

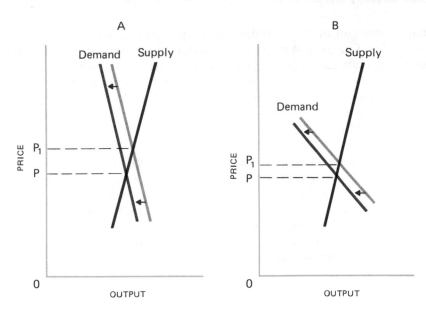

importance of the commodity in consumers' budgets. The elasticity of demand for commodities like pepper and salt may be quite low. Typical consumers spend a very small portion of their income on pepper and salt, and the quantity they demand may not be influenced much by changes in price within a reasonable range. However, although a tendency of this sort is often hypothesized, there is no guarantee that it always exists.

LENGTH OF THE PERIOD. Every market demand curve pertains, you will recall, to a certain time interval. In general, *demand is likely to be more sensitive to price over a long period than over a short one.* The longer the period, the easier it is for consumers and business firms to substitute one good for another. If, for example, the price of oil should decline relative to other fuels, oil consumption in the month after the price decline would probably increase very little. But over a period of several years, people would have an opportunity to take account of the price decline in choosing the type of fuel to be used in new and renovated houses and businesses. In the longer period of several years, the price decline would have a greater effect on the consumption of oil than in the shorter period of one month.

PRICE ELASTICITY AND TOTAL MONEY EXPENDITURE

Many important decisions hinge on the price elasticity of demand for a commodity. One reason why this is so is that the price elasticity of demand determines whether a given change in price will increase or decrease the amount of money spent on a commodity—often a matter of basic importance to firms and government agencies. Let's look more closely at how the price elasticity of demand determines the effect of a price change on the total amount spent on a commodity.

As a first step, we must define three terms: price elastic, price inelastic, and unitary elasticity. The demand for a commodity is *price elastic* if the price elasticity of demand is *greater than 1.* The demand for a commodity is *price inelastic* if the price elasticity of demand is *less than 1.* And the demand for a commodity is of *unitary elasticity* if the price elasticity of demand *equals 1.* As we will see, the effect of a price change on the total amount spent on a commodity depends on whether the demand for the commodity is price elastic, price inelastic, or of unitary elasticity. Let's consider each case.

Case 1: Demand Is Price Elastic

In this case, if the price of the commodity is *reduced,* the total amount spent on the commodity will *increase.* To see why, suppose that the price elasticity of demand for stereo sets is 2 and that the price of the stereo sets is reduced by 1 percent. Because the price elasticity of demand is 2, the

1 percent reduction in price results in a 2 percent increase in the quantity of stereo sets demanded. Since the total amount spent on stereo sets equals the quantity demanded times the price, the 1 percent reduction in price will be more than offset by the 2 percent increase in quantity demanded. The result of the price cut will be an increase in the total amount spent on stereo sets.

On the other hand, if the price of the commodity is *increased,* the total amount spent on the commodity will *fall.* For example, if the price of stereo sets is raised by 1 percent, this will reduce the quantity demanded by 2 percent. The 2 percent reduction in the quantity demanded will more than offset the 1 percent increase in price, the result being a decrease in the total amount spent on stereo sets.

Case 2: Demand Is Price Inelastic

In this case, if the price is *reduced,* the total amount spent on the commodity will *decrease.* To see why, suppose that the price elasticity of demand for corn is 0.5 and the price of corn is reduced by 1 percent. Because the price elasticity of demand is 0.5, the 1 percent price reduction results in a ½ percent increase in the quantity demanded of corn. Since the total amount spent on corn equals the quantity demanded times the price, the ½ percent increase in the quantity demanded will be more than offset by the 1 percent reduction in price. The result of the price cut will be a decrease in the total amount spent on corn.

On the other hand, if the price of the commodity is *increased,* the total amount spent on the commodity will *increase.* For example, if the price of corn is raised by 1 percent, this will reduce quantity demanded by ½ percent. The 1 percent price increase will more than offset the ½ percent reduction in quantity demanded, the result being an increase in the total amount spent on corn.

Case 3: Demand Is of Unitary Elasticity

In this case, a price increase or decrease results in no difference in the total amount spent on the commodity. Why? Because a price decrease (increase) of a certain percentage always results in a quantity increase (decrease) of the same percentage, so that the product of the price and quantity is unaffected. Table 17.3 summarizes the results of this section. It should help you review our findings.

Commodity's price elasticity of demand	Effect on total expenditure of:	
	Price decrease	Price increase
Price elastic (which means that elasticity is greater than 1)	Increase	Decrease
Price inelastic (which means that elasticity is less than 1)	Decrease	Increase
Unitary elasticity (which means that elasticity equals 1)	No change	No change

Table 17.3
Effect of an Increase or Decrease in the Price of a Commodity on the Total Expenditure on the Commodity

THE DEMAND CURVE FOR AUTOMOBILES: A CASE STUDY

Some congressional committees have asserted that important industries in the American economy have tended to underestimate the price elasticity of demand, so that they have not been sufficiently prone to reduce prices. According to the critics, the industries in question should, in their own interest as well as the public's, reduce their prices. Among those charged with such an underestimation is the automobile industry, unquestionably one of the biggest industries in the entire American economy.

How great is the price elasticity of demand for automobiles? This is a very important question both to the automobile industry and to those, like the congressional committees, who have some responsibility for evaluating our economy's overall performance. Perhaps the first major study of this question was carried out in 1939 by C. F. Roos and V. von Szeliski for the General Motors Corporation. On the basis of data for 1919–37, their statistical analysis indicated that the price elasticity of demand for new automobiles was about 1.5. In other words, a 1 percent reduction in price would result in about a 1.5 percent increase in the quantity demanded of new automobiles.

Several more recent studies of the price elasticity of demand for automobiles have been carried out by academic economists. Although there has been some controversy over particular aspects of these investigations, they seem to indicate that the price elasticity of demand for automobiles is at least 1.2. In other words, a 1 percent reduction in price brings about at least a 1.2 percent increase in the quantity demanded. Thus these studies, carried out by L. J. Atkinson, Gregory Chow, and D. B. Suits, seem generally to agree rather well with the earlier study by Roos and von Szeliski.

On the basis of the available evidence, it is difficult to tell conclusively whether the automobile manufacturers have tended to underestimate the price elasticity of demand for their product. But suppose for the sake of argument that they have. Why should anyone care? The answer is that both the automobile manufacturers and the general public should care, because by underestimating the price elasticity of demand, the companies are underestimating the potential gain in sales from a price reduction. Thus they are inclined to maintain car prices at too high a level, possibly to the detriment of their own profits as well as the consumer's pocketbook.

INDUSTRY AND FIRM DEMAND CURVES

Up to this point, we have been dealing with the market demand curve for a commodity. *The market demand curve for a commodity is not the same as the market demand curve for the output of a single firm that produces the commodity, unless, of course, the industry is composed of only a single firm.* If the industry is composed of more than one firm, as is usually the case, the demand curve for the output of each firm producing the commodity will usually be quite different from the demand curve for the commodity. The demand curve for the output of Farmer Brown's wheat is quite different from the market demand curve for wheat.

In particular, the demand curve for the output of a particular firm is generally more price elastic than the market demand curve for the commodity, because the products of other firms in the industry are close substitutes for the product of this firm. As pointed out earlier, products with many close substitutes have relatively high price elasticities of demand.

If there are many firms selling a homogeneous product, the individual firm's demand curve becomes *horizontal,* or essentially so. To see this, suppose that 100,000 firms sell a particular commodity and that all of these firms are of equal size. If any one of these firms were to triple its output and sales, the total industry output would change by only .002 percent—too small a change to have any perceptible effect on the price of the commodity. Consequently, each firm can act as if variations in its output—within the range of its capabilities—will have no real impact on market price. In other words, the demand curve facing the individual firm is horizontal, as in Figure 17.4.

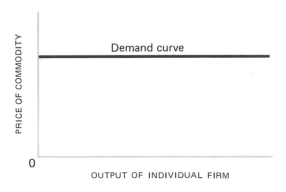

**Figure 17.4
Demand Curve for Output of an Individual Firm: The Case of a Great Many Sellers of a Homogeneous Commodity**
If there are many firms selling a homogeneous product, the demand curve facing an individual firm is horizontal.

INCOME ELASTICITY OF DEMAND

So far this chapter has dealt almost exclusively with the effect of a commodity's price on the quantity demanded of it in the market. But price is not, of course, the only factor that influences the quantity demanded of the commodity. Another important factor is the level of money income among the consumers in the market. The sensitivity of the quantity demanded to the total money income of all of the consumers in the market is measured by the *income elasticity of demand*, which is defined as the percentage change in the quantity demanded resulting from a 1 percent increase in total money income (all prices being held constant).

A commodity's income elasticity of demand may be positive or negative. For many commodities, increases in income result in increases in the amount demanded. Such commodities, like steak or caviar, have positive income elasticities of demand. For other commodities, increases in income result in decreases in the amount demanded. These commodities, like margarine and poor grades of vegetables, have negative income elasticities of demand. However, be careful to note that the income elasticity of demand of a commodity is likely to vary with the level of income under consideration. For example, if only families at the lowest income levels are considered, the income elasticity of demand for margarine may be positive.

Luxury items tend to have higher income elasticities of demand than necessities. Indeed, one way to define luxuries and necessities is to say that luxuries are commodities with high income elasticities of demand, and necessities are commodities with low income elasticities of demand.

CROSS ELASTICITY OF DEMAND

Besides the price of the commodity and the level of total money income, the quantity demanded of a commodity also depends on the prices of other commodities. Suppose the price of butter is held constant. The amount of butter demanded will be influenced by the price of margarine. The *cross elasticity of demand*, defined as the percentage change in the quantity demanded of one commodity resulting from a 1 percent change in the price of another commodity, is used to measure the sensitivity of the former commodity's quantity demanded to changes in the latter commodity's price.

Pairs of commodities can be classified as *substitutes* or *complements*, depending on the sign of the cross elasticity of demand. *If the cross elasticity of demand is positive, two commodities are substitutes.* Butter and margarine are substitutes because a decrease in the price of butter will result in a decrease in the quantity demanded of margarine. *On the other hand, if the cross elasticity of demand is negative, two commodities are complements.* For example, gin and tonic may be complements since a decrease in the price of gin may increase the quantity demanded of tonic. The reduction in the price of gin will increase the quantity demanded of gin, thus increasing the quantity demanded of tonic since gin and tonic tend to be used together.

Many studies have been made of the cross elasticity of demand for various pairs of commodities. After all, it frequently is very important to know how a change in the price of one commodity will affect the sale of another commodity. For example, what would be the effect of a 1 percent increase in the price of pork on the quantity demanded of beef? According to estimates by Herman Wold, a distinguished Swedish economist, the effect would be a .28 percent increase in the quantity demanded of beef, since he estimates that the cross elasticity of demand for these two commodities is 0.28. What effect would a 1 percent increase in the price of butter have on the quantity demanded of margarine? According to Wold, the effect would be a .81 percent increase in the quantity demanded of margarine, since he estimates that the cross elasticity of demand for these two commodities is 0.81.

EXPLORING FURTHER: THE FARM PROBLEM

Agriculture is an enormously important sector of the American economy. Even though its size has been decreasing steadily for many decades, agriculture still employs about 3 million Americans. Its importance, moreover, cannot be measured entirely by its size. You need only think about how difficult it would be to get along without food to see the strategic role agriculture plays in our economic life. Also, agriculture is one of the most technologically progressive parts of the American economy. The efficiency of American agriculture is admired throughout the world.

Nonetheless, American farmers have had serious problems. Perhaps the clearest indication of these problems emerges from a comparison of American farmers' per capita income with per capita income among the rest of the population. Until the past fifteen years, farm incomes have tended to be much lower than nonfarm incomes. In 1970, per capita income on the farms was about 20 percent below that for the nonfarm population. Moreover, a large proportion of the rural population is poor. Thus the National Advisory Commission on Rural Poverty found in 1967 that "rural proverty is so widespread, and so acute, as to be a national disgrace."[3] Of course, this does not mean that all farmers are poor; on the contrary, many do very well indeed. But a large percentage of the nation's farmers are poor by any standard.

This farm problem is nothing new. Farmers did enjoy relatively high prices and high incomes during the first two decades of the twentieth century. But in 1920 the country experienced a sharp depression that jolted agriculture as well as the rest of the economy. Whereas the Roaring Twenties saw a recovery and boom in the nonfarm sector of the

Wisconsin farmers dumping milk during the Depression

economy, agriculture did not recover as completely, and the 1930s were dreadful years; the Great Depression resulted in a sickening decline in farm prices and farm incomes. World War II brought prosperity to agriculture, but in the postwar period, farm incomes have consistently been well below nonfarm incomes. From 1973 to 1975, prosperity returned to the farms, but the late 1970s and 1980s saw renewed complaints by

[3]National Advisory Committee on Rural Poverty, *The People Left Behind*, Washington, D.C., 1967.

farmers about prices and incomes. All in all, agriculture has been experiencing difficulties for several decades.

Characteristics of Demand and Supply Curves for Farm Products

Let's start with the market demand curve for farm products. This market demand curve must have two important characteristics. First, *its shape must reflect the fact that food is a necessity and that the quantity demanded will not vary much with the price of food—in other words, the demand curve is price inelastic.* Second, *the market demand curve for food is unlikely to shift to the right very much as per capita income rises,* because consumption of food per capita faces natural biological and other limitations. In other words, consumption of food is income inelastic as well.

Next, consider the market supply curve for farm products. Again, you should be aware of two important characteristics of this market supply curve. First, *the quantity of farm products supplied tends to be relatively insensitive to price* (i.e., price inelastic) because the farmers have only limited control over their output. (Weather, floods, insects, and other factors are important.) Second, because of rapid technological change, *the market supply curve has been shifting markedly and rapidly to the right.*

Decline in Relative Price of Food Products

If you understand these simple characteristics of the market demand curve and market supply curve for farm products, it is no trick to understand why we have had the sort of farm problem just described. Figure 17.5 shows the market demand and market supply curves for farm products at various points in time. As you would expect, the market demand curve for farm products shifts rather slowly to the right as incomes (and population) grow over time. Specifically, the market demand curve shifted from D in the first period to D_1 in the second period to D_2 in the third period. On the other hand, the market supply curve for farm products shifted rapidly to the right as technology improved over time. It shifted from S in the first period to S_1 in the second period to S_2 in the third period.

What was the consequence of these shifts in the market demand and supply curves for food products? Clearly, *the equilibrium price of food products fell (relative to other products).* Specifically, the equilibrium price fell from OP to OP_1 to OP_2 in Figure 17.5. This price decrease was, of course, a large part of the farm problem. If we correct for changes in the general level of prices (which have tended to rise over time), there was, in general, a declining trend in farm prices. Agricultural prices gener-

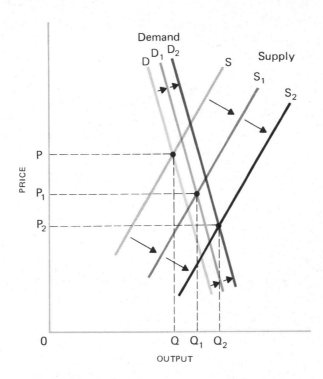

Figure 17.5
Shifts over Time in Market Demand and Supply Curves for Farm Products
The market demand curve has shifted rather slowly to the right (from D to D_1 to D_2), whereas the market supply curve has shifted rapidly to the right (from S to S_1 to S_2), with the result that the equilibrium price has declined (from OP to OP_1 to OP_2).

ally fell, relative to other prices, in the last 60 years. Moreover, *given this fall in farm prices, farm incomes tended to fall, because, although lower prices were associated with greater amounts sold, the reduction in price was much greater than the increase in quantity sold,* as we can see in Figure 17.5.[4]

Thus the simple model of market behavior described in previous chapters makes it possible to explain the fact that farm prices and farm incomes have tended to fall in the United States. Certainly there is nothing mysterious about these trends. Given the nature and characteristics of the market demand curve and market supply curve for farm products, our simple model shows that these trends are as much to be expected as parades on the Fourth of July.

Slow Exit of Resources

However, one additional fact must be noted to understand the farm problem: *people and nonhuman resources have been relatively slow to move out of agriculture in response to these trends.* The price system uses such trends—lower prices and lower incomes—to signal producers that they

[4]The amount farmers receive is the amount they sell times the price. Thus, in Figure 17.5, the amount farmers receive in income is $OP \times OQ$ in the first period, $OP_1 \times OQ_1$ in the second period, and $OP_2 \times OQ_2$ in the third period. Clearly, since the price is decreasing much more rapidly than the quantity is increasing, farm incomes are falling.

*An abandoned
North Carolina farm*

should use their resources elsewhere. Farmers have been loath to move out of agriculture (even though they often could make more money elsewhere), and this has been a primary cause of the farm problem that has existed over most of the past 40 years. If more people and resources had left farming, agricultural prices and incomes would have risen, and ultimately farm incomes would have come closer to nonfarm incomes. (Poor education and color were, of course, significant barriers to migration.)

Nonetheless, even though farmers have been slow to move out of agriculture, the long run shows that they have left the farm. In 1930 the farm population was about 30 million, or 25 percent of the total population; in 1950, it was about 23 million, or 15 percent of the total population; and in 1981, it was about 6 million, or 3 percent of the total population. Thus the price system has had its way. Resources have been moving out of agriculture in response to the signals and pressures of the price system. This movement of people and nonhuman resources unquestionably has contributed to greater efficiency and production for the nation as a whole. But during most of the past 40 years, we have continued to have a "surplus" of farmers, and this has been the root of the farm problem.

Government Aid to Agriculture

Traditionally, farmers have had a disproportionately large influence in Congress. When faced with declining economic fortunes, they have appealed to the government for help. They have extolled the virtues of rural life, emphasized that agriculture is a competitive industry, and claimed that it was unfair for their prices to fall relative to the prices they have had to pay. In addition, they have pointed out that the movement of resources out of agriculture has entailed large human costs, since this movement, although beneficial to the nation as a whole, has been traumatic for the farm population. For reasons of this sort, they have argued that the government should help farmers; and in particular, the government should act to bolster farm prices and farm incomes.

The Concept of Parity

Their voices were heard. In the Agricultural Adjustment Act of 1933, the Congress announced the concept of parity as the major objective of

American farm policy. This concept has since acquired great importance, and must be clearly understood. Put in its simplest terms, the concept of *parity* holds that a farmer should be able currently to exchange a given quantity of his output for as much in the way of nonfarm goods and services as he could at some time in the past. For example, if a farmer could take a bushel of wheat to market in 1912 and get enough money to buy a pair of gloves, today he should be able to get enough money for a bushel of wheat to buy a pair of gloves.

To see what the concept of parity implies for farm prices, suppose that the price of gloves triples. Obviously, if parity is to be maintained, the price of wheat must triple too. Thus the concept of parity implies that farm prices must increase at the same rate as the prices of the goods and services farmers buy. Of course, farmers buy lots of things besides gloves, so in actual practice the parity price of wheat or other farm products is determined by the changes over time in the average price of all the goods and services farmers buy.

Two major points should be noted about parity. First, to use this concept, one must agree on some base period, such as 1912 in the example above, during which the relationship of farm to nonfarm prices is regarded as equitable. Obviously, the higher farm prices were relative to nonfarm prices in the base period, the higher farm prices will be in subsequent periods if parity is maintained. It is significant that 1910–14 was used for many years as the base period. Since this was a period of relatively high farm prices and of agricultural prosperity, the farm bloc must have wielded considerable political clout on this issue. Second, note that the concept of parity is an ethical, not a scientific, proposition. It states what the relative economic position of a bushel of wheat ought to be—or, more precisely, it states one particular view of what the relative economic position of a bushel of wheat should be. Based on purely scientific considerations, there is no way to prove (or disprove) this proposition, since it is based on one's values and political preferences. Using the terminology in Chapter 1, it is a proposition in normative, not positive, economics.

Price Supports and Surplus Controls

During the four decades up to 1973, the concept of parity was the cornerstone of a system of government price supports. It is true that the government did not support all farm prices at the full 100 percent of parity. For example, Congress sometimes enacted bills saying that the secretary of agriculture could establish a price of wheat, corn, cotton, or some other product within a certain range, say between 65 and 90 percent of parity. But whatever the exact level of farm price supports, the idea behind them was perfectly simple: it was to maintain farm prices above the level that would result in a free market.

Using the simple supply-and-demand model, we can see more clearly the effects of these price supports. The situation is shown in Figure 17.6. A support price, OP', was set by the government. Since this support price

Figure 17.6
**Effects of Farm
Price-Support
Program**
The support price,
OP', is above the
equilibrium price,
OP, so the public
buys *OQ₂*, farmers
supply *OQ₁* units of
output, and the
government buys
the difference
(OQ₁ − OQ₂).

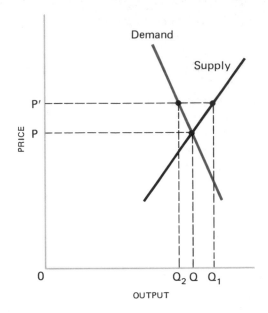

was above the equilibrium price, *OP*, the public bought *less* of farm products (*OQ₂* rather than *OQ*) and paid a *higher* price for them. Farmers
gained from the price supports, since the amount they received for their
crop under the price support was equal to $OP' \times OQ_1$, a greater amount
than what they would have received in a free market, which was $OP \times OQ$.

Note, however, that since the support price exceeded the equilibrium
price, the quantity supplied of the farm product, OQ_1, exceeded the quantity demanded, OQ_2. That is, *there was a surplus of the farm product in
question,* which the government had to purchase, since no one else would.
These surpluses were an embarrassment, both economically and politically. They showed that society's scarce resources were being utilized to
produce products consumers simply did not want at existing prices. Moreover, the cost of storing these surpluses was very large indeed: in some
years, these storage costs alone hit the $1-billion mark.

Policies to Cut Surpluses

To help reduce these surpluses, the government followed two basic strategies. First, *it tried to restrict output of farm products.* In particular, the
government established an acreage allotment program, which said that
farmers had to limit the number of acres they planted in order to get price
supports on their crops. The Department of Agriculture estimated how
much of each product would be demanded by buyers (other than the
government) at the support price, and tried to cut back the total acreage
planted with this crop to the point where the quantity supplied equaled

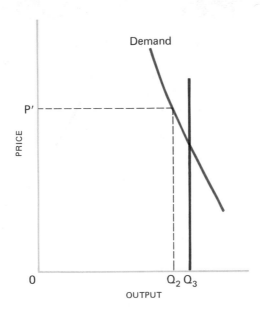

Figure 17.7
Effects of Price Supports and Output Restrictions
The government restricts output to OQ_3, with the result that it buys $(OQ_3 - OQ_2)$ units of output.

the quantity demanded. These output restrictions did not eliminate the surpluses, because farmers managed to increase the yields from acreage they were allowed to plant, but undoubtedly they reduced the surpluses. Under these restrictions, the situation was as shown in Figure 17.7, where $0Q_3$ was the total output that could be grown on the acreage that could be planted with the crop. Because of the imposition of this output control, the surplus—which the government had to purchase—was reduced from $(0Q_1 - 0Q_2)$ to $(0Q_3 - 0Q_2)$. Farmers continued to benefit from price supports because the amount they received for their crop, $0P' \times 0Q_3$, was still greater than they would have received in a free market, because the amount demanded of farm products was not very sensitive to their price.

Second, *the government tried to shift the demand curve for farm products to the right.* An effort was made to find new uses for various farm products. Also, various antipoverty programs, such as the food-stamp program, used our farm surpluses to help the poor. In addition, the government tried to expand the export markets for American farm products. Western Europe and Japan increased their demand for food, and the Communist countries purchased our farm products to offset their own agricultural deficiencies. Moreover, the less developed countries were permitted by Public Law 480 to buy our farm products with their own currencies, rather than dollars. The result was a reduction in farm surpluses, as shown in Figure 17.8. Since the market demand curve for farm products shifted to the right, the surplus was reduced from $(0Q_3 - 0Q_2)$ to $(0Q_3 - 0Q_4)$. Because of these demand-augmenting and output-restricting measures, surpluses during the late 1960s and early 1970s were considerably smaller than they were during the late 1950s and early 1960s.

Figure 17.8
Effects of Price Supports, Output Restrictions, and a Shift to the Right in the Demand Curve for Farm Products
By shifting the demand curve to the right, the government reduces the surplus from $(OQ_3 - OQ_2)$ to $(OQ_3 - OQ_4)$ units of output.

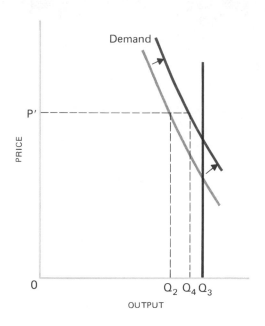

Post-1973 Developments

In 1973, farm prices increased markedly, due partly to very great increases in foreign demand for American agricultural products. This increase in foreign demand was due partly to poor harvests in the Soviet Union, Australia, Argentina, and elsewhere, as well as to devaluations of the dollar. (In 1972–73, the Soviet Union alone bought over $1 billion of grain—on terms that provoked considerable controversy in the United States.) As a result, farm incomes reached very high levels, farm surpluses disappeared, and for the first time in 30 years the government was trying to stimulate farm production rather than restrict it.

Farmers protest in Washington against falling prices

Taking advantage of this new climate, Congress passed a new farm bill which ended price supports. This bill, the Agriculture and Consumer Protection Act of 1973, aimed at reducing government involvement in agriculture and at a return to freer markets. Specifically, agricultural prices were allowed to fluctuate freely in accord with supply and demand. However, the government made cash payments to farmers if prices fell below certain "target" levels established by the law. These target levels were above the prices that generally prevailed in the past, but they were below the high levels of prices prevailing in 1973. A program of this kind was originally proposed in 1949 by Charles F. Brannan, who was secretary of agriculture under President Harry Truman.

By 1975, it appeared to many knowledgeable observers that the farm sector no longer was suffering from overcapacity, and that, in this respect at least, an equilibrium had been achieved. However, this attitude did not last long. During 1976 and 1977, U.S. farmers harvested bumper crops, with the result that prices fell considerably. The price of wheat, which had been about $3.50 per bushel in 1975, fell to about $2.30 per bushel in 1977. Farmers protested, and exerted political pressure for increased government price and income supports. In 1985, the Reagan administration talked repeatedly about the government's lessening its intervention in agriculture, but many observers were skeptical.

Indeed, in late 1985, the trend seemed to be in the opposite direction. A substantial number of farmers were reported to be unable to pay their debts, and farm groups (and banks) were pressing for government help. Congress passed a $169 billion spending bill covering five years.

SUMMARY

1. The market demand curve, which is the relationship between the price of a commodity and the amount of the commodity demanded in the market, is one of the most important and frequently used concepts in economics. The shape and position of a product's market demand curve depend on consumers' tastes, consumer incomes, the price of other goods, and the number of consumers in the market.

2. The price elasticity of demand, defined as the percentage change in quantity demanded resulting from a 1 percent change in price, measures the sensitivity of the amount demanded to changes in price. Whether a price increase results in an increase or decrease in the total amount spent on a commodity depends on the price elasticity of demand.

3. The market demand curve for a commodity is not the same as the demand curve for the output of a single firm that produces the commodity, unless the industry is composed of only one firm. In general, the demand curve for the output of a single firm will be more elastic than the market demand curve for the commodity. Indeed, if there are many firms selling a homogeneous commodity, the individual firm's demand curve becomes horizontal.

4. The income elasticity of demand, defined as the percentage change in quantity demanded resulting from a 1 percent increase in total money income, measures the sensitivity of the amount demanded to changes in total income. A commodity's income elasticity of demand may be positive or negative. Luxury items are generally assumed to have higher income elasticities of demand than necessities.

5. The cross elasticity of demand, defined as the percentage change in the quantity demanded resulting from a 1 percent change in the price of another commodity, measures the sensitivity of the amount demanded to changes in the price of another commodity. If the cross elasticity of demand is positive, two commodities are substitutes; if it is negative, they are complements.

*6. American agriculture has been plagued by relatively low incomes. The demand for farm products grew slowly, while rapid technological change meant that the people and resources currently in agriculture could supply more and more farm products. Because people and resources did not move out of agriculture as rapidly as the price system dictated, farm incomes tended to be relatively low.

*7. In response to political pressures from the farm blocs, the government set in motion a series of programs to aid farmers. A cornerstone of these programs was the concept of parity, which held that the prices farmers receive should increase at the same rate as the prices of the goods and services farmers buy. The government instituted price supports to keep farm prices above their equilibrium level. But since the support prices exceeded the equilibrium prices, there was a surplus of the commodities that the government had to purchase and store. To help reduce these surpluses, the government tried to restrict the output of farm products and expand the demand for them.

*8. In 1973, farm prices increased greatly, due partly to very great increases in foreign demand for U.S. agricultural products. By 1975, many people felt that American agriculture no longer was suffering from overcapacity. But in recent years, farmers have complained bitterly of low prices and their need for government assistance.

*The starred items refer to material covered in the section, "Exploring Further."

CHAPTER 18

★ ★ ★ ★ ★ ★ ★ ★ ★

Economic Efficiency, Market Supply, and Perfect Competition

LEARNING OBJECTIVES

In this chapter, you should learn:

★ The conditions that define a perfectly competitive market structure

★ The "golden rule" of output determination for a perfectly competitive firm

★ The concept of economic profits

★ The long-run equilibrium position for a perfectly competitive firm

Even a country as rich as the United States cannot afford to waste resources, particularly when much of the world is hungry. One of the important determinants of how a society's resources are used is how its markets are organized. If the market for wheat contained few sellers rather than many, it would use resources quite differently. Or if 20 firms provided telephone service in Chicago, resources would be used differently. Economists do not have any simple formulas that will eliminate all social waste. But based on existing models and evidence, some forms of market organization tend to minimize social waste whereas other forms seem to promote it.

In this chapter, we examine the way resources are allocated and prices are set under *perfect competition*. This type of market organization—or market structure, as it is often called—is a polar case that seldom, if ever,

★ 360
Economic
Efficiency, Market
Supply, and
Perfect
Competition

occurs in a pure form in the real world. But it is an extremely useful model that sheds much light on a market structure's effects on resource allocation. Anyone who wants to understand how markets work in a capitalistic economy, or why our public policies toward business are what they are, must understand perfect competition, as well as the other market structures we take up later.

MARKET STRUCTURE AND ECONOMIC PERFORMANCE

Many economists have come to the conclusion, based on their studies of the workings of markets, that certain kinds of market organization are better, from society's point of view, than others. This is a much stronger statement than merely saying, as we did in the previous section, that market structure influences market behavior. This statement is based on some set of values and preferences, explicit or implicit, and on certain economic models that predict that "better" behavior is more likely if markets are organized in certain ways. Although there is considerable controversy on this score, many economists believe that, from society's point of view, market structures should be as close as possible to perfect competition.

Economists have generally found it useful to classify markets into four broad types: *perfect competition, monopoly, monopolistic competition*, and *oligopoly*. Each of these terms describes a particular type of market structure or organization. Table 18.1 provides a capsule description of each of these types. Before looking in detail at each of them, let's go over this table to see how these market structures differ.

Table 18.1
Types of Market
Structure

Market structure	Examples	Number of producers	Type of product	Power of firm over price	Barriers to entry	Nonprice competition
Perfect competition	Parts of agriculture are reasonably close	Many	Standardized	None	Low	None
Monopolistic competition	Retail trade	Many	Differentiated	Some	Low	Advertising and product differentiation
Oligopoly	Autos, steel, machinery	Few	Standardized or differentiated	Some	High	Advertising and product differentiation
Monopoly	Public utilities	One	Unique product	Considerable	Very high	Advertising

Number of Firms

The economist's classification of market structures is based to an important extent on the number of firms in the industry that supplies the product.

In perfect competition and monopolistic competition, there are *many* sellers, each of which produces only a small part of the industry's output. In monopoly, on the other hand, the industry consists of only a *single* seller. Oligopoly is an intermediate case where there are a *few* sellers. For example, Consolidated Edison, if it is the only supplier of electricity in New York City, is a monopoly. And since there are only a small number of computer manufacturers, the market for computers is an oligopoly.

Control over Price

Market structures differ considerably in the extent to which an individual firm has control over price. A firm under perfect competition has no control over price. For example, a wheat farm (which is close to being a perfectly competitive firm) has no control over the price of wheat. On the other hand, a monopolist is likely to have *considerable control* over price. Thus, in the absence of public regulation, Consolidated Edison would have considerable control over the price of electricity in New York City. A firm under monopolistic competition or oligopoly is likely to have *more* control over price than a perfectly competitive firm and *less* control over price than a monopolist.

Type of Product

These market structures also differ in the extent to which the firms in an industry produce standardized (that is, identical) products. Firms in a perfectly competitive market all produce *identical* products. Thus Farmer Brown's corn is essentially the same as Farmer Smith's. In a monopolistic competitive industry like dress manufacturing, firms produce *somewhat different* products. One firm's dresses differ in style and quality from another firm's dresses. In an oligopolistic industry, firms *sometimes,* but not always, produce identical products. And in a monopolistic industry, there can be *no difference* among firms in their products, since there is only one firm.

Barriers to Entry

The ease with which firms can enter the industry differs from one market structure to another. In perfect competition, barriers to entry are *low*. Thus only a small investment is required to enter many parts of agriculture. Similarly, there are *low* barriers to entry in monopolistic competition. But in oligopolies such as autos and steel, there tend to be *very considerable* barriers to entry because, among other reasons, it is so expensive to build an auto or steel plant. In monopoly, entry is blocked; once another firm enters, the monopolist is an ex-monopolist.

★ 362
**Economic
Efficiency, Market
Supply, and
Perfect
Competition**

Nonprice Competition

These market structures also differ in the extent to which firms compete on the basis of advertising and differences in product characteristics, rather than price. In perfect competition, there is *no* nonprice competition. In monopolistic competition, there is *considerable emphasis* on nonprice competition. Dress manufacturers compete by trying to develop better styles and by advertising their product lines. Oligopolies also tend to rely *heavily* on nonprice competition. For example, auto firms try to increase their sales by building better and more attractive cars and by advertising. Monopolists also engage in advertising to increase their profits, although this advertising is not directed at reducing the sales of other firms in the industry, since no other firms exist.

PERFECT COMPETITION

When business executives speak of a highly competitive market, they often mean one in which each firm is keenly aware of its rivalry with a few others and in which advertising, styling, packaging, and other such commercial weapons are used to attract business away from them. In contrast, the basic feature of the economist's definition of perfect competition is its *impersonality.* Because there are so many firms in the industry, no firm views another as a competitor, any more than one small tobacco farmer views another small tobacco farmer as a competitor. A market is perfectly competitive if it satisfies the following three conditions.

HOMOGENEITY OF PRODUCT. The first condition is that *the product of any one seller must be the same as the product of any other seller.* This condition ensures that buyers do not care from which seller they purchase the goods, so long as the price is the same. This condition is met in many markets. As pointed out in the previous section, Farmer Brown's corn is likely to be essentially the same as Farmer Smith's.

MANY BUYERS AND SELLERS. The second condition is that there must be a large number of buyers and sellers. *Each participant in the market, whether buyer or seller, must be so small in relation to the entire market that he or she cannot affect the product's price.* All buyers and sellers must be "price takers," not "price makers." A firm under perfect competition faces a *horizontal demand curve,* since variations in its output—within the range of its capabilities—will have no effect on market price.

MOBILITY OF RESOURCES. The third condition is that *all resources must be able to switch readily from one use to another, and consumers, firms, and resource owners must have complete knowledge of all relevant economic and technological data.*

No industry in the real world, now or in the past, satisfies all these conditions completely; thus no industry is perfectly competitive. Some agricultural markets may be reasonably close, but even they do not meet all the requirements. But this does not mean that it is useless to study the behavior of a perfectly competitive market. The conclusions derived from the model of perfect competition have proved very helpful in explaining and predicting behavior in the real world. Indeed, as we shall see, they have permitted a reasonably accurate view of resource allocation in many important segments of our economy.

THE OUTPUT OF THE FIRM

What determines the output rate in the short run of a perfectly competitive firm? Since the firm is perfectly competitive, it cannot affect the price of its product, and it can sell any amount it wants at this price. Since we are concerned with the short run, the firm can expand or contract its output rate by increasing or decreasing its utilization of its variable, but not its fixed, inputs. (The situation in the long run will be considered in a later section.)

What Is the Profit at Each Output Rate?

To see how a firm determines its output rate, suppose that your aunt dies and leaves you her business, the Allegro Piano Company. Once you take over the business, your first problem is to decide how many pianos (each of which has a price of $1,000) the firm should produce per week. Having a good deal of economic intuition, you instruct your accountants to estimate the company's *total revenue* (defined as price times output) and total costs (as well as, separately, fixed and variable costs) at various output levels. They estimate the firm's total revenue at various output rates and its total cost function (as well as its total fixed cost function and total variable cost function), with the results shown in Table 18.2. Subtracting the total cost at a given output rate from the total revenue at this output rate, you obtain the total profit at each output rate, which is shown in the last column of Table 18.2.

Output per week (pianos)	Price	Total revenue (price × output)	Total fixed cost (dollars)	Total variable cost	Total cost	Total profit
0	1,000	0	1,000	0	1,000	−1,000
1	1,000	1,000	1,000	200	1,200	− 200
2	1,000	2,000	1,000	300	1,300	700
3	1,000	3,000	1,000	500	1,500	1,500
4	1,000	4,000	1,000	1,000	2,000	2,000
5	1,000	5,000	1,000	2,000	3,000	2,000
6	1,000	6,000	1,000	3,200	4,200	1,800
7	1,000	7,000	1,000	4,500	5,500	1,500
8	1,000	8,000	1,000	7,200	8,200	− 200

Table 18.2
Costs and Revenues, Allegro Piano Company

★ 364
Economic
Efficiency, Market
Supply, and
Perfect
Competition

Finding the Maximum-Profit Output Rate

As the output rate increases from 0 to 4 pianos per week, the total profit *rises.* As the output rate increases from 5 to 8 pianos per week, the total profit *falls.* Thus the *maximum* profit is achieved at an output rate between 4 and 5 pianos per week.[1] (Without more detailed data, one cannot tell precisely where the maximum occurs, but this is close enough for present purposes.) Since the maximum profit is obtained at an output of between 4 and 5 pianos per week, this is the output rate you choose.

Figure 18.1 gives a more vivid picture of the firm's situation by plotting the relationship between total revenue and total cost, on the one hand, and output on the other. At each output rate, the vertical distance between the total revenue curve and the total cost curve is the amount of profit the firm earns. Below an output rate of about 1 piano per week and above a rate of about 8 pianos per week, the total revenue curve lies *below* the total cost curve, indicating that profits are negative—that is, there are losses. Both Table 18.2 and Figure 18.1 show that the output rate that will maximize the firm's profits is between 4 and 5 pianos per week. At this output rate, the firm will make a profit of over $2,000 per week, which is more than it can make at any other output rate.

Figure 18.1
Costs, Revenues,
and Profits,
Allegro Piano
Company
Profit equals the vertical distance between the total revenue curve and the total cost curve. This distance is maximized when the output rate is between 4 and 5 pianos per week. At this output rate, profit (measured by the vertical distance) is somewhat more than $2,000.

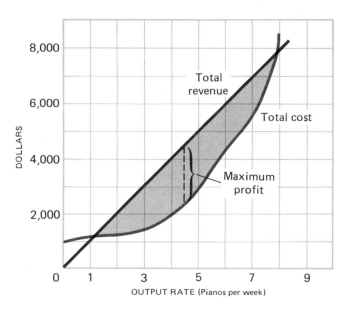

There is an alternative way to analyze the firm's situation. Rather than looking at total revenue and total cost, let's look at price and marginal cost. Table 18.3 and Figure 18.2 show the product price and marginal cost at each output rate. It turns out that the maximum profit is achieved at the

[1]This assumes that the output rate can be varied continuously and that there is a single maximum. These are innocuous assumptions.

Table 18.3
Marginal Cost and Price, Allegro Piano Company

Output per week (pianos)	Marginal cost (dollars)	Price
0		1,000
	200	
1		1,000
	100	
2		1,000
	200	
3		1,000
	500	
4		1,000
	1,000	
5		1,000
	1,200	
6		1,000
	1,300	
7		1,000
	2,700	
8		1,000

output rate where price equals marginal cost. In other words, both Table 18.3 and Figure 18.2 indicate that price equals marginal cost at the profit-maximizing output rate of between 4 and 5 pianos per week. This raises a question. Will price usually equal marginal cost at the profit-maximizing output rate, or is this merely a coincidence?

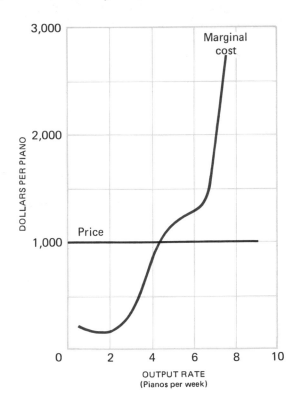

Figure 18.2
Marginal Cost and Price, Allegro Piano Company
At the profit-maximizing output rate of between 4 and 5 pianos per week, marginal cost (which is $1,000 when the output rate is between 4 and 5) equals price ($1,000). Recall from Figure 16.11 that marginal cost is plotted at the midpoint of the range of output to which it pertains.

★ 366

**Economic
Efficiency, Market
Supply, and
Perfect
Competition**

The Golden Rule of Output Determination

Readers familiar with television scripts and detective stories will have recognized that the question just posed can only be answered in one way without ruining the plot. The equality of marginal cost and price at the profit-maximizing output rate is no mere coincidence. It will usually be true if the firm takes the price of its product as given. Indeed, the Golden Rule of Output Determination for a perfectly competitive firm is: *Choose the output rate at which marginal cost is equal to price.*

To prove that this rule maximizes profits, consider Figure 18.3, which shows a typical short-run marginal cost function. Suppose that the price is OP_1. At any output rate less than OQ_1, price is greater than marginal cost. This means that increases in output will increase the firm's profits since they will add more to total revenues than to total cost. Why? Because an extra unit of output adds an amount equal to price to total revenue and an amount equal to marginal cost to total cost. Thus, since price exceeds marginal cost, an extra unit of output adds more to total revenue than to total cost. This is the case for the Allegro Piano Company when it is producing 3 pianos per week. As shown in Table 18.3, the extra cost of producing a fourth piano is $500, while the revenue brought in by producing and selling it is $1,000. Consequently, it pays the Allegro Piano Company to produce more than 3 pianos per week.

At any output rate above OQ_1, price is less than marginal cost. This means that decreases in output will increase the firm's profits since they will subtract more from total costs than from total revenue. This happens because one less unit of output subtracts an amount equal to price from

**Figure 18.3
Short-Run Average
and Marginal Cost
Curves**
If price is OP_1, the
profit-maximizing
output rate is OQ_1.
If price is OP_2, the
profit-maximizing
output rate is OQ_2,
even though the
firm will incur a loss.
If the price is below
OP_3, the firm will
discontinue
production. (Note,
that, regardless of
what the price is,
the demand curve
facing the firm is a
horizontal line at
this price.)

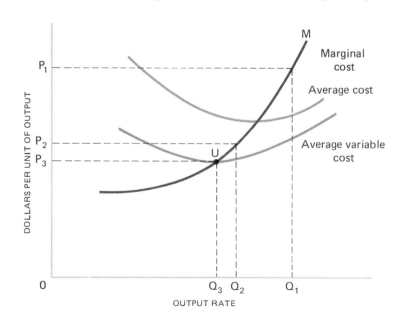

total revenue and an amount equal to marginal cost from total cost. Thus since price is less than marginal cost, one less unit of output subtracts more from total cost than from total revenue. Such a case occurs when the Allegro Piano Company is producing 7 pianos per week. As shown in Table 18.3, the extra cost of producing the seventh piano is $1,300, while the extra revenue it brings in is $1,000. So it pays the Allegro Piano Company to produce less than 7 pianos per week.

Since increases in output will increase profits if output is less than $0Q_1$, and decreases in output will increase profits if output is greater than $0Q_1$, it follows that profits must be maximized at $0Q_1$, the output rate at which price equals marginal cost. After all, if increases in output up to this output ($0Q_1$) result in increases in profit and further increases in output result in decreases in profit, $0Q_1$ must be the profit-maximizing output rate. For the Allegro Piano Company, this output rate is between 4 and 5 pianos per week, as we saw above.

Does It Pay to Be a Dropout?

All rules, even the Golden Rule we just mentioned, have exceptions. Under some circumstances, the perfectly competitive firm will not maximize its profits if it sets marginal cost equal to price. Instead, it will maximize profits only if it becomes an economic dropout by discontinuing production. Let's demonstrate that this is indeed a fact. The first important point is that, even if the firm is doing the best it can, it may not be able to earn a profit. If the price is $0P_2$ in Figure 18.3, short-run average cost exceeds the price, $0P_2$, at all possible output rates. Thus the firm cannot earn a profit whatever output it produces. Since the short run is too short for the firm to alter the scale of its plant, it cannot liquidate its plant in the short run. Its only choice is to produce at a loss or discontinue production.

Under what conditions will the firm produce at a loss, and under what conditions will it discontinue production? *If there is an output rate where price exceeds average variable costs, it will pay the firm to produce, even though price does not cover average total cost. If there is no such output rate, the firm is better off to produce nothing at all.* This is true because even if the firm produces nothing it must pay its fixed cost. If the loss resulting from production is less than the firm's fixed cost, the firm is better off producing than not producing. On the other hand, if the loss resulting from production is greater than the firm's fixed cost, the firm is better off not to produce.

Dropping Out: Illustrative Cases

To illustrate the conditions under which it pays a firm to drop out, suppose that the cost functions of the Allegro Piano Company are as shown in Table 18.4. In this case, there exists no output rate such that average

★ **368**

Economic
Efficiency, Market
Supply, and
Perfect
Competition

variable cost is less than price, which, you will recall, is $1,000 per piano. Thus, according to the results of the last paragraphs, the Allegro Piano Company should discontinue production under these conditions. The wisdom of this course of action is shown by the last column of Table 18.4, which demonstrates that the profit-maximizing—or, what amounts to the same thing, the loss-minimizing—output rate is zero.

Table 18.4
Costs and
Revenues, Allegro
Piano Company

Output per week (pianos)	Price	Total revenue	Total fixed cost	Total variable cost	Average variable cost	Total cost	Total profit
				(dollars)			
0	1,000	0	1,000	0	—	1,000	−1,000
1	1,000	1,000	1,000	1,200	1,200	2,200	−1,200
2	1,000	2,000	1,000	2,600	1,300	3,600	−1,600
3	1,000	3,000	1,000	4,200	1,400	5,200	−2,200
4	1,000	4,000	1,000	6,000	1,500	7,000	−3,000
5	1,000	5,000	1,000	8,000	1,600	9,000	−4,000
6	1,000	6,000	1,000	10,200	1,700	11,200	−5,200
7	1,000	7,000	1,000	12,600	1,800	13,600	−6,600
8	1,000	8,000	1,000	15,200	1,900	16,200	−8,200

Sometimes, as in the present case, the best thing to produce is nothing. The situation is analogous to the common experience of leaving a movie after finding in the first ten minutes that it is not going to be a good one. One ignores the fixed costs (the non-refundable admission price), and finding that the variable cost (the pleasure gained from activities that would be forgone by seeing the rest of the show) is going to exceed the benefits of staying, one leaves.

In 1973, many meat-processing plants discontinued production for essentially this reason. The federal government, in an attempt to control inflation, froze the price of their product, but allowed the prices of the inputs they used to go up. The result was that their average variable costs exceeded price at all possible output levels. The consequence, as our theory would predict, was that many plants closed down. In Chicago, the American Meat Institute announced that 16 plants closed down in the second quarter of 1973. As the president of Detroit's Crown Packing Company put it, "Frankly, we closed down so that we would lose less money."

The Market Supply Curve

In Chapters 2 and 16 we described some of the factors underlying a commodity's market supply curve, but we could not go into much detail. Now we can, because our Golden Rule of Output Determination underlies the market supply curve. As a first step, let's derive the *firm's supply curve*, which shows how much the firm will want to produce at each price.

The Firm's Supply Curve

Since the firm takes the price of its product as given (and can sell all it wants at that price), we know from the previous sections that the firm will choose the output level at which price equals marginal cost. Or if the price is below the firm's average variable cost curve at every output level, the firm will produce nothing. These results are all we need to determine the firm's supply curve.

Suppose that the firm's short-run cost curves are as shown in Figure 18.3. The marginal cost curve must intersect the average variable cost curve at the latter's minimum point, U. If the price of the product is less than OP_3, the firm will produce nothing, because there is no output level where price exceeds average variable cost. If the price of the product exceeds OP_3, the firm will set its output rate at the point where price equals marginal cost. If the price is OP_1, the firm will produce OQ_1; if the price is OP_2, the firm will produce OQ_2; and so forth. Consequently, *the firm's supply curve is exactly the same as the firm's marginal cost curve for prices above the minimum value of average variable cost* (OP_3). For prices at or below the minimum value of average variable cost, the firm's supply curve corresponds to the price axis, the desire to supply at these prices being uniformly zero. Thus the firm's supply curve is $OP_3 UM$.

DERIVING THE MARKET SUPPLY CURVE

Our next step is to derive the market supply curve from the supply curves of the individual firms. If one assumption (which we will consider shortly) holds, *the* **market supply curve** *can be regarded as the horizontal summation of the supply curves of all the firms producing the product.* If there were three firms in the industry and their supply curves were as shown in Figure 18.4, the market supply curve would be the horizontal summation of their three supply curves. Since these three supply curves show that firm 1 would supply 25 units of output at a price of $2 per unit, that firm 2 would supply 40 units at this price, and that firm 3 would supply 55 units at this price, the market supply curve shows that 120 units of output will be supplied if the price is $2 per unit. Why? Because the market supply curve shows the *total* amount of the product that all of the firms together would supply at this price—and $25 + 40 + 55 = 120$. If there were only three firms, the market would not be perfectly competitive, but we can ignore this inconsistency. Figure 18.4 is designed to illustrate the fact that the market supply curve is the horizontal summation of the firm supply curves, at least under one important assumption.

The assumption underlying this construction of the short-run market supply curve is that *increases or decreases in output by all firms simultaneously do not affect input prices.* This is a convenient simplification, but it is not always true. Although changes in the output of one firm alone often

Figure 18.4
**Horizontal
Summation of
Short-Run Supply
Curves of Firms**
If each of the three
firms' supply curves
are as shown here
(and if each firm
supplies nothing if
the price is below
OH), the market
supply curve is the
horizontal
summation of the
firms' supply curves,
assuming that input
prices are not
influenced by the
output of the
industry.

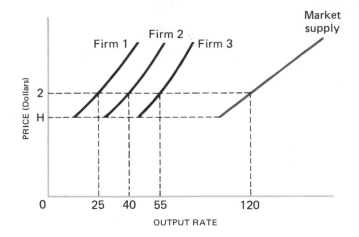

cannot affect input prices, the simultaneous expansion or contraction of output by all firms may well alter input prices, so that the individual firm's cost curves—and supply curve—will shift. For instance, an expansion of the whole industry may bid up the price of certain inputs, with the result that the cost curves of the individual firms will be pushed upward. A sudden expansion of the aerospace industry, for instance, might well increase the price of such inputs as the services of aerospace scientists and engineers.

If, contrary to the assumption underlying Figure 18.4, input prices *are* increased by the expansion of the industry, one can still derive the short-run market supply curve by seeing how much the industry will supply in the short run at each price of the product. But it is then incorrect to assume that the market supply curve is the horizontal summation of the firm supply curves.

PRICE AND OUTPUT: THE MARKET PERIOD

How much of a particular product will be produced if the market is perfectly competitive, and what will the price be? The answers depend on the length of the time period being considered. To begin with, let's consider the relatively short period of time when the supply of the relevant good is *fixed*. This period of time is called the **market period**. In the market period, as in the short and long runs, the price of a good in a perfectly competitive market is determined by the market demand and market supply curves. However, in the market period, the market supply curve is a vertical line, as shown in Figure 18.5.

Thus in the market period output is unaffected by price. In Figure 18.5, output is *0Q*—and regardless of price, it cannot be changed. The equilibrium price depends on the position of the demand curve. Price is OP_1 if the demand curve is *A*, and OP_2 if the demand curve is *B*.

The role of price as a rationing device is particularly obvious in the market period, where this is the major function of price. Consumers who

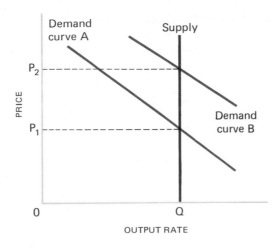

Figure 18.5
Price
Determination in
the Market Period
In the market
period, supply is
fixed at *OQ*.
Equilibrium price is
OP₁ if the demand
curve is demand
curve *A* and *OP₂* if
the demand curve is
demand curve *B*.

are willing to pay the equilibrium price get some of the product; others do without.

PRICE AND OUTPUT: THE SHORT RUN

Let's turn now to the short run, the period during which each firm's plant and equipment are fixed. What determines the price and output of a good in a perfectly competitive market in the short run? The answer once again is the market demand and market supply curves. However, the position and shape of these curves will generally be different in the short run than in the market period. In particular, the market supply curve in the short run will not be a vertical line; it will generally slope upward to the right, as in panel B of Figure 18.6. Thus, *in the short run, price influences, as well as rations, the amount supplied.* In panel B of Figure 18.6, the equilibrium price and output in the short run are *OP* and *OQ*.

To illustrate the nature of the short-run supply curve, consider the bituminous coal industry, which in many respects has (at least in the past) come reasonably close to perfect competition. According to Hubert Risser

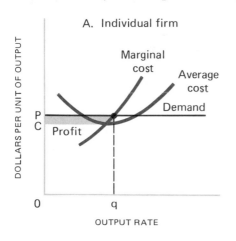

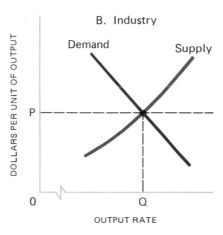

Figure 18.6
Short-Run
Competitive
Equilibrium
In the short run,
equilibrium price is
OP, and the
equilibrium output of
the industry is *OQ*,
since (as shown in
panel B) the industry
demand and supply
curves intersect at
this price and
output.

★ 372
Economic
Efficiency, Market
Supply, and
Perfect
Competition

of the University of Kansas, the short-run supply curve for bituminous coal has been very price elastic, so long as output stays within the range of existing capacity.[2] In other words, if output is less than existing capacity, small variations in price will result in large variations in output. Thus the situation in the short run is quite different from that in the market period, where output is fixed and unaffected by price. But the basic fact remains that equilibrium price and equilibrium output are determined by the intersection of the relevant demand and supply curves, in both the market period and the short run.

Returning to Figure 18.6, panel A shows the behavior of an individual firm in short-run equilibrium. Since OP is the price, the demand curve facing the firm is a horizontal line at OP, as shown in panel A. To maximize profit, the firm produces an output of Oq, because price equals marginal cost at this output. In short-run equilibrium, firms may be making either profits or losses. In the particular case described in panel A, the firm earns a profit equal to the shaded area shown there. Since the profit per unit of output equals CP, total profit equals CP multiplied by Oq, which is this shaded area.

Taken together, the two panels of Figure 18.6 bring out the following important point. To the *individual* firm, the price of the product is taken as given. If the price is OP, the firm in panel A reacts to this price by setting an output rate of Oq units. It cannot alter the price; it can only react to it. But *as a group* the reactions of the firms are a major determinant of the price of the product. The supply curve in panel B shows the total amount that the entire group of firms will supply at each price. It summarizes the reactions of the firms to various levels of the price. But briefly, the equilibrium price is viewed by the individual firm as being beyond its control; yet the supply decisions of all firms taken as a group are a basic determinant of the equilibrium price.

PRICE AND OUTPUT: THE LONG RUN

In the long run, what determines the output and price of a good in a perfectly competitive market? In the long run, a firm can change its plant size, which means that established firms may *leave* an industry if it has below-average profits, or that new firms may *enter* an industry with above-average profits. Suppose that textile firms can earn up to (but not more than) a 15 percent rate of return by investing their resources in other industries. If they can earn only 12 percent by keeping these resources invested in the textile industry, they will leave the textile industry. On the other hand, if a rate of return of 18 percent can be earned by investing in the textile industry, firms in other industries, attracted by this relatively high return, will enter the textile industry.

[2]H. Risser, *The Economics of the Coal Industry,* Lawrence: University Press of Kansas, 1958, p. 155.

Equilibrium: Zero Economic Profit

Equilibrium is achieved in the long run when enough firms—no more, no less—are in the industry so that *economic profits*—defined as the excess of a firm's profits over what it could make in other industries—are zero. This condition is necessary for long-run equilibrium because, as we have seen, new firms will enter the industry if there are economic profits, and existing firms will leave if there are economic losses. This process of entry and exit is the key to long-run equilibrium.

Note that the existence of economic profits or losses in an industry brings about a shift in the industry's short-run supply curve. If there are economic profits, new firms will enter the industry, and so will shift the short-run supply curve to the right. On the other hand, if there are economic losses in the industry (if the industry's profits are less than could be obtained elsewhere), existing firms will leave the industry, causing the short-run supply curve to shift to the left. Only if economic profits are zero will the number of firms in the industry—and the industry's short-run supply curve—be stable. Putting this equilibrium condition another way, *the long-run equilibrium position of the firm is at the point at which its long-run average costs equal price.* If price exceeds average total costs, economic profits are being earned; if price is less than average total costs, economic losses are being incurred.

Equilibrium: Maximum Economic Profit

Going a step further, *long-run equilibrium requires that price equal the lowest value of long-run average total costs.* In other words, firms must be producing at the *minimum point* on their long-run average cost curves, because to maximize their profits, as we have seen, they must operate where price equals long-run marginal cost; at the same time they also have to operate where price equals long-run average cost. But if both these conditions are satisfied, long-run marginal cost must equal long-run average cost, since both equal price. And we know from Chapter 16 that long-run marginal cost equals long-run average cost only at the point at which long-run average cost is a minimum.[3] Consequently, if long-run marginal cost equals long-run average cost, the firm must be producing at the minimum point on the long-run average cost curve.

This equilibrium position is illustrated in Figure 18.7. When all adjustments are made, price equals *0P*. The equilibrium output of the firm is *0q*, and its plant corresponds to the short-run average and marginal cost curves in Figure 18.7. At this output and with this plant, long-run marginal cost equals short-run marginal cost equals price. This ensures that the firm

[3]The previous discussion of this point concerned short-run cost functions, but the argument applies just as well to long-run cost functions.

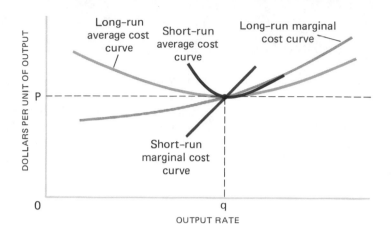

Figure 18.7 Long-Run Equilibrium of a Perfectly Competitive Firm In long-run equilibrium, output is *Oq* and the firm's plant corresponds to the short-run average and marginal cost curves shown here.

is maximizing profit. Also, long-run average cost equals short-run average cost equals price. This ensures that economic profits are zero. Since long-run marginal cost and long-run average cost must be equal, the firm is producing at the minimum point on its long-run average cost curve.

To illustrate the process of entry and exit in an industry that approximates perfect competition, let's return to the bituminous coal industry. Entry into this industry is relatively easy, but exit is relatively difficult, for at least two reasons. First, it is costly to shut down a mine and reopen it later. Second, because of corrosion and water damage, it is hard to shut down a mine for longer than two years unless it is to be abandoned entirely. For these reasons, mines tend to stay open and produce even though short-term losses are incurred. In the period before World War II, the demand for coal fell substantially, but although the industry suffered substantial losses, mines were slow to close down. Nonetheless, the competitive process had its way. Slowly but surely, the number of mines fell markedly in response to these losses.[4] Thus, despite the barriers to rapid exit, firms eventually left the industry, just as the model would predict.

THE ALLOCATION OF RESOURCES UNDER PERFECT COMPETITION: A MORE DETAILED VIEW

At this point, it is instructive to describe the process by which a perfectly competitive economy—one composed of perfectly competitive industries —would allocate resources. In earlier chapters we stressed that the allocation of resources among alternative uses is one of the major functions of any economic system. Equipped with the concepts we have learned since, we can now go much further in describing how a perfectly competitive economy shifts resources in accord with changes in tastes, technology, and other factors.

[4]J. B. Hendry, "The Bituminous Coal Industry," in W. Adams, *The Structure of American Industry,* New York: Macmillan, 1961.

CASE STUDY 18.1 PRICE CEILINGS AND PRICE SUPPORTS

During national emergencies, the government sometimes puts a lid on prices, not allowing them to reach their equilibrium levels. For example, during World War II, the government did not allow the prices of various foodstuffs to rise to their equilibrium levels, because it felt that this would have been inequitable (and highly unpopular). Thus the quantity demanded of a product exceeds the quantity supplied.

Since the price system is not allowed to perform its rationing function, some formal system of rationing or allocating the available supply of the product may be required. Thus in World War II families were issued ration coupons that determined how much they could buy of various commodities. And in 1979, when the Organization of Petroleum Exporting Countries cut back oil production and reduced exports of oil to the United States, there was serious talk that gasoline and oil might be rationed in a

Rent control was adopted in part to stem inflation

similar way. Such rationing schemes may be justified in emergencies (of reasonably short duration), but they can result eventually in serious distortions, since prices are not allowed to do the job normally expected of them.

To illustrate the sorts of problems that can arise when price ceilings are imposed, consider the rent ceilings that exist on some apartments in New York City. Originally imposed to prevent dwelling costs from soaring during World War II, these ceilings have been defended on the ground that they help the poor, at least in the short run. Although this may be so, they have also resulted in a shortage of housing in New York City. Because they have pushed the price of housing below the equilibrium price, less housing has been supplied than has been demanded. The depressed price of housing has discouraged investors from building new housing, and has made it unprofitable for some owners of existing housing to maintain their buildings. Although it would be socially desirable to channel more resources into New York housing, the rent ceilings have prevented this from occurring.

Government authorities may also impose price floors—or price supports, as they are often called. These floors are generally defended on the ground that they enable the producers of the good in question to make a better living. For example, the federal government has imposed price supports on a wide range of agricultural commodities, the purpose being to increase farm incomes. The result, as we saw in the section, "Exploring Further," in Chapter 17, is that the quantity supplied exceeds the quantity demanded at the support price. Thus there is a surplus of the commodity and, in the case of agricultural commodities, the government has had to buy up and store these surpluses. As in the case of a price ceiling, the result is that the price system is not allowed to do the job expected of it.

Whether price ceilings or floors are socially desirable depends on whether the loss in social efficiency resulting from them is exceeded by the gain in equity they achieve. Their purpose is to help or protect parts of the population that would be treated inequitably by the unfettered price system.

☆ ☆ ☆ ☆ ☆ ☆ ☆ ☆ ☆ ☆ ☆ ☆ ☆

★ 376
Economic
Efficiency, Market
Supply, and
Perfect
Competition

Consumers Turn from Corn to Wheat

To be specific, suppose that a change occurs in tastes. Consumers become more favorably disposed toward wheat and less favorably disposed toward corn than in the past.[5] In the short run, the increase in the demand for wheat increases the price of wheat and results in some increase in the output of wheat. However, the output cannot be increased very substantially because the industry's capacity cannot be expanded in the short run. Similarly, the fall in the demand for corn reduces the price of corn and results in some reduction in output. But the output will not be curtailed greatly because firms will continue to produce as long as they can cover variable costs.

Prices Signal Resource Reallocation

The change in the relative prices of wheat and corn tells producers that a reallocation of resources is called for. Because of the increase in the price of wheat and the decrease in the price of corn, wheat producers are earning economic profits and corn producers are showing economic losses. This will trigger a new deployment of resources. If some variable inputs in corn production can be used as effectively in the production of wheat, they may be switched from corn production to wheat production. Even if no variable inputs are used in both wheat and corn production, adjustments can be made in various interrelated markets, with the result that wheat production gains resources and corn production loses resources. (For example, some resources may move from corn production to manufacturing, and others may move from manufacturing to wheat production.) When short-run equilibrium is attained in both the wheat and corn industries, the reallocation of resources is not yet complete, since there has not been enough time for producers to build new capacity or liquidate old capacity. In particular, neither industry is operating at minimum average cost. The wheat producers are operating at greater than the output level where average cost is a minimum; and the corn producers are operating at less than this level.

Effects in the Long Run

What will happen in the long run? The shift in consumer demand from corn to wheat will result in greater adjustments in production and smaller adjustments in price than in the short run. In the long run, existing firms can leave corn production and new firms can enter wheat production.

[5]Since we assume here that the markets for wheat and corn are perfectly competitive, it is also assumed that there is no government intervention in these markets.

Because of short-run economic losses in corn production, some corn land and related equipment will be allowed to run down, and some firms engaged in corn production will be liquidated. As firms leave corn production, the supply curve shifts to the left, causing the price to rise above its short-run level. The transfer of resources out of corn production will stop when the price has increased, and costs have decreased, to the point where losses are avoided.

While corn production is losing resources, wheat production is gaining them. The prospect of positive economic profits in wheat production will cause new firms to enter the industry. The increased demand for inputs will raise input prices and cost curves in wheat production, and the price of wheat will be depressed by the movement to the right of the supply curve because of the entry of new firms. Entry ceases when economic profits are no longer being earned. At this point, when long-run equilibrium is achieved, more resources will be used in the industry than in the short run. (Note that if corn land and equipment can be converted to the production of wheat, some of the entry may occur through existing farmers' shifting of their crop mix toward wheat and away from corn.)

Finally, long-run equilibrium is established in both industries, and the reallocation of resources is complete. It is important to note that this reallocation can affect industries other than wheat and corn. If corn land and equipment can be easily adapted to the production of wheat, corn producers can simply change to wheat production. If not, the resources used in corn production are converted to some use other than wheat, and the resources that enter wheat production come from some use other than corn production.

SUMMARY

1. Economists generally classify markets into four types: perfect competition, monopoly, monopolistic competition, and oligopoly. Perfect competition requires that the product of any seller be the same as the product of any other seller, that no buyer or seller be able to influence the price of the product, and that resources be able to switch readily from one use to another.

2. If it maximizes profit, a perfectly competitive firm should set its output rate in the short run at the level where marginal cost equals price, so long as price exceeds average variable cost. If there is no output rate at which price exceeds average variable cost, the firm should discontinue production.

3. The firm's supply curve coincides with its marginal cost curve for prices exceeding the minimum value of average variable cost. For prices that are less than or equal to the minimum value of average variable cost, the firm's supply curve coincides with the price axis.

★ 378
Economic
Efficiency, Market
Supply, and
Perfect
Competition

4. As a first approximation, the market supply curve can be viewed as the horizontal summation of the supply curves of all of the firms producing the product. This assumes that increases or decreases in output by all firms simultaneously do not affect input prices.

5. Price and output under perfect competition are determined by the intersection of the market supply and demand curves. In the market period, supply is fixed; thus price plays the role of the allocating device. In the short run, price influences as well as rations the amount supplied.

6. In the long run, equilibrium is achieved under perfect competition when enough firms—no more, no less—are in the industry so that economic profits are eliminated. In other words, the long-run equilibrium position of the firm is at the point where its long-run average cost equals price. But since price must also equal marginal cost (to maximize profit), it follows that the firm must be operating at the minimum point on the long-run average cost curve.

7. In a perfectly competitive economy, prices are the signals that are used to guide the reallocation of resources in response to changes in consumer tastes, technology, and other factors.

CHAPTER 19

★ ★ ★ ★ ★ ★ ★ ★ ★

Monopoly and Its Regulation

LEARNING OBJECTIVES

In this chapter, you should learn:

★ The conditions that define a monopolistic market structure and their causes

★ The "golden rule" of output determination for a monopolistic firm

★ How the prices and outputs set under monopoly compare with those under perfect competition

★ The case against monopolies, and how they can be regulated

★ *(Exploring Further)* How monopoly power has been defended

At the opposite extreme from perfect competition is monopoly. Under a monopolistic market structure, what sorts of behavior can we expect? How much of the product will be produced, and at what level will its price be set? What are the social disadvantages of monopoly? In what ways have government commissions attempted to regulate industries whose market structures approximate monopoly? These are some of the major questions dealt with in this chapter.

To begin with, recall what is meant by *monopoly*: *a market where there exists one, and only one, seller.* Monopoly, like perfect competition, seldom corresponds more than approximately to conditions in real industries, but it is a very useful model. In several respects, monopoly and perfect competition stand as polar opposites. The firm in a perfectly competitive market has so many rivals that competition becomes entirely impersonal. The firm is a price taker, an inconspicuous seller in a sea of inconspicuous sellers. Under monopoly, on the other hand, the firm has no direct competitors at all; it is the sole supplier.

However, even the monopolist is affected by certain indirect and potential forms of competition. Suppose a firm managed to obtain a monopoly on wheat production. It would have to worry about competition from corn and other agricultural commodities that could be substituted for wheat. Moreover, the wheat monopolist would also have to take into account the possibility that new firms might arise to challenge its monopoly if it attempted to extract conspicuously high profits. Thus even the monopolist is subject to some restraint imposed by competitive forces.

CAUSES OF MONOPOLY

There are many reasons why monopolies, or market structures that closely approximate monopoly, may arise.

Patents

A firm may acquire a monopoly over the production of a good by having patents on the product or on certain basic processes used in its production. The patent laws of the United States give an inventor the exclusive right to make a certain product or to use a certain process for 17 years. The purpose of the patent system is to encourage invention and innovation and to discourage industrial secrecy. Many firms with monopoly power achieved it in considerable part through patents. For example, the United Shoe Machinery Company became the sole supplier of certain important kinds of shoemaking equipment through control of basic patents.

Control of Inputs

A firm may become a monopolist by obtaining control over the entire supply of a basic input required to manufacture a product. The International Nickel Company of Canada controls about nine-tenths of the proven nickel reserves in the world—obviously, a strong monopoly position. Similarly, the Aluminum Company of America (Alcoa) kept its dominant position for a long time by controlling practically all the sources of bauxite, the ore used to make aluminum. However, Alcoa's monopoly was broken in 1945 when the Supreme Court decided that Alcoa's control of practically all the industry's output violated the antitrust laws.

Government Action

A firm may become a monopolist because it is awarded a market franchise by a government agency. The government may give a particular firm the franchise to sell a particular product in a public facility. Or it may give a particular company the right to provide a service, such as electrification, to people in a particular area. In exchange for this right, the firm agrees to allow the government to regulate certain aspects of its operations. The form of regulation does not matter here; the important point is that the monopoly is created by the government.

Declining Cost of Production

A firm may become a monopolist because the average costs of producing the product reach a minimum at an output rate that is large enough to satisfy the entire market (at a price that is profitable). In a case like this, a firm obviously has an incentive to expand until it produces all the market wants of the good. (Its costs fall as it continues to expand.) Thus competition cannot be maintained in this case. If there are a number of firms in the industry, the result is likely to be economic warfare and the survival of a single victor, the monopolist.

Cases where costs behave like this are called *natural monopolies.* When an industry is a natural monopoly, the public often insists that its behavior be regulated by the government. For example, electric power is an industry where there seem to be great economies of scale, and thus decreasing average costs. Fuel consumed per kilowatt hour is lower in larger power generating units, and there are economies in combining generating units at a single site. Because of these factors, there has been little attempt to force competition in the industry, since it would be wasteful. Instead, the market for electric power in a particular area is a regulated monopoly.[1]

DEMAND CURVE AND MARGINAL REVENUE UNDER MONOPOLY

Before we can make any statements about the behavior of a monopolistic market, we must point out certain important characteristics of the demand curve facing the monopolist. Since the monopolist is the only seller of the commodity, the demand curve it faces is the market demand curve

[1]However, it is worth noting that technological developments in this industry may permit more competition in the future. See L. Weiss, "Antitrust in the Electric Power Industry," in A. Phillips, *Promoting Competition in Regulated Markets,* Washington, D.C.: The Brookings Institution, 1975.

Table 19.1
Demand and
Revenue of a
Monopolist

Quantity	Price	Total revenue (dollars)	Marginal revenue
1	100	100	
			80
2	90	180	
			60
3	80	240	
			40
4	70	280	
			20
5	60	300	
			0
6	50	300	
			−20
7	40	280	
			−40
8	30	240	

for the product. Since the market demand curve is almost always downward-sloping to the right, the monopolist's demand curve must also be downward-sloping to the right. This is quite different from perfect competition, where the firm's demand curve is horizontal. To illustrate the situation faced by a monopolist, consider the hypothetical case in Table 19.1. The price at which each quantity (shown in column 1) can be sold by the monopolist is shown in column 2. The firm's *total revenue*—its total dollar sales volume—is shown in column 3. Obviously, column 3 is the product of the first two columns. Column 4 contains the firm's *marginal revenue, defined as the addition to total revenue attributable to the addition of one unit to sales.* Thus if $R(q)$ is total revenue when q units are sold and $R(q - 1)$ is total revenue when $(q - 1)$ units are sold, the marginal revenue between q units and $(q - 1)$ units is $R(q) - R(q - 1)$.

Marginal revenue is very important to the monopolist. We can estimate it from the figures in the first three columns of Table 19.1. The marginal revenue between 1 and 2 units of output per day is $180 − $100, or $80; the marginal revenue between 2 and 3 units of output per day is $240 − $180, or $60; the marginal revenue between 3 and 4 units of output per day is $280 − $240, or $40; and so on. The results are shown in column 4 of the table (and are plotted in Figure 19.1). Note that marginal revenue is analogous to marginal cost (and marginal utility and marginal product, for that matter). Recall that marginal cost is the extra cost resulting from an extra unit of production. Substitute "revenue" for "cost" and "sales" for "production" in the previous sentence, and what do you get? A perfectly acceptable definition of marginal revenue.

Marginal revenue will always be less than price if the firm's demand curve is downward-sloping (as it is under monopoly and other market structures that are not perfectly competitive). In Table 19.1, the extra revenue from the second unit of output is $80 whereas the price of this unit is $90. *The basic reason is that the firm must reduce the price of all units of output, not just the extra unit, in order to sell the extra unit.* Thus in Table 19.1 the extra revenue from the second unit of output is $80

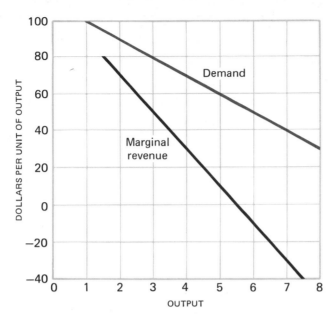

Figure 19.1
Marginal Revenue and Demand Curves
The demand curve comes from Table 19.1. Each value of marginal revenue is plotted at the midpoint of the range of output to which it pertains. Since the demand curve is downward-sloping, marginal revenue is always less than price, for reasons discussed in the text.

because, while the price of the second unit is $90, the price of the first unit must be reduced by $10 in order to sell the second unit. Thus the extra revenue (that is, marginal revenue) from selling the second unit of output is $90 − $10, or $80, which is less than the price of the second unit.

Similarly, the marginal revenue from selling the third unit of output ($60, according to Table 19.1) is less than the price at which the third unit can be sold ($80, according to Table 19.1). Why? Because to sell the third unit of output, the price of the first two units of output must be reduced by $10 each (that is, from $90 to $80). Thus the extra revenue (that is, marginal revenue) from selling the third unit is not $80, but $80 less the $20 reduction in the amount received for the first two units.

PRICE AND OUTPUT: THE SHORT RUN

We are now in a position to determine how output and price behave under monopoly. If the monopolist is free to maximize its profits, it will choose the price and output rate at which the difference between total revenue and total cost is greatest. Suppose that the firm's costs are as shown in Table 19.2 and that the demand curve it faces is as shown in Table 19.1. Based on the data in these two tables, the firm can calculate the profit that it will make at each output rate. To do so, it subtracts its total cost from its total revenue, as shown in Table 19.3. What output rate will maximize the firm's profit? According to Table 19.3, profit *rises* as its output rate increases from 1 to 3 units per day, and profit *falls* as its output rate increases from 4 to 8 units per day. Thus the *maximum* profit is achieved at an output rate between 3 and 4 units per day.[2] (Without more detailed

[2]This assumes that the output rate can vary continuously and that there is a single maximum. These are innocuous assumptions.

**Table 19.2
Costs of a
Monopolist**

Quantity	Total variable cost	Total fixed cost (dollars)	Total cost	Marginal cost
0	0	100	100	
				40
1	40	100	140	
				30
2	70	100	170	
				40
3	110	100	210	
				40
4	150	100	250	
				50
5	200	100	300	
				60
6	260	100	360	
				90
7	350	100	450	
				100
8	450	100	550	

**Table 19.3
Profits of a
Monopolist**

Quantity	Total revenue	Total cost	Total profit
		(dollars)	
1	100	140	−40
2	180	170	10
3	240	210	30
4	280	250	30
5	300	300	0
6	300	360	−60
7	280	450	−170
8	240	550	−310

data, one cannot tell precisely where the maximum occurs, but this is close enough for present purposes.) Figure 19.2 shows the same thing graphically.

What price will the monopolist charge? To maximize its profit, it must charge the price that results in its selling the profit-maximizing output, which in this case is between 3 and 4 units per day. Thus, according to Table 19.1, it must charge between $70 and $80 per unit. Why? Because if it charges $70, it will sell 4 units per day; and if it charges $80, it will sell 3 units per day. Consequently, to sell the profit-maximizing output of between 3 and 4 units per day, it must charge a price of between $70 and $80 per unit.

The Golden Rule of Output Determination

In Chapter 18, we set forth the Golden Rule of Output Determination for a perfectly competitive firm. We can now formulate a Golden Rule of

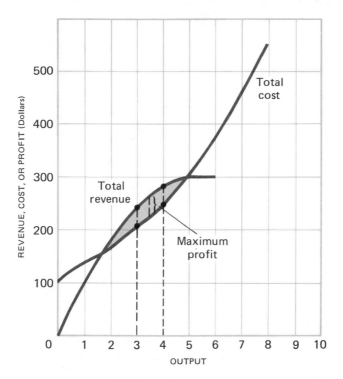

Figure 19.2
Total Revenue, Cost, and Profit of Monopolist
The output rate that will maximize the firm's profit is between 3 and 4 units per day. At this output rate, profit (which equals the vertical distance between the total revenue and total cost curves) is over $30 per day. Based on the demand curve for its product (shown in Table 19.1), the firm must set a price of between $70 and $80 to sell between 3 and 4 units per day.

Output Determination for a monopolist: *set the output rate at the point where marginal revenue equals marginal cost.* Table 19.4 and Figure 19.3 show that this rule results in a maximum profit in this example. It is evident from Table 19.4 that marginal revenue equals marginal cost at the profit-maximizing output of between 3 and 4 units per day. Figure 19.3 shows the same thing graphically.

Quantity	Total profit	Marginal cost	Marginal revenue
		(dollars)	
1	−40		
		30	80
2	10		
		40	60
3	30		
		40	40
4	30		
		50	20
5	0		
		60	0
6	−60		
		90	−20
7	−170		
		100	−40
8	−310		

Table 19.4
Marginal Cost and Marginal Revenue of a Monopolist

Figure 19.3
**Marginal Cost and
Marginal Revenue
of Monopolist**
At the
profit-maximizing
output rate of
between 3 and 4
units per day,
marginal cost (which
is $40 between an
output rate of 3 and
4 units per period)
equals marginal
revenue (which also
is $40 between an
output rate of 3 and
4 units per period).
Both marginal cost
and marginal
revenue are plotted
at the midpoints of
the ranges of output
to which they
pertain.

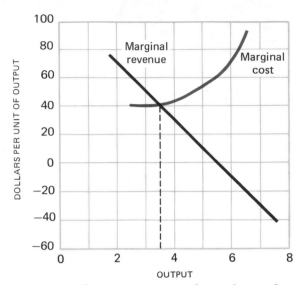

Why is this rule generally a necessary condition for profit maximization? At any output rate at which marginal revenue *exceeds* marginal cost, profit can be increased by *increasing* output, since the extra revenue will exceed the extra cost. At any output rate at which marginal revenue is *less than* marginal cost, profit can be increased by *reducing* output, since the decrease in cost will exceed the decrease in revenue. Thus since profit will *not* be a maximum when marginal revenue exceeds marginal cost or falls short of marginal cost, *it must be a maximum only when marginal revenue equals marginal cost.*

The Monopolist's Equilibrium Position

Figure 19.4 shows the equilibrium position of a monopolist in the short run. Short-run equilibrium will occur at the output, *OQ*, where the marginal cost curve intersects the marginal revenue curve (the curve that

Figure 19.4
**Equilibrium
Position of
Monopolist**
The monopolist sets
its output rate at
OQ, where the
marginal revenue
curve intersects the
marginal cost curve.
At this output, price
must be *OP*. And
profit per unit of
output equals *CP*,
since average cost
equals *OC*.

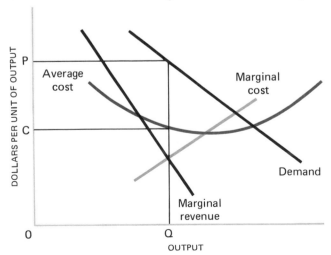

shows the firm's marginal revenue at each output level). And if the monopolist is to sell OQ units per period of time, the demand curve shows that it must set a price of OP. Thus the equilibrium output and price are OQ and OP, respectively.

It is interesting to compare the Golden Rule of Output Determination for a monopolist (set the output rate at the point where marginal revenue equals marginal cost) with that for a perfectly competitive firm (set the output rate at the point where price equals marginal cost). The latter is really the same as the former because, *for a perfectly competitive firm, price equals marginal revenue.* Since the perfectly competitive firm can sell all it wants at the market price, each additional unit sold increases the firm's total revenue by the amount of the price. Thus *for both the monopolist and the perfectly competitive firm, profits are maximized by setting the output rate at the point where marginal revenue equals marginal cost.*

PRICE AND OUTPUT: THE LONG RUN

In contrast to the situation under perfect competition, the long-run equilibrium of a monopolistic industry may not be marked by the absence of economic profits. If a monopolist earns a short-run economic profit, it will not be confronted in the long run with competitors, unless the industry ceases to be a monopoly. The entrance of additional firms into the industry is incompatible with the existence of monopoly. Thus the long-run equilibrium of an industry under monopoly may be characterized by economic profits.

On the other hand, if the monopolist incurs a short-run economic loss, it will be forced to look for other, more profitable uses for its resources. One possibility is that the firm's existing plant is not optimal and that it can earn economic profits by appropriate alterations to its scale and characteristics. If so, the firm will make these alterations in the long run and remain in the industry. However, *if there is no scale of plant that will enable the firm to avoid economic losses, it will leave the industry in the long run.* The mere fact of having a monopoly over the production of a certain commodity does not mean that the firm must be profitable. A monopoly over the production of cut-glass spittoons would be unlikely to catapult a firm into financial glory—or even allow it to avoid losses.

To illustrate the long-run behavior of a monopolist, consider the prewar policy of the Aluminum Company of America (Alcoa). Until after World War II, Alcoa was virtually the sole producer of aluminum in the United States. According to various observers, Alcoa recognized the dangers involved in potential competition, and it adopted a policy of keeping its price low enough to ward off potential entrants. Naturally, it wanted to make money—and it did. But it was smart enough to see that if it charged very high prices, it might encourage other firms to enter the aluminum industry. So it set a price high enough to permit it to make plenty of economic profits, but not so high that it would have to wrestle with competitors. Some other firms with monopoly power think the same way and act accordingly, but by no means all are so clever. On the contrary, some monopolists, like some newlyweds, think the *status quo* will last forever. And just as for newlyweds, sometimes it does, but sometimes it doesn't.

PERFECT COMPETITION AND MONOPOLY: A COMPARISON

At the beginning of the previous chapter, we said that a market's structure would be likely to affect the behavior of the market; in other words, a market's structure would influence how much was produced and the price that would be set. If we could perform an experiment in which an industry was first operated under conditions of perfect competition and then under conditions of monopoly (assuming that the demand for the industry's product and the industry's cost functions would be the same in either case),[3] we would find that the equilibrium price and output would differ under the two sets of conditions.

Higher Price and Less Output Under Monopoly

Specifically, if the product demand curve and the industry's cost functions are the same, *the output of a perfectly competitive industry tends to be greater and the price tends to be lower than under monopoly.* We see this in Figure 19.5, which shows the industry's demand and supply curves if it is perfectly competitive. Since price and output under perfect competition are given by the intersection of the demand and supply curves, OQ_C is the industry output and OP_C is the price. But what if all of the competitive firms are bought up by a single firm, which operates as a pure monopolist? Under these conditions, what formerly was the industry's

Figure 19.5
Comparison of Long-Run Equilibria: Perfect Competition and Monopoly
Under perfect competition, OQ_C is the industry output and OP_C is the price. Under monopoly, OQ_M is the industry output, OP_M is the price. Clearly, output is higher and price is lower under perfect competition than under monopoly.

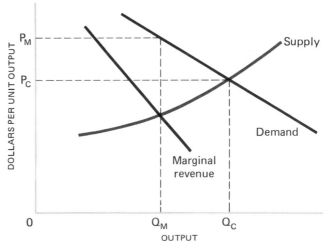

[3]However, the cost and demand curves need not be the same. For example, the monopolist may spend money on advertising, thus shifting the demand curve. It should be recognized that the assumption that they are the same is more significant than it appears at first glance.

supply curve is now the monopolist's marginal cost curve.[4] And what formerly was the industry's demand curve is now the monopolist's demand curve. Since the monopolist chooses the output where marginal cost equals marginal revenue, the industry output will be OQ_M and the price will be OP_M. Clearly, OQ_M is less than OQ_C, and OP_M is greater than OP_C—which is what we set out to prove.

Of course, all this is theory. But there is plenty of evidence that monopolists restrict output and charge higher prices than firms under competition. Take the case of tungsten carbide, which sold for $50 per pound until a monopoly was established in 1927 by General Electric. Then the price went to between $225 and $453 per pound, until the monopoly was broken by the antitrust laws in 1945. The price then dropped back to between $27 and $45 per pound.[5] This case was extreme, but by no means unique. Indeed, for centuries people have observed that, when monopolies are formed, output tends to be restricted and price tends to be driven up.

Monopoly and Resource Allocation

Moreover, it has long been felt that the allocation of resources under perfect competition is socially more desirable than under monopoly. Society might be better off if more resources were devoted to producing the monopolized good in Figure 19.5 and if the competitive, not the monopolistic, output were produced. For example, in the *Wealth of Nations*, published about 200 years ago, Adam Smith stressed that when competitive forces are thwarted by "the great engine . . . of monopoly," the tendency for resources to be used "as nearly as possible in the proportion which is most agreeable to the interest of the whole society" is thwarted as well.

Why do many economists believe that the allocation of resources under perfect competition is more socially desirable than that under monopoly? This is not a simple question, and like most hard questions it can be answered at various levels of sophistication. Put most simply, many economists believe that firms under perfect competition are induced to produce quantities of goods that are more in line with consumer desires, and that firms under perfect competition are induced to use the least costly methods of production. In the following section, we will indicate in detail why economists believe that these things are true.

[4]The monopolist will operate the various plants that would be independent under perfect competition as branches of a single firm. The marginal cost curve of a multiplant monopoly is the horizontal sum of the marginal cost curves of the individual plants. (To see why, suppose that a monopoly has two plants, A and B. The total amount that the monopoly can produce at a particular marginal cost is the sum of (1) the amount plant A can produce at this marginal cost, and (2) the amount plant B can produce at this marginal cost.) This is also the supply curve of the industry if the plants are operated as separate firms under perfect competition.

[5]W. Adams, *The Structure of American Industry*, 5th ed., New York: Macmillan, 1977, p. 485.

THE CASE AGAINST MONOPOLY

Many people oppose monopolies on the grounds that they "gouge" the consumers by charging a higher price than would otherwise exist—a price that can be sustained only because monopolists artificially limit the supply.

CASE STUDY 19.1 JOHN D. ROCKEFELLER AND STANDARD OIL OF OHIO

In the mid-nineteenth century, the nascent oil industry was characterized by competition. With thousands of small-scale prospectors, drillers, and refiners competing, the supply of oil was plentiful. Prices were low, but so were profits. This was the oil industry John D. Rockefeller saw after the Civil War. He was doing well as a produce wholesaler, but he thought he could do better in oil. Not searching for it or drilling it, but refining it.

The offices of Standard Oil in the 1900s

By 1865 Rockefeller had built two refineries. He borrowed all he could, paid any interest, and invested it all in expanding his refineries' capacity. By 1869 he had the largest refinery in the country, and a year later Standard Oil of Ohio was born. A firestorm of competition in oil refining during the 1870s made prices erratic, and squeezed profit margins. Rockefeller responded by squeezing the competition. Willing competitors were bought. Unwilling competitors were liable to find railroads and pipelines closed to their oil shipments, or their credit cut off. The more completely Rockefeller dominated the industry, the higher his profits, and the more pressure he could bring to bear on would-be competitors.

By 1879 Rockefeller and Standard Oil controlled, directly and indirectly, 90 to 95 percent of the nation's crude oil supplies, refining capacity, and oil product sales. Under Rockefeller's "guidance," the industry quickly became less crowded. As competition dropped and then disappeared, Rockefeller set prices where he thought they should be, for the good of Standard and, in his opinion, the good of the industry and the nation. He became a price maker. More than twenty years and four presidents were to pass before Standard Oil was broken up under the Sherman Antitrust Act of 1890.

N.B.

In other words, these people claim that monopolists reap higher profits than would be possible under perfect competition and that these profits come at the expense of consumers, who pay higher prices than under perfect competition. Is their claim accurate? As we have just seen, a monopolist will reap higher profits than under perfect competition and consumers will pay higher prices under monopoly than under perfect competition. But is this bad?

To the extent that the monopolist is rich and the consumers are poor, we are likely to answer yes. Also, to the extent that the monopolist is less deserving than the consumers, we are likely to answer the same thing. But suppose the monopolist is a selfless philanthropist who gives to the poor. Is monopoly still socially undesirable? The answer remains yes, because *monopoly imposes a burden on society by misallocating resources. In the presence of monopoly, the price system cannot be relied on to direct the allocation of resources to their most efficient use.*

The Misallocation of Resources

To see more precisely how monopoly interferes with the proper functioning of the price system, suppose that all industries other than the shoe industry are perfectly competitive. The shoe industry, however, has been monopolized. How does this cause a misallocation of resources? Under fairly general circumstances, a good's price can be taken as a measure of the social value of an extra unit of the good. Thus if the price of a pair of socks is $1, the value to the consumer of an extra pair of socks can be taken to be $1. Moreover, under fairly general circumstances, a good's marginal cost can be taken as a measure of the cost to society of an extra unit of the good. Thus, if the marginal cost of a pair of shoes is $30, the cost to society of producing an extra pair of shoes can be taken to be $30.

In perfectly competitive industries, price is set equal to marginal cost, as we saw in Chapter 18. Thus each of the competitive industries produces up to the point where the social value of an extra unit of the good (which equals price) is set equal to the cost to society of producing an extra unit of the good (which equals marginal cost). This is the amount each of these industries should produce—the output rate that will result in an optimal allocation of resources.

Why Is the Competitive Output Optimal?

To see that the competitive output rate is the optimal one, consider what happens when an industry produces up to the point where the social value of an extra unit of the good is *more* than the cost to society of producing an extra unit. This isn't the socially optimal output rate because a one-unit increase in the output rate will increase the social value of output by more than the social cost of production, which means that it will increase social welfare. Thus since a one-unit increase in the output rate will increase social welfare, the existing output rate cannot be optimal.

Next, consider what happens when an industry produces up to the point where the social value of an extra unit of the good is *less* than the cost to society of producing the extra unit. This isn't the socially optimal output rate because a one-unit decrease in the output rate will decrease the social value of output by less than the social cost of production, which means that it will increase social welfare. Thus since a one-unit decrease in the output rate will increase social welfare, the existing output rate cannot be optimal.

Putting together the results of the previous two paragraphs, it follows that the socially optimal output rate must be at the point where the social value of an extra unit of the good *equals* the social cost of producing an extra unit of the good. Why? Because if the output rate is not optimal when the social value of an extra unit of the good exceeds or falls short of the cost to society of producing the extra unit, it must be optimal only when the two are equal.

The Monopolist Produces Too Little

Now let's return to the monopolistic shoe industry. Is the shoe industry producing the optimal amount of shoes? The answer is no. Like any monopolist, it produces at the point where marginal revenue equals marginal cost. And since marginal revenue is *less* than price (as was proved above), the monopolist produces at a point where price is *greater* than marginal cost. Consequently, *the monopolistic industry produces at a point where the social value of an extra unit of the good (which equals price) is greater than the cost to society of producing the extra unit (which equals marginal cost).* As we saw in a previous paragraph, this means that the monopolist's output rate is too small. A one-unit increase in the output of shoes will increase the social value of output by more than the social cost of production.

Here lies the economist's principal complaint against monopoly: it results in a misallocation of resources. Too little is produced of the monopolized good. Society is less well off, in terms of its own tastes and potentialities, than it could be. The price system, which would not lead to, or tolerate, such waste if all industries were perfectly competitive, is not allowed to perform as it should.

Income Distribution

Misallocation of resources is only part of the economist's case against monopoly. As we have already pointed out, *monopoly redistributes income in favor of the monopolists.* In other words, monopolists can fatten their own purse by restricting their output and raising their price. Admittedly, there is no scientific way to prove that monopolists are less deserving than the rest of the population, but it is also pretty difficult to see why they are more deserving.

Efficiency

Since monopolists do not have to face direct competition, they are likely to be less diligent in controlling costs and in using resources efficiently. As the economist Sir John Hicks put it, "The best of all monopoly profits is a quiet life."[6] Certainly we all dream at times of being able to take life easy. It would be strange if monopolists, having succeeded in insulating themselves from direct competition, did not take advantage of the opportunity—not open to firms in perfectly competitive markets—to relax a bit and worry less about pinching pennies. For this reason, economists fear that, to use Adam Smith's pungent phrase, "Monopoly . . . is a great enemy to good management."

Technological Change

Further, *it is often claimed that monopolists are slow to innovate and adopt new techniques and products.* This lethargy stems from the monopolist's freedom from direct competition. Innovation tends to be disruptive, while old ways, like old shoes, tend to be comfortable. The monopolist may be inclined, therefore, to stick with "time-honored" practices. Without question, competition is an important spur to innovation and to the rapid diffusion of innovations. But there are well-known arguments on the other side as well. Some economists argue (as we will see in the section, "Exploring Further," in this chapter) that substantial monopoly power promotes innovation and technological change.

PUBLIC REGULATION OF MONOPOLY

One way that society has attempted to reduce the harmful effects of monopoly is through *public regulation.* Suppose that the long-run cost curve in a particular industry is such that competition is not feasible. In such a case, society may permit a monopoly to be established. But a commission or some other public body is also established to regulate the monopoly's behavior. Among the many such regulatory commissions in the United States are the Federal Energy Regulatory Commission, the Federal Communications Commission, and the Interstate Commerce Commission. They regulate the behavior of firms with monopoly power in the electric power, transportation, and other industries. These industries are big as well as important, accounting for about 10 percent of the national output. Thus we need to know how these commissions operate and make decisions on prices and other matters.

[6]J. Hicks, "Annual Survey of Economic Theory: The Theory of Monopoly," *Econometrica,* 1935.

Regulatory commissions often set the price—or the maximum price—at the level at which it equals average total cost, including a "fair" rate of return on the firm's investment. In Figure 19.6, the price would be established by the commission at *OP*, where the demand curve intersects the average total cost curve (which includes what the commission regards as a fair profit per unit of output). Needless to say, there has been considerable controversy over what constitutes a fair rate of return. Frequently, commissions have settled on 8 to 10 percent. In addition, there has been a good deal of controversy over what should be included in the company's "investment" on which the fair rate of return is to be earned. A company's assets can be valued at **historical cost** or at **reproduction cost**: at what the company paid for them or at what it would cost to replace them. If the price level does not change much, these two approaches yield much the same answer. But if prices are rising, as they have been during most of the past 40 years, replacement cost will be greater than historical cost, with the result that the company will be allowed higher profits and rates if replacement cost is used. Most commissions now use historical cost.

Figure 19.6
Regulation of
Monopoly
The price established by a commission might be *OP,* where the demand curve intersects the average total cost curve. (Costs here include what the commission regards as a fair profit per unit of output.) In the absence of regulation, the monopolist would set a price of *OP_M.* For price to equal marginal cost, price would have to equal *OP_u.*

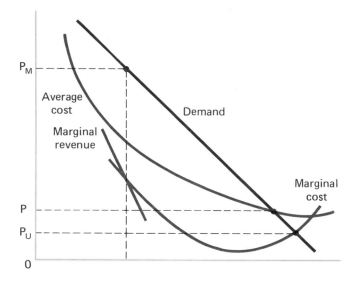

Does Regulation Affect Prices?

The regulatory commissions and the principles they use have become extremely controversial. *Many observers feel that the commissions are lax and that they tend to be captured by the industries they are supposed to regulate.* Regulated industries, recognizing the power of such commissions, invest considerable time and money in attempts to influence the commissions. The public, on the other hand, often has only a foggy idea of what the commissions are doing, and of whether or not it is in the public interest. According to some critics like Ralph Nader, "Nobody seriously challenges the fact that the regulatory agencies have made an accommodation with the businesses they are supposed to regulate—and they've

CASE STUDY 19.2 AT&T AND THE KINGSBURY AGREEMENT

The patent the government gave Alexander Graham Bell on the first telephone in 1884 gave him a seventeen-year monopoly on the new invention. With other patented inventions Bell Telephone connected first neighbors, then the whole country, in a coast-to-coast communications network. But as Bell's patents expired after the turn of the century, other companies began wiring the nation's cities and towns, and competition broke out. Almost every city had two telephone systems, some had three. Webs of telephone wire darkened the skies of America's cities. Only by having two or three phones could you be sure of being able to call all around town. But as it had in the oil industry, competition meant lower prices, and lower profits.

Bell Telephone connects the country in this early advertisement

Bell fought back. It slashed rates to undercut some competitors, bought others out, and tried to deny financing and equipment to others. Bell had another weapon: Lots of small companies could buy some telephones and wire, hire operators, and go into business. But only Bell had—and only Bell could afford—the national network that made long-distance calls possible. An independent local phone company that was refused interconnection by Bell was cut off from the rest of the country. Wounded phone companies began asking the government to take Bell to court under antitrust laws, the way it had Standard Oil. In 1914, rather than endure lengthy court battles, AT&T's president, Theodore Vail, sent AT&T vice president Nathan C. Kingsbury to Washington, D.C., to work out a compromise. The Kingsbury agreement forestalled any attempt to break up AT&T but did subject the natural monopoly to regulation. For the next seventy years, AT&T was *the* phone company.

N.B.

☆ ☆ ☆ ☆ ☆ ☆ ☆ ☆ ☆ ☆ ☆ ☆ ☆

done so at the expense of the public." For these and other reasons, some economists believe that regulation has little effect on prices.

It is difficult to isolate and measure the effects of regulation on the average level of prices. Some well-known economists have conducted studies that suggest that regulation has made little or no difference in this regard. George Stigler and Claire Friedland of the University of Chicago compared the levels of rates charged for electricity by regulated and unregulated electric power companies. They found that there was no significant difference between the average rates charged by the two sets of firms.[7] Other economists challenge Stigler's and Friedland's interpretation of their factual findings, and much more research on this topic is needed. Nonetheless, it seems fair to conclude that, although the simple model of the regulatory process presented above would predict that regulated prices would be lower, on the average, than unregulated prices (of the same item), the evidence in support of this prediction is much weaker than might be supposed.

Whether or not regulation has a significant effect on the *average* level of prices, it certainly has an effect on *particular* prices charged by regulated firms. In some cases, it has reduced the price of a product. There seems to be general agreement that the Federal Energy Regulatory Commission kept the price of natural gas (in interstate commerce) below what this price would have been during the 1970s in the absence of regulation. In other cases, it has increased the price of a product.

EFFICIENCY INCENTIVES

As we have stressed, competitive markets provide considerable incentives for a firm to increase its efficiency. Firms that are able to push their costs below those of their competitors reap higher profits than their competitors. As a simple illustration, suppose that firms A and B both have contracts to produce 100 airplanes, and that the price they will get for each airplane is $25,000. Firm A's management, which is diligent, imaginative, and innovative, gets the cost per airplane down to $10,000, and thus makes a healthy profit of $1,500,000. Firm B's management, which is lazy, unimaginative, and dull, lets the cost per airplane rise to $30,000, and thus loses $500,000. Clearly, firm A is rewarded for its good performance, while firm B is penalized for its poor performance.

No Incentive for Efficiency

One of the primary purposes of regulators is to prevent a monopoly from earning excessive profits. The firm is allowed only a "fair" rate of return on its investment. One problem with this arrangement is that the firm is guaranteed this rate of return regardless of how well it performs. If the regulators decide that the Sleepy Hollow Electric and Gas Company should receive a 10 percent rate of return on its investment, this is the rate of return it will receive regardless of whether the Sleepy Hollow Electric and Gas Company is managed well or poorly. Why is this a problem? Because, unlike the competitive firms discussed in the previous paragraph, there is no incentive for the firm to increase its efficiency.

The available evidence indicates that if a firm is guaranteed a fixed amount of profit for a job (regardless of how efficiently it does this job), the

---

[7]G. Stigler and C. Friedland, "What Can Regulators Regulate? The Case of Electricity," *The Journal of Law and Economics,* 1962. For another point of view, see H. Trebing, "The Chicago School versus Public Utility Regulation," *Journal of Economic Issues,* March 1976.

firm will tend to be less efficient than if the amount of profit it receives is directly related to its efficiency. The Department of Defense has found that when it bought goods or services on a cost-plus-fixed-fee basis, these goods and services were not produced as cheaply as when it bought them in a competitive market. This is reasonable. It takes time, energy, and lots of trouble to make a firm more efficient. Why should a firm's managers bother to induce added efficiency if the firm's profits are the same, regardless of how efficient or inefficient it is?

EXPLORING FURTHER: THE DEFENSE OF MONOPOLY POWER

Not all economists agree that monopoly power is a bad thing. On the contrary, some respected voices in the economics profession have been raised to praise monopoly power. In discussing the social problems due to monopoly earlier in this chapter, we assumed that the rate of technological change is independent of an industry's market structure. Some economists like Joseph Schumpeter and John Kenneth Galbraith challenge this assumption. *They assert that the rate of technological change is likely to be higher in an imperfectly competitive industry (monopoly, oligopoly, and so on) than in a perfectly competitive industry.* Since the rate of technological change affects productivity and living standards, in their view a perfectly competitive economy is likely to be inferior in a dynamic sense to an economy containing many imperfectly competitive industries.

Arguments by Schumpeter and Galbraith

But is their assertion true? This question has been debated at great length. On the one hand, Schumpeter and Galbraith argue that firms under perfect competition have fewer resources to devote to research and experimentation than do firms under imperfect competition. Because profits are at a relatively low level, it is difficult for firms under perfect competition to support large expenditures on research and development. Moreover, they argue that unless a firm has sufficient control over the market to reap the rewards from an innovation, the introduction of the innovation may not be worthwhile. If competitors can imitate the innovation very quickly, the innovator may be unable to make any money from it.

Rejoinders to Schumpeter and Galbraith

Defenders of perfect competition retort that there is likely to be less pressure for firms in imperfect markets to introduce new techniques and products, since such firms have fewer competitors. Moreover, firms in imperfect markets are better able to drive out entrants who, uncommitted to present techniques, are likely to be relatively quick to adopt new ones.

(Entrants, unlike established producers, have no vested interest in maintaining the demand for existing products and the profitability of existing equipment.) Also, there are advantages in having a large number of independent decision-making units. There is less chance that an important technological advance will be blocked by the faulty judgment of a few people.

It is very difficult to obtain evidence to help settle the question, if it is posed in this way, since perfect competition is a hypothetical construct that does not exist in the real world. However, it does seem unlikely that a perfectly competitive industry (if such an industry could be constructed) would be able in many areas of the economy to carry out the research and development required to promote a high rate of technological change. Moreover, if entry is free and rapid, firms in a perfectly competitive industry will have little motivation to innovate. Although the evidence is not at all clear-cut, at least this much can be granted the critics of perfect competition.

Monopoly Power, Big Business, and Technological Change

Some economists go much further than the assertion that a certain amount of market imperfection will promote a more rapid rate of technological change. *They say that an industry composed of or dominated by a few large companies is the best market structure for promoting rapid technological change.* Galbraith has said that the "modern industry of a few large firms [is] an almost perfect instrument for inducing technical change."[8] And in some circles, it is accepted as an obvious fact that giant firms with their financial strength and well-equipped laboratories are absolutely necessary to maintain a rapid rate of technological change.

Suppose that, for a market of given size, we could replace the largest firms by a larger number of somewhat smaller firms—and thus reduce the extent to which the industry is dominated by the largest firms. Is there any evidence that this would decrease the rate of technological change, as is sometimes asserted? The evidence currently available does not indicate that such a decrease in industrial concentration would reduce the rate of technological change in most industries.

Specifically, the available studies do not show that total research and development expenditures in most industries would decrease if the largest firms were replaced by somewhat smaller ones. Nor do they indicate that the research and development expenditures carried out by the largest firms are generally more productive (or more ambitious or more risky) than those carried out by somewhat smaller firms. Moreover, they do not suggest that greater concentration of an industry results in a faster diffusion of innovations. However, if innovations require a large amount of capital, they do suggest that the substitution of a larger number of smaller

[8]John Kenneth Galbraith, *American Capitalism,* Boston: Houghton Mifflin, 1952, p. 91.

Thus, *contrary to the allegations of Galbraith and others, there is little
evidence that industrial giants are needed in most industries to ensure
rapid technological change and rapid utilization of new techniques.* This
does not mean that industries composed only of small firms would necessarily be optimal for the promotion and diffusion of new techniques. On
the contrary, there seem to be considerable advantages in a diversity of
firm sizes. Complementarities and interdependencies exist among large
and small firms. There is often a division of labor. Smaller firms may focus
on areas requiring sophistication and flexibility and cater to specialized
needs, while bigger firms concentrate on areas requiring large production,
marketing, or technical resources. However, there is little evidence in
most industries that firms considerably smaller than the biggest firms are
not big enough for these purposes.

How Much Monopoly Power Is Optimal?

The discussion in previous sections makes it clear that the case against
monopoly power is not open and shut. A certain amount of monopoly
power is inevitable in practically all real-life situations, since perfect competition is a model that can only be approximated in real life. Moreover,
a certain amount of monopoly power may be needed to promote desirable
technological change. The difficult problem is to determine how much
monopoly power is optimal under various circumstances (and how this
power is to be measured). Some economists (like Galbraith) are convinced
that a great deal of monopoly power is both inevitable and desirable.
Others believe the opposite. And the economic arguments are not strong
enough to resolve the differences of opinion. Much more will be said on
this in the following chapter.

SUMMARY

1. A pure monopoly is a market with one, and only one, seller. Monopolies may occur because of patents, control over basic inputs, and government action, as well as decreasing average costs up to the point where the
market is satisfied.

2. If average costs reach their minimum at an output rate large enough
to satisfy the entire market, perfect competition cannot be maintained;
the public often insists that the industry (a natural monopoly) be regulated
by the government.

[9]E. Mansfield, *Technological Change,* New York: Norton, 1971, and the literature cited
there. Also, see E. Mansfield, J. Rapoport, A. Romeo, E. Villani, S. Wagner, and F. Husic,
The Production and Application of New Industrial Technology, New York: Norton, 1977.

3. Since the monopolist is the only seller of the product, the demand curve facing the monopolist is the market demand curve, which slopes downward (rather than being horizontal as in perfect competition).

4. The unregulated monopolist will maximize profit by choosing the output where marginal cost equals marginal revenue, marginal revenue being defined as the addition to total revenue attributable to the addition of one unit to sales. This rule for output determination also holds under perfect competition, where price equals marginal revenue.

5. If monopolists cannot prevent losses from exceeding fixed costs, they, like perfect competitors, will discontinue production. In contrast to the case in perfect competition, the long-run equilibrium of a monopolistic industry may not be marked by the absence of economic profits.

6. The output of a monopoly tends to be smaller and the price tends to be higher than under perfect competition. Economists tend to believe that society would be better off if more resources were devoted to the production of the good than under monopoly, the competitive output often being regarded as best.

7. One way that society has attempted to reduce the harmful effects of monopoly is through public regulation. Commissions often set price at the level at which it equals average total cost, including a "fair" rate of return on the firm's investment.

8. There is a great deal of controversy over current practices of the regulatory commissions. Many economists view them as lax or ill-conceived. According to many studies, their decisions have resulted in substantial costs and inefficiencies.

9. Regulatory commissions try to prevent a monopoly from earning excessive profits; the firm is allowed only a "fair" rate of return on its investment. One difficulty with this arrangement is that, since the firm is guaranteed this rate of return (regardless of how well or poorly it performs), there is little incentive for the firm to increase its efficiency.

*10. In defense of monopoly power, some economists, including John Kenneth Galbraith, have asserted that the rate of technological change is likely to be greater in an imperfectly competitive industry than under perfect competition. It does seem unlikely that a perfectly competitive industry would be able—and have the incentive—to carry out the research and development required to promote a rapid rate of technological change in many sectors of the economy.

*11. Contrary to the allegations of Galbraith and others, there is little evidence that giant firms are needed to ensure rapid technological change in a great many sectors of the economy. The situation is much more complex than such statements indicate, and the contributions of smaller firms are much greater than is commonly recognized.

*Starred items refer to material covered in the section, "Exploring Further."

CHAPTER 20

★ ★ ★ ★ ★ ★ ★ ★ ★

Monopolistic Competition, Oligopoly, and Antitrust Policy

LEARNING OBJECTIVES

In this chapter, you should learn:

★ The conditions that define monopolistic competition, and those that define oligopoly

★ How the prices and outputs set under monopolistic competition compare with those set under monopoly

★ How oligopolies are organized

★ How prices and outputs under oligopoly compare with those under perfect competition

★ The nature of the major antitrust laws and their effectiveness

The industries encountered in the real world are seldom perfectly competitive or monopolistic. Although perfect competition and monopoly are very useful models that shed much valuable light on the behavior of markets, they are polar cases. Economists have developed other models that portray more realistically the behavior of many modern industries. The model of monopolistic competition helps to explain market behavior **401 ★**

in such industries as retail drug stores and barber shops, while the model of oligopoly pertains to industries like steel, oil, and automobiles.

In this chapter, we examine how resources are allocated and prices are set under monopolistic competition and oligopoly. The results are of considerable significance, both because they give us a better understanding of how many markets work and because they provide valuable information on the social desirability of monopolistic competition and oligopoly.

MONOPOLISTIC COMPETITION AND OLIGOPOLY: THEIR MAJOR CHARACTERISTICS

To begin with, we must recall what monopolistic competition and oligopoly are. **Monopolistic competition** *occurs where there are many sellers (as in perfect competition) but where there is product differentiation. In other words, the firms' products are not the same.* It does not matter whether the differences among products are real or imagined. What is important is that the consumer regards the products as different.

Oligopoly *occurs in markets where there are few sellers.* There are two types of oligopolies, one where all sellers produce an indentical product, and one where the sellers produce somewhat different products. Examples of the first type, *pure oligopoly*, are the markets for steel, cement, tin cans, and petroleum. Examples of the second type, *differentiated oligopoly*, are the markets for automobiles and machinery.

In contrast to the extremes of perfect competition and monopoly, monopolistic competition and oligopoly are intermediate cases that include an element of competition and of monopoly—and so are more realistic than the two extremes.

MONOPOLISTIC COMPETITION

The key feature of monopolistic competition is *product differentiation*. In contrast to perfect competition, where all firms sell an identical product, firms under monopolistic competition sell somewhat different products. Producers differentiate their product from that of other producers. This is the case in many American markets. In many parts of retail trade, producers can differentiate their product by altering the product's physical makeup, the services they offer, and other such variables. Other differences which may be spurious are based on brand name, image making, advertising claims, and so on. In this way, the producers gain some monopoly power; but it usually is small, because the products of other firms are very similar.

In perfect competition, the firms included in an industry are easy to identify because they all produce the same product. But if product differentiation exists, it is no longer easy to define an industry, since each firm produces a somewhat different product. Nevertheless, it is useful to group together firms that produce similar products and call them a *product*

product groups is bound to be somewhat arbitrary, since there is no way
to decide how close a pair of substitutes must be to belong to the same
product group. But it is assumed that meaningful product groups can be
established.

Besides product differentiation, other conditions must be met for an
industry to qualify as a case of monopolistic competition. First, *there must
be a large number of firms in the product group.* In other words, the
product must be produced by perhaps 50 to 100 or more firms, with each
firm's product a fairly close substitute for the products of the other firms
in the product group. Second, *the number of firms in the product group
must be large enough so that each firm expects its actions to go unheeded
by its rivals and is unimpeded by possible retaliatory moves on their
part.* If there is a large number of firms, this condition will normally be
met. Third, *entry into the product group must be relatively easy, and there
must be no collusion, such as price fixing or market sharing, among firms
in the product group.* If there is a large number of firms, collusion generally is difficult, if not impossible.

PRICE AND OUTPUT UNDER MONOPOLISTIC COMPETITION

Under monopolistic competition, what determines how much output a
firm will produce, and what price it will charge? If each firm produces a
somewhat different product, it follows that the demand curve facing each
firm slopes downward to the right. That is, if the firm raises its price
slightly it will lose some, but by no means all, of its customers to other
firms. And if it lowers its price slightly, it will gain some, but by no means
all, of its competitors' customers. This is in contrast to perfect competition,
where the demand curve facing each firm is horizontal.

Figure 20.1 shows the short-run equilibrium of a monopolistically competitive firm. The firm in the short run will set its price at OP_0 and its
output rate at OQ_0, since this combination of price and output will maximize its profits. We can be sure that this combination of price and output
maximizes profit because marginal cost equals marginal revenue at this
output rate. In the situation shown in Figure 20.1, economic profits will
be earned because price, OP_0, exceeds average total costs, OC_0, at this
output rate.

What will the equilibrium price and output be in the long run? One
condition for long-run equilibrium is that each firm be making no economic profits or losses, since entry or exit of firms will occur otherwise—
and entry and exit are incompatible with long-run equilibrium. Another
condition for long-run equilibrium is that each firm be maximizing its
profits. At what price and output will both these conditions be fulfilled?
Figure 20.2 shows that long-run equilibrium is at a price of OP_1 and an
output of OQ_1. The zero-economic-profit condition is met at this combina-

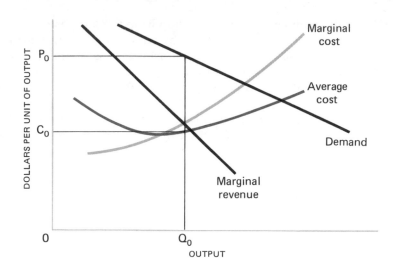

Figure 20.1
Short-Run Equilibrium: Monopolistic Competition
The firm will set price at OP_0 and its output rate at OQ_0 since marginal cost equals marginal revenue at this output. It will earn a profit of C_0P_0 per unit of output.

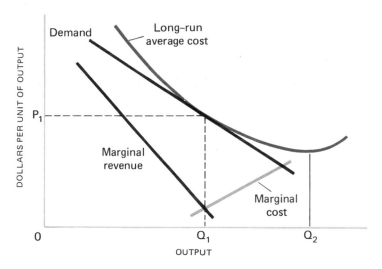

Figure 20.2
Long-Run Equilibrium: Monopolistic Competition
The long-run equilibrium is at a price of OP_1 and an output of OQ_1. There are zero profits since long-run average cost equals price. Profits are being maximized since marginal cost equals marginal revenue at this output.

tion of price and output since the firm's average cost at this output equals the price, OP_1. And the profit-maximization condition is met, since the marginal revenue curve intersects the marginal cost curve at this output rate.[1]

Comparisons with Perfect Competition and Monopoly

Market structure is important because it influences market behavior. We need to know how the behavior of a monopolistically competitive industry

[1]For the classic work on monopolistic competition, see E. Chamberlin, *The Theory of Monopolistic Competition*, Cambridge, Mass.: Harvard University Press, 1933.

differs from that of a perfectly competitive industry or a monopoly. Suppose that there exists a magician who can transform an industry's structure by a wave of a wand. (John D. Rockefeller was a real-life magician who transformed the structure of the oil industry in the late 1800s—but he seemed to favor mergers, mixed with some ungentlemanly tactics, over wands. See Case Study 19.1.) Suppose that the magician makes an industry monopolistically competitive, rather than perfectly competitive or monopolistic. What difference would it make in the behavior of the industry? Or, to take a less fanciful case, what difference would it make if government action or technological change resulted in such a change in an industry's market structure? It is difficult to say how the industry's behavior would be affected, because output would be heterogeneous in one case and homogeneous in the other, and its cost curves would probably vary with its organization. But many economists seem to believe that differences of the following kind can be expected.

1. *The firm under monopolistic competition is likely to produce less, and charge a higher price, than under perfect competition.* The demand curve confronting the monopolistic competitor slopes downward to the right. Consequently, as we saw in the previous chapter, marginal revenue must be less than price. Thus under monopolistic competition, marginal cost must also be less than price, since marginal revenue must equal marginal cost at the firm's profit-maximizing output rate. But if marginal cost is less than price, the firm's output rate must be smaller—and the price higher —than if marginal cost equals price, which is the case under perfect competition. On the other hand, *relative to monopoly, monopolistically competitive firms are likely to have lower profits, greater output, and lower price.* The firms in a product group might obtain positive economic profits if they were to collude and behave as a monopolist. Such an increase in profits resulting from the monopoly would benefit the producers. Consumers would be worse off because of the higher prices and smaller output of goods.

2. *A firm under monopolistic competition may be somewhat inefficient.* As shown in Figure 20.2, it produces a smaller-than-minimum-cost output. (It produces OQ_1 units of output; the output where average cost is a minimum is OQ_2 units of output.) Consequently, more firms exist than if average costs were minimized; this results in some overcrowding of the industry. Inefficiencies of this sort would not be expected under perfect competition.

3. *Firms under monopolistic competition will offer a wider variety of styles, brands, and qualities than firms under perfect competition. Moreover, they will spend much more on advertising and other selling expenses than a perfectly competitive firm would.* Whether this diversity is worth its cost is hard to say. Some economists are impressed by the apparent waste in monopolistic competition. They think it results in too many firms, too many brands, too much selling effort, and too much spurious product differentiation. But if the differences among products are real and are understood by consumers, the greater variety of alternatives available

under monopolistic competition may be very valuable to consumers. The proper evaluation of the social advantages and disadvantages of product differentiation is a problem economists have not solved.[2]

OLIGOPOLY

Oligopoly (domination by a few firms) is a common and important market structure in the United States; many industries, including steel, automobiles, oil, and electrical equipment, are oligopolistic. An example of an oligopolist is General Motors. *The key characteristic of oligopoly is interdependence, actual and perceived, among firms.* Each oligopolist formulates its policies with an eye to their effect on its rivals. Since an oligopoly contains a small number of firms, any change in one firm's price or output influences the sales and profits of its competitors. Moreover, since there are only a few firms, each must recognize that changes in its own policies are likely to result in changes in the policies of its rivals as well.

What factors are responsible for oligopoly? First, in some industries, *low production costs cannot be achieved unless a firm is producing an output equal to a substantial portion of the total available market,* with the consequence that the number of firms will tend to be rather small. Second, *there may be economies of scale in sales promotion* in certain industries, and this too may promote oligopoly. Third, entry into some industries may be blocked by *the requirement that a firm build and maintain a large, complicated, and expensive plant, or have access to patents or scarce raw materials.* Only a few firms may be in a position to obtain all these prerequisites for membership in the club.

OLIGOPOLY BEHAVIOR AND THE STABILITY OF PRICES

Unlike perfect competition, monopoly, and monopolistic competition, there is no single unified model of oligopoly behavior. Instead, *there are a number of models, each based on a somewhat different set of assumptions concerning the relationships among the firms that make up the oligopoly.* Basically, no single model exists because economists have not yet been able to devise one that would cover all the relevant cases adequately.

---

[2]Before leaving the subject of monopolistic competition, it should be recognized that Professor Chamberlin's theory has been subjected to considerable criticism. As a case in point, the definition of the product group is ambiguous. See G. Stigler, *Five Lectures on Economic Problems,* London: Longmans Green, 1949.

The Kinked Oligopoly Demand Curve

Let's start with a model that sheds light on the stability of oligopolistic prices. Empirical studies of pricing in oligopolistic markets have often concluded that prices in such markets tend to be rigid. A classic example occurred in the sulphur industry. From 1926 to 1938, the price of sulphur remained at $18 a ton, despite great shifts in demand and production costs.[3] This example is somewhat extreme, but it illustrates the basic point: prices in oligopolistic industries commonly remain unchanged for fairly long periods. A well-known model designed to explain this price rigidity was advanced by Paul Sweezy, who asserted that, *if an oligopolist cuts its price, it can be pretty sure that its rivals will meet the reduction. On the other hand, if it increases its price, its rivals may not change theirs.*

Figure 20.3 shows the situation. The oligopolist's demand curve is represented by *DAD'* and the current price is *OP*. There is a "kink" in the demand curve because, *under the postulated circumstances, the demand curve for the oligopolist's product is much less elastic for price decreases than for price increases.* Why is this? Because price decreases will be met by the firm's rivals, which means that the firm will not be able to take any appreciable amount of sales away from its rivals by such decreases. The effect of such decreases will be to increase the quantity demanded of the firm's product, since the total quantity demanded of the entire industry's product will increase because of the price reduction. But the increase in the quantity demanded of the firm's product will be relatively modest. On the other hand, if the firm raises its price, it is assumed that its rivals will not follow suit, and the quantity demanded of the firm's product will fall considerably.

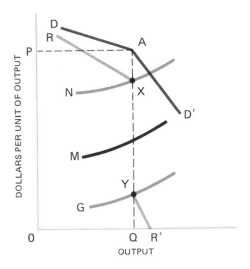

[3]Marshall Colberg, William Bradford, and Richard Alt, *Business Economics: Principles and Cases*, Homewood, Ill.: Irwin, 1957, p. 276.

**Figure 20.3
The Kinked
Oligopoly Demand
Curve**
Because of the kink in the demand curve, the marginal revenue curve consists of two segments *RX* and *YR'*. Since the marginal cost curve is *M*, the most profitable output is *OQ*. Moreover, it remains the most profitable output— and *OP* the most profitable price— even if the marginal cost curve shifts to *N* or to *G* or if the demand curve shifts considerably (within limits).

Prediction: Rigid Prices

Because of the kink in the demand curve, the marginal revenue curve in Figure 20.3 is not continuous. It consists of two segments, *RX* and *YR'*. Given that the firm's marginal cost curve is *M*, the most profitable output is *OQ*, where the marginal cost curve intersects the vertical line, *XY*. Moreover, OQ *remains the most profitable output—and* OP *the most profitable price—even if the marginal cost curve shifts considerably (even to* N *or* G) *or if the demand curve shifts (within limits).* One would expect price to be quite rigid under these circumstances, since many types of changes in cost and demand will not alter the price that maximizes profits.

This theory, although useful in explaining why price tends to remain at a certain level (*OP* in Figure 20.3), is of no use at all in explaining why this level, rather than another, currently prevails. It simply takes the current price as given. Thus this theory is an incomplete model of oligopoly pricing. Nonetheless, it seems to explain some of the relevant facts.

COLLUSION AND CARTELS

How Firms Collude

Collusion occurs when firms get together and agree on price and output. Up to this point, we have assumed that oligopolists do not collude, but conditions in oligopolistic industries tend to promote collusion, since the number of firms is small and the firms recognize their interdependence. The advantages of collusion to the firms seem obvious: increased profits, decreased uncertainty, and a better opportunity to prevent entry.

Not all collusion is disguised from the public or secret. In contrast to illicit collusion, a *cartel* is an open, formal collusive arrangement among firms. In many countries in Europe, cartels have been common and legally acceptable. In the United States, most collusive arrangements, whether secret or open cartels, were declared illegal by the Sherman Antitrust Act, which was passed in 1890.

However, this does not mean that such arrangements do not exist. Widespread collusion to fix prices occurred among American electrical equipment manufacturers during the 1950s, and when the collusion was uncovered a number of high executives were tried, convicted, and sent to jail. (See Case Study 20.1.) Moreover, collusion of this sort is not limited to a single industry, or a single country. Some cartels, like that in quinine in the early 1960s are international in scope.[4] A particularly famous international cartel is the Organization of Petroleum Exporting Countries

---

[4]See "Collusion among Electrical Equipment Manufacturers" and "Quinine: An International Cartel," in E. Mansfield, ed., *Microeconomics: Selected Readings,* 4th ed., New York: Norton, 1982.

(OPEC), which consists of thirteen oil-producing countries, including Saudi Arabia and Iran.

Price and Output of a Cartel

If a cartel is established to set a uniform price for a particular product, what price will it charge? As a first step, the cartel must estimate the marginal cost curve for the cartel as a whole. Then it must find the output where its marginal cost equals its marginal revenue, since this output maximizes the total profit of the cartel members. In Figure 20.4, this output is *OQ*. Thus if it maximizes cartel profits, the cartel will choose a price of *OP*, which is the monopoly price. In short, *the cartel acts like a monopolist with a number of plants or divisions, each of which is a member firm.*

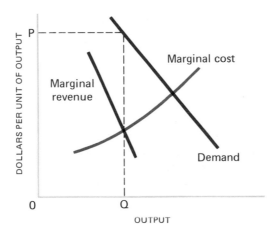

Figure 20.4
Price and Output of a Cartel
The marginal cost curve shows the marginal cost for the cartel as a whole. Based on the demand curve for the industry's product, the cartel can derive the marginal revenue curve. The output that maximizes the total profit of the cartel members is *OQ*. The corresponding price is *OP*.

How will the cartel allocate sales among the member firms? If its aim is to maximize cartel profits, it will allocate sales to firms in such a way that the sum of the firms' costs is minimized. But this allocation is unlikely to occur in reality. The allocation process is a bargaining process, and firms with the most influence and the shrewdest negotiators are likely to receive the large sales quotas, even though this decreases the total profits of the cartel. Moreover, high-cost firms are likely to receive larger sales quotas than would be the case if total cartel profits were maximized, since they would be unwilling otherwise to stay in the cartel. In practice, it appears that cartels often divide markets geographically or in accord with a firm's level of sales in the past.

BARRIERS TO COLLUSION

The fact that oligopoly often can lead to collusion is not new. Back in 1776, Adam Smith warned that "people of the same trade seldom meet together even for merriment and diversion, but the conversation ends in a conspiracy against the public, or in some contrivance to raise prices." However, it must be borne in mind that collusive arrangements are often difficult to accomplish and maintain for long. In particular, there are several important barriers to collusion.

Legal Problems

The antitrust laws, discussed in detail later in this chapter, forbid outright collusion and price fixing. This does not mean that firms do not break those laws; witness the electrical equipment manufacturers described in Case Study 20.1. But the antitrust laws are an important obstacle to collusion.

Technical Problems

Collusion is often difficult to achieve and maintain because an oligopoly contains an unwieldy number of firms, or the product is quite heterogeneous, or the cost structures of the firms differ considerably. It is clear that a collusive agreement will be more difficult to achieve and maintain if there are a dozen oligopolists than if there are three or four. Moreover, if the products sold by the oligopolists differ substantially, it will probably be more difficult for them to find a common price strategy that will be acceptable to all. Similarly, if the firms' cost structures differ, it will be more difficult to get agreement, since the low-cost firms will be more inclined to cut price. For example, National Steel, after introducing low-cost continuous strip mills in the 1930s, became a price cutter in the steel industry.

Cheating

There is a constant temptation for oligopolists to cheat on any collusive agreement. If other firms stick to the agreement, any firm that cheats— by cutting its price below that agreed to under the collusive arrangement —can take a lot of business away from the other firms and increase its profits substantially, at least in the short run. This temptation is particularly great when an industry's sales are depressed and its profits are low. Every firm is hungry for business, and it is difficult to resist. Moreover, one firm may be driven to cheating because it hears that another firm is doing so, with the eventual result that the collusive agreement is torn apart.

To illustrate the problems of maintaining a collusive agreement, let's return to the electrical equipment manufacturers described in Case Study 20.1. As the *Wall Street Journal* summed it up:

> One of the great ironies of the conspiracies was that no matter how hard the participants schemed, no matter how friendly their meetings and communications might be, there was an innate tendency to compete. Someone was always violating the agreements to get more business and this continually called for

CASE STUDY 20.1 THE ELECTRICAL CONSPIRACY

To illustrate how firms collude, consider electrical equipment manufacturers. During the 1950s, there was widespread collusion among about 30 firms selling turbine generators, switchgear, transformers, and other products with total sales of about $1.5 billion per year. Representatives of these firms got together and agreed upon prices for many products. The available evidence indicates that both prices and profits tended to be increased by the collusive agreements, or at least until the firms were prosecuted under the antitrust laws by the Department of Justice. The following statement by F. M. Scherer of Swarthmore College is a good description of some of the procedures used by these firms:

> Some of the most elaborate procedures were devised to handle switchgear pricing. Each seller agreed to quote book prices in sales to private buyers, and meetings were held regularly to compare calculations for forthcoming job quotations. Sealed-bid competitions sponsored by government agencies posed a different set of problems, and new methods were worked out to handle them. Through protracted negotiation, each seller was assigned a specific share of all sealed-bid business, e.g., General Electric's share of the high voltage switchgear field was set at 40.3 percent in late 1958, and Allis-Chalmers' at 8.8 percent. Participants then coordinated their bidding so that each firm was lowest bidder in just enough transactions to gain its predetermined share of the market. In the power switching equipment line, this was achieved for a while by dividing the United States into four quadrants, assigning four sellers to each quadrant, and letting the sellers in a quadrant rotate their bids. A "phases of the moon" system was used to allocate low-bidding privileges in the high voltage switchgear field, with a new seller assuming low-bidding priority every two weeks. The designated bidder subtracted a specified percentage margin from the book price to capture orders during its phase, while others added various margins to the book price. The result was an ostensibly random pattern of quotations, conveying the impression of independent pricing behavior.*

*Kefauver Assails Identical Bids
To T. V. A. and Other Utilities*

General Electric, Westinghouse, and the other conspirators were found guilty of violating the antitrust laws. Some of the executives were sentenced to jail on criminal charges, and the firms had to pay large amounts to customers to make up for the overcharges. In particular, 1,800 triple damage suits against the firms resulted in payments estimated at between $400 and $600 million.

*F.M. Scherer, *Industrial Market Structure and Economic Performance*, p. 160.

new illegal plans. For example, price-cutting in sales of power switching equipment to government agencies was getting out of hand in late 1958. This led to the "quadrant" system of dividing markets.

As one executive of General Electric complained, "No one was living up to the agreement and we . . . were being made suckers. On every job someone would cut our throat; we lost confidence in the group." Given that these agreements were illegal, it is remarkable that such a complaint was uttered with a straight face.

PRICE LEADERSHIP

In order to coordinate their behavior without outright collusion, some industries contain a *price leader.* It is quite common in oligopolistic industries for one or a few firms to set the price and for the rest to follow their lead. Two types of price leadership are the dominant-firm model and the barometric-firm model. *The* **dominant-firm** *model applies to cases where the industry has a single large dominant firm and a number of small firms.* The dominant firm sets the price for the industry, but it lets the small firms sell all they want at that price. *The* **barometric-firm** *model applies to cases where one firm usually is the first to make changes in price that are generally accepted by other firms in the industry.* The barometric firm may not be the largest, or most powerful, firm. Instead, it is a reasonably accurate interpreter of changes in basic cost and demand conditions in the industry as a whole. According to some authorities, barometric price leadership often occurs as a response to a period of violent price fluctuation in an industry, during which many firms suffer and greater stability is widely sought.

In the past, the steel industry has been a good example of price leadership of the dominant-firm variety. The largest firm in the industry is U.S. Steel, which was formed in 1901 by the merger of a number of companies. Judge Elbert Gary, the first chairman of the board of U.S. Steel, sought the cooperation of the smaller firms in the industry. He inaugurated a series of so-called "Gary dinners," attended by all the major steel producers, which made declarations of industry policy on pricing and other matters. Since any formal pricing agreements would have been illegal, they made no such agreements. But, generally speaking, U.S. Steel set the pricing pattern and other firms followed. Moreover, this relationship continued long after Judge Gary had gone to his final reward. According to Walter Adams of Michigan State University, U.S. Steel typically set the pace, "and the other companies follow in lockstep—both in their sales to private customers and in their secret bids on government contracts."[5]

Illustrating the attitude of other firms was the statement by the president of Bethlehem Steel to a congressional committee in 1939 that "in the main we . . . await the (price) schedules of the [U.S.] Steel Corporation." However, there was some secret price cutting, particularly during depres-

[5]W. Adams, *The Structure of American Industry,* New York: Macmillan, 1961, p. 168.

sions. On at least one occasion, U.S. Steel responded to such price cutting by announcing publicly that it would meet any price reduction it heard of. In this way, it attempted to discourage under-the-counter price cutting. In more recent times, U.S. Steel no longer seems to be the price leader it once was. In 1962, it drew a great deal of criticism from President Kennedy for being the first steel firm to raise prices. Subsequently, smaller steel firms have often been the first. Indeed, in 1968 the world was treated to the amusing spectacle of Bethlehem announcing a price cut in order to counter some secret price cutting by the former price leader, U.S. Steel.

NONPRICE COMPETITION

Oligopolists tend to compete more aggressively through advertising and product differentiation than through direct price reductions. In other words, when we observe the behavior of major oligopolies, we find that firms try hard to get business away from their rivals by outdoing them with better advertising campaigns and with improvements in the product; but it is less common for oligopolists to slug it out, toe to toe, with price reductions. This is an important characteristic of oligopoly. In contrast to the case of perfect competition, nonprice competition plays a central role in oligopoly. It is worthwhile, therefore, to note a few salient points about the advertising and product development strategies of oligopolists.

Advertising

Advertising is a very big business. In 1983 over $75 billion per year was spent on it in the United States. One important purpose of advertising is to convince the consumer that one firm's product is better than another's. In industries where there is less physical differentiation of the product, advertising expenditures often are larger than in industries where the product varies more. Thus the cigarette, liquor, and soap industries spend over 10 percent of their gross revenues (excluding excise taxes) on advertising, whereas the automobile industry spends less than 1 percent of its gross revenue on advertising.

The social desirability of much of this advertising is debatable, and much debated. While advertising can serve an important purpose by keeping the consumer better informed, some advertising is more misleading than informative. Unfortunately, it is difficult to make reliable estimates of the extent to which oligopolists may be overinvesting, from society's point of view, in advertising.

Product Development

The development of new and improved products is also a very big business in the United States. Currently firms spend over $40 billion per year on research and development. In many industries, R and D is a central part

CASE STUDY 20.2 HOW FORD BECAME NUMBER TWO AND GENERAL MOTORS BECAME NUMBER ONE

Henry Ford didn't invent the car, and he didn't invent the assembly line. But he brought the two together and gave America its first mass-produced car. Ford was an inventor and mechanic by trade, and no effort was spared to improve the car and the process by which it was built. The Tin Lizzie looked the same year after year, but Ford's mechanical genius made it run better each year than the last. His industrial genius made it cheaper to build and to buy. He paid the highest wages in industry, $5 a day, and he made a car his workers could afford to buy. It seemed as though he had devised the perfect competitive product: It never wore out, it kept getting cheaper—and it was never out of style.

The Model T wasn't the only car on the road. Americans were driving Pierce Arrows, Stutz Bearcats, and Deusenbergs, as well as the Chevrolets, Buicks, Oldsmobiles, and Cadillacs made by Ford's number one competitor, General Motors, headed by

An early GM advertisement

SECURE IN THEIR SMARTNESS, the strikingly handsome new La Salles provide their fortunate owners with all that extra ride-easy roominess and luxury which distinguish the Unisteel Body as decidedly as do its Fisher No Draft Ventilation and silent, weave-proof, shock-proof solidity.

Alfred P. Sloan. Sloan once said, "The primary object of the corporation is to make money, not just to make motor cars. The core of the GM product policy lies in the concept of mass producing a full line of cars graded upward in quality and price." Sloan saw that even if GM could produce for less than Ford, it couldn't *increase* profits by *decreasing* prices. So to do battle with Ford's black Model Ts, GM's massive research and development effort produced a brand for every pocketbook—Chevrolets, Pontiacs, Buicks, and Cadillacs—a color for every taste, and a wish list of options. Every year brought a new edition. GMs were old, not when they wore out, but when they went out of style.

Any business decision is a kind of gamble. Henry Ford bet that America wanted a car that would last forever, was cheap and easy to fix, and never went out of style. Alfred Sloan bet that there was something more attractive to American drivers than a low price, that they were ready to have some fun with their cars, and that GM advertising could join their desires and GM's cars, at a profit to GM. Henry Ford knew cars, but Alfred Sloan knew the consumer, and he knew the twenties. By the time the Great Depression started in 1929 Henry Ford had yielded to reality and started varying his cars. But he had lost the 50 percent share of the market he had commanded, and had to settle for second place.

N.B.

of oligopolistic competition. For example, a spectacular case in the drug industry was the effect of American Cyanamid's Achromycin tetracycline, introduced in 1953, on sales of Aureomycin chlortetracycline, which had been marketed since late 1948. After an almost continuous upward trend in 1950-53, Aureomycin sales dropped by nearly 40 percent during the first full year of the sale of Achromycin. Hardly a typical case, this nonetheless illustrates how one firm can take sales away from its rivals through new product development.

It is important to add, however, that much of industry's R and D is aimed at fairly minor improvements in products and processes. Moreover, a good deal of the engineering efforts of many important industries is aimed largely at style changes, not basic improvements in the product. A case in point is the automobile industry, which spends an enormous amount to produce the model changes that are familiar to car buyers throughout the land. Specifically, according to three economists—Frank Fisher, Zvi Griliches, and Carl Kaysen—such model changes in the automobile industry cost about $5 billion per year during the late 1950s.[6] From society's point of view, it is not at all clear that such huge expenditures are justifiable.

Perhaps the main reason why oligopolists would rather compete through advertising and product differentiation than through price is that a firm's rivals can easily and quickly match a price reduction, whereas they may find it difficult to match a clever advertising campaign or an attractive product improvement. Thus oligopolists tend to feel that they have a better chance of improving their long-run profits at the expense of their rivals in the arena of nonprice competition than by price cutting.

COMPARISON OF OLIGOPOLY WITH PERFECT COMPETITION

We have seen that economists have constructed a number of types of models of oligopoly behavior: the Sweezy model, the cartel models, price leadership models, and others. But there is no agreement that any of these models is an adequate general representation of oligopoly behavior. For this reason, it is difficult to estimate the effects of an oligopolistic market structure on price, output, and profits. Nonetheless, if a perfectly competitive industry were turned overnight into an oligopoly, it seems likely that certain changes would occur.

1. *Price would probably be higher than under perfect competition.* The difference between the oligopoly price and the perfectly competitive price will depend on the number of firms in the industry and the ease of entry. The larger the number of firms and the easier it is to enter the industry, the closer the oligopoly price will be to the perfectly competitive

[6]F. Fisher, Z. Griliches, and C. Kaysen, "The Costs of Automobile Model Changes since 1949," *Journal of Political Economy*, 1962. For more recent data, see L. White, *The Automobile Industry Since 1945*, Cambridge, Mass.: Harvard University Press, 1971.

level. Also, prices will tend to be more inflexible under oligopolistic conditions than under perfect competition.

2. If the demand curve is the same under oligopoly as under perfect competition, it also follows that *output will be less under oligopoly than under perfect competition.* However, it is not always reasonable to assume that the demand curve is the same in both cases, since the large expenditures for advertising and product differentiation incurred by some oligopolies may tend to shift the demand curve to the right. Consequently in some cases both price and output may tend to be higher under oligopoly than under perfect competition.

3. *Oligopolistic industries tend to spend more on advertising, product differentiation, and style changes than perfectly competitive industries.* The use of some resources for these purposes is certainly worthwhile, since advertising provides buyers with information, and product differentiation allows greater freedom of choice. Whether oligopolies spend too much for these purposes is an open question. However, there is a widespread feeling among economists, based largely on empirical studies (and hunch), that in some oligopolistic industries such expenditures have been expanded beyond socially optimal levels.

4. One might expect on the basis of the models presented in this chapter that *the profits earned by oligopolists would be higher, on the average, than the profits earned by perfectly competitive firms.* This conclusion is supported by some statistical evidence. Joe Bain of the University of California has found that firms in industries in which the largest few firms had a high proportion of total sales tended to have higher rates of return than firms in industries in which the largest few firms had a small proportion of total sales.[7]

THE ANTITRUST LAWS

National policies are too ambiguous and rich in contradictions to be summarized neatly and concisely. Consequently, it would be misleading to say that the United States has adopted a policy of promoting competition and controlling monopoly. To a large extent, it certainly is true that "competition is our fundamental national policy," as the Supreme Court said in 1963. But it is also true that we have adopted many measures to promote monopoly and to limit competition. On balance, however, we probably

[7]J. Bain, "Relation of Profit Rate to Industry Concentration: American Manufacturing, 1936-1940," *Quarterly Journal of Economics,* August 1951. However, there has been much disagreement on this score. According to some recent evidence, a firm is likely to have higher-than-average profits if it has a relatively big share of the market, regardless of whether or not the industry as a whole is highly concentrated. For some relevant discussion, see L. Weiss "The Concentration-Profits Relationship and Antitrust," in H. Goldschmid, H. J. Mann, and J. F. Weston, *Industrial Concentration, The New Learning,* Boston: Little Brown, 1974; and H. Demsetz, "Industry Structure, Market Rivalry, and Public Policy," *Journal of Law and Economics,* April 1973.

have gone further in promoting competition than other major industrialized countries, and the principal pieces of legislation designed to further this objective are the *antitrust laws.*

417 ★
The Antitrust Laws

The Sherman Act

In 1890, the first antitrust law, the Sherman Act, was passed by Congress. Although the common law had long outlawed monopolistic practices, it appeared to many Americans in the closing years of the nineteenth century that legislation was required to discourage monopoly and to preserve and encourage competition. The formation of "trusts"—monopolistic combines that colluded to raise prices and restrict output—brought the matter to a head. The heart of the Sherman Act lies in the following two sections:

An early cartoon opposing the trusts

Section 1. Every contract, combination in the form of trust or otherwise, or conspiracy, in restraint of trade or commerce among the several states or with foreign nations, is hereby declared to be illegal. Every person who shall make any such contract or engage in any such combination or conspiracy, shall be deemed guilty of a misdemeanor. . . .

Section 2. Every person who shall monopolize, or attempt to monopolize or combine or conspire with any other person or persons to monopolize, any part of the trade or commerce among the several States, or with foreign nations shall be deemed guilty of a misdemeanor.

The Clayton Act

The first 20 years of experience with the Sherman Act were not very satisfying to its supporters. The ineffectiveness of the Sherman Act led in 1914 to passage by Congress of two additional laws: the Clayton Act and the Federal Trade Commission Act. The Clayton Act tried to be more specific than the Sherman Act in identifying certain practices that were illegal because they would "substantially lessen competition or tend to create a monopoly." In particular, the Clayton Act outlawed unjustified price discrimination, a practice whereby one buyer is charged more than another buyer for the same product. It also outlawed the use of a tying contract, which makes the buyers purchase other items to get the product they want. Further, it outlawed mergers that substantially lessen competition; but since it did not prohibit one firm's purchase of a competitor's plant and equipment, it really could not stop mergers. In 1950, this loophole was closed by the Celler-Kefauver Anti-Merger Act.

The Federal Trade Commission Act

The Federal Trade Commission Act was designed to prevent undesirable and unfair competitive practices. Specifically, it created a Federal Trade Commission to investigate unfair and predatory practices and to issue cease-and-desist orders. The act stated that "unfair methods of competition in commerce are hereby declared unlawful." However, the commission—composed of five commissioners, each appointed by the president for a term of seven years—was given the unenviable task of defining exactly what was "unfair." Eventually, the courts took away much of the commission's power; but in 1938, the commission acquired the function of outlawing untrue and deceptive advertising. Also, the commission has authority to carry out economic investigations of the structure and conduct of American business.

THE ROLE OF THE COURTS

The antitrust laws, like any laws, are enforced in the courts. Typically, charges are brought against a firm or group of firms by the Antitrust Division of the Department of Justice, a trial is held, and a decision is reached by the judge. In key cases, appeals are made that eventually reach the Supreme Court. The real impact of the antitrust laws depends on how the courts interpret them. And the judicial interpretation of these laws has changed considerably over time.

The first major set of antitrust cases took place in 1911 when the Standard Oil Company and the American Tobacco Company were forced to give up a large share of their holdings of other companies. In these cases, the Supreme Court put forth and used the famous *rule of reason*: that only unreasonable combinations in restraint of trade, not all trusts, required conviction under the Sherman Act. In 1920, the rule of reason was used by the Supreme Court in its finding that U.S. Steel had not violated the antitrust laws even though it had tried to monopolize the industry—since the Court said it had not succeeded. Moreover, U.S. Steel's large size and its potential monopoly power were ruled beside the point since "the law does not make mere size an offense. It . . . requires overt acts."

During the 1920s and 1930s the courts, including the Supreme Court, interpreted the antitrust laws in such a way that they became as toothless as a new-born babe. Although Eastman Kodak and International Harvester controlled very substantial shares of their markets, the Court, using the rule of reason, found them innocent on the grounds that they had not built up their near-monopoly position through overt coercion or predatory practices. Moreover, the Court reiterated that mere size was not an offense, no matter how great the unexerted monopoly power might be.

In the late 1930s, this situation changed very greatly, with the prosecution of the Aluminum Company of America (Alcoa). This case, decided in 1945 (but begun in 1937), reversed the decisions in the *U.S. Steel* and *International Harvester* cases. Alcoa had achieved its 90 percent share of the market by means that would have been considered "reasonable" in the earlier cases: keeping its price low enough to discourage entry, building capacity to take care of increases in the market, and so forth. Nonetheless, the Court decided that Alcoa, because it controlled practically all the industry's output, violated the antitrust laws. Thus to a considerable extent, *the Court used market structure rather than market conduct as a test of legality.*

THE ROLE OF THE JUSTICE DEPARTMENT

The impact of the antitrust laws is determined by the vigor with which the Antitrust Division of the Justice Department prosecutes cases. If the Antitrust Division does not prosecute, the laws can have little effect. Like the judicial interpretation of the laws, the extent to which the Justice Department has prosecuted cases has varied from one period to another. Needless to say, the attitude of the political party in power had been an important determinant of how vigorously antitrust cases have been prosecuted. When the Sherman Act was first passed, it was of singularly little value. President Grover Cleveland's attorney general did not agree with the law and would not prosecute under it. "Trust-busting" was truly a neglected art until President Theodore Roosevelt devoted his formidable energies to it. In 1903, he established the Antitrust Division of the Justice Department. Moreover, his administration started the major cases that led to the *Standard Oil, American Tobacco,* and *U.S. Steel* decisions.

Subsequently, there was a long lull in the prosecution of antitrust cases, reflecting the Supreme Court's rule-of-reason doctrine and a strong conservative tide in the nation. The lull continued for about 25 years, until 1937, when there was a significant upsurge in activity on the antitrust front. Led by Thurman Arnold, the Antitrust Division entered one of the most vigorous periods of antitrust enforcement to date. Arnold went after the glass, cigarette, cement, and other industries, the most important case being that against Alcoa. The Antitrust Division attempted in this period to reopen cases that were hopeless under the rule-of-reason doctrine. With the change in the composition of the Supreme Court, Arnold's activism turned out to be effective.

THE EFFECTIVENESS OF ANTITRUST POLICY

How effective have the antitrust laws been? Obviously it is difficult to tell with any accuracy, since there is no way to carry out an experiment in which American history is rewritten to show what would have happened if the antitrust laws had not been on the books. Many experts seem to feel that the antitrust laws have not been as effective as they might—or should —have been, largely because they do not have sufficient public support and there is no politically powerful pressure group pushing for their enforcement.

But this does not mean that the antitrust laws have had no effect. As Edward Mason of Harvard University has pointed out, their effectiveness is due "not so much to the contribution that particular judgments have made to the restoring of competition as it is to the fact that the consideration of whether or not a particular course of action may or may not be in violation of the antitrust acts is a persistent factor affecting business judgment, at least in large firms."[8] This same idea is summed up in the old saying that the ghost of Senator Sherman sits as an *ex officio* member of every firm's board of directors.

In 1982, two of the biggest antitrust cases in history were decided. According to one settlement, American Telephone and Telegraph Company divested itself of 22 companies that provide most of the nation's local telephone service, and kept its Long Lines Division, Western Electric, and the Bell Laboratories. According to the other settlement, a huge antitrust case against IBM Corporation, begun in 1969, was dropped by the government because it was "without merit." Although there is considerable skepticism in some quarters concerning the beneficial effects of the antitrust laws, these two cases show that they continue to play an important role in American economic life.

SUMMARY

1. Monopolistic competition occurs where there are many sellers whose products are somewhat different. The demand curve facing each firm slopes downward to the right. The conditions for long-run equilibrium are that each firm is maximizing profits and that economic profits are zero.

2. The firm under monopolistic competition is likely to produce less, and charge a higher price, than under perfect competition. Relative to pure monopoly, monopolistically competitive firms are likely to have lower profits, greater output, and lower prices. Firms under monopolistic competition will offer a wider variety of styles, brands, and qualities than will firms under perfect competition.

3. Oligopoly is characterized by a small number of firms and a great deal of interdependence, actual and perceived, among them. Oligopoly is a common market structure in the United States.

[8]Edward Mason, preface to Carl Kaysen and Donald Turner, *Antitrust Policy* (and reprinted in E. Mansfield, *Monopoly Power and Economic Performance*, 4th ed. New York: Norton, 1978).

4. According to empirical studies, prices tend to be rigid in oligopolistic industries. A well-known theory designed to explain this phenomenon is Sweezy's model, based on the kinked demand curve.

5. Conditions in oligopolistic industries tend to promote collusion. A cartel is an open, formal, collusive arrangement. A profit-maximizing cartel will act like a monopolist with a number of plants or divisions, each of which is a member firm. In practice, it appears that the members of a cartel often divide markets geographically or in accord with each firm's level of sales in the past.

6. Price leadership is quite common in oligopolistic industries, one or a few firms apparently setting the price and the rest following their lead. Two types of price leadership are the dominant-firm model and the barometric-firm model. An example of the former kind of price leadership was the steel industry until a decade or two ago.

7. Relative to perfect competition, it seems likely that both price and profits will be higher under oligopoly. Moreover, oligopolistic industries will tend to spend more on advertising, product differentiation, and style changes than perfectly competitive industries.

8. In 1890, the Sherman Act was passed. It outlawed any contract, combination, or conspiracy in restraint of trade and made it illegal to monopolize or attempt to monopolize. In 1914, Congress passed the Clayton Act, and the Federal Trade Commission was created. A more recent antitrust development was the Celler-Kefauver Anti-Merger Act of 1950.

9. The real impact of the antitrust laws depends on the interpretation placed on these laws by the courts. In its early cases, the Supreme Court put forth and used the famous rule of reason: that only unreasonable combinations in restraint of trade, not all trusts, required conviction under the Sherman Act. The situation changed greatly in the 1940s when the Court decided that Alcoa, because it controlled practically all of the nation's aluminum output, was in violation of the antitrust laws.

10. Many observers seem to feel that the antitrust laws have not been as effective as they might—or should—have been, largely because they do not have sufficient public support. At the same time, many feel that the evidence, although incomplete and unclear, suggests that they have had a noteworthy effect on business behavior and markets. Two important recent cases involved AT&T and IBM.

CHAPTER 21

★ ★ ★ ★ ★ ★ ★ ★ ★

Pollution and the Environment

LEARNING OBJECTIVES

In this chapter, you should learn:

★ What external diseconomies are, and how they clarify the economic problem of pollution

★ The distinction between private costs and social costs

★ The relation of pollution to economic growth

★ The goals and methods of public policy toward environmental quality

According to many scientists and social observers, one of the costs of economic growth is environmental pollution. For many years, people in the United States paid relatively little attention to the environment and what they were doing to it. But this attitude changed markedly in the last twenty years. The public became genuinely concerned about environmental problems. However, in the effort to clean up the environment, choices are not always clear, nor solutions easy. In particular, the energy crisis of the 1970s brought home the fact that a cleaner environment is not costless. For example, many measures that would reduce pollution would increase the demand for energy.

OUR ENVIRONMENTAL PROBLEMS

Water Pollution

To see what we mean by environmental pollution, let's begin with one of

the most important parts of man's environment: our water supplies. A broad range of human activities results in the discharge of large amounts of pollutants into streams, lakes, and the sea. Chemical wastes are released by industrial plants and mines, as well as by farms and homes when fertilizers, pesticides, and detergents run off into waterways. Oil is discharged into the waters by tankers, sewage systems, oil wells, and other sources. Organic compounds enter waterways from industrial plants and farms, as well as from municipal sewage plants; and animal wastes, as well as human wastes, contribute substantially to pollution.

Obviously, we cannot continue to increase the rate at which we dump wastes into our streams, rivers, and oceans. A river, like everything else, can bear only so much. The people of Cleveland know this well. In 1969, the Cuyahoga River, which flows through Cleveland, literally caught fire, so great was its concentration of industrial and other wastes. Of course, the Cuyahoga is an extreme case, but many of our rivers, including the Hudson and the Ohio, are badly polluted. Water pollution is a nuisance and perhaps a threat.

Air Pollution

If clean water is vital to man's survival, so too is clean air. Yet the battle being waged against air pollution in most of our major cities has not been won. Particles of various kinds are spewed into the air by factories that utilize combustion processes, grind materials, or produce dust. Motor vehicles release lead compounds from gasoline and rubber particles worn from tires, helping to create that unheavenly condition known as smog. Citizens of Los Angeles are particularly familiar with smog, but few major cities have escaped at least periodic air pollution. No precise measures have been developed to gauge the effects of air pollution on public health and enjoyment, but some rough estimates suggest that perhaps 25 percent of all deaths from respiratory disease could be avoided by a 50 percent reduction in air pollution.

One of the most important contributors to air pollution is the combustion of fossil fuels, particularly coal and oil products: by-products of combustion make up about 85 percent of the total amount of air pollutants in the United States. Most of these pollutants result from impure fuels or inefficient burning. Among the more serious pollutants are sulphur dioxide, carbon monoxide, and various oxides of nitrogen. At present, the automobile is the principal source of air pollution in the United States. According to some estimates, human activities pump into the air over 200 million tons of waste each year, and automobiles can be credited with the dubious honor of contributing about 40 percent of this figure.

THE IMPORTANT ROLE OF EXTERNAL DISECONOMIES

The reason why our economic system has tolerated pollution of the environment lies largely in the concept of external diseconomies. An *external diseconomy* occurs when one person's (or firm's) use of a resource damages other people who cannot obtain proper compensation. When this occurs, a market economy is unlikely to function properly. The price system is based on the supposition that the full cost of using each resource is borne by the person or firm that uses it. If this is not the case and if the user bears only part of the full costs, then the resource is not likely to be directed by the price system into the socially optimal use.

To understand why, we might begin by reviewing briefly how resources are allocated in a market economy. Resources are used in their socially most valuable way because they are allocated to the people and firms who find it worthwhile to bid most for them, assuming that prices reflect true social costs. Under these circumstances, a firm that maximizes its profits will produce the socially desirable output and use the socially desirable amounts of labor, capital, and other resources. Under these circumstances, there is no problem.

Private Cost Does Not Equal Social Cost

Suppose, however, that because of the presence of external diseconomies people and firms do not pay the true social costs for resources. For example, suppose that some firms or people can use water and air for nothing, but that other firms or people incur costs as a consequence of this prior use. In this case, the *private costs* of using air and water differ from the *social costs: the price paid by the user of water and air is less than the true cost to society.* In a case like this, users of water and air are guided in their decisions by the private cost of water and air: by the prices they pay. Since they pay less than the true social costs, water and air are artificially cheap to them, so that they will use too much of these resources, from society's point of view.

Note that the divergence between private and social cost occurs if, and only if, the use of water or air by one firm or person imposes costs on other firms or persons. Thus, if a paper mill uses water and then treats it to restore its quality, there is no divergence between private and social cost. But when the same mill dumps harmful wastes into streams and rivers (the cheap way to get rid of its by-products), the towns downstream that use the water must incur costs to restore its quality. The same is true of air pollution. If an electric power plant uses the atmosphere as a cheap and convenient place to dispose of wastes, people living and working nearby may incur costs as a result, since the incidence of respiratory and other diseases may increase. In such cases, there may be a divergence between private and social cost.

We said above that pollution-causing activities that result in external diseconomies represent a malfunctioning of the market system. At this point, the nature of this malfunctioning should be clear. *Firms and people dump too much waste material into the water and the atmosphere. The price system does not provide the proper signals because the polluters are induced to use our streams and atmosphere in this socially undesirable*

*way by the artificially low price of disposing of wastes in this manner.
Moreover, because the polluters do not pay the true cost of waste disposal,
their products are artificially cheap, so that too much of them is produced.*

ECONOMIC GROWTH AND ENVIRONMENTAL POLLUTION

According to many authorities, economic growth—defined as increases in
total economic output per capita—has been associated with increases in
the level of environmental pollution. This is not very surprising, since
practically all the things that are produced must eventually be thrown
away in one form or another. Thus, as output per capita goes up, the level
of pollution is likely to go up as well. For example, as we grow more
affluent and increase the number of automobiles per capita, we also increase the amount of such air pollutants as nitrogen oxide and tetraethyl
lead, both of which are emitted by automobiles.

But it is important to recognize that *pollution is not tied inextricably
to national output.* Although increases in national output in the past have
been associated with increases in pollution, there is no reason why this
correlation must continue unchanged in the future. We can produce
things that are heavy polluters of the environment—like electric power
and automobiles—or we can produce things that do not pollute the environment nearly so much—like pianos and bicycles.

In recent years, some people have suggested that we curtail our economic growth in order to reduce pollution. ***Zero economic growth*** is their
goal. Very few economists seem to favor such a policy. Opponents of zero
economic growth point out that more productive capacity would help
produce the equipment required to reduce pollution. As we shall see, this
equipment will not be cheap. Moreover, with proper public policies, we
should be able to increase output without increasing pollution, if this is
what our people want. In addition, as pointed out by the economist Walter
Heller of the University of Minnesota:

> Short of a believable threat of extinction, it is hard to believe that the public
> would accept the tight controls, lowered material living standards, and large
> income transfers required to create and manage a (no-growth) state. Whether
> the necessary shifts could be accomplished without vast unemployment and
> economic dislocation is another question. It may be that the shift to a no-growth
> state would throw the fragile ecology of our economic system so out of kilter as
> to threaten its breakdown. Like it or not, economic growth seems destined to
> continue.[1]

Some people have also argued that technological change is the real villain
responsible for pollution, and that the rate of technological change should

[1]W. Heller, "Economic Growth and Ecology—An Economist's View," *Monthly Labor Review,* November 1971.

☆ ☆ ☆ ☆ ☆ ☆ ☆ ☆ ☆ ☆ ☆ ☆ ☆

CASE STUDY 21.1 RESERVE MINING: THE PRICE OF CLEANER WATER

Shortly after World War II, some far-sighted entrepreneurs decided there was money to be made in a rock called taconite, found in abundance beside the famous Mesabi iron range in Minnesota. Taconite contains iron—not a lot of iron, but enough to make a profit if you know how to crush it into sand-sized particles and separate the grains of iron from the rest of the rock. And that's what the Reserve Mining Company set out to do in the early 1950s. Since the refining process requires vast amounts of

*Taconite tailings
flowing from the
Reserve Mining
Company*

water, Reserve decided to mine the rock near Babbit, Minnesota, and transport it on their own railway to a processing plant 40 miles away, on the shores of the largest fresh-water lake in the Americas, Lake Superior. The costs of the operation are the same as for most industries—rents, wages, capital costs, debt service—but in Reserve's case, there is a hidden cost as well.

For every ton of iron pellets Reserve manufactures, it also produces two tons of waste, taconite tailings, and for fifteen years, Reserve was able to dump these tailings into Lake Superior at no cost to itself. Reserve's original idea was that the tailings could be dumped into a deep trough in the lake, and that they would settle to a depth of 400 feet or more where they couldn't harm anybody or do any damage to the lake. But in fact no one really knew what was happening to those tailings or whether they posed any real hazard to the lake or to humans living around it. It was only a matter of time before Reserve's dumping practices came under fire. Environmentalists charged that Reserve was ruining Lake Superior. Reserve denied the charges but by late 1969 found itself involved in a court battle that would take seven years to resolve. One of the most hotly debated issues in the case was the discovery of asbestos-like fibers in the water supply of Duluth, Minnesota.

The court battle was resolved in 1977. Reserve was granted the necessary permits to begin construction of a new dumping facility. The cost of this new facility, by Reserve's calculations, was some $387 million. The costs of the new dumping site were absorbed in a number of ways: tax breaks, lower profits, higher prices. Today, there's little doubt that Lake Superior is a cleaner lake than it was ten years ago. Scientific analysis indicates that the asbestos levels have dropped by 90 percent.

N.B.

☆ ☆ ☆ ☆ ☆ ☆ ☆ ☆ ☆ ☆ ☆ ☆ ☆

be slowed. Certainly, technological change has made people more inter-dependent, and has brought about more and stronger external diseconomies. Technological change also results in ecological changes, some of which are harmful. For example, detergents containing phosphate have induced water pollution by causing heavy overgrowths of algae.

But technological change is also a potential hero in the fight against pollution, because the creation of new technology is an important way to reduce the harmful side effects of existing techniques—assuming, of course, that we decide to use our scientists and engineers to this end. Contrary to some people's views, *pollution is not the product of some mindless march of technology, but of human action and inaction.* There is no sense in blaming technology, when pollution is due basically to economic, social, and political choices and institutions.

Finally, it is frequently suggested that as our population increases we must expect more pollution. Many who advocate a policy of *zero population growth* advance the argument that it would help reduce the level of pollution. The available evidence indicates some relationship between a nation's population and its pollution levels. But there are important differences in the amount of pollution generated by people in various countries. The average American is responsible for much more pollution than the average citizen of most other countries, because the average American is a much bigger user of electric power, detergents, pesticides, and other such products. It has been estimated that the United States, with less than one-tenth of the world's population, produces about one-third of the wastes discharged into the air and water. Much more than economics is involved in the discussion of the optimal level of population. Although it is only one of a number of important factors, a nation's population does affect the level of pollution; but as we shall see in subsequent sections, pollution can be re-duced considerably even if our population continues to grow.

PUBLIC POLICY TOWARD POLLUTION

Pollution is caused by defects in our institutions, not by malicious intent, greed, or corruption. In cases where waste disposal causes significant ex-ternal diseconomies, economists generally agree that government inter-vention may be justifiable. But how can the government intervene? Per-haps the simplest way is through *direct regulation:* the issuance of certain enforceable rules for waste disposal. For example, the government can prohibit the burning of trash in furnaces or incinerators, or the dumping of certain materials in the ocean; and it can make any person or firm that violates these restrictions subject to a fine, or perhaps even imprisonment. Also, the government can ban the use of chemicals like the harmful pesti-cide DDT, or require that all automobiles meet certain regulations for the emission of air pollutants. Further, the government can establish quality standards for air and water.

The government can also intervene by establishing effluent fees. An *effluent fee* is a fee a polluter must pay to the government for discharging waste. In other words, a price is imposed on the disposal of wastes into the environment; the more firms or individuals pollute, the more they must pay. The idea behind the imposition of effluent fees is that they can bring the private cost of waste disposal closer to the true social costs. Faced with a closer approximation to the true social costs of their activities, polluters will reduce the extent to which they pollute the environment. Needless to say, many practical difficulties are involved in carrying out this seemingly simple scheme, but many economists believe that this is the best way to deal with the pollution problem.

Still another way for the government to intervene is to establish *tax credits* for firms that introduce pollution-control equipment. There are, of course, many types of equipment that a plant can introduce to cut down on pollution—for example, "scrubbers" for catching poisonous gases, and electrostatic precipitators for decreasing dust and smoke. But such pollution-control equipment costs money, and firms are naturally reluctant to spend money on purposes where the private rate of return is so low. To reduce the burden, the government can allow firms to reduce their tax bill by a certain percentage of the amount they spend on pollution-control equipment. Tax incentives of this sort have been discussed widely in recent years, and some have been adopted.

POLLUTION-CONTROL PROGRAMS IN THE UNITED STATES

In recent decades, there has been considerable growth in government programs designed to control pollution. To take but one example, federal expenditures to reduce water pollution increased in the period from the mid-1950s to 1970 from about $1 million to $300 million annually. To curb water pollution, the federal government has for years operated a system of grants-in-aid to state, municipal, or regional agencies to help construct treatment plants; and grants are made for research on new treatment methods. In addition, the 1970 Water Quality Improvement Act authorized grants to demonstrate new methods and techniques and to establish programs to train people in water control management. (The federal government has also regulated the production and use of pesticides.) The states, as well as the federal government, have played an important role in water pollution control. They have set standards for allowable pollution levels, and many state governments have provided matching grants to help municipalities construct treatment plants.

In 1969, the Congress established a new agency, the Council on Environmental Quality, to oversee and plan the nation's pollution-control programs. Modeled to some extent on the Council of Economic Advisers, the Council on Environmental Quality, which has three members, is supposed to gather information on considerations and trends in the quality of the environment, review and evaluate the federal government's programs in this area, develop appropriate national policies, and conduct needed surveys and research on environmental quality. The tasks assigned to the council are obviously important ones.

In 1970, the federal government established another new agency, the Environmental Protection Agency (EPA). Working with state and local officials, this agency establishes standards for desirable air and water quality, and devises rules for attaining these goals. The 1970 Clean Air Amendments directed EPA to establish minimum ambient standards for air quality, and it set limits on the emission of carbon monoxide, hydrocarbons, and nitrous oxides from automobiles. But after a number of clashes between EPA and the auto makers, the EPA relaxed the deadlines by which these limits were supposed to be met. In 1972, amendments to the Water Pollution Act authorized EPA to set up effluent standards for both privately and publicly owned plants. A stated goal of the amendments was to eliminate the discharge of pollutants into water by 1985, but, for reasons discussed in the next section, this goal was unrealistically stringent. In general, recent legislation has emphasized direct regulation, although there has been some study of the use of effluent fees. For example, the government has considered imposing a fee on the emission of sulphur oxide into the air.

Some people believe that public policy is moving too rapidly in this area; others believe that it is moving too slowly. It is not easy to determine how fast or how far we should go in attempting to reduce pollution. Those who will bear the costs of reducing pollution have an understandable tendency to emphasize (and perhaps inflate) the costs and discount the benefits of such projects. Those who are particularly interested in enjoying nature and outdoor recreation (like the Sierra Club) are understandably inclined to emphasize (and perhaps inflate) the benefits and discount the costs of such projects. Politics inevitably plays a major role in the outcome of such cases. The citizens of the United States must indicate, through the ballot box as well as the marketplace, how much they are willing to pay to reduce pollution.

HOW CLEAN SHOULD THE ENVIRONMENT BE?

One of the most fundamental questions about pollution control is: How clean do we want the air, water, and other parts of our environment to be? At first glance, it may seem that we should restore and maintain a pristine pure environment, but this is not a very sensible goal, since the costs of achieving it would be enormous. The Environmental Protection Agency has estimated that it would cost about $60 billion to remove 85 to 90 percent of water pollutants from industrial and municipal sources. This is hardly a trivial amount, but it is far less than the cost of achieving zero discharge of pollutants, which would be about $320 billion—a truly staggering sum.

Fortunately, however, there is no reason to aim at so stringent a goal. *It seems obvious that, as pollution increases, various costs to society increase as well.* Some of these costs were described at the beginning of this chapter. For example, we pointed out that increases in air pollution result in increased deaths, and increases in water pollution reduce the recreational value of rivers and streams. Suppose that we could get accurate data on the cost to society of various levels of pollution. Of course, it is extremely difficult to get such data, but if we could, we could determine the relationship between the amount of these costs and the level of pollution. It would look like the hypothetical curve in Figure 21.1. The greater the level of pollution, the higher these costs will be.

Figure 21.1
Costs to Society
of Pollution
The costs to society
of pollution increase
with the level of
pollution.

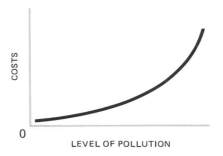

But these costs are not the only ones that must be considered. *We must also take into account the costs of controlling pollution.* In other words, we must look at the costs to society of maintaining a certain level of environmental quality. These costs are not trivial, as we saw at the beginning of this section. To maintain a very low level of pollution, it is necessary to invest heavily in pollution-control equipment and to make other economic sacrifices.[2] If we could get accurate data on the cost to society of controlling pollution, we could find the relationship between the amount of these costs and the level of pollution. It would look like the hypothetical curve in Figure 21.2; the lower the level of pollution, the higher these costs will be.

Figure 21.2
Costs to Society
of Pollution
Control
The more pollution
is reduced, the
higher are the costs
to society of
pollution control.

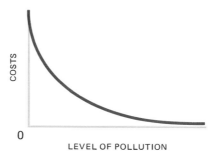

[2]It is important to recognize that the costs of pollution control extend far beyond the construction of more and better water treatment plants, or the more extensive control of gas emission, or other such steps. A serious pollution-control program can put firms out of business, put people out of work, and bring economic trouble to entire communities. Further, a pollution-control system can result in a redistribution of income. For example, automobiles, electric power, and other goods and services involving considerable pollution are likely to increase in price relative to other goods and services involving little pollution. To the extent that polluting goods and services play a bigger role in the budgets of the poor than of the rich, pollution controls hurt the poor and help the rich.

CASE STUDY 21.2 LEADED GAS AND COST-BENEFIT ANALYSIS

In the 1930s, oil refiners discovered that the addition of a very small amount of lead (one or two grams per gallon) increased a gasoline's performance. As automobile engines got larger and more sophisticated, the use of lead increased for yet another reason: its unique lubricating properties, which reduced friction inside the engine and increased the lifetime of valves and pistons. Then, as the number of cars increased, so did the amount of lead polluting the air. Lead, above certain levels, was known to be a poison, causing damage to the kidney, the liver, the reproductive system, and brain function. Studies have shown that children living in high-traffic areas have more blood-lead than many believe to be safe. Clean-air legislation in the 1970s ordered a change: new cars had to be designed to run cleaner. This reduction in airborne lead had dramatic benefits.

Students demonstrating for clean-air legislation

The next question was: How much benefit could be derived from reducing the levels of lead even further? And it was that question that the Environmental Protection Agency was assigned to explore. In accordance with Executive Order 12–291, EPA did a comprehensive cost-benefit analysis asking how much it would cost to remove lead from gasoline entirely, as opposed to a ''very low lead'' option that would lower lead in gasoline by about 90 percent. EPA determined that it was more cost-effective to go with the very low lead (VLL) versus the no lead (NL) option. The costs of VLL were estimated at $503 million. These costs would be borne by the manufacturing process, primarily new refining equipment and changes in gasoline engines. The benefits—largely due to better health for people and longer lifetimes for spark plugs, mufflers, and catalytic converters—were estimated at about $800 million. The costs of the NL option were estimated at $691 million, whereas the benefits were estimated to be only marginally greater than the VLL option. In March 1985, the EPA revised its rules and reduced the limit of 1.1 grams of lead per gallon to 0.5 gram per gallon by July 1, 1985, and to 0.1 by 1986.

N.B.

☆ ☆ ☆ ☆ ☆ ☆ ☆ ☆ ☆ ☆ ☆ ☆ ☆

A Goal of Zero Pollution?

At this point, it should be obvious why we should not try to achieve a zero level of pollution. *The sensible goal for our society is to minimize the sum of the costs of pollution and the costs of controlling pollution.* In other words, we should construct a graph, as shown in Figure 21.3, to indicate the relationship between the sum of these two types of costs and the level of pollution. Then we should choose the level of pollution at which the sum of these two types of costs is a minimum. Thus in Figure 21.3, we should aim for a pollution level of *A*. There is no point in trying for a lower level; such a reduction would cost more than it would be worth. For example, the cost of achieving a zero pollution level would be much more than it would be worth. Only when the pollution level exceeds *A* is the extra cost to society of the additional pollution greater than the cost of preventing it. For example, the cost of allowing pollution to increase from *A* to *B* is much greater than the cost of prevention.

Figure 21.3
Determining Optimal Level of Pollution
The optimal level of pollution is at point *A*, since this is where the total costs are a minimum. Below point *A*, the cost to society of more pollution is less than the cost of preventing it. Above point *A*, the cost to society of more pollution is greater than the cost of preventing it.

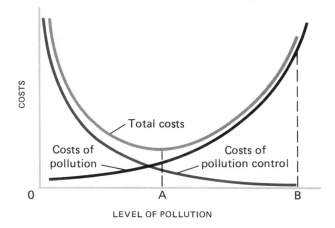

It is easy to draw hypothetical curves, but not so easy actually to measure these curves. Unfortunately, no one has a very clear idea of what the curves in Figure 21.3 really look like—although we can be sure that their general shapes are like those shown here. Thus no one really knows just how clean we should try to make the environment. Under these circumstances, expert opinion differs on the nature and extent of the programs that should be carried out. Moreover, as pointed out in a previous section, political considerations and pressures enter in. But one thing is certain: we will continue to live with some pollution, and that, for the reasons just given, will be the rational thing to do.

Recent Directions of Environmental Policy

In the late 1970s and early 1980s, policy makers became increasingly concerned that regulatory agencies like EPA had been paying too little attention to the costs involved in reducing pollution. For example, a government study found that a relaxation of EPA's 1977 standard for water-pollution control in the steel industry *with no change in its more stringent 1983 standard* would allow the industry savings in capital costs of $200 million. As President Carter's Council of Economic Advisers pointed out, "In making regulatory decisions on the speed of attaining standards, we should explicitly make a qualitative judgment about whether the gains from earlier attainment are worth the costs."

Going a step further, some experts, like Lester Lave and Gilbert Omenn of the Brookings Institution, have concluded from their studies that the Clean Air Act has not been very effective. In their view, "the application of pollution controls to existing plants and older cars has been limited, and costs have been excessive, largely because Congress has failed to confront [many of] the difficult issues."

During the 1980s, environmentalists and others charged that the Reagan administration was dismantling, or at least emasculating, EPA. Anne Gorsuch resigned in 1983 as head of EPA, as criticism of the agency continued to build. James Watt, former Secretary of the Interior, also angered environmentalists. Administration officials responded to such criticism by claiming that they were trying to promote and restore balance between environmental objectives and economic growth.

SUMMARY

1. One of the major social issues of the 1980s is environmental pollution. To a considerable extent, environmental pollution is an economic problem. Waste disposal and other pollution-causing activities result in external diseconomies.

2. Firms and individuals that pollute the water and air (and other facets of the environment) often pay less than the true social costs of disposing of their wastes in this way. Part of the true social cost is borne by other firms and individuals, who must pay to clean up the water or air or who must live with the consequences.

3. Because of the divergence of private from social costs, the market system does not result in an optimal allocation of resources. Firms and individuals create too much waste and dispose of it in excessively harmful ways. Because the polluters do not pay the full cost of waste disposal, their products are artificially cheap, with the result that they produce too much of these products.

4. The government can intervene in several ways to help remedy the breakdown of the market system in this area. One way is to issue regulations for waste disposal and other activities influencing the environment. Another is to establish effluent fees, charges a polluter must pay to the government for discharging wastes. In recent decades, there has been considerable growth in government programs designed to control pollution.

5. It is extremely difficult to determine how clean the environment should be. The sensible goal for society is to permit the level of pollution that minimizes the sum of the costs of pollution and the costs of controlling pollution; but no one has a very clear idea of what these costs are, and to a large extent the choices must be made through the political process.

PART 5

☆☆☆☆☆☆☆☆☆☆☆☆☆☆

The Distribution
of Income

CHAPTER 22

★ ★ ★ ★ ★ ★ ★ ★

The Supply and Demand for Labor

LEARNING OBJECTIVES

In this chapter, you should learn:

★ How the firm's demand curve for labor can be derived

★ The nature of the market demand curve for labor

★ How the equilibrium wage and quantity of labor are determined

★ The role of labor unions in the American economy

★ How unions affect the wages earned by workers

Everyone has a healthy—indeed, sometimes an unhealthy—interest in income. Organizations as holy as the church and as unholy as the Mob are interested in this subject. Surely we all need to look carefully at the social mechanisms underlying the distribution of income in our society.

Economists frequently classify inputs into three categories: labor, capital, and land. The disadvantage of this simple classification is that each category contains an enormous variety of inputs. Consider the services of labor, which include the work of a football star like Eric Dickerson, a salesman like Willy Loman, and a knight like Don Quixote. But this classification does have the important advantage of distinguishing between different types of inputs. In this chapter, we are concerned with the determinants of the price of labor. The next chapter will deal with the determinants of the prices of capital and land, as well as profits.

THE LABOR FORCE AND THE PRICE OF LABOR

At the outset it is important to note that, to the economist, labor includes a great deal more than the organized labor that belongs to trade unions. The secretary who works at General Motors, the young account executive at Merrill Lynch, the auto mechanic at your local garage, the professor who teaches molecular biology, all put forth labor. Table 22.1 shows the occupational distribution of the labor force in the United States. You can see that almost two-thirds of the people employed are white-collar workers (such as salesmen, doctors, secretaries, or managers) and service workers (such as waiters, bartenders, or cooks), while only about one-third are blue-collar workers (such as carpenters, mine workers, or foremen) and farm workers.

**Table 22.1
Occupational
Composition of the
Employed Labor
Force, United
States,
August 1984[a]**

		Percent of employed labor force
Managerial and professional workers		22.9
Executive	11.0	
Professional	11.9	
Technical, sales, and administrative support workers		30.9
Technicians	3.0	
Sales	12.1	
Administrative support	15.8	
Service workers		13.4
Private household	0.9	
Protective service	1.6	
Other service	10.8	
Precision production, craft, repair workers		12.8
Operators, fabricators, and laborers		16.1
Machine operators	7.6	
Transportation and material moving	4.2	
Handlers and laborers	4.3	
Farming, forestry, and fishing		3.9
Total		100.0

[a]Because of rounding errors, figures may not sum to total.
Source: Bureau of Labor Statistics.

It is also worthwhile to preface our discussion with some data concerning how much people actually get paid. As shown in Table 22.2, average weekly earnings vary considerably from one industry to another. For example, in 1984, workers in manufacturing averaged about $373 a week, while construction workers averaged $455 a week, and workers in retail trade averaged $177 a week. Also, average weekly earnings vary considerably from one period to another. Table 22.2 shows that average weekly earnings in manufacturing in 1965 were only $108, as contrasted with $373 in 1984. In subsequent sections, we will investigate the reasons for these differences in wages, both among industries and over periods of time.

Year	Manufacturing	Construction	Retail trade
1955	76	91	49
1960	90	113	58
1965	108	138	67
1970	134	195	82
1975	190	265	108
1980	289	368	147
1984	373	455	177

Table 22.2
Average Weekly
Earnings, Selected
Industries, 1955–84
(Dollars)

Source: U.S. Department of Labor.

More broadly, we will be concerned in subsequent sections with the price of labor, which includes a great many forms of remuneration other than what we commonly regard as wages. As noted above, economists include as labor the services performed by professional people (such as lawyers, doctors, and professors) and self-employed businessmen (such as electricians, mechanics, and barbers). Thus the amount such people receive per unit of time is included here as a particular sort of price of labor, even though these amounts are often called fees or salaries rather than wages.

Finally, it is important to distinguish between *money* wages and *real* wages. Whereas the money wage is the amount of money received per unit of time, the real wage is the amount of real goods and services that can be bought with the money wage. The real wage depends on the price level for goods and services as well as on the magnitude of the money wage. In recent years, the inflation we have experienced has meant that real wages have increased less than money wages; thus the increases in earnings in Table 22.2 exaggerate the increase in real wages. In subsequent sections, since we will assume that product prices are held constant, our discussion will be in terms of real wages.

THE EQUILIBRIUM WAGE AND EMPLOYMENT UNDER PERFECT COMPETITION

The Firm's Demand Curve for Labor

Let's begin by discussing the determinants of the price of labor under perfect competition. We assume that firms take the prices of their products, as well as the prices of all inputs, as given; and we assume that owners of inputs take input prices as given. Under these circumstances, what determines how much labor an individual firm will hire (at a specified wage rate)? Once we answer this question, we can derive a firm's demand curve for labor. A *firm's demand curve for labor* is the relationship between the price of labor and the amount of labor utilized by the firm. That is, it shows, for each price, the amount of labor that the firm will use.

The Profit-Maximizing Quantity of Labor

Let's assume that we know the firm's production function, and that labor is the only variable input. Given the production function, we can determine the marginal product of labor when various quantities are used. (Recall that the marginal product of labor is the additional output resulting from an extra unit of labor.) The results of such a calculation are as shown in Table 22.3. If the price of the firm's product is $10, let's determine the value to the firm of each additional worker it hires per day.[1] According to Table 22.3, the firm achieves a daily output of 7 units when it hires the first worker; and since each unit is worth $10, this brings the firm's daily revenues up to $70. By hiring the second worker, the firm increases its daily output by 6 units; and since each unit is worth $10, the resulting increase in the firm's daily revenues is $60. Similarly, the increase in the firm's daily revenues from hiring the third worker is $50, the increase from hiring the fourth worker is $40, and so on.

Table 22.3
The Firm's Demand for Labor under Perfect Competition

Number of workers per day	Total output per day	Marginal product of labor	Value of marginal product (dollars)
0	0		
		7	70
1	7		
		6	60
2	13		
		5	50
3	18		
		4	40
4	22		
		3	30
5	25		

How many workers should the firm hire per day if it wants to maximize profit? It should hire more workers as long as the extra workers result in at least as great an addition to revenues as they do to costs. If the price of a worker is $50 per day, it is profitable for the firm to hire the first worker, since this adds $70 to the firm's daily revenues but only $50 to its daily costs. Also, it is profitable to hire the second worker, since this adds $60 to the firm's daily revenues but only $50 to its daily costs. The addition of the third worker does not reduce the firm's profits. But beyond 3 workers per day, it does not pay the firm to hire more labor. (The addition of a fourth worker adds $50 to the firm's daily costs but only $40 to its daily revenues.)

[1]For simplicity, we assume that the number of workers that the firm hires per day must be an integer, not a fraction. This assumption is innocuous and can easily be relaxed.

The Value of the Marginal Product of Labor

Thus the optimal number of workers per day for this firm is 3. Table 22.3 shows that this is the number of workers at which the value of the marginal product of labor is equal to the price of labor. What is the *value of the marginal product of labor?* It is the marginal product of labor multiplied by the product's price. In Table 22.3, the value of the marginal product of labor is $70 when between 0 and 1 workers are used per day. Why? Because the marginal product of labor is 7 units of output, and the price of a unit of output is $10. Thus this product, 7 times $10, equals $70.

To maximize profit, the value of the marginal product of labor must be set equal to the price of labor, because if the value of the marginal product is greater than labor's price, the firm can increase its profit by increasing the quantity used of labor; while if the value of the marginal product is less than labor's price, the firm can increase its profit by reducing the quantity used of labor. Thus *profits must be at a maximum when the value of the marginal product is equal to the price of labor.*

Given these results, it is a simple matter to derive the firm's demand curve for labor. Specifically, its demand curve must be the value-of-marginal-product schedule in the last column of Table 22.3. If the daily wage of a worker is between $51 and $60, the firm will demand 2 workers per day; if the daily wage of a worker is between $41 and $50, the firm will demand 3 workers per day; and so forth. Thus *the firm's demand curve for labor is its value-of-marginal-product curve,* which shows the value of labor's marginal product at each quantity of labor used. This curve is shown in Figure 22.1.[2]

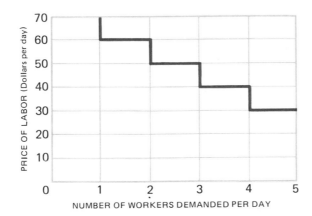

**Figure 22.1
The Firm's Demand Curve for Labor under Perfect Competition**
The firm's demand curve for labor is the firm's value-of-marginal-product curve, which shows the value of labor's marginal product at each quantity of labor used. The data for this figure come from Table 22.3.

[2]Strictly speaking, the firm's demand curve is the same as the curve showing the value of the input's marginal product only if this input is the only variable input. For a discussion of the more general case, see E. Mansfield, *Microeconomics: Theory and Applications,* 5th ed., New York: Norton, 1985, Chap. 12.

THE MARKET DEMAND CURVE FOR LABOR

In previous sections, we were concerned with the demand curve of a single firm for labor. But many firms, not just one, are part of the labor market, and the price of labor depends on the demands of all of these firms. The situation is analogous to the price of a product, which depends on the demands of all consumers. *The market demand curve for labor shows the relationship between the price of labor and the total amount of labor demanded in the market. That is, it shows, for each price, the amount of labor that will be demanded in the entire market.* The market demand curve for labor, like any other input, is quite analogous to the market demand curve for a consumer good, which we discussed in detail in Chapter 17.

But there is at least one important difference. *The demand for labor and other inputs is a* **derived demand,** *since inputs are demanded to produce other things, not as an end in themselves.* This fact helps to explain why the price elasticity of demand is higher for some inputs than for others. In particular, the higher the price elasticity of demand for the product the input helps produce, the higher the price elasticity of demand for the input. (In addition, the price elasticity of demand for an input is likely to be greater in the long run than in the short run, and greater if other inputs can readily be substituted for the input in question.)

THE MARKET SUPPLY CURVE FOR LABOR

We have already seen that a product's price depends on its market supply curve as well as its market demand curve. This is equally true for labor. *The* **market supply curve for labor** *is the relationship between the price of labor and the total amount of labor supplied in the market.* When individuals supply labor, they are supplying something they themselves can use, since the time that they do not work can be used for leisure activities. Because of this fact, the market supply curve for labor, unlike the supply curve for inputs supplied by business firms, may be **backward bending,** particularly for the economy as a whole. That is, *beyond some point, increases in price may result in smaller amounts of labor being supplied.*

An example of a backward-bending supply curve is provided in Figure 22.2. What factors account for a curve like this? Basically, the reason is that, as the price of labor increases, individuals supplying the labor become richer. And when they become richer, they want to increase their amount of leisure time, which means that they want to work less. Even though the amount of money per hour they give up by not working is greater than when the price of labor was lower, they nonetheless choose to increase their leisure time. This sort of tendency has shown up quite

PRICE OF LABOR

0   QUANTITY OF LABOR SUPPLIED

Figure 22.2
Backward-Bending Supply Curve for Labor
Beyond some point, increases in the price of labor may result in smaller amounts of labor being supplied. The reason for a supply curve of this sort is that, as the price of labor increases, the individual supplying the labor becomes richer and wants to increase his amount of leisure time.

clearly in the last century. As wage rates have increased and living standards have risen, the average work week has tended to decline.

Note that there is no contradiction between the assumption that the supply curve of labor or other inputs *to an individual firm* is horizontal under perfect competition and the fact that the *market* supply curve for the input may not be horizontal. For example, unskilled labor may be available to any firm in a particular area at a given wage rate in as great an amount as it could possibly use. But the total amount of unskilled labor supplied in this area may increase relatively little with increases in the wage rate. The situation is similar to the sale of products. As we saw in Chapter 18, any firm under perfect competition believes that it can sell all it wants at the existing price. Yet the total amount of the product sold in the entire market can ordinarily be increased only by lowering the price.

EQUILIBRIUM PRICE AND QUANTITY OF LABOR

Labor's price (or wage rate) is determined under perfect competition in essentially the same way that a product's price is determined: by supply and demand.

The price of labor will tend toward equilibrium at the level where the quantity of labor demanded equals the quantity of labor supplied. Thus, in Figure 22.3, the equilibrium price of labor is *OP*. If the price were higher than *OP*, the quantity supplied would exceed the quantity demanded and there would be downward pressure on the price. If the price were lower than *OP*, the quantity supplied would fall short of the quantity demanded and there would be upward pressure on the price. By the same token, *the equilibrium amount of labor utilized is also given by the intersection of the market supply and demand curves.* In Figure 22.3, *OQ* units of labor will be utilized in equilibrium in the entire market.

Graphs such as Figure 22.3 are useful, but it is important to look behind

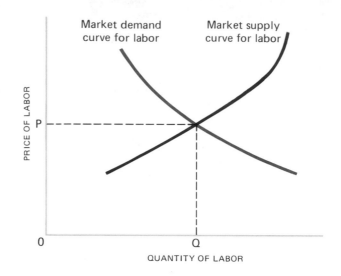

Figure 22.3
Equilibrium Price and Quantity of Labor
The equilibrium price of labor is *OP*, and the equilibrium quantity of labor used is *OQ*.

the geometry and to recognize the factors that lie behind the demand and supply curves for labor. Consider the market for surgeons and that for unskilled labor. As shown in Figure 22.4, the demand curve for the services of surgeons is to the right of the demand curve for unskilled labor (particularly at high wage rates). Why is this so? Because an hour of a surgeon's services is worth more to people than an hour of an unskilled laborer's services. In this sense, surgeons are more productive than unskilled laborers. Also, as shown in Figure 22.4, the supply curve for the services of surgeons is far to the left of the supply curve for unskilled labor. Why is this so? Because very few people are licensed surgeons, whereas practically everyone can do unskilled labor. In other words, surgeons are much more scarce than unskilled laborers.

For these reasons, surgeons receive a much higher wage rate than do unskilled laborers. As shown in Figure 22.4, the equilibrium price of labor

Figure 22.4
The Labor Market for Surgeons and Unskilled Labor
The wage for surgeons is higher than for unskilled labor because the demand curve for surgeons is farther to the right and the supply curve for surgeons is farther to the left than the corresponding curves for unskilled labor.

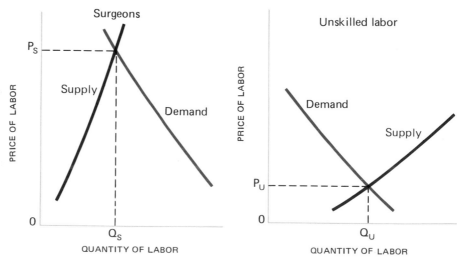

for surgeons is much higher than that for unskilled labor. If unskilled laborers could quickly and easily turn themselves into competent surgeons, this difference in wage rates would be eliminated by competition, since unskilled workers would find it profitable to become surgeons. But unskilled workers lack the training and often the ability to become surgeons. Thus surgeons and unskilled labor are examples of *noncompeting groups.* Wage differentials can be expected to persist among noncompeting groups because people cannot move from the low-paid to the high-paid jobs.

LABOR UNIONS

About 1 in 6 nonfarm workers in the United States belongs to a union, and the perfectly competitive model does not apply to these workers. There are about 200 national unions in the United States; the biggest are the Teamsters, the National Education Association, and the Food and Commercial Workers, each with 1.3 million members or more. Next come the United Auto Workers, the United Steel Workers, the Electrical Workers, the Machinists, the Carpenters, the State, County, and Municipal Employees, and the Service Employees, each with over 800,000 members.

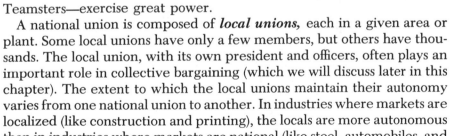

Logo of the United Auto Workers

The *national unions*[3] are of great importance in the American labor movement. The supreme governing body of the national union is the convention, which is held every year or two. The delegates to the convention have the authority to set policy for the union. However, considerable power is exercised by the national union's officers. Union presidents— men like Owen Bieber of the Auto Workers and Jackie Presser of the Teamsters—exercise great power.

A national union is composed of *local unions,* each in a given area or plant. Some local unions have only a few members, but others have thousands. The local union, with its own president and officers, often plays an important role in collective bargaining (which we will discuss later in this chapter). The extent to which the local unions maintain their autonomy varies from one national union to another. In industries where markets are localized (like construction and printing), the locals are more autonomous than in industries where markets are national (like steel, automobiles, and coal).

Finally, there is the AFL-CIO, a federation of national unions created

[3]Sometimes they are called international unions because some locals are outside the United States—for example, in Canada.

by the merger of the American Federation of Labor and the Congress of Industrial Organizations in 1955. The AFL-CIO does not include all national unions. The United Mine Workers refused to join the AFL-CIO, the Auto Workers left it in 1968, and the Teamsters were kicked out (because of corruption). The AFL-CIO is a very important spokesman for the American labor movement; but because the national unions in the AFL-CIO have given up relatively little of their power to the federation, its authority is limited.

THE AMERICAN LABOR MOVEMENT

Early History of American Labor Unions

To understand the nature and behavior of labor unions, let's look briefly at the history of the American labor movement. Unions arose because workers recognized that acting together gave them more bargaining power than acting separately. They frequently felt that they were at the mercy of their employers, and they formed fraternal societies and unions to promote economic and social benefits for the members. However, until the 1930s unions in the United States were not very strong, partly because of employers' efforts to break up unions, and partly because the courts held that the unions' attempts to increase wages and influence working conditions were conspiracies in restraint of trade.

During the early 1930s, the tide began to turn. To a great extent, this was because of government encouragement of unions, in which the first important step was the *Norris-La Guardia Act* of 1932. This act made it much more difficult for courts to issue injunctions (cease-and-desist orders, to prevent striking or picketing) against unions, and it made *yellow-dog contracts*— agreements in which workers promised their employers not to join a union—unenforceable in federal courts. The next important step occurred in 1935, when Congress passed the *Wagner Act*, which made it an unfair labor practice for employers to refuse to bargain collectively with unions representing a majority of their workers, or to interfere with their workers' right to organize. In addition, this act established the *National Labor Relations Board* to investigate unfair labor practices, to issue orders enforceable in federal courts, and to hold elections to determine which, if any, union would represent various groups of employees. The Wagner Act was a very important factor in encouraging the growth of labor unions in the United States—so important that it has often been called American labor's Magna Carta.

The 1930s were years of spectacular union growth. Aided by the prounion attitude of the Roosevelt administration, new legislation, and the energy of its leaders, total union membership rose from less than 3 million in 1933 to more than 10 million in 1941. World War II witnessed further growth in total union membership. Stimulated by the increase in total employment and the government's favorable attitude toward their growth, unions increased their membership from over 10 million in 1941 to almost 15 million—or about 36 percent of all nonfarm workers—in 1945. The government helped unions gain recognition in exchange for union cooperation in promoting war production. By the end of World War II, labor unions were conspicuous and powerful features of the economic landscape.

The Structure of the AFL-CIO

The AFL-CIO is organized along the lines indicated in Figure 22.5. The constitution of the AFL-CIO puts supreme governing power in the hands of a biennial convention. The national unions are represented at these conventions on the basis of their dues-paying membership. Between conventions, the AFL-CIO's business is directed by its president (Lane Kirkland in 1985) and secretary-treasurer, as well as by various committees and councils composed of representatives of various national unions or people elected at the convention. The AFL-CIO contains seven trade and industrial departments, such as building trades, food and beverage trades, maritime trades, and so forth. Also, as indicated by Figure 22.5, a few local unions are not affiliated with a national union, but are directly affiliated with the AFL-CIO.

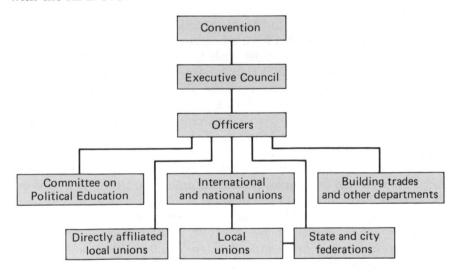

**Figure 22.5
Structure of
AFL-CIO**
The AFL-CIO is organized with the governing power in the hands of a biennial convention.

Internal Problems in Labor Unions

As unions have grown older and more secure and powerful, there has been more and more concern about the nature of their internal practices and leadership. After all, they are no longer the underdogs that they were 50 years ago. They are huge organizations with immense power. Both in this country and in Europe, observers have charged that unions are often far from democratic. Members are frequently apathetic, for there is less interest in union affairs now than in the early days when unions were fighting for survival; and the leadership of some unions has become entrenched and bureaucratic. Moreover, there are frequent charges that unions engage in racial and other forms of discrimination.

Another problem is *corruption within labor unions.* In the 1950s, a Senate committee (the McClellan Committee) conducted lengthy and revealing investigations that showed that the leaders of the Teamsters Union had misused union funds, had questionable relations with the underworld, and had "shamefully betrayed their own members." Other unions were also accused of corrupt practices. It is important, however, to avoid smearing the entire labor movement. Although racketeering and fraud unquestionably are problems, they tend to be localized in relatively few industries—particularly the building trades, trucking, longshoring, laundries, and hotels. Many responsible and honest leaders of the labor movement have tried hard to rid the labor movement of these unsavory practices.

Postwar Labor Legislation

After World War II, public sentiment turned somewhat against unions. Strikes and higher prices got under the skin of the consumer as well as the employer, and there began to be a lot of talk in Congress and elsewhere about the prewar Wagner Act having been too one-sided, giving too many advantages to labor in its contest with the employer. In 1947, despite bitter labor opposition, the *Taft-Hartley Act* was passed with the purpose of redressing the balance between labor and employers. The act established standards of conduct for unions as well as employers, defined unfair union practices, and stated that unions could be sued for acts of their agents. Also, the act outlawed the closed shop, which requires that firms hire only workers who are already union members, and stipulated that, unless the workers agree in writing, the **checkoff** is illegal. (The checkoff is a system in which the employer deducts union dues from each worker's pay and hands them over to the union.)

In addition, the act tried to increase protection against strikes in which the public's safety and health are involved. If the president decides that an actual or impending strike imperils the national health or safety, he can appoint a fact-finding committee to investigate the situation. After receiving the committee's report, he can tell the attorney general to obtain an injunction forbidding a strike for 80 days, during which the parties can continue to negotiate. A Federal Mediation Service was established to help the parties settle such negotiations. The act does not forbid a strike at the end of the 80 days, if no agreement has been reached.

In response to the evidence of union corruption presented by the McClellan Committee, Congress passed the *Landrum-Griffin Act* in 1959. This act attempts to protect the rights of individual union members from abuse by union leaders. It contains a "bill of rights" for labor, guaranteeing that each member can participate in union elections, that elections be held by secret ballot, and that other steps be taken to protect the rights of the members. It also requires unions to file financial reports, forbids payments (beyond wages) by employers to union representatives, and prohibits loans exceeding $2,000 by unions to union officials.

HOW UNIONS INCREASE WAGES

Unions wield considerable power, and economists must include them in their analysis if they want their models of the labor market to be accurate. Let's begin to see how this is done by supposing that a union wants to increase the wage rate paid its members. How can it accomplish this objective? In other words, how can it alter the market supply curve for labor, or the market demand curve for labor, so that the price of labor—its wage—will increase?

1. *The union may try to shift the supply curve of labor to the left.* It may shift the supply curve, as shown in Figure 22.6, with the result that the price of labor will increase from OP to OP_1. How can the union cause this shift in the supply curve? Craft unions have frequently forced employers to hire only union members, and then restricted union membership by high initiation fees, reduction in new membership, and other devices. In addition, unions have favored legislation to reduce immigration, shorten working hours, and limit the labor supply in other ways.

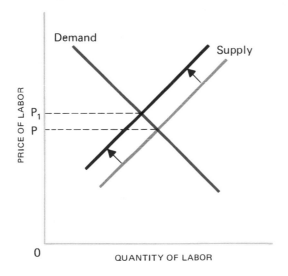

**Figure 22.6
Shift of Supply
Curve for Labor**
A union may shift
the supply curve to
the left by getting
employers to hire
only union members
and then restricting
union membership,
or by other
techniques.

2. *The union may try to get the employers to pay a higher wage, while allowing some of the supply of labor forthcoming at this higher wage to find no opportunity for work.* In Figure 22.7, the union may exert presure on the employers to raise the price of labor from OP to OP_1. At OP_1, not all of the available supply of labor can find jobs. The quantity of labor supplied is OQ_2, while the amount of labor demanded is OQ_1. The effect is the same as in Figure 22.6, but in this case the union does not limit the

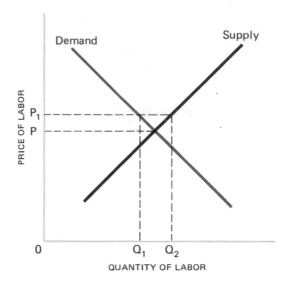
supply directly. It lets the higher wage reduce the opportunity for work. Strong industrial unions often behave in this fashion. Having organized practically all the relevant workers and controlling the labor supply, the union raises the wage to OP_1. This is a common and important case.

3. *The union may try to shift the demand curve for labor upward and to the right.* If it can bring about the shift described in Figure 22.8, the price of labor will increase from OP to OP_2. To cause this shift in the demand for labor, the union may resort to *featherbedding:* It may try to restrict output per worker in order to increase the amount of labor required to do a certain job. (To cite but one case, the railroad unions have insisted on much unnecessary labor.) Unions also try to shift the demand curve by helping the employers compete against other industries, or by encouraging Congress to pass legislation that protects the employers from foreign competition.

Figure 22.8
Shift in Demand Curve for Labor
A union may shift the demand curve for labor to the right by featherbedding or other devices, thus increasing the wage from *OP* to *OP*₂.

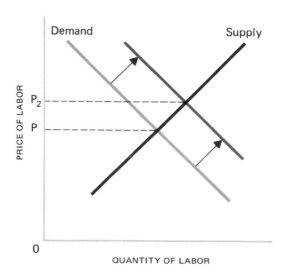

COLLECTIVE BARGAINING

Collective bargaining is the process of negotiation between the union and management over wages and working conditions. Representatives of the union and management meet periodically to work out an agreement or contract. Typically, each side asks at first for more than it expects to get, and compromises must be made to reach an agreement. The union representatives take the agreement to their members, who must vote to accept or reject it. If they reject it, they may vote to strike or to continue to negotiate.

Collective bargaining agreements vary greatly. Some pertain to only a single plant while others apply to an entire industry. However, an agreement generally contains the following elements. It specifies the extent and kind of recognition that management gives the union, the level of wage rates for particular jobs, the length of the work week, the rate of overtime pay, the extent to which seniority will determine which workers will be first to be laid off, the nature and extent of management's prerogatives, and how grievances between workers and the employer will be handled.

Historically, industries and firms have extended recognition to unions by accepting one of three arrangements: the closed shop, the union shop, or the open shop. In a *closed shop,* workers must be union members before they can be hired. This gives the union more power than if there is a *union shop,* in which the employer can hire nonunion workers who must then become union members in a certain length of time after being hired. In an *open shop,* the employer can hire union or nonunion labor, and nonunion workers need not, once employed, join the union. As we have seen, the closed shop was banned by the Taft-Hartley Act. The Taft-Hartley Act also says that the union shop is legal unless outlawed by state laws; and in about 20 states there are "right to work" laws that make the union shop illegal. Right-to-work laws are opposed by organized labor, which regards them as a threat to its security and effectiveness.

Basic Forces at Work

Collective bargaining is a power struggle. At each point in their negotiations, both the union and the employer must compare the costs (or benefits) of agreeing with the other party with the costs (or benefits) of continuing to disagree. The costs of disagreement are the costs of a strike, while the costs of agreement are the costs of settling on terms other than one's own. These costs are determined by basic market forces. For example, during periods when demand is great, employers are more likely to grant large wage increases because the costs of disagreement seem higher (a strike will prove more costly) than those of settlement. The outcome of the negotiations will depend on the relative strength of the parties. The strength of the employers depends on their ability to withstand a strike. The strength of the unions depends on their ability to keep out nonunion

CASE STUDY 22.1 THE CLOSING OF THE HERALD TRIBUNE

In 1965, New York City newspapers and their union employees were feeling the bite of computer technology. It took a linotype operator an hour to set 200 lines of newspaper type. A new machine called the Teletypesetter could do the same work in as little as half an hour, and computerized typesetting equipment on the drawing board would be able to do it in 17 seconds. The new technology would increase productivity and save labor—and thus displace printers.

The International Typographical Union's Local Six ("Big Six") had the bargaining power to keep the new technology out or to let it in. The union did not seek to stand in the way of progress; although automated and computerized typesetting machinery could cost the jobs of union printers, higher wages without the increased productivity of automation could force less profitable papers to merge or even close—and that would cost jobs too. Big Six wanted only to ensure that the new equipment would be operated by union members, so that the technology would not be used for union busting, and to protect its members and apprentices.

Six months of complicated maneuvering resulted in a contract without a strike. In addition to a pay raise, Big Six got what was in effect a veto over the introduction of automated equipment. The contract allowed the papers to use punch tape printing equipment, but set up a fund equal to 100 percent of the direct labor savings from the introduction of the new technology—a fund under the union's control and to be used to protect printers put out of work by the new equipment. The union had opened the door to automation, but it took most of what was saved and required the same wages and benefits from big, profitable papers as from unprofitable ones.

In less than a year, the new contract and the competitive New York newspaper business claimed their first victims. Profitable papers like the *New York Times* and the *News* could afford to pay the price because they would save so much from automating. But three unprofitable papers, the *Herald Tribune,* the *Journal American,* and the *World Telegram,* merged into a new corporation, the World Journal Tribune Inc. Almost half the three papers' 4,700 employees lost their jobs, and about 400 Big Six printers were laid off.

April 25, 1966, was to have seen the first edition of the new *Herald Tribune,* but was instead the first day of another strike. But this strike was different. When Big Six had struck some papers in 1963, the others had shut down in solidarity. This time, the *Times,* the *News,* and the *Post* were on the stands as usual. And while Big Six had signed a contract with the World Journal Tribune by the end of May, the other unions had not, and the printers followed union tradition and refused to cross the picket lines. For 113 days the *Herald Tribune* presses were silent, and on August 16, John Hay Whitney, publisher of the *Herald Tribune,* announced its closing.

N.B.

workers and to enlist the support of other unions, as well as on the size of their financial reserves.

In the early 1980s, many important unions cut back on their wage requests. In the automobile industry, American firms were finding it difficult to compete with their Japanese rivals, and many experts attributed this partly to the very high wages in the U.S. auto industry. In the trucking industry, unionized firms were finding it increasingly difficult to compete with nonunion firms. More and more union members in industries like autos, trucking, steel, rubber, and airlines began to worry about the effects of hefty wage increases on whether or not they would have jobs. The climate for collective bargaining was quite different from earlier years.

SUMMARY

1. Assuming perfect competition, a firm will employ each type of labor in an amount such that its marginal product times the product's price equals its wage. In other words, the firm will employ enough labor so that the value of the marginal product of labor equals labor's price.

2. The firm's demand curve for labor—which shows, for each price of labor, the amount of labor the firm will use—is the firm's value-of-marginal-product curve (if labor is the only variable input). The market demand curve for labor shows the relationship between its price and the total amount of labor demanded in the market.

3. Labor's price depends on its market supply curve as well as on its market demand curve. Labor's market supply curve is the relationship between the price of labor and the total amount of labor supplied in the market. (Labor's market supply curve may be backward bending.)

4. An input's price is determined under perfect competition in essentially the same way that a product's price is determined: by supply and demand. The price of labor will tend in equilibrium to the level at which the quantity of labor demanded equals the quantity of labor supplied. By the same token, the equilibrium amount of labor utilized is also given by the intersection of the market supply and demand curves.

5. There are about 200 national unions in the United States, the biggest being the Teamsters. Each national union is composed of local unions, which operate within the context of the constitution of the national union.

6. The AFL-CIO is a federation of national unions created by the merger in 1955 of the American Federation of Labor and the Congress of Industrial Organizations. It is an important spokesman for the labor movement, but because the national unions in the AFL-CIO have given up relatively little of their power to the federation, its authority is limited.

7. Unions can increase wages by shifting the supply curve of labor to the left, by shifting the demand curve for labor to the right, and by influencing the wage directly. Collective bargaining is the process of negotiation between union and management over wages and working conditions.

★ ★ ★ ★ ★ ★ ★ ★

CHAPTER 23

Interest, Rent, and Profits

LEARNING OBJECTIVES

In this chapter, you should learn:

★ How the interest rate is determined, and the economic functions it performs

★ The nature and importance of the present value of future income

★ The definition of rent

★ The nature of profit and its function in a capitalistic economic system

Not all income is received in the form of wages. The school teacher who has a savings account at the Bank of America receives income in the form of *interest.* The widow who rents out 100 acres of rich Iowa land to a farmer receives income in the form of *rent.* And the engineer who founds and owns a firm that develops a new type of electronic calculator receives income in the form of *profit.* All of these types of income—interest, rent, and profit—are forms of property income. That is, they are incomes received by owners of property. In this chapter, we are concerned with the determinants of interest, rent, and profit. Also, we try to explain the social functions of each of these types of property income.

THE NATURE OF INTEREST

Charles Lamb, the English essayist, said, "The human species, according
to the best theory I can form of it, is composed of two distinct races, the

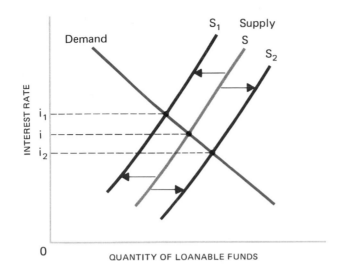

Figure 23.3
Effects on the Equilibrium Interest Rate of Federal Reserve Policies Influencing the Supply Curve for Loanable Funds
When the Federal Reserve pushes the supply curve to the right (from *S* to S_2), the equilibrium interest rate falls from *i* to i_2. When the Federal Reserve pushes the supply curve to the left (*S* to S_1), the equilibrium interest rate increases from *i* to i_1.

curve for loanable funds to the right. On the other hand, when the Federal Reserve pursues a policy of tight money, interest rates generally tend to rise in the short run because the Fed is pushing the supply curve for loanable funds to the left. (See Figure 23.3.)

The government is also an important factor on the demand side of the market for loanable funds, because it is a big borrower, particularly during wartime. Between 1941 and 1945, it borrowed almost $200 billion to help finance World War II. In 1984, total federal debt (excluding the debt of state and local governments) held by the public exceeded $1.1 trillion.

FUNCTIONS OF THE INTEREST RATE

Interest has often been a relatively unpopular and somewhat suspect form of income. Even the great Greek philosopher Aristotle, who was hardly noted for muddle-headedness, felt that money was "barren" and that it was improper to charge interest. In real life and in fiction, the money lender is often the villain, almost never the hero. Yet *interest rates serve a very important function. They allocate the supply of loanable funds.*

At a given point in time, funds that can be used to construct new capital goods are scarce, and society faces the problem of allocating these scarce funds among alternative possible uses. One way to allocate the loanable funds is through freely fluctuating interest rates. When such funds are relatively scarce, the interest rate will rise, with the result that only projects with relatively high rates of return will be carried out since the others will not be profitable. On the other hand, when such funds are relatively plentiful, the interest rate will fall, and less productive projects will be carried out because they now become profitable.

Choosing the Most Productive Projects

The advantage of using the interest rate to allocate funds is that only the most productive projects are funded. To see why, assume that all investments are riskless. *If firms can borrow all the money they want (at the prevailing interest rate), and if they maximize their profits, they will buy all capital goods and accept all investment opportunities where the rate of return on these capital goods or investment opportunities exceeds the interest rate at which the firms can borrow.*[2] The reason for this is clear enough. If one can borrow money at an interest cost that is less than the rate of return on the borrowed money, clearly one can make money. Thus, if you borrow $1,000 at 3 percent per year interest and buy a $1,000 machine that has a rate of return of 4 percent per year, you receive a return of $40 per year and incur a cost of $30 per year. Since you make a profit of $10 per year, it obviously pays to buy this machine.

At a particular point in time, there are many possible capital goods that can be produced and investment projects that can be carried out. Their rates of return vary a great deal; some goods or projects have much higher rates of return than others. Suppose that we rank the capital goods or projects according to their rates of return, from highest to lowest. If only a few of the goods or projects can be accepted, only those at the top of the list will be chosen. But as more and more can be accepted, society and private investors must go further and further down the list, with the consequence that projects with lower and lower rates of return will be chosen. How many of these capital goods and investment projects will be carried out? As noted above, firms will continue to invest as long as the rate of return on these goods or projects exceeds the interest rate at which they can borrow. Thus it follows that *the most productive projects—all those with rates of return exceeding the interest rate—will be carried out.*

CAPITALIZATION OF ASSETS

In a capitalist economy, each asset has a market value. How can we determine what this value is? How much money is a particular asset worth? To keep things reasonably simple, suppose that you can get 5 percent on various investments open to you; specifically, you can get 5 percent by investing your money in the stock of a local firm. That is, for every $1,000 you invest, you will receive a permanent return of $50 a year, and this is the highest return available. Now suppose that you have an opportunity to buy a piece of equipment that will yield you a permanent return of

[2]We assume here that the investment opportunities are independent in the sense that the rate of return from each opportunity is not influenced by whether some other opportunity is accepted.

$1,000 per year. This piece of equipment is worth $1,000 ÷ .05 = $20,000 to you. Why? Because this is the amount you would have to pay for any other investment open to you that yields an equivalent amount, $1,000, per year. (If you must invest $1,000 for every $50 of annual yield, $20,000 must be invested to obtain an annual yield of $1,000.)

In general, if a particular asset yields a permanent amount, X dollars, each year, how much is this asset worth? In other words, how much should you be willing to pay for it? If you can get a return of $100 \times r$ percent per year from alternative investments, you would have to invest $X \div r$ dollars in order to get the same return as this particular asset yields. Consequently, this asset is worth

$$\frac{\$X}{r}.$$

Thus, if the rate of return on alternative investments had been 3 percent rather than 5 percent in the example above, the worth of the piece of equipment would have been $1,000 ÷ .03 = $33,333 (since $X = $1,000 and $r = .03$). This is the amount you would have to pay for any other investment open to you that yields an equivalent amount, $1,000, per year. To see this, note that if you must invest $1,000 for every $30 (not $50, as before) of annual yield, $33,333 (not $20,000, as before) must be invested to obtain an annual yield of $1,000.

This process of computing an asset's worth is called *capitalization.* Note one important point about an asset's capitalized value. Holding constant an asset's annual returns, the asset's worth is higher, the lower the rate of return available on other investments. Thus the piece of equipment discussed above was worth $33,333 when you could get a 3 percent return on alternative investments, but worth only $20,000 when you could get a 5 percent return on alternative investments. This makes sense. After all, the lower the rate of return on alternative investments, the more you must invest in them in order to obtain annual earnings equivalent to those of the asset in question. Thus the more valuable is the asset in question.

This principle helps to explain why in securities markets bond prices fall when interest rates rise, and rise when interest rates fall. A *bond* is a piece of paper that states that the borrower will pay the lender a fixed amount of interest each year (and the principal when the bond comes due). Suppose that this annual interest is $100, and that the interest rate equals $100 \times r$ percent per year. Then, applying the results of the previous paragraphs, this bond will be worth $100 ÷ r$ dollars, if the bond is due a great many years hence. Suppose the interest rate is 5 percent. Then it is worth $2,000. But if the interest rate rises to 10 percent, it will be worth only $1,000; and if the interest rate falls to 4 percent, it will be worth $2,500. Securities dealers make these sorts of calculations all the time, for they recognize that the value of the bond will fall when interest rates rise, and rise when interest rates fall.

THE PRESENT VALUE OF FUTURE INCOME

In the previous section, we determined the value of an asset that yields a perpetual stream of earnings. Now let's consider a case where an asset will provide you with a single lump sum at a certain time in the future. Suppose that you are the heir to an estate of $100,000, which you will receive in two years. How much is that estate worth now?

To answer this question, we must recognize the basic fact that *a dollar now is worth more than a dollar later.* Why? Because one can always invest money that is available now and obtain interest on it. If the interest rate is 6 percent, a dollar received now is equivalent to $1.06 received a year hence. Why? Because if you invest the dollar now, you'll get $1.06 in a year. Similarly, a dollar received now is equivalent to $(1.06)^2$ dollars two years hence. Why? Because if you invest the dollar now, you'll get $1.06 in a year; and if you reinvest this amount for another year at 6 percent, you'll get $(1.06)^2$ dollars.

Consequently, if the interest rate is 6 percent, the estate is worth $100,000 \div (1.06)^2$ dollars now. Since $(1.06)^2 = 1.1236$, it is worth

$$\frac{\$100,000}{1.1236} = \$88,100.$$

In general, *if the interest rate is 100 $\times$ r percent per year, a dollar received now is worth 1 $\div$ (1 + r)^2 dollars two years from now.* Thus, whatever the value of the interest rate may be, the estate is worth

$$\frac{\$100,000}{(1 + r)^2}.$$

The principle that a dollar now is worth more than a dollar later is of fundamental importance. If you don't understand it, you don't understand a basic precept of the world of finance. Although the example considered in previous paragraphs pertains only to a two-year period, this principle remains valid no matter how long the period of time we consider. Table 23.1 shows the present value of a dollar received at various points of time

Table 23.1
Present Value of a
Future Dollar

| Number of years hence (that dollar is received) | Interest rate (percent) | | | |
	4	6	8	10
		(cents)		
1	96.2	94.3	92.6	90.9
2	92.5	89.0	85.7	82.6
3	89.0	83.9	79.4	75.1
4	85.5	79.2	73.5	68.3
5	82.3	74.7	68.1	62.0
10	67.6	55.8	46.3	38.5
15	55.5	41.7	31.5	23.9
20	45.6	31.1	21.5	14.8

in the future. Its present value declines with the length of time before the dollar is received (so long as the interest rate remains constant).

RENT: NATURE AND SIGNIFICANCE

Besides interest, another type of property income is rent. To understand rent, one must understand what economists mean by land. *Land* is defined by economists as *any input that is fixed in supply, its limits established by nature.* Since certain types of minerals and natural resources are in relatively fixed supply, they are included in the economist's definition of land. Suppose that the supply of an input is completely fixed. Increases in its price will not increase its supply and decreases in its price will not decrease its supply. Following the terminology of the classical economists of the nineteenth century, *the price of such an input is rent.* Note that rent means something quite different to an economist than to the man in the street, who considers rent the price of using an apartment or a car or some other object owned by someone else.

If the supply of an input is fixed, its supply curve is a vertical line, as shown in Figure 23.4. Thus the price of this input, its rent, is determined entirely by the demand curve for the input. If the demand curve is D_0, the rent is OP_0; if the demand curve is D_1, the rent is OP_1. Since the supply of the input is fixed, the price of the input can be lowered without influencing the amount supplied. Thus *a rent is a payment above the minimum necessary to attract this amount of the input.*[3]

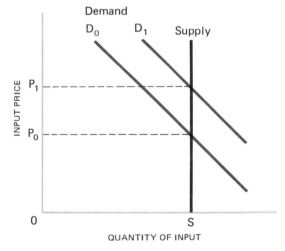

Demand

QUANTITY OF INPUT

Figure 23.4
Rent
Rent is the price of an input in fixed supply. Since its supply curve is vertical, the price of such an input is determined entirely by the demand curve for the input. If the demand curve is D_0, the rent is OP_0; if the demand curve is D_1, the rent is OP_1.

[3]In recent years, there has been a tendency among economists to extend the use of the word *rent* to encompass all payments to inputs above the minimum required to make these inputs available to the industry or to the economy. To a great extent these payments are costs to individual firms; the firms must make such payments to attract and keep these inputs, which are useful to other firms in the industry. But if the inputs have no use in other industries, these payments are not costs to the industry as a whole (or to the economy as a whole) because the inputs would be available to the industry whether or not these payments are made.

Why is it important to know whether a certain payment for inputs is a rent? Because a reduction of the payment will not influence the availability and use of the inputs if the payment is a rent; if it is not a rent, a reduction of the payment is likely to change the allocation of resources. If the government imposes a tax on rents, there will be no effect on the supply of resources to the economy.

The Views of Henry George

In 1879, Henry George (1839–97) published a book, *Progress and Poverty,* in which he argued that rents should be taxed away by the government. In his view, owners of land were receiving substantial rents simply because their land happened to be well situated, not because they were doing anything productive. Since this rent was unearned income and since the supply of land would not be influenced by such a tax, George felt that it was justifiable to tax away such rent. Indeed, he argued that a tax of this sort should be the only tax imposed by the government.

Critics of George's views pointed out that land can be improved, with the result that the supply is not completely price inelastic. Moreover, they argued that if land rents are unearned, so are many other kinds of income. In addition, they pointed out that it was unrealistic to expect such a tax to raise the needed revenue. George's single-tax movement gained a number of adherents in the last decades of the nineteenth century, and he even made an unsuccessful bid to become mayor of New York. Arguments in favor of a single tax continue to surface from time to time.

PROFITS

Besides interest and rent, another important type of property income is *profit.* The economist's concept of profit varies from the accountant's concept. According to accountants, profit is the amount of money the owner of a firm has left after paying wages, interest, and rent—and after providing proper allowance for the depreciation of buildings and equipment. Economists dissent from this view; their position is that the opportunity costs of the labor, capital, and land contributed by the owner should also be deducted.

Profit Statistics

Available statistics concerning profits are based on the accountant's concept, not the economist's. Before taxes, corporation profits average about 10 percent of gross national product. Profits, expressed as a percentage of either net worth or sales, vary considerably from industry to industry and from firm to firm. (For example, the drug industry's profits in the postwar period have frequently been about 15–20 percent of net worth—considerably higher than in most other manufacturing industries.) Also, profits vary greatly from year to year, and are much more erratic than wages. They fall more heavily in recessions and rise more rapidly in recoveries than wages do. Table 23.2 shows profit as a percentage of stockholders' equity in manufacturing in the United States in 1980–84.

Year	All manufacturing Corporations	Durable goods Industries	Nondurable goods Industries
		(percent)	
1980	13.9	11.2	16.3
1981	13.6	11.9	15.2
1982	9.2	6.1	11.9
1983	10.6	8.1	12.7
1984	11.9	11.3	12.4

Table 23.2
Annual Profit (after Taxes) as a Percentage of Stockholders' Equity, United States, 1980–84

Source: *Economic Report of the President*, 1985. The 1984 figures pertain to the third quarter.

Innovation, Uncertainty, and Monopoly Power

Why do profits, as economists define them, exist? Three important factors are innovation, uncertainty, and monopoly power. Suppose that an economy was composed of perfectly competitive industries, that entry was completely free, and that no changes in technology—no new processes, no new products, or other innovations—were permitted. Moreover, suppose that everyone could predict the future with perfect accuracy. Under these conditions, there would be no profits, because people would enter industries where profits exist, thus reducing these profits eventually to zero, and leave industries where losses exist, thus reducing these negative profits eventually to zero. This sort of no-profit equilibrium has already been discussed in Chapter 18.

But in the real world, innovations of various kinds are made. For example, Du Pont introduces a new product like nylon, or Henry Ford introduces the assembly line, or Marconi introduces the radio. The people who carry out these bold schemes are the *innovators,* those with vision and the daring to back it up. The innovators are not necessarily the inventors of new techniques or products, although in some cases the innovator and the inventor are the same. Often the innovator takes another's invention, adapts it, and introduces it to the market. According to economists like the late Joseph Schumpeter of Harvard, profits are the rewards earned by innovators. The profits derived from any single innovation eventually erode with competition and imitation, but other innovations replace them, with the result that profits from innovation continue to be made.

In the real world, uncertainty also exists. Indeed, one of the real hazards in attempting to be an innovator is the *risk* involved. According to a theory set forth several decades ago by Frank Knight of the University of Chicago, all economic profit is due to uncertainty. Profit is the reward for risk bearing. Assuming that people would like to avoid risk, they will prefer relatively stable, sure earnings to relatively unstable, uncertain earnings—*if the average level of earnings is the same.* Consequently, to induce people to take the risks involved in owning businesses in various industries, a profit—a premium for risk—must be paid to them.

Still another reason for the existence of profits is the fact that markets are not perfectly competitive. Under perfect competition, there will be a tendency in the long run for profits to disappear. But, as we have seen, this will not be the case if an industry is a monopoly or oligopoly. Instead, profits may well exist in the long run in such imperfectly competitive industries. Much of our entire economy is composed of imperfectly competitive industries. Monopoly profits are fundamentally the result of "contrived scarcities." Since a firm's demand curve is downward-sloping if competition is imperfect, it pays the firm to take account of the fact that the more it produces, the smaller the price it will receive. In other words, the firm realizes that it will spoil the market if it produces too much. Thus it pays firms to limit their output, and this contrived scarcity is responsible for the existence of the profits they make as a consequence.

THE FUNCTIONS OF PROFITS

To many people, profit seems to be "something for nothing." They do not recognize the innovative or risk-bearing functions of the owners of the firm, and consequently see no reason for the existence of profits. Other people, aware that profits arise because of imperfect competition, ignore the other functions of profit and regard it as entirely the ill-gotten gain of fat monopolists who smoke big cigars and sport a rapacious leer. But no group is more hostile to profits than the followers and disciples of Karl Marx. According to Marx, laborers in a capitalist system receive a wage that is barely enough to cover the minimum amount of housing, food, clothing, and other commodities needed for survival. The difference between the amount the employers receive for their products and the amount they pay the laborers that produce them is "surplus value." And, according to Marx, this "surplus value," which includes what we would call profit, is a measure of, and a consequence of, exploitation of labor by owners of firms.

Marx's views and those of others who look on profits with suspicion and even distaste are rejected by most economists, who feel that profits play a legitimate and very important role in a capitalistic system. In such a system, consumers, suppliers of inputs, and firms try to advance their own interests. Workers try to maximize their earnings, capitalists look for the highest interest returns, landlords try to get the highest rents, and firm owners seek to maximize their profits. At first glance, this looks like a chaotic, dog-eat-dog situation; but, as we have seen, it actually turns out to be an orderly and efficient system—if competition is present.

Profits and Losses: Mainsprings of a Capitalistic System

Profits and losses are mainsprings of this system for several reasons.

1. *They are signals that indicate where resources are needed and where they are too abundant.* When there are economic profits in an industry, this is the signal for resources to flow into it; when economic losses exist in an industry, this is the signal for resources to leave it.

2. *Profits are very important incentives for innovation and for betting on the future.* For an entrepreneur like Joseph Wilson of Xerox, profits are the bait society dangles before him to get him to take the risks involved in marketing a new product, like xerography. If his judgment turns out to be faulty, losses—negative profits—are the penalties society imposes on him.

3. *Profits are society's reward for efficiency.* Firms that use inefficient techniques or produce an inappropriate amount or type of product are penalized by losses. Firms that are particularly alert, efficient, and adaptive receive profits. Further, profits enable firms to embark on new projects. Thus the profits that Xerox earned on xerography are currently being used to support its new ventures into other types of business machines.

The importance of profits in a free-enterprise economy is clear enough. However, this does not mean that all profits are socially justified or that the system as a whole cannot be improved. Monopoly profits may not be socially justified, and a competitive system, despite its advantages, may produce some socially undesirable effects—such as an undesirable income distribution. (More will be said about this in Chapter 24.)

THE FUNCTIONAL DISTRIBUTION OF INCOME

In this and the previous chapter, we have been concerned with wages, interest, rent, and profit. How is the total income of the nation as a whole divided among these categories? In other words, what proportion of all income goes to employees? What proportion goes for interest? For rent? For profits? In this section, we take up these questions.

Table 23.3 shows the proportion of national income going for (1) wages and salaries, (2) proprietors' income, (3) corporate profits, (4) interest, and (5) rents.[4] It is clear that wages and salaries are by far the largest of these five income categories. In 1984, about three-fourths of national income went for wages and salaries (including employer contributions to Social Security and pensions). Moreover, this is an understatement of the share of employee compensation in national income, because part of proprie-

[4]The concept of rent on which these figures are based is different from the one presented in this chapter, but this does not affect the conclusions presented below.

Table 23.3
Percentage Shares
of National Income,
1900–84

Period	Wages and salaries	Proprietors' Income	Corporate profits	Interest	Rent	Total
1900–09	55	24	7	5	9	100
1910–19	54	24	9	5	8	100
1920–29	60	18	8	6	8	100
1930–39	67	15	4	9	5	100
1939–48	65	17	12	3	3	100
1949–58	67	14	13	3	3	100
1963–70	70	12	11	4	3	100
1984	73	5	10	10	2	100

Source: I. Kravis, "Income Distribution: Functional Share," International Encyclopedia of the Social Sciences, New York: Macmillan, 1968, and Annual Reports of the Council of Economic Advisers. These figures may not be entirely comparable over time, but they are sufficiently accurate for present purposes.

tors' income is really wages. As we pointed out in an earlier section, a portion of what the proprietor of the corner drugstore or the local shoe-store makes is compensation for the proprietor's labor, not profit as defined by the economist.

The figures in Table 23.3 indicate a marked reduction over time in the proportion of national income going to proprietors, and a marked increase over time in the proportion going for wages and salaries. Part of this shift is due to the fact that the corporation has become a more dominant organizational form, with the result that many people who would have been individual proprietors owning their own small businesses 50 years ago now work as employed managers for corporations. Another fact that may help to explain this shift is the long-term shift from agriculture (where labor's share of income is low) to manufacturing and services (where labor's share is higher).

Some economists are impressed by the constancy of the share of national income going to labor. Using definitions that are somewhat different than those underlying Table 23.3, they come up with numbers indicating that labor's share has not varied much over time. Other economists, using somewhat different definitions, conclude that labor's share has varied considerably. But one thing is for sure. There is no evidence that a bigger share of the economic pie is going to capitalists in the form of interest, rent, or profits. Perhaps the figures in Table 23.3 exaggerate the extent to which labor's share has increased, but there is certainly no evidence that it has decreased.

SUMMARY

1. Interest is a payment for the use of money. Interest rates vary a great deal, depending on the nature of the borrower and the type and riskiness of the loan. One very important function of interest rates is to allocate the supply of loanable funds.

2. The pure interest rate—the interest rate on riskless loans—is, like any price, determined by the interaction of supply and demand. However, because of the influence of the government on both the demand and supply sides of the market, it is clear that the pure interest rate is to a considerable extent a matter of public policy.

3. In a capitalist system, each asset has a market value that can be determined by capitalizing its earnings. Holding constant an asset's annual return, the asset's worth is higher, the lower the rate of return available on other investments.

4. Any asset has a rate of return, which indicates its net productivity. An asset's rate of return is the interest rate earned on the investment in the asset. If firms maximize profits, they must carry out all projects where the rate of return exceeds the interest rate at which they can borrow.[5]

5. Rent is the return derived from inputs that are fixed in supply. Since the supply of the input is fixed, its price can be lowered without influencing the amount supplied. Thus, if the government imposes taxes on rents, there will be no effect on the supply of resources to the economy.

6. Another important type of property income is profits. Available statistics on profits are based on the accountant's concept, not the economist's, with the result that they do not exclude the opportunity costs of the labor, capital, and land contributed by the owners of the firm. Profits play a very important and legitimate role in a free enterprise system.

7. Two of the important factors responsible for the existence of profits are innovation and uncertainty. Profits are the rewards earned by innovators and a payment for riskbearing. Still another reason for the existence of profits is monopoly power; because of contrived scarcity, profits are made by firms in imperfectly competitive markets.

---

[5]In practice, firms often base their decisions on discounted cash flow rather than rates of return. The present discussion is necessarily simplified. For a more complete discussion, see E. Mansfield, *Microeconomics: Theory and Applications*, 5th ed.

CHAPTER 24

★ ★ ★ ★ ★ ★ ★ ★ ★

Poverty, Income Inequality, and Discrimination

LEARNING OBJECTIVES

In this chapter, you should learn:

★ The extent of income inequality in the United States

★ How the tax structure affects the distribution of income in the United States

★ The nature of the Social Security program

★ The nature and limitations of the major anti-poverty programs

★ The economic effects of discrimination

Although the United States is one of the richest countries on earth, it is not a land of milk and honey to all its inhabitants. Some Americans are poor—so poor that they suffer from malnutrition—and while poverty may not be a sin, it is no less a problem to the poor. Given the affluence of American society, one is led to ask why poverty exists and whether it cannot be abolished by proper public policies. One purpose of this chapter is to examine these questions.

HOW MUCH INEQUALITY OF INCOME?

We don't have to be very perceptive social observers to recognize that there are great differences in income levels in the United States. But our idea of what the distribution of income looks like depends on the sort of family and community we come from. A child brought up in Lake Forest, a wealthy suburb of Chicago, is unlikely to be as aware of the incidence of poverty as a child brought up on Chicago's poor South Side. For a preliminary glimpse of the extent of income inequality in the United States, scan Table 24.1, which shows the percentage of all families in the United States that were situated in various income classes in 1983. According to the table, the bottom fifth of the nation's families received an income of less than $11,629 in 1983. On the other hand, the top fifth of the nation's families received an income of $41,824 or more in 1983.

Money income (dollars)	Percent of all families	Percent of total income received
Under 11,629	20	5
11,629–20,059	20	11
20,060–29,203	20	17
29,204–41,823	20	24
41,824–67,325	15	27
67,326 and over	5	16
Total	100	100

Source: Department of Commerce.

Table 24.1
Percentage
Distribution of
Families, by Income,
1983

It may come as a surprise to some that so large a percentage of the nation's families made less than $11,629. The image of the affluent society projected in the Sunday supplements and on some television programs is strangely out of tune with these facts. Yet, to put these figures in world perspective, it should be recognized that Americans are very rich relative to other peoples. This fact is shown clearly by Table 24.2, which gives for various countries the 1983 level of income per person, which is the total income of each nation divided by its population. The United States is among the leaders in this table.

I. Countries with income per capita exceeding $6,000		
United States	Denmark	Sweden
Australia	France	Japan
Canada	Germany	Switzerland
II. Countries with income per capita between $2,500 and $6,000		
Argentina	Greece	Yugoslavia
Ireland	Hong Kong	Italy
Soviet Union	United Kingdom	Venezuela
III. Countries with income per capita between $1,000 and $2,500		
Algeria	Congo	Guatemala
Brazil	Malaysia	Turkey
IV. Countries and regions with income per capita less than $1,000		
India	El Salvador	Most of Africa
Indonesia	Haiti	Much of Asia

Table 24.2
Selected Countries
Grouped by
Approximate Level
of Income per
Capita, 1983.

ªWhere 1983 figures are not yet published, the most recent available data are used. All figures are in 1975 dollars.

WHY INEQUALITY?

Nonetheless, recognizing that our poor are better off than the bulk of the population in many other countries, the fact remains that there is substantial inequality of income in this country. Why is this the case? Based on our discussion of labor and property incomes in previous chapters, this question is not hard to answer. One reason is that some people possess greater abilities than others. Since Ozzie Smith and Dave Winfield have extraordinary skill as baseball players, it is easy to understand why they make a lot of money. Another reason is differences in the amount of education and training people receive. Thus physicians or lawyers must receive a higher income than people in occupations requiring little or no training. (Otherwise it would not pay people to undergo medical or legal training.) Still another reason is that some people own large amounts of property. Thus, because of a shrewd choice of ancestry, current members of the Ford, Rockefeller, and Mellon families get high incomes from inherited wealth. Still other reasons are that some people have managed to obtain monopoly power, and others have had an extraordinary string of good luck.

EFFECTS OF THE TAX STRUCTURE ON INCOME INEQUALITY

So far we have looked at the distribution of before-tax income. But we must also consider the effect of the tax system on income inequality.

A tax is *progressive* if the rich pay a higher proportion of their income for the tax than do the poor. A tax is *regressive* if the rich pay a smaller proportion of their income for the tax than do the poor.

Needless to say, people who feel that the tax system should promote a redistribution of income from rich to poor favor progressive, not regressive, taxes. Besides the personal income tax, other progressive taxes are inheritance or estate taxes. (The federal government levies a gift tax to prevent wealthy people from circumventing the estate tax by giving their money away before death.) State governments also levy inheritance taxes (on persons who inherit money) and estate taxes (on the deceased's estate). All of this is applauded by reformers who oppose accumulation and preservation of inherited wealth. But, as in the case of the personal income tax, the portion of an estate subject to taxes can be reduced through clever use of various loopholes, all quite legal. Thus the estate tax is not as progressive as it looks.

Not all taxes are progressive; examples of regressive taxes are not hard to find. General sales taxes of the sort used by most states and some cities are regressive, since high-income people pay a smaller percentage of their income in sales taxes than do low-income people. The Social Security and payroll tax is also regressive. It is difficult to tell whether the corporation income tax is progressive or regressive. At first glance, it seems progressive because the owners of corporations—the stockholders—tend to be wealthy people; and to the extent that the corporate income tax is paid from earnings that might otherwise be paid to the stockholders, one might conclude that it is progressive. But this ignores the possibility that the corporation may pass the tax on to the consumer by charging a higher price; in this case the tax may not be progressive.

INCOME INEQUALITY: THE PROS AND CONS

The Case against Income Inequality

Many distinguished social philosophers have debated the merits and demerits of making the income distribution more equal. We cannot consider all the subtler points, but those who favor greater equality make four main arguments.

1. *They say that inequality of income lessens total consumer satisfaction, because an extra dollar given to a poor man provides him with more extra satisfaction than the loss of a dollar takes away from a rich man.* According to the British economist A. C. Pigou, "It is evident that any transference of income from a relatively rich man to a relatively poor man of similar temperament, since it enables more intense wants to be satisfied at the expense of less intense wants, must increase the aggregate sum of satisfactions."[1] A problem in this very appealing argument is its assumption that the rich man and the poor man have the same capacities to gain enjoyment from income. Most economists believe that there is no scientific way to make such comparisons. They deny that the satisfaction one person derives from an extra dollar of income can be measured against the satisfaction another person derives from an extra dollar. Although such comparisons may be drawn, they rest on ethical, not scientific, grounds.

2. *It is argued that income inequality is likely to result in unequal opportunities for young people to gain advanced education and training.* The children of the rich can get an education, while the children of the poor often cannot. The result is that some able and productive people may be denied an education simply because their parents are poor. This is a waste of resources.

3. *It is argued that income inequality is likely to lead to political inequality.* The rich may well influence legislation and political decisions more heavily than the poor, and there is likely to be one kind of justice for the rich and another kind for the poor.

4. In the past few years, the arguments for income equality have been carried a step forward by John Rawls, the Harvard philosopher. He says that, *if people were framing a constitution for society without knowing what their class position would be, they would opt for equality.* And he argues that "all social values . . . are to be distributed equally unless an

[1]A. C. Pigou, *Economics of Welfare*, 4th ed., London: Macmillan, 1948, p. 89.

unequal distribution . . . is to everyone's advantage"—that is, unless an unequal distribution is to the advantage of society's least privileged group. Although Rawls's book, *A Theory of Justice,* has had considerable impact, many economists have pointed out that his prescription for society might not appeal to people who were willing to take risks. Suppose that you could establish a society that guaranteed every family $15,000 a year (no more, no less) or one where 99 percent of all families would receive $20,000 and 1 percent would receive $12,000. You might choose the latter kind of society because, although there is a small chance that you would do worse than in the egalitarian case, the chance of doing better seems worth this risk.

The Case for Income Inequality

In general, people who favor income inequality also make four arguments.

1. *They argue that income inequality is needed to give people an incentive to work and create.* After all, if everyone receives the same income, why bother to increase your production, or to try to invent a new process, or to work overtime? Whatever you do, your income will be the same. This is an important point, though it overlooks the fact that nonmonetary incentives like pride in a job well done can be as important as monetary incentives.

2. *Advocates of income inequality claim that it permits greater savings, and thus greater capital formation.* Although this seems reasonable, it is not hard to cite cases where countries with greater inequality of income invest less, not more, than countries with less inequality of income. Thus some Middle Eastern countries with great income inequality have not had relatively high investment rates.

3. *Advocates of income inequality say that the rich have been important patrons of new and high-quality products that benefit the entire society.* They argue that there are social advantages in having certain people with the wherewithal to pioneer in consumption and to support art and culture. In their view, a completely egalitarian society would be rather dull.

4. *Advocates of income inequality point out that, even if everyone received the same income, the poor would not be helped a great deal, because the wealthy are relatively few.* If the riches of the rich were transferred to the poor, each poor person would get only a little, because there are so many poor and so few rich.

THE TRADEOFF BETWEEN EQUALITY AND EFFICIENCY

In trying to decide how much income inequality you favor, it is important to recognize that measures taken to reduce inequality are likely to decrease economic efficiency. In other words, *if we reduce inequality, we may well cut society's total output.* Why? Because, as pointed out in the previous section, people are likely to have less incentive to produce if their incomes are much the same regardless of how much they produce. This does not mean that all measures designed to reduce income inequality are bad. What it does mean is that, if you want to reduce income inequality, you should be sensitive to the effects on output. In particular, you should try to find policies that will attain a given reduction in inequality at a minimum cost in terms of reduced output.

In view of the strong feelings of many advocates and opponents of reduced income inequality, it is not surprising that they sometimes make extreme statements about the nature of the tradeoff between equality and efficiency. Some egalitarians deny that there is any tradeoff at all. They claim that inequality can be reduced without any cut in output. Some opponents of reductions in income inequality assert that there will be a catastrophic fall in output if the existing income distribution is tampered with. Although far too little is known about the quantitative character of this tradeoff, there seems to be general agreement among economists that the truth lies somewhere between these two extremes.

People vary considerably in their evaluation of how much society should pay (in terms of decreased total output) for a particular reduction in income inequality. The late Arthur Okun of the Brookings Institution suggested that to characterize your own feelings on this score, it is useful to view money as a liquid and to visualize a bucket that carries money from the rich to the poor.[2] The bucket is leaky, so only part of what is taken from the rich can be given to the poor. If the leak is very small, a dollar taken from the rich may result in 99 cents going to the poor. Many people would accept a loss of this magnitude. If the leak is very large, a dollar taken from the rich may result in only 5 cents going to the poor. Few people would accept this big a loss. How big a loss would you accept? The larger the leak that you would find acceptable, the more willing you are to accept output losses in order to attain decreases in income inequality.

The argument between the advocates and opponents of reduced income inequality involves much more than economics. Whether you favor greater or less income inequality depends on your ethical and political beliefs. It is not a matter economics alone can settle. What economists can do is assess the degree of income inequality in a country and suggest ways to alter the gap between the haves and have-nots in accord with the dictates of the people or their leaders. In recent years, economists in and out of government have devoted much effort to designing programs aimed at reducing poverty. To understand these programs, we must discuss what poverty is, and who the poor are.

---

[2] Arthur Okun, *Equality and Efficiency,* Washington, D.C.: Brookings Institution, 1975. For an excerpt from this book, see E. Mansfield, *Principles of Microeconomics: Readings, Issues, Cases,* 4th ed., New York: Norton, 1983.

WHAT IS POVERTY?

Some people are fond of saying that everything is relative. Certainly this is true of poverty. Moreover, poverty is certainly subjective. Consider the average young executive making $60,000 a year. After a bad day at the office or a particularly expensive family shopping spree, he is likely to tell anyone who will listen that he is as poor as a church mouse.

There is no well-defined income level that can be used in all times and places as a touchstone to define poverty. Poverty is partly a matter of how one person's income stacks up against that of others. What most people in America today regard as stark poverty would have seemed like luxury to many Americans of 200 years ago—and would seem like luxury in parts of Asia and Africa today. Consequently, one must be careful not to define poverty in such a way that it cannot be eliminated, and then try to eliminate it. If poverty is defined as being in the bottom 10 percent of the income distribution, how can a war against poverty ever be won? Regardless of what measures are taken, there will always be a bottom 10 percent of the income distribution, unless all income inequality is eliminated (which is highly unlikely).

Perhaps the most widely accepted definition of *poverty* in the United States today is the one developed by the Social Security Administration, which began by determining the cost of a *minimal* nutritionally sound food plan (given by the Department of Agriculture). Then, since low-income families spend about one-third of their incomes on food, this food cost was multiplied by 3 to obtain an income level that was used as a criterion for poverty. Families with less income were regarded as "living below the poverty level."

Based on such computations, an urban family of four needed an income of about $10,178 to make it barely over the Social Security Administration's poverty line in 1983. (Since farm families typically have lower food costs, the estimates for them are somewhat lower.) Although one could quarrel with this figure on various counts, most people probably would agree that families with income below this level are poor.[3]

Declining Incidence of Poverty

According to estimates made by the federal government in 1984, about 15 percent of the population in the United States was below the Social Security Administration's poverty line. In absolute terms, this means that

[3]The basic figures come from the Department of Commerce's *Current Population Reports,* which explain in detail the way in which these figures are derived. The method described in the text is crude, but it provides results that are quite close to those of more complicated methods. Since 1969, the poverty line has been calculated on the basis of the Consumer Price Index, not the price of food.

over 35 million people were poor enough to fall below the criterion described above.

Fortunately, the incidence of poverty (measured by this criterion) generally has been declining in the United States. In 1947 about 30 percent, in 1960 about 20 percent, and in 1977 about 12 percent of the people were poor by this definition. This is what we would expect. As the average level of income rises, the proportion of the population falling below the poverty line (which is defined by a relatively fixed dollar amount of income) will tend to decrease. Nonetheless, the fact that poverty is being eliminated in the United States does not mean that this process is going on as fast as it should. Many observers feel, as we shall see in subsequent sections, that poverty could and should be eradicated more rapidly.

Characteristics of the Poor

Naturally, the poor are not confined to any particular demographic group, but some types of families are much more likely than others to be below the poverty line. In particular, *nonwhites are much more likely to be poor than whites*. In 1983, 36 percent of nonwhites were poor, whereas 12 percent of whites were poor. Also, *families headed by females are much more likely to be poor than families headed by males*. In addition, very large families (seven persons and over) are much more likely than others to be poor.

Reasons for Poverty

To a considerable extent, the reasons why families are poor lie beyond the control of the families themselves. About one-third of poor adults have suffered a disability of some sort, or the premature death of the family breadwinner, or family dissolution. Some have had to face a smaller demand for their occupation (because of technological or other change) or the decline of their industry or geographical area. Some have simply lived "too long": their savings have given out before their minds and bodies have. Another instrumental factor in making some families poor is discrimination of various kinds. The most obvious type is racial, but others exist as well: discrimination based on sex, religion, age, residence, education, and seniority. In addition, some people are poor because they have very limited ability or little or no motivation. These factors should not be overlooked.

There are important barriers which tend to separate the poor from the rest of society. As the University of Wisconsin's Robert Lampman points out:

> Barriers, once established, tend to be reinforced from the poverty side by the alienated themselves. The poor tend to be cut off from not only opportunity but even from information about opportunity. A poverty subculture develops which

sustains attitudes and values that are hostile to escape from poverty. These barriers combine to make events nonrandom; e.g., unemployment is slanted away from those inside the feudalistic walls of collective bargaining, disability more commonly occurs in jobs reserved for those outside the barriers, the subculture of poverty invites or is prone to self-realizing forecasts of disaster.[4]

Judging from the available evidence, poverty tends to be self-perpetuating. Families tend to be poor year after year, and their children tend to be poor. Because the families are poor, the children are poorly educated, poorly fed, and poorly cared for, and poverty is transmitted from one generation to the next. It is a vicious cycle.

SOCIAL INSURANCE

Old-Age Insurance

Until about 50 years ago, the federal government played little or no role in helping the poor. Private charity was available in limited amounts and state and local governments provided some help, but the general attitude was "sink or swim." Self-reliance and self-support were the watchwords. The Great Depression of the 1930s, which changed so many attitudes, also made a marked change in this area. In 1935, with the passage of the *Social Security Act*, the federal government established a social insurance system providing compulsory old-age insurance for both workers and self-employed people, as well as unemployment insurance. By 1984, about 36 million Americans were receiving well over $100 billion in benefits from the resulting system of old-age and survivors' insurance.

Every wage earner covered under the Social Security Act pays a tax, which in 1984 amounted to 7 percent of the first $37,800 of his or her annual earnings. The employer also pays a tax, which is equal to that paid by the employee. The amount that one can expect to receive each month in *old-age insurance* benefits depends on one's average monthly earnings. Also, the size of the benefits depends on the number of years one has worked. Table 24.3 shows the maximum monthly benefits in 1984. The benefits in the table are a retirement annuity. In other words, they are

Table 24.3
Maximum Initial
Social Security
Benefits, 1984

	Monthly payment
Retired worker alone	
65 years old	$703
62 years old	559
Retired worker with wife	
65 years old	908
62 years old	821

[4]Robert Lampman, "Approaches to the Reduction of Poverty," *American Economic Review*, May 1965.

paid to the wage earner from the date of retirement to the time he or she dies. In addition, when a wage earner dies, Social Security provides payments to his or her spouse, to dependent parents, and to children until they are about 18 years of age (21 if they are in school). Further, payments are made to a wage earner (and dependents) if he or she is totally disabled and unable to work.

Controversies over Social Security

There are a number of controversial aspects of the Social Security program.

1. *If you work past the retirement age of 65, you can be penalized considerably.* For every dollar in wages that you earn above and beyond $6,960 in 1984, you lose 50 cents in Social Security benefits. Thus, since you must pay taxes on your earnings, you get to keep well under one-half of every extra dollar that you earn in wages (over $6,960 per year). But you can earn any amount of interest or dividends or pensions without your Social Security benefits being reduced. To some observers, this is unfair discrimination against older people who want to hold down jobs.

2. *The Social Security tax is regressive,* since those with annual earnings above $37,800 pay a smaller proportion of their income in Social Security taxes than do those with annual earnings below $37,800. For this and other reasons, many observers believe that the system is not as generous to the poor as it should be.

A 1981 protest against cuts in Social Security

3. *Some people are disturbed that the Social Security system is not really an ordinary insurance system at all.* An ordinary insurance program must have assets that are sufficient to finance all of the benefits promised to the people in the program. This is not the case for Social Security. But this does not mean that you won't receive your Social Security. What it does mean is that the Social Security system is a means of transferring income each year from the working young and middle-aged to the retired old people. It will be up to future Congresses to determine what these benefits will be. (In 1983 Congress made a number of important changes: for example, up to half of the Social Security benefits of the well-to-do will be taxable under the personal income tax.) Perhaps you will receive much more than the amounts in Table 24.3—but then again, perhaps you won't. Only time will tell.

4. *Some people are disturbed that Social Security is mandatory.* Milton

CASE STUDY 24.1 JOB TRAINING PROGRAMS AND THE WAR ON POVERTY

The Affluent Society, the best-selling book by President Kennedy's friend, the economist John Kenneth Galbraith, focused the president's attention on one of America's most serious problems: poverty. Galbraith pointed out that, while everybody recognized the need for investment in factories and equipment, society was neglecting the need for investment in people, in education and training. The concept of structural unemployment was discussed widely during the Kennedy administration. (Recall from Chapter 4 that structural unemployment occurs when new goods and new technologies call for new skills, and workers with old skills cannot find jobs.) Although the tax cut of 1964—as well as the additional federal measures that reduced unemployment to 3.8 percent in 1966—weakened some of the arguments regarding the importance of structural unemployment, plans were made for job training programs. These programs would be unlike those of the 1930s, when unemployment reflected a cyclical downturn rather than the poor job skills of the participants; and unlike Social Security and other programs designed to reduce the symptoms of poverty, these would be designed to reduce its causes.

A Job Corps recruiting poster

Bug Us...
About
Job Corps

JOB TRAINING PROGRAM • PAID LIVING EXPENSES • G.E.D. CLASSES • AGE 16-21

WOMEN IN COMMUNITY SERVICE, INC. **WICS** 1-800-JOB-CORP

President Johnson picked up the war on poverty that Kennedy had begun. Defense Secretary McNamara had observed high illiteracy rates among low-income military recruits and draftees, and advocated training through the military as the answer. In 1967, the McNamara idea was developed into a program called the Job Corps, which was the key training program in the War on Poverty bill. Under the program, teenagers, mostly high school dropouts, would receive education and vocational training at Job Corps camps around the country. The effectiveness of the Job Corps proved controversial, although its supporters could point to many success stories. Twenty years later, conservatives in particular argued that the Job Corps' results were not worth the cost.

N.B.

Friedman is concerned that the government interferes with an individual's freedom to plan for the future by forcing him or her to be a member of the Social Security system. (Workers might be able to obtain larger pensions by investing the money that they contribute to Social Security in investments of their own choosing.) Other observers retort that without a mandatory system, some workers would make inadequate provision for their old age and might become public charges.

5. *Some people are concerned that Social Security is an impediment to saving and capital formation.* Martin Feldstein, former chairman of President Reagan's Council of Economic Advisers, feels that Americans save relatively little because they depend on Social Security to take care of their old age. This, he believes, tends to depress capital formation in the United States, since savings can be used to build factories, expand old plants, and add in various ways to the nation's stock of capital. He favors a slowdown in the rate of growth of Social Security, and more reliance on private pensions and personal savings.

Medicare, Unemployment Insurance, and Other Programs

In 1965, the Congress extended the Social Security program to include *Medicare,* a compulsory hospitalization insurance plan plus a voluntary insurance plan covering doctors' fees for people over 65. The hospitalization insurance pays for practically all the hospital costs of the first 90 days of each spell of illness, as well as some additional costs. The plan covers about 80 percent of doctors' fees after the first $60. The cost of the compulsory insurance is included in the taxes described above. This program is also an important factor in preventing and alleviating poverty. The incidence of illness is relatively high among the elderly; with the rapid rise in medical costs, it has become more difficult for them to afford decent care.

Besides instituting old-age, survivors, and medical insurance, the Social Security Act also encouraged the states to set up systems of *unemployment insurance*. Such systems now exist in all states, financed by taxes on employers. Once an insured worker is unemployed, he can obtain benefits after a short waiting period, generally a week. The average weekly benefits differ from state to state; in 1980 they ranged from about $120 in Ohio and Wisconsin to about $70 in Mississippi and Florida. (Since these benefits are not subject to income taxes, these figures understate the value of the benefit to the recipient.) In most states, there is a 26-week ceiling on the duration of benefits, but in 1975, there was a temporary extension of benefits to a maximum duration of 65 weeks. Clearly, unemployment insurance is another important device to keep people from falling below the poverty line.

ANTIPOVERTY PROGRAMS

According to the eighteenth-century English poet and essayist Samuel Johnson, "A decent provision for the poor is the true test of civilization."

There is general agreement that our social insurance programs, although useful in preventing and alleviating poverty, are not an adequate or complete antipoverty program. For one thing, they focus largely on the elderly, which means that they do not aid many poor people. They do not help the working poor; and even for the unemployed, they provide only limited help for a limited period of time.

Consequently, the government has started a number of additional programs specifically designed to help the poor, although many of them are aimed more at the symptoms of poverty than at its basic causes. There are programs that provide goods and services to the poor. Perhaps the most important of these are the *food programs,* which distribute food to the needy families. The federal government gives stamps that can be used to buy food to local agencies, which sell them (at less than the equivalent of market prices) or give them to low-income families. In 1983, the cost of this program to the federal government exceeded $11 billion. On the whole, this program has reached people who were truly needy, but critics have pointed out that some recipients, for example, college students from well-off families, have qualified for the program and have received this subsidy.

More important in quantitative terms than programs that give particular commodities to the poor are programs that provide them with cash. These are what people generally have in mind when they refer to *welfare.* There are advantages to cash payments. They allow a family to adapt its purchases to its own needs and circumstances. There are obvious disadvantages too, since the money may be spent on liquor and marijuana rather than on food and milk. The most important single program of cash payments gives *aid to families with dependent children.* In 1983, this program alone paid out over $13 billion.

To qualify for this program, a family must include dependent children who are without the support of a parent (usually the father) through death, disability, or absence (and in some states, through unemployment as well). The amount paid to a family under this program varies from state to state. Each state administers its own program, sets its own schedule of payments, and contributes part of the cost of the program, with the federal government providing the balance. In 1980, the average payment was about $3,400, but it was higher in states like New York and Massachusetts and lower in states like Mississippi and Alabama. To determine eligibility, the family's affairs are examined, and while receiving aid the family may be under the surveillance of a social worker who supervises its housekeeping and child care.

In 1981, President Reagan cut back the food stamp program, aid to families with dependent children, and other such programs. With regard to aid for families with dependent children, the changes reduced or eliminated the benefits for some low-income people who work. With regard to food stamps, the changes stiffened income eligibility requirements. Liberals tended to be angry at these cuts; many conservatives tended to view them as overdue.

The Negative Income Tax

There is widespread dissatisfaction with current antipoverty—or welfare —programs. The cost of these programs has risen alarmingly; the programs themselves are judged by many experts to be inefficient; and, in some people's view, the welfare recipients are subjected to unnecessary meddling and spying. Moreover, there is little incentive for many people to get off welfare. Both Republicans and Democrats seem to agree that current welfare programs need improvement. What changes might be made? One suggestion that has received serious consideration is the negative income tax, an idea proposed by two Nobel laureates: Stanford University's Milton Friedman (an adviser to presidential candidate Barry Goldwater in 1964 and to President Nixon) and Yale's James Tobin (an adviser to President Kennedy).

A *negative income tax* would work as follows. Just as families with reasonably high incomes *pay* taxes, families with low incomes would *receive* a payment. In other words, the poor would pay a *negative* income tax. Figure 24.1 illustrates how a negative income tax might work; it shows the amount a family of four would pay, or receive, in taxes for incomes at various levels. According to Figure 24.1, $4,000 is the **break-even income:** the income at which a family of four neither pays nor receives income taxes. Above $4,000, a family pays taxes. Thus a family with an income of $6,000 pays $500 in taxes. Below $4,000 a family receives a payment. Thus a family with an income of $1,000 is paid $1,500.

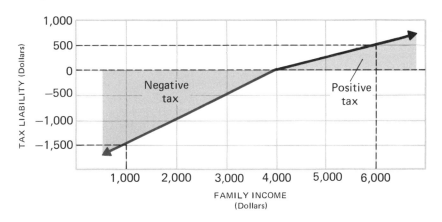

Figure 24.1
Example of Negative Income Tax
A family with more than $4,000 in income pays taxes. Thus a family with an income of $6,000 pays $500 in taxes. A family with an income less than $4,000 receives a payment. Thus a family with an income of $1,000 is paid $1,500.

There are several advantages of a negative income tax.

1. It would give people on welfare more incentive to work. As indicated in Figure 24.1, for every extra dollar it earns, the family receives only 50 cents less from the government under this kind of negative income tax. Thus the family gets to keep half of every extra dollar (up to $4,000) it earns, which is a larger portion of this extra dollar than under the present system.

CASE STUDY 24.2 THE FAMILY ASSISTANCE PLAN

Aid to Dependent Children was initially a state and local program for widows with children. The federal government became involved in 1935. In the 1950s, it was expanded to include support payments for mothers as well as children, and was renamed Aid to Families with Dependent Children (AFDC). It is now the largest of the welfare programs.

Dissatisfaction with the perverse effects of this and other poverty programs became increasingly widespread. Some programs created huge disincentives to work, since a welfare recipient who takes a job can lose more than a dollar's worth of benefits for every additional dollar he or she makes. Moreover, in-kind (as opposed to cash) transfer payments distort people's decisions as to how to spend their income. And the high rate of taxation that is partially due to the cost of welfare programs may distort economic incentives and the allocation of resources, inhibiting overall economic growth.

The rural poor in North Carolina

The expanding costs of welfare, the increase in AFDC cases despite a downturn in unemployment in 1963–64, and the growing awareness of welfare dependency prompted efforts by the Nixon administration to rationalize the welfare programs under the Family Assistance Plan (FAP). FAP would, in essence, pay a certain amount to each needy family each month, depending on family size. If earnings from work raised family income beyond the cut off point, partial benefits would still be paid. Allowing the working poor to keep some benefits would, unlike some earlier programs, give them an incentive to work.

The Nixon plan passed in the House but ran into trouble in the Senate. Some argued that under FAP the poor would get less than they needed, perhaps less than they were already getting. Moreover, although FAP did provide work incentives, it had no work requirement—an omission that raised opposition to the plan. Compromises were struck in the congressional debate, but the plan was ultimately defeated.

N.B.

2. There would be no intrusion into the internal affairs of families on welfare and no regulations that cut off welfare payments if the husband remains with his family. In the past, the welfare system has given families an incentive to break up, and has encroached on the dignity of poor people.

3. It might cost less to administer the negative income tax than the present system, and differences among states in benefits might be reduced.

Despite these advantages, many citizens remain skeptical about the negative income tax. For one thing, they are antagonistic to the idea of giving people an income without requiring any work in return. They also are unwilling to transfer large amounts from rich to poor. This amount would depend on how high the break-even income was set and on the negative tax rates. In the late 1960s, it was estimated that a negative income tax based on the sort of plan described in Figure 24.1 would have meant that those above the break-even income level would transfer about $25 billion to those below the break-even level. Despite the attractive features of a negative income tax, a transfer of this magnitude has proved unacceptable in many quarters.

Also, some economists regard the results of the experiments with a negative income tax in Seattle and Denver to have been somewhat disappointing. These experiments, carried out with a sample of households, seem to indicate that under a negative income tax people work less, apparently because they are more willing to quit work, and less willing to search hard for a new job.

Has the War on Poverty Been Won?

The official government statistics concerning the incidence of poverty do not recognize the fact that many people below the official poverty line receive noncash benefits from the government, such as food stamps, subsidized school lunches, public housing, Medicaid (provision of health services for the poor), and Medicare. These benefits accounted in 1980 for more than two out of every three dollars of government assistance. According to a report published by the U.S. Bureau of the Census in 1984, the percentage of the U.S. population below the poverty line is much smaller than the official statistics indicate, when these government noncash benefits are taken into account. Specifically, the figure according to official statistics is about 10 percent. When underreporting of incomes is taken into consideration, some economists conclude that only about 4 percent of the population have fallen below the poverty line in recent years.

Based on these statistics, some observers claim that the war on poverty in the United States has been won. But it is important to recognize that, even if only 4 percent fall below the poverty line, this means that about 9 million people remain poor. And among blacks, the percentage of poor people is much higher than 4 percent. Also, the statistics themselves are subject to many limitations and should be viewed with caution. Although they suggest that considerable progress against poverty has been made, these statistics do not indicate that poverty is no longer of concern to the American people.

THE PROBLEMS OF DISCRIMINATION

Racial Discrimination

Poverty, *discrimination,* and race are closely intertwined. Despite recent improvements, the sad fact is that racial discrimination occurs in many walks of life in many areas of the United States. Table 24.4 shows certain aspects of the relative position of the white and nonwhite populations in the United States. The average income of nonwhites is only about two-thirds that of whites. About one-quarter of the nonwhite population is below the poverty line, compared with only about one-tenth of the white population. On the average, whites complete more years of schooling than nonwhites, and a larger percentage of whites than of nonwhites are college graduates.

**Table 24.4
Economic
Characteristics of
Whites and
Nonwhites, United
States, 1983**

	White	Nonwhite
Median family income (dollars)	25,757	14,506
Percent of persons in poverty	12.1	35.7
Percent unemployed (males)	6.4	16.4
Percent unemployed (females)	6.5	15.4
Percent unemployed (male teenagers)	16.8	42.7
Percent of people (25 years and over) with		
4 years or more of college	19.5	9.5

Source: *Economic Report of the President,* 1985, and World Almanac. Unemployment rates pertain to 1984.

There is considerable agreement that at least part of these economic differences is the result of discrimination. Nonwhites are often prevented from reaching certain occupational or managerial levels. It is rare to find a black in the higher reaches of management in a major corporation. To a considerable extent they are cut off from job opportunities at this level by lack of education. But even at much lower levels, they are kept out of certain occupations by union policy (the building trades are a good example); and even when nonwhites do essentially the same kind of work as whites, there is sometimes a tendency to pay nonwhites less.

Effects of Discrimination

Some important effects of racial discrimination can be demonstrated by using the theory of wages. (The general point of this discussion holds true whether discrimination is on racial or other grounds.) The important thing to recognize at the outset is that nonwhite labor is not allowed to compete with white labor. This results in two different labor markets, one for whites and one for nonwhites. As shown in Figure 24.2, the demand curve for nonwhite labor is quite different from the demand curve for white labor, reflecting the fact that nonwhites are not allowed to enter many of the more productive occupations. Because of the difference in the demand (and supply) curves, the equilibrium wage for nonwhites, P_B, is lower than for whites, P_W.

A. The case of discrimination

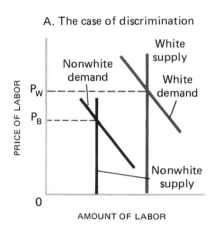

B. No discrimination

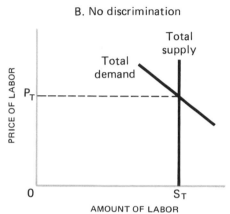

Figure 24.2 Racial Discrimination Under discrimination, the demand curve for white labor is quite different from that for nonwhite labor, and the supply curve of white labor is quite different from that of nonwhite labor, so that the equilibrium wage for nonwhites, P_B, is lower than for whites, P_W. If there were no discrimination, the wage for all labor, nonwhite or white, would be P_T.

How does this equilibrium differ from a situation of no discrimination? If nonwhites and whites competed in the same labor market, the total demand for labor—regardless of color—and the total supply of labor—regardless of color—would be as shown in panel B of Figure 24.2; the wage for all labor—regardless of color—would be P_T. A comparison of P_T with P_B shows that the wage rate of nonwhites would increase considerably. A comparison of P_T with P_W shows that the wage rates of whites would decrease slightly. The slight cut in white wages would be much smaller than the considerable increase in nonwhite wages, since the nation's total production (and income) would increase because nonwhites could be put to more productive use.

Thus the effect of discrimination is to exploit nonwhites, by reducing their wages relative to whites, and to lower the nation's total output. Fortunately, there is evidence that racial discrimination is lessening. In part because of changing attitudes among whites, the growing restiveness of nonwhites, and the coming of age of new leadership, the old patterns of segregation and discrimination are breaking down. Blacks are now being recruited actively by many prestigious colleges, and they are being hired and promoted to responsible positions in firms where formerly they remained at a relatively menial level. The ratio of nonwhite to white average income rose from about 50 percent in the 1950s to about 60 percent in the 1980s. Progress is slow, but it unquestionably exists.

Discrimination against Women

Needless to say, discrimination is not limited to nonwhites: blacks, Puerto Ricans, Mexican-Americans, and Native Americans. There is some discrimination against older workers. Even more widespread is discrimination against women. Holding age and education constant, women earn much less than men. To some extent, this difference in earnings arises because women work shorter hours and often have less experience in their jobs than men. But even after adjusting for factors such as education, work experience during the year, and lifetime work experience, there remains a differential of about 20 percent between the earnings of men and women. To a considerable extent, this differential is probably the result of discrimination, the nature of which has been described by the Council of Economic Advisers:

> There is clearly prejudice against women engaging in particular activities. Some patients reject women doctors, some clients reject women lawyers, some customers reject automobile saleswomen, and some workers reject women bosses. Employers also may have formulated discriminatory attitudes about women, exaggerating the risk of job instability or client acceptance and therefore excluding women from on-the-job training which would advance their careers. In fact, even if employers do estimate correctly the average job turnover of women, women who are strongly committed to their jobs may suffer from "statistical discrimination" by being treated as though their own behavior resembled the average. The extent to which this type of discrimination occurs depends on how costly it is for employers to distinguish women who will have a strong job commitment from those who will not. Finally, because some occupations restrict the number of newcomers they take in and because women move in and out of the labor force more often, more women than men tend to fall into the newcomer category and to be thus excluded. For example, restrictive entry policies may have kept women out of the skilled crafts.
>
> On the other hand, some component of the earnings differential and of the occupation differential stems from differences in role orientation which start with differences in education and continue through marriage, where women generally are expected to assume primary responsibility for the home and subordinate their own outside work to their household responsibilities. It is not now possible to distinguish in a quantitative way between the discrimination which bars women from jobs solely because of their sex, and the role differentiation whereby women, either through choice or necessity, restrict their careers because of the demands of their homes. Some may label the latter as a pervasive social discrimination which starts in the cradle; nonetheless, it is useful to draw the distinction.[6]

In various ways, the government has set out to discourage discrimination against women. The Equal Pay Act of 1963 requires employers to pay

[6] *The Economic Report of the President*, 1973, pp. 106–7.

men and women equally for the same work, and Title VII of the Civil Rights Act of 1964 bars discrimination in hiring, firing, and other aspects of employment. In addition, a number of women have been appointed to high-ranking government jobs, including economists Juanita Kreps (who has been secretary of commerce), Marina Whitman (who has served as a member of the president's Council of Economic Advisers), Alice Rivlin (who has headed the Congressional Budget Office), and Nancy Teeters (who has been a member of the Federal Reserve Board). All these measures undoubtedly will have a beneficial effect, but it must be recognized that eliminating discrimination of this kind will require basic changes in the attitudes of both males and females. The problem of discrimination against women is likely to be with us for a long time.

SUMMARY

1. Many factors are responsible for existing income differentials. Some people are abler, better educated, or luckier than others. Some people have more property, or more monopoly power, than others.

2. Critics of income inequality argue that it lessens total consumer satisfaction because an extra dollar given to the poor provides them with more extra satisfaction than the loss of a dollar taken away from the rich. Also, they argue that income inequality leads to social and political inequality.

3. Defenders of income inequality point out that it is scientifically impossible to make interpersonal comparisons of utility, and argue that income inequality is needed to provide incentives for people to work and create, and that it permits greater capital formation.

4. There is no well-defined income level that can be used in all times and all places to determine poverty. Perhaps the most widely accepted definition of poverty in the United States today is the one developed by the Social Security Administration, according to which about 15 percent of the population in the United States—over 35 million people—fall below the poverty line. Compared with 25 years ago, the incidence of poverty has declined in the United States.

5. Nonwhite families, families headed by a female, and very large families are more likely than others to be poor. To a considerable extent, the reasons for their poverty lie beyond the control of the poor people. About one-third of poor adults have suffered a disability of some sort, or the premature death of the family breadwinner, or family dissolution. Most heads of poor families do not have jobs.

6. Because private charity is judged to be inadequate, the nation has authorized its government to carry out various public programs to aid the poor. There are programs to provide them with goods and services: food-stamp programs, for instance. Other programs, like aid to families with dependent children, give them cash. When these programs are taken into account, the percentage of the population falling below the poverty line is reduced considerably.

7. There is widespread dissatisfaction with existing antipoverty—or welfare—programs. They are judged to be inefficient; their costs have increased at an alarming rate; and they provide little incentive for people to get off welfare. One suggestion to remedy these problems is a negative income tax. In most of the forms put forth it involves a transfer of income that may be beyond the realm of political feasibility.

8. Despite recent improvements, the sad fact is that racial discrimination occurs in many walks of life in many areas of the United States. Nonwhites often are cut off from educational and job opportunities; and even when nonwhites do essentially the same kind of work as whites, there is sometimes a tendency to pay them less. The effects of discrimination are to reduce the wages of nonwhites relative to whites and to lower the nation's total output.

9. There is also much discrimination against women, making them less likely than men to enter better-paying occupations. Even after adjusting for factors such as education and work experience, women earn about 20 percent less than men.

PART 6
☆☆☆☆☆☆☆☆☆☆☆☆☆☆☆☆

Growth, the Government, and International Economics

CHAPTER 25

★ ★ ★ ★ ★ ★ ★ ★ ★

Economic Growth

LEARNING OBJECTIVES

In this chapter, you should learn:

★ What economic growth is, and how it is measured

★ The role of diminishing marginal returns in economic growth

★ The effects of investment on economic growth

★ The role of public policy in promoting economic growth

Until fairly recently in human history, poverty was the rule, not the exception. As Sir Kenneth Clark puts it in his famous lectures on *Civilisation,*

> Poverty, hunger, plagues, disease: they were the background of history right up to the end of the nineteenth century, and most people regarded them as inevitable—like bad weather. Nobody thought they could be cured: St. Francis wanted to sanctify poverty, not abolish it. The old Poor Laws were not designed to abolish poverty but to prevent the poor from becoming a nuisance. All that was required was an occasional act of charity.[1]

Clearly, the human condition has changed considerably during the past century, at least in the industrialized nations of the world. Rising living standards have brought a decline in poverty, though by no means its disappearance. How has this increase in per capita output been achieved?

[1] K. Clark, *Civilisation,* New York: Harper and Row, 1970.

This question has fascinated economists for a long time. Although we still are far from completely understanding the process of economic growth, our knowledge has increased considerably through the efforts of economic researchers, here and abroad. In this chapter, we discuss the process of economic growth in industrialized countries.

WHAT IS ECONOMIC GROWTH?

There are two common measures of the rate of *economic growth.* The first is the rate of growth of a nation's real gross national product (or net national product),[2] which tells us how rapidly the economy's total real output of goods and services is increasing. The second is the rate of growth of *per capita* real gross national product (or net national product), which is a better measure of the rate of increase of a nation's standard of living. We will use the second measure unless we state otherwise. Two aspects of the rate of growth of per capita real gross national product should be noted from the start.

1. *This measure is only a very crude approximation to the rate of increase of economic welfare.* For one thing, gross national product does not include one good that people prize most highly: leisure. For another, gross national product does not value accurately new products and improvements in the quality of goods and services, and does not allow properly either for noneconomic changes in the quality of life or for the costs of environmental pollution. Nor does gross national product take account of how the available output is distributed. Clearly, it makes a difference whether the bulk of the population gets a reasonable share of the output, or whether it goes largely to a favored few.

2. *Small differences in the annual rate of economic growth can make very substantial differences in living standards a few decades hence.* For example, per capita GNP in the United States was about $15,000 in 1984. If it grows at 2 percent per year, it will be about $20,600 (1984 dollars) in the year 2000, whereas if it grows at 3 percent per year, it will be about $24,100 (1984 dollars) in the year 2000. Thus an increase of 1 percentage point in the growth rate means a $3,500—or 17 percent—increase in per capita GNP in the year 2000. Even an increase of one-quarter of one percentage point can make a considerable difference. If the growth rate increases from 1¾ percent to 2 percent per year, per capita GNP in the year 2000 will increase from $19,800 to $20,600.

ECONOMIC GROWTH AS A POLICY OBJECTIVE

Following World War II, governments throughout the world became much more involved in trying to stimulate economic growth. In the United States, the government was not much inclined to influence the

[2]Either net national product or gross national product will do. As pointed out in Chapter 3, NNP has certain conceptual advantages, but GNP is more frequently used. It makes little difference since they do not differ by much. We use gross national product in this chapter, because data on GNP are more easily available.

growth rate before the war. Of course, the government did many things that had some effect on the rate of economic growth, and in a general sort of way was interested in promoting economic growth. But it was normally taken for granted that, left to its own devices, our economy would manage to grow at more or less the proper rate.

Whether or not the government should increase the rate of economic growth is, of course, a political decision; and your opinion of such a government policy will depend on many things, including your attitude toward present sacrifice for future material gain. As we shall see in subsequent sections, *a more rapid rate of growth can often be achieved only if consumers are willing to give up some consumption now so that they and their children can have more goods and services in the future.* To the extent that you believe that private decisions place too little weight on the future and too much weight on the present, you may be inclined to support a government policy designed to increase the growth rate. Otherwise you may not favor such a policy.

THOMAS MALTHUS AND POPULATION GROWTH

A nation's rate of economic growth depends on, among other things, how much the quantities of inputs of various kinds increase. To illuminate the nature of the growth process, we discuss the effect on the rate of economic growth of increasing each kind of input, holding the others constant. We begin by looking at the effects of changes in the quantity of labor. Economists have devoted a great deal of attention to the effects of population growth on the rate of economic growth. The classic work was done by Thomas Malthus (1776–1834), a British parson who devoted his life to academic research. The first professional economist, he taught at a college established by the East India Company to train its administrators—and was called "Pop" by his students behind his back. Whether "Pop" stood for population or not, Malthus's fame is based on his theories of population growth.

Thomas Malthus

Malthus believed that the population tends to grow at a geometric rate. In his *Essay on the Principle of Population,* published in 1798, he pointed out the implications of such a constant rate of growth:

If any person will take the trouble to make the calculation, he will see that if the necessities of life could be obtained without limit, and the number of people could be doubled every twenty-five years, the population which might have been produced from a single pair since the Christian era, would have been sufficient, not only to fill the earth quite full of people, so that four should stand in every square yard, but to fill all the planets of our solar system in the same way, and not only them but all the planets revolving around the stars which are visible to the naked eye, supposing each of them . . . to have as many planets belong to it as our sun has.[3]

In contrast to the human population, which tends to increase at a geometric rate,[4] the supply of land can increase slowly if at all. And land, particularly in Malthus's time, was the source of food. Consequently, it seemed to Malthus that the human population was in danger of outrunning its food supply: "Taking the whole earth," he wrote, ". . . and supposing the present population to be equal to a thousand millions, the human species would increase as the numbers 1, 2, 4, 8, 16, 32, 64, 128, 256, and subsistence as 1, 2, 3, 4, 5, 6, 7, 8, 9. In two centuries, the population would be to the means of subsistence as 256 to 9; in three centries as 4096 to 13, and in two thousand years the difference would be incalculable."[5]

A Bleak Prospect

Certainly, Malthus's view of humanity's prospects was bleak; as he himself acknowledged, "the view has a melancholy hue." Gone is the optimism of Adam Smith. According to Malthus, the prospect for economic progress was very limited. Given the inexorable increase in human numbers, the standard of living will be kept at a minimum level required to keep body and soul together. If it exceeds this level, the population will increase, driving the standard of living back down. On the other hand, if the standard of living is less than this level, the population will decline because of starvation. Certainly, the long-term prospects were anything but bright. Thomas Carlyle, the famous historian and essayist, called economics "the dismal science." To a considerable extent, economics acquired this bad name through the efforts of Parson Malthus.

Malthus's theory can be interpreted in terms of the law of diminishing marginal returns. (Recall Chapter 15.) Living in what was still largely an agricultural society, he emphasized the role of land and labor as resources, and assumed a relatively fixed level of technology. Since land is fixed, increases in labor—due to population growth—will eventually cause the marginal product of labor to get smaller and smaller because of the law

[3]T. Malthus, *Essay on the Principle of Population*, as quoted by R. Heilbroner, *The Worldly Philosophers*, 5th ed., New York: Simon and Schuster, 1980, p. 71. For those who would like to read more concerning the history of economic thought, Heilbroner's book is highly recommended.

[4]Of course, it does not matter to Malthus's argument whether the population doubles every 25 years or every 40 years. The important thing is that it increases at a geometric rate.

[5]T. Malthus, "The Principle of Population Growth," reprinted in E. Mansfield, *Principles of Macroeconomics: Readings, Issues, and Cases*, 4th ed., New York: Norton, 1983.

of diminishing marginal returns. (Recall from Chapter 22 that the marginal product of labor is the additional output resulting from an extra unit of labor.) In other words, because of this law, the marginal product of labor will behave as shown in Figure 25.1, with the result that continued growth of the labor force will ultimately bring economic decline—that is, a reduction in output per worker. This happens because, as the marginal product of labor falls with increases in the labor force, the average product of labor will eventually fall as well—and the average product of labor is another name for output per worker.

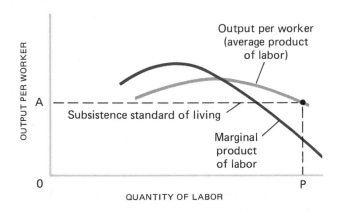

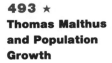

Figure 25.1 Diminishing Marginal Returns and the Effect of Population Growth According to Malthus, the labor force will tend to OP because, if output per worker exceeds OA, population will increase, and if output per worker is less than OA, starvation will reduce the population.

Of course, Malthus recognized that various devices could keep the population down: war, famine, birth-control measures, among others. In fact, he tried to describe and evaluate the importance of various checks on population growth. For example, suppose that population tends to grow to the point where output per worker is at a subsistence level—just sufficient to keep body and soul together. If this is the case, and if the subsistence level of output per worker is OA, then the labor force will tend to equal OP in Figure 25.1. Why? Because, as noted above, Malthus believed that if the standard of living rises appreciably above OA, population will increase, thus forcing it back toward OA. On the other hand, if the standard of living falls below OA, some of the population will starve, thus pushing it back toward OA.

Effects of Population Growth

Was Malthus right? Among the less developed nations of the world, his analysis seems very relevant today. During the past 40 years, the population of the less developed nations has grown very rapidly, in part because of the decrease in death rates attributable to the transfer of medical advances from the industrialized countries to the less developed countries. Between 1940 and 1970, the total population of Asia, Africa, and Oceania almost doubled. There has been a tendency for growing populations to push hard against food supplies in some of the countries of Africa,

CASE STUDY 25.1 THE CLUB OF ROME'S "LIMITS TO GROWTH" REPORT

In 1974, an M.I.T.-based group produced a pessimistic analysis called the Club of Rome's "Limits to Growth" report. The report concluded that if the world's burgeoning population were to consume resources at the rate of the United States, many critical resources, minerals especially, would soon become very scarce; and that with scarcity, prices would rise to unacceptable levels, and economic and industrial growth would slow down.

The notion was not new. Thomas Malthus in 1798 had considered that population growth, and hence consumption, would soon undermine growth—indeed, civilization itself—in Europe. In 1908, President Roosevelt worried about a diminishing supply of raw materials, and gathered a commission to ponder the future of an America without minerals and metals. More resources were quickly found. In 1944, there was another review, and 21 commodities were placed on the endangered list. By now, those commodities should have been exhausted. None has been. What has repeatedly pulled us back from the pessimists' brink of doom?

Copper has often been listed as a mineral due for future scarcity. It is subject to fluctuating prices. In peak-price years, there is a flurry of exploration, and new low-grade porphyries across the world are added to the tonnage in reserve. But in those peak-price years, before new mines have time to develop, another factor comes into play: It becomes cost-effective for users to find substitutes for copper, using aluminum or plastics instead. And once substitutes are found, copper consumption does not return to its original levels. The telecommunications industry is a recent example where massive substitution has taken place, as fiber optics have come to the fore in intracity communications.

So the Club of Rome doomsayers would seem to be discredited on two counts: Increased prices generate greater supplies through improved exploration and mining technology, and increased prices encourage substitution of other materials (and the recycling of scrap) to satisfy demand.

But aren't the planet's mineral resources finite? They are, although the geochemical cycle that creates minerals is virtually infinite. Not much gets off the planet, and we have hardly scratched the surface in our search for greater supplies. The costs of extraction from deep within the earth's crust or the ocean floor might look excessively expensive today, but they looked astronomical a century ago, and the relative cost of minerals has remained roughly constant, hardly increasing even with diminishing returns. Basic raw materials, then, will not run out for centuries. Our growth will continue, less dependent on supplies than on our technological ability and the wisdom of our investment.

N.B.

Latin America, and Asia; the Malthusian model can explain important elements of the situation.

However, Malthus's theory seems far less relevant or correct for the industrialized countries. In contrast to his model, population has not increased to the point where the standard of living has been pushed down to the subsistence level. On the contrary, the standard of living has increased dramatically in all of the industrialized nations. The most important mistake Malthus made was to underestimate the extent and importance of technological change. Instead of remaining fixed, the marginal-product-of-labor curve in Figure 25.1 moved gradually to the right, as new methods and new products increased the efficiency of agriculture. In other words, the situation was as shown in Figure 25.2. Thus as population increased, the marginal product of labor did not go down. Instead, technological change prevented the productivity of extra agricultural workers from falling.

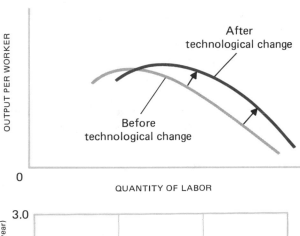

Figure 25.2
Shift over Time in the Marginal Product of Labor Technological change has shifted the marginal-product-of-labor curve to the right.

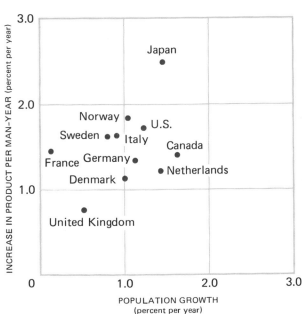

Figure 25.3
Relationship between Population Growth and Increases in National Product per Man-Year, 11 Industrialized Nations, 1913–59 In industrialized nations, there is little or no relationship between a nation's rate of population growth and its rate of economic growth.

Among the industrialized nations, have countries with relatively high rates of growth of population had relatively low—or relatively high—rates of economic growth? In general, there seems to be little or no relationship between a nation's rate of population increase and its rate of economic growth. Figure 25.3 plots the rate of population increase against the rate of growth of output per man-year in 11 industrialized nations between 1913 and 1959. The results suggest that there is little or no relation between them; and the relationship that exists appears to be direct rather than inverse.

DAVID RICARDO AND CAPITAL FORMATION

A contemporary and good friend of Malthus's who also contributed to the theory of economic growth was David Ricardo (1772–1823). Of all the titans of economics, he is probably the least known to the general public. Smith, Malthus, Marx, and Keynes are frequently encountered names. Ricardo is not, although he made many brilliant contributions to economic thought. An extremely successful stockbroker who retired at the age of 42 with a very large fortune, he devoted much of his time to highly theoretical analyses of the economic system and its workings. In contrast to Malthus, who was reviled for his pessimistic doctrines, Ricardo and his writings were widely admired in his own time. He was elected to England's House of Commons and was highly respected there.

Ricardo on Income Distribution

Ricardo was concerned in much of his work with the distribution of income. Unlike Adam Smith, who paid much less attention to the conflict among classes, Ricardo emphasized the struggle between the industrialists —a relatively new and rising class in his time—and the landowners—the old aristocracy that resisted the rise of the industrial class. This clash was reflected in the struggle in Britain around 1800 over the so-called Corn Laws (*corn* being a general term covering all types of grain). Because of the increase of population, the demand for grain increased in Britain, causing the price of grain to rise greatly. This meant higher profits for the landowners. But the industrialists complained bitterly about the increase in the price of food, because higher food prices meant that they had to pay higher wages. As the price of grain increased, merchants began to import cheap grain from abroad. But the landowners, who dominated Parliament, passed legislation, the Corn Laws, to keep cheap grain out of Britain. In effect the Corn Laws imposed a high tariff or duty on grain.

According to Ricardo's analysis, the landlords were bound to capture most of the benefits of economic progress, unless their control of the price of grain could be weakened. As national output increased and population expanded, poorer and poorer land had to be brought under cultivation to produce the extra food. As the cost of producing grain increased, its price would increase, and so would the rents of the landlords. The workers and the industrialists, on the other hand, would benefit little, if at all. As the price of grain increased, the workers would have to get higher wages— but only high enough to keep them at a subsistence level (since Ricardo agreed entirely with his friend Malthus on the population issue). Thus the workers would be no better off; neither would the industrialists, who would wind up with lower profits because of the increase in wage rates.

Ricardo felt that the Corn Laws should be repealed and that free trade in grain should be permitted. In a beautiful piece of theoretical analysis that is still reasonably fresh and convincing 170 years after its publication, he laid out the basic principles of international trade and pointed out the benefits to all countries that can be derived by specialization and free trade. For example, suppose that England is relatively more efficient at producing textiles, and France is relatively more efficient at producing wine. Then, on the basis of Ricardo's analysis, it can be shown that each country is likely to be better off by specializing in the product it is more efficient at producing—textiles in England, wine in France—and trading this product for the one the other country specializes in producing.

Ricardo's View of Capital Formation

Let's turn to the effect on economic growth of increases in physical capital, holding other inputs and technology fixed. Ricardo constructed some interesting theories concerning the effects of *capital formation*—that is, investment in plant and equipment—on economic growth. Other things held constant, a nation's output depends on the amount of plant and equipment that it has and operates. Moreover, one can draw a curve showing the marginal product of capital—the extra output that would result from an extra dollar's worth of capital—under various assumptions about the total amount of capital in existence. This curve will slope downward to the right, as shown in Figure 25.4, because of the law of diminishing marginal returns. As more and more capital is accumulated, its marginal product eventually must decrease. For example, if $100 billion is the

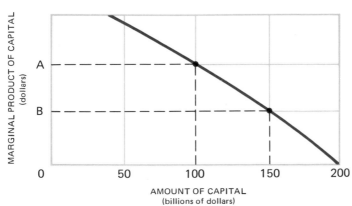

Figure 25.4
Marginal Product of Capital
This curve shows the marginal product of capital, under various assumptions concerning the total amount of capital. For example, if there is $100 billion of capital, the marginal product of capital is $A, whereas if there is $150 billion of capital, the marginal product of capital is $B.

total investment in plant and equipment (or total capital), the extra output to be derived from an extra dollar of investment is worth $A;$ if the total investment is increased to $150 billion, however, the economy must resort to less productive investments, and the extra output to be derived from an extra dollar of investment is only worth $B.$

The curve in Figure 25.4 leads to the conclusion that investment in plant and equipment, although it will increase the growth rate up to some point, will eventually be unable to increase it further. As more and more is invested in new plant and equipment, less and less productive projects must be undertaken. Finally, when all the productive projects have been carried out, further investment in plant and equipment will be useless. At this point—$200 billion of total capital in Figure 25.4—further investment in plant and equipment will not increase output at all.

This kind of analysis led Ricardo to the pessimistic conclusion that the economy would experience decreases in the profitability of investment in plant and equipment, and the eventual termination of economic growth.

Was Ricardo Right?

Have we seen decreases in the profitability of investment in plant and equipment, and eventual termination of economic growth? No. Ricardo, like Malthus, was led astray by underestimating the extent and impact of future changes in technology. Suppose that, because of the development of major new products and processes, lots of new opportunities for profitable investment arise. Obviously, the effect on the curve in Figure 25.4 is to shift it to the right, because there are more investment opportunities than before above a certain level of productivity. But if this curve shifts to the right, as shown in Figure 25.5, we may be able to avoid Ricardo's pessimistic conclusions.

To see how this can occur, note that if X in Figure 25.5 is the relevant curve in a particular year and if $100 billion is the total amount of capital, an extra dollar of investment in plant and equipment would have a marginal product of $C.$ A decade later, if Y is the relevant curve and if the total amount of capital has grown to $150 billion, the marginal product of

**Figure 25.5
Effects of
Technological
Change on the
Marginal Product
of Capital**
Technological
change has shifted
the marginal-
product-of-capital
curve to the right.
(Actually, Ricardo's
variable input was a
combined dose of
capital and labor.)

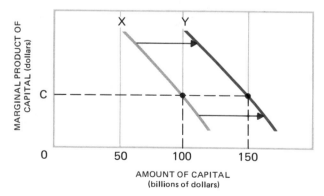

an extra dollar of investment in plant and equipment is still C. Thus there is no reduction in the productivity of investment opportunities despite the 50 percent increase in the total amount of capital. Because of technological change and other factors, productive and profitable new investment opportunities are opened up as fast as old ones are invested in.

The history of the United States is quite consistent with this sort of shift in investment opportunities over time. Even though we have poured an enormous amount of money into new plant and equipment, we have not exhausted or reduced the productivity or profitability of investment opportunities. The rate of return on investment in new plant and equipment has not fallen. Instead, it has fluctuated around a fairly constant level during the past 70 years.

CAPITAL FORMATION AND ECONOMIC GROWTH

To see more clearly the role of investment in the process of economic growth, let's extend the model we discussed in Chapter 5. Suppose we ignore the government and consider only the private sector of the economy. Suppose that the full-employment, noninflationary NNP this year is $1,000 billion, and that the consumption function is such that consumption expenditure is $900 billion if NNP is $1,000 billion. If intended investment this year is $100 billion, with the result that NNP is in fact $1,000 billion, *next year's full-employment NNP will increase because this year's investment will increase the nation's productive capacity.* In other words, this year's investment increases next year's full-employment NNP. The amount of the increase in full-employment NNP depends on the *capital-output ratio,* which is the number of dollars of investment (or extra capital goods) required to produce an extra dollar of output. For example, if the capital-output ratio is 2, $2 of investment is required to increase full-employment NNP by $1.

Effect of Investment on Full-Employment NNP

Let's look more closely at the effect of investment on full-employment NNP. If the capital-output ratio is 2, full-employment NNP will increase by $50 billion as a consequence of the $100 billion of investment. Thus full-employment NNP next year is $1,050 billion. On the other hand, suppose that this year's investment is $200 billion rather than $100 billion, and that the consumption function is such that consumption expenditure is $800 billion rather than $900 billion if NNP is $1,000 billion. What will full-employment NNP be next year? If the capital-output ratio is 2, it will be $1,100 billion. Why? Because the $200 billion in investment will increase full-employment NNP by $100 billion—from $1,000 billion to $1,100 billion.

Thus the full-employment NNP will be larger if investment is $200 billion than if it is $100 billion. Similarly, full-employment NNP will be larger if investment is $300 billion than if it is $200 billion. If the capital-output ratio is 2, full-employment NNP will be $1,150 billion next year, if investment is $300 billion. Why? Because the $300 billion in investment will increase full-employment NNP by $150 billion—from $1,000 to $1,150 billion.

In general, the greater the percentage of NNP that the society devotes to investment this year, the greater will be the increase in its full-employment NNP. Thus *so long as the economy sustains noninflationary full employment and the capital-output ratio remains constant, the rate of growth of national output will be directly related to the percentage of NNP devoted to investment.*[6]

Some Evidence Concerning the Effects of Investment

Certainly, this result seems sensible enough. If a country wants to increase its growth rate, it should produce more blast furnaces, machine tools, and plows, and fewer cosmetics, household furniture, and sports cars. But all this is theory. What do the facts suggest? Table 25.1 shows the rate of investment and the growth rate in six major industrialized nations of the non-Communist world in the 1970s. The investment rate was highest in Japan; so was the growth rate. The investment rates were lowest in the United States and the United Kingdom, and their growth rates were among the lowest. Of course, this does not prove that there is any simple cause-and-effect relationship between the investment rate and the growth rate, but it certainly is compatible with the view that investment influences growth.

Table 25.1
Rate of Growth of Output (1978–80) and Investment as Percentage of Output (1970–77)

Nation	Rate of growth of output (percent)	Percent of output invested
	Annual average	
France	2.8	18.8
Germany	3.3	18.7
Canada	2.4	19.3
Japan	5.0	26.7
United Kingdom	1.0	17.6
United States	2.6	14.5

Source: *Economic Report of the President*, 1982.

[6]It can be shown that the rate of growth of NNP equals s/b, where s is the proportion of NNP that is saved (and invested), and b is the capital-output ratio, assuming that both s and b are constant and that full employment is maintained. For example, if b is 2 and $s = .10$, NNP will grow at 5 percent per year, since $.10/2 = .05$. This result is part of the so-called Harrod-Domar growth model developed by the late Sir Roy Harrod of Oxford and Evsey Domar of M.I.T. Although useful, this result must be used with caution since it is based on highly simplified assumptions.

THE ROLE OF HUMAN CAPITAL

A nation's rate of economic growth is influenced by the rate at which it invests in human capital as well as physical capital. It may seem odd to speak of *human* capital, but every society builds up a certain amount of human capital through investments in formal education, on-the-job-training, and health programs. You often hear people talk about investing in their children's future by putting them through college. For the economy as a whole, the expenditure on education and public health can also be viewed—at least partly—as an investment, because consumption is sacrificed in the present in order to make possible a higher level of per capita output in the future.

The United States invests in human capital on a massive scale. In 1960 expenditures for schools at all levels of education were about $25 billion, or about 5 percent of our gross national product. Moreover, our total investment in the education of the population—the "stock" of educational capital—has grown much more rapidly than has the stock of plant and equipment. Whereas the stock of physical capital was about 4 times as big in 1956 as in 1900, the stock of educational capital was about 8 times as big. These enormous and rapidly growing investments in human capital have unquestionably increased the productivity, versatility, and adaptability of our labor force. They have certainly made a major contribution to economic growth.

Income tends to rise with a person's education. Using this relationship to measure the influence of education on a person's productivity, some economists, notably University of Chicago's Nobel laureate Theodore Schultz and Gary Becker, have tried to estimate the profitability, both to society and to the person, of an investment in various levels of education. Becker has tried to estimate the rate of return from a person's investment in a college education. According to his estimates, the typical urban white male in 1950 received about a 10 percent return (after taxes) on his investment in tuition, room, books, and other college expenses (including the earnings he gave up by being in college rather than at work). This was a relatively high return—much higher, for example, than if the student simply put the equivalent amount of money in a savings bank or in government bonds.

By the mid-1970s, however, the return from the investment in a college education seemed to have fallen considerably. According to Richard Freeman of Harvard University and Herbert Hollomon of M.I.T., it declined from about 11 or 12 percent in 1969 to about 7 or 8 percent in 1974. In part, this was due to the increase in college tuition, as well as the recession experienced by the economy that year. Also, the income differential between college-educated and other workers seems to have narrowed. In 1969, full-time male workers with four years of college earned 53 percent more than male workers with only four years of high school, but in 1974, the differential was only about 40 percent. Whether this decrease in the return from a college education is temporary is hard to say.

THE ROLE OF TECHNOLOGICAL CHANGE

A nation's rate of economic growth depends on the rate of *technological change,* as well as on the extent to which quantities of inputs of various kinds increase. Indeed, the rate of technological change is perhaps the most important single determinant of a nation's rate of economic growth. Recall from Chapters 1 and 11 that technology is knowledge concerning

CASE STUDY 25.2 COMPUTER-ASSISTED DESIGN AND MANUFACTURE AT BOEING AIRCRAFT

Twenty, and even ten years ago, the design and manufacture of a Boeing 727 or 747 were far from smooth processes. Drawings were hand-done, and passed from hand to hand with each requested improvement. And when designs got to the shop floor, often they did not quite fit. Parts had to be rejigged, shaved, and modified here and there. The manufacturing process was full of fits and starts—beautiful and safe in the end, but inefficient and expensive getting there.

In 1978 and 1979, work began on the Boeing 767 and 757, the airbuses. Sophisticated interactive computer graphics were developed for drafting the designs. Each part, each point on every surface, was built into a mathematical program and stored on computer to be manipulated for any slight change. A set of drawings could now be changed in a day, rather than a week, and with more accuracy that before. Computer-assisted design (CAD) had arrived in the aircraft industry. In the back rooms, productivity and growth increased.

The effect was felt on the assembly line too. Fewer modifications had to be made on the shop floor. Costs were reduced because the designs could be applied more accurately at lower tolerances. Airplane components fit together better. And computer-assisted manufacturing (CAM) controlled equipment precisely, turning out wing-skins, spare assemblies, and dozens of delicate rivets for quality in flight.

It all took some time to go through the learning process, but Boeing now experiences less overtime in rework and fewer delays in start-up. For the next generation of planes, productivity will be enhanced even more as computers are more fully linked in design and manufacture. Technology will continue to increase growth in output per hour.

N.B.

the industrial and agricultural arts. Thus technological change often takes the form of new methods of producing existing products; new designs that make it possible to produce goods with important new characteristics; and new techniques of organization, marketing, and management. Two examples of technological change are new ways of producing power (for example, atomic energy) and new fibers (for example, nylon or Dacron).

We have already seen that technological change can shift the curves in both Figures 25.2 and 25.5, thus warding off the law of diminishing marginal returns. But note that new knowledge by itself has little impact. *Unless knowledge is applied, it has little effect on the rate of economic growth.* A change in technology, when applied for the first time, is called an *innovation,* and the firm that first applies it is called an *innovator.* Innovation is a key stage in the process leading to the full evaluation and utilization of a new process or product. The innovator must be willing to take the risks involved in introducing a new and untried process, good, or service; and in many cases, these risks are high. Once a change in technology has been applied for the first time, the *diffusion process*—the process by which the use of the innovation spreads from firm to firm and from use to use—begins. How rapidly an innovation spreads depends heavily on its economic advantages over older methods or products. The more profitable the use of the innovation is, the more rapidly it will spread.

Joseph Schumpeter, Harvard's distinguished economist and social theorist, stressed the important role played by innovators in the process of economic growth. In Schumpeter's view, innovators are the mainspring of economic progress, the people with the foresight to see how new things can be brought into being and the courage and resourcefulness to surmount the obstacles to change. For this trouble, innovators receive profit; but this profit eventually is whittled down by competitors

Bill Gates, a young entrepreneur in computer software

who imitate the innovators. The innovators push the curves in Figures 25.2 and 25.5 to the right, and once their innovations are assimilated by the economy, other innovators may shove these curves somewhat farther to the right. For example, one innovator introduces vacuum tubes, a later innovator introduces semiconductors; one innovator introduces the steam locomotive, a later innovator introduces the diesel locomotive. This process goes on and on, and is a main source of economic growth.

ENTREPRENEURSHIP AND THE SOCIAL ENVIRONMENT

Still another set of basic factors influencing a nation's level of potential output and its rate of economic growth is the economic, social, political, and religious climate of the nation. It is difficult, if not impossible, to measure the effect of these factors, but there can be no doubt of their importance. Some societies despise material welfare and emphasize the glories of the next world. Some societies are subject to such violent political upheavals that it is risky, if not foolish, to invest in the future. Some societies are governed so corruptly that economic growth is frustrated. And some societies look down on people engaged in industry, trade, or commerce. Obviously, such societies are less likely to experience rapid economic growth than others with a more favorable climate and conditions.

The relatively rapid economic growth of the United States was undoubtedly stimulated in part by the attitude of its people toward material gain. It is commonplace to note that the United States is a materialistic society, a society that esteems business success, that bestows prestige on the rich, that accepts the Protestant ethic (which, crudely stated, is that work is good), and that encourages individual initiative. The United States has been criticized over and over again for some of these traits, often by nations frantically trying to imitate its economic success. Somewhat less obvious is the fact that, because the United States is a young country whose people came from a variety of origins, it did not inherit many feudal components in the structure of society. This too was important in promoting economic growth.

The United States has also been characterized by great economic and political freedom, by institutions that have been flexible enough to adjust to change, and by a government that has encouraged competition in the marketplace. This has meant fewer barriers to new ideas. Also, the United States has for a long time enjoyed internal peace, order, and general respect for property rights. There have been no violent revolutions since the Civil War, and for many years we were protected from strife in other lands by two oceans—which then seemed much broader than they do now. All these factors undoubtedly contributed to rapid economic growth.

The American economy also seems to have been able to nurture a great many entrepreneurs and a vast horde of competent business executives. During the twentieth century, American entrepreneurs were responsible for such basic innovations as the automobile assembly line, pioneered by Henry Ford. (See Case Study 25.3.) In many areas, the United States gained a technological lead over other nations, which was maintained for many years. Much of this lead came from superior management as well as superior technological resources. For example, the Organization for Economic Cooperation and Development concluded in 1968: "In the techniques of *management,* including the management of research, and of combined technological and market forecasting, the United States appears to have a significant lead."[7] In the past decade, according to many observers, our technological lead has been reduced considerably. This has caused concern among American government officials and business executives.

---

[7]Organization for Economic Cooperation and Development, *Technology Gap: General Report,* Paris, 1968, p. 25.

CASE STUDY 25.3 THE FORD ASSEMBLY LINE

At the turn of the century, there were dozens of different models of automobiles. Made in tiny machine shops, they were all designed and made differently, some gas-driven, some stream-driven, some electric. With car prices at around $5,000, the embryonic industry was supported by the New England wealthy. In Michigan machine shops, however, there was another idea: getting a car on the road for $1,000.

By 1908, the first Model T rolled off Henry Ford's plant in Highland Park, Detroit. That year, Ford led the industry in the number of cars sold and turned a $3 million profit. Yet in a country of 89 million people, there were still fewer than 200,000 automobiles. To sell more cars, there had to be further reduction in price. Ford and his friends figured out that a $600 car would tap this market.

Between 1912 and 1914, the new Highland Park factory was completely reorganized. Before then, a worker spent half his day walking about to get small components for the assembly of the main component, which stayed in one place until assembly was complete. Ford's idea was to place the machine tools in such a way that the car parts could move past the equipment to complete sub-assembly; then these partially assembled parts would move past other lines of tools to final assembly. Stationary workers would help the line along.

Ford's Highland Park factory, 1913

To attain this goal, Ford had first to rationalize work-tasks and routines. He invested in labor; his stunning $5 a day wage rate doubled the Michigan average overnight, and his workforce also stabilized overnight, from a terrible 60 percent turnover rate per month. A second requirement was a standard design; cars must come off the line as alike as pins at a pin factory. But above all, Ford had to risk a heavy investment in machine tools and the moving assembly plant. In 1914, the Highland Park factory represented $3.6 million in new plant and $2.8 million in machine tool equipment. Although these tools were complicated, they were called "farmer's tools," because they allowed even green farmhands to produce large quantities of high-quality work.

Output per worker shot up. Labor hours per engine dropped from 35 to 23; a man who made 35 magnetos in a day could now produce 95; and most radical of all, the endless chain-driven conveyor for chassis production meant that a chassis was turned out in one and a half man-hours, compared with twelve and a half man-hours before. Each worker had more equipment around him, and although his wages had doubled, his output increased even more. Sales of the Model T rose from 78,000 to 500,000, and the price came down to $600 per car—then to $360 per car in 1916.

N.B.

☆ ☆ ☆ ☆ ☆ ☆ ☆ ☆ ☆ ☆ ☆ ☆ ☆

THE GAP BETWEEN ACTUAL AND POTENTIAL OUTPUT

Up to this point, our discussion of economic growth has centered on the factors that determine how rapidly a nation's potential output grows: factors like technological change, increased education, investment in plant and equipment, and increases in the labor force. Now we must examine the factors that determine how close a nation's actual output comes to its potential output. As we already know, a nation's potential output is its output under full employment. Thus, as we also know, whether or not the economy operates close to full employment is determined by the level of the $C + I + G$ line. If the $C + I + G$ line is too low, the economy will operate with considerable unemployment, and actual output will be substantially below potential output. (Recall Chapter 6.) Or, in terms of the equation of exchange, if $M \times V$ is too small, the economy will operate with considerable unemployment, and actual output will be substantially below potential output. (Recall Chapter 13.)

From previous chapters, we also know how the government can use fiscal and monetary policies to push actual output close to potential output. Cuts in tax rates, increases in government spending, incentives for private investment in plant and equipment, increases in the money supply, reductions in interest rates—all these devices can be used to push actual output closer to potential output. Such devices promote economic growth, in the sense that actual per capita output is increased. However, only so much growth can be achieved by squeezing the slack out of the economy. For example, if there is a 7 percent unemployment rate, output per capita can be increased by perhaps 6 percent simply by reducing the unemployment rate to 5 percent. *But this is a one-shot improvement.* To get any further growth, the nation must increase its potential output.

This doesn't mean that it isn't important to maintain the economy at close to full employment. On the contrary, one of the major objectives of public policy must be high employment, and a reduction of unemployment will have a significant effect on the rate of economic growth in the short run. (Much of the economic growth in the United States in the early 1960s was caused by the transition to full employment.) But the point we are making is that, once the economy gets to full employment, no further growth can occur by this route. If a nation wants further growth, it must influence the factors responsible for the rate of growth of potential output.

SUMMARY

1. Economic growth is measured by the increase of per capita real gross national product, an index that does not measure accurately the growth of economic welfare but is often used as a first approximation.

2. One factor that may influence a nation's rate of economic growth is the rate at which its population grows. In Malthus's view, population growth, unless checked in some way, ultimately meant economic decline, since output could not grow in proportion to the growth in population. The law of diminishing marginal returns ensured that beyond some point, increases in labor, holding the quantity of land constant, would result in smaller and smaller increments of output. However, Malthus under-estimated the extent and importance of technological change, which offset the law of diminishing marginal returns.

3. Another factor that determines whether per capita output grows rapidly or slowly is the rate of expenditure on new plant and equipment. Without technological change, more and more of this sort of investment would result in increases in the amount of capital per dollar of output and decreases in the profitability of investment in plant and equipment, as Ricardo pointed out. But because of technological change, none of these things has occurred. According to the available evidence, a nation's rate of economic growth seems directly related to its rate of investment in plant and equipment.

4. To a considerable extent, economic growth here and abroad has resulted from technological change. A change in technology, when ap-plied for the first time, is called an innovation, and the firm that first applies it is called an innovator. Innovation is a key stage in the process leading to the full evaluation and utilization of a new process or product. Unless knowledge is used, it has little effect on the rate of economic growth.

5. Another factor with an important effect on a nation's rate of economic growth is the rate at which it invests in human capital. The United States invests in human capital on a massive scale, and these enormous and rapidly growing investments have unquestionably increased the produc-tivity, versatility, and adaptability of our labor force.

6. Still another set of basic factors influencing the rate of economic growth is the economic, social, and political climate of the nation. Some societies despise material welfare, are subject to violent political upheav-als, and are governed by corrupt groups. Such societies are unlikely to have a high rate of economic growth.

7. Finally, the rate of economic growth is also affected by the extent and behavior of the gap between actual and potential GNP. However, once a nation gets to full employment, it cannot grow further by reducing this gap.

CHAPTER 26

Public Goods and the Role of the Government

LEARNING OBJECTIVES

In this chapter, you should learn:

★ The nature and extent of the government's role in the economy

★ The characteristics of a public good

★ The nature and importance of externalities

★ What determines the incidence of a tax

★ The purposes of the tax system

To state that the United States is a mixed capitalist system, in which both government decisions and the price system play important roles, is hardly to provoke a controversy. But going a step beyond takes us into areas where viewpoints often diverge. The proper functions of government and the desirable size and nature of government expenditures and taxes are not matters on which all agree. Indeed, the question of how big government should be, and what its proper functions are, is hotly debated by conservatives and liberals throughout the land. In Chapters 6 through 14 we discussed the role of the government in stabilizing economic fluctuations. In this chapter we consider other roles for the government in the economy.

WHAT FUNCTIONS SHOULD THE GOVERNMENT PERFORM?

In Chapter 2 we discussed the limitations of the price system. Although it is generally agreed that there is a role for the government to redistribute income in favor of the poor, provide public goods, and offset the effects of external economies and diseconomies, there is considerable disagreement over how far the government should go in these areas, and what additional areas the government should be responsible for. Some people feel that "big government" is already a problem, that government is doing too much. Others believe that the public sector of the economy is being undernourished and that government should be allowed to do more. This is a fundamental question, and one that involves a great deal more than economics.

Conservative View

On the one hand, conservatives, such as Stanford University's Nobel laureate, Milton Friedman, believe that the government's role should be limited severely. They feel that economic and political freedom is likely to be undermined by excessive reliance on the state. Moreover, they tend to be skeptical about the government's ability to solve the social and economic problems at hand. They feel that the prevailing faith in the government's power to make a substantial dent in these problems is unreasonable, and they call for more and better information concerning the sorts of tasks government can reasonably be expected to do—and do well. They point to the slowness of the government bureaucracy, the difficulty in controlling huge government organizations, the inefficiencies political considerations can breed, and the difficulties in telling whether government programs are successful or not. On the basis of these considerations, they argue that the government's role should be carefully circumscribed.

The flavor of the conservative position on this question is evident in the remarks of George Stigler, a Nobel laureate at the University of Chicago:

> I consider myself courageous, or at least obtuse, in arguing for a reduction in governmental controls over economic life. You are surely desirous of improving this world, and it assuredly needs an immense amount of improvement. No method of displaying one's public-spiritedness is more popular than to notice a problem and pass a law. It combines ease, the warmth of benevolence, and a suitable disrespect for a less enlightened era. What I propose is, for most people, much less attractive: close study of the comparative performance of public and private economy, and the dispassionate appraisal of special remedies that is involved in compassion for the community at large.[1]

[1]G. Stigler, "The Government of the Economy," *A Dialogue on the Proper Economic Role of the State*, University of Chicago, Graduate School of Business, Selected Paper no. 7,

(continued)

Liberal View

To such remarks, liberals respond with very telling salvos of their own. Just as conservatives tend to be skeptical of the government's ability to solve important social and economic problems, so liberals tend to be skeptical about the price system's ability to solve these problems. They point to the important limitations of the price system, and they assert that the government can do a great deal to overcome these limitations, by regulating private activity and by subsidizing and providing goods and services that the private sector produces too little of.

According to some distinguished liberals, like Harvard's John Kenneth Galbraith, the public sector of the economy has been starved of needed resources, while the private sector has catered to relatively unimportant wants. In his best-selling book, *The Affluent Society,* Galbraith argued that consumers are led by advertising and other promotional efforts to purchase more and more goods of marginal significance to them. On the other hand, in his opinion, the nation is suffering because too little is spent on government services like education, transportation, and urban renewal.[2]

Liberals tend to be less concerned than conservatives about the effects on personal freedom of greater governmental intervention in the economy. They point out that the price system also involves a form of coercion by awarding the available goods and services to those who can pay their equilibrium price. In their view, people who are awarded only a pittance by the price system are coerced into discomfort and malnutrition.[3]

ESTABLISHING "RULES OF THE GAME"

Although there is considerable disagreement over the proper role of the government, both conservatives and liberals agree that it must do certain things. The first of these is to establish the "rules of the game"—a legal, social, and competitive framework enabling the price system to function as it should.

Maintaining a Legal and Social Framework

Specifically, *the government must see to it that contracts are enforced, that private ownership is protected, and that fraud is prevented.* Clearly, these

reprinted in E. Mansfield, *Principles of Microeconomics: Readings, Issues, and Cases,* 4th ed., New York: Norton, 1983. Also, see M. Friedman, *Capitalism and Freedom,* Chicago: University of Chicago Press, 1962.
[2]J. K. Galbraith, *Affluent Society,* 3d rev. ed., New York: New American Library, 1978.
[3]See P. Samuelson, "The Economic Role of Private Activity," *A Dialogue on the Proper Economic Role of the State,* University of Chicago, Graduate School of Business, Selected Paper no. 7, in E. Mansfield, *Principles of Microeconomics: Readings, Issues, and Cases.*

matters must be tended to if the price system is to work properly. Also, *the government must maintain order (through the establishment of police and other forces), establish a monetary system (so that money can be used to facilitate trade and exchange), and provide standards for the weight and quality of products.*

As an example of this sort of government intervention, consider the Pure Food and Drug Act. This act, originally passed in 1906 and subsequently amended in various ways, protects the consumer against improper and fraudulent activities on the part of producers of foods and drugs. It prohibits the merchandising of impure or falsely labeled food or drugs, and it forces producers to specify the quantity and quality of the contents on labels. These requirements strengthen the price system. Without them, the typical consumer would be unable to tell whether food or drugs are pure or properly labeled. Unless consumers can be sure that they are getting what they pay for, the basic logic underlying the price system breaks down. Similar regulations and legislation have been instituted in fields other than food and drugs, and for similar reasons.

Maintaining a Competitive Framework

Besides establishing a legal and social framework that will enable the price system to do its job, *the government must also see to it that markets remain reasonably competitive.* Only if markets are competitive will prices reflect consumer desires properly. If, on the other hand, markets are dominated by a few sellers (or a few buyers), prices may be "rigged" by these sellers (or buyers) to promote their own interests. For example, if a single firm is the sole producer of aluminum, it is a safe bet that this firm will establish a higher price than if there were many aluminum producers competing among themselves. In Chapters 19 and 20, we studied the social problems due to monopoly.

REDISTRIBUTION OF INCOME

We have already noted the general agreement that the government should redistribute income in favor of the poor. In other words, *it is usually felt that help should be given to people who are ill, handicapped, old and infirm, disabled, or unable for other reasons to provide for themselves.* To some extent, the nation has decided that income—or at least a certain minimum income—should be divorced from productive services. Of course, this doesn't mean that people who are too lazy to work should be given a handout. It does mean that people who cannot provide for themselves should be helped. To implement this principle, various payments are made by the government to needy people—including the aged, the handicapped, the unemployed, and pensioners.

These welfare payments are to some extent a "depression baby," for they grew substantially during the Great Depression of the 1930s, when relief payments became a necessity. But they also represent a feeling shared by a large segment of the population that human beings should be assured that, however the wheel of fortune spins and whatever number comes up, they will not starve and their children will not be deprived of a healthy environment and basic schooling. Of course, someone has to pay for this. Welfare payments allow the poor to take more from the nation's output than they produce. In general, the more affluent members of society contribute some of their claims on output to pay for these programs, their contributions being in the form of taxes. By using its expenditures to help certain groups and by taxing other groups to pay for these programs, the government accomplishes each year, without revolt and without bayonets, a substantial redistribution of income. This is a crucial aspect of the government's role in our economy.

PROVIDING PUBLIC GOODS

As we have indicated, the government provides many public goods. Let's consider the nature of public goods in more detail.

What Is a Public Good?

One hallmark of a **public good** *is that it can be consumed by one person without diminishing the amount that other people consume of it.* Public goods tend to be relatively indivisible; they often come in such large units that they cannot be broken into pieces that can be bought or sold in ordinary markets. Also, *once such goods are produced, there often is no way to bar certain citizens from consuming them.* Whether or not citizens contribute toward their cost, they benefit from them. This means that the price system cannot be used to handle the production and distribution of such goods.

An oft-cited example of a public good is a lighthouse. There might be general agreement that the cost of building a particular lighthouse would be more than justified by the benefits (saving of lives, fewer shipwrecks, cheaper transportation). Nonetheless, no private firm or person might build and operate such a lighthouse because they might be unable to charge the ships using the lighthouse for the service.[4] Nor would any single user gain enough from the lighthouse to warrant constructing and operating it. Moreover, voluntary contributions are very unlikely to support such a lighthouse because individual users are likely to feel that their contribution will not affect whether or not it is built, and that they will be able to use the lighthouse whether or not they contribute. Consequently,

---

[4]Under some circumstances, lighthouses have been able to charge users. For example, English lighthouses sometimes assessed the shipowners at the docks. Ordinarily only one ship was in sight of the lighthouse at a particular point in time. The light would not be shown if the ship (which was identified by its flag) had not paid.

National Defense: A Major Example

National defense is another example of a public good. The benefits of
expenditure on national defense extend to the entire nation. Extension of
the benefits of national defense to an additional citizen does not mean that
any other citizen gets less of these benefits. Also, there is no way of preventing citizens from benefiting from them, whether they contribute to
their cost or not. Thus there is no way to use the price system to provide
for national defense. Since it is a public good, national defense, if it is to
reach an adequate level, must be provided by the government.

Decision Making Regarding Public Goods

Essentially, deciding how much to produce of a public good is a political
decision. The citizens of the United States elect senators and congressmen
who decide how much should be spent on national defense, and how it
should be spent. These elected representatives are responsive to special-
interest groups, as well as to the people as a whole. Many special-interest
groups lobby hard for the production of certain public goods. For example,
an alliance of military and industrial groups presses for increased defense
expenditures.

The tax system is used to pay for the production of public goods. In
effect, the government says to each citizen, "Fork over a certain amount
of money to pay for the expenses incurred by the government." The
amount particular citizens are assessed may depend on their income (as
in the income tax), the value of all or specific types of their property (as
in the property tax), the amount they spend on certain types of goods and
services (as in the sales tax), or on still other criteria. In the 1980s, the tax
system has often been the object of enormous controversy. Much more
will be said about the tax system, and the controversies swirling around
it, in a later section of this chapter.

EXTERNALITIES

It is generally agreed that *the government should encourage the production of goods and services that entail external economies and discourage
the production of those that entail external diseconomies.* Take the pollution of air and water discussed in Chapter 21. When a firm or individual
dumps wastes into the water or air, other firms or individuals often must
pay all or part of the cost of putting the water or air back into a usable
condition. Thus the disposal of these wastes entails external diseconomies.
Unless the government prohibits certain kinds of pollution, or enforces air

and water quality standards, or charges polluters in accord with the amount of waste they dump into the environment, there will be socially undesirable levels of pollution.

Effects of External Diseconomies

To see how such externalities affect the social desirability of the output of a competitive industry, consider Figure 26.1, where the industry's demand and supply curves are contained in the top left-hand panel. As shown there, the equilibrium output of the industry is OQ_0. If the industry results in no external economies or diseconomies, this is likely to be the socially optimal output. But what if the industry results in external diseconomies, such as the pollution described above? Then the industry's supply curve does not fully reflect the true social costs of producing the product. The supply curve that reflects these social cost is S_1, which, as shown in the top right-hand panel of Figure 26.1, lies to the left of the industry's supply curve. The optimal output of the good is OQ_1, which is less than the competitive output, OQ_0.

What can the government do to correct the situation? There are many ways that it can intervene to reduce the industry's output from OQ_0 to OQ_1. For example, it can impose taxes on the industry. If these taxes are of the right type and amount, they will result in the desired reduction of output.

**Figure 26.1
Effect of External
Economies and
Diseconomies on
the Optimal Output
of a Competitive
Industry**
The optimal output
is OQ_0 if neither
external economies
nor diseconomies
are present. If there
are external
diseconomies, curve
S_1 reflects the true
social costs of
producing the
product, and OQ_1 is
the optimal output.
If there are external
economies, curve
D_1 reflects the true
social benefits of
producing the
product, and OQ_2 is
the optimal output.

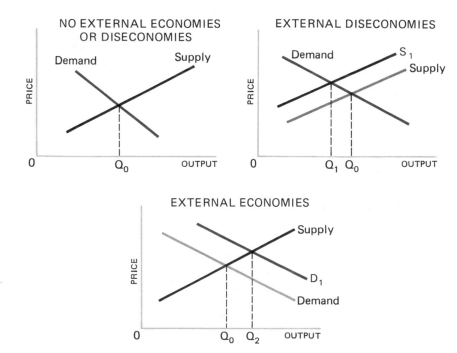

CASE STUDY 26.1 THE TENNESSEE VALLEY AUTHORITY

The Great Mississippi Flood of 1927 left 800,000 homeless and focused national attention on the federal government's responsibility for flood control. Such control had been considered for years on the Tennessee River. Senator Norris of Nebraska campaigned for federal support for river control in the 1920s and 1930s, but his attempts were unsuccessful—largely because local utilities feared that by building dams, the federal government would be providing not only flood control but electric power as well.

The debate continued until in 1933 the Roosevelt administration created the Tennessee Valley Authority (TVA). The TVA was foremost a construction project that would create jobs in a depressed economy, but it was also created for regional development that would yield benefits for many years to come. In addition to its responsibility for flood control and for improving the navigability of the Tennessee's waters, the TVA built housing, worked on agricultural development, and provided electric power to the depressed area. And the local utilities challenged the TVA all the way.

The TVA dam at Fort Loudoun

By 1954 the TVA was well established and requested funds from Congress to build a steam-driven electric plant. Congress rejected the proposal because it did not feel that the TVA should be expanded further into a federal power facility not exclusively hydroelectric, nor should it be made into a business larger than it already was.

Why is it proper for the government to provide for flood control, but not proper for it to build steam-driven electric power plants? The rationale for the government to provide a service is a breakdown of the free market—that is, when the private sector will not provide the proper quantity of certain goods and services. Flood control and navigation are clearly public goods, and insofar as electrification is a by-product of flood control, it is reasonable for the government to provide this service too. But the proposed steam-driven electrical generators could have been as easily provided by the private sector as by the government.

N.B.

Effects of External Economies

What if the industry results in external economies? For example, what if the manufacture of one industrial product makes it cheaper to produce other products? Then the industry's demand curve underestimates the true social benefits of producing the product. The demand curve that reflects these social benefits correctly is D_1, which, as shown in the bottom panel of Figure 26.1, lies to the right of the industry's demand curve. The optimal output of the good is OQ_2, which is greater than the competitive output, OQ_0.

As in the case where the industry results in external diseconomies, the government can intervene in various ways to change the industry's output. But in this case, the object is to increase, not decrease, its output. To accomplish this, the government can, among other things, grant subsidies to the industry. If they are of the right type and amount, they can be used to increase the industry's output from OQ_0 to OQ_2.

THE THEORY OF PUBLIC CHOICE

According to many economists interested in the theory of public choice, many factors induce the government to make decisions that are not efficient from an economic point of view. Just as the price system suffers from certain limitations, so the government has shortcomings as a mechanism for promoting economic welfare. These factors, discussed below, often result in expanded government expenditures.

Special-Interest Groups

It is no secret that politicians try to stay in office. In some cases, they must decide whether or not to adopt a policy that benefits a small number of people each of whom will gain a great deal at the expense of a very large number of people each of whom will lose very little. The small group of gainers (the special-interest group) is likely to be well organized, well financed, and vocal. The large group of losers is likely to be unaware of its losses and more indifferent to the outcome of this decision, since each member of this group has little at stake. In a case of this sort, a politician will be inclined to adopt the policy favoring the special-interest group. Why? Because the politician, by not adopting this policy, would lose the support of this group. On the other hand, by adopting this policy, the politician is unlikely to lose the support of the large group of people that are hurt by it because they are much more interested in other issues where they have more at stake.

There are many cases where politicians have adopted policies favoring special-interest groups, even though the total gains to the special-interest group are less than the total losses to other segments of society. Whereas such policies are unsound economics, they have been regarded as good politics. One example is the enactment of tariffs and quotas that reduce domestic competition and result in consumers paying higher prices. Government services that benefit special-interest groups often are expanded, to the detriment of society at large.

Bureaucratic Inefficiency

Many observers contend that government agencies are less efficient than private firms. As we have seen in previous chapters, the price system establishes strong incentives for firms to minimize their costs. If firms can lower their costs, they can increase their profits, at least temporarily. Government officials, on the other hand, often have less incentive to reduce costs. Indeed, it is sometimes claimed that there is an incentive to increase costs since an agency's power and influence is directly related to the size of its budget. Unfortunately, we do not have a great deal of evidence concerning whatever differences exist between the efficiency of government agencies and of private firms, largely because of the difficulties in measuring the efficiency or inefficiency of government agencies. For example, how efficient is the Environmental Protection Agency? Because it is so difficult to measure EPA's output, and because it is so difficult to find a standard against which to measure its performance, this question is exceedingly difficult to answer.

One area where there has been evidence of inefficiency has been the development and production of new weapons by the Department of Defense and its contractors. There have been spectacular overruns in development and production costs. To some extent, such cost increases reflect the fact that new weapons systems tend to push the state of the art, so that problems must be expected. But in addition, the firms that develop and produce these weapons systems often submit unrealistically low bids to get a contract, knowing that they are likely to get approval for cost increases later on. According to some observers, like Merton J. Peck of Yale University and F. M. Scherer of Swarthmore College, these cost overruns have also been due to "inadequate attention to the efficient utilization of technical, production, and administrative manpower—areas in which major cost reductions are possible."[5]

Nonselectivity

Another point made by public-choice theorists is that when citizens vote for their elected officials, they vote for a "bundle" of political programs. For example, in a particular election, the two candidates may be John

[5]M. J. Peck and F. M. Scherer, *The Weapons Acquisition Process,* Cambridge, Mass.: Harvard University Press, 1962, p. 594.

Brown, who favors increased defense spending, reduced capital gains taxes, and the development of nuclear power, and Jane Smith, who opposes all of these things. If you favor increased defense spending and the development of nuclear power, but oppose reduced capital gains taxes, there is no way that you can elect a candidate who mirrors your preferences. All that you can do is vote for the candidate whose bundle of programs is closest to your preferences.

In contrast, citizens, when making choices in the marketplace, are better able to pick a set of goods and services that is in accord with their preferences, since they do not have to buy items that they do not want. If you want a green shirt and a purple tie, you can buy them without having to buy a pair of socks as well. Since citizens cannot be so selective with regard to goods and services in the public sector, public-choice theorists hold that the provision of such goods and services tends to be inefficient.

To conclude this brief section on the theory of public choice, it is important to recognize that no one is accusing government officials of being stupid, lazy, or corrupt. Some undoubtedly are, but this is true of business executives as well. The point is that the incentives faced by government officials and the nature of the political process result in decision making that can be suboptimal from an economic point of view. This helps to explain why the government, like the price system, can bungle the job of organizing the nation's economic activities. Neither is a panacea.

PRINCIPLES OF TAXATION

As we saw in Chapters 6 and 12, the government finances most of its expenditures through taxation. According to the English political philosopher Edmund Burke, "To tax and to please, no more than to love and to be wise, is not given to men." What constitutes a rational tax system? Are there any generally accepted principles to guide the nation in determining who should pay how much? The answer is that there are some principles most people accept, but they are so broad and general that they leave plenty of room for argument and compromise. Specifically, two general principles of taxation command widespread agreement.

Benefit Principle

The first principle is that *people who receive more from a certain government service should pay more in taxes to support it.* Certainly few people would argue with this idea. However, it is frequently difficult, if not impossible, to apply. For example, there is no good way to measure the amount of the benefits received by a particular taxpayer from many public services, such as police protection.

Ability-to-Pay Principle

The second principle is that *people should be taxed so as to result in a socially desirable redistribution of income.* In practice, this has ordinarily meant that the wealthy have been asked to pay more than the poor. This idea, too, has generally commanded widespread assent—although this, of course, has not prevented the wealthy from trying to avoid its application to them.

Applications of These Principles

It follows from these principles that if two people are in essentially the same circumstances (their income, purchases, utilization of public services are the same), then they should pay the same taxes. This is an important rule, innocuous though it may seem. It says that equals should be treated equally; *whether one is a Republican and the other is a Democrat, or whether one is a friend of the president and the other is his enemy, or whether one has purely salary income and the other has property income, they should be treated equally.* Certainly, this is a basic characteristic of an equitable tax system.

It is easy to relate most of the taxes in our tax structure to these principles. For example, the first principle, the benefit principle, is the basic rationale behind taxes on gasoline and license fees for vehicles and drivers. Those who use the roads are asked to pay for their construction and upkeep. Also, the property tax, levied primarily on real estate, is often supported on these grounds. It is argued that property owners receive important benefits—fire and police protection, for example—and that the extent of the benefits is related to the extent of their property.

The personal income tax is based squarely on the second principle: ability to pay. A person with a large income pays a higher proportion of income in personal income taxes than does a person with a smaller income. In 1984, if a couple's income (after deductions and exemptions) were $16,000, their federal income tax would be $1,741, whereas if their income were $60,000, their federal income tax would be $15,168. Also, estate and inheritance taxes hit the rich much harder than the poor.

The principles cited above are useful and important, but they do not take us very far toward establishing a rational tax structure. They are too vague and leave too many questions unanswered. If I use about the same amount of public services as you do, but my income is twice yours, how much more should I pay in taxes? Twice as much? Three times as much? Fifty percent more? These principles throw no real light on many of the detailed questions that must be answered by a real-life tax code.

THE PERSONAL INCOME TAX

The federal *personal income tax* brings in over $350 billion a year. Yet many people are unaware of just how much they are contributing because it is deducted from their wages each month or each week, so that they owe little extra when April 15 rolls around. (Indeed, they may even be due a refund.) This pay-as-you-go scheme reduces the pain, but, of course, it does not eliminate it; taxes are never painless.

The Tax Schedule

Obviously, how much a family has to pay in personal income taxes depends on the family's income. The tax schedule (as of 1984) is as shown in Table 26.1. The second column shows how much a couple would have to pay if their income was the amount shown in the first column. At an income of $29,900, their income tax would be $4,790; at an income of $109,400, their income tax would be $36,630. Clearly, the percentage of income owed in income tax increases as income increases, but this percentage does not increase indefinitely. The percentage of income going for personal income taxes never exceeds 50 percent, no matter how much money the couple makes.

Table 26.1
Federal Personal
Income Tax, Couple
without Children,
1984

Income—after deductions and personal exemptions (dollars)	Personal income tax (dollars)	Average tax rate (percent)	Marginal tax rate (percent)
5,500	231	4.2	12
16,000	1,741	10.9	18
29,900	4,790	16.0	28
60,000	15,168	25.3	42
109,400	36,630	33.5	49
1,000,000	481,400	48.1	50

The Marginal Tax Rate

It is instructive to look further at how the "tax bite" increases with income. In particular, let's ask ourselves what proportion of an *extra* dollar of income the couple will have to pay in personal income taxes. In other words, what is the *marginal tax rate*: the tax on an extra dollar of income? The fourth column of Table 26.1 shows that the marginal tax rate is 12 percent if the couple's income is $5,500, 18 percent if their income is $16,000, 42 percent if their income is $60,000, and 50 percent if their income is $1 million. The greater the couple's income, the greater the proportion of an extra dollar that goes for personal income taxes.

CASE STUDY 26.2 EQUITY AND SIMPLICITY IN THE INCOME TAX CODE

Lawyers and accountants like to distinguish between tax *avoidance* and tax *evasion*. Tax avoidance occurs when taxpayers take legal steps to minimize their tax bill. Tax evasion occurs when taxpayers misreport their income or take other illegal steps to cut down on what they actually pay Uncle Sam.

Tax avoidance is a particularly profitable pastime of the well-to-do. With the help of a good lawyer or accountant, one frequently can cut one's income taxes considerably. To illustrate, consider the actual case of a wealthy socialite who took a job as an editor. The job allows her to deduct many expenses that she would have incurred anyhow. For example, if she takes a trip to Europe, many of her expenses may be deductible, if she can argue (convincingly) that the trip is somehow related to the

Congressman Jack Kemp

development of a book. A deduction is an item that is subtracted from one's income to obtain the net income figure on which the amount of income tax is figured. If you can deduct an expense that otherwise would not be deductible, this reduces your income tax by an amount equal to your marginal income tax rate times the expense. Thus, in the case of the socialite, if she spends $5,000 on a trip to Europe, and if her marginal tax rate is 50 percent, she will save $2,500 in income taxes (that is, .50 × $5,000) if she can convince the Internal Revenue Service that the trip pertained to her business interests.

Many economists feel that the tax system would be more equitable if the tax code were simplified and if many of these ways to avoid income taxes were eliminated. In December 1984, the U.S. Treasury proposed a major revision of the tax laws which would call for only three tax rates, the highest being 35 percent. No deductions would be allowed for state and local income taxes, charitable contributions would be deductible only under certain circumstances, and deductions for interest on second-home mortgages, auto loans, and personal loans would be limited. The Treasury hailed this proposal as a major attempt to simplify the tax code and to make it more equitable.

Other proposals have been put forth as well. In 1983, Congressman Jack Kemp (N.Y.) and Senator Robert Kasten (Wis.) introduced a bill for a "flat tax" whereby the tax rate would be a flat 25 percent for families with incomes exceeding $3,500. Congressmen Richard Gephardt (Mo.) and Senator Bill Bradley (N.J.) introduced a rival bill that would simplify the tax code but maintain lower tax rates for lower-income families. Without question, the mid-1980s were a time when many politicians as well as economists were clamoring for more equity and simplicity in the tax code.

☆ ☆ ☆ ☆ ☆ ☆ ☆ ☆ ☆ ☆ ☆ ☆ ☆

The Corporate Income Tax

The federal government imposes a tax on the incomes of corporations as well as of people. If a corporation's profits exceed $100,000, the corporate income tax equals $25,750 plus 46 percent of the amount by which the corporation profits exceed $100,000. A corporation with annual profits of $150,000 would pay $48,750 in corporate income tax: $25,750 plus $23,-000 (46 percent of $50,000).[6] The corporate income tax involves double taxation. The federal government taxes a corporation's earnings both through the corporate income tax (when the corporation earns the profits) and through the personal income tax (when the corporation's earnings are distributed to the stockholders as dividends).

It is generally agreed that the personal income tax is paid by the person whose income is taxed; he or she cannot shift this tax to someone else. But the incidence of the corporate income tax is not so clear. To some extent, corporations may pass along some of their income tax bill to customers in the form of higher prices or to workers in the form of lower wages. Some economists feel that a corporation shifts much of the tax burden in this way; others disagree. This is a controversial issue that has proved very difficult to resolve.

THE PROPERTY TAX AND THE SALES TAX

The *property tax* is the fiscal bulwark of our local governments. The way it works is simple enough. Most towns and cities estimate the amount they will spend in the next year or two, and then determine a property tax based on the assessed property values in the town or city. If there is $500 million in assessed property values in the town and the town needs to raise $5 million, the tax rate will be 1 percent of assessed property value. In other words, each property owner will have to pay 1 percent of the assessed value of his property. There are well-known problems in the administration of the property tax. First, assessed values of property often depart significantly from actual market values; the former are typically much lower than the latter. And the ratio of assessed to actual value is often lower among higher-priced pieces of property; thus wealthier people tend to get off easier. Second, there is widespread evasion of taxes on personal property: securities, bank accounts, and so on. Many people simply do not pay up. Third, the property tax is not very flexible; assessments and rates tend to change rather slowly.

The *sales tax*, of course, is a bulwark of state taxation. It provides a high

---

[6]If a corporation's profits are less than $100,000, the corporate income tax equals 15 percent of the first $25,000 of annual profits, 18 percent of the second $25,000 of annual profits, 30 percent of the third $25,000 of annual profits, and 40 percent of the fourth $25,000 of annual profits.

CASE STUDY 26.3 PROPOSITION 13

The combination of inflation and a housing shortage led to a rapid increase in land values in California in the late 1970s. This in turn resulted in steadily increasing property taxes. Homes that sold for $600 after World War II were selling for $60,000 in the late 1970s, and it was not unusual for homeowners to be paying over $2,000 per year in property taxes. Many homeowners felt that the burden of local taxes was

Supporters celebrate the passage of Proposition 13

too much and that it was time to cut government expenditures. The taxpayers' revolt, led by Howard Jarvis, began with the collection of over a million signatures, more than enough to place Proposition 13 on the California state ballot. Proposition 13 would limit property taxes to 1 percent —a 60 percent rollback that would wipe out some $7 billion of local government funds. At the polls, Proposition 13 easily passed with 65 percent of the vote.

The cut in property taxes helped stimulate a statewide economic upsurge. Local government spending leveled out throughout the state, and local government services suffered. Public employees were laid off, and services such as summer school classes, library services, and garbage collection were curtailed. Some of the other consequences came as a surprise to voters. For example, of the $7 billion tax rollback, corporations got the lion's share.

Jarvis was back in 1980 with a new initiative: Proposition 9, which would have cut state income taxes by 50 percent. This time, however, Jarvis's opponents focused on equity issues. Amid widespread charges that Proposition 9 might simply let the rich get richer at the expense of the less well-to-do, Jarvis was defeated and the tax revolt fever began to cool down.

N.B.

☆ ☆ ☆ ☆ ☆ ☆ ☆ ☆ ☆ ☆ ☆ ☆ ☆

yield with relatively low collection costs. Most of the states have some form of general sales tax, the rate being usually between 3 and 6 percent. For example, New York has a 4 percent sales tax, and California has a 4¾ percent sales tax. Retailers add to the price of goods sold to consumers an amount equal to 3 to 6 percent of the consumer's bill. This extra amount is submitted to the state as the general sales tax. Some states exempt food purchases from this tax, and a few exempt medical supplies. Where they exist, these exemptions help reduce the impact of the sales tax on the poor;

but in general the sales tax imposes a greater burden relative to income on the poor than on the rich, for the simple reason that the rich save a larger percentage of their income. Practically all of a poor family's income may be subject to sales taxes; a great deal of a rich family's income may not be, because it is not spent on consumer goods, but is saved.

Who really pays the property tax or the sales tax? To what extent can these taxes be shifted to other people? The answer is not as straightforward as one might expect. For the property tax, the owner of unrented residential property swallows the tax, since there is no one else to shift it to. But the owner of rented property may attempt to pass along some of the tax to the tenant. In the case of a general sales tax, it is generally concluded that the consumer pays the tax. But if the tax is imposed on only a single commodity, the extent to which it can be shifted to the consumer depends on the demand and supply curves for the taxed commodity. The following section explains in some detail why this is the case.

TAX INCIDENCE

Suppose that a sales or excise tax is imposed on a particular good, say beer. In Figure 26.2, we show the demand and supply curves for beer before the imposition of the tax. With no tax, the equilibrium price of a case of beer is $6, and the equilibrium quantity is 100 million cases. If a tax of $1 is imposed on each case produced, what is the effect on the price of each case? Or to see it from the beer guzzler's perspective, how much of the tax is passed on to the consumer in the form of a higher price?

Since the tax is collected from the sellers, *the supply curve is shifted upward by the amount of tax,* as shown in Figure 26.2. For example, if the pretax price had to be $5 a case to induce sellers to supply 80 million cases of beer, the posttax price would have to be $1 higher, or $6 a case, to induce the same supply. Similarly, if the pretax price had to be $6 a case to induce sellers to supply 100 million cases of beer, the posttax price

**Figure 26.2
Effect of a $1.00
Tax on a Case of
Beer**
The tax shifts the supply curve upward by $1.00. Since the demand curve is unaffected, the equilibrium price of beer increases from $6.00 to $6.50 per case.

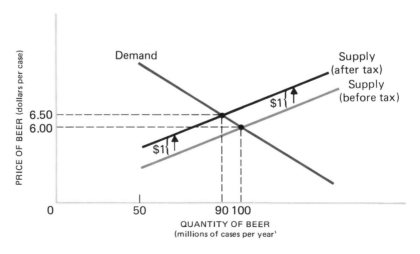

would have to be $1 higher, or $7 a case, to induce the same supply. The reason why the sellers require $1 more per case to supply the pretax amount is that they must pay the tax of $1 per case to the government. To wind up with the same amount as before (after paying the tax), they require the extra $1 per case.

Who Pays the Tax?

Figure 26.2 shows, that after the tax is imposed, the equilibrium price of beer is $6.50, an increase of $.50 over its pretax level. Consequently, in this case half of the tax is passed on to consumers, who pay $.50 per case more for beer. And half of the tax is swallowed by the sellers, who receive (after they pay the tax) $.50 per case less for beer. But it is not always true that sellers pass half of the tax on to consumers and absorb the rest themselves. On the contrary, in some cases, consumers may bear almost all of the tax (and sellers may bear practically none of it), while in other cases consumers may bear almost none of the tax (and sellers may bear practically all of it). The result will depend on how sensitive the quantity demanded and the quantity supplied are to the price of the good.

Sensitivity of Demand to Price

In particular, holding the supply curve constant, *the less sensitive the quantity demanded is to the price of the good, the bigger the portion of the tax that is shifted to consumers.* To illustrate this, consider Figure 26.3, which shows the effect of a $1-per-case tax on beer in two markets, one (panel B) where the quantity demanded is much more sensitive to price than in the other case (panel A). As is evident, the price increase to consumers resulting from the tax is much greater in the latter case than in the former. And the amount of the tax that is absorbed by producers is much less in the latter case (panel A) than in the former (panel B).

Figure 26.3
Effect on Tax Incidence of the Sensitivity of the Quantity Demanded to Price
The supply curve is the same in panel A as in panel B. The quantity demanded is more sensitive to price in panel B than in panel A. Before the tax the equilibrium price is OP_0 in both panels. After the tax the equilibrium price is OP_2 in panel A and OP_1 in panel B. The increase in price to the consumer is greater if the quantity demanded is less sensitive to price (panel A) than if it is more sensitive (panel B).

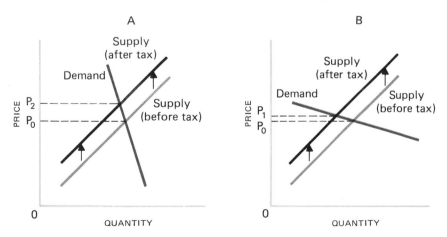

Sensitivity of Supply to Price

It can also be shown that, holding the demand curve constant, *the less sensitive the quantity supplied is to the price of the good, the bigger the portion of the tax that is absorbed by producers.* To illustrate this, consider Figure 26.4, which shows the effect of a $1-per-case tax on beer in two markets, one (panel A) where the quantity supplied is much more sensitive to price than in the other (panel B). As is evident, the price increase to consumers resulting from the tax is much greater in the former case than in the latter. And the amount of the tax that is absorbed by producers is much less in the former case (panel A) than in the latter case (panel B).

Figure 26.4
Effect on Tax Incidence of the Sensitivity of the Quantity Supplied to Price
The demand curve is the same in panel A as in panel B. The quantity supplied is more sensitive to price in panel A than in panel B. Before the tax the equilibrium price is OP_3 in both panels. After the tax the equilibrium price is OP_5 in panel A and OP_4 in panel B. The increase in price to the consumer is greater if the quantity supplied is more sensitive to price (panel A) than if it is less sensitive (panel B).

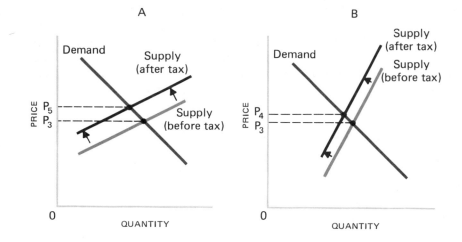

Effect of Tax on Quantity

Finally, note that the tax reduces the equilibrium quantity of the good that is taxed: beer in this case. One reason why governments impose taxes on goods like cigarettes and liquor is that they are regarded (in some circles at least) as socially undesirable. Clearly, the more sensitive the quantity demanded and quantity supplied are to price, the larger the reduction in the equilibrium quantity. Thus, if the government imposes a tax of this sort to reduce the quantity consumed of the good, the effect will be greater if both the quantity demanded and the quantity supplied are relatively sensitive to price.

SUMMARY

1. To a considerable extent, the government's role in the economy has developed in response to the limitations of the price system. There is considerable agreement that the government should redistribute income

in favor of the poor, provide public goods, and offset the effects of external economies and diseconomies. Also, it is generally felt that the government should establish a proper legal, social, and competitive framework for the price system.

2. Beyond this, however, there are wide differences of opinion on the proper role of government in economic affairs. Conservatives tend to be suspicious of "big government" while liberals are inclined to believe that the government should do more.

3. Basically, the amount that the government spends on various activities and services must be decided through the nation's political processes. Voting by ballots must be substituted for dollar voting.

4. Just as the price system suffers from limitations, so does the government. Special-interest groups sometimes gain at the expense of society as a whole. Government agencies sometimes have little incentive to increase efficiency. Citizens find it difficult to be selective in their choice of goods and services in the public sector. In recent years, economists seem to have put more emphasis on these (and other) limitations of the public sector.

5. It is generally agreed that people who receive more in benefits from a certain government service should pay more in taxes to support it. It is also generally agreed that people should be taxed so that the result is a socially desirable redistribution of income, and that equals should be treated equally. But these general principles, although useful, cannot throw light on many of the detailed questions a real-life tax code must answer.

6. The personal income tax is a very important source of federal revenues, the sales tax is an important source of state revenues, and the property tax is an important source of local revenues. In recent years, there has been a surge of interest in simplifying the personal income tax and making it more equitable.

7. If a tax is imposed on a single commodity, the extent to which it can be shifted to the consumer depends on the demand and supply curves for the taxed commodity. If the quantity demanded is relatively insensitive to the price of the good, or if the quantity supplied is relatively sensitive to the price, a large portion of the tax is shifted to consumers.

CHAPTER 27

★ ★ ★ ★ ★ ★ ★ ★ ★

International Trade

LEARNING OBJECTIVES

In this chapter, you should learn:

★ The definition of comparative advantage and its relation to international trade

★ What tariffs and quotas are

★ The impact of tariffs and quotas on international trade

★ The arguments for and against tariffs and quotas

Practically all people realize that they are not islands unto themselves, and that they benefit from living with, working with, and trading with other people. Exactly the same is true of nations. They too must interact with one another, and they too benefit from trade with one another. No nation can be an island unto itself—not even the United States. To understand how the world economy functions, you must grasp the basic economic principles of international trade.

AMERICA'S FOREIGN TRADE

America's foreign trade, although small relative to our national product, plays a very important role in our economic life. Many of our industries depend on other countries for markets or for such raw materials as coffee, tea, or tin. Our *exports*—the things we sell to other countries—amount to about 10 percent of our gross national product, which seems small relative to other countries like Germany, France, Italy, and the United Kingdom, where exports are about 15 to 20 percent of gross national product. But this is because our domestic market is so large. In absolute terms, our exports (and imports) are bigger than those of any other nation. Without question, our way of life would have to change considerably if we could not trade with other countries.

When we were a young country, we exported raw materials primarily. During the 1850s about 70 percent of our exports were raw materials and foodstuffs. But the composition of our exports has changed with time. More are now finished manufactured goods and fewer are raw materials. Machinery and industrial supplies now account for much of our merchandise exports.

What sorts of goods do we buy from abroad? About 10 percent of our *imports* are agricultural commodities like coffee, sugar, bananas, and cocoa. About 20 percent are petroleum and its products. But a considerable proportion is neither raw materials nor foodstuffs. Over one-half of our imports are manufactured goods like bicycles from England or color TVs from Japan.

SPECIALIZATION AND TRADE

Why do we trade with other countries? Do we, and our trading partners, benefit from this trade? And if so, what determines the sorts of goods we should export and import? These are very important questions, among the most fundamental in economics. The answers are not new. They have been well understood for considerably more than a century, from the work of such great economists as David Hume, David Ricardo, Adam Smith, and John Stuart Mill.

Why Do Individuals Trade?

As a first step, it is useful to recognize that the benefits *nations* receive through trade are essentially the same as those *individuals* receive through trade. Consider the hypothetical case of John Barrister, a lawyer, with a wife and two children. The Barrister family, like practically all families, trades continually with other families and with business firms. Since Mr. Barrister is a lawyer, he trades his legal services for money which he and his wife use to buy the food, clothing, housing, and other goods and services his family wants. Why does the Barrister family do this? What advantages does it receive through trade? Why doesn't it attempt to be self-sufficient?

To see why the Barrister family is sensible indeed to opt for trade rather than self-sufficiency, let's compare the current situation—where Mr. Barrister specializes in the production of legal services and trades the money he receives for other goods and services—with the situation if the Barrister family attempted to be self-sufficient. In the latter case, the Barristers would have to provide their own transportation, telephone service, food-stuffs, clothing, and a host of other things. Mr. Barrister is a lawyer—a well-trained, valuable, productive member of the community. But if he were to try his hand at making automobiles—or even bicycles—he might be a total loss. If the Barrister family attempted to be self-sufficient, it might be unable to provide many of the goods it now enjoys.

Why Do Nations Trade?

Trade permits specialization, and specialization increases output. This is the advantage of trade, both for individuals and for nations. In our hypothetical case, it is obvious that, because he can trade with other families and with firms, Mr. Barrister can specialize in doing what he is good at: law. Consequently, he can be more productive than if he were forced to be a Jack-of-all-trades, as he would have to be if he could not trade with others. The same principle holds for nations. Because the United States can trade with other nations, it can specialize in the goods and services it produces particularly well. Then it can trade them for goods that other countries are especially good at producing. Thus both we and our trading partners benefit.

Some countries have more and better resources of certain types than others. Saudi Arabia has oil, Canada has timber, Japan has skilled labor, and so on. *International differences in resource endowments, and in the relative quantity of various types of human and nonhuman resources, are important bases for specialization.* Consider countries with lots of fertile soil, little capital, and much unskilled labor. They are likely to find it advantageous to produce agricultural goods, while countries with poor soil, much capital, and highly skilled labor will probably do better to produce capital-intensive high-technology goods. We must recognize, however, that the bases for specialization do not remain fixed over time. Instead, as technology and the resource endowments of various countries change, the pattern of international specialization changes as well. As we saw in the previous section, the United States specialized more in raw materials and foodstuffs about a century ago than it does now.

ABSOLUTE ADVANTAGE

To clarify the benefits of trade, consider the following example. Suppose that the United States can produce 2 electronic computers or 5,000 cases of wine with 1 unit of resources. Suppose that France can produce 1 electronic computer or 10,000 cases of wine with 1 unit of resources. Given the production possibilities in each country, are there any advantages in trade between the countries? And if so, what commodity should each country export, and what commodity should each country import? Should France export wine and import computers, or should it import wine and export computers?

To answer these questions, assume that the United States is producing a certain amount of computers and a certain amount of wine—and that France is producing a certain amount of computers and a certain amount of wine. If the United States shifts 1 unit of its resources from producing wine to producing computers, it will increase its production of computers by 2 computers and reduce its production of wine by 5,000 cases of wine. If France shifts 1 unit of resources from the production of computers to the production of wine, it will increase its production of wine by 10,000 cases and reduce its production of computers by 1 computer.

Table 27.1 shows the *net* effect of this shift in the utilization of resources on *world* output of computers and of wine. World output of computers increases (by 1 computer) and world output of wine increases (by 5,000 cases) as a result of the redeployment of resources in each country. Thus *specialization increases world output.*

Table 27.1
Case of Absolute Advantage

| | Increase or decrease in output of: | |
	Computers	Wine (thousands of cases)
Effect of U.S.'s shifting 1 unit of resources from wine to computers	+2	−5
Effect of France's shifting 1 unit of resources from computers to wine	−1	+10
Net effect	+1	+5

Moreover, if world output of each commodity is increased by shifting 1 unit of American resources from wine to computers and shifting 1 unit of French resources from computers to wine, it follows that world output of each commodity will be increased further if each country shifts *more* of its resources in the same direction. This is because the amount of resources required to produce a unit of each good is assumed to be constant, regardless of how much is produced.

Thus in this situation, one country—the United States—should specialize in producing computers, and the other country—France—should specialize in producing wine. This will maximize world output of both wine and computers, permitting a rise in both countries' standards of living. Complete specialization of this sort is somewhat unrealistic, since countries often produce some of both commodities, but this simple example illustrates the basic principles involved.

COMPARATIVE ADVANTAGE

The case just described is a very special one, since one country (France) has an absolute advantage over another (the United States) in the production of one good (wine), whereas the second country (the United States) has an absolute advantage over the first (France) in the production of another good (computers). What do we mean by the term *absolute advantage?* Country A has an ***absolute advantage*** over Country B in the production of a good when Country A can produce a unit of the good with fewer resources than can Country B. Since the United States can produce a computer with fewer units of resources than France, it has an absolute advantage over France in the production of computers. Since France requires fewer resources than the United States to produce a given amount of wine, France has an absolute advantage over the United States in the production of wine.

But what if one country is more efficient in producing both goods? If the United States is more efficient in producing both computers and wine, is there still any benefit to be derived from specialization and trade? At first glance, you are probably inclined to answer no. But if this is your inclination, you should reconsider—because you are wrong.

A Numerical Example

To see why specialization and trade have advantages even when one country is more efficient than another at producing both goods, consider the following example. Suppose the United States can produce 2 electronic computers or 5,000 cases of wine with 1 unit of resources, and France can produce 1 electronic computer or 4,000 cases of wine with 1 unit of resources. In this case, the United States is a more efficient producer of both computers and wine. Nonetheless, as we shall see, world output of both goods will increase if the United States specializes in the production of computers and France specializes in the production of wine.

Table 27.2 demonstrates this conclusion. If 2 units of American resources are shifted from wine to computer production, 4 additional computers and 10,000 fewer cases of wine are produced. If 3 units of French resources are shifted from computer to wine production, 3 fewer computers and 12,000 additional cases of wine are produced. Thus the combined effect of this redeployment of resources in both countries is to increase

Table 27.2
Case of
Comparative
Advantage

	Increase or decrease in output of:	
	Computers	Wine (thousands of cases)
Effect of U.S.'s shifting 2 units of resources from wine to computers	+4	−10
Effect of France's shifting 3 units of resources from computers to wine	−3	+12
Net effect	+1	+2

world output of computers by 1 computer and to increase world output of wine by 2,000 cases. Even though the United States is more efficient than France in the production of both computers and wine, world output of both goods will be maximized if the United States specializes in computers and France specializes in wine.

Basically, this is so because, although the United States is more efficient than France in the production of both goods, it has a greater advantage in computers than in wine. It is twice as efficient as France in producing computers, but only 25 percent more efficient than France in producing wine. To derive these numbers, recall that 1 unit of resources will produce 2 computers in the United States, but only 1 computer in France. Thus the United States is twice as efficient in computers. On the other hand, 1 unit of resources will produce 5,000 cases of wine in the United States, but only 4,000 cases in France. Thus the United States is 25 percent more efficient in wine.

Trade Depends on Comparative Advantage

A nation has a *comparative advantage* in those products where its efficiency relative to other nations is highest. Thus in this case the United States has a comparative advantage in the production of computers and a comparative disadvantage in the production of wine. So long as a country has a comparative advantage in the production of some commodities and a comparative disadvantage in the production of others, it can benefit from specialization and trade. A country will specialize in products where it has a comparative advantage, and import those where it has a comparative disadvantage. The point is that *specialization and trade depend on comparative, not absolute, advantage.* One of the first economists to understand the full significance of this fact was David Ricardo, the English economist of the early nineteenth century.

THE TERMS OF TRADE

The *terms of trade* are defined as the quantity of imported goods that a country can obtain in exchange for a unit of domestic goods. Thus, in our previous example, the terms of trade are measured by the ratio of the price of a computer to the price of a case of wine—since this ratio shows how many cases of French wine the U.S. can get in exchange for an American computer. It is important to note that this ratio must be somewhere between 2,500:1 and 4,000:1. By diverting its own resources from computer production to wine production, the United States can exchange a computer for 2,500 cases of wine. Since this is possible, it will not pay the United States to trade a computer for less than 2,500 cases of wine. Similarly, since France can exchange a case of wine for $1/4{,}000$ of a computer by diverting its own resources from wine to computers, it clearly will not be willing to trade a case of wine for less than $1/4{,}000$ of a computer.

But where will the price ratio lie between 2,500:1 and 4,000:1? The answer depends on *world supply and demand for the two products.* The stronger the demand for computers (relative to their supply) and the weaker the demand for wine (relative to its supply), the higher the price ratio. On the other hand, the weaker the demand for computers (relative to their supply) and the stronger the demand for wine (relative to its supply), the lower the price ratio.

Incomplete Specialization

In our numerical example, the United States should specialize completely in computers, and France should specialize completely in wine. This result stems from the assumption that the cost of producing a computer or a case of wine is constant. If, on the other hand, the cost of producing each good increases with the amount produced, the result is likely to be incomplete specialization. In other words, although the United States will continue to specialize in computers and France will continue to specialize in wine, each country will also produce some of the other good as well. This is a more likely outcome, since specialization generally tends to be less than complete.

INTERNATIONAL TRADE AND INDIVIDUAL MARKETS

We have emphasized that nations can benefit by specializing in the production of goods for which they have a comparative advantage and trading these goods for others where they have a comparative disadvantage.[1] But how do a nation's producers know whether they have a comparative advantage or disadvantage in the production of a given commodity? They do not call up the local university and ask the leading professor of economics (although that might not always be such a bad idea). Instead, as we shall see in this section, the market for the good provides the required signals.

To see how this works, let's consider a new (and rather whimsical) product: bulletproof suspenders. Suppose that the Mob, having run a scientific survey of gunmen and policemen, finds that most of them wear their suspenders over their bulletproof vests. As a consequence, the Mob's

[1]The principle of comparative advantage is useful in explaining and predicting the pattern of world trade, as well as in showing the benefits of trade. For example, consider the exports of Great Britain and the United States. Robert Stern of the University of Michigan compared British and American exports of 39 industries. In 21 of the 24 industries where our labor productivity was more than three times that of the British, our exports exceeded British exports. In 11 of the 15 industries where our labor productivity was less than three times that of the British, our exports were less than British exports. Thus in 32 out of 39 industries, the principle of comparative advantage, as interpreted by Stern, predicted correctly which country would export more. This is a high batting average, since labor is not the only input and labor productivity is an imperfect measure of true efficiency. Moreover, as we shall see in subsequent sections, countries raise barriers to foreign trade, preventing trade from taking place in accord with the principle of comparative advantage.

gunmen are instructed to render a victim immobile by shooting holes in his suspenders (thus making his trousers fall down and trip him). Naturally, the producers of suspenders will soon find it profitable to produce a new bulletproof variety, an innovation that, it is hoped, will make a solid contribution to law and order. The new suspenders are demanded only in the United States and England, since the rest of the world wears belts. The demand curve in the United States is as shown in panel A of Figure 27.1, and the demand curve in England is as shown in panel B. Suppose further that this product can be manufactured in both the United States and England. The supply curve in the United States is as shown in panel A, and the supply curve in England is as shown in panel B.

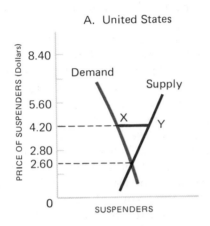
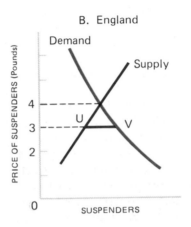

Figure 27.1 Determination of Quantity Imported and Exported under Free Trade Under free trade, price will equal $4.20, or £3. The United States will export *XY* units, the English will import *UV* units, and *XY* = *UV*.

Take a closer look at Figure 27.1. Note that prices in England are expressed in pounds (£) and prices in the United States are expressed in dollars ($). This is quite realistic. Each country has its own currency, in which prices in that country are expressed. As of 1985 £1 was equal to about $1.40. In other words, you could exchange a pound note for $1.40, or $1.40 for a £1 note. For this reason, the two panels of Figure 27.1 are lined up so that a price of $2.80 is at the same level as a price of £2, $4.20 is at the same level as £3, and so on.

No Foreign Trade

To begin with, suppose that bulletproof suspenders cannot be exported or imported, perhaps because of a very high tariff (tax on imports) imposed on them in both the United States and England. (One can readily imagine members of both Congress and Parliament defending such a tariff on the grounds that a capacity to produce plenty of bulletproof suspenders is important for national defense.) If this happens, the price of bulletproof suspenders will be $2.60 in the United States and £4 in England. Why? Because, as shown in Figure 27.1, these are the prices at which each country's demand curve intersects its supply curve.

Foreign Trade Permitted

Next, suppose that international trade in this product is permitted, perhaps because both countries eliminate the tariff. Now what will happen? Since the price is lower in the United States than in England, people can make money by sending this product from the United States to England. After all, they can buy it for $2.60 in this country and sell it for £4 (= $5.60) in England. But they will not be able to do so indefinitely. As more and more suspenders are supplied by the United States for the English market, the price in the United States must go up (to induce producers to produce the additional output) and the price in England must go down (to induce consumers to buy the additional quantity).

When an equilibrium is reached, *the price in the United States must equal the price in England.* If this did not happen, there would be an advantage in increasing American exports (if the price in England were higher) or in decreasing American exports (if the price in the United States were higher). Thus only if the prices are equal can an equilibrium exist.

At what level will this price—which is common to both countries—tend to settle? Obviously, *the price must end up at the level where the amount of the good one country wants to export equals the amount the other country wants to import.* In other words, it must settle at $4.20 or £3 (since this is the price where $XY = UV$). Otherwise, the total amount demanded in both countries would not equal the total amount supplied in both countries. And any reader who has mastered the material in Chapter 2 knows that such a situation cannot be an equilibrium.

The Signal of Market Forces

At this point, we can see how market forces indicate whether a country has a comparative advantage or a comparative disadvantage in the production of a certain commodity. *If a country has a comparative advantage, it turns out—after the price of the good in various countries is equalized and total world output of the good equals total world demand for it—that the country exports the good under free trade and competition.* In Figure 27.1, it turns out that the United States is an exporter of bulletproof suspenders under free trade, because the demand and supply curves in the United States and England take the positions they do. The basic reason why the curves take these positions is that the United States has a comparative advantage in the production of this good. To put things in a nutshell, a nation's producers can tell (under free trade) whether they have a comparative advantage in the production of a certain commodity by seeing whether it is profitable for them to export it. If they can make a profit, they have a comparative advantage.

TARIFFS AND QUOTAS

What Is a Tariff?

Despite its advantages, not everyone benefits from free trade. On the contrary, the well-being of some firms and workers may be threatened by foreign competition; and they may press for a *tariff*, a tax the government imposes on imports. The purpose of a tariff is to cut down on imports in order to protect domestic industry and workers from foreign competition. A secondary reason for tariffs is to produce revenue for the government.

To see how a tariff works, consider the market for wristwatches. Suppose that the demand and supply curves for wristwatches in the United States are as shown in panel A of Figure 27.2, and that the demand and supply curves for wristwatches in Switzerland are as shown in panel B. Clearly, Switzerland has a comparative advantage in the production of wristwatches, and under free trade the price of a wristwatch would tend toward $10 in the United States and toward 25 Swiss francs in Switzerland. (Note that 1 Swiss franc is assumed to equal 40 cents.) Under free trade, the United States would import 10 million wristwatches from Switzerland.

Now if the United States imposes a tariff of $10 on each wristwatch imported from Switzerland, the imports will completely cease. Any importers who buy watches in Switzerland at the price (when there is no foreign trade) of 15 Swiss francs—which equals $6.00—must pay a tariff of $10; this makes their total cost $16.00 per watch. But this is more than the price of a watch in the United States when there is no foreign trade (which is $15). Consequently, there is no money to be made by importing watches —unless Americans can be persuaded to pay more for a Swiss watch than for an identical American watch.

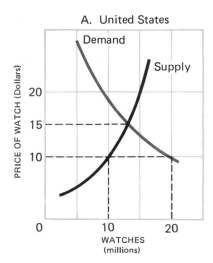

A. United States

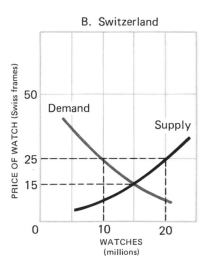

B. Switzerland

Figure 27.2
Effect of a Tariff on Swiss Watches Under free trade, price would equal $10, or 25 Swiss francs. If a tariff of $10 is imposed on each watch imported from Switzerland, there will be a complete cessation of imports. Price in the United States will increase to $15, and price in Switzerland will fall to 15 Swiss francs.

The Social Costs of Tariffs

What is the effect of the tariff? The domestic watch industry receives a higher price—$15 rather than $10—than it would without a tariff. And the workers in the domestic watch industry may have more jobs and higher wages than without the tariff. The victim of the tariff is the American consumer, who pays a higher price for wristwatches. Thus the domestic watch industry benefits at the expense of the rest of the nation. But does the general public lose more than the watch industry gains? In general, the answer is yes. The tariff reduces the welfare of the nation as a whole.

The tariff in Figure 27.2 is a *prohibitive tariff*: a tariff so high that it stops all imports of the good in question. Not all tariffs are prohibitive. (If they were, the government would receive no revenue at all from tariffs.) In many cases, the tariff is high enough to stop some, but not all, imports; and, as you would expect, the detrimental effect of a nonprohibitive tariff on living standards is less than that of a prohibitive tariff. But this does not mean that nonprohibitive tariffs are harmless. On the contrary, they can do lots of harm to domestic consumption and living standards.

What Is a Quota?

Besides tariffs, other barriers to free trade are *quotas*, which many countries impose on the amount of certain commodities that can be imported annually. The United States sets import quotas on sugar and exerts pressure on foreigners to get them to limit the quantity of steel and textiles that they will export to us. To see how a quota affects trade, production, and prices, let's return to the market for wristwatches. Suppose the United States places a quota on the import of wristwatches: no more than 6 million wristwatches can be imported per year. Figure 27.3 shows the effect of the

Figure 27.3
Effect of a Quota on Swiss Watches
Before the quota is imposed, the price is $10, or 25 Swiss francs. After a quota of 6 million watches is imposed, the price in the United States rises to $12, and the price in Switzerland falls to 20 Swiss francs.

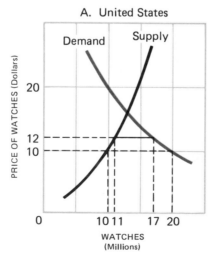
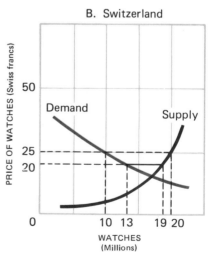

Swiss francs), and the United States imported 10 million wristwatches
from Switzerland. The quota forces the United States to reduce its imports
to 6 million.

What will be the effect on the U.S. price? The demand curve shows that
if the price is $12, American demand will exceed American supply by 6
million watches; in other words, we will import 6 million watches. Thus
once the quota is imposed, the price will rise to $12, since *this is the price
that will reduce our imports to the amount of the quota.* A quota—like a
tariff—increases the price of the good. (Note too that the price in Switzerland will fall to 20 Swiss francs. Thus the quota will reduce the price in
Switzerland.)

The Social Costs of Quotas

Both a quota and a tariff reduce trade, raise prices, protect domestic
industry from foreign competition, and reduce the standard of living of
the nation as a whole. But most economists tend to regard quotas with
even less enthusiasm than they do tariffs. Under many circumstances, a
quota insulates local industry from foreign competition even more effectively than a tariff does. Foreigners, if their costs are low enough, can
surmount a tariff barrier; but if a quota exists, there is no way they can
exceed the quota. Moreover, a (nonprohibitive) tariff provides the government with some revenue, while quotas do not even do that. The windfall
price increase from a quota accrues to the importer who is lucky enough
or influential enough (or sufficiently generous with favors and bribes) to
get an import license. (However, if the government auctions off the import
licenses, it can obtain revenue from a quota.)

Export Subsidies and Other Nontariff Barriers to Free Trade

Finally, **export subsidies**, another means by which governments try to
give their domestic industry an advantage in international competition,
are also a major impediment to free trade. Such subsidies may take the
form of outright cash disbursements, tax exemptions, preferential financing or insurance arrangements, or other preferential treatment for
exports. Export subsidies and other such measures frequently lead to
countermeasures. Thus to counter foreign export subsidies on goods sold
here, the U.S. government has imposed tariff duties on such goods.

Other nontariff barriers to free trade include licensing requirements
and unreasonable product quality standards. By granting few licenses
(which are required in some countries to import goods) and by imposing
unrealistically stringent product quality standards, governments discourage imports.

ARGUMENTS FOR TARIFFS AND QUOTAS

Given the disadvantages to society at large of tariffs and other barriers to free trade, why do governments continue to impose them? There are many reasons, some sensible, some irrational.

The National Defense Argument

One of the most convincing arguments is the desirability of maintaining a domestic industry for purposes of *national defense.* Thus even if Sweden had a comparative advantage in producing airplanes, we would not allow free trade to put our domestic producers of aircraft out of business if we felt that a domestic aircraft industry was necessary for national defense. Although the Swedes are by no means unfriendly, we would not want to import our entire supply of such a critical commodity from a foreign country, where the supply might be shut off for reasons of international politics. (Recall the Arab oil embargo of the 1970s.)

This is a perfectly valid reason for protecting certain domestic industries, and many protective measures are defended on these grounds. To the extent that protective measures are in fact required for national defense, economists go along with them. The restrictions entail social costs (some of which were described in previous sections), but these costs may well be worth paying for enhanced national security. The trouble is that many barriers to free trade are defended on these grounds when in fact they protect domestic industries only tenuously connected with national security. Moreover, even if there is a legitimate case on defense grounds for protecting a domestic industry, subsidies are likely to be a more straightforward and efficient way to do so than tariffs or quotas.

Other Arguments for Tariffs

Besides national defense, several other arguments for tariffs or quotas can make sense.

1. *Tariffs or other forms of protection can be justified to foster the growth or development of young industries.* Suppose that Japan has a comparative advantage in the production of a certain semiconductor, but Japan does not presently produce this item. It may take Japanese firms several years to become proficient in the relevant technology and to take advantage of the relevant economies of scale. While this industry is "growing up," Japan may impose a tariff on such semiconductors, thus shielding its young industry from competition it cannot yet handle. This "infant industry" argument for tariffs has a long history; Alexander Hamilton was one of its early exponents. Needless to say, it is *not* an argument for *permanent* tariffs, since infant industries are supposed to grow up—and

CASE STUDY 27.1 RESTRICTIONS ON U.S. IMPORTS OF JAPANESE AUTOS

When the first Japanese cars arrived on the West Coast in the 1970s, no one saw them as a threat to American jobs. Although they were cheaper and more fuel-efficient than American-made cars, most Americans couldn't be bothered; with gasoline at thirty cents a gallon, the difference between a car that got thirty miles per gallon and one that got ten might be as little as $300, even for someone who drove a lot.

But all this changed with the Arab oil embargo of 1973. As gas prices climbed, Americans took another look at small foreign cars. With expensive American labor and outmoded facilities on one side, and Japanese efficiency and management techniques on the other, Japan seemed to be winning the war in the showroom.

While imports may create as many jobs as they consume in the long run, in the short run many smokestack industry workers can be left permanently unemployed or underemployed. Worried American workers wanted protection, and they found a strong advocate in Representative John Dingell, one of the leaders of an emerging protectionist movement in Congress. Dingell spoke with President Reagan and Trade Representative William Brock, and urged that if voluntary restrictions on Japanese auto imports weren't adopted, Congress would impose mandatory ones. Faced with this choice, the Japanese agreed in negotiations to voluntary restrictions.

Workers rally to fight foreign competition

The restrictions worked. As the number of Japanese auto imports dropped between 1981 and 1982, domestic auto industry employment rose. But the cost of saving hundreds of *thousands* of American jobs was restricted choice and higher prices for hundreds of *millions* of American consumers. Hefty dealer markups were imposed on the scarcer but still-popular imports, and as sticker prices rose on Toyotas and Datsuns, General Motors, Ford, and Chrysler found that they could raise prices too.

The combined price paid by consumers for trade restrictions is very high; it has been estimated that each job protected from foreign competition with quotas or tariffs costs consumers about $160,000 in higher prices—more than enough to support the holder of that job. While trade restrictions may save jobs in the short run, they lock inefficiencies into the American economy and merely delay needed efforts to divert people and assets into areas of the economy in which the United States has a competitive advantage—and which therefore offer long-term employment and profit possibilities.

N.B.

the sooner the better. (Moreover, a subsidy for the industry would probably be better and easier to remove than a temporary tariff, according to many economists.)

2. *Tariffs sometimes may be imposed to protect domestic jobs and to reduce unemployment at home.* In the short run this policy may succeed, but we must recognize that other nations are likely to retaliate by enacting or increasing their own tariffs, so that such a policy may not work very well in the long run. A more sensible way to reduce domestic unemployment is to use the tools of fiscal and monetary policy described elsewhere in this book rather than tariffs. If workers are laid off by industries that cannot compete with foreign producers, proper monetary and fiscal policy, together with retraining programs, should enable these workers to switch to other industries that can compete. (See Case Study 27.1.)

3. *Tariffs sometimes may be imposed to prevent a country from being too dependent on only a few industries.* Consider a Latin American country that is a major producer of bananas. Under free trade, this country might produce bananas and little else, putting its entire economy at the mercy of the banana market. If the price of bananas fell, the country's national income would decrease drastically. To promote industrial diversification, this country may establish tariffs to protect other industries—for example, certain types of light manufacturing. In a case like this, the tariff protects the country from having too many of its eggs—or bananas—in a single basket.

4. *Tariffs may sometimes improve a country's terms of trade—that is, the ratio of its export prices to its import prices.* The United States is a major importer of bananas. If we impose a tariff on bananas, thus cutting down on the domestic demand for them (because the tariff will increase their price), the reduction in our demand is likely to reduce the price of bananas abroad. Consequently, foreign producers of bananas will really pay part of the tariff. However, other countries may retaliate; and if all countries pursue such policies, few, if any, are likely to find themselves better off.

SUMMARY

1. International trade permits specialization, and specialization increases output. This is the advantage of trade, both for individuals and for nations.

2. Country A has an absolute advantage over Country B in the production of a good when Country A can produce a unit of the good with fewer resources than can Country B. Trade can be mutually beneficial even if one country has an absolute advantage in the production of all goods.

3. Specialization and trade depend on comparative, not absolute, advantage. A nation is said to have a comparative advantage in those products where its efficiency relative to other nations is highest. Trade can be mutually beneficial if a country specializes in the products where it has a comparative advantage and imports the products where it has a comparative disadvantage.

4. If markets are relatively free and competitive, producers will automatically be led to produce in accord with comparative advantage. If a country has a comparative advantage in the production of a certain good, it will turn out—after the price of the good in various countries is equalized and total world output of the good equals total world demand—that this country is an exporter of the good under free trade.

5. A tariff is a tax imposed by the government on imports, the purpose being to cut down on imports in order to protect domestic industry and workers from foreign competition. Tariffs benefit the protected industry at the expense of the general public, and, in general, a tariff costs the general public more than the protected industry (and its workers and suppliers) gains.

6. Quotas are another barrier to free trade. They too reduce trade, raise prices, protect domestic industry from foreign competition, and reduce the standard of living of the nation as a whole.

7. Tariffs, quotas, and other barriers to free trade can sometimes be justified on the basis of national security and other noneconomic considerations. Moreover, tariffs and other forms of protection can sometimes be justified to protect infant industries, to prevent a country from being too dependent on only a few industries, and to carry out other national objectives.

CHAPTER 28

★ ★ ★ ★ ★ ★ ★ ★ ★

Exchange Rates and the Balance of Payments

LEARNING OBJECTIVES

In this chapter, you should learn:

★ What exchange rates are

★ The workings of the gold standard, fixed exchange rates, and flexible exchange rates

★ The definition of a balance-of-payments deficit and balance-of-payments surplus

★ The factors underlying recent problems in the international monetary system

In late 1984, the financial pages of newspapers around the world trumpeted that the value of the dollar had reached its highest level in over a decade. (*Business Week,* for example, published a cover story on the "superdollar.") American tourists visiting other countries and U.S. importers were happy because a dollar was worth more German marks, Japanese yen, or Swiss francs. The situation was quite different from 1978, when the value of the dollar plunged, also resulting in headline news.

To understand these developments, we must consider several questions. What are exchange rates, and how are they determined? How are international business transactions carried out? Should there be fixed or flexible exchange rates? What is a balance-of-payments deficit, and what is its significance? What problems have afflicted the international monetary system in recent years? These questions, which are both fundamental and timely, are taken up in this chapter.

THE EFFECTS OF FOREIGN TRADE ON NNP

Before considering these questions, we must look at a related, and important, topic. In Chapters 5 and 6, we discussed how the level of net national product is determined. As a first approximation, it seemed adequate to ignore exports and imports in our discussion there. Now we must take account of exports and imports and see how they affect NNP. Recall from Chapter 3 that net national product = consumption expenditure + net investment + government spending + net exports, where net exports equal exports minus imports. In other words, $Y = C + I + G + X$, where Y is NNP, C is consumption expenditure, I is investment, G is government spending, and X is net exports. Recall too that *the equilibrium level of NNP will be at the point where intended spending on NNP equals NNP.*

Thus in Figure 28.1 the equilibrium level of NNP must be $500 billion, since this is the level at which the $C + I + G + X$ line intersects the 45-degree line. To see this, note that we are merely carrying out a straight-forward extension of the analysis in Chapter 6, where we assumed that net exports were zero. Once this assumption is relaxed, intended net exports must be added to the $C + I + G$ line to get total intended spending, and the equilibrium level of NNP is at the point where the resulting total-intended-spending line, $C + I + G + X$, intersects the 45-degree line.

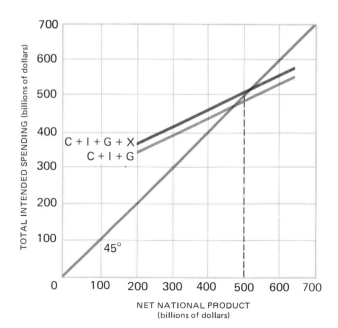

**Figure 28.1
Effects of Foreign Trade on Net National Product**
The equilibrium level of NNP is at the point where the $C + I + G + X$ line intersects the 45-degree line; in this case, $500 billion.

**Figure 28.2
Effect of Increase
in Net Exports on
Net National
Product**
If net exports
increase from X to
X', the equilibrium
level of NNP
increases from $500
billion to $550
billion.

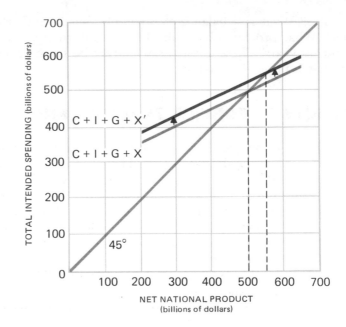

It is clear why governments during the 1930s wanted to increase their exports and decrease their imports. Spending on net exports results in increases in NNP. If intended spending on net exports increases from X to X', as shown in Figure 28.2, the equilibrium level of NNP increases from $500 billion to $550 billion. Moreover, *increases in spending on net exports have a multiplier effect,* which is like the multiplier effect for investment or government spending. Thus a $1 increase in intended spending on net exports results in more than a $1 increase in NNP.[1] Since governments during the 1930s wanted desperately to increase their NNP to reduce unemployment, it is clear why they tried to increase their net exports. However, all that resulted was a reduction in international trade, because of retaliatory measures.

INTERNATIONAL TRANSACTIONS AND EXCHANGE RATES

Having taken up the effects of foreign trade on NNP, let's turn now to the nature of exchange rates. Suppose you want to buy a book from a German publisher, and the book costs 20 marks. (The German currency consists of marks, not dollars.) To buy the book, you must somehow get marks to pay the publisher, since this is the currency in which the publisher deals. Or,

[1]If we assume that exports, government expenditures, and tax receipts are the same at all levels of NNP, then a $1 increase in intended spending on net exports will result in an increase in equilibrium NNP of $1 \div (\text{MPS} + \text{MPI})$ dollars, where MPS is the marginal propensity to save and MPI is the marginal propensity to import. (The *marginal propensity to import* is the proportion of an extra dollar of income that is spent on imports.) Note that the multiplier is smaller now than in the case of a closed economy (where MPI equals zero).

if the publisher agrees, you might pay in dollars; but the publisher would then have to exchange the dollars for marks, since its bills must be paid in marks. Whatever happens, either you or the publisher must somehow exchange dollars for marks, since international business transactions, unlike transactions within a country, involve two different currencies.

If you decide to exchange dollars for marks to pay the German publisher, how can you make the exchange? The answer is simple. You can buy German marks at a bank, just as you might buy lamb chops at a butcher shop. Just as the lamb chops have a price (expressed in dollars), so the German marks have a price (expressed in dollars). The bank may tell you that each mark you buy will cost you $.40. This makes the *exchange rate* between dollars and marks .4 to 1, since it takes .4 dollars to purchase 1 mark.

In general, *the exchange rate is simply the number of units of one currency that exchanges for a unit of another currency.* The obvious question is: What determines the exchange rate? Why is the exchange rate between German marks and American dollars what it is? Why doesn't a dollar exchange for 10 marks, rather than 2½ marks? This basic question will occupy us in the next several sections.

EXCHANGE RATES UNDER THE GOLD STANDARD

As a starter, let's see how exchange rates were determined under the *gold standard*, which prevailed before the 1930s. *If a country was on the gold standard, a unit of its currency was convertible into a certain amount of gold.* Before World War I the dollar was convertible into one-twentieth of an ounce of gold, and the British pound was convertible into one-quarter of an ounce of gold. Thus, since the pound exchanged for 5 times as much gold as the dollar, the pound exchanged for $5. The currency of any other country on the gold standard was convertible into a certain amount of gold in the same way; *to see how much its currency was worth in dollars, you divided the amount of gold a unit of its currency was worth by the amount of gold (one-twentieth of an ounce) a dollar was worth.*

Why did the exchange rate always equal the ratio between the amount of gold a foreign currency was worth and the amount of gold a dollar was worth? Why did the price of a British pound stay at $5 before World War I? To see why, suppose that the price (in dollars) of a pound rose above this ratio—above $5. Instead of exchanging their dollars directly for pounds, Americans would have done better to exchange them for gold and then exchange the gold for pounds. By this indirect process, Americans could have exchanged $5 for a pound, so they would have refused to buy pounds at a price above $5 per pound.

Similarly, if the price of a pound fell below $5, the British would have refused to sell pounds, since they could have obtained $5 by converting the pound into gold and the gold into dollars. Thus *because Americans would refuse to pay more than $5, and the British would refuse to accept* *less, the price of a pound had to remain at about $5. (In practice, the pound could be a few cents above or below $5, because it costs money to transport gold in order to carry out the conversion.)*

Balance between Exports and Imports

But what ensured that this exchange rate, dictated by the gold content of currencies, would result in a rough equality of trade between countries? If one pound exchanged for $5, perhaps the British might find our goods so cheap that they would import a great deal from us, while we might find their goods so expensive that we would import little from them. Under these circumstances, the British would have to ship gold to us to pay for the excess of their imports from us over their exports to us, and eventually they could run out of gold. Could this happen? If not, why not? These questions occupied the attention of many early economists. The classic answers were given by David Hume, the Scottish philosopher, in the eighteenth century.

Hume pointed out that under the gold standard a mechanism ensured that trade would be brought into balance and that neither country would run out of gold. This mechanism worked as follows. If, as we assumed, the British bought more from us than we bought from them, they would have to send us gold to pay for the excess of their imports over their exports. As their gold stock declined, their price level would fall. (Recall the quantity theory of money discussed in Chapter 13.) As our gold stock increased, our price level would rise. Thus, because of our rising prices, the British would tend to import less from us; because of their falling prices, we would tend to import more from them. Consequently, the trade between the two countries would tend toward a better balance. Eventually when enough gold had left Britain and entered the United States, prices here would have increased enough and prices in Britain would have fallen enough to put imports and exports in balance.

THE FOREIGN EXCHANGE MARKET

The gold standard is long gone; and after many decades of fixed exchange rates (discussed in a later section), the major trading nations of the world began to experiment with flexible exchange rates in early 1973. Let's consider a situation where exchange rates are allowed to fluctuate freely, like the price of any commodity in a competitive market. In a case of this sort, exchange rates, like any price, are determined by supply and demand. There is a market for various types of foreign currency—German marks, British pounds, French francs, and so on—just as there are markets for various types of meat.

In the case of the German mark, the demand and supply curves may look like those shown in Figure 28.3. The demand curve shows the amount of German marks that people with dollars will demand at various prices

Figure 28.4
Effect of Shift in
Demand Curve for
German Marks
Because of the
demand curve's
shift to the right, the
equilibrium price of
a German mark
increases from $.40
to $.44.

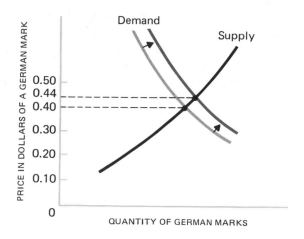

means that more marks will be supplied at a given price (in dollars) of the mark. Given the posited increase in Germand demand for American goods, such a shift in the supply curve would be expected.

Appreciation and Depreciation of a Currency

Two terms frequently encountered in discussions of the foreign exchange market are *appreciation* and *depreciation*. When Country A's currency becomes more valuable relative to Country B's currency, Country A's currency is said to appreciate relative to that of Country B, and Country B's currency is said to depreciate relative to that of Country A. In Figure 28.4, the mark appreciated relative to the dollar and the dollar depreciated relative to the mark. This use of terms makes sense. Since the number of dollars commanded by a mark increased, the mark became more valuable relative to the dollar and the dollar became less valuable relative to the mark.

Note that such a change in exchange rates would not have been possible under the gold standard. Unless a country changed the amount of gold that could be exchanged for a unit of its currency, exchange rates were fixed under the gold standard. Sometimes governments did change the amount of gold that could be exchanged for their currencies. For example, in 1933 the United States increased the price of gold from $21 an ounce to $35 an ounce. When a country increased the price of gold, this was called a *devaluation of currency*.

Determinants of Exchange Rates

In a previous section, we saw that flexible exchange rates are determined by supply and demand. But what are some of the major factors determining the position of these supply and demand curves?

RELATIVE PRICE LEVELS. In the long run, the exchange rate between any two currencies may be expected to reflect differences in the price of a mark. The supply curve shows the amount of German marks that people with marks will supply at various prices of a mark. Since the amount of German currency supplied must equal the amount demanded in equilibrium, *the equilibrium price (in dollars) of a German mark is given by the intersection of the demand and supply curves.* In Figure 28.3, this intersection is at $.40.

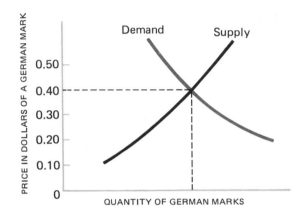

Figure 28.3
Determination of the Exchange Rate between Dollars and German Marks under Freely Fluctuating Exchange Rates Under freely fluctuating exchange rates, the equilibrium price of a German mark would be $.40 if the demand and supply curves for marks are as shown here.

The Demand and Supply Sides of the Market

Let's look in more detail at the demand and supply sides of this market. On the *demand* side are people who want to import German goods (like the book you want to buy) into the United States, people who want to travel in Germany (where they'll need German money), people who want to build factories in Germany, and others with dollars who want German currency. The people on the *supply* side are those who want to import American goods into Germany, Germans who want to travel in the United States (where they'll need American money), people with marks who want to build factories in the United States, and others with marks who want American currency.

When Americans demand more German cameras or Rhine wine (causing the demand curve to shift upward and to the right), the price (in dollars) of the German mark will tend to increase. Thus, if the demand curve for marks shifts as shown in Figure 28.4, the result will be an increase in the equilibrium price (in dollars) of a mark from $.40 to $.44. Conversely, *when the Germans demand more American cars or computers (resulting in a shift of the supply curve downward and to the right), the price (in dollars) of the German mark will tend to decrease.*

To see why an increase in German demand for American cars or computers shifts the supply curve downward and to the right, recall that the supply curve shows the amount of marks that will be supplied at each price of a mark. Thus a shift downward and to the right in the supply curve levels in the two countries. To see why, suppose that Germany and the United States are the only exporters or importers of automobiles, and that automobiles are the only product they export or import. If an automobile costs $4,000 in the United States and 10,000 marks in Germany, what must be the exchange rate between the dollar and the mark? Clearly, a mark must be worth 0.40 dollars, because otherwise the two countries' automobiles would not be competitive in the world market. If a mark were set equal to 0.60 dollars, this would mean that a German automobile would cost $6,000 (that is, 10,000 times $0.60), which is far more than what an American automobile would cost. Thus foreign buyers would obtain their automobiles in the United States.

Based on this theory, one would expect that, *if the rate of inflation in Country A is higher than in Country B, Country A's currency is likely to depreciate relative to Country B's.* Suppose that costs double in the United States but increase by only 25 percent in Germany. After this burst of inflation, an automobile costs $8,000 (that is, 2 times $4,000) in the United States and 12,500 marks (that is, 1.25 times 10,000 marks) in Germany. Thus, based on the purchasing-power parity theory, the new value of the mark must be 0.64 dollars, rather than the old value of 0.40 dollars. (Why 0.64 dollars? Because this is the exchange rate that makes the new cost of an automobile in the United States, $8,000, equivalent to the new cost of an automobile in Germany, 12,500 marks.) Because the rate of inflation is higher in the United States than in Germany, the dollar depreciates relative to the mark.

RELATIVE RATES OF GROWTH. Although relative price levels may play an important role in the long run, other factors tend to exert more influence on exchange rates in the short run. In particular, *if one country's rate of economic growth is higher than the rest of the world, its currency is likely to depreciate.* If a country's economy is booming, this tends to increase its imports. If there is a boom in the United States, Americans will tend to import a great deal from other countries. If a country's imports tend to grow faster than its exports, its demand for foreign currency will tend to grow more rapidly than the amount of foreign currency that is supplied to it. Consequently, its currency is likely to depreciate.

RELATIVE INTEREST-RATE LEVELS. If the rate of interest in Germany is higher than in the United States, banks, multinational corporations, and other investors in the United States will sell dollars and buy marks in order to invest in the high-yielding Germany securities. Also, German investors (and others) will be less likely to find American securities attractive. Thus the mark will tend to appreciate relative to the dollar, since the demand curve for marks will shift to the right and the supply curve for marks will shift to the left. In general, *an increase in a country's interest rates leads to an appreciation of its currency, and a decrease in its interest rates leads to a depreciation of its currency.* In the short run, interest-rate differentials can have a major impact on exchange rates, since there is estimated to be over $100 billion in funds that are moved from country to country in response to differentials in interest rates.

The Adjustment Mechanism under Flexible Exchange Rates

Under flexible exchange rates, what ensures a balance in the exports and imports between countries? The situation differs from that described by David Hume, since Hume assumed the existence of the gold standard. Under flexible exchange rates, the balance is achieved through changes in exchange rates. Suppose that for some reason Britain is importing far more from us than we are from Britain. This will mean that the British, needing dollars to buy our goods, will be willing to supply pounds more cheaply. In other words, the supply curve for British pounds will shift downward and to the right, as shown in Figure 28.5. This will cause the price of a pound to decline from P_1 dollars to P_2 dollars. Or, from Britain's point of view, the price (in pounds) of a dollar will have been bid up by the swollen demand for imports from America.

**Figure 28.5
Adjustment
Mechanism**
If Britain imports more from us than we do from Britain, the supply curve for British pounds will shift downward and to the right, resulting in a decline of the price of the pound from P_1 to P_2 dollars. If Britain tries to maintain the price at P_1 dollars, the British government will have to exchange dollars for $(Q_S - Q_D)$ pounds.

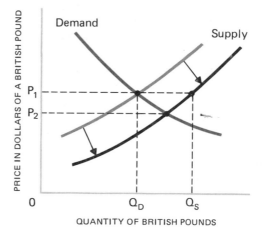

Because of the increase in the price (in pounds) of a dollar, our goods will become more expensive in Britain. Thus the British will tend to reduce their imports of our goods. At the same time, since the price (in dollars) of a pound has decreased, British goods will become cheaper in the United States, and this will stimulate us to import more from Britain. Consequently, as our currency appreciates in terms of theirs—or, to put it another way, as theirs depreciates in terms of ours—the British are induced to import less and export more. Thus there is an automatic mechanism (just as there was under the gold standard) to bring trade between countries into balance.

FIXED EXCHANGE RATES

Although many economists believed that exchange rates should be allowed to fluctuate, very few exchange rates really did so in the period from the end of World War II up to 1973. Instead, *most exchange rates were fixed by government action and international agreement.* Although they may have varied slightly about the fixed level, the extent to which they were allowed to vary was small. Every now and then, governments changed the exchange rates, for reasons discussed below; but for long periods of time, they remained fixed.

If exchange rates remain fixed, the amount demanded of a foreign currency may not equal the amount supplied. Consider the situation in Figure 28.6. If A is the demand curve for German marks, the equilibrium price of a mark is $.40. But suppose the fixed exchange rate between dollars and marks is .35 to 1—that is, each mark exchanges for $.35. Unless the government intervenes, more German marks will be demanded at a price of $.35 per mark than will be offered. Specifically, the difference between the quantity demanded and the quantity supplied will be $Q_D - Q_S$. Unless the government steps in, a black market for German marks may develop, and the real price may increase toward $.40 per mark.

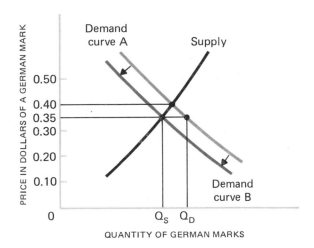

QUANTITY OF GERMAN MARKS

**Figure 28.6
Fixed Exchange Rate**
The equilibrium price of a German mark is $.40, if A is the demand curve. If $.35 is the fixed exchange rate, the U.S. government may try to shift the demand curve for marks from A to B, thus bringing the equilibrium exchange rate into equality with the fixed exchange rate.

Types of Government Intervention

To maintain exchange rates at their fixed levels, governments can intervene in a variety of ways. For example, they may reduce the demand for foreign currencies by reducing defense expenditures abroad, by limiting the amount that their citizens can travel abroad, and by curbing imports from other countries. Thus, in the case depicted in Figure 28.6, the American government might adopt some or all of these measures to shift the demand curve for German marks downward and to the left. If the demand curve can be pushed from A to B, the equilibrium price of a German mark can be reduced to $.35, the fixed exchange rate. For the time being, there will no longer be any mismatch between the quantity of marks demanded and the quantity supplied.

When exchange rates are fixed, mismatches of this sort cannot be eliminated entirely and permanently. To deal with such temporary mismatches, governments enter the market and buy and sell their currencies in order to maintain fixed exchange rates. Take the case of post-World War II Britain. At times the amount of British pounds supplied exceeded the amount demanded. Then the British government bought up the excess at the fixed exchange rate. At other times, when the quantity demanded exceeded the amount supplied, the British government supplied the pounds desired at the fixed exchange rate. As long as the equilibrium exchange rate was close to (sometimes above and sometimes below) the fixed exchange rate, the amount of its currency the government sold at one time equaled, more or less, the amount it bought at another time.

But in some cases governments have tried to maintain a fixed exchange rate far from the equilibrium exchange rate. The British government tried during the 1960s to maintain the price (in dollars) of the pound at $2.80, even though the equilibrium price was about $2.40. The situation was as shown in Figure 28.7. Since the quantity of British pounds supplied exceeded the quantity demanded at the price of $2.80, the British government had to buy the difference. That is, it had to buy ($Q_S - Q_D$) pounds with dollars. Moreover, it had to keep on exchanging dollars for pounds in these quantities for as long as the demand and supply curves remained in these positions. Such a situation could not go on indefinitely, since the British government eventually had to run out of dollars. How long it could go on depended on how big Britain's reserves of gold and foreign currency were.

Figure 28.7
Balance-of-Payments Deficit
Because the British pound is overvalued at $2.80, the quantity of pounds demanded (Q_D) is less than the quantity supplied (Q_S). The shortfall —that is, ($Q_S - Q_D$) pounds—is the balance-of-payments deficit.

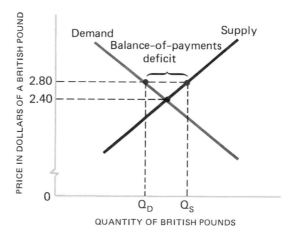

BALANCE-OF-PAYMENTS DEFICITS AND SURPLUSES

Under a system of fixed exchange rates, economists and financial analysts look at whether a country has a balance-of-payments deficit or surplus to see whether its currency is above or below its equilibrium value. What is a *balance-of-payments deficit?* What is a *balance-of-payments surplus?* It is important that both of these terms be understood.

Balance-of-Payments Deficit

If a country's currency is *overvalued* (that is, if its fixed price exceeds the equilibrium price), the quantity supplied of its currency will exceed the quantity demanded. Let's return to the case where the price of the British pound was set at $2.80. Under these circumstances, the quantity supplied of pounds exceeds the quantity demanded by $(Q_S - Q_D)$ pounds, as shown in Figure 28.7. This amount—$(Q_S - Q_D)$ pounds—is Britain's balance-of-payments deficit. (See Figure 28.7.) As pointed out in the previous section, it is the number of pounds that Britain's central bank, the Bank of England, must purchase. To pay for these pounds, the Bank of England must give up some of its *reserves* of foreign currencies or gold.

In a situation of this sort, there may be a "run" on the overvalued currency. Suppose that speculators become convinced that the country with the balance-of-payments deficit cannot maintain the artificially high price of its currency much longer because its reserves are running low. Because they will suffer losses if they hold on to a currency that is devalued, the speculators are likely to sell the overvalued currency (in Figure 28.7, the British pound) in very large amounts, thus causing an even bigger balance-of-payments deficit for the country with the overvalued currency. Faced with the exhaustion of its reserves, the country is likely to be forced to allow the price of its currency to fall.

Balance-of-Payments Surplus

If a country's currency is *undervalued* (that is, if its price is less than the equilibrium price), the quantity demanded of its currency will exceed the quantity supplied. During the early 1970s, the price of the German mark was set at $0.35, even though its equilibrium price was about $0.40. As shown in Figure 28.8, the quantity of marks demanded exceeds the quantity supplied by $(Q'_D - Q'_S)$ marks under these circumstances. This

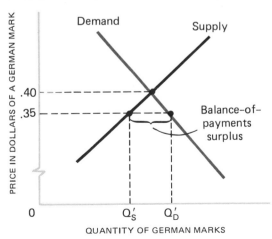

QUANTITY OF GERMAN MARKS

**Figure 28.8
Balance-of-
Payments Surplus**
Because the German mark is undervalued at $.35, the quantity of marks demanded (Q'_D) is greater than the quantity supplied (Q'_S). The surplus—that is, $(Q'_D - Q'_S)$ marks— is the balance-of-payments surplus.

amount—$(Q'_D - Q'_S)$ marks—is Germany's balance-of-payments surplus. (See Figure 28.8.) Germany can keep the price of the mark at $0.35 only if it provides these $(Q'_D - Q'_S)$ marks in exchange for foreign currencies and gold. By doing so, it increases its reserves.

Whereas a country with an overvalued currency is likely to be forced by the reduction in its reserves to reduce the price of its currency, a country with an undervalued currency is unlikely to be forced by the increase in its reserves to increase the price of its currency. And a country with an undervalued currency often is reluctant to increase the price of its currency because of political pressures by its exporters (and their workers) who point out that such a revaluation would make the country's goods more expensive in foreign markets and thus would reduce its exports. Consequently, when exchange rates were fixed, countries with undervalued currencies were less likely to adjust their exchange rates than countries with overvalued currencies.

Measuring Deficits and Surpluses

If we are given the demand and supply curves for a country's currency, it is a simple matter to determine the deficit or surplus in its balance of payments. All that we have to do is subtract the quantity demanded of the currency from the quantity supplied. However, since we do not observe these demand and supply curves in the real world, this method of determining the deficit or surplus, while fine in principle, is not practical. The available data show only the total amount of the country's currency bought and the total amount of the country's currency sold. Since each unit of the country's currency that is bought must also be sold, it is evident that the total amount bought must equal the total amount sold. Given that this is the case, how can one identify and measure a balance-of-payments deficit or surplus?

The answer lies in the transactions of the country's central bank. If the central bank's purchases or sales of currency make up for the difference between the quantity demanded and the quantity supplied, it will purchase currency if there is a balance-of-payments deficit and sell currency if there is a balance-of-payments surplus. The amount it purchases or sells measures the size of the deficit or surplus. In other words, the official transactions of this country's government with other governments are used to measure the deficit or surplus. Roughly speaking, this is how a balance-of-payments deficit or surplus has been measured. However, beginning in May 1976, the U.S. government stopped publishing figures on the deficit or surplus in our balance of payments. Under the current regime of flexible exchange rates, changes in demand and supply for foreign exchange generally show up as changes in exchange rates, rather than in the transactions of the central bank. Thus figures regarding the deficit or surplus in our balance of payments have lost much of their previous meaning.

EXCHANGE RATES: PRE-WORLD WAR II EXPERIENCE

Now that we are familiar with a balance-of-payments deficit and surplus we can begin to see how various types of exchange rates have worked out. What has been our experience with the gold standard? With fixed exchange rates? With flexible exchange rates?

During the latter part of the nineteenth century, the gold standard seemed to work very well, but serious trouble developed after World War I. During the war, practically all of the warring nations went off the gold standard to keep people from hoarding gold or from sending it to neutral countries. After the war, some countries tried to re-establish the old rates of exchange. Because the wartime and postwar rates of inflation were greater in some countries than in others, under the old exchange rates the goods of some countries were underpriced and those of other countries were overpriced. According to the doctrines of David Hume, this imbalance should have been remedied by increases in the general price level in countries where goods were underpriced and by reductions in the general price level in countries where goods were overpriced. But wages and prices proved to be inflexible, and, as one would expect, it proved especially difficult to adjust them downward. When the adjustment mechanism failed to work quickly enough, the gold standard was abandoned.

During the 1930s, governments tried various schemes. This was the time of the Great Depression, and governments were trying frantically to reduce unemployment. Sometimes a government allowed the exchange rate to be flexible for a while, and, when it found what seemed to be an equilibrium level, fixed the exchange rate there. Sometimes a government depreciated the value of its own currency relative to those of other countries in an attempt to increase employment by making its goods cheap to other countries. When one country adopted such policies, others retaliated, causing a reduction in international trade and lending, but little or no benefit for the country that started the fracas.

CASE STUDY 28.1 THE ABANDONMENT OF THE GOLD STANDARD

During the 40 years before World War I, world trade prospered under a system of exchange rates such that currencies were pegged to gold and fixed relative to one another. During World War I, however, as countries expanded their money supplies rapidly to pay for the war effort, every country experienced sharp inflation—and different relative rates of inflation. The previous fixed exchange rates could not have been honored, so the payment of gold for currency was suspended for the war's duration.

Although relative rates of inflation had changed radically during the war, in 1925 the United Kingdom decided to fix the pound to gold at the prewar level. The primary reason was to preserve the value of bonds and other fixed income securities, which had lost value during the wartime inflation. Wealthy and influential bondholders pressured the government to reverse the inflation, and pegging the price of the pound to gold was the first step in trying to re-establish the prewar price level.

Countries that had undervalued currencies, such as France and the United States, prospered during the 1920s. France in particular had "export-led" growth, and it accumulated vast reserves of foreign exchange and gold. The British economy, however, stagnated for the six years that it was on the gold standard at the prewar rate. The United Kingdom found itself importing too much, and could not compete against foreign producers because its own goods were much higher priced than foreign goods. Only by either devaluating the pound or by forcing wages down could the United Kingdom compete. If it failed to do either, it would constantly be sending out more pounds than it was collecting in foreign currencies. Foreigners would then exchange those pounds for gold, draining gold from the country.

Sterling weakened in July 1930, and despite efforts to arrange foreign financing to defend the pound and a hike in the U.K. discount rate, gold withdrawals accelerated by September. On September 21, Britain abandoned the gold standard. The pound fell from $4.86 to $3.25 within a few days but recovered to about $3.50.

Pressure shifted to the dollar as the French withdrew gold from the United States. The United States raised its discount rate from 1.5 percent to 3.5 percent in October 1930, and this was not offset by open market operations. Bank failures spread. The U.S. money supply, commodity prices, security prices, imports, and (to a lesser extent) industrial production declined faster after the British devaluation than before. The United States lost gold throughout 1932, and the early-1933 banking crises worsened the outflow.

On March 4, President Roosevelt closed the banks and let the dollar float. The dollar fell vis-à-vis the pound, and it was not until 1936 that a stabilization of the dollar, the pound, and the franc was worked out.

N.B.

THE GOLD-EXCHANGE STANDARD

In 1944, the Allied governments sent representatives to Bretton Woods, New Hampshire, to work out a more effective system for the postwar era. It was generally agreed that competitive devaluations, such as occurred in the 1930s, should be avoided. Out of the Bretton Woods conference came the ***International Monetary Fund*** (IMF), which was set up to maintain a stable system of fixed exchange rates and to ensure that, when exchange rates had to be changed because of significant trade imbalances, disruption was minimized.

The system developed during the postwar period was generally labeled the *gold-exchange standard,* as opposed to the gold standard. Under this system, the dollar—which had by this time taken the place of the British pound as the world's key currency—was convertible (for official monetary purposes) into gold at a fixed price. And since other currencies could be converted into dollars at fixed exchange rates, other currencies were convertible indirectly into gold at a fixed price.

U.S. BALANCE-OF-PAYMENTS DEFICITS, 1950–72

During the early postwar period, the gold-exchange standard worked reasonably well. However, it was not long before problems began to develop. As noted in a previous section, when exchange rates are fixed, a U.S. balance-of-payments deficit is evidence of pressure on the dollar in foreign exchange markets. Figure 28.9 shows that, *during the period from 1950 to 1972 (the last full year when exchange rates were fixed), the United States showed a chronic deficit in its balance of payments.* This chronic deficit caused considerable uneasiness and concern, both here and abroad. Several factors were responsible for it.

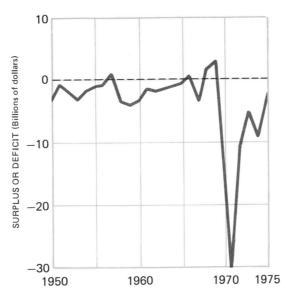

Figure 28.9
Deficit or Surplus in U.S. Balance of Payments 1950–75
From 1950 to 1972, the United States showed a chronic deficit in its balance of payments.

POSTWAR RECOVERY OF WESTERN EUROPE AND JAPAN. As the Western European and Japanese economies recovered from the devastation of World War II, they adopted new technology, and became tough competitors. To cite but one example, the Japanese were particularly adept at absorbing modern electronic technology and at producing electronic goods for civilian markets. In many areas of technology, the United States continued to enjoy a lead, but the gap seemed to be narrowing. As productivity in Western Europe and Japan rose more rapidly than ours, their costs fell relative to ours, and they were able to undersell us much more in their markets, third markets, and sometimes even our own market.

MILITARY AND FOREIGN AID. We spent enormous amounts abroad for military purposes and for foreign aid. Our military expenditures abroad were particularly high during the Vietnam War. They were about $4.5 billion in 1968 alone. Not only did this war take a heavy toll in lives and in social disruption; it also helped keep our balance of payments in deficit. Note, however, that some of our government spending abroad has involved the use of "tied" funds, which can be used only to buy American goods. Since these programs result in exports that would not otherwise be made, the elimination of some of these programs would not reduce the deficit. If government spending were cut, the exports it financed would be cut as well.

PRIVATE INVESTMENT ABROAD. American firms invested enormous amounts of money abroad. U.S. investors acquired oil refineries, assembly lines, and hundreds of other types of plants. The rate of private investment abroad increased spectacularly during the 1950s and 1960s. In the early 1950s, new American private investment abroad was about $2 billion per year; in the late 1950s, over $3 billion per year; in the early 1960s, over $4 billion per year; and in the late 1960s, over $8 billion per year. The reason for this growth is fairly obvious. The markets of Western Europe (and other parts of the world) were growing rapidly and the construction of plants abroad was a profitable move. To help reduce our balance-of-payments deficit, the government introduced a voluntary program to limit such investment abroad in 1965, and made the program compulsory in 1968. (It lapsed in the 1970s.)

INFLATION AND DISCRIMINATION. A number of other factors, including inflation in the United States and discrimination abroad against U.S. products, also contributed to our balance-of-payments deficits. Clearly, inflation in the United States made our exports more expensive abroad. It is true that inflation in the United States was not as great as in many other countries, but in many industries, like steel, our prices rose relative to those abroad. Also, foreigners maintained various quotas, tariffs, and other devices to keep out American exports. Many of these discriminatory regulations were enacted during earlier days when such policies were more understandable than during the period under consideration.

DEMISE OF THE BRETTON WOODS SYSTEM

In 1971 the dollar was depreciated relative to all major foreign currencies, and a new system of fixed exchange rates was approved by representatives of the major trading nations at a meeting at the Smithsonian Institution. Although President Nixon hailed the Smithsonian agreement as "the greatest international monetary agreement in the history of the world," events were to prove it unequal to the tasks it faced. In February 1973, scarcely more than a year after the agreement, the United States felt obliged to devalue the dollar again, as the outflow of dollars to other countries continued. Then, in March 1973, representatives of the major trading nations met in Paris to establish a system of fluctuating exchange rates, thus abandoning the Bretton Woods system of fixed exchange rates. This was a major break with the past, and one that was greeted with considerable apprehension as well as hope.

FIXED VERSUS FLEXIBLE EXCHANGE RATES

Why, until 1973, did most countries fix their exchange rates, rather than allow them to fluctuate? One important reason was the feeling that flexible exchange rates might vary so erratically that it might be difficult to carry out normal trade. Thus American exporters of machine tools to Britain might not know what British pounds would be worth six months later, when they would collect a debt in pounds. According to the proponents of fixed exchange rates, fluctuating rates would increase uncertainties for people and firms engaged in international trade and thus reduce the volume of such trade. Moreover, they argued that the harmful effects of speculation over exchange rates would increase if exchange rates were flexible, because speculators could push a currency's exchange rate up or down, and destabilize the exchange market. Further, they argued that flexible exchange rates might promote more rapid inflation, because countries would be less affected by balance-of-payments discipline.

Many economists disagreed, feeling that flexible exchange rates would work better. They asked why flexible prices are used and trusted in other areas of the economy, but not in connection with foreign exchange. They pointed out that a country would have more autonomy in formulating its fiscal and monetary policy if exchange rates were flexible, and they claimed that speculation regarding exchange rates would not be destabilizing. But until 1973, the advocates of flexible exchange rates persuaded few of the world's central bankers and policy makers.

HOW WELL HAVE FLOATING EXCHANGE RATES WORKED?

Since 1973, exchange rates have been flexible, not fixed. However, there has been some intervention by central banks to keep the movement of exchange rates between broad bounds, but this intervention generally has not been very great. The result has been considerable volatility in exchange rates. The exchange rate between the dollar and the German mark has sometimes varied by 2 percent or more from one day to the next, and by 15 percent or more over a period of several months.

Unquestionably, the variations in exchange rates, some of which are erratic and without fundamental economic significance, have made international transactions more difficult. Thus Renault, the French auto manufacturer, is reported to have hesitated to launch an export drive into the

U.S. market because of the erratic behavior of the dollar-franc exchange rate. However, businesses seem to have coped rather successfully with such exchange rate variation, as reflected in the following statement in late 1975 by the National Foreign Trade Council: "Floating exchange rates have . . . responded well to the shocks of the fast-moving developments of recent years . . . although at times business has been unfavorably affected by sharp fluctuations of key currencies."

One of the greatest "shocks" of recent years was the increase in oil prices at the beginning of 1974. This sharp price increase meant that oil-importing countries suddenly had to pay unprecedented bills to the oil-producing countries, with the result that massive strain was put on the international financial system. Although the difficulties were not surmounted easily, the new system of floating exchange rates seems to have shown the required resilience to overcome this crisis.

A crisis of another sort occurred in 1977 and 1978, when the value of the dollar dropped dramatically. Between September 1977 and March 1978, and again between June and October 1978, the value of the dollar fell by about 10 percent, in part because of our unfavorable balance of trade[2] (because we pursued a more expansionary policy than our major trading partners) and because interest rates were higher abroad than here.

During the early 1980s, the dollar staged a very impressive rebound. Between 1980 and 1983, its value rose by about 50 percent. In large part, this was due to the fact that inflation in the United States seemed to have moderated, real interest rates here were higher than in other countries (partly the result of huge government borrowing to finance its deficits),

World leaders at the 1985 Economic Summit: (from left) Prime Minister Brian Mulroney (Canada), President Ronald Reagan (United States), Prime Minister Yasuhiro Nakasone (Japan), Prime Minister MargaretThatcher (Great Britain), Chancellor Helmut Kohl (West Germany), President Francois Mitterrand (France), and Premier Bettino Craxi (Italy).

and the rates of return from investments here seemed relatively high. This marked appreciation of the dollar hurt American exporters, since their goods became very expensive to foreigners, but it helped to keep a lid on inflation, since imported goods were relatively cheap, and many American firms could not raise their own prices very much without losing business to imported goods.

Although there is no indication that flexible exchange rates will be forsaken (and fixed exchange rates restored), some observers feel that central banks should intervene to a greater extent to influence exchange rates. For example, in September 1985, the United States, Britain, France, Germany, and Japan agreed to intervene to help bring down the value of the dollar.

[2] A nation is said to have a *favorable* balance of merchandise trade if its exports of merchandise are more than its imports of merchandise, and an *unfavorable* balance of merchandise trade if its exports of merchandise are less than its imports of merchandise.

SUMMARY

1. The equilibrium level of NNP is where intended spending on NNP —which equals intended consumption expenditure plus intended investment plus government spending plus intended net exports—equals NNP.

2. An important difference between international business transactions and business transactions within a country is that international business transactions involve more than one currency. The exchange rate is the number of units of one currency that exchanges for a unit of another currency.

4. Under a system of flexible exchange rates, the market for foreign exchange functions like any other free market, the exchange rate being determined by supply and demand. Under such a system, exchange rates tend to move in a way that removes imbalances among countries in exports and imports. The price of a country's currency tends to fall (rise) if its inflation rate and growth rate are relatively high (low) or if its interest rate is relatively low (high).

5. Until 1973, when exchange rates became more flexible, most exchange rates were fixed by government action and international agreement. They were allowed to vary slightly, but only slightly, about the official rate.

6. If exchange rates are fixed, the amount of a foreign currency demanded may not equal the amount supplied. To maintain exchange rates at the official levels, governments enter the market and buy and sell their currencies as needed. They also intervene by curbing imports, limiting foreign travel, and other measures.

7. Under a system of fixed exchange rates, a country will have a balance-of-payments deficit if its currency is overvalued and a balance-of-payments surplus if its currency is undervalued. A balance-of-payments deficit is the difference between the quantity supplied and quantity demanded of the currency. A balance-of-payments surplus is the difference between the quantity demanded and quantity supplied of the currency.

8. The United States experienced a chronic balance-of-payments deficit during the 1950s, 1960s, and 1970s. This deficit was the result of the growing productivity of other economies, our large investments abroad, and our military and foreign aid expenditures abroad. In 1973, the system of fixed exchange rates was abandoned.

9. In recent years, the variation in exchange rates, some of which are erratic and without fundamental economic significance, have made international transactions more difficult. Although there was no indication that flexible exchange rates would be forsaken, some observers seemed to feel in late 1985 that central banks should intervene to a greater extent to influence exchange rates.

Glossary of Terms

Absolute advantage the ability of one country to produce a commodity more cheaply than another country.

Aggregate demand curve a curve, sloping downward to the right, that shows the level of real national output that will be demanded at various economy-wide price levels.

Aggregate production function the relationship between the amount used of each of the inputs available in the economy and the resulting amount of potential output, i.e., the most output that existing technology permits the economy to produce from various quantities of all available inputs.

Aggregate supply curve a curve, sloping upward to the right, that shows the level of real national output that will be supplied at various economy-wide price levels.

Aid to Families with Dependent Children (AFDC) an antipoverty program that provides cash payments to families with children who are without the support of a parent through death, disability, or absence.

Alternative cost the value of what cer-

tain resources could have produced had they been used in the best alternative way; also called **opportunity cost.**

American Federation of Labor-Congress of Industrial Organizations (AFL-CIO) a federation of national labor unions formed in 1955 by the merger between the American Federation of Labor (originally a federation of unions organized along craft lines) and the Congress of Industrial Organizations (originally a federation of unions organized along industrial lines).

Antitrust laws legislation (such as the Sherman Act, the Clayton Act, and the Federal Trade Commission Act) intended to promote competition and control monopoly.

Appreciation of currency an increase in the value of one currency relative to another.

Automatic stabilizers structural features of the economy that tend by themselves to stabilize national output, without the help of legislation or government policy measures.

Average fixed cost the firm's total fixed cost divided by its output.

Average product of an input total output divided by the amount of input used to produce this amount of output.

Average product of labor total output per unit of labor.

Average propensity to consume the fraction of total disposable income that is spent on consumption; equal to personal consumption expenditure divided by disposable income.

Average total cost the firm's total cost divided by its output; equal to average fixed cost plus average variable cost.

Average variable cost the firm's total variable cost divided by its output.

Backward-bending supply curve for labor a supply curve for labor inputs showing that, beyond some point, increases in price may result in smaller amounts of labor being supplied.

Balance-of-payments deficit the difference between the quantity supplied and the quantity demanded of a currency when the currency is overvalued (i.e., priced above its equilibrium price).

Balance-of-payments surplus the difference between the quantity demanded and the quantity supplied of a currency when the currency is undervalued (i.e., priced below its equilibrium price).

Balanced budget a budget in which tax revenues cover government expenditures.

Barometric firm in an oligopolistic industry, any single firm that is the first to make changes in prices, which are then generally accepted by other firms.

Base year a year chosen as a reference point for comparison with some later or earlier year.

Budget a statement of the government's anticipated expenditures and tax revenues for a fiscal year.

Budget deficit a budget in which tax revenues fall short of government expenditures.

Budget surplus a budget in which tax revenues exceed government expenditures.

Business cycle the cyclical fluctuations in national output over time.

$C + I + G$ line a curve showing total intended spending (the sum of intended consumption expenditure, investment expenditure, and government expenditure) at various levels of net national product; for simplicity, net exports are omitted.

Capital resources (such as factory buildings, equipment, raw materials, and inventories) that are created within the economic system for the purpose of producing other goods.

Capital consumption allowance the value of the capital (i.e., the plant, equipment, and structures) that is worn out in a year; also called **depreciation.**

Capital formation investment in plant and equipment.

Capital goods output consisting of plant and equipment that are used to make other goods.

Capital-output ratio the ratio of the total capital stock to annual national output.

Capitalism an economic system characterized by private ownership of the tools of production; freedom of choice and of enterprise whereby consumers and firms can pursue their own self-interest; competition for sales among producers and resource owners; and reliance on the free market.

Capitalization of assets a method of computing the value of an asset by calculating the present value of the expected future income this asset will produce.

Cartel an open formal collusive arrangement among firms.

Central bank a government-established

agency that controls the supply of money and supervises the country's commercial banks; the central bank of the United States is the Federal Reserve.

Checkoff a system whereby an employer deducts union dues from each worker's pay and hands them over to the union.

Closed shop a situation where firms can hire only workers who are already union members.

Collective bargaining a process of negotiation between union and management over wages and working conditions.

Collusion a covert arrangement whereby firms agree on price and output levels in order to decrease competition and increase profits.

Commercial banks financial institutions that hold demand and other checkable deposits and permit checks to be written on them, and lend money to firms and individuals.

Comparative advantage the law that states that a nation should produce and export goods which it can produce at *relatively* lower costs than other countries.

Compensation of employees the wages and salaries paid by firms and government agencies to the suppliers of labor, including supplementary payments for employee benefits (such as payments into public and private pension and welfare funds).

Complements commodities that tend to be consumed together, i.e., commodities with a negative cross elasticity of demand such that a decrease in the price of one will result in an increase in the quantity demanded of the other.

Constant dollar amounts amounts measured in base-year dollars (i.e., according to the purchasing power of the dollar in some earlier year), in order to express value in a way that corrects for changes in the price level.

Constant returns to scale a long-run situation where, if the firm increases the amount of all inputs by the same proportion, output increases by the same proportion as each of the inputs.

Consumer an individual or household that purchases the goods and services produced by the economic system.

Consumer goods output consisting of items that consumers purchase, such as clothing, food, and drink.

Consumer Price Index a measure of U.S. inflation, calculated by the Bureau of Labor Statistics, originally intended to measure changes in the prices of goods and services purchased by urban wage earners and clerical workers; in 1978, expanded to cover all urban consumers.

Consumption function the relationship between consumption spending and disposable income, i.e., the amount of consumption expenditure that will occur at various levels of disposable income.

Corporate profits the net income of corporations (i.e., corporate profits before income taxes), including dividends received by the stockholders, retained earnings, and the amount paid by corporations as income taxes.

Corporation a fictitious legal person separate and distinct from the stockholders who own it, governed by a board of directors elected by the stockholders.

Cost function the relationship between cost and a firm's level of output, i.e., what a firm's costs will be at various levels of output.

Council of Economic Advisers a group established by the Employment Act of 1946, whose function is to help the president formulate and assess the economic policies of the government.

Craft union a labor union that includes all the workers in a particular craft (such as machinists or carpenters).

Creeping inflation an increase in the

general price level of a few percent per year that gradually erodes the value of money.

Cross elasticity of demand the percentage change in the quantity demanded of one commodity resulting from a one percent change in the price of another commodity; may be either positive or negative.

Crowding-out effect the tendency for an increase in public sector expenditure to result in a cut in private sector expenditure.

Crude quantity theory of money and prices the theory that if the velocity of circulation of money remains constant and real net national product remains fixed at its full-employment level, it follows from the equation of exchange $(MV=PQ)$ that the price level will be proportional to the money supply.

Cyclical unemployment joblessness that occurs because of business cycle fluctuations.

Decreasing returns to scale a long-run situation where, if the firm increases the amount of all inputs by the same proportion, output increases by a smaller proportion than each of the inputs.

Deflating the conversion of values expressed in current dollars into values expressed in constant dollars, in order to correct for changes in the price level.

Demand curve for loanable funds a curve showing the quantity of loanable funds that will be demanded at each interest rate.

Demand curve for money a curve representing the quantity of money that will be demanded at various interest rates (holding net national product constant).

Demand deposits checking accounts; bank deposits subject to payment on demand.

Demand-pull inflation an increase in the general price level that occurs

when there is too much aggregate spending, too much money chasing too few goods; also called **demand-induced inflation**.

Depreciation the value of the capital (i.e., plant, equipment, and structures) that is worn out in a year; also called a **capital consumption allowance**.

Depreciation of currency a decrease in the value of one currency relative to another.

Depression a period when national output is well below its potential (i.e., full-employment) level; a severe recession.

Derived demand demand for labor and other inputs not as ends in themselves, but as means to produce other things.

Devaluation of currency under the gold standard, a decrease in the value of a currency as a consequence of an increase in the price of gold.

Differentiated oligopoly a market structure (such as those for automobiles and machinery) where there are only a few sellers of somewhat different products.

Diffusion process the process by which the use of an innovation spreads from firm to firm and from use to use.

Direct regulation government issue of enforceable rules concerning the conduct of firms.

Discount rate the interest rate the Federal Reserve charges for loans to commercial banks.

Discretionary fiscal policy government tax and spending programs that supplement the effects of the automatic stabilizers in managing the economy.

Disposable income the total amount of income people can keep after taxes.

Dominant firm in an oligopolistic industry, a single large firm that sets the price for the industry but lets the small firms sell all they want at that price.

Easy monetary policy a monetary policy that increases the money supply and reduces interest rates.

Economic profits the excess of a firm's profits over what it could make in other industries.

Economic resources resources that are scarce and thus command a nonzero price.

Economics the study of how resources are allocated among alternative uses to satisfy human wants.

Economies of scale efficiencies that result from carrying out a process (such as production or sales) on a large scale.

Effluent fee a fee that a polluter must pay to the government for discharging waste.

Equation of exchange a way of restating the definition of the velocity of circulation of money, such that the amount received for the final goods and services during a period equals the amount spent on those final goods and services during the same period (that is, $MV=PQ$).

Equilibrium a situation in which there is no tendency for change.

Equilibrium level of net national product the value of national output at which the flow of income generated by this level of output results in a level of spending precisely sufficient to buy this level of output.

Equilibrium price a price that shows no tendency for change, because it is the price at which the quantity demanded equals the quantity supplied; the price toward which the actual price of a good always tends to move.

Exchange rate the number of units of one currency that can purchase a unit of another currency.

Excise tax a tax imposed on each unit sold of a particular product, such as cigarettes or liquor.

Expansion the phase in the business cycle after the trough during which national output rises.

Explicit cost the cost of resources for which there is an explicit payment.

Exports the goods and services that a nation sells to other nations.

External diseconomy a situation that occurs when consumption or production by one person or firm results in uncompensated costs to another person or firm.

External economy a situation that occurs when consumption or production by one person or firm results in uncompensated benefits to another person or firm.

Featherbedding a practice whereby a union restricts output per worker in order to increase the amount of labor required to do a certain job.

Federal Open Market Committee (FOMC) a group, composed of the seven members of the Federal Reserve Board plus five presidents of Federal Reserve Banks, which makes decisions concerning the purchase and sale of government securities, in order to control bank reserves and the money supply.

Federal Reserve Board the Board of Governors of the Federal Reserve System, composed of seven members appointed by the president for 14-year terms, whose function is to promote the nation's economic welfare by supervising the operations of the U.S. money and banking system.

Federal Reserve System a system established by Congress in 1913 that includes the member banks (commercial banks, both national and state), the twelve Federal Reserve Banks, and the seven-member Board of Governors of the Federal Reserve System.

Final goods and services goods and services that are destined for the ultimate user (such as flour purchased for family consumption).

Firm an organization that produces a good or service for sale in an attempt to make a profit.

Firm's demand curve for labor a curve showing the relationship between the price of labor and the amount of labor demanded by a firm, i.e., the amount of labor that will be demanded by a firm at various wage rates.

Firm's supply curve a curve, usually sloping upward to the right, showing the quantity of output a firm will produce at each price.

Fixed input a resource used in the production process (such as plant and equipment) whose quantity cannot be changed during the particular period under consideration.

Food programs federal antipoverty programs that distribute food to the poor, either directly from surpluses produced by farm programs or indirectly via stamps that can be exchanged for food.

45-degree line a line that contains all points where the amount on the horizontal axis equals the amount on the vertical axis.

Fractional-reserve banking the practice whereby banks hold less cash than the amount they owe their depositors.

Free resources resources (such as air) that are so abundant that they can be obtained without charge.

Frictional unemployment temporary joblessness, such as that occurring among people who have quit jobs, people looking for their first job, and seasonal workers.

Full employment the minimum level of joblessness that the economy could achieve without undesirably high inflation, recognizing that there will always be some frictional and structural unemployment.

Full-employment budget the difference between tax revenues and government expenditures that would result if the economy were operating at full employment.

Functional finance a budgetary policy whereby the government's budget is set to promote the socially optimal combination of unemployment and inflation, even if this means that the budget is unbalanced over considerable periods of time.

Gold exchange standard an exchange rate system developed after World War II, under which the dollar was directly convertible into gold at a fixed price, and other currencies, since they could be converted into dollars at fixed exchange rates, were thus indirectly convertible into gold at a fixed price.

Gold standard a method of exchange rate determination prevailing until the 1930s, under which currencies were convertible into a certain amount of gold.

Government purchases federal, state, and local government spending on final goods and services, excluding transfer payments.

Gross national product (GNP) the value of the total amount of final goods and services produced by the economy during a period of time; this value can be measured either by the expenditure on the final goods and services, or by the income generated by the output.

Gross private domestic investment all additions to the nation's stock of investment goods, i.e., all investment spending by firms, including purchases of tools, equipment, and machinery, all construction expenditures, and the change in total inventories.

Historical cost of assets what a firm actually paid for its assets.

Implicit cost the cost (for which there may not be an explicit payment) of the resources that are provided by the owner of a firm, measured by what these resources could bring if they were used in their best alternative employment.

Imports the goods and services that a nation buys from other nations.

Income elasticity of demand the percentage change in the quantity demanded of a commodity resulting from a one percent increase in total money income (all prices being held constant).

Income tax a federal, state, or local tax imposed on personal income and corporate profits.

Incomes policy a policy to control inflation that sets some targets for wages and prices in the economy as a whole; gives particular firms and industries detailed guides for making wage and price decisions; and provides some inducements for firms and unions to follow these guidelines.

Increasing returns to scale a long-run situation where, if a firm increases the amount of all inputs by the same proportion, output increases by a larger proportion than each of the inputs.

Indirect business taxes taxes (such as general sales taxes, excise taxes, and customs duties) that are imposed not directly on the business itself but on its products or services, and hence are treated by firms as costs of production.

Individual demand curve a curve showing the relationship between individual consumer demand and prices, i.e., how much of a good an individual consumer will demand at various prices.

Industrial union a labor union that includes all the workers in a particular plant or industry (such as autos or steel).

Inflation an increase in the general level of prices economy-wide.

Innovation the first commercial application of a new technology.

Innovator a firm that is first to apply a new technology.

Input any resource used in the production process.

Interest the payment of money by borrowers to suppliers of money capital.

Interest rate the annual amount that a borrower must pay for the use of a dollar for a year.

Intermediate good a good that is not sold to the ultimate user, but is used as an input in producing final goods and services (such as flour to be used in manufacturing bread).

Keynesians economists who share many of the beliefs of John Maynard Keynes. His principal tenet was that a capitalist system does not automatically tend toward a full-employment equilibrium (due in part to the rigidity of wages). Keynesians tend to believe that a free-enterprise economy has weak self-regulating mechanisms that should be supplemented by activist fiscal (and other) policies.

Labor human effort, both physical and mental, used to produce goods and services.

Labor force the number of people employed plus the number of those unemployed (i.e., actively looking for work and willing to take a job if one were offered).

Labor productivity the amount of output divided by the number of units of labor employed.

Laffer curve a curve representing the relationship between the amount of income tax revenue collected by the government and the marginal tax rate, i.e., how much revenue will be collected at various marginal tax rates.

Land natural resources, including minerals as well as plots of ground, used to produce goods and services.

Law of diminishing marginal returns the principle that if equal increments of a given input are added (the quantities of other inputs being held constant), the resulting increments of product obtained from the extra unit of input (i.e., the marginal product) will begin to decrease beyond some point.

Law of diminishing marginal utility the principle that if a person consumes additional units of a given commodity (the consumption of other commodities being held constant), the resulting increments of utility derived from the extra unit of the commodity (i.e., the commodity's marginal utility) will begin to decrease beyond some point.

Law of increasing costs the principle that as more and more of a good is produced, the production of each additional unit of the good is likely to entail a larger and larger opportunity cost.

Legal reserve requirements regulations, imposed by the Federal Reserve System in order to control the money supply, requiring banks (and other institutions) to hold a certain fraction of deposits as cash reserves.

Liabilities the debts of a firm.

Loanable funds funds (including those supplied by households and firms that find the rate of interest high enough to get them to save) that are available for borrowing by consumers, businesses, and government.

Long run the period of time during which all of a firm's inputs are variable, i.e., during which the firm could completely change the resources used in the production process.

Long-run average cost function the minimum average cost of producing various output levels when any desired type or scale of plant can be built.

M-1 narrowly defined money supply, which includes coins, currency, demand deposits, and other checkable deposits.

M-2 broadly defined money supply, which includes savings deposits, small time deposits, money market mutual fund balances, and money market deposit accounts, as well as the components of the narrowly defined money supply, M-1 (coins, currency, demand deposits, and other checkable deposits).

Marginal cost the addition to total cost resulting from the addition of the last unit of output.

Marginal product of an input the addition to total output that results from the addition of an extra unit of input (the quantities of all other inputs being held constant).

Marginal product of labor the additional output resulting from the addition of an extra unit of labor.

Marginal propensity to consume the fraction of an extra dollar of disposable income that is spent on consumption.

Marginal propensity to save the fraction of an extra dollar of disposable income that is saved.

Marginal revenue the addition to total revenue that results from the addition of one unit to the quantity sold.

Marginal tax rate the proportion of an extra dollar of income that must be paid in taxes.

Marginal utility the additional satisfaction derived from consuming an additional unit of a commodity.

Market a group of firms and individuals that are in touch with each other in order to buy or sell some good or service.

Market demand curve a curve, usually sloping downward to the right, showing the relationship between a product's price and the quantity demanded of the product.

Market demand curve for labor a curve showing the relationship between the price of labor and the total amount of labor demanded in the market.

Market period the relatively short period of time during which the supply of a particular good is fixed and output is unaffected by price.

Market structure the type or organization of a market. Markets differ with ragard to the number and size of buyers and sellers in the market, the ease with which new firms can enter, the extent of product differentiation, and other factors.

Market supply curve a curve, usually sloping upward to the right, showing the relationship between a product's price and the quantity supplied of the product.

Market supply curve for labor a curve showing the relationship between the price of labor and the total amount of labor supplied in the market.

Markup in cost-plus pricing, an addition to a product's estimated average cost that is meant to include certain costs that cannot be allocated to any specific product, and to provide a return on the firm's investment.

Medicare a compulsory hospitalization program plus a voluntary insurance plan for doctors' fees for people over 65, included under the Social Security program.

Member banks the commercial banks (all of the national banks and many of the larger state banks) that belong to the Federal Reserve System.

Model a theory composed of assumptions that simplify and abstract from reality, from which conclusions or predictions about the real world are deduced.

Monetarists economists generally sharing the belief that business cycle fluctuations are due largely to changes in the money supply. Many monetarists think that a free-enterprise economy has effective self-regulating mechanisms that activist fiscal and monetary policies tend to disrupt. Some monetarists, like Milton Friedman, advocate a rule for stable growth in the money supply of 3 to 5 percent per year.

Monetary base the reserves of Federal Reserve member banks plus currency outside of the member banks.

Monetary policy the exercise of the central bank's control over the quantity of money and the level of interest rates in order to promote the objectives of national economic policy.

Money anything that serves as a medium of exchange and a standard and store of value; the unit in which the prices of goods and services are measured.

Money income income measured in current dollars (i.e., actual money amounts).

Monopolistic competition a market structure in which there are many sellers of somewhat differentiated products, where entry is easy, and where there is no collusion among sellers. Retailing seems to have many of the characteristics of monopolistic competition.

Monopoly a market structure (such as those for public utilities) in which there is only one seller of a product.

Monopsony a market structure (such as that for the single firm that employs all the labor in a company town) in which there is only a single buyer.

Moral suasion the Federal Reserve's practice of exhorting member banks to go along with its wishes, in the absence of any actual power to force the banks' compliance.

Multinational firm a firm that makes direct investments in other countries, and produces and markets its products abroad.

National banks commercial banks chartered by the federal government.

National debt the amount owed by the government. To cover the difference between expenditures and tax revenues, the government sells bonds, notes, and other forms of IOUs.

Natural monopoly an industry in which the average costs of producing the product reach a minimum at an output rate large enough to satisfy the entire market, so that competition among firms cannot be sustained and one firm becomes a monopolist.

Near-money assets (such as government bonds) that can be converted into cash, though not quite as easily as time and savings accounts.

Negative income tax a system whereby families with incomes below a certain break-even level would receive, rather than make, a government income tax payment.

Net exports the amount spent by foreigners on a nation's goods and services (exports) minus the amount a nation spends on foreign goods and services (imports).

Net national product (NNP) gross national product minus depreciation. (Depreciation equals the value of the plant, equipment, and structures that are worn out during the relevant period of time.)

Nominal expressed in current dollars (i.e., actual money amounts).

Normative economics economic propositions about what ought to be, or about what a person, organization, or nation ought to do.

Old-age insurance benefits paid under the Social Security program to retired workers, from taxes imposed on both workers and employers.

Oligopoly a market structure (such as those for autos and steel) in which there are only a few sellers of products that can be either identical or differentiated.

Open market operations the purchase and sale of U.S. government securities on the open market by the Federal Reserve in order to control the quantity of bank reserves.

Open shop a situation where a firm can hire both union and nonunion workers, with no requirement that nonunion workers ever join a union.

Opportunity cost the value of what certain resources could have produced had they been used in the best alternative way; also called **alternative cost.**

Overvaluation of currency the setting of a currency's price above the equilibrium price.

Parity the principle that a farmer should be able to exchange a given quantity of farm output for the same quantity of nonfarm goods and services he would have been able to purchase at some point in the past; in effect, the principle that farm prices should increase at the same rate as the prices of the goods and services that farmers buy.

Partnership a form of business organization whereby two or more people agree to own and conduct a business, with each party contributing some proportion of the capital and/or labor and receiving some proportion of the profit or loss.

Peak the point in the business cycle where national output is highest relative to its potential (i.e., full-employment) level.

Perfect competition a market structure in which there are many sellers of identical products, where no one seller or buyer has control over the price, where entry is easy, and where resources can switch readily from one use to another. Many agricultural markets have many of the characteristics of perfect competition.

Personal consumption expenditures the spending by households on durable goods, nondurable goods, and services.

Phillips curve a curve representing the relationship between the rate of increase in wages and the level of unemployment.

Positive economics descriptive statements, propositions, and predictions about the economic world that are generally testable by an appeal to the facts.

Potential gross national product the total amount of goods and services that could have been produced had the economy been operating at full capacity or full employment.

Precautionary demand for money the demand for money because of uncertainty about the timing and size of future disbursements and receipts.

Price discrimination the practice whereby one buyer is charged more than another buyer for the same product.

Price elastic the demand for a good if its price elasticity of demand is greater than one.

Price elasticity of demand the percentage change in quantity demanded resulting from a one percent change in price; by convention, always expressed as a positive number.

Price elasticity of supply the percentage change in quantity supplied resulting from a one percent change in price.

Price index the ratio of the value of a set of goods and services in current dollars to the value of the same set of goods and services in constant dollars.

Price inelastic the demand for a good if its price elasticity of demand is less than one.

Price leader in an oligopolistic industry, a firm that sets a price that other firms are willing to follow.

Price supports price floors imposed by the government on a certain good.

Price system a system under which every good and service has a price, and which in a purely capitalistic economy carries out the basic functions of an economic system (determining what goods and services will be produced, how the output will be produced, how much of it each person will receive, and what the nation's growth of per capita income will be).

Primary inputs resources (such as labor and land) that are produced outside of the economic system.

Private cost the price paid by the individual user for the use of a resource.

Product differentiation the process by which producers create real or apparent differences between products that perform the same general function.

Product group a group of firms that produce similar products that are fairly close substitutes for one another.

Product market a market where products are bought and sold.

Production function the relationship between the quantities of various inputs used per period of time and the maximum quantity of output that can be produced per period of time, i.e., the most output that existing technology permits the firm to produce from various quantities of inputs.

Production possibilities curve a curve showing the combinations of amounts of various goods that a society can produce with given (fixed) amounts of resources.

Profit the difference between a firm's revenue and its costs.

Progressive tax a tax whereby the rich pay a larger proportion of their income for the tax than do the poor.

Prohibitive tariff a tariff so high that it prevents imports of a good.

Property tax a tax imposed on real estate and/or other property.

Proprietors' income the net income of unincorporated businesses (i.e., proprietorships and partnerships).

Proprietorship a firm owned by a single individual.

Prosperity a period when national output is close to its potential (i.e., full-employment) level.

Public goods goods and services that can be consumed by one person without diminishing the amount of them that others can consume. Often there is no way to prevent citizens from consuming public goods whether they pay for them or not.

Public sector the governmental sector of the economy.

Pure oligopoly a market structure (like those for steel, cement, tin cans, and petroleum) in which there are only a few sellers of an identical product.

Pure rate of interest the interest rate on a riskless loan.

Quota a limit imposed on the amount of a commodity that can be imported annually.

Rate of return the annual profit per dollar invested that businesses can obtain by building new structures, adding new equipment, or increasing their inventories; the interest rate earned on the investment in a particular asset.

Rational expectations theory the theory put forth by Robert Lucas, Thomas Sargent, and others that markets clear quickly and expectations are rational. Under these circumstances, predictable macroeconomic policies may not influence real output or unemployment.

Real expressed in constant dollars.

Real income income measured in constant dollars (i.e., the amount of goods and services that can be bought with the income).

Recession the phase in the business cycle after the peak during which national output falls.

Regressive tax a tax whereby the rich pay a smaller proportion of their income for the tax than do the poor.

Rent in the context of Chapter 23, the return derived from an input that is fixed in supply.

Reproduction cost of assets what the firm would have to pay to replace its assets.

Resource market a market where resources are bought and sold.

Resources inputs used to produce goods and services.

Retained earnings the total amount of profit that the stockholders of a corporation have reinvested in the business, rather than withdrawing as dividends.

Rule of reason the principle that not all trusts, but only unreasonable combinations in restraint of trade, require conviction under the antitrust laws.

Runaway inflation a very rapid increase in the general price level that wipes out practically all of the value of money.

Sales tax a tax imposed on the goods consumers buy (with the exception, in some states, of food and medical care).

Saving the process by which people give up a claim on present consumption goods in order to receive consumption goods in the future.

Saving function the relationship between total saving and disposable income, i.e., the total amount of saving that will occur at various levels of disposable income.

Say's Law the principle that the production of a certain amount of goods and services results in the generation of an amount of income precisely sufficient to buy that output.

Short run the period of time during which at least one of a firm's inputs (generally its plant and equipment) is fixed.

Social Security a program that imposes taxes on wage earners and employers, and provides old-age, survivors, disability, medical, and unemployment benefits to workers covered under the Social Security Act.

Stagflation a simultaneous combination of high unemployment and high inflation.

State banks commercial banks chartered by the states.

Structural unemployment joblessness that occurs when new goods or new technologies call for new skills, and workers with older skills cannot find jobs.

Substitutes commodities with a positive cross elasticity of demand (that is, a decrease in the price of one commodity will result in a decrease in the quantity demanded of the other commodity).

Supply curve for loanable funds a curve showing the relationship between the quantity of loanable funds supplied and the pure interest rate.

Supply-side economics a set of propositions concerned with influencing the aggregate supply curve through the use of financial incentives such as tax cuts.

Tariff a tax imposed by the government on imported goods (designed to cut down on imports and thus protect domestic industry and workers from foreign competition).

Tax avoidance legal steps taken by taxpayers to reduce their tax bill.

Tax evasion misreporting of income or other illegal steps taken by taxpayers to reduce their tax bill.

Technological change new methods of producing existing products, new designs that make it possible to produce new products, and new techniques of organization, marketing, and management.

Technology society's pool of knowledge concerning how goods and services can be produced from a given amount of resources.

Terms of trade the ratio of an index of export prices to an index of import prices.

Tight monetary policy a monetary policy that restrains or reduces the money supply and raises interest rates.

Total cost the sum of a firm's total fixed cost and total variable cost.

Total fixed cost a firm's total expenditure on fixed inputs per period of time.

Total revenue a firm's total dollar sales volume.

Total variable cost a firm's total expenditure on variable inputs per period of time.

Transactions demand for money the holding of money in cash or in checking accounts in order to pay for final goods and services.

Transfer payments payments made by the government or private business to individuals who do not contribute to the production of goods and services in exchange for them.

Trough the point in the business cycle where national output is lowest relative to its potential (i.e., full-employment) level.

Tying contract the practice whereby

buyers must purchase other items in order to get the product they want.

Undervaluation of currency the setting of a currency's price below the equilibrium price.

Unemployment according to the definition of the Bureau of Labor Statistics, joblessness among people who are actively looking for work and would take a job if one were offered.

Unemployment rate the number of people who are unemployed divided by the number of people in the labor force.

Union shop a situation where firms can hire nonunion workers who must then become union members within a certain length of time after being hired.

Unitary elasticity a price elasticity of demand equal to one.

Utility a number representing the level of satisfaction that a consumer derives from a particular good or group of goods.

Value-added the amount of value added by a firm or industry to the total worth of a product.

Value of the marginal product of labor the marginal product of labor (i.e., the additional output resulting from the addition of an extra unit of labor) multiplied by the product's price.

Variable input a resource used in the production process (such as labor or raw material) whose quantity can be changed during the particular period under consideration.

Velocity of circulation of money rate at which the money supply is used to make transactions for final goods and services, i.e., the average number of times per year that a dollar is used to buy the final goods and services produced. It equals nominal NNP divided by the money supply.

Wage and price controls limits imposed by the government on the amount by which wages and prices can increase, in order to reduce the inflation rate at a given unemployment rate.

Wage-price spiral a series of steps whereby higher wage demands by workers prompt firms to raise their prices to consumers, which in turn raises the general cost of living and prompts workers to make yet higher wage demands.

Wage rate the price of labor.

Index

absolute advantage, 530–31
accelerated depreciation, 225
accelerationists, 201–5
actual GNP, gap between potential GNP and, 150
actual price, 41
  equilibrium price and, 41
Adams, Walter, 412
advertising industry, 413
Affluent Society, The (Galbraith), 478, 510
AFL-CIO (American Federation of Labor and Congress of Industrial Organizations), 443–44
  structure of, 445
aggregate demand, 77–78
  fiscal policy and, 141–43
  inflation and, 150–56
aggregate demand curves, 78–80
  income-expenditure analysis and, 112–13
  monetary policy and, 194
  money supply and, 194
  shape of, 79–80
  shifts in, 93–96, 141
  shifts of, in World War II, 84–85
aggregate supply, 77–78
  see also potential GNP
aggregate supply curves, 80–82
  constants in construction of, 80
  horizontal (Keynesian) range of, 81, 94, 141
  income-expenditure analysis and, 112–13
  output level and, 82
  positively sloped range of, 82, 95
  under Reagan administration, 227–28
  shape of, 81–82
  shifts in, 96–97
  stagflation and, 202
  vertical (classical) range of, 81–82, 94–95
Agricultural Adjustment Act (1933), 352–53

Agriculture and Consumer Protection Act (1973), 356–57
Agriculture Department, U.S., 33, 354–55, 474
agriculture industry, *see* farm industry
Aid to Families with Dependent Children (AFDC), 480, 482
air pollution, 423
Alaska, use of land in, 14
Alaska National Interest Lands Conservation Act (1980), 14
Alaska Statehood Act (1958), 14
allocation:
  of food stamps, 48
  under monopoly, 390, 391–92
  under perfect competition, 374–77
  price system and, 43–45
  wage and price controls in, 205
alternative cost, *see* opportunity cost
Aluminum Company of America (Alcoa), 33
Amacher, Peter, 32, 292
American Cyanamid, 415
American Economics Association, 280
American Meat Institute, 368
American Telephone & Telegraph (AT&T), 395, 420
American Tobacco Company, 418
Andrus, Cecil, 14
anti-inflationary fiscal policy, 142–43
  stagflation and, 197–213
  wage and price controls in, 205
antipoverty programs, 479–84
antitrust laws, 380, 408, 410, 416–20
anti-unemployment fiscal policy, 141
anti-usury laws, 456
appreciation of currency, 550
Appropriations Committee, 131
arc elasticity of demand, 341
Aristotle, 457

Armco, 208
Arnold, Thurman, 419
assets, capitalization of, 458–59
AT&T (American Telephone & Telegraph), 395, 420
Atkinson, L. J., 346
automatic stabilizers, 132–34
  corporate dividends as, 134
  family saving as, 134
  farm programs as, 134
  tax revenues as, 132
  unemployment compensation as, 132–34
  welfare payments as, 132–34, 135
automobile assembly line, 504–5
automobile industry, 207
  demand curves in, 346
  see also General Motors Corporation
average cost function, long-run, 332–33
average costs:
  marginal cost functions and, 330–32
  short-run, 326–28
average fixed cost, 326
average product of input, 303
average propensity to consume, 103
average total cost, 327–28
average variable cost, 326–27

baby boom, 139
backward-bending supply curve, 440–41
balance-of-payments deficit, 554–56, 559–60
balance-of-payments surplus, 555–56
balance sheets:
  of banks, 166–67
  left-hand (assets) side of, 166
  right-hand (liabilities) side of, 166–67
banking system, 159–78
  fractional-reserve, 167–69
  government and, 170–71
  money and, 159–78
Bank of America, 166–67
banks:
  balance sheet of, 166–67
  cash vs. deposits in, 167
  central, 183–84
  commercial, 164, 185
  excess reserves in, 173–77
  failure of, 165–66, 170–71, 172–73
  legal reserve requirements of, see legal
    reserve requirements
  liquidity of, 165–66
  managers of, 170
  member, 182–83, 265
  money created by, 171–76
  mutual savings, 164
  national, 182
  operation of, 164–66
  profit-making motive in, 165
  "runs" on, 170–71, 172–73
  safety of, 170–71
  secondary reserves of, 170
  state, 182
  see also Federal Reserve Banks; specific banks
Barney, Charles T., 172–73
barometric-firm model, 412
barter, 160
base year, GNP-adjustment and, 59
Becker, Gary, 501
Bell, Alexander Graham, 395
Bethlehem Steel, 412–13
Bieber, Owen, 443
bituminous coal industry, 371–72, 374

Blough, Roger M., 208
bonds, 165
  defined, 459
  interest rate and price of, 254, 256
booms, baby, 139
Boskin, Michael, 285
Bradley, Bill, 521
Brannan, Charles F., 357
break-even income, 481
Bretton Woods System, 558–59, 560–61
Brock, William, 541
budget:
  balancing of, 232–34, 237
  federal, 240–42
  full-employment, 234–35
  price elasticity of demand and, 342–44
  see also deficit, U.S.
Budget Committee (House of Representatives), 131, 242
Budget Committee (Senate), 131, 242
Bureau of Economic Analysis (Commerce Department, U.S.), 56
Bureau of Labor Statistics, 86, 146–47, 218
Burns, Arthur F., 133, 181, 190, 261
business fluctuations, 74–85
  depressions in, 76
  expansion period in, 76
  individualistic nature of, 77
  peaks in, 76
  prosperity period in, 76
  recessions in, 76
  troughs in, 76
  unemployment and, 283

California, drought in, 319
capital, 10–11
  human, 501–2
capital consumption allowance, 72
capital formation, 496–500
  economic growth and, 499–500
capital formation theory (Ricardo), 496–99
  conclusions of, 497–98
  feasibility of, 498–99
  income distribution in, 496–97
capital goods:
  defined, 28
  durability of, 114–15
  production possibilities curve and, 28
capitalism, 90
  mainsprings of, 465
capitalization of assets, 458–59
capital-labor ratio, 219
capital-output ratio, 499
capital stock, 69
Carlyle, Thomas, 492
cartels:
  defined, 408
  collusion and, 408–9
  price and output of, 409
Carter, Jimmy, 14, 223, 235, 268, 286
Carter administration:
  fiscal policy of, 244–45
  oil-price controls under, 331
  technology policy of, 223
Census Bureau, U.S., 483
central banks, 183–84
Chase Manhattan Bank, 186
checkable deposits, 162–63
checkoff, 446
Chow, Gregory, 346
Civilisation (Clark), 489

Civil Rights Act (1964), 487
Civil War, 153, 238, 249, 250
Clark, Sir Kenneth, 489
classical economics:
    Keynes's criticisms of, 113
    unemployment in, 88–89
classical range of aggregate supply curves,
    81–82, 94–95
Clayton Act (1914), 417–18
Clean Air Amendments (1970), 429
Cleveland, Grover, 419
Cleveland, Ohio, 423
closed shop, 449
Club of Rome's "Limits to Growth" report, 494
Coca-Cola Company, 304
cocaine, 52
coins, 161
collective bargaining, 449–51
collusion:
    barriers to, 409–12
    cartels and, 408–9
    defined, 408
    in electrical industry, 411
    "phases of the moon" system in, 411
Commerce Department, U.S., 56, 58, 67
commercial banks, 164
    loans to, 185
Committee for Economic Development, 133
communism, 90–91
comparative advantage, 531–33
complements, cross elasticity of demand and,
    348–49
computer-assisted design (CAD), 502
Congress, U.S., 17, 130, 131, 135–37, 151, 187,
    190, 223, 240–43, 270, 446–47
Congressional Budget Office, 131, 240–42
Consolidated Edison, 361
constant dollars, 61
    current dollars vs., 57–59, 258
constant returns to scale, 333
construction industry, 193
consumer behavior, 42, 311–22
    aggregate U.S. data on, 313–14
    equilibrium market basket and, 317–19
    marginal propensity to consume, 102–3
    marginal propensity to save, 105
    marginal utility and, 315–17
    model of, 314–17
consumer expenditures, 312–14
    marginal propensity to consume, 102–3
"consumer finance" companies, 164
consumer goods:
    defined, 28
    production possibilities curve and, 28
Consumer Price Index (CPI), 146–47, 197
consumers, 31–32
    defined, 32
    market demand and income level of, 35
consumption expenditures:
    aggregate flows of income and, 108–11
    in consumption function, 100–103, 107
    NNP and, 126–27
    tradeoff between economic growth and, 491
consumption function, 100–103
    average propensity to consume, 103
    defined, 100
    disposable income in, 100–103, 107
    marginal propensity to consume, 102–3
    nonincome determinants of, 118–21
    shifts in, 118–21
    shifts in saving function and, 120

shifts in, vs. movements along, 119–20
    slope of, 102–3
Continental Illinois Bank, 171
Coolidge, Calvin, 292
Corn Laws, 496–97
corporate dividends, 134
corporate income taxes, 140, 522
corporate profits, 71
corporations, 299–300
cost functions, 323–26
    average, in long run, 332–33
    average and marginal, 330–32
cost-push inflation, 198–99
    accommodation of, 212
    demand-pull inflation vs., 199
    Fed and, 212
    wage-price spiral in, 198
costs, 322–34
    average fixed, 326
    average total, 327–28
    average variable, 326–27
    historical vs. reproduction, 394
    implicit, 323
    marginal, in short run, 328–32
    opportunity, see opportunity costs
    private vs. social, 424–25
    total, 325–26
    total fixed, 323–24
    total variable, 324–25
Council of Economic Advisers (CEA), 65, 91,
    130, 131–32, 136, 147, 151, 198, 205, 206–7,
    208, 219, 241, 271, 486
Council on Environmental Quality, 428–29
CPI (Consumer Price Index), 146–47, 197
$C+I+G$ line, 124–26, 128–30, 152, 201, 255,
    506, 545–46
creeping inflation, 145–46
    output and, 149–50
cross elasticity of demand, 348–49
crude quantity theory, 260–63
    assumptions of, 271
    evaluation of, 262–63
    full employment and, 260–61
    nominal NNP in, 262
    price level and money supply in, 261–62
currency, 161–62, 248
    appreciation and depreciation of, 550
    devaluation of, 550
    overvalued, 554–55
    undervalued, 555–56
current dollars, constant dollars vs., 57–59, 255
curves:
    Laffer, 226–27
    money demand, 252–53
    Phillips, 153–54
    see also aggregate demand curves; aggregate
        supply curves; demand curves; market
        demand curves; production possibilities
        curves; supply curves
Cuyahoga River, 423
cyclical unemployment, 86

decreasing returns to scale, 333
Defense Department, U.S., 224, 309, 397
defense spending, 48–49, 513
    in 1965 vs. 1966, 151
deficit, U.S.:
    balance-of-payments, 554–56, 559–60
    defined, 231
    under Eisenhower administration, 234–35
    expansionary effects of, 236

deficit (*continued*)
  financing of, 231, 232–34, 235–36
  in 1980s, 230
deflating, 59–60
demand:
  aggregate, *see* aggregate demand
  changes in quantity demanded vs. changes in,
    36–37
  derived, 440
  effective, 48
  elasticity of, *see* elasticity of demand; price
    elasticity of demand
  excess, 41
  market, *see* market demand
demand curves, 312–22
  aggregate, *see* aggregate demand curves
  constant elements in, 34
  consumer's, 320
  firm, 346–47
  individual, 320
  industry, 346–47
  kinked oligopoly, 407–8
  for loanable funds, 453–55
  marginal revenue and, under monopoly,
    381–83
  market vs. individual, 320
  for money, 252–53
  rightward vs. leftward shifts in, 37, 50–51
  shifts in, 49–51
  shifts in, vs. movements along, 36–37
  slope of, 33–34, 78–79
demand deposits, 162–63, 248
demand-induced inflation, 152
demand-pull inflation, 151, 153
  cost-push inflation vs., 199
Denison, Edward, 216
depreciation, 71–72, 225
  accelerated, 225
  of currency, 550
  NNP and, 63
Depression, Great, 26, 67, 83–84, 87, 92, 130,
    277
  anti-unemployment fiscal policy in, 141
  cause of, 193–95
  Friedman-Schwartz interpretation of, 194–95,
    271
  welfare payments in, 511–12
depressions:
  defined, 76
  monetary policy in, 277
derived demand, 440
devaluation of currency, 550
differentiated oligopoly, 402
diffusion process, 503
Dillon, Douglas, 136
diminishing marginal returns, law of, 306–7,
    324–25, 329–30
  Malthus's theory in terms of, 492–93
diminishing marginal utility, law of, 316–17
Dingell, John, 541
direct relationships, inverse relationships vs.,
    20–21
discount rate, 189–91
"discount window," 191
discretionary fiscal policy, 134–37
discrimination, 484–87
  effects of, 484–85
  racial, 484
  against women, 486–87
diseconomies, external, *see* external
  diseconomies

disposable income:
  in consumption function, 100–103, 107
  defined, 100
  in saving function, 104–5
distribution, 20
  income, *see* income distribution
dividends, corporate, 134
dollar, U.S., current vs. constant, 57–59
Domestic Policy Review on Industrial
    Innovation, 223
dominant-firm model, 412
drought in California, 319
durable goods, 68
Durant, William C., 292–93, 296

Eastman Kodak, 418
Eccles, Marriner, 190
economic profits, 373–74
Economic Report of the President, 131
economic resources, 10–11
  free resources, vs., 10
economics:
  central questions of, 11–12
  classical, *see* classical economics
  defined, 9
  impact on society of, 15–17
  measurements in, 19–20
  methodology of, 18–21
  positive vs. normative, 17
  supply-side, 226–28, 285–88
economic stabilization, 211–12
Economic Stabilization Agency, 205
economic systems, tasks of, 21–22
economies, external, *see* external economies
effective demand, 48
efficiency:
  under monopoly, 393
  per capita income growth and, 45
  reduction of income inequality and loss of,
    471–72
efficiency incentives, 396–97
effluent fees, 427–28
Eisenhower, Dwight D., 133, 237
Eisenhower administration, 206, 234–35
elasticity of demand:
  arc, 341
  cross, 348–49
  income, 347–48
  price, *see* price elasticity of demand
Employment Act (1946), 130, 131
"Engine of Inflation," 190
England, 161
entrepreneurship, 503–5
Environmental Protection Agency (EPA), 429,
    431, 432–33
Equal Pay Act (1963), 486–87
equation of exchange, 259–60
equilibrium, 39–41
  defined, 39
  in long run, under perfect competition,
    373–74
  under monopolistic competition, 403–6
  under monopoly, 386–87
  of national output and price levels, 82–85
  NNP at, 107–11, 113–14, 257
  pure interest rate at, 455
equilibrium market basket, 317–19
equilibrium price, 39–41
  actual price and, 41
  defined, 39–40, 41
  quantity of labor and, 441–43

Essay on the Principle of Population (Malthus), 491–92
Europe, 26
excess demand, 41
excess reserves, 173–77
excess supply, 40
exchange rate, 544–54
  determinants of, 550–51
  fixed, 552–54
  fixed vs. flexible, 561
  flexible, 552
  under gold standard, 547–48
  government intervention and, 553–54
  growth rates and, 551
  import-export balance and, 548
  interest rate and, 551
  international transactions and, 546–47
  relative price levels and, 550–51
excise taxes, 140
expansion period, defined, 76
expected rate of return, 106–7
exports, 528–29
  net, 70, 546
export subsidies, 539
external diseconomies, 49
  government and, 513–15
  pollution and, 423–24
  private vs. social costs and, 424–25
external economies, 49
  government and, 513–14, 516

Family Assistance Plan (FAP), 482
family saving, 134
farm industry, 349–57
  automatic stabilizers in, 134
  characteristics of demand and supply curves in, 350
  government aid to, 352
  parity in, 352–53
  policies to cut surplus in, 354–55
  post-1973 developments in, 356–57
  price supports and surplus controls in, 353–54
  relative price of food products in, 350–51
  slow exit of resources in, 351–52
farm prices, instability of, price elasticity of demand and, 343
farm programs, 134
FCC (Federal Communications Commission), 393
FDIC (Federal Deposit Insurance Corporation), 166, 171
featherbedding, 448
Fed (Federal Reserve System), 179–96, 268–69
  Board of Governors of, 183
  check collection facilities of, 184
  coordination between executive branch and, 269–70
  cost-push inflation and, 212
  discount rate of, 189–91
  "discount window" of, 191
  districts of, 183
  emphasis on inflation vs. unemployment of, 270
  establishment of, 182
  forecasting by, 269
  functions of, 183–84
  independence of, 190
  interest-rate ceilings of, 193
  interest rate vs. money supply in policy-making of, 265–66
  lags in policy-effect of, 267, 269

long-term growth targets of, 182
  member banks of, 182–83
  monetary policy of, *see* monetary policy
  money supply rule for, 270–71, 279–80
  moral suasion and, 193
  1975 policy of, 261
  notes issued by, 161, 184, 185
  open market operations of, 185–87
  performance of, 269–70
  reserve requirements of, 169
  securities bought and sold by, 185–86
  "stop-go" policies of, 271
Federal Advisory Council, 183
federal budget, 240–42
Federal Communications Commission (FCC), 393
Federal Deposit Insurance Corporation (FDIC), 166, 171
Federal Energy Regulatory Commission (FERC), 393, 396
Federal Open Market Committee (FOMC), 181, 183, 187, 268–69
Federal Reserve Banks, 182–83
  assets of, 184–85
  consolidated balance sheet of, 184–85
  as fiscal agents, 184
  member bank reserves of, 184
  of Minneapolis, 284
Federal Reserve Board, 183, 192
Federal Reserve notes, 161, 184, 185
Federal Trade Commission Act (1914), 417–18
Feldstein, Martin, 241, 479
FERC (Federal Energy Regulatory Commission), 393, 396
fiat money, 161–62
final goods and services, 56
Finance Committee (Senate), 131
Financial Reform Act (1980), 169, 193
firm demand curves, 346–47
firms, 31–32, 291–310
  American, characteristics of, 296–97
  capacity utilization by, 115
  corporations, 299–300
  costs to, *see* costs
  defined, 32
  demand curve for labor in, 437–38
  dropping out by, 367–68
  inflationary wage and price decisions of, 206
  as influenced by income policy, 206
  inputs of, *see* inputs
  law of diminishing marginal returns and, 306–7
  in long run, 302–3
  motivation of, 300
  net worth of, 166
  output of, 363–69
  partnerships, 298–99
  price system and technology of, 45–46
  production function of, 301
  proprietorships, 297–98
  returns to scale of, 333–34
  in short run, 302–3
  supply curve of, 368–69
  technology and, 300
  total revenue of, 382
fiscal policy, 123–43
  aggregate demand and, 141–43
  anti-inflationary, 142–43
  anti-unemployment, 141
  automatic stabilizers in, 132–34
  of Carter administration, 244–45

fiscal policy (*continued*)
changes in public attitude and, 234
coordinating monetary policy with, 281
deficit and surplus financing in, 231–34
discretionary, 134–37
expansionary, 204
of Ford administration, 244
functional finance as, 234
in Great Depression, 141
imminent recession and, 231
inflationary pressures from, 210
inflationary signals and, 231–32
interest rate vs. money supply in, 265–66
lag in, 267, 269
makers of, 131–32
monetary policy and, 180
nature and objectives of, 129–31
of Nixon administration, 243–44
NNP and, 123–43
policy menu in, 154–55
of Reagan administration, 245
supply-side, 226–28
unemployment and, 130–31
Fisher, Frank, 415
fixed costs:
average, 326
total, 323–24
fixed exchange rate, 552–54
flexible exchange rate vs., 561
fixed input, 301–2
fixed money income, 148
flexible exchange rates, 552
fixed exchange rate vs., 561
performance of, 561–62
floating exchange rate, *see* flexible exchange rate
FOMC (Federal Open Market Committee), 181,
183, 187, 268–69
food programs, 480
Food Stamp Act (1964), 48
food stamp program, 48
Ford, Gerald R., 141, 244, 261
Ford, Henry, 44, 414, 504–5
foreign exchange market, 548–52
demand and supply sides of, 549–50
45-degree line, 111, 255
Fox, Karl, 340
fractional-reserve banking, 167–69
defined, 168
origins of, 168
franchises, 381
Freeman, Richard, 501
free resources, economic resources vs., 10
frictional unemployment, 86
Friedland, Claire, 395–96
Friedman, Milton, 134, 192, 194–95, 201,
225–27, 257, 258, 270–71, 277–78, 279–80,
481, 509
full employment, 25, 75, 130
crude quantity theory and, 260–61
defined, 89–91
in vertical range of aggregate supply curves,
82
full-employment budget, 234–35
full employment NNP, investment and, 499–500
functional finance, 234

Galbraith, John Kennedy, 397–99, 478, 510
Gary, Elbert, 412
gas, leaded, 431
General Electric, 411–12
General Motors Corporation, 32, 186, 253,
292–97, 406, 414

early years of, 292–93
profit history of, 295–96
reorganization of, 293–94
stock of, 299
*General Theory of Employment, Interest, and
Money* (Keynes), 92, 284
geometric rate, 491–92
George, Henry, 462
Gephardt, Richard, 521
Germany, Federal Republic of, 156
Germany, Nazi, 145, 250, 262–63
GNP (gross national product), 55–73
adjusting of, for price changes, 57–62
at-cost valuation in, 56–57
base year in adjusting of, 59
capital consumption allowance in, 72
changes in quality of goods and, 64–65
compensation to employees in, 70–71
corporate profits in, 71
current vs. constant dollars in, 57–59
deflating of, 59–60
depreciation and, 71–72
double counting in, 56
expenditures approach to, 66–70
first estimates of, 56, 58
government purchases of goods and services
in, 69
gross private domestic investment in,
68–69
income approach to, 66, 70–73
indirect business taxes in, 72–73
interest in calculation of, 71
inventory change in, 68–69
leisure in, 64
limitations of, 64–65
net exports in, 70, 546
net private domestic investment in, 69
in 1983 vs. 1984, 55
nonmarket transactions in, 57
nonproductive transactions in, 57
personal consumption expenditures in, 68
population and, 64
potential, *see* potential GNP
price indexes in adjustment of, 59–62
proprietors' income in, 71
R and D in, 219, 221–22
real, 59, 75
rents in, 71
secondhand goods in, 57
social costs in, 65
value-added in calculation of, 62–63
value and distribution in, 65
GNP gap, 150
Goldberg, Arthur, 207
gold certificates, 184
Golden Rule of Output Determination, 366–67,
368, 384–86, 387
gold-exchange standard, 558–59
gold standard, 161–62
abandonment of, 557–58
exchange rate under, 547–48
Goldwater, Barry, 481
goods:
consumer, *see* consumer goods
durable vs. nondurable, 68
intermediate vs. final, 56
secondhand, 57
Gordon, Robert, 195
government:
bureaucratic inefficiency of, 517
conservative vs. liberal views on, 509–10
externalities and, 513–16

in maintaining a competitive framework, 510–11
in maintaining legal and social framework, 510–11
proper functions of, 509–10
redistribution of income by, 511–12
revenue at federal, state, and local levels, 140–41
size of, 137–38
special-interest groups and, 516–17
government debt, 236–43
externally held, 239–40
future generations and, 239
internally held, 240
government purchases, in GNP, 69
government spending:
at federal level, 138–40
at local level, 139, 140
multiplier and, 126
NNP and, 124–26
on schooling, 139
size of, 137–38
at state level, 139, 140
in Vietnam, 192
government transfer payments, 57, 137–38
graphs, 20–21
Great Crash, *see* Stock Market Crash
Great Mississippi Flood (1927), 515
Greece, ancient, 160–61
Griliches, Zvi, 415
gross private domestic investment, 68–69
growth, economic, 489–507
capital formation and, 499–500
defined, 490
entrepreneurship in, 503–5
human capital and, 501–2
as policy objective, 490–91
pollution and, 425–27
in pre-World War II period, 26
price system and, 45–46
production possibilities curve and, 26–28
technological change and, 45–46, 502–3
zero, 425
growth, population, 493–96
effects of, 493–96
guns and butter, production of, 26
Gwynn, Tony, 470

Hamilton, Alexander, 540
Heady, Earl, 308–9
Heinze, Frederick, 172
Heller, Walter W., 136, 151, 425
Heraclitus, 49
Herald Tribune, 450
Hicks, Sir John, 393
historical costs, 394
Hollomon, Herman, 501
horizontal range of aggregate supply curves, 81, 94, 141
House of Representatives, U.S., 131, 242–43
Howrey, Phillip, 285
human capital, 501–2
human wants, defined, 9–10
Hume, David, 529, 557
Hymans, Saul, 285

IBM Corporation, 420
ICC (Interstate Commerce Commission), 393
IMF (International Monetary Fund), 558–59
implicit costs, 323

imports, 529
income:
break-even, 481
disposable, *see* disposable income
distribution of, *see* income distribution
fixed money, 148
future, present value of, 460–61
market demand and level of, 35
money vs. real, 147–48
NNP as determinant of, 108
price system and distribution of, 47
proprietors', 71
as spending determinant, 108
income, per capita, 22
growth of resources and efficiency in, 45
income distribution:
in capital formation theory, 496–97
functional, 465–66
under monopoly, 392
production possibilities curve and, 27–28
income elasticity of demand, 347–48
income-expenditure analysis, 112–13
income inequality, 468–73
cause of, 470
efficiency lost in reduction of, 472–73
pros and cons of, 471–72
tax structure and, 470–71
incomes policies, 206–10
elements of, 206
firms influenced by, 207
Kennedy-Johnson guidelines in, 206–10
tax-based, 210
wage and price targeting in, 206
income tax, *see* taxes, taxation
increasing returns to scale, 333
indexes, price, *see* price indexes
indirect business taxes, 72–73
individual demand curves, 320
market demand curve vs., 320
industry demand curves, 346–47
inflation, 144–57
aggregate demand and, 150–56
as arbitrary "tax," 149
borrowers and, 148–49
cost-push, *see* cost-push inflation
creeping, 145–46
defined, 144–45
demand-induced, 152
demand-pull, *see* demand-pull inflation
elderly and, 148
FOMC (1979) policy for, 268–69
impact of, 147–50
lenders and, 148–49
measurement of, 146–47
output and, 149–50
policy menu and, 154–55
recession in stopping of, 286–87
redistributive effects of, 147–49
runaway, 145, 255, 262–63
quantity of money and, 250
savers and, 149
speculation and, 145, 149
unemployment and, 154–55, 156
in wartime, 153
inflationary gap, 152
Inland, 208
innovation, defined, 503
innovation rate, 114, 220–21
differences among sectors of economy and, 220–21
evidence of decline in, 220
general economic climate and, 225–27

innovation rate (*continued*)
    investment in plant and equipment in, 224–25
    see also technology
innovators, 463, 503
inputs, 300–302
    average product of, 303
    control of, 380
    defined, 300–301
    fixed, 301–2
    marginal product of, 303–6
    market supply and price of, 39
    optimal, 307–8
    variable, 302
insurance companies, 164
interest, in GNP calculation, 71
interest rate, 247–75, 452–61
    ceilings on, 193
    choosing productive projects and, 458
    defined, 106
    demand curve for loanable funds and, 453–55
    demand curve for money and, 252–53
    determination of, 453–57
    exchange rate and, 551
    functions of, 457–58
    investment and, 106–7
    monetary policy and, 247–75
    money supply and, 253–55, 257, 265–66
    price level and, 79
    price of bonds and, 254, 256
    pure, 453
    real vs. nominal, 264–65
    short-term, 264–65
    supply curve for loanable funds and, 455–57
    total output and, 79–80
intermediate goods, 56
International Harvester, 418
International Monetary Fund (IMF), 558–59
International Nickel Company of Canada, 380
international trade, 528–44
    absolute advantage in, 530–31
    comparative advantage in, 531–33
    export subsidies in, 539
    incomplete specialization in, 534
    individual markets and, 534–36
    NNP and, 545–46
    specialization and, 529–30
    tariffs and quotas in, 537–42
International Typographical Union's Local Six
    (Big Six), 450
Interstate Commerce Commission (ICC), 393
inventories, 68–69
inverse relationships, direct relationships vs.,
    20–21
investment:
    determinants of, 105–6
    expected rate of return in, 106–7
    Great Crash and, 117
    intended, changes in, 115–16
    interest rate and, 106–7
    NNP and, 105–7
    in plant and equipment, 224–25
    positive vs. negative, 68–69
    spending chain and, 115
    volatility of, 114–15
investment bankers, 164
investment function, 254–55, 257

Japan, 156, 215–16
    automobiles imported from, 541
Jarvis, Howard, 523
Job Corps, 478

job training programs, 478
Johnson, Lyndon B., 141, 151, 478
Johnson, Samuel, 479
Johnson administration, 48
    incomes policy of, 206–10
Joint Economic Committee of Congress, 131,
    271
Justice Department, U.S., 411, 418, 419

Kaiser, 208
Kapital, Das (Marx), 90
Kasten, Robert, 521
Kaysen, Carl, 415
Kemp, Jack, 521
Kennedy, John F., 136, 141, 151, 206–10, 237,
    413, 478
Kennedy administration, 192
    incomes policy of, 206–10
Keynes, John Maynard, 81, 92, 113, 130, 277,
    279, 284, 285
Keynesian model:
    business fluctuations in, 278
    fiscal policy in, 123–43
    investment function in, 254–55, 257
    monetarists vs., 257–58, 277–84
    monetary rule in, 280
    money supply in, 253–57
    NNP in, 99–122
    price flexibility in, 282
    private spending in, 280–82
    rational expectations theory and, 282–84
    rules vs. activism in, 282
    stabilization policy in, 279
Keynesian range of aggregate supply curves, 81,
    94, 141
Kingsbury, Nathan C., 395
Kingsbury Agreement, 395
kinked oligopoly demand curves, 407–8
Kirkland, Lane, 445
Klein, Lawrence, 120
Knickerbocker Trust, 172–73
Knight, Frank, 463
Korean War, 147, 205
Kreps, Juanita, 487
Kuznets, Simon, 56, 58

labor, 10, 435–51
    "bill of rights" for, 446–47
    early history of, 444–45
    equilibrium price and quantity of, 441–43
    firm's demand curve for, 437–38
    legislation on, in post-World War II period,
       446–47
    marginal product of, 303–6, 439
    market demand curve for, 440
    market supply curve for, 440–41
    profit-maximizing quantity of, 438
labor force, 86–87
    increase in proportion of youths and women
       in, 219
    occupational composition of, 436
    price of labor and, 436–37
labor productivity:
    in automobile industry, 207
    defined, 154–55
labor unions, 133, 443–51
    corruption in, 444, 446
    featherbedding by, 448
    growth of, in World War II, 444–45
    growth of, under Roosevelt administration, 444
    internal problems of, 445–46

local, 443
national, 443
wages increased by, 447–48
Laffer, Arthur, 226–27
Laffer curves, 226–27
La Follette, Robert M., 58
Lamb, Charles, 452–53
Lampman, Robert, 475–76
land, 10, 461–62
use of, in Alaska, 14
Landrum-Griffin Act (1959), 446–47
law of diminishing marginal returns, 306–7,
    324–25, 329–30
    Malthus's theory in terms of, 492–93
law of diminishing marginal utility, 316–17
legal reserve requirements, 169, 176–77
    changes in, 187–89
    decrease in, 189
    increase in, 188–89
Leo XIII, Pope, 85
liability:
    of corporations, 299
    of partnerships, 298
    of proprietorships, 298
Lincoln, Abraham, 297
lines:
    $C+I+G$, 124–26, 128–30, 152, 201, 255, 506,
        545–46
    45-degree, 111, 255
liquidity, of banks, 165–66
loanable funds:
    allocating supply of, 457–58
    demand curve for, 453–55
    supply curve for, 455–57
loans:
    to commercial banks, 185
local unions, 443
long run, 302–3
    defined, 302
    equilibrium under perfect competition in,
        373–74
    price and output under monopoly in, 387–
        88
    price and output under perfect competition
        in, 372–74
    short run vs., 323
long-run average cost function, 332–33
Lucas, Robert, 283

McNamara, Robert S., 478
Malthus, Thomas, 491–96
Mansfield, Edwin, 70, 420, 439, 510
marginal cost:
    average cost functions and, 330–32
    increase of, diminishing returns and, 324–25,
        329–30
    in short run, 328–32
marginal product of input, 303–6
marginal product of labor, 303–6, 439
    population growth and, 492–93
    value of, 439
marginal propensity to consume (MPC), 102–3
    average propensity to consume vs., 103
    defined, 102
    geometric interpretation of, 102–3
marginal propensity to save (MPS), 105
    multiplier and, 116–18
marginal revenue, demand curve and, under
    monopoly, 381–83
marginal tax rate, 520

marginal utility, 315–17
    defined, 315
    diminishing, law of, 316–17
mark, German, 145, 548–51, 553, 555
market basket, 146
    equilibrium, 317–19
market demand, 33–37, 336–58
    consumer tastes in, 34
    income level of consumers and, 35
    price elasticity and, 336–58
    substitution and, 35–36
market demand curves, 33, 336–38
    derivation of, 321–22
    individual demand curve vs., 320
    for labor, 440
    measuring of, 337–38
market period, 370–71
markets, 31–53
    defined, 32
    demand side of, *see* market demand
    prices and, 31–53
    product, 46–47
    resource, 46–47
    supply side of, *see* market supply
    variations in, 32–33
    see also monopolistic competition; monopoly;
        oligopoly; perfect competition
market structure, 360–62
    barriers to entry and, 361
    control over price in, 361
    nonprice competition in, 362
    number of firms in, 360–61
    type of product in, 361
market supply, 37–39
    input prices and, 39
market supply curve, 37–38, 368–70
    derivation of, 369–70
    for labor, 440–41
    technology and, 38
Marshall, Alfred, 259
Martin, William McChesney, 136, 181
Marx, Karl, 90–91, 92, 464
Mason, Edward, 420
maximum-profit output rate, 364–65
Medicare, 479
member banks, 182–83, 265
Merrill Lynch, Pierce, Fenner, and Smith, 186
microelectronics industry, 221
Mill, John Stuart, 529
Miller, G. William, 181, 190
Minarik, Joseph, 148
mini-mills, 44
models, 18–19
    best vs. good prediction by, 18–19
    defined, 18
    purpose of, 18
    quantification of, 20
    simplification of real situation in, 18
    see also specific models
Modigliani, Franco, 280, 284
M_1 money, 162–64
monetarist model:
    business fluctuations in, 278
    Keynesians vs., 257–58, 277–84
    monetary rule in, 279–80
    price flexibility in, 282
    private spending in, 280–82
    rational expectations theory and, 282–84
    rules vs. activism in, 282
    stabilization policy in, 279
monetary base, defined, 265

monetary policy, 179–96, 247–75
  aggregate demand curve and, 194
  aims of, 180
  coordinating fiscal policy with, 281
  in depressions, 277
  efficiency of, 195
  expansionary, 204
  fiscal policy and, 180
  formulation of, 266–67
  inflationary pressures from, 210
  interest rate and, 247–75
  interest-rate ceilings in, 193
  lag in, 267, 269
  makers of, 181–82
  moral suasion in, 193
  in 1960s, 192
  in recession, 180–81
  reserves and, 180–81
  stabilization in, 211–12
  "stop-go," 192, 271
  tight vs. easy, 263–65, 267–68
money:
  banking system and, 159–78
  circular flows of, 46–47
  coins, 161
  as created by banks, 171–76
  crude quantity theory of prices and, 260–63
  currency, 161–62
  defined, 159–61
  demand for, 251–53
  equation of exchange of, 259–60
  fiat, 161–62
  importance of, 263
  inflation and quantity of, 250
  interest rate and demand curve for, 252–53
  as medium of exchange, 160
  M_1, 162–64
  M_2, 163–64
  NNP and demand for, 252–53
  paper, invention of, 161
  price level and value of, 248–49
  as social invention, 160–61
  as standard of value, 160–61
  as store of value, 160–61
  value of, 248–49
  velocity of, see velocity of money
money income:
  fixed, 148
  real income vs., 147–48
money supply, 161–64
  aggregate demand curve and, 194
  broadly defined, 163–64
  checkable deposits in, 162–63
  decrease in, 256–57
  demand deposits in, 162–63, 248
  determinants of, 251
  increase in, 253–55, 263
  interest rate and, 253–55, 257
  interest rate vs., in policy-making, 265–66
  legal reserve requirements and, 169
  narrowly defined, 161–63
  NNP and, 253–57, 263
  nominal NNP and, in quantity theory, 272
  in post-World War II period, 162–63
  price level and, in crude quantity theory,
    261–62
  rapid increase of, 250
  rate of increase of, 265
  unemployment and, 250–51
monopolistic competition, 360, 361, 401–6
  defined, 402
  equilibrium under, 403–6

monopoly vs., 404–6
  perfect competition vs., 404–6
  price and output under, 403–6
  product differentiation under, 402–3
monopoly, 360, 361, 379–400
  causes of, 380–81
  defined, 379
  demand curve and marginal revenue under,
    381–83
  efficiency incentives under, 396–97
  efficiency under, 393
  equilibrium under, 386–87
  Golden Rule of Output Determination under,
    384–86, 387
  government action and, 381
  income distribution under, 392
  long-run price and output under, 387–88
  monopolistic competition vs., 404–6
  natural, 381
  perfect competition vs., 379–80, 388–90
  power of, as optimal, 399
  production under, 392
  public regulation of, 393–96
  resource allocation under, 390, 391–92
  short-run price and output under, 382–87
  technology under, 393, 398–99
moral suasion, 193
Morgan, J. P., 172–73
Morse, Charles, 172
MPC, see marginal propensity to consume
MPS (marginal propensity to save), 105, 116–18
M_2 money, 163–64
multiplier, 116–18
  defined, 117
  government expenditure and, 126
mutual savings banks, 164

Nader, Ralph, 394–96
Nathan, Robert, 227
National Advisory Committee on Rural Poverty,
  349
National Aeronautics and Space Administration
  (NASA), 224
national banks, 182
National Bureau of Economic Research, 56, 58,
  241
national debt:
  defined, 236
  size of, 238–39
National Foreign Trade Council, 562
national income accounts, defined, 56
national income and product accounting, see
  GNP
National Labor Relations Board, 444
national output, see NNP
national unions, 443
natural monopolies, 381
negative income tax, 481–83
negative investments, 69
negotiable order of withdrawal (NOW) accounts,
  162
net exports, 70, 546
net national product, see NNP
net private domestic investment, 69
net worth, defined, 166
Nixon, Richard M., 48, 135, 235, 237, 560
Nixon administration:
  Family Assistance Plan under, 482
  fiscal policy of, 243–44
NNP (net national product), 63, 99–122
  automatic stabilizers and, 132–34
  capacity utilization and, 115

changes in money supply and, 253–57
consumption expenditure and, 126–27
consumption expenditure and net investment
  in, 100
consumption function in, 100–103
crude quantity theory and, 262
decreased government expenditure and, 126
defined, 63
durability of capital goods and, 114–15
equilibrium level, graphical determination of,
  110–11
equilibrium level of, 107–11, 113–14, 257
fiscal policy and, 123–43
flow of income in, 107
full employment, investment and, 499–500
government expenditure and, 124–26
as income determinant, 108
increased government expenditure and, 175
inflationary gap and, 152
innovation rate and, 114
international trade and, 545–46
investment and, 105–7
investment volatility and, 114–15
limitations of, 64–65
money demand and, 252–53
money supply and, 253–57, 263
multiplier and, 116–18
net exports and, 546
in 1957 vs. 1958, 234–35
nominal, *see* nominal NNP
precautionary demand for money and, 252
price level and, 82–85
saving function in, 104–5
shift to services from goods in, 219
spending and, 107–10
spending chain in, 115–16
taxation and, 126–29
transactions demand for money and, 252
see also consumption function; disposable
  income
nominal interest rate, real interest rate vs.,
  264–65
nominal NNP, 258
  in crude quantity theory, 262
  money supply and, in quantity theory, 272
noncompeting groups, 443
nondurable goods, 68
nonprice competition, under oligopoly, 413–15
nonselectivity, 517–18
Nordhaus, William, 65
normative economics, 17
  positive economics vs., 17
Norris-La Guardia Act (1932), 444
NOW (negotiable order of withdrawal) accounts,
  162

OECD (Organization for Economic Cooperation
  and Development), 504
Office of Management and Budget (OMB), 131,
  240
oil embargo (1973–74), 331
oil prices, 198–99, 331
Okun, Arthur, 149, 473
old-age insurance, 476–77
oligopoly, 360, 361, 401–2, 406–8
  nonprice competition under, 413–15
  perfect competition vs., 415–16
  price leadership in, 412–13
  price stability and, 406–8
  pure vs. differentiated, 402
OMB (Office of Management and Budget), 131,
  240

OPEC (Organization of Petroleum Exporting
  Countries), 331, 375, 408–9
open market operations, 185–87
open shop, 449
opportunity cost, 12–15, 322
  defined, 12, 15
Organization for Economic Cooperation and
  Development (OECD), 504
Organization of Petroleum Exporting Countries
  (OPEC), 331, 375, 408–9
output, 21–22, 24, 363–69
  actual and potential, gap between, 506
  Golden Rule for determination of, 366–67,
    368, 384–86, 387
  inflation and, 149–50
  interest rate and, 79–80
  maximum-profit, 364–65
  national, *see* NNP
  optimal rate of, 391–92
  per capita, growth of, 215–17
  profit correlated to, 363
  research and development and increase in,
    27–28
  slope of aggregate supply curves and, 82
  see also production possibilities curve

Parker Pen company, 338
partnerships, 298–99
patents, 220
  as cause of monopoly, 380
peak, defined, 76
Peck, Merton J., 517
Penner, Rudolph, 242
Penn Square Bank of Oklahoma City, 165,
  171
perfect competition, 33, 359–78
  allocation of resources under, 374–77
  defined, 359–60
  dropping out of, 367–68
  equilibrium wage and employment under,
    437–39
  homogeneity of product in, 362
  impersonality of definition of, 362
  long-run price and output under, 372–74
  market period and, 370–71
  mobility of resources in, 362–63
  monopolistic competition vs., 404–6
  monopoly vs., 379–80, 388–90
  number of buyers and sellers in, 362
  oligopoly vs., 415–16
  short-run price and output under, 371–72
personal consumption expenditures, 68
Phelps, Edmund, 201
Phillips, A. W., 154
Phillips curves, 153–54
  defined, 154
  instability of, 199–201
  long-run, 201–5
  shifts in, 202–5
  short-run, 203–5
Pigou, A. C., 471
planning horizon, *see* long run
plant and equipment, investment in, 224–25
policy menu, 155–56
pollution, 422–34
  air, 423
  direct regulation and, 427
  economic growth and, 425–27
  effluent fees and, 427–28
  external diseconomies and, 423–24
  public policy toward, 427–28
  recent directions of policy on, 432–33

pollution (*continued*)
  tax credits for control of, 428
  U.S. programs for control of, 428–29
  water, 422–23, 426
  zero, 432
positive economics, 17
  normative economics vs., 17
positive investments, 68–69
positively sloped range of aggregate supply
    curves, 82, 95
post-World War I period:
  Germany in, 145, 150, 250, 262–63
  productivity in, 214
  real GNP in, 75
post-World War II period:
  creeping inflation in, 145–46, 147
  economic growth as policy objective in,
    490–91
  evolution of fiscal policy in, 123
  exchange rates in, 552–53
  GNP gap in, 150
  labor legislation in, 446–47
  narrowly defined money supply in, 162–63
  peaks and troughs in, 76–77
  productivity in, 214
  recovery of Europe and Japan in, 559
  size of military in, 137
  unemployment in, 87, 133
potential GNP, 75, 89
  gap between actual GNP and, 150
poverty, 474–84
  declining incidence of, 474
  defined, 474
  among families headed by females vs. males,
    475
  reasons for, 475–76
  among whites vs. non-whites, 475, 484
precautionary demand for money, 252
present value of future income, 460–61
presidency, U.S., 15–17, 240–42
Presser, Jackie, 443
price ceilings, 375
price controls, 205, 243–44
price elastic, 344–45
  defined, 344
price elasticity of demand, 336–58
  calculation of, 340–41
  consumers' budget and, 342–44
  defined, 339
  determinants of, 341–44
  instability of farm prices and, 343
  market demand and, 336–58
  in relative vs. absolute terms, 339
  substitutes and, 342
  time period and, 344
  total money expenditure and, 344–45
price indexes:
  applications of, 61–62
  defined, 59
  expressed as percentage, 60
  GNP-adjustment and, 59–62
price inelastic, 345
  defined, 344
price leadership, 412–13
price level:
  money supply and, in crude quantity theory,
    261–62
  national output and, 82–85
  value of money and, 248–49
  in wartime, 248–49
price rigidity, 407–8

prices, 31–53
  actual, 41
  crude quantity theory of money and, 260–63
  equilibrium, *see* equilibrium price
  of input, market supply and, 39
  markets and, 31–53
  oligopoly and stability of, 406–8
  public regulation and, 394–96
  substitution and market demand in, 35–36
price supports, 353–54, 375
price system, 41–49
  allocation and, 43–45
  circular flows of money and products in, 46–47
  determination of what is produced in, 41–42
  in determining how goods are produced, 43
  distribution of income in, 47
  economic growth and, 45–46
  limitations of, 47–49
  public goods and, 48–49
private costs, 424–25
private transfer payments, 57
product differentiation, under monopolistic
    competition, 402–3
product group, defined, 402–3
production, 22
  declining cost of, 381
  under monopoly, 392
  price system and methods of, 43
  price system in determining level of, 41–42
  spending and, 107
production function, 301
production possibilities curves, 22–28
  defined, 23
  in determining how goods are produced,
    24–27
  in determining what is produced, 22–24
  full employment of resources and, 25
  growth and, 26–28
  income distribution and, 27–28
  inside vs. on, 25–27
  production of capital vs. consumer goods and,
    28
  technology and, 27–28
  unemployment and, 24–25
productivity, 214–29
  slowdown of, 217–19
  technological change and, 216–17
product markets, 46
products, circular flows of, 46–47
profit maximization, 300
profits, 462–65
  economic, 373–74
  functions of, 464–65
  output correlated to, 363
profit statistics, 462–63
Progress and Poverty (George), 462
progressive tax, 470–71
prohibitive tariff, 538
property tax, 522–24
Proposition 13, 523
proprietorships, 297–98
proprietors' income, 71
prosperity period, defined, 76
Protestant ethic, 504
public choice theory, 516–18
public goods, 48–49, 512–13
  defined, 512
Public Law 480, 355
public regulation, 393–96
  prices and, 394–96
public works, 134–35

pure oligopoly, 402
pure rate of interest, 453, 455

quantity demanded, 35, 36–37
    changes in demand vs. changes in, 36–37
quantity theory, 271–73
    crude, *see* crude quantity theory
    money supply and nominal NNP in, 272
quotas, 538–42
    arguments for, 540
    social costs of, 539

race discrimination, 484
R and D, *see* research and development
rate of return, 106
    defined, 454
    expected, 106–7
rational expectations, 282–84
ratios:
    capital-labor, 219
    capital-output, 499
    reserve to deposit, *see* legal reserve
        requirements
Rawls, John, 471–72
Reagan, Ronald, 223, 241, 242, 281, 286–87, 478,
    480, 541
Reagan administration, 48
    aggregate supply curve under, 227–28
    agriculture policy of, 357
    anti-inflationary policy of, 142–43, 281
    fiscal policy of, 245
    technology policy of, 223
real GNP, 59
    in post-World War I period, 75
real income, money income vs., 147–48
real interest rate, nominal interest
    rate vs., 264–65
real terms, defined, 61
recession:
    defined, 76
    monetary policy in, 180–81
    in 1957–58, 198, 237
    in 1974–75, 77, 244, 250–51
    in 1981–82, 77, 245
    stopping inflation with, 286–87
Regan, Donald, 241
regressive tax, 470–71
Regulation Q, 193
rent, 461–62
    in GNP, 71
reproduction costs, 394
research and development (R and D):
    in federal laboratories, 224
    funding of, 217
    in GNP, 219, 221–22
    increased output and, 27–28
    "in house" expenditures for, 223
    as nonprice competition, 413–15
    tax credits for, 222–24
    Vietnam War and, 222
Reserve Mining Company, 426
reserves:
    excess, 173–77
    fractional, 167–69
    monetary policy and, 180–81
    required, *see* legal reserve requirements
    secondary, 170
resource markets, 46–47
resources:
    defined, 9–10
    economic vs. free, 10

full employment of, 25
    market supply and price of, 39
    mobility of, in perfect competition, 362–63
    reallocation of, 376–77
returns to scale, 333–34
    constant, 333
    increasing vs. decreasing, 333
Revolutionary War, 153, 248, 250
Ricardo, David, 496–99, 529
right-to-work laws, 449
Ripken, Cal, Jr., 470
risk, 463–64
Risser, Hubert, 371–72
Rivlin, Alice, 487
Rockefeller, John D., 389
Rome, ancient, 161
Roos, C. F., 346
Roosevelt, Franklin D.:
    TVA created by, 515
    union growth under, 444
Roosevelt, Theodore, 419, 494
rule-of-reason doctrine, 418–19
runaway inflation, 145, 255, 262–63

sales tax, 522–24
Samuelson, Paul, 510
Sargent, Thomas, 283
Saturday Night Special, 268–69
saving function, 104–5
    disposable income in, 104–5
    marginal propensity to save in, 105
    shifts in, 118–21
    shifts in consumption function and, 170
    shifts in vs. movements along, 119–20
savings and loans associations, 164
Say, J. B., 88
Say's Law, 88
Scherer, F. M., 411, 517
Schultz, Theodore, 501
Schumpeter, Joseph, 397–98, 463, 503
Schwartz, Anna, 194–95
secondary reserves, 170
secondhand goods, 57
selective credit control, 193
semi-dwarf wheats, 38
Senate, U.S., 130, 131, 242
sex discrimination, 486–87
Sherman Antitrust Act (1890), 408, 417
short run, 302–3
    average costs in, 326–28
    cost functions in, 323–26
    defined, 302
    long run vs., 323
    marginal cost in, 328–32
    price and output under monopoly in, 382–87
    price and output under perfect competition
        in, 371–72
Sloan, Alfred P., 293, 414
slope:
    of consumption function, 102–3
    of demand curves, 33–34, 78–79
    of supply curve, 38, 80
Smith, Adam, 16, 227, 390, 393, 409–10, 492,
    496, 529
Smithsonian Institution, 560
social costs, 424–25
social insurance, 476–79
socialism, 90
Social Security, 476–79
    controversies over, 477–79
Social Security Act (1935), 476

Social Security Administration, 474–75
Social Security tax, 477
space program, U.S., 222
special-interest groups, 516–17
specialization, incomplete, 534
speculation, inflation and, 145, 149
spending:
    autonomous vs. induced changes in, 115
    income as determinant of, 108
    NNP and, 107–10
    production and, 107
    see also consumer expenditures; government
      spending
spending chain, 115
stabilization policy, 211–12, 276–89
    feasibility of, 283
    monetarist vs. Keynesian views of, 279
    monetary rule as, 270–71, 279–80
    price flexibility and, 282
    private spending and, 280–82
    rational expectations theory and, 282–84
    rules vs. activism in, 282
    supply-side economics in, 285–88
stagflation, 197–213
    aggregate supply curve and, 202
    anti-inflationary measures and, 197–213
    etymology of, 202
Standard Oil of Ohio, 389, 418
state banks, 182
steel industry, 44, 207–8
Stigler, George, 395–96, 509
Stockman, David, 478
Stock Market Crash (1929), 83–84
    investment and, 117
"stop-go" policies, 192, 271
structural unemployment, 86
Studebaker, 295
substitutes:
    cross elasticity of demand and, 348–49
    price elasticity of demand and, 342
substitution, market demand and, 35–36
Suits, D. B., 346
sulphur industry, 407
supply:
    aggregate, 77–78
    excess, 40
    market, *see* market supply
supply curves, 322–33
    aggregate, *see* aggregate supply curves
    assumptions of, 37–38
    backward-bending, 440–41
    for loanable funds, 455–57
    rightward vs. leftward shifts in, 39, 51–52
    shifts in, 51–52
    slope of, 38, 80
supply-side economics, 226–28, 285–88
    demand management in, 287–88
Supreme Court, U.S., 416, 418–19
surplus:
    anti-inflationary effects of, 236
    balance-of-payments, 555–56
    defined, 231
surplus controls, 353–54
surplus financing, 231–34, 235–36
surplus value theory, 464
Sweezy, Paul, 407

Taft-Hartley Act (1947), 446, 449
targeting:
    price levels in, 356–57
    of wages and prices in incomes policy, 206

tariffs, 537–42
    arguments for, 540–42
    prohibitive, 538
    social costs of, 538
tastes and preferences, market demand and, 34
tax credits:
    for pollution-control measures, 428
    for research and development, 222–24
tax cuts, 128–29
    in 1964, 136
    in 1975, 244
    in 1981, 226–27, 288
    in supply-side economic policy, 285
taxes, taxation, 518–26
    ability-to-pay principle in, 519
    as automatic stabilizer, 132
    benefit principle in, 518, 519
    corporate income, 140, 522
    equity and simplicity in, 521
    excise, 140
    increase of, 128
    indirect business, 72–73
    legislative process for setting level of, 242–43
    marginal rate of, 520
    negative income, 481–83
    NNP and, 126–29
    personal income, 520
    progressive, 470–71
    property, 522–24
    regressive, 470–71
    sales, 522–24
    schedule of, 520
tax incidence, 524–26
    sensitivity of demand to price in, 525
    sensitivity of supply to price in, 526
tax revenues, 132
tax simplification, 242
tax surcharge of 1968, 151
Teamsters Union, 443–44, 446
technology:
    choice and, 11
    civilian, federal support for, 222–24
    economic growth and, 45–46, 502–3
    firms and, 300
    market supply curve and, 38
    under monopoly, 393, 398–99
    NNP and, 114
    production possibilities curve and, 27–28
    productivity and, 216–17
    U.S. lead in, 221
    see also innovation rate
Teeters, Nancy, 487
Temin, Peter, 195
Tennessee Valley Authority (TVA), 515
terms of trade, 533–34
Theory of Justice, A (Rawls), 472
Tobin, James, 65, 281, 481
Torrio, Joseph, 91–93
total cost, 325–26
    average, 327–28
total fixed cost, 323–24
total variable cost, 324–25
trade, international, *see* international trade
transactions demand for money, 252
transfer payments:
    government, 137–38
    government vs. private, 57
Treasury Department, U.S., 131, 182, 242,
    521
Treasury deposits, 185
trough, defined, 76

Truman, Harry S., 130, 357
Truman administration, 206
TVA (Tennessee Valley Authority), 515

Udall, Morris, 14
unemployment, 85–93
  business fluctuations and, 283
  classical view of, 88–89
  collective bargaining by, 449–51
  cyclical, 86
  economic vs. noneconomic costs of, 87–93
  fiscal policy and, 130–31
  frictional, 86
  inflation and, 154–55, 156
  Marx on, 90–91
  natural rate of, 201–3
  in post-World War II period, 87, 133
  production possibilities curve and, 24–25
  quantity of money and, 250–51
  rational expectations and, 283
  structural, 86
  see also Phillips curves
unemployment compensation, 132–34, 479
unemployment rate, 86–87
  among racial minorities, 93
  in West Germany, 156
unions, labor, *see* labor unions
union shop, 449
unitary elasticity, 345
  defined, 344
United Shoe Machinery Company, 380
United States Steel Corporation, 207–8, 253,
  412–13
utility:
  defined, 315
  marginal, *see* marginal utility
  total, 316

Vail, Theodore, 395
value-added:
  in calculation of GNP, 62–63
  defined, 62
value of the marginal product of labor, 439
variable costs:
  average, 326–27
  total, 324–25
variable input, 302

variables:
  average relationships between, 20
  direct vs. inverse relationships between, 20–21
velocity of money, 259–60, 261
  in quantity theory, 271–73
vertical range of aggregate supply curves, 81–82,
  94–95
"Victory" program, 67
Vietnam War, 135, 147, 151, 153, 222, 243, 560
Volcker, Paul A., 181, 190, 268, 287
von Szeliski, V., 346

wage controls, 205, 243–44
wage-price spiral, 198
wages, 70–71
  money vs. real, 437
  unions in increasing of, 447–48
Wagner Act (1935), 444, 446
Wallace, Neil, 283
Wallich, Henry, 210
Wall Street Journal, 410–12
Walters of San Diego, 312–13
War of 1812, 248
water, conservation of, 319
water pollution, 422–23, 426
Water Quality Improvement Act (1970), 428
Ways and Means Committee (House of
  Representatives), 131, 242–43
Wealth of Nations, The (Smith), 16, 390
welfare payments, 132–34, 135, 480
  in Great Depression, 511–12
Westinghouse, 411
wheat industry, 33–34, 37–38, 51
Whitman, Marina, 487
Wilson, Joseph, 465
Wold, Herman, 348–49
World War I, 249
  see also post-World War I period
World War II, 84–85, 249
  GNP estimates in, 67
  size of military before vs. after, 137
  union growth in, 444–45
  wage and price controls during, 205
  see also post-World War II period

yellow-dog contracts, 444

zero economic growth, 425
zero population growth, 427